Contemporary Britain

Contemporary Britain

An Annual Review 1990

Edited by
PETER CATTERALL

Published for the
Institute of Contemporary British History
by Basil Blackwell

British Library Cataloguing in Publication Data

Contemporary Britain: an annual review. 1990–
1. Great Britain, Social conditions.
I. Institute of Contemporary British History
941.0859

ISBN 0–631–17237–8
ISSN 0957–5960

Typeset in 10 on 12pt Times
by the Institute of Contemporary British History
Printed in Great Britain by
T. J. Press Ltd, Padstow, Cornwall

Contents

Preface

This is the first of a new series that will annually review events, trends and policies in contemporary Britain. These will both describe and critically assess current affairs and the prevailing issues and themes in British society and politics. The object is to provide an authoritative record of the year just past that will serve both as an indispensable current guide and a valuable point of reference for future historians. Each of the ensuing essays surveys an important aspect of British life or policy and examines the major themes that have characterized 1989. The essays are supported by detailed chronologies recording the development of the issues, the significant reports and the other notable occurrences of the past year.

This series forms part of the work of the Institute of Contemporary British History, which was founded in September 1986 with the aim of promoting the study of all aspects of post-war British history at every level. To that end the Institute publishes books and a quarterly journal, *Contemporary Record*; it organizes seminars and conferences for school students, undergraduates, researchers and teachers of post-war history and also runs a number of research projects. A central objective of this series is to provide the material with which an informed assessment of the contemporary state of and the future agenda for Britain can be made.

I would like to thank Anthony Seldon, the Director of the Institute, for initiating this project. The efforts and the helpful suggestions of the contributors to this volume, who have done their best to mitigate the editorial problems posed by such a task, must not pass without comment. Nor should the support and advice of Alyn Shipton, Caroline Bundy and Jeff Borer of Basil Blackwell and of Katrin Barlow of Oryx Systems. Above all, I must thank my colleague Stephanie Maggin who has borne the brunt of the task of typesetting and subediting this volume. We hope that this book neither flatters nor condemns but that it provides a recognizable picture of Britain in 1989; one which provokes both memories of the recent past and questions as to where Britain is going in the 1990s.

List of Contributors

* ARTHUR, Paul. Lecturer in Politics at the University of Ulster at Jordanstown and the author of several books on Northern Ireland, including *The Government and Politics of Northern Ireland* and *Northern Ireland since 1968*, Basil Blackwell, 1988.
* BALSOM, Dr Denis. Lecturer in Political Science, Department of International Politics, University College of Wales, Aberystwyth. A well known commentator on Welsh affairs for the BBC, ITV and press and also author of numerous academic articles concerning Wales.
* BAYLIS, Dr John. Reader in International Relations, Department of International Politics, University College of Wales, Aberystwyth. His current research interests include British foreign and defence policies in the 1940s and 1950s, post-war Anglo-American defence relations, and contemporary problems of European security. His most recent publication is *British Defence Policy: Striking the Right Balance*, Macmillan, 1989 and he co-authored *Britain, NATO and Nuclear Weapons: Alternative Defence v Alliance Reform*, Macmillan, 1989.
* BILSBOROUGH, Peter. Senior Assistant Director, Centre for Physical Education and Sports Development, University of Stirling. He has written on the history of Scottish physical education and sport and in 1989 published *A Hundred Years of Scottish Swimming*, Scottish Amateur Swimming Association.
* BLOWERS, Andrew. Professor of Social Sciences and Pro-Vice-Chancellor (Degree Studies), The Open University. He is a county councillor in Bedfordshire specializing in environmental issues. Recent books include *Nuclear Power in Crisis*, co- authored with David Pepper and the forthcoming title, *International Politics of Nuclear Waste*, co-authored with David Lowry and Barry Soloman.
* BUDD, Professor Alan. Economic Adviser to Barclays Bank plc. He was previously Professor of Economics and Director of the Centre for Economic Forecasting at the London Business School, where he still holds a Visiting Chair. He worked in HM Treasury from 1970–74.
* BUTLER, Dr David. Is a Fellow of Nuffield College, Oxford. He has been associated with the Nuffield Election Studies since 1945. His most recent book is *British General Elections since 1945*, Basil Blackwell, 1989.

* CATTERALL, Dr Peter. Executive Director, Institute of Contemporary British History. He is the author of the forthcoming *British History 1945–1987: An Annotated Bibliography*, Basil Blackwell, forthcoming.
* CHERRY, Gordon. Professor of Urban and Regional Planning and Head of the School of Geography at the University of Birmingham. He is a past President of the Royal Town Planning Institute, specializes in planning history and is Chairman of the Planning History Group, an international body of scholars working in that field. His latest book *Cities and Plans* was published in 1988.
* DAVIE, Dr Grace. A sociologist of religion, holding an honorary research fellowship in the Department of Sociology, University of Exeter. She has carried out a number of studies for the Church of England and has published *Inner City God*, Hodder and Stoughton, 1987.
* DAVIES, Alan. Head of Barclays Bank Economics Department. Most of his career has been with Barclays primarily in the Economics Department, where he has specialized in UK economic, banking and financial matters.
* DAVIES, Gary. MFI Professor of Retail Marketing at Manchester Polytechnic. He has published widely on distribution and retailing including two texts, *Positioning Strategy in Retailing* and *The Independent Retailer*.
* GEORGE, Dr Stephen. Lecturer in Politics, University of Sheffield. His research specialisms are the politics of policy making in the European Community and British policy towards the EC. He has published widely and his latest work is *An Awkward Partner: Britain in the European Community*, OUP, 1990. He is presently working on *Britain and European Integration*, Basil Blackwell, forthcoming 1990.
* GOODWIN, Dr P. B. Director of the Transport Studies Unit and Reader in Transport Studies at Oxford University. Member of SACTRA, the statutory body advising the Secretary of State for Transport on trunk road assessment methods, also a member of the Dover Harbour Board. Has published articles and books on transport topics for twenty years, and frequently advises national and local government and transport companies.
* HALSEY, A. H. Professor of Social and Administrative Studies, University of Oxford and Fellow of Nuffield College. He is the author of *Change in British Society*, OUP, 1986 and editor of *British Social Trends since 1900*, Macmillan, 1988.
* HARDMAN, David. Senior Lecturer in Resources/Tourism and Head of the BSc (Hons) Environmental Management Degree in the Department of Environmental and Geographical Studies, Manchester Polytechnic. Extensive experience in tourism lecturing. Particular interests include National Parks as tourist attractions, mining and quarrying as a basis for tourism and urban tourism initiatives.
* HARLOW, Carol. Professor of Law at the London School of Economics. Author of *Compensation and Government Torts*, *Politics and Public Law* and

(with Richard Rawlings) *Law and Administration.* She is currently working on a book on pressure through law, she is also vice-chair of the Legal Action Group.

* HENNESSY, Dr Peter. Visiting Professor of Government at Strathclyde University and author of *Cabinet*, Basil Blackwell, 1986, and *Whitehall*, Secker and Warburg, hardback, 1989; Fontana, paperback, 1990.

* HEWISON, Robert. Author of four books on Ruskin, and of the trilogy *The Arts in Britain 1939–75*. His most recent books are *The Heritage Industry*, 1987, and *Future Tense*, 1990. He has written on the theatre for the *Sunday Times* since 1981, and is a regular presenter of the 'Issues' edition of Radio Three's 'Third Ear'.

* HILL, Dr Christopher. Lecturer in International Relations at the London School of Economics, where he specializes in British foreign policy, the external relations of the European Community, and theories of foreign policy making. He is the author of a forthcoming book on *Cabinet Decisions in Foreign Policy*, and editor/joint author of *National Foreign Policies and European Political Cooperation*, 1983.

* HIORNS, Dr Brennan. Joined Grieveson Grant in 1974 as an investment analyst and subsequently became a partner in 1983. In 1987 he became Head of Kleinwort Benson Securities' UK equity research department after Grieveson Grant joined the Kleinwort Benson group. He was appointed Deputy Managing Director in January 1990.

* HOLDERNESS, Dr B. A. Reader in Economic and Social History, Department of Economics and Social Studies, University of East Anglia. A farmer's son, he has written numerous works on agricultural history since the eighteenth- century, including *British Agriculture since 1945*, MUP, 1985. He is currently working on a book on British agriculture in the twentieth-century.

* HYMAN, Professor Richard. Convenor of graduate studies at the Industrial Relations Research Unit, University of Warwick. He has written extensively on industrial relations; the fourth edition of *Strikes*, and a new study of *The Political Economy of Industrial Relations*, were both published by Macmillan in 1989.

* JUDGE, Ken. Director of King's Fund Institute since 1986. He is a former Chairman of Camden and Islington Family Practitioner Committee and was an adviser to Sir Roy Griffiths during his review of community care. His publications include *Rationing Social Services*, *Charging for Social Care* and *Care in the Community: The First Steps*. He was editor of the *Journal of Social Policy* from 1980 and 1986 and is the series editor for *Studies in Social Policy* published by Macmillan.

* KELLAS, James G. Professor in Politics, University of Glasgow. Author of *The Scottish Political System*, CUP, 4th edition, 1989.

* KENWARD, Michael. Editor, *New Scientist*, 1979–90. He is a physicist and science journalist and a member of the Committee on the Public Understanding of Science.
* LAYTON-HENRY, Dr Zig. He is a Senior Lecturer in the Department of Politics, University of Warwick. He has recently edited *The Political Rights of Migrant Workers in Western Europe* and is currently writing *Immigration and Race in Britain since 1945*, Basil Blackwell, forthcoming.
* MACLURE, Stuart. Visiting Fellow at the Policy Studies Institute, 1989–90. From 1954–69 he was editor of *Education*, and from 1969–1989, of the *Times Educational Supplement*.
* McRAE, Dr Susan. Senior Fellow and Women's Employment Programme Leader at the Policy Studies Institute, London. Her main publications include *Cross-Class Families*, Clarendon Press, 1986; *Young and Jobless*, PSI, 1987; and *Working Time and Family Life*, PSI, 1989. She is currently working on a national survey of women that focuses on maternity rights and benefits and on employment changes over childbirth.
* MORGAN, David. After researching twentieth-century poetry at Birkbeck College, London, he is now teaching English at Bancroft's School.
* MORRIS, Terence. Professor of Social Institutions at the London School of Economics and a specialist in the areas of criminology and criminal justice policy. He is the author of, among other works, *The Criminal Areas*, 1957, *Pentonville: The Sociology of an English Prison*, 1963, *Deviance and Control: The Secular Heresy*, 1976, and *Crime and Criminal Justice since 1945*, 1989.
* MURIE, Alan. He is Professor of Planning and Housing at Heriot-Watt University, Edinburgh. He is editor of *Housing Studies* and joint author with P. Malpass of *Housing Policy and Practice*, Macmillan. He is also joint author with R. Forrest of *Selling the Welfare State*, Routledge, and with R. Forrest and P. Williams, *Home Ownership: Differentiation and Fragmentation*, Unwin Hyman.
* NORTON, Professor Philip. Professor of Government at the University of Hull. His publications include *Dissensions in the House of Commons*, 2 vols: 1975, 1980; *The Commons in Perspective*, 1981; *The Constitution in Flux*, 1982; *The British Polity*, 1984, 2nd ed. 1990; *Parliament in the 1980s*, (ed.), 1985; *Parliament in Perspective*, 1987; *Legislatures*, (ed.), 1990, and *Parliaments and Executives in Western Europe*, (ed.), 1990.
* PINTO-DUSCHINSKY, Dr Michael. Senior Lecturer in Government at Brunel University. His books include *British Political Finance, 1830–1980*, American Enterprise Institute, 1981. He is currently conducting research on the foreign funding of political parties for the Foreign Office.
* REID, Margaret. A freelance financial journalist and author. Once a Treasury official she has worked for the *Financial Times* and the *Investors Chronicle* (of which she was Finance Editor), and has been Journalist Research Fellow at Nuffield College, Oxford. Her latest book, *All- Change in the City*, was

published in 1988 and followed her earlier title *The Secondary Banking Crisis, 1972–75*.

* REINER, Dr Robert. Law Department, London School of Economics. He was formerly Reader in Criminology at the University of Bristol and at Brunel University. He is author of *The Blue-Coated Worker, The Politics of the Police*, and numerous articles and chapters in books. He is currently completing a study of contemporary chief constables.

* SEYMOUR-URE, Colin. Professor of Government, Rutherford College, University of Kent. He has written widely on political communication and the mass media and is currently writing a history of the mass media in Britain since 1945 for Basil Blackwell and preparing a study of Prime Ministers and Presidents relations with the news media in the UK, other parliamentary systems and the USA.

* SINCLAIR, Dr Peter. He is a Fellow and Tutor in Economics at Brasenose College, Oxford, and currently Visiting Professor at Queen's University, Canada. He is a managing editor of *Oxford Economic Papers*. His most recent books include *Modern International Economics* (with S. A. Heffernan) 1990, and *Unemployment: Economic Theory and Evidence*, 1987.

* STONE, Graham. Principal Lecturer in Tourism in the Department of Hotel, Catering and Tourism Management, Manchester Polytechnic. Extensive experience in lecturing to undergraduate and post-graduate tourism students and consultancy to the Industry.

* SUTTON, Kathy. She is the Wages Rights Officer at the Low Pay Unit. She has previously been employed as Women's Rights Unit Team Leader at the National Council for Civil Liberties, Low Pay Campaign Officer for Leicester City Council and Welfare Rights Team Lead for the West Midlands County Council. She writes here in a personal capacity.

* WALDEN, Neil. Lectured at Manchester Polytechnic in industrial economics and later in science and technology policy before moving to the University of Strathclyde, Department of Marketing, where he is pursuing teaching and research in the area of Marketing and Social Responsibility.

* WALSH, Kieron. Senior Lecturer, INLOGOV, University of Birmingham. Currently doing research on the impact of competitive tendering on local authority management. Author of a number of books and articles on public sector management, most recently *Marketing and Local Government*, Longmans, 1989.

* WEBB, Adrian. Professor of Social Policy and Pro-Vice-Chancellor, Loughborough University. He is also a member of the Council on Tribunals.

List of Abbreviations

ACAS	Arbitration and Conciliation Advisory Service
ACPO	Association of Chief Police Officers
AEU	Amalgamated Engineering Union
AGRs	advanced gas-cooled reactors
AIDS	Acquired Immune Deficiency Syndrome
AMMA	Assistant Masters and Mistresses Association
APEX	Association of Professional, Executive, Clerical and Computer Staff
ASLEF	Associated Society of Locomotion Engineers and Firemen
AUT	Association of University Teachers
AWACs	Airborne Warning and Control Systems
BAAS	British Association for the Advancement of Science
BBC	British Broadcasting Corporation
BEd	Bachelor of Education
BMA	British Medical Association
BP	British Petroleum
BR	British Rail
BSB	British Satellite Broadcasting
BT	British Telecom
CAA	Civil Aviation Authority
CAP	Common Agricultural Policy
CBI	Confederation of British Industry
CCPR	Central Council of Physical Recreation
CCT	Compulsory Competitive Tendering
CEGB	Central Electricity Generating Board
CERN	European Laboratory for Particle Physics
CF	cystic fibrosis
CFCs	chlorofluoro hydrocarbons
CIPs	Cost Improvement Programmes
CLP	Constituency Labour Party
COHSE	Confederation of Health Service Employees
CPSA	Civil Service Union
CPS	Crown Prosecution Service
CSA	Campaign for a Scottish Assembly
DES	Department of Education and Science
DESO	Defence Export Services Organization

DHSS	Department of Health and Social Security
DOE	Department of the Environment
DOH	Department of Health
DM	Deutschmark
DNA	deoxyribonucleic acid
DPP	Director of Public Prosecutions
DSS	Department of Social Security
DTI	Department of Trade and Industry
DUP	Democratic Unionist Party
EC	European Community
EDM	early day motion
EETPU	Electrical, Electronic, Telecommunications & Plumbing Union
EFTA	European Free Trade Association
ELC	European Legislative Committee
EMS	European Monetary System
ENO	English National Opera
ERM	exchange rate mechanism
ET	Employment Training
ETB	English Tourist Board
FA	Football Association
FIFA	International Federation of Football Associations
FPS	Family Practitioner Services
FSA	Financial Services Act
GCHQ	Government Communication Headquarters
GCSE	General Certificate of Secondary Education
GDP	Gross Domestic Product
GEC	General Electric Company
GHS	General Household Survey
GIAs	General Improvement Areas
GLC	Greater London Council
GMB	General, Municipal and Boilermakers Union
GMSC	General Medical Services Committee
GNP	Gross National Product
GP	General Practitioner
HAAs	Housing Action Areas
HAC	Home Affairs Committee
HAT	Housing Action Trust
HCHS	Hospital and Community Health Services
HIV	Human Immuno Deficiency Virus
HMI	Her Majesty's Inspectorate
HMIC	Her Majesty's Inspectorate of Constabulary
HMS	Her Majesty's Ship
HMSO	Her Majesty's Stationery Office

HRA	Housing Revenue Account
IBA	Independent Broadcasting Authority
ICC	International Cricket Conference
ICI	Imperial Chemicals Industries
ILA	Interim Licensing Authority
ILEA	Inner London Education Authority
ILO	International Labour Organization
IMF	International Monetary Fund
INF	Intermediate Nuclear Force
IPD	interest profits and dividends
IRA	Irish Republican Army
ISC	International Signals Corporation
ISE	International Stock Exchange
IT	Information Technology
ITV	Independent Television
IVF	in-vitro fertilization
JESSI	Joint European Submicron Silicon Project
JET	Joint European Torus
LEP	Large Electron Positron
LIFFE	London International Financial Futures Exchange
LS	longitudinal study
LWT	London Weekend Television
MBA	Master of Business Administration
MEP	Member European Parliament
MI5	Military Intelligence Branch 5
MMC	Monopolies and Mergers Commission
MOD	Ministry of Defence
MORI	Market and Opinion Research International
MP	Member of Parliament
MPQM	money plus quasi money
MRC	Medical Research Council
MSF	Manufacturing, Science and Finance Union
NACAB	National Association of Citizens Advice Bureaux
NACRO	National Association for the Care and Rehabilitation of Offenders
NAHA	National Association of Health Authorities
NAHT	National Association of Head Teachers
NALGO	National and Local Government Officers
NAS/UWT	National Association of Schoolmasters/Union of Women Teachers
NATFHE	National Association of Teachers in Further and Higher Education
NATO	North Atlantic Treaty Organization

NCC	National Consumer Council
NEC	National Executive Committee (of the Labour Party)
NEDO	National Economic Development Office
N-FFO	non-fossil fuel obligation
NHS	National Health Service
NI	National Income
NICs	National Insurance Contributions
NUM	National Union of Mineworkers
NUPE	National Union of Public Employees
NUR	National Union of Railwaymen
NUT	National Union of Teachers
NVQ	National Vocational Qualification
OECD	Organization of Economic Co-operation and Development
Ofgas	Office of Gas Supply
Oftel	Office of Telecommunications
OLS	Ordinary Least Squares
OPCS	Office of Population, Censuses and Surveys
P&O	Peninsular & Oriental Steam Navigation Company
PAT	Professional Association of Teachers
PCA	Police Complaints Authority
PCBs	polychlorinated biphenyl
PGCE	Post-graduate Certificate of Education
PLC	public limited company
PLO	Palestine Liberation Organization
PLP	Parliamentary Labour Party
PQ	parliamentary questions
PR	Proportional Representation
PSDR	Public Sector Debt Repayment
PSS	Personal Social Services
PWR	pressurized water reactor
QC	Queen's Counsel
RAAs	Regional Arts Associations
RAF	Royal Air Force
RCGO	Royal College of Gynaecologists and Obstetricians
RHM	Rank Hovis Macdougall
RIBA	Royal Institute of British Architects
RN	Royal Navy
RPI	Retail Price Index
RSC	Royal Shakespeare Company
RUC	Royal Ulster Constabulary
SAEF	securities automated execution facility
SAS	Special Air Services
SDA	Scottish Development Agency

SDLP	Social Democratic and Labour Party
SDP	Social Democratic Party
SEAQ	stock exchange automatic quotation
SEM	Single European Market
Serplan	The London and South East Regional Planning Conference
SF	Sinn Fein
SHA	Secondary Heads Association
SIB	Securities and Investment Board
SITC	Standard Industrial Trade Classification
SLC	Stanford Linear Collider
SLD	Social and Liberal Democrats
SMRs	standardized mortality ratios
SNCF	Sociétè Nationale de Chemins de Fer
SNF	Short-range Nuclear Forces
SNP	Scottish National Party
SRAM	Short-range Attack Missile
SROs	Self-Regulating Organizations
SSI	Social Services Inspectorate
SSP	Statutory Sick Pay
TACs	TAURUS Account Controllers
TAURUS	Transfer and Automated Registration of Uncertificated Stock
TECs	Training and Enterprise Councils
TGV	Train de Grand Vitesse
TGWU	Transport and General Workers Union
TPFR	total period fertility rate
TSB	Trustee Savings Bank
TUC	Trades Union Congress
UDM	Union of Democratic Mineworkers
UDR	Ulster Defence Regiment
UEFA	Union of European Football Associations
UFC	University Funding Council
UGC	University Grants Committee
UMIST	University of Manchester Institute of Science and Technology
UN	United Nations
USDAW	Union of Shop, Distributive and Allied Workers
USM	Unlisted Securities Market
UUP	Ulster Unionist Party
UUUC	United Ulster Unionist Coalition
VAT	value added tax
V&A	Victoria and Albert Museum
WRU	Welsh Rugby Union
YTS	Youth Training Scheme

Introduction: The Year in Perspective

PETER CATTERALL

Contemporary history embarrasses a writer not only because he knows too much but also because what he knows is too undigested, too unconnected, too atomic. It is only after close and prolonged reflection that we begin to see why things happened as they did, and to write history instead of newspapers.
R. G. Collingwood[1]

Establishing the profile of a year such as 1989 is not an easy task. As Collingwood points out, our knowledge of it remains both too intimate and too fragmentary. There is considerable difficulty in putting the many issues that have emerged in the course of the year into perspective because we do not, in most cases, as yet know the outcome. This difficulty does not however mean that we should feel constrained to wait many years before attempting to assess the trends, events and atmosphere shaping Britain in 1989.

The First Rough Draft of History

Attempting to delineate the character of these events and trends and setting them within their context and their significance for the future is indeed a historian's task. The story of history is the story of how people have confronted the future in the circumstances in which they find themselves and its task is to provide the consciousness of the society it serves. The essays in this volume will not perhaps completely explain the how and why of Britain's circumstances in 1989. They will however provide a first rough draft, seeking to locate the current state of contemporary Britain and the issues confronting it. The kaleidoscope of newspaper headlines and the speculations of the political and economic forecasters and commentators of course have a place in this, for the consciousness-forming efforts of the media played as important a role in creating the atmosphere and providing the bar-room conversation pieces in 1989 as they have ever done. The object of this volume is not merely to summarize and assess critically the current state of policy and trends but also to preserve an image of the atmosphere, interests and concerns of Britain in 1989.

The Events of 1989

The most dramatic events of 1989 were not in Britain but were behind the rapidly disintegrating iron curtain in Eastern Europe. The changes taking place raised problems in the West for both Communist parties and policy-makers. On the spectrum of response the British government was one of those on the pragmatic and cautious extreme. Whilst the cracking of Communist rule in East Germany and the demolition of the Berlin Wall under popular pressure led Chancellor Kohl of West Germany to suggest a way forward to the reunification of the two Germanies, the question of German reunification remained one which the British government refused to discuss. It was enthusiastic about economic aid to the Eastern Bloc countries, Poland and Hungary, where progress towards genuine democracy had proceeded furthest. Whether this aid will eventually take the form of some kind of Marshall Aid, for which certain commentators were calling by the end of the year,[2] remains to be seen.

The government's delight at what it saw as the people of Eastern Europe struggling towards economic and political freedom certainly did not lead to any major reappraisal of foreign and defence policy. The argument was that a stable international climate was a necessary condition for the development of the Eastern Bloc countries towards full democracy. In its continuing emphasis on the military threat of the Warsaw Pact and its calls for vigilance the government was somewhat at variance with many of its NATO colleagues. Within the context of an emphasis on stability there was a cautious welcome of the winds of change in Eastern Europe, the continuing East–West dialogue between Presidents Gorbachev and Bush and the Conventional Forces in Europe negotiations in Vienna.[3]

Some issues have remained continually at the forefront of the news, and as a result, of the public mind throughout 1989. Environmental issues have continually been addressed since Mrs Thatcher's speech to the Royal Society in September 1988 and the publication of a Green Bill in November at the start of the new Parliamentary session ensured that they would remain prominent for the foreseeable future. In the process the significance of problems such as the hole in the ozone layer has become more widely and readily grasped. The significance of the other issue which, in 1989, refused to go away, however much Edwina Currie at times seemed to wish that it would do so, was much more easy to comprehend. As with environmental issues the importance of food quality issues throughout the year can be traced back to a high profile statement late in 1988, in this case to then junior health minister Mrs Currie's unguarded remark in December 1988 that most eggs were infected with salmonella. The allegations at the time of Conservative backbenchers and the egg industry that this charge was irresponsible and alarmist should be set in the context of the hundreds of thousands of salmonella-infected chickens the Ministry of Agriculture has since felt obliged to slaughter. Even if it was a gaffe it was clearly not without substance. It has also helped to ensure that, as with environmental issues, food quality has become a matter of urgent concern to policy-makers, as well as the press and the public. The Food Safety Bill and the Green Bill were both pieces of reactive policy making which seem certain to win by far the most bi-partisan support of all the fifteen bills announced in the Queen's speech in November 1989.

Another important issue in 1989 was the changes proposed to the Health Services and the introduction of an internal market. The publication of the White Paper on the issue in January provoked a vocal campaign of opposition from most parts of the medical profession in the same way that the Mackay Green Paper stirred up the legal professions. These campaigns looked set to continue with the publication of Bills on the subjects at the end of the year. In the process the question of the amount of hours worked by the junior doctors and their campaign to establish a statutory maximum working week of 72 hours, which had been much in the news at the start of the year, became totally overshadowed even though the issue itself remained far from resolved.

Education meanwhile remained a controversial area of policy innovation. The government in November introduced a Bill to enable the Secretary of State to introduce student loans in higher education. In the universities this was seen as being more likely to restrict rather than to help achieve the government's objective of increasing access to higher education.[4]

The Muslim response to Salman Rushdie's *The Satanic Verses* and the issues it raised for a pluralist society in which toleration and free speech are guiding principles was another enduring issue, the effects of which were felt in a whole range of areas from foreign policy to race relations. The ferocity of much of the Muslim agitation seemed to stem from a determination to avoid compromising with secular society in the way that they felt Christianity had done. Thus Shabbir Akbhar of the Bradford Council of Mosques said that the affair had shown Christians that it is a matter of shame to tolerate blasphemy[5] (though many Christians might feel this is a misreading of the nature of a religion whose Founder said, even on the cross, 'Father forgive them for they know not what they do'). The government, whilst acknowledging the offence the book caused, rejected Muslim demands for changes in the blasphemy laws. There was however much soul-searching about the implications of the affair and the need to balance the demands of free speech with the outraged feelings of a religious minority.

Other issues which emerged either in late 1988 or at the turn of the year do not yet seem to have evoked a coherent policy response. Transport, in which the interwoven issues of environmental impact, safety and the economic cost of congestion coincide, has been constantly in the news in 1989. Improving the transport infrastructure so as to ensure that Britain is not left on the periphery of Europe in the run-up to 1992 is increasingly urgent as groups such as the CBI sought to point out.[6] The government's plans are by no means as far-reaching as the CBI would like. The plans for major road improvements, announced in the May White Paper, *Roads for Prosperity*, may deal with the costs of congestion but will increase the environmental impact of the motor vehicle. On reducing the environmental cost of such vehicles the government, despite its much vaunted green credentials, has followed rather than led EC policy.

Meanwhile the rail services seem to have remained largely out of favour with the government. The resulting incoherence of policy has been most visible in the case of the Channel Tunnel link, which denied the public money provided for the road building programme announced in May, was in November put into abeyance by British Rail. This contrasted with the increasing emphasis on building high-speed rail links in the rest of Europe. It is not surprising, in the light of this and of the questions about safety raised by periodic transport disasters throughout the year, that the attack on the government's transport policy was one of the most effective aspects of the Opposition front bench's performance in 1989.

Politics and the Economy

The revival of the Labour Party in Parliament and in the opinion polls has been fuelled both by the policy review and by the government's introduction of unpopular policies. The fact that the highest profile items in the government's programme in 1989, the poll tax, the National Health Service proposals and the electricity and water privatizations, were also widely unpopular even amongst Conservative supporters (not to mention accident-prone), greatly assisted Labour. The government meanwhile began to seem vulnerable in what was formerly one of its strongest suits, its handling of the economy. This was not merely because of the differences of opinion between Nigel Lawson and Mrs Thatcher which repeatedly unsettled the financial markets; nor even because of the trade deficit and the decline of sterling in the course of the year. The latter difficulties not only suggested that the economy had been over-inflated by the loosening of fiscal policy since about 1985. They also called into question the extent to which the Thatcher years can be described as years of economic revival.

The pressure on the pound and the need to slow an over-heated economy suggested that assumptions that Britain had broken out of the post-war economic cycle into a period of high, sustainable growth were premature. As with all previous engineered booms it collapsed under the imports sucked in by the demand generated and which British industry failed to meet. The balance of trade in the process revealed the weakness of British industry. In most of the main industrial classifications Britain has a trade deficit and in major industrial categories such as consumer electronics or semi-conductors there is little British industry to speak of.[7] Whatever economic revival may have taken place during the Thatcher years the long term prospects of the economy remain bleak whilst manufacturing industry in so many important sectors remains weak or non-existent.

Meanwhile the consumer boom which followed the loosening of fiscal policy in 1987–8 showed that progress towards the enterprise and investment culture of which the government dreamed was still strictly limited. Nevertheless the government's emphasis on value for money had certainly started to infect the administration of universities and other public services.

Short-termism in the City and the preference for quick profits over long term economic recovery remained another major problem. This short-termism is partly institutional. The requirement that pension funds, a major source of investment, should report quarterly puts pressure on these major investors regularly to show results that please their beneficiaries. The leveraged buyouts that were a feature of 1989 do satisfy these beneficiaries and shareholders, though whether they do much for the economic health of the country is another matter. It certainly seems likely that the bid speculation that is a major engine of stock market activity does little for the companies that become targets. Indeed the buying up of their own shares by companies as protection against bids increased company indebtedness when investment was already becoming depressed by high interest rates.

This short-termism also operated on the foreign exchange markets. The government's reliance on interest rates to protect the currency encouraged speculators to put pressure on sterling in order to encourage rises in the interest rates. The climate of steady and high investment clearly remained a long way off. Progress on improving the supply-side of the economy meanwhile also began to appear chimeric. Concern about training began to be particularly acute in the light of the declining number of school-leavers expected in the 1990s. Despite the claims of a professed government of supplysiders the skills gap relative to competitor economies and the relative disadvantages in other areas such as transport or research and development have been but little dented in the Thatcher years.[8]

These circumstances have given Labour the opportunity to appear to have a more vigorous attitude to some of the problems confronting Britain than the government. The government's approach to the debate over the future of Europe has also enabled a newly pro-European Labour Party to appear in a favourable light.

Britain and Europe

The proposals that emerged in 1989 on the future of Europe concerned economic issues. The reaction of the British government was however dominated by its reading of the political implications. Whatever the apparent issue the real issue as far as the government was concerned was sovereignty. In its concern about this its position was not very different from that of Labour. This similarity, and the fact that their misgivings over aspects of the Delors programme were shared by European partners such as the West Germans were however obscured by the confrontational approach adopted by the British government.

The government's interest in 1992 and indeed in the EC in general is sustained by a vision of a supranational free market which it hopes to influence in the direction of free trade externally as well as internally. Other EC tendencies, such as the Social Charter, which to the government seemed to threaten a return to the dark days of union power in the 1970s they had striven so long and hard to dispel for ever, repelled the government. So did the hidden agenda of supranationalism it perceived in the further proposals for economic and monetary union. This undoubtedly lay behind Mrs Thatcher's reluctance to countenance an early entry to the European Exchange Rate Mechanism (ERM) which was such a contentious issue throughout the year, though by the end of 1989 the entry of sterling into the ERM seemed increasingly likely to take place in the coming year. This battle was fought by the Prime Minister essentially on the issue of sovereignty rather than on the question of the economic benefits. This does not seem to have been consistent with the best interests of the City or of British industry in a year in which the threat of European competition to the City has been a persistent theme in the financial pages.

In the process Mrs Thatcher latched onto the same attitude to sovereignty as those who opposed entry to Europe in the 1970s. Her emphasis was on the erosion of a specifically British sovereignty, an inevitable consequence of developments such as the 1986 Single European Act to which she acceded. She did not seem to share the vision of the pro-marketeers of the 1970s of an enhanced sovereignty through playing a positive role in EC affairs. The public image of Mrs Thatcher's relationship with Europe in 1989 remained that of implacable opposition to many of the policies and ideas emanating from Brussels.

Society and Culture

The evidence for social attitudes is necessarily circumstantial and impressionistic. There is for instance little hard evidence for the oft-repeated charge that Britain has become more selfish and greedy during the Thatcher years. It is however clear that in striving to create the circumstances in which an enterprise culture can be established the government has also created the circumstances in which greed can flourish. Because of its *laissez-faire* approach to public morality the government, beyond widely misinterpreted rhetoric about Victorian values, has only created the circumstances and not stressed the virtues which are necessary to make such a culture work.

The received image that has resulted as the latest bout of Church criticism (the 'Cry for the Poor' campaign launched in December), indicated, is of a government insufficiently concerned about people at the margins of society. These people find it increasingly difficult to pay the ever rising entry price to join the property-owning democracy that the government wishes to create. The changes in social security introduced in April 1988 tended to increase their plight, particularly in the case of the homeless, who became increasingly evident on the streets of London. As surveys throughout the year showed, too many of the homeless population – especially the younger – drift into crime and prostitution.[9] The failings of the Care in the Community programme have also resulted in large numbers of people formerly in mental health institutions being on the streets. The difficulty of securing social security and the tendency, if they are caught begging, for them to be taken to court and presented with absurd (because unpayable) fines under the archaic 1824 Vagrancy Act does little to halt this drift and reintegrate them into society. A society which operates in this fashion does seem in danger of allowing the development of an underclass as numerous commentators during the Thatcher years have warned.[10]

The government expansion of the Youth Training Scheme to the point where it is close to being able to fulfil the dream of the 1918 Education Act that either education or useful training should be available for all young people up to the age of 18 does not seem to be stemming the growing numbers of young homeless people. This presents a major policy dilemma for a government which would rather fund young people through providing them with training on the YTS, and thus provide them with at least a basis for economic independence, than support them on social security. It however first needs to reintegrate the young homeless into society. The indications by the end of 1989 were that the government was prepared to make some relaxations of the social security rules and provide extra funding in an attempt to deal with the problem of the homeless.

In at least aiming to create a basis of economic independence the government have perhaps not been as far from the founding ideals of the Welfare State, in which the emphasis was on the creation of an inclusive society in which welfare would provide the circumstances which would enable people to live fulfilled, happy and socially responsible and useful lives, as some commentators have suggested. These ideals, the *raison d'être* of the Welfare State, have not always been emphasized in the post-war years. Perhaps it was not thought necessary to emphasize them. Bernard Shaw, in his play *Major Barbara*, described poverty as the only sin and assumed that with its solution the creation of a society of morally responsible beings was assured. In fact the Welfare State has too often created the dependency cultures of which the opponents of Shaw and his fellow Fabians, the Bosanquets of the Charity Organisation Society warned and which the Thatcher government abhors. The ideals of the Welfare State, *pace* Shaw, do need to be reiterated. The unquantifiable nature of ideals does not mean that they are not important.

Britain and the Future

Various changes designed to increase effectiveness, choice and value for money, three of the guiding principles of the Thatcher government, such as to the management and finance of the NHS, were proposed in 1989. They did not go unchallenged. The government indeed ended 1989 appearing rather vulnerable, with the Prime Minister's authority having been tested for the first time by her own Party. It also faced a Labour Party revived in morale and performance. The government has had mid-term difficulties before and may well surmount them again. In doing so it will have to start to evolve a new agenda. The government has spent the 1980s fighting the union power, overloaded government and economic decline that were the demons of the 1970s. In 1989 the need to adjust to new issues, particularly the environment but also to the changing international scene, not least in Eastern Europe, became increasingly clear. The environment is not a mid-term issue but a major and intractable problem for Britain as for the rest of the world. The government has clearly grasped the increasing urgency of protecting the planet and the eco-system but its rhetoric in 1989 outshone its actions. For instance, Mrs Thatcher was the only leader to oppose the $18 billion Planet Protection Fund proposed by Rajiv Gandhi at the Commonwealth Heads of Government meeting in Kuala Lumpur in October. The Gandhi agenda included the need for some recompense from the West to ensure that any reductions in emissions of greenhouse gases in the developed world are not more than replaced in the process of industrialization in the Third World. Whether the government can reconcile the claims of such programmes and the need to reduce emissions of greenhouse gases from British industry with its original objective of British economic revival remains to be seen.

Notes

1. R. G. Collingwood, *Speculum Mentis,* Clarendon, 1924, p. 82.
2. Ben Pimlott, 'Administrative socialism is dead', *Samizdat,* 7 Nov/Dec 1989, pp. 1–2.
3. Mark Urban, 'Britain out of step with Nato over military spending', *The Independent,* 2 December 1989.
4. Lord Flowers, speech at the Royal Albert Hall, 13 December 1989. This concern was supported by the survey, 'Opportunity Lost' National Union of Students 1989.
5. The Independent, 23 November 1989.
6. Trade Roads to the Future, CBI, 1989.
7. Paul Ormerod and Will Hutton, 'Britain's economy: What is to be done,' *Samizdat,* 7 Nov/Dec 1989, pp. 3–5.
8. Science and Public Expenditure 1989: A Report to the Secretary of State for Education and Science from the Advisory Board for the Research Councils Department of Education and Science 1989 and Annual Review of Government-Funded Research and Development 1989, HMSO, 1989.
9. *One Day I'll have My Own Place to Stay,* Shelter/Central London Social Security Advisers' Forum 1989, *Raising the Roof on Housing Myths,* Shelter, 1989 and *Young Runaways . . . Findings from Britain's First Safe House,* Church of England Children's Society, 1989.
10. Terence Morris, *Crime and Criminal Justice since 1945,* argues that an underclass has already emerged, Basil Blackwell, 1989, p. 168.

Central Administration

PETER HENNESSY

Introduction

The year in Whitehall was dominated by two themes: one displayed in technicolour; the other not as visible as it deserved to be. This was the year of the great debate about Mrs Thatcher's style as Prime Minister. That old faithful of the examination paper – prime ministerial versus Cabinet government – came to preoccupy political discussion in a fashion rare for constitutional issues. It was triggered by a trio of events: the tenth anniversary of Mrs Thatcher's premiership in May; her extensive and unexpectedly dramatic Cabinet reshuffle in July; and the resignation of Nigel Lawson from the Treasury in October over both the content of exchange rate policy and the Prime Minister's methods of making it.

Less spectacularly, but, almost certainly more importantly for the way in which Britain is governed in the long term, the *Next Steps* programme for hiving-off large chunks of government activity into freestanding 'executive agencies' proceeded apace. With every passing month, the prospect grew stronger of a Whitehall transformed in its pay, recruitment, financial and work practices by the end of the century which, if it actually happens, will amount to a revolution without precedent in the peacetime history of the modern Civil Service.

Looking to the future in a different sense, the Labour Party began to prepare for a return to power. Plans were announced to beef-up the status and power of the Department of Trade and Industry relative to the Treasury in Whitehall. Labour also pledged an elected Scottish Assembly in Edinburgh with substantial delegated powers and its own administrative back-up. A leading member of the Shadow Cabinet, Dr John Cunningham, raised the possibility of a change in a small number of top posts in Whitehall in the event of a Labour government in instances where civil servants were thought to be too close to the policies of the Conservative administration.

The Next Steps

Though the *Next Steps* report was conceived as an idea in 1986 by Mrs Thatcher's then Efficiency Adviser, Sir Robin Ibbs, presented to her in 1987 and published in 1988, only in 1989 did its full significance become apparent in qualitative, if not yet quantitative terms.

By the time the government reported progress to Parliament at the end of October (in Cm 841, the latest of a series of replies to reports from the all-party House of Commons Select Committee on the Treasury and the Civil Service), 10 agencies were up and running with a further 40 blocks of work identified as candidates for agency treatment (see chart). By the summer of 1990 it was expected that the number of operational agencies would have doubled. By the end of the century, it was predicted, three- quarters of Civil Service manpower could be working in them. From the variety of pay, recruitment, financial and management systems agreed by the Treasury, the Cabinet Office (from where the project was managed) and the sponsoring department and incorporated in the charters (or 'framework agreements') of the new agencies, it was already apparent by the winter of 1989 that the old wiring systems of Whitehall budgeting and Treasury control, established 70 years earlier by David Lloyd George and Sir Warren Fisher, were being dug-up and replaced on the grand scale. So far and so fast has change proceeded that some Whitehall figures wondered privately if the concept of a unified Civil Service would survive in anything but name.

It was the government's position that it would and, as Cm 841 put it, it 'expects Agencies to combine the very best in the public sector traditions of fairness and impartiality with a continuing commitment to improve the quality of service offered to the public'. Both the head of the Home Civil Service, Sir Robin Butler, and the *Next Steps* project manager, Peter Kemp, put their views of the new philosophy on record before the Commons Treasury and Civil Service Committee and in press interviews.

Sir Robin regarded the *Next Steps* reforms as a much-needed recognition that Whitehall was a federation of departments, comparable in its way to a multinational company with a small headquarters staff (in this case the Cabinet Office and the Treasury) to which subsidiaries were answerable for their overall stewardship. One benefit of devolved responsibility for pay, recruitment and the patten of work to agency chief executives and line managers was that employees no longer had to assume the permanent secretary was responsible for everything, requiring them to look over their shoulders before taking any initiative involving public expenditure.[1]

For his part, Mr Kemp saw the concept of *Next Steps* as 'a new idea of getting the best of both worlds, filling a gap in the management armoury of this country... It's a public sector owner and broad public sector rules with a private sector approach to running businesses because that's what many Civil Service activities are.'[2]

There was open recognition in Whitehall that the testing-ground for the *Next Steps* would not be any of the terrain covered by the first wave of agency creations. That would come when the biggest Civil Service businesses received the agency treatment such as the Employment Service and the social security benefits system. As one of his last acts as Secretary of State for Social Security, John Moore announced that the benefits system would be broken up into two or possibly three agencies (benefits, information technology and, maybe, contributions). Much of 1989 was taken up by planning the details of the huge transition which will put 70,000 staff and Whitehall's biggest budget (£50 billions) into a Benefit Agency by the spring of 1990 and a 3,000-strong Information Technology Services Agency a year before that. Nick Montagu, Principal Establishments Officer at the Department of Social Security, admitted: 'We're the showpiece. If we succeed in the biggest executive operation, we can succeed with almost any operation.'[3]

Executive Agencies established	Staff*
Vehicle Inspectorate	1,550
Companies House	1,150
Her Majesty's Stationery Office	3,200
National Weights and Measures Laboratory	50
Warren Spring Laboratory	300
Resettlement Agency	550
Civil Service College	200
Queen Elizabeth II Conference Centre	50
Historical Royal Palaces	350
Laboratory of the Government Chemist	300
TOTAL	7,700

Executive Agency candidates announced	
Air Office Training (Defence Support)	2,000†
Building Research Establishment	650
Cadw	200
Central Office of Information	800
Central Statistical Office	1,000
Central Veterinary Laboratory	550
Civil Service Commission	300
Defence Research Agency	12,000
Department of the Registers of Scotland	950
Director General of Defence Accounts (Defence Support)	2,100
Driver Testing and Training	2,000
Drive Vehicle Licensing Directorate	5,400
Employment Service	35,000
Forensic Science Service	550
Fuel Suppliers Branch (Crown Suppliers)	under 50
Her Majesty's Land Registry	10,500
Historical Buildings and Monuments Directorate	500

Hydrographer of the Navy (Defence Support)	900†
Insolvency Service	1,400
Intervention Board for Agricultural Produce	800
Meteorological Office	2,250
Military Survey (Defence Support)	800†
National Engineering Laboratory	600
National Physical Laboratory	750
Occupational Health Service	100
Passport Department	1,100
Patent Office	1,300
Planning Inspectorate	500
Property Holdings	1,600
Radiocommunications Division	450
Royal Parks	550
Service Children Education Authority (Defence Support)	1,300‡
Social Security Operations Benefits	77,000
Social Security Operations IT Services	2,900
Training Agency	11,800
Vehicle Component Approval Division	100
Veterinary Medicines Directorate	50
TOTAL	180,700

*   Figures are based on staff in post as at 1 July 1989
†   Figure does not include Service personnel
‡   Figure does not include locally recruited staff

Cabinet Government

In the dying days of 1988, Sir Leon Brittan, about to depart for Brussels as an EC Commissioner, told a seminar on 'Constitutional Development' at the Policy Studies Institute in London that he had 'no intention of entering the increasingly moribund debate about whether the present Prime Minister is any more or less powerful than others'.[4] 'Moribund' it was not in 1989. It glowed at the time of the summer reshuffle when Sir Geoffrey Howe was transferred from the Foreign Office to become Leader of the House of Commons and Deputy Prime Minister (that office 'unknown to the constitution' as commentators like to put it each time someone is awarded it).

It well and truly caught fire when Nigel Lawson resigned as Chancellor of the Exchequer over the role of Professor Sir Alan Walters, Mrs Thatcher's Downing Street economic adviser. Accusations of 'one person' government, obituaries for 'the death of Cabinet government' revived *fortissimo*, surpassing even the Westland furore in 1986. There were echoes in Mr Lawson's resignation speech in the House of Commons of Michael Heseltine's complaint in 1986 that his European solution to the problems of the Westland helicopter company had not received the full collective discussion it merited in Cabinet or Cabinet committee.[5]

Another sensitive European issue – whether or not Britain should join the Exchange Rate Mechanism (ERM) of the European Monetary System – was Mr Lawson's on 31 October. The implication of his words was that, for all its centrality to the government's overall economic strategy, the ERM had not in recent months reached the agenda of the Cabinet. A key question of economic policy, Mr Lawson told the Commons:

is where the exchange rate fits in. Is it to be part of the maximum practicable market freedom or is it to be part, indeed a central part, of the necessary financial discipline?

I recognize a case can be made for either approach. No case can be made for seeming confusion or apparent vacillation between these two positions.

Moreover, for our system of Cabinet government to work effectively, the prime minister of the day must appoint ministers that he or she trusts and then leave them to carry out the policy. When differences of view emerge, as they are bound to do from time to time, they should be resolved privately and, wherever appropriate, collectively.[6]

As with Westland there were calls from within the Conservative Party for more of a team approach to policy-making. Douglas Hurd, transferred from the Home to the Foreign Office as part of the post-Lawson ministerial dispositions, reminded the public in his first television interview as Foreign Secretary of what he had said after Mr Heseltine's departure, 'I think it is very important that people should see that we are under Cabinet government.'[7]

Like Westland before it, the Lawson affair stimulated Mrs Thatcher to make a vigorous defence of her prime ministerial style:

A leader must lead, must lead firmly, have firm convictions, and see that those convictions are reflected in every piece of policy.

How can I change Margaret Thatcher? I am what I am.[8]

I am not an 'I' person, I am not an 'I did this in my government', 'I did that'. I have never been an 'I' person so I talk about 'We' – the government. I cannot do things alone so it has to be 'we'. It is a Cabinet 'we'.[9]

Yes, I do lead from the front. Yes, I do have fundamental convictions . . . But we do have very lively discussions because that's the way I operate . . . then we reach collective decisions. That's collective responsibility.[10]

Is it? Such questions cannot be answered emphatically without allowing in the contaminant of prejudice. But 'moribund' the debate was not. For about a month the political nation spoke of little else.

The Cabinet
Prime Minister and First Lord of the Treasury
 Rt Hon Margaret Thatcher MP
Secretary of State for Foreign and Commonwealth Affairs
 Rt Hon Sir Geoffrey Howe QC MP

Rt Hon John Major MP (24 July 1989)
Rt Hon Douglas Hurd CBE MP (27 Oct 1989)
Chancellor of the Exchequer
Rt Hon Nigel Lawson MP
Rt Hon John Major MP (27 Oct 1989)
Lord Chancellor
Rt Hon The Lord Mackay of Clashfern
Secretary of State for the Home Office
Rt Hon Douglas Hurd CBE MP
Rt Hon David Waddington QC MP (27 Oct 1989)
Secretary of State for Wales
Rt Hon Peter Walker MBE MP
Secretary of State for Defence
Rt Hon George Younger TD MP
Rt Hon Tom King MP (24 July 1989)
Secretary of State for Employment
Rt Hon Norman Fowler MP
Secretary of State for Northern Ireland
Rt Hon Tom King MP
Rt Hon Peter Brooke MP (24 July 1989)
Secretary of State for the Environment
Rt Hon Nicholas Ridley MP
Rt Hon Christopher Patten MP (24 July 1989)
Secretary of State for Trade and Industry
Rt Hon The Lord Young of Graffham
Rt Hon Nicholas Ridley MP (24 July 1989)
Chancellor of the Duchy of Lancaster
Rt Hon Anthony Newton OBE MP
Rt Hon Kenneth Baker MP (24 July 1989)
Minister of Agriculture, Fisheries and Food
Rt Hon John MacGregor OBE MP
Rt Hon John Selwyn Gummer MP (24 July 1989)
Secretary of State for Scotland
Rt Hon Malcolm Rifkind QC MP
Secretary of State for Transport
Rt Hon Paul Channon MP
Rt Hon Cecil Parkinson MP (24 July 1989)
Secretary of State for Health
Rt Hon Kenneth Clarke QC MP
Secretary of State for Social Security
Rt Hon John Moore MP
Rt Hon Anthony Newton OBE MP
Lord President of the Council and Leader of the House of Commons
Rt Hon John Wakeham MP
Rt Hon Sir Geoffrey Howe QC MP (24 July 1989)
Lord Privy Seal and Leader of the House of Lords
Rt Hon The Lord Belstead JP DL

Secretary of State for Energy
    Rt Hon Cecil Parkinson MP
    Rt Hon John Wakeham MP (24 July 1989)
Chief Secretary of the Treasury
    Rt Hon John Major MP
    Rt Hon Norman Lamont MP (24 July 1989)

Labour Plans for Power

Labour's improved showing in the polls, the publication of its policy review in the Spring plus the government's difficulties of various kinds, shifted attention to what the Opposition might do it if acquired power after the next election. Its policy document, *Meet the Challenge, Make the Change*, placed especial emphasis on 'the need for a medium-term industrial strategy administered by a transformed Department of Trade and Industry.'[11]

John Smith, the Shadow Chancellor, explained in a newspaper interview that 'The Treasury shouldn't be running industrial policy. It has enough to do running macro-economic policy.' Looking back to 1964 when Harold Wilson had established the Department of Economic Affairs to live in 'creative tension' with the Treasury, Mr Smith went on:

The Department of Economic Affairs was not a success because it was a co-ordinating department. It didn't have its own territory, standing or weight. That was an error which led us to the view that the new ministry should be a strengthened Department of Trade and Industry. We very much deplore the loss of power and status of the DTI in recent years. We want much more of a powerhouse ministry, not subordinate to the Treasury but equal with it.[12]

The need for parity of esteem between the Treasury and the DTI was a theme common to Labour's economic shadow ministers. Where they did not speak with one voice was on the future of top people in Whitehall. John Smith saw no need to change the mix in the Treasury. 'I don't have any doubts about their intellectual calibre,' he said.[13]

By contrast, Dr John Cunningham as Shadow Environment Minister raised doubts publicly about his ability to work with Sir Terence Heiser, Permanent Secretary at the Department of the Environment:

... there would either have to be a remarkable change of attitude towards local government and the exercise of power by Mr Heiser or he'd have to go. Frankly, from what I know of his views and attitudes over the last five years, I couldn't see he and I working together if I was to be Secretary of State for the Environment.[14]

Another member of the Shadow Cabinet, Michael Meacher, welcomed the creation of *Next Steps* agencies as 'Cracking the monolith would allow us to ditch the pretence of a non-political service even at the highest policy levels. Most permanent secretaries are now deeply imbued with the values of Thatcherism, even those in less overtly "political" areas.[15]

The opinion that really counts, however, is Neil Kinnock's. He hasn't updated it, in public at least, since a television interview in 1985 in which he said: 'I don't know about the permanent secretaries. We obviously have to examine the degree of enthusiasm and loyalty that they are prepared to demonstrate in support of a Labour government and in the implementation of the policy of that government. I'm prepared to work on . . . the conventional basis, which has stood us in good stead in Britain, about the way in which civil servants are prepared to work.'[16]

Footnote

As I complete this chapter in early December 1989, the possibility of a public and dramatic change in the way senior civil servants work was beginning to become apparent. The televizing of Parliament and its select committees looked set to put permanent secretaries in the limelight not just in exceptional circumstances, but routinely. Footage of Sir Peter Gregson, Permanent Secretary to the Department of Trade and Industry, defending the financial background of the sale of Rover to British Aerospace before the Public Accounts Committee, was a star item on the news bulletins of all major television channels on the evening of Monday, 4 December. It was the shape of things to come.

Notes

1. *The Independent*, 31 July 1989.
2. *The Independent*, 13 February 1989.
3. *The Independent*, 9 October 1989.
4. Leon Brittan, *Discussions on Policy*, Policy Studies Institute, 1989, p. 75. Sir Leon's remarks were delivered during an after dinner presentation at PSI on 5 December 1988.
5. Michael Heseltine, 'When I knew I had to go', *Observer*, 12 January 1986.
6. Stephen Goodwin, 'Britain must join ERM "as soon as practicable"', *The Independent*, 1 November 1989.
7. Mr Hurd first delivered this judgement on London Weekend Television's 'Weekend World', 26 January 1986. He repeated it on 'Panorama', BBC1, 30 October 1989.
8. Jean Rook, 'Who dares to say that I'm finished?', *Daily Express*, 28 October 1989.
9. Robin Oakley, 'By popular acclaim I am happy to carry on as the party leader', *The Times*, 24 November 1989.
10. BBC1, 'Panorama', 27 November 1989.
11. *Meet the Challenge, Make the Change*, Labour Party, 1989, p. 10.
12. Peter Hennessy, 'Whitehall Watch: Enhancing the status of industry', *The Independent*, 13 November 1989.
13. Ibid.
14. Peter Hennessy, 'Whitehall Watch: Why new masters could mean wholesale change', *The Independent*, 9 January 1989.

15. Colin Brown, 'Labour "set to break power of mandarins"', *The Independent*, 28 November 1989.
16. Mr Kinnock was interviewed by Peter Jay on 'A Week in Politics', Brook Productions, Channel 4 Television, 24 May 1985.

Chronology

9 Jan: Labour frontbencher Dr John Cunningham attacks the politicization of the higher Civil Service and states that a number of senior civil servants appointed by Thatcher would not be acceptable to a future Labour government.

9 Feb: The government announces that 34,000 Whitehall jobs are to be shifted to the regions.

19 Feb: The Property Services Agency is severely censured for management failures by the Public Accounts Committee.

1 Mar: Lord Young launches a £600,000 advertising campaign to promote temporary job swaps between the Civil Service and industry (the DTI's Bridge Programme).

20 Mar: Announcement that Britain's four main non-nuclear defence research establishments are to become a self- supporting agency in Spring 1991 taking work from the private sector and foreign countries under the government's *Next Steps* programme.

5 Apr: Sir Leon Brittan reopens the Westland Affair by blaming 10 Downing Street for giving approval for the leak designed to damage Michael Heseltine.

Nigel Lawson becomes the minister responsible for the Central Statistical Office. Its powers are widened to embrace the production of nearly all Great Britain's key economic indicators, as a result of a Cabinet Office inquiry into how to improve Great Britain's highly inaccurate economic statistics.

10 Apr: Peter Walker criticizes the government's economic record, prompting media speculation, eventually proved to be unfounded, that he will be sacked from the Welsh Office later in the year.

19 Apr: The Civil Service Commission reports difficulties in recruiting executive officers for the South East and in specialist areas.

2 May: A report on 'Top Management Information Systems' in Whitehall is published.

Sir Alan Walters returns as Mrs Thatcher's personal economic adviser.

4 May: The tenth anniversary of Mrs Thatcher's coming to power.

5 May: Announcement that Sir David Hancock, the permanent secretary at the DES, is to be replaced by John Cairnes on 1 July.

17 May: John Moore announces moves to turn the Social Security service into two or three agencies.

5 June: Bob Kemp's report on the Export Credit Guarantee Department suggests that its Insurance Service Group should be privatized and the rest moved from its costly city headquarters.

24 July: Seventeen men moved in Thatcher's Cabinet reshuffle. A reshuffle of the lower levels of government also begins.

2,500 Inland Revenue officials are to move out of London from 1992, mostly to Nottingham.

25 July: Controversy begins as it is revealed that Mrs Thatcher offered Sir Geoffrey Howe the Home Secretaryship in her efforts to reshuffle him, prompting feeling that both he and Douglas Hurd had been shabbily treated.

Commons Treasury and Civil Service committee *Developments in the Next Steps Programme*, HC Paper 348 published.

17 Aug: Commons Treasury and Civil Service Committee *The Presentation of Information on Public Expenditure* published.

28 Aug: 'Panorama' on BBC Television accuses the government of using its advertising budget for Party political purposes.

3 Sept: The Institution of Professional and Civil Servants is relaunched as the Institution of Professionals, Managers and Specialists.

8 Oct: Calls for an independent watchdog on government statistical services made.

25 Oct: Reports that Professor Bernard Benjamin's report *Accessibility and other problems relating to statistics used by social scientists*, which questions the integrity of official statistics, has been buried by the Economic and Social Research Council.

26 Oct: Nigel Lawson resigns as Chancellor of the Exchequer because his economic policy has not received the full support of the Prime Minister since Sir Alan Walters returned as her personal economic adviser in the summer. Later in the evening Walters also resigned. In the ensuing reshuffle John Major moved to the Exchequer, being replaced at the Foreign Office by Douglas Hurd who was in turn replaced at the Home Office by David Waddington, formerly the Chief Whip.

28 Oct: Speech by Sir Geoffrey Howe is taken to indicate that he and certain Cabinet colleagues are prepared to stand up to the Prime Minister's adamant opposition to the EMS.

30 Oct: Downing Street lunch with senior Ministers and backbenchers at which the Prime Minister was apparently warned to curb her authoritarian style and restore Cabinet government.

Leading social scientists launch a campaign to establish an independent watchdog to monitor and analyse government statistics.

31 Oct: Full-scale denunciation of the style and substance of Mrs Thatcher's leadership and of her policies on the EMS made by Lawson in his first Commons speech since his resignation.

2 Nov: Bernard Porter, *Plots and Paranoia: A History of Political Espionage in Britain 1790–1988*, Unwin Hyman, argues that Britons have been spied on more in the 1980s than at any other time in their history.

Nigel Lawson on LWT's 'The Walden Interview' rebuts the Thatcher version of his resignation.

14 Nov: The creation of a head office of the NHS at Leeds, enabling the Department of Health to concentrate on policy-making, is announced.

15 Nov: Relocation of 1,700 customs and excise jobs from the South-East to the North-West announced.

21 Nov: Privatization of the Crown Suppliers announced in the Queen's speech.

23 Nov: Announcement that the Royal Mint is to become a free standing executive agency from April 1990.

1 Dec: Announcement that the Employment Service is to become a semi-independent government agency in spring 1990.

5 Dec: National Audit Office Publicity Services for Government Departments, HMSO, criticizes inefficiency and financial waste in government publicity.

6 Dec: Second reading of the Property Services Agency and Crown Suppliers Bill, privatizing both agencies, is passed in the Commons by 237 to 181.

13 Dec: Criticism of inefficient financial management by government departments in the National Audit Office's annual report.

14 Dec: White Paper published on *The Financing and Accountability of Next Steps Agencies*, HMSO.

Parliament

PHILIP NORTON

House of Commons

The parliamentary year witnessed some glaring high points: the appearance of Edwina Currie before the Select Committee on Agriculture in February and the resignation speech of former Chancellor of the Exchequer, Nigel Lawson, in November, among them. Members of Parliament (MPs) continued to demonstrate some independent voting behaviour, as they had done in previous sessions, though not to the extent that threatened the government's majority. However, the two most significant features of the session were not to be found in the more publicly noteworthy of *particular* activities by prominent MPs. What was significant was, first, the growing recognition of challenges faced by the House and, second, the sheer extent of members' activities. The first constituted an opportunity for the House, the second a problem.

Two Principal Challenges

During 1989, there was a growing realization by MPs that they faced two major challenges. One was presented by the consequences of the Single European Act, the other by television.

The Single European Act came into effect in 1987. Parliament had discussed and approved the measure – a treaty amendment – in 1986. The motivation for approving the measure was essentially economic: it was a mechanism for helping achieve completion of the Single European Market (SEM). Only in the past year or so, prompted especially by the Bruges Speech of the Prime Minister in September 1988, have MPs become exercized by the constitutional implications of the Act. The Act extended provision for weighted majority voting in the Council of Ministers and introduced the co-operation procedure for European Community (EC) legislation. The effect was to shift the power relationship not only *within* the institutions of the EC but also *between* the institutions of the EC and the institutions of the member states. A greater decision-making competence was transferred to Brussels. How was Parliament to deal with the changed situation? It had taken considerable time to respond to initial membership of the Community. A European Legislation Committee (ELC) had been established in 1974. The new Select Committees created in 1979 were – and remain – able to consider any EC matters drawn to their attention by the ELC. However, the ELC does not enjoy as wide a remit as the European Communities Committee of the House of Lords, nor does it indulge in the extensive evidence-taking indulged in by the Lords Committee.[1] Investigations by the departmentally-related select committees have been sporadic, with practice varying from committee to committee. The consequences of the Single European Act have highlighted what is increasingly an unsatisfactory situation.

As a response to the changed conditions wrought by the Single European Act, the Select Committee on Procedure began an investigation into how the House might respond in order to ensure a greater input into Community policy-making. During the year, the Committee held a number of evidence-taking sessions, its witnesses including former Leader of the House, John Biffen, Leader of the European Democratic Group in the European Parliament, Christopher Prout (who provided committee members with an invaluable summary of the EC legislative process), MEP-turned-MP Joyce Quin, and the Chairman of the Commons' Liaison Committee, Terence Higgins. The hearings demonstrated both the extent to which the links between the Westminster and European Parliaments remain tenuous (not least in comparison with the experience of other member states) and the opportunity afforded by the new conditions to develop closer, more formally-recognized links. Various proposals were advanced: a Grand European Committee of the Commons, the departmentally-related Select Committees having power to appoint sub-committees to consider EC business, MEPs being empowered to take part in the proceedings of the Commons or its committees, and – an idea put in the public domain by Michael Heseltine, but beyond the remit of the Procedure Committee – a second chamber of the European Parliament with members drawn from Parliaments of the member states. The Committee reported at the end of the year. There were two strands running through its report: one was the need to enhance scrutiny of proposed EC legislation, the other was to build links with EC institutions, not least MEPs. To achieve the former, it recommended especially the creation of five special standing committees, each with responsibility to scrutinize EC documents in particular sectors, and the extension of the terms of reference of the existing scrutiny committee to encompass broad trends in EC policy. To achieve the latter, it urged in effect a new attitude towards the changed conditions, encouraging select committees in particular to develop links with both the Commission and MEPs.[2] Though the report was not as ambitious as some observers had hoped for, its tone was essentially positive rather than defensive, recognizing there were new opportunities for the House to exploit.

The second challenge arises from the televising of proceedings in the House of Commons. On 9 February 1988, the Commons voted – to the surprise of many commentators – in favour of an experimental period of televised broadcasting. A select committee was appointed to make recommendations on how the experiment should be conducted. The lengthy deliberations of the committee ensured that the experiment did not begin, as some proponents hoped it would, with the Queen's Speech at the opening of the 1988–9 session. The committee reported in May and the House debated its recommendations on 12 June. The recommendations on camera shots in the chamber were well summarized by the then Leader of the House, John Wakeham: 'We . . . propose a number of specific guidelines for the director to observe, chief among which are the designation of a standard head and shoulders shot, limited use of wide-angle shots, a strict limitation on the use of reaction shots and a prohibition of the use of split-screen and panning shots.'[3] The House approved the Committee's report by 293 votes to 69 and the televising of the House began when the House returned for the new session on 21 November. The Commons thus followed in the footsteps of the House of Lords, which has permitted televised broadcasting of its proceedings since 1985.

In the initial stages, televising proceedings is problematic. For many members, the rules governing camera shots – though not as limiting in practice as many feared would be the case – are unnecessarily restrictive. It will take some time for broadcasters to determine whether they have achieved, in terms of time and focus, coverage that proves attractive to viewers. However, in the long term, the opportunities afforded by the experiment are likely to prove substantial. By widening public knowledge of parliamentary debates, the House may acquire new political muscle. Coverage of select committees – already more extensive than many observers expected – provides a major opportunity both to enhance the reputation of the House and to increase Committee influence. There is also the likelihood of a greater emphasis on the role of the individual MP, already apparent in the coverage given by regional news and current affairs programmes. Though the radio broadcasting of proceedings has not been successful, the first two months of televising proceedings suggests that, as with the House of Lords, the entry of the cameras is likely to prove a notable success.

The House of Commons is thus in a position where, if it exploits both challenges to the full, it can enhance its political clout in policy making, both at national and supranational level. If members treat both as threats rather than challenges, there is a very real danger that parliamentary influence will decline. Which direction the House takes will, ultimately, be determined by MPs themselves.

A More Active House

Over the past two decades, the House of Commons has become a more active House. In part, this increased activity is the product of greater demands being made of it. There has been a substantial legislative load. Bills have not necessarily been more numerous, but they have often been substantial in length and contentious in nature. The past session witnessed a record number of bills – ten – being guillotined.

However, the increased activity has also been the produce of supply. MPs have made far greater use of the mechanisms available to raise issues and question government. The most observable and quantifiable indicators of this development are the number of parliamentary questions (PQs) tabled, the number of letters sent by MPs to ministers, and the number of Early Day Motions (EDMs) tabled.

Parliamentary questions are tabled for a variety of purposes: to keep ministers on their toes, to raise particular issues with the departments, to pursue constituency grievances, to embarrass the government, and often concomitantly to raise the profile of the questioning members. Some – especially written questions – actually seek information, either for the member or for a constituent or outside group. In most of the parliamentary sessions of the 1970s, fewer than 40,000 questions (written or oral) were tabled. In an average length session today, the number is closer to 50,000. (In the long session of 1987–8, the number was just over 74,000.) In the past session, the number exceeded 63,472.

Of probably greater importance, in terms of effectiveness, is the correspondence that takes place between MPs and those of their number who are ministers. Writing letters to ministers is a well-used method for pursuing constituency casework; it is more popular than tabling questions and generally judged by MPs to be more effective.[4] Letters from members receive priority within a department and replies carry ministerial signatures. Replies are often detailed and in most cases will tend to provide the explanation sought. Letter writing, once rarely indulged in, is not a significant part of an MP's activity. Extensive by the beginning of the 1980s, it has shown a further notable increase over the past few years. A survey of departments, carried out through a series of written PQs in 1982, found that approximately 10,000 letters in one month (January 1982) were written by MPs to ministers. A series of written PQs, tabled just before the 1989 summer recess by James Cran, the Member for Beverley, revealed an increase over 1982 of approximately 50 per cent: in January 1989 more than 15,000 letters were written. For the session up to the summer recess (an eight-month period), the total exceeded 100,000. Departments with a particularly heavy parliamentary mailbag included Environment, Social Security, Home Office, Foreign Office, and Health.

Early Day Motions constitute a form of parliamentary notice board. Technically they are motions for debate 'on an early day'. As time is usually never available, the motions serve instead to demonstrate the strength of opinion on a range of issues: MPs who agree with the motion add their signatures to it. In the past, the practice has been for departments to monitor such motions and for ministers to advise the Leader of the House of how to respond should reference be made to a particular EDM during the weekly business questions. Occasionally an EDM has attracted so many signatures that it has influenced government action. However, the order paper in recent years has been subject to a proliferation of EDMs. A number are frivolous (congratulating a football team for example), others are highly detailed; an increasing number are used for partisan point-scoring. A decade ago, three or four hundred EDMs would normally be tabled in one session. Today, more than 1,000 are tabled. The 1988–9 session saw a total of 1,420 motions appearing on the order paper. A consequence of the number, as well as the nature, of EDMs now appearing is that departments now spend little if any time monitoring them. A motion attracting a large number of signatories will continue to attract attention – the most recent example being that, towards the end of the year, on the issue of war widows' pensions; others are now largely ignored.

The reasons for this greater activity on the part of members are, in part, the greater competition among MPs to raise their political profiles in order to achieve political advancement and, more especially, the greater expectations of constituents. Recent years have witnessed a significant increase in constituency casework for members. This is reflected in the letters received from constituents. A survey by the Letter Writing Bureau in 1986 found that most MPs each received more than 100 letters a week; a separate survey in 1987 found that for some MPs this represented a doubling of the number they received in 1984.[5] MPs have responded by spending more time in their constituencies and by pursuing constituents' grievances through the various parliamentary mechanisms available. For the members, there is an opportunity cost: the time that could be spent scrutinizing government policy. At the same time, especially for new members, there is a potential reward. There is increasing evidence that there is some electoral payoff from constituency work, greater than was previously presumed to be the case; first-term incumbents who were active in their constituencies did significantly better than other members in the 1987 general election.[6] However, from the perspective of the House as a whole there is a problem. In terms of usage, Question Time and EDMs – and to some degree, correspondence with ministers – are now reaching saturation point. EDMs are now close to being killed through over-use. Hence, there is what may be termed parliamentary overload. Overload – unlike the Single European Act and televising proceedings – presents no obvious opportunity by which the House can actually improve its capacity to influence public policy. There is a clear problem; for the House, it is a case of deciding how best to manage the problem. There are no obvious solutions under immediate discussion and likely to be implemented in the near future. The situation is likely to get worse before it gets better.

The House of Lords

The Upper House witnessed a notable increase in activity (and voting independence) in the 1970s. The number of peers attending increased significantly, as did the number of defeats imposed on the government. (The Labour government of 1974–9 suffered the embarrassment of 347 defeats.) These changes have been attributed to the growth in the number of life peers an to the realization among peers that – following the abandonment of the Parliament (No. 2) Bill in 1969 – reform of the House was not likely to occur in the near future; hence they might as well make the most of the existing framework.[7]

The 1980s witnessed a continuation of both activity and independence. The average number of questions tabled for written answer in a session more than doubled in the 1980s compared with the 1970s. Despite a preponderance of Conservative peers, succeeding Parliaments witnessed government defeats. In ten years, the Thatcher government witnessed more than 130 defeats. Several of these took place in the 1988–9 session, principally in May and November on the government's privatization measures for water and electricity, thus allaying the fears of some Opposition peers that the opportunities to defeat the government had disappeared. The activity of the House was also reflected in work off the floor of the House. The two sessional committees of the House – on the European Communities and on Science and Technology – continued their work and were joined by an *ad hoc* committee, the Select Committee on Murder and Life Imprisonment. Appointed in July 1988 to consider the scope and definition of the offence of murder, and whether life imprisonment should remain a mandatory rather than a maximum penalty for murder, the Committee took extensive evidence from a wide range of bodies and even from a number of prisoners; various meetings of the Committee were held in HM Prisons. The report of the Committee (recommending a statutory definition of murder and that mandatory life sentences should be abolished) was published in October and debated by the House in November.[8] The work of this and the sessional committees show the Upper House at its best, allowing for thorough scrutiny of particular topics through a number of detached (and often dedicated) peers examining evidence presented by those with expert knowledge or those most affected by the matter under consideration.

The past session was, for the House, a fairly full and reasonably productive one. Nonetheless, various problems were apparent. The House subjects legislation to scrutiny often more extensively than is possible in the Commons. That scrutiny is valuable but the extent of the legislation that the House now considers is such that an increasing proportion of the time of the House is taken up with legislative scrutiny. Whereas before 1980, sometimes less than 40 per cent of the time of the House was devoted to such scrutiny, in an average session in the late 1980s it exceeded 50 per cent, occasionally reaching 60 per cent. There is thus less time for general debates, thus reducing the opportunity for peers to raise and debate issues that might otherwise be ignored. This debating function is an important and distinctive one, and by concentrating more on legislative scrutiny there is the danger the House will emulate more the House of Commons. The increase in legislative scrutiny also points to the increasing burden on the House, which has been apparent for a number of years. To get through scrutiny of government Bills, which will often reach the Lords late in the session, the House will normally sit a week or so longer than the Commons when the latter rises for the summer recess and return a week earlier than the Commons in October. The year 1989 was no exception. In the second week of October, Conservative peers had a choice of attending the House or the Conservative Party Conference, a dilemma never faced by Conservative MPs. In 1986, pressure on the House was such that the then Leader of the House, Viscount Whitelaw, established a Working Party to determine whether any reforms of procedure were necessary. The Working Party – which reported in 1987 – contended that 'the current procedures are, in the main, satisfactory'.[9] In 1989, the House coped with the business placed before it. It did so despite growing worries on both sides of the House about the limited number of new or young peers capable of carrying on much of the necessary work of the House. Following the July ministerial reshuffle, the government was unable to fill one of the vacancies for a whip in the Lords; by the end of the year, the position was still unfilled. A heavy legislative load, coupled with a failure to recruit peers to carry some of the essential burdens imposed by that load, is likely to create strains that may be relieved only by procedural reforms and the creation of new peers.

Conclusion

The two Houses of Parliament in 1989 operated well under increasing pressures. Both face problems of parliamentary overload. The paradox of the situation is that the problem of overload is largely the product of success: by doing what is expected of them, more is expected of them. Both face new challenges, the House of Commons in particular. How they respond to these challenges will largely determine the future role of Parliament in the British polity.

Notes
1. See C. M. Grantham and C. Moore Hodgson, 'The House of Lords: structural changes', in P. Norton (ed), *Parliament in the 1980s*, Oxford, Basil Blackwell, 1985, pp. 114–35, and the evidence of Baroness Serota to the Select Committee on Procedure, *The Scrutiny of European Legislation, Minutes of Evidence, 19 July 1989*, HC368–ix, London, HMSO, 1989, pp. 122–31.
2. The Fourth Report from the Select Committee on Procedure, Session 1988/89, *The Scrutiny of European Legislation, Vol.I: Report and Proceedings of the Committee*, HC 622–I, London, HMSO, 1989.
3. HC Deb. 154, col.609. See also *First Report from the Select Committee on Televising of Proceedings of the House, Session 1988-89*, HC141–1, London: HMSO, 1989.
4. R. Gregory and A. Alexander, 'Our Parliamentary Ombudsman Pt.2: development and the problem of identity', *Public Administration*, 51(1), 1973, p. 48; a more recent survey by the study group on Parliamentary Questions of the Study of Parliament Group (1989) found that most of the MPs who were sampled, judged letters more effective than questions. See also P. Norton, '"Dear Minister . . ." the importance of MP-to-Minister correspondence', *Parliamentary Affairs*, 35(1), 1982, pp. 59–72.
5. C. Miller, *The Government Report*, London, Public Policy Consultants, 1987, p. 9.
6. P. Norton and D. Wood, 'MPs constituency service by British MPs: does it contribute to a personal vote?', *Parliamentary Affairs*, 1990 (forthcoming).
7. N. D. J. Baldwin, 'The House of Lords: behavioural changes', in P. Norton, (ed), *Parliament in the 1980s*, Oxford, Basil Blackwell, 1985, pp. 96–113.

8. *Report of the Select Committee on Murder and Life Imprisonment, Session 1988–89,* HL78–I, London, HMSO, 1989.
9. House of Lords, *Report by the Group on the Working of the House,* Session 1987–88, HL9, London, HMSO, 1987, p. 22.

Recent Publications

1989 saw the publication of two major volumes focusing on the procedures of Parliament:

Erskine May's *Treatise on The Law, Privileges, Proceedings and Usage of Parliament,* 21st edition, C. J. Boulton (ed), London, Butterworths, 1989.

J.A.G. Griffith and M. Ryle, *Parliament: Functions, Practices and Procedures,* London, Sweet and Maxwell, 1989.

Chronology

3 Jan: Edwina Currie refuses to testify on the salmonella in eggs issue before the Commons select committee on agriculture.

30 Jan: *Hansard* announces trials of computer-aided transcription of parliamentary debates.

1 Feb: Eighteen Tory MPs support an amendment to the Official Secrets Bill allowing a public interest defence, defying a three-line whip.

7 Feb: Commons Agriculture Committee votes nine to one to compel Currie to testify and she agrees after three previous refusals.

8 Feb: Currie stonewalls before the Agriculture Select Committee.

9 Feb: Tory backbench protests led by Edward Heath against the proposed guillotine of the Official Secrets Bill.

13 Feb: Fourteen Conservative backbenchers rebel against the guillotine on the committee stage of the Official Secrets Bill.

Dale Campbell-Savours suspended from the Commons after clashing with the Speaker over allegations that six Tory MPs were security risks.

16 Feb: Further Conservative rebellions fail to amend the Official Secrets Bill.

22 Feb: Third reading given to the Official Secrets Bill after an angry debate.

13 Mar: Questions asked in the Commons over the issue of a parliamentary pass to Pamella Bordes.

21 Mar: Parliamentary security to be tightened in the wake of the Bordes affair. 4 Apr: Four Tory rebels vote with the Opposition on the third reading of the Water Bill.

18 Apr: An all-party Space Committee set up in the Commons.

24 Apr: Nineteen Conservatives rebel in the Commons over the government decision to freeze child benefit.

3 May: Commons Procedure Committee suggests measures to abolish the worst cases of filibustering.

8 May: Guidelines for the televising of the Commons approved.

15 May: Government defeated on the Water Bill when the Lords vote by 81 to 47 to back an Opposition amendment to impose a legally binding target of September 1993 by which British water must comply with EC standards.

16 May: Government defeated on an amendment to the Electricity Bill in the Lords by 126 to 114.

17 May: BBC and ITV attack the rules laid down for experiment in televising the Commons as unduly restrictive.

5 June: Second defeat for the government on an amendment to the Electricity Bill in the Lords by 112 to 104.

12 June: Commons approves the rules for the experiment in televising its proceedings from November by 293 to 69. But proposals for more strictly limited shots are rejected by 243 to 109. A suggestion that there should be a dedicated channel was defeated by 274 to 98.

22 June: Government defeated in the Lords as peers vote to raise child benefit by 115 to 94.

27 June: Fifteen Conservatives rebel in the Commons on the second reading of the Football Supporters Bill.

29 June: Representation of the People Bill given a second reading by 162 to 19. It allows people who left the country up to 25 years ago the right to vote (the previous limit was five years).

5 July: Thirteen Tory rebels in the Lords vote to include an amendment in the Electricity Bill to prevent higher rates in rural areas after privatization.

11 July: Five Tories rebel over child benefit in the Commons.

19 July: Nineteen Tories rebel over child benefit in the Commons.

24 July: Tam Dalyell suspended from the Commons for refusing to withdraw an allegation that the Prime Minister lied over the Westland Affair in 1986.

5 Nov: Announcement of a pay rise for MPs of 10.7 per cent.

8 Nov: Timothy Raison resigns as chairman of the Commons Education Select Sommittee after months of political bickering in the Committee and personal criticism from some of his fellow Tories.

11 Nov: Polls of MPs for the Channel 4 programme 'The Commons Touch' show that they feel that they have insufficient opportunity to scrutinize European legislation and that there is also substantial feeling that select committees should have greater powers to require ministers to answer questions.

21 Nov: State opening of Parliament. Televising of the Commons begins.

30 Nov: Commons *Select Committee on Procedure Fourth Report: The Scrutiny of European Legislation*, HMSO, demands five new standing committees on agriculture, trade and industry, the treasury, transport and the environment and urges that two full days of debate should be allocated to EC topics prior to EC summits.

Political Parties

MICHAEL PINTO-DUSCHINSKY

This chapter will describe developments in the organization and policies of the main national parties during 1989. It will not cover the fortunes of extremist parties and factions, of parties in Northern Ireland, or of nationalist parties in Scotland and Wales.

The Parties at Mid-Term

Although the prime purpose of British party organizations is to fight general election campaigns, they staff their headquarters and local offices and maintain programmes in electoral peacetime as well. Indeed, it is these routine activities which consume the lion's share of party funds during the course of a parliamentary cycle. Nevertheless, there are certain patterns and changes in pace at different points of the normal four-year period between one election and the next. At the mid-point between general election campaigns, party organizations are staffed at a slightly lower level, new officials are recruited to replace some members of the team responsible for the previous election, and central party incomes are generally lower (especially in the Conservative Party). In the second year of a new Parliament, the Opposition party often starts to gain ground in the public opinion polls and carries out a thorough review of party policy. Another common feature of party politics in mid-cycle is that the Leader of the Opposition, who has a personal staff at the House of Commons but no ministerial apparatus, remains relatively close to his party headquarters whereas the Prime Minister of the day is usually more remote from the party bureaucracy. It is important to bear these points in mind when attempting to interpret developments during 1989. For instance, was the Labour Party's policy review a landmark or was it an example of the exercises undertaken by most oppositions? Were the political setbacks of the Conservatives part of the characteristic midterm slump experienced by many governments? Are they likely to be followed by the usual recovery of the ruling party as the next election approaches (as in 1958–9, 1982–3, and 1986–7)? Or do Labour's advances mark the beginning of a major breakthrough (as in 1961–3)?

At the time of writing, it would be rash to offer answers to these questions. But four assertions can be made: first, the Labour Party emerged in 1988–9 as a serious contender for power. After the Conservatives' third election victory in 1987 (as after their third successive win in 1959), it became fashionable to comment that Labour could never hope to regain power and that it was in long term decline. Even the party's pollster, Robert Worcester of Market and Opinion Research International (MORI), suggested in July 1988 that 'the Labour Party has now very little possibility of holding office'. Some saw the desertion from Labour in Britain as part of an international trend. Mrs Thatcher, who had warned in the general election campaign of 1983 that the Labour Party would never die, seemed confident after her third victory in 1987 that the danger from the Left had receded at last. By the end of 1989, no one could write off Labour's chances. The bookmakers showed Labour as the narrow favourite to win the coming election. Though the state of the economy was a key factor in determining shifts in public opinion, Labour's rising popularity also stemmed from measures taken by the Labour leadership to modernize the organization and to present a new image of Labour policy.

Second, 1988–9 witnessed the disastrous effects of the split in the Alliance between the Social Democrats and the Liberals. By their internal quarrels following the 1987 elections, the centre parties squandered the political gains of the previous fifteen years. Faction fighting and falling popularity led to organizational crisis.

Third, the elections to the European Parliament held in June 1989, though serving as an important indicator of the improved popularity of Labour and of the Greens, were preceded by relatively minor efforts by the national and local party organizations. The campaign was fought on the scale of local government elections rather than of a general election to the House of Commons.

Fourth, the level of political activity in the constituencies remained low. The main parties had a combined membership of less than one and a half million – about 3 per cent of the electorate.

The Conservative Party

As Robert McKenzie argued in his classic book, *British Political Parties*, the Conservative Central Office, in strictly constitutional terms, is the personal machine of the party leader. Whereas the Labour Party constitution lays down procedures for the election of the national executive committee and for the appointments of the General Secretary, the Conservative leader is free to appoint whomever she wishes to the party chairmanship and to other senior posts. It is the leader who has the formal responsibility for party policy. The leader's power over the Conservative Party is not just constitutional fiction. For example, the Conservative campaign for the elections to the European Parliament, held in June 1989, bore Mrs Thatcher's stamp. However, it is unrealistic to regard the Conservative headquarters as a mere personal organization. Mrs Thatcher's closest advisers have been situated in No. 10 Downing Street and, arguably, in some Conservative-oriented think-tanks and to a lesser extent, in the party offices at 32

Smith Square. Under many Conservative premiers there has been a certain distance and, occasionally, tension between the leader's staff and the Central Office. This is partly because No. 10 Downing Street and the party headquarters have different functions. The Prime Minister is too busy with affairs of State to be involved in the day-to-day tasks of party management. Moreover, there is always a possibility that the party chairman – even if he has been appointed as a leader's agent – will use his position to establish an independent power base.

A succession of articles, books and memoirs reporting disagreements between Mrs Thatcher and her former party chairman, Norman Tebbit, appeared after the general election of 1987. Despite Mr Tebbit's background as a staunch backer of the premier, his period in control of the party organization apparently witnessed rifts. Immediately after the Conservative victory in June 1987, Mr Tebbit left the Cabinet and, soon afterwards, the party chairmanship. The party's advertising agency, Saatchi and Saatchi, whose position in the election campaign had been a subject of comment, announced that it would no longer represent the party. This brought to an end an association which had lasted through the general elections of 1979, 1983 and 1987 and which had contributed to the advertising company's meteoric rise.

During 1988–9, the new party chairman, Peter Brooke, together with his deputy chairman and fellow Member of Parliament, Peter Morrison, concentrated on a low key reorganization of the headquarter staff. In spring 1989, Brendan Bruce was recruited from the advertising agency DMB & B to act as Director of Communications. He was responsible for commissioning political advertisements, for other aspects of marketing and for relationships with the media. Failure to agree on a similar coordinator before the 1987 election had been a source of friction at that time. As a temporary measure, the advertising agency Alan Brady and Marsh was given the account for the party's publicity in the European elections. In late 1989 Central Office still had not chosen its advertising agency for the next general election.

John Lacy, who had been Director of Campaigning in the 1987 campaign, now assumed the title of General Director of Campaigning with responsibilities for the former departments of organization (formerly headed by Sir Anthony Garner) and of campaigning. The research department remained under the directorship of Robin Harris until his departure in the summer of 1989 for a position in the Policy Unit at No. 10 Downing Street. Mr Harris was among several members of the research department who took up positions as special advisers to ministers or to the Prime Minister. The use of the research department as a recruiting ground for ministerial advisers is not a new phenomenon but it has led to a rapid turnover of staff. In part, this may indicate that the department's functions are more crucial when the party is in opposition. An innovation of 1989 was the research department's publication of a 600–page campaign guide for the 1989 European elections.

As in 1983–7, Mrs Thatcher placed the Central Office in the hands of a relatively junior minister during the first half of the Parliament. In the reshuffle of July 1989,

Peter Brooke entered the Cabinet as Secretary of State for Northern Ireland, and his position as party chairman was taken by Kenneth Baker, the former education minister. Lord Young, who resigned from the Cabinet, became deputy chairman though his responsibilities in this role were uncertain.

Central Office's income between April 1988 and March 1989 (net of direct funding costs) totalled £8 million and expenditure was £7.8 million. Though less than the £15 million collected in the election year 1987–8, it was a very healthy performance for a year following the election. At the equivalent stage of the previous parliamentary cycle, 1984–5, Conservative central income was only £4.3 million and expenditure was £5.6 million. This financial success in 1988–9 made it possible to undertake an extensive and expensive modernization of the headquarters building during 1989. The party continued to raise funds by various commercial schemes and by some direct mail appeals but these 'modern' methods remained relatively unimportant. Apart from £1.2 million contributed by constituency associations, the bulk of income came from corporate and individual donations. The year 1989 saw adverse press comment about company payments to Conservative Central Office, and the House of Lords voted in January 1989 to amend company law to control corporate political payments, a proposal later overturned by the government in the House of Commons.

At the local level, there were nearly 300 full-time constituency agents in 1989. Questionnaires returned by 200 constituency associations indicated that they had a total of 400,000 members. Central Office estimated on this basis – maybe optimistically – that there were about one million members, though it should be noted that membership subscriptions are lower and more flexible in the Conservative Party than in the other main parties. A membership drive in 1988–9 reportedly yielded over 100,000 new members, but it is unclear whether they compensated for those whose subscriptions had lapsed. Though the Conservatives are the best organized party at the local level, the number of members has remained a cause for concern.

The Labour Party

Neil Kinnock's consistent aim following the 1987 election was to abandon the 'old unrealism' in Labour's policy and organization. The modernization of the party was seen to require the reformulation of policy, control over the hard-left wing, reform of the party's constitution and a continuing emphasis on Labour Head Office's role as a campaigning force.

The priority given to electoral appeal over socialist doctrine was hardly likely to please the left. The Labour leader's moves to modify the party's unilateral stance on nuclear disarmament led in June 1988 to the resignation of the party's defence spokesman, Denzil Davies. Tony Benn's left-wing challenge to Mr Kinnock's leadership failed in October 1988, with Mr Benn obtaining only 11.4 per cent of electoral college votes. The deputy leader, Roy Hattersley, also comfortably survived, gaining 66.8 per cent of electoral college votes. These results meant that by 1989 Mr Kinnock enjoyed an unchallenged ascendancy over the party at all levels. His prestige grew with Labour's good performance in the European elections and in the opinion polls. Improving political prospects meant that proportional representation, favoured by some of the Shadow Cabinet, became even less attractive to Mr Kinnock.

A policy document comprising seven major reports by party review groups was launched in May 1989 and debated at the party conference in October. In order to secure its approval, the party's National Executive and Conference Committees ruled that each section of the review had to be accepted or rejected in its entirety; no amendments were to be permitted. Despite some opposition, particularly from the Transport and General Workers' leader, Ron Todd, the new policies were duly endorsed by the conference.

The review document, *Meet the Challenge: Make the Change*, confirmed the party's gradual reversal on British membership of the European Community. Far from wishing to withdraw, Labour was attracted by the social measures being spearheaded from Brussels (a development particularly welcomed by British trade union leaders). The electorally damaging commitment to unilateral nuclear disarmament was dropped. Tax increases were proposed for the rich. The top marginal rate of income tax was to be raised from 40 per cent to 50 per cent, considerably lower than during Labour's last term of office. The party would no longer aim at wide-scale nationalization. Though British Telecom and the major utilities privatized by the Conservatives were to return to social control, shareholders could retain minority holdings. The Conservative's trade union legislation would only partly be overturned.

The Conservatives were not slow to point out the radical parts of what they termed a 'red fudge'. Though the 1989 Labour Conference abandoned unilateralism, it voted for a drastic reduction in defence spending. The details of Labour's nuclear policy – according to the Conservatives – meant that the effectiveness of the nuclear deterrent would be sacrificed. The underlying policy remained effectively unilateralist.

If Labour's proposals for income tax seemed moderate, there would be other new taxes – a wealth tax, a tax on investment income and new local taxes. Private schooling would be subject to taxation and the assisted places scheme dropped.

Apart from presenting policies designed to appeal to the political middle ground, Mr Kinnock continued his attack on the far left influences within the party. The 1989 National Executive Committee (NEC) report contains accounts of investigations and disciplinary proceedings against alleged supporters of the Militant Tendency in the Southwark–Bermondsey, Glasgow Pollock and Liverpool Broadgreen constituency Labour parties as well as proceedings against individual Militants elsewhere.

The determination to avoid the selection of extreme or potentially unpopular candidates led to the adoption in 1988 of a rule allowing the NEC to intervene directly in the selection of candidates for parliamentary by-elections. This power was used to select a candidate for the Vauxhall by-election against the wishes of the local party. As the constituency included a high proportion of black voters, the Vauxhall party wished to short-list black candidates. The Vauxhall affair was linked with a running controversy, still unresolved after the 1989 party conference, about the proposed formation of separate 'Black Sections' of the Party.

Several constitutional changes were introduced or agreed in 1988 and 1989. The most far-reaching was the decision at the 1989 party conference to reform the time-honoured system of union block-votes. The two largest unions both favoured a change and it was the General and Municipal Workers' leader, John Edmonds, who declared, 'The block vote must go. Trade unions of course should retain influence but we must surrender control.'

Another reform, implemented by the NEC in 1989, gave votes to individual constituency members in elections of the party leader and deputy. It was also proposed to permit individual members to vote for constituency representatives on the NEC.

A gradual diminution of trade union power and an increasing role for individual members was widely favoured as part of a programme of modernization. The changes have yet to be implemented and their effects observed. Historically, the constituency parties have often been more left-wing than the unions.

In terms of central organization, Neil Kinnock continued to work with the young team which had fought the 1987 election, with Larry Whitty as General Secretary and Peter Mandelson as Director of Campaigns and Communications. A serious financial deficit had made it necessary to impose staff cuts after the 1987 general election. In 1988 (the last year for which information is available) Head Office income amounted to £5.6 million and nearly balanced expenditure. But the Head Office remained £1.1 million in the red. Amid the financial pressures, a high priority seems to have been given to the professional presentation of Party materials and broadcasts.

At the constituency level, there were some 50 full-time agents serving 62 constituencies. Yet individual membership fell in 1988 by 7.7 per cent to 265,927, the largest fall since comparable records began in 1981. A mass membership campaign was run in 1989.

The aim of reducing dependence on the trade unions by attracting a mass individual membership remained far from being fulfilled. But the party succeeded in presenting a more acceptable image to the public.

Another organizational development is worth noting. After the 1987 election, the government agreed to a 70 per cent raise in the grants to Opposition parties in the House of Commons (the 'Short Money'). Labour was the main beneficiary receiving £840,000 a year. The grant now provides a significant supplement to opposition parties' central funds and, in particular, adds to the resources available to party leaders' and whips' offices. Only a small portion of Labour's share of the 'Short Money' (£189,000) is included in the National Executive Committee accounts.

The Labour Party
Leader
    Rt Hon Neil Kinnock MP
Deputy Leader, Home Affairs
    Rt Hon Roy Hattersley MP
Chief Whip
    Derek Foster MP
Chairman of the Parliamentary Labour Party
    Rt Hon Stan Orme MP
Trade and Industry
    Bryan Gould MP
    Gordon Brown MP (Nov 1989)
Energy
    John Prescott MP
    Frank Dobson MP (Nov 1989)
Employment
    Michael Meacher MP
    Tony Blair MP (Nov 1989)
Foreign and Commonwealth Affairs
    Rt Hon Gerald Kaufman MP
Treasury and Economic Affairs
    Rt Hon John Smith MP
Defence and Disarmament
    Martin O'Neill MP
Transport
    John Prescott MP
Health and Social Security
    Robin Cook MP to Nov 1989
    Robin Cook MP – Health (Nov 1989)
    Michael Meacher MP – Social Security (Nov 1989)
Scotland
    Donald Dewer MP
Leader of the House and Campaign Co-ordinator
    Frank Dobson MP
    Dr John Cunningham MP (Nov 1989)
Chief Secretary to the Treasury
    Gordon Brown MP
    Margaret Beckett MP (Nov 1989)
Environment
    Dr John Cunningham MP
    Bryan Gould MP (Nov 1989)
Women
    Jo Richardson MP

Agriculture and Rural Affairs
    Dr David Clark MP
Education
    Jack Straw MP
Wales
    Barry Jones MP
Northern Ireland
    Kevin McNamara MP
Arts
    Mark Fisher MP
Development and Co-operation
    Joan Lester MP
    Ann Clwyd MP (Nov 1989)
Disabled People
    Rt Hon Alf Morris MP
Legal Affairs
    Rt Hon John Morris MP
Science and Technology
    Dr Jeremy Bray MP
Secretary to the Committee
    Bryan Davies
Leader of the Labour Peers
    Rt Hon Lord Cledwyn
Opposition Chief Whip, Lords
    Lord Ponsonby
Labour Peers Representative
    Lord Dean of Beswick

Labour NEC elected at 1989 party conference
TU section (12 places)
    Eddie Hayes (TGWU) 5,324,000
    Andy Dodds (NUR) 5,250,000
    Tom Barkinson (GMB) 5,050,000
    Tony Clarke (UCW) 4,951,000
    Ted O'Brien (Sogat) 4,813,000
    Syd Tierney (USDAW) 4,756,000
    Jack Rodgers (UCATT) 4,744,000
    Tom Sawyer (NUPE) 4,588,000
    Gordon Colling (NGA) 4,414,000
    Peter Burns (AEU) 4,250,000
Constituency sections (7 places)
    David Blunkett 485,000
    Robin Cook 404,000
    John Prescott 300,000
    Tony Benn 387,000
    Dennis Skinner 358,000

Bryan Gould 329,000
Jo Richardson 319,000
Socialist societies (1 place)
John Evans 48,000
Women's section (5 places)
Joan Lestor 5,096,000
Diana Jeuda 4,922,000
Clare Short 3,794,000
Margaret Beckett 3,786,000
Anne Davis 3,093,000
Treasurer
Sam McCluskie 5,415,000

The Social and Liberal Democrats

The new party was launched on 3 March 1988 as a fusion of the Liberal Party and the Social Democratic Party. In effect it constituted a Liberal takeover of the SDP. To its protagonists, fusion would succeed in producing a unity in the centre of British politics which the former Liberal–SDP Alliance had lacked. The events of 1988 and 1989 were to demonstrate the error of this judgement.

Although the original decision to form the new party was taken by a large majority at the Liberals' Special Assembly on 24 January 1988 (2,099 votes to 385), SDP members voted only narrowly to accept (57.4 per cent to 42.6 per cent). Negotiations about the terms of the union were acrimonious. The Liberal leader and architect of merger, David Steel, decided that he would not stand for the position of leader of the new party. In a ballot of SLD members, two Liberal MPs contested the leadership. Paddy Ashdown defeated Alan Beith by 41,401 votes to 16,202.

Mr Ashdown's attempts to establish a strong personal image and a distinctive theme of 'citizenship' politics were submerged beneath political and organizational difficulties. First, and most important, the SDP leader, David Owen, refused to join the new party and formed a rump SDP. The fact that the SDP could field rival candidates at parliamentary by-elections made it harder for the SLD to achieve those spectacular victories which had boosted the Liberals and Social Democrats during their previous years of electoral cooperation. The SLD would have nearly taken Epping from the Conservatives in December 1988 and would have won Richmond in February 1989 had the 'Alliance' vote not been split by the SDP. Second, a group of diehard Liberals, under former MP Michael Meadowcroft, remained hostile to the new Party.

Third, there was damaging confusion about the new party's name. 'SLD' (itself a product of wrangling) proved too complicated and led to the nickname 'Salads'. Mr Ashdown persuaded the 1988 party con ference to adopt the abbreviated title 'The Democrats'. This was unwelcome to a number of MPs who had won their seats under the Liberal banner and were unwilling to desert the name of their ancient party. In late 1989, a postal ballot of members was held and 70 per cent voted to change the name once again to 'Liberal Democrats'.

Fourth, the constitutional structure of the new party was unwieldy. National functions were divided between a federal party and separate English, Scottish and Welsh parties. There were to be two federal conferences a year and separate English, Scottish and Welsh conferences.

Fifth, the merger made it necessary to form a new party bureaucracy. The Chief Executive was a former Liberal official, Andrew Ellis, but the headquarters building was that of the SDP in Cowley Street. The removal of papers from the Liberal headquarters and the recreation of membership lists was itself a major disruption.

Mr Ashdown hoped that a well-staffed, well-funded party would make a strong electoral impact and would thus absorb the SDP. The plan in 1988 was to employ a central staff of 60 to raise an income higher than the combined incomes of the Liberals and the SDP. By spring 1989 it was already proving hard to meet these targets, especially in view of the policy of investing heavily in by-election campaigns.

In May 1989 the senior party committee accepted the recommendations of a special review group to restructure the staff in order to place much greater emphasis on management, finance and administration and to tackle the burgeoning deficit. This led to Andrew Ellis' resignation as Chief Executive and to the appointment of Graham Elson to a new post of General Secretary. The party's abysmal showing in the Euro-elections in June 1989 led to a sharp fall in renewals of membership and to a financial crisis, requiring staff cuts and savings of £400,000.

In the ten months of its existence to December 1988, the federal party's and English party's incomes combined (net of fundraising costs) totalled £0.8 million. Spending came to £1.1 million. In September 1989 a document presented to the party conference gave a proposed budget for 1990 including both the federal and English parties, based on an income of £0.8 million and expenditure of only £.05 million. Pressure on resources at the Cowley Street headquarters meant that its staff was reduced to 15 and the organization became more dependent on the parliamentary Party's share of the 'Short Money', which amounted to an additional £0.2 million a year.

By October 1989 the shock waves resulting from the Euro-elections appeared to have been absorbed and membership had stabilized at about 80,000. The Liberal Democrats, unlike the SDP did not need to fear extinction, although earlier hopes of changing the mould of British politics had been disappointed and the party had been forced to reduce its level of activity.

The Social Democrats

The problem faced by David Owen's rump party were desperate. There were only three SDP members of Parliament, compared with 19 SLD MPs. Most of the headquarters staff of the old SDP opted for the SLD, and the few Owenites were reduced to smuggling out membership lists. Few SDP local government councillors dared to remain under the party's banner. The main assets of the SDP were Dr Owen's public profile and the financial support of David Sainsbury.

It was decided to create a new headquarters, which was to be funded by membership subscriptions. Donations from Mr Sainsbury and his fellow Trustees were reserved for special projects such as party conferences and by-elections. The party invested heavily in preparations for the Richmond by-election held in February 1989. The SDP candidate not only succeeded in beating the SLD candidate but fell only 2,600 votes short of winning the seat from the Tories. It had been hoped that a spectacular by-election performance would improve the party's status, help recruitment and make it possible to pressure an electoral pact with the SLD. Negotiations with the SLD continued through 1989. They proved fruitless.

By March 1989 it became apparent from the slow pace of membership renewals that the party's support was much lower than previously calculated and that there were only 11,000 SDP members. In the county council elections in England and Wales held in May 1989, the SDP won only 11 seats (compared with 515 won by the SLD). In order to save electoral deposits and to avoid further humiliation, the party decided to field candidates in only 16 constituencies in the European elections in June. They all lost their deposits.

In September 1989 the party managed to attract 800 people to its annual conference which was an achievement in the circumstances. In order to avoid awkward publicity about the party's organizational decline, no financial accounts were published. By October 1989 the SDP had a headquarters staff of four, no regional staff and no professional agents outside the constituencies of the party's three MPs. Additional staff, funded by the 'Short Money' and by MPs' allowances, served the party's parliamentary office. The two tasks of the party were to save its three seats in the House of Commons and to continue negotiations with other parties, albeit from a position of weakness.

The Greens

With the decline of the SLD and the SDP, there was no obvious home for protest voters. Both the Scottish and Welsh Nationalists made some gains. However, the Greens were the main beneficiaries.

The party had been founded as the People's Party in 1973 and changed its name to the Ecology Party in 1975. In 1985 it became the Green Party, echoing the name of similar parties in West Germany and other European countries. The strong

European connection seems to have been a source of both moral and organizational support, as shown by the importance of the party's international committee. A large British contingent were among the 1,500 attending the fifth congress of the European Greens held in Paris in April 1989 and the British party maintained close links with the Green group in the European Parliament.

The Greens contested every constituency in the Euro-election of June 1989. The Party's success in winning 15 per cent of the vote produced a notable improvement in the income from subscriptions. Membership rose from 7,466 in 1988 to 14,432 by July 1989. (The party's central income in 1988 was £107,000.) The party's conference held in Wolverhampton, September 1989, received wide media coverage, whereas the previous year's event had been virtually ignored.

Sudden political success brought problems as well as opportunities. The absence of a party leadership and the reliance on 'co-chairs' produced, in the words of a report to the 1989 conference, 'acrimony' and 'polarization' on matters of policy as well as personality clashes. By the end of 1989 it was not yet apparent whether the Greens would be able to build a solid following from their success in June 1989.

Chronology

9 Jan: Publication of the Fabian Tract *Working for Common Security*. This anti-unilateralist tract was widely seen as as piece of kite-flying by the party leadership.

13 Jan: Eight members of Glasgow Cathcart CLP are expelled as members of Militant.

16 Jan: TGWU suggest that the trade union block vote at the Labour Party conference should be reduced from 90 per cent to 75 per cent of the total votes.

30 Jan: Government defeated in the Lords by an amendment to the Companies Bill which would give shareholders the right to block donations to political parties by 106 to 93. Neil Kinnock calls for a 'Social Europe' and criticizes the government for failures in its preparations for 1992, thus signalling a more positive attitude towards the EC in the Labour Party.

30–31 Jan: Labour's defence review committee visits Moscow.

8 Feb: SLD launches a new statement of values; *Our Different Vision*.

9 Feb: In a television interview Kinnock confirms his shift away from unilateralism.

10 Feb: Mr Kinnock signs the European socialist manifesto prepared for the summer's European elections, but put his reservations about a federal Europe on record.

8 Feb: Three more Militants expelled in Glasgow.

24 Feb: Paddy Ashdown, leader of the SLD, in the wake of the Richmond by-election, renews his call for the Owenites to merge with the SLD.

27 Feb: David Owen rejects a by-election pact urged by Ashdown.

3 Mar: The right captures the leadership of the Young Conservatives.

7 Mar: Expulsion of two councillors in Vale of Glamorgan mars the Conservative preparations for the impending by-election.

8 Mar: An attempt to revive the Liberal Party by diehard Liberals opposed to the SLD is launched.

20 Mar: It is revealed that Inland Revenue inspectors are examining documents detailing a system for funding the Conservative cause proposed in letters seeking donations from companies sent out before the 1987 general election.

Mr Kinnock makes an emphatic commitment to the market economy in a speech in Nottingham.

21–23 Mar: Labour's defence review committee visits the USA.

6 May: Labour's defence review paper marks a shift away from unilateralism.

8 May: Labour's National Executive Committee (NEC) begins considering the party's policy review documents. The trade and industry (marking a move away from nationalization), taxation and benefits, consumer, education and constitution papers are approved.

9 May: The rejection of unilateralism is endorsed by Labour's NEC by 17 to 8.

13 May: SDP announce decision to cut electoral role and spending.

14 May: Dr Owen pins hopes of future for SDP on getting Labour to accept proportional representation.

15 May: SDP launch scaled-down European elections campaign after a scaled-down campaign in the county council elections, marking a general reduction in SDP activities. A reorganization of the key posts in the SLD takes place in an attempt to improve its campaigning.

16 May: Lords' amendment to the Companies Bill giving new powers to shareholders to challenge corporate politi cal donations is overturned in the Commons.

17 May: The Labour leadership infuriated black supporters and imposed the white Kate Hoey as candidate for the Vauxhall by-election after local party activists abandoned the selection meeting to demand a black candidate.

18 May: Labour's *Meet the Challenge, Make the Change*: Final Report of Labour's Policy Review for the 1990s published.

22 May: National Union of Public Employees vote to support Mr Kinnock's new line on defence.

25 May: Mr Kinnock loses temper in interview on economic policy on BBC radio. Trident should be retained 'as long as necessary' according to the SLD's new defence document *After the Cold War: Social and Liberal Democrats Policies on East–West Relations in the 1990s*.

29 May: Labour concern over a possible smear campaign by the intelligence services after a BBC report.

30 May: Edward Heath accuses Peter Brooke, the Conservative Party Chairman, of lying about a dirty tricks cam paign Mr Heath alleges was mounted by Conservative Central Office to discredit and stop Heath speaking during the European elec tions campaign.

31 May: Communist Party issues *Manifesto for New Times: A Communist Party Strategy for the 1990s*. A black Methodist minister becomes the second black candidate selected to stand against Kate Hoey in the Vauxhall by-election.

2 June: William Waldegrave, Minister of State at the Foreign Office, repudiates BBC report (see 29 May) which suggests the Russians recently expelled for spying had been trying to bribe Labour MPs.

6 June: John Edmonds, General Secretary of the General and Municipal Boilermakers wins unanimous support from his union for the document *Meeting the Challenge* which outlines plans to dismantle the Labour Party block vote and reform the party's decision making process.

12 June: Strategy statement for the forthcoming left-wing Socialist conference denounces the Labour leadership as 'new men with old ideas'.

17–18 June: Socialist conference held in Sheffield ends by agreeing to establish itself on a more permanent footing.

19 June: Departure of Andy Ellis as Chief Executive of the SLD.

21 June: SLD MPs call for change of name to Liberal Democrat.

27 June: TGWU conference votes to retain unilateralist policy, a rebuff to Mr Kinnock.

28 June: Tory MEPs begin their attempt to join the Christian Democrat group in the European Parliament.

29 June: Giles Radice's *Labour's Path to Power: The New Revisionism* published by Macmillan.

5 July: Draft review of the Parliamentary Labour Party issued.

19 July: PLP approves a rule change which increases the size of the Shadow Cabinet from 15 to 18 and requires that at least three votes must be cast for women candidates in a move to increase the number of women in the Shadow Cabinet.

4 Aug: SLD to cut its 30-strong headquarters staff, disband its network of 11 area agents and make other redundancies in face of financial crisis.

3 Sept: In a car crash in Dublin Kinnock escapes unhurt.

7 Sept: Mr Ashdown publishes *Citizen's Britain*.

9 Sept: Poll in *The Independent* shows Dr Owen is the most popular leader for a centre party even among SLD members and that there is continued support for a party of the centre but dissatisfaction with the SLD in that role.

10 Sept: Dr Owen offers to revive former Alliance and serve under Mr Ashdown in the Commons. This is rejected by Mr Ashdown.

11 Sept: Labour's transport policy document goes before NEC.

SLD conference supports EC Social Charter, seeks reduction in arms exports, supports the EC Lingua programme, and suggests the need for a state-assisted accident compensation scheme.

12 Sept: SLD managers attacked at the SLD conference over the party's budget crisis. The conference called for action on Cambodia and approved a multilateral nuclear defence policy.

13 Sept: Launch of the Islamic Party of Britain.

SLD conference supports Britain joining the EMS, condemns pornography and calls for powers for local councils to remove sex offenders and not their victims from the home, and demands the replacement of the poll tax with local taxation related to income.

14 Sept: SLD conference rejects a call to withdraw from the political honours system, calls for a boost to British research and development, approves proposals for a Bill of Rights, the lowering of the voting age to 16, and a common age of consent for homosexual and heterosexual acts, and demands more recycling and other environmental measures.

15 Sept: SLD conference calls for large scale aid to Poland, right of abode for British passport holders from Hong Kong and a speeding up of the democratization process in the colony, and pressure on Brazil and its neighbours to stop the destruction of the rainforests. The proposals for televising Parliament are also criticized.

18 Sept: Drastic retrenchment of the SDP's campaigning efforts drawn up by the leadership. Mr Kinnock contradicts his trade and industry spokesman, Bryan Gould, on the handling of privatized utilities under a future Labour government.

20 Sept: Green Party conference begins.

22 Sept: Greens drop their target of reducing the population to 30–40 million but remain committed to population reductions, vote to give more rights to travellers, condemn the

sending back of the Vietnamese boat people and vote for a health policy which scraps prescription charges and gives a more devolved health service. The Scottish Greens become a separate organization.

24 Sept: Greens conference rejects proposals for a pre-election pact with the SLD and Labour designed to secure proportional representation.

25 Sept: Conservatives launch a new party logo.

Two Militant members expelled from Labour in Newport, Gwent.

SDP conference opens. Leadership plans to scale down activities are criticized as defeatist. The conference condemns UK food and drink regulations as inadequate, calls for separate agriculture and food ministries and an increase in environmental health officers, agrees to run candidates in Northern Ireland and calls for less emphasis on road transport and an end to under-funding of the railways.

26 Sept: SDP conference calls for an inquiry into security at military establishments, backs the ambulancemen in their dispute, demands repeal of Section 28 of the Local Government Act which bans the promotion of homosexuality by local authorities, rejects moves to lower the age of majority to 16 and to extend the law of blasphemy to cover all faiths, calls for entry of the EMS and more investment in skill training and in manufacturing industry, supports the idea of a football pools levy to fund ground improvements, and opposes the government's plans to lift restrictions on the working hours of 16–18 year olds.

27 Sept: SDP conference rejects leadership proposals to adapt the poll tax and relate it to ability to pay, and approves the integration of the tax and benefit system, the exemption from tax of all forms of saving and investment, the introduction of a separate health tax to support the NHS and the scrapping of regional health authorities, to be replaced with greater local autonomy and district health trusts.

The Labour NEC votes to set up a black socialist society as a compromise in an attempt to solve the row over the party's black sections.

2 Oct: Labour Party conference opens against a growing background of calls for the party to opt for PR. The presence of Gerry Adams, the Sinn Fein president, invited to speak at a fringe meeting by the unofficial Labour Committee on Northern Ireland, angers party leaders. Meanwhile in the conference hall the policy review document Productive and Competitive Economy, which proposes a full employment target, a strengthened DTI to steer strategic investment, a nationwide IT cable network, anti-inflation measures and the regaining of majority shareholdings in privatized utilities was approved. So was the Britain in the Modern World policy review, which proposed the cancellation of one of the four planned Trident submarines, the introduction of British nuclear weapons into international arms talks, no modernization of short-range nuclear missiles in Europe, the abandonment of NATO's flexible response strategy, the elimination of all nuclear weapons by 2000 and no first use of British nuclear weapons. Other decisions included the rejection of a call to phase out nuclear power stations within 15 years and of Labour's former policy of unilateralism, the reduction of defence spending to the West European average, and the rejection of moves to make the European Parliament the principal legisla tive body of the EC.

3 Oct: Labour conference approves the Economic Equality policy review which proposes to end the tax on childcare, introduce a minimum wage, set up income tax levels graduated from below 20 per cent to 50 per cent, increase child benefit, tax gift and inheritance at the point of receipt, close down tax loopholes, raise pensions

immediately, introduce a new disability benefit, simplify income support rules and retain mortgage tax relief. Other decisions were to allow retirement for both men and women on full pensions at 60, with an option to take early retirement at 55, a restoration of cuts in young people's benefits and a quota of 40 per cent for women's representation on all party committees. The conference also rejected both the idea of black sections and the leadership's compromise proposals for a black socialist society.

4 Oct: Labour conference approves the People at Work policy review, which proposes to replace Tory legislation with positive rights, to allow sympathy actions, a review of the use of interim injunctions to prevent disputes, the restoration of trade union immunities for certain kinds of secondary action, an end to the sequestration of trade union assets, a Charter of Employee Rights, an expansion of childcare facilities and full rights for part-time workers. The conference also approved the Physical and Social Environment policy document which proposes the establishment of a Ministry of Environmental Protection and an independent Environmental Protection Executive, a wildlife and countryside service, a Clean Water Act, a 'polluter pays' principle, a ban on the import and export of toxic waste and a major housing programme. Other decisions included a call to immediately renationalize any land sold off by privatized water companies.

5 Oct: Labour conference approves the Consumers and the Community policy review, which proposes a Department of Consumer Affairs, funding for local, regional and national consumer groups, quality and standards controls in local government, health and education services, the replacement of the Audit Commission with a Quality Commission and the creation of a Education Standards Council and a Health Quality Commission, increasing preventative medicine, a flexible national curriculum and records of achievements for pupils. The conference also approved the Democracy and the Individual policy review which proposes to replace the Lords with an elected second chamber, devolution for Scotland, Wales and the English regions, the unification of Ireland only by the consent of the majority in the North, a Freedom of Information Act, a Ministry of Women, a Department of Legal Administration to run the courts, an exten sion of legal aid, integrated childcare facilities for the under-fives and a Children's Commissioner as an ombudsman on children's rights. The conference also rejected by a large majority a proposal to set up a working party to consider options on PR and electoral reform.

6 Oct: Labour conference condemns the privatization of security at defence establishments, instructs the NEC to prepare a scheme for widening party democracy and streamlining conference procedures, rejects a call for the next Labour government to introduce a Bill of Rights and supports a reduction in the age of consent for homosexual acts to 16.

10 Oct: On the opening day of the Conservative conference Sir Peter Lane, the chairman of the National Union Executive Committee agrees, in view of conference votes, to recommend the affiliation to the party of a model Conservative association set up in North Down.

16 Oct: SLD changes its short name to Liberal Democrats.

17 Oct: *Negotiating the Rapids: Socialist Policies for the 1990s* Socialist Society, calls for the left to support PR.

25 Oct: Allegations aired on BBC television programme 'Despatches' that Tory anti-semitism played a part in the campaign against Edwina Currie after her gaffe about salmonella in eggs in 1988.

1 Nov: New Labour Shadow Cabinet elected: Gordon Brown (162 votes), John Smith (153), Robin Cook (141), Tony Blair (138), Gerald Kaufman (134), Joan Lestor (129), Jo Richardson (126), Jack Cunningham (125), Bryan Gould (124), Frank Dobson (118), John Prescott (116), Michael Meacher (115), David Clark (111), Ann Clwyd (111), Donald Dewar (109), Barry Jones (108), Margaret Beckett (106), Jack Straw (104).

5 Nov: Interview with Mrs Thatcher in *The Sunday Correspondent* suggests for the first time that the next election will be the last that she fights as leader of the Conservative Party.

7 Nov: Attempt to include in the Companies Bill the right for shareholders to veto company donations to political parties is overturned in the Lords by 223 to 110.

15 Nov: Labour's policy review is critically assessed in Mike Craven's *Labour and Business: The Implications for Industry of a Labour Government's Legislative Programme* Market Access International.

24 Nov: Sir Anthony Meyer confirms he will definitely stand against Mrs Thatcher in the Tory Party leadership election.

25 Nov: Mrs Thatcher indicates determination to fight two more general elections in an interview on US television.

5 Dec: In the Conservative Party leadership election Mrs Thatcher wins 314 votes, Sir Anthony Meyer 33 and 27 abstained.

8 Dec: Frank Field MP is deselected as Labour candidate in Birkenhead in favour of local TGWU official Paul Davies.

15 Dec: John Hughes MP is deselected as Labour candidate in Coventry NW in favour of Bob Ainsworth.

21 Dec: Home Office consultation paper on election expenses published.

Elections in Britain

DAVID BUTLER

There are many ways in which politicians take the pulse of the nation. General elections provide the ultimate measure, but between those quinquennial events, every indicator is eagerly scrutinized. The year 1989 was notable for a major switch in party support. A long period of Conservative predominance came to an end: the party dismissed its ill fortune as a mid-term slump but Labour spokesmen hailed it as the turn of the tide.

The year 1989 provided the one full nationwide test of voter allegiance due during the third Thatcher Parliament. On 15 June, British electors were asked, for the third time, to choose their representatives for a five-year European Parliament. The campaign was low-key. For once Labour managed to sound more pro-European than the Conservatives. Some Conservative MEPs indicated their distaste for the way in which Mrs Thatcher took over the campaign and distanced herself from European idealism.

When it came to the vote only 36.5 per cent of the electorate went to the polls (but that was 5 per cent more than in 1984 or 1979). Their ballots demonstrated a marked swing to Labour, exactly reversing the majority at Strasbourg from 45 Conservative and 32 Labour to 45 Labour and 32 Conservative. The swing to Labour compared to the 1985 Euro-election was 4.4 per cent; set against the 1987 general election it was 9.1 per cent. The Conservatives lost their last two seats in Scotland, as well as four in the North, three in the Midlands and three in London. It was the first time Mrs Thatcher had led her party to defeat at the polls.

But the most sensational aspect of the result was the upsurge of the Greens and the downfall of the centre parties. The Green vote jumped from almost nothing to 14.9 per cent and the Centre parties' vote collapsed from 19.5 per cent to 6.5 per cent. These percentage changes match the largest ever recorded in Britain (the Conservative fall of 14 per cent in 1945 and the Liberal/Alliance rises of 12 per cent in 1974 and 12 per cent in 1983) and provide the only other instances since 1931 of a party's nationwide vote increasing or decreasing by over 10 per cent.

The Greens came ahead of the Centre candidate in every seat except Devon and Cornwall and actually pushed Labour into third place in six South of England constituencies. In the extreme North, Mrs Ewing easily held onto Highlands and Islands for the Scottish National Party. Two of the three Northern Ireland seats, decided by proportional representation, went to the only Westminster members to

Table 1. Euro-Election results, 15 June 1989

	Seats (UK) 1989 (1985)	Votes % (GB) 1989 (1985)	Votes % (GB) 1987
Conservative	32 (45)	34.7 (40.8)	43.3
Labour	45 (32)	40.1 (36.5)	31.5
Centre	– (–)	6.7 (19.5)	23.1
Green	– (–)	14.9 (0.6)	0.3
Other	4 (4)	3.6 (2.7)	1.8

stand for Europe – Ian Paisley (Democratic Unionist) and John Hume (SDLP); the third seat was held by an official Unionist.

Opinion polls make the most continuous dent on party morale. From 1987 to early 1989 the Conservatives maintained a better poll position than any previous government had managed in the 18 months after a general election. They stayed continuously in the lead and their average rating of 45 per cent seemed to presage a healthy future for Mrs Thatcher.

But during 1989 the mood changed. The economy failed to respond to Mr Lawson's medicine and, as interest rates and balance of payments deficits went up while inflation refused to fall, disillusion set in. Labour's abandonment of its 'unacceptable' defence and trade union stances must have helped; and Mrs Thatcher certainly suffered first from the clumsy hype of her tenth anniversary in

Table 2. Opinion polls 1989 (monthly average of nationwide published polls)

	Con	Lab	Dem	SDP	Green
Jan	45	38	10	4	
Feb	40	39	10	6	
Mar	42	40	8	6	
Apr	41	40	8	6	
May	43	42	7	3	
Jun	36	45	6	3	6
Jul	36	45	5	4	7
Aug	37	45	6	3	7
Sep	37	44	6	3	8
Oct	38	48	5	2	5
Nov	37	49	6	3	4
Dec					

Table 3. Parliamentary by-elections 1989 (%)

Turnout		Con	Lab	SLD	SDP	Green	Nat	Others
62.0 Pontypridd	Lab Hold	13.5	53.4	3.9	3.1	–	25.3	0.8
–14.8 Feb 23		–6.0	–2.9	–11.9		–	+20.0	+0.8
64.2 Richmond (Yorks)	Con Hold	37.2	4.9	22.0	32.2	2.8	–	0.9
–7.9 Feb 23		–24.0	–6.9	+27.2		+2.8	–	+0.9
70.7 Vale of Glamorgan	Lab Gain	36.3	48.9	4.2	2.3	2.0	3.5	2.8
–8.6 May 4		–10.5	+14.2	–10.2		+2.0	+1.7	+2.8
52.9 Glasgow Central	Lab Hold	7.6	54.6	1.5	1.0	3.8	30.2	1.2
–12.7 June 15		–5.4	–9.9	–8.0		+2.9	+20.2	0.0
44.4 Vauxhall	Lab Hold	8.8	52.8	17.5	–	6.1	–	4.8
–19.6 June 15		–10.2	+2.6	–0.7	–	+4.3	–	+4.0

office in May and then from the mishandled reshuffle of July and the Lawson resignation in October. For the second half of the year the Conservatives stayed well behind Labour in the polls. The Centre vote fell to its lowest since the 1970s and the deserters seem to have divided fairly evenly between Conservative, Labour and the Greens. But the Greens never recorded support comparable to their 14.9 per cent vote in the Euro-elections and the Democrats never matched the 20 per cent they gained on average in local elections.

The by-elections continued to be infrequent. Only eight took place in the first 30 months after the 1987 general election; five of these occurred in 1989, three caused by death and two by Euro-appointments. Three of them were masked by being held simultaneously with local or European elections.

The contests in the Labour strongholds of Pontypridd in February and of Glasgow Central in June were mainly notable for the upsurge of the Nationalists vote which, in each case, advanced by 20 per cent, raising their candidate from fourth to second place. However, after the loss of Glasgow Govan to the SNP in November 1988, Labour was relieved to get back in each seat with well over 50 per cent of the vote. The other fight in a safe Labour seat, Vauxhall, seemed to presage trouble for the party when the National Executive overturned the selection of a black nominee – but the dissidents made no impact and the Labour vote increased: this by-election provided the first parliamentary context in which a Green candidate passed the deposit-saving threshold of 5 per cent.

The two by-elections that caused most stir were those in Richmond and in the Vale of Glamorgan. In Richmond in February, the Conservative vote slumped by 24 per cent and the seat would have been lost but for the even division of the vote between the Liberal candidate and Dr Owen's SDP – and even so the SDP

Table 4. Shire county elections May 4 (change from 1985)

	Seats	Votes %			Council majorities	
Con	1298	+77	40.5	+4.3	9	+7
Lab	1450	+67	32.2	+0.6	12	+4
Dem	479	−112	19.7	⎫	1	−
SDP	14	−22	1.3	⎬ −5.5	−	−
Others	257	−20	6.3	⎭ +0.6	3	−
No control					12	−11

candidate, a well-known local councillor, ran the Conservatives close. The SDP achievement was the party's only electoral success – but it was a major setback for Mr Ashdown's Democrats. The Vale of Glamorgan saw Labour win a seat that had been Conservative since 1951. It was only the fourth by-election gain by Labour since 1970. Coming on the day of Labour's local election successes (and the tenth anniversary of Mrs Thatcher's taking office) and at a time when at last the party had reached level terms with the Conservatives in the opinion polls, this victory seemed to mark the turn of the tide for Labour.

The Shire county elections on Thursday, 4 May, affected only half the nation. London, the old Metropolitan counties, and Scotland had no contests. The Shires had last voted in 1985, at a relatively bad time for the government; thus there was less scope for Opposition gains than in past years.

In fact all parties found some comfort in the outcome. The Alliance vote slumped and they lost their balance of power position in ten counties. But they forfeited only a fifth of the seats won in 1985, far fewer than they had feared, and they continued to control the Isle of Wight and to have a balancing position in ten other counties. Labour could rejoice in 67 net gains compared to 1985 and in winning control of Humberside, Lancashire, Northumberland, and Clwyd.

The Conservatives, prepared for disaster, found that they had recovered full control from hung councils in seven counties and that they had won 77 more seats than in 1985.

Although each of the large parties had cause for relief, it was a minor party that had most reason to celebrate. The average vote for Green candidates was 8 per cent. They only won one seat but they demonstrated for the first time that they were a nationwide force.

Commentators, adding up the votes in marginal constituencies, or applying the nationwide swing to the 1987 general election results, concluded that on such a division of strength Labour would have been within a hairsbreadth of a clear

Table 5. Local government by-elections 1989

	Conservative		Labour		Centre +	
	won	net change	won	net change	won	net change
Jan–Mar	29	−9	24	+1	27	+10
Apr–Jun	91	−21	94	+24	41	−
Jul–Sep	25	−25	27	+8	21	−
Oct–Dec	36	−36	47	+8	17	−4

+Centre combines the Democrats and the SDP (throughout 1989 the SDP lost 8 seats and gained none in by-elections. *The* Democrats could thus claim a net gain of 14 not 6). David Cowling of ITN provided the data for this table.

Table 6. Northern Ireland council results

	1985		1987	
	Seats	Votes	Seats	Votes
OUP	190	29.5	194	30.1
DUP	142	24.3	110	18.6
SDLP	101	17.8	121	20.8
Sinn Fein	59	11.8	43	11.1
Alliance	34	7.1	38	6.9
Workers Party	4	1.6	4	2.2
Others	36	4.4	56	10.3
Turnout	−	60%	55%	

parliamentary majority. But the Conservatives could point to what happened in the 1987 general election after an even worse result in the 1985 county contests.

Local government by-elections can supplement opinion polls in offering a continuous measure of the ups and downs of party support. About 250 occur every year, spread out week by week. Despite low turnout they do offer a valuable political barometer. It is notable that the centre parties have never fared as badly in these contests as in the opinion polls. Over 1989 as a whole, the Liberal Democrats made a net gain in seats even while their poll rating was being halved.

One quite separate set of local elections took place on 18 May in Northern Ireland. For the first time since 1985 the people of the six counties had a chance to vote for the 26 District Councils which cover the province. The voting was by proportional representation.

The control of councils changed only in a few cases. After the election, Unionists of some sort had a clear majority in 17 councils (18 in 1985), while five contained a majority of Catholic councillors (eight in 1985). Four councils were deadlocked between Orange and Green (two in 1985).

Electoral legislation is rare. But July 1989 saw the Royal Assent to a new Representation of the People Act. Its provisions were hardly earthshaking. The right of British citizens living overseas to vote (exercised by only 13,000 of the half million potentially eligible in 1987) was extended from five years to 25 years. The government estimated that 60,000 of the two million who would be eligible would take advantage of the facility. A threefold increase in the legal limit on expenses was also permitted – but only for by-elections where, it was agreed, all parties had been guilty of flagrant overspending.

Local Government

KIERON WALSH

Introduction

The last decade has been a time of great change in local government, with financial constraint, legislative change and debate about the proper relationship between the public and private sectors. The governments of 1979 to 1987 made substantial revisions to the local government finance system, introduced rate-capping, abolished the Greater London Council and the metropolitan counties and introduced council house sale amongst many other changes. But the previous developments were relatively minor compared with the proposals for change that have been introduced since Mrs Thatcher's third election victory in 1987. Between 1979 and 1987 the basic patterns of operation of local government largely continued unchanged, and, while individual authorities introduced new approaches, there was no widespread acceptance that radical change was needed.

The legislation that has been introduced since 1987 has raised fundamental questions about the future of local government and the way that it should operate. The traditional understanding about the nature of the public service and local authority management is being questioned both by right and left. Local government has traditionally been self-sufficient, hierarchically controlled and professionally dominated, but it is becoming more concerned with working with other agencies, decentralizing control and emphasizing management more than professionalism.

The changes that are being made in the organization and management of local government are paralleled by changes in the approach to the organization of the Civil Service and the National Health Service (NHS). In both cases there are attempts to develop more accountable management, delegate financial responsibility and control, and introduce commercial attitudes. The Civil Service, for example, has experienced a great deal of competitive tendering, and the *Next Steps* report proposes the development of agencies working on a commercial basis. In the NHS the changes proposed in *Working for Patients* are largely based on concepts of internal trading and commercial management styles. The changes in local government are part of fundamental changes in the culture of the public service and the concept of public administration.

The Framework of Change

Between 1987 and 1989 legislation has been introduced to change the way that education, housing, economic development and local government finance will operate. Competitive tendering has been introduced for a range of local authority services. Legislation has been introduced, following the Widdicombe Report, on the conduct of local authority business. Most recently the government has given a commitment to implement the Griffiths Report on the future of community care and has published a White Paper detailing its proposals. Each of these developments on its own involves major change, together they will require an almost total reorganization of the way that local authorities work. Behind the various individual changes lies the assumption that market principles, commercialization and an entrepreneurial style of management will improve the way that local authorities work.

Education

The Education Reform Act 1988 has significantly reduced the power of the local authority to control education through a combination of the centralization and decentralization of control. Powers have been concentrated in the hands of the Secretary of State for Education and devolved from the local education authority to the school and to parents. The local authority is largely left with a monitoring, quality control and resource allocation role. Further education colleges have been given greater autonomy and polytechnics and some colleges of higher education have been given complete freedom from local government, granted corporate status and are now funded through the Polytechnics and Colleges Funding Council. In primary and secondary education changes have been made in what is to be taught, the financing of schools, processes of entry to school, school autonomy and the rights of schools to move out of local authority control altogether.

A national curriculum is to be introduced covering ten subjects to be taught to all pupils and attainment targets are to be set and children tested at the ages of 7, 11, 14 and 16. The local education authority's role in the curriculum will largely be limited to ensuring that the national curriculum is implemented in schools, though formal responsibility for the curriculum is rather uneasily shared between the authority, the school and the Secretary of State for Education. Schools are to be given control of their own budgets for the great proportion of their expenditure, only a relatively small amount being retained centrally by the local authority for the provision of common services. Schools will have considerable freedom over whether they use the local authority's services, for example, for cleaning or grounds maintenance. The local authority is required to determine the budget for each school according to a formula largely dependent upon the number of pupils weighted according to age. The system of delegated financial control is to be phased in from 1990 and will apply to all except the smaller primary schools. Parents are to be allowed to send their child to the school of their choice as long as there is physical space to do so, and the system of admission limits is to be abandoned. Schools are to be allowed to opt out of the local authority system and become grant-maintained, being funded directly by central government if they so wish, and a small number have already chosen to do so. A number of schools – city technology colleges – have been established which are wholly outside the control of the local authority. Industry has been unwilling to provide funds for city technology colleges and it is unlikely that many more will be established. In 1989 local authorities have largely been preparing for the introduction of the new system that will begin to have its effect from 1990 onwards.

Housing

The major developments in housing before 1987 were the cuts in the level of public funding and the sales of council houses. Housing has been the service most affected by financial cutbacks. The aim of the Local Government and Housing Act is to move local authorities even further from direct provision towards a strategic role with other agencies, notably housing associations, being the main providers. Tenants are to be allowed to pick their own landlords, and a few authorities have already passed the responsibility for their stock over to a housing association, normally established with the co-operation of the authority itself. The government has proposed that a small number of poor estates should be taken over by Housing Action Trusts, funded directly by central government and operating much like Urban Development Corporations, a proposal which has aroused much antagonism on the estates involved. The finance of local authority housing is to change with the Housing Revenue Account being 'ring-fenced', that is, receiving no subsidy from the rate fund. The system of financial support for poorer tenants is to be changed so that more of the cost is likely to be met from within the Housing Revenue Account itself, which is likely to lead to higher rents in many authorities.

Social Services

The Griffiths Report in 1988 proposed that the primary responsibility for ensuring that the elderly and people with mental and physical disabilities receive adequate care should lie with local authorities, though they should not necessarily be the major providers of services. The existing system, as the Audit Commission's damning study had shown, is ineffective and wasteful because responsibility is fragmented and contradictory. Griffiths argued that the local authority should hold the care budgets, be responsible for letting contracts for provision by the private sector and voluntary agencies, and for monitoring the standards of provision. After much agonizing the government has accepted this proposal. Detailed legislation has yet to be produced and the process of reform, given the massive changes that have already been proposed for the NHS, will be complex. Much will also depend upon the adequacy of the money that is made available. Community care is not a cheap option.

Finance

There were many changes to the local government finance system between 1979 and 1987 as the government attempted to control local expenditure. There were a number of local government finance acts and increasing confrontations between central and local government often ending in the courts. As local government finance became more complex and more constrained financial management became more difficult. Local authorities searched for new sources of finance and developed more sophisticated approaches to management. In large part these developments were the natural result of the increasing tightness of the financial system. The uncertainty that was created sometimes led to extremely complex problems over the legality of action, as in the case of interest rate swaps.

The complexity of local government finance is likely to grow in future. It will be compounded by the Local Government Finance Act 1988 which introduced a fundamental reorganization of the system. Domestic rates are to be replaced by the community charge, a flat rate tax levied on everybody over the age of 18. The community charge has generated considerable antagonism in Scotland where it has already been introduced, and seems likely to be at least as unpopular in England and Wales. (Nobody seems yet to have seen it as appropriate for Northern Ireland.) The potential impact of the community charge in some Conservative constituencies has led the government to abolish the safety net, by which lower spending authorities would subsidize higher spenders, after the first year of operation. Subsidy will be provided directly by the Treasury.

The 'business' rate is to be replaced by the national non-domestic rate, which will involve the same level of payment all over the country, with central government distributing the proceeds to local authorities according to population. There has been a revaluation of commercial and industrial property which has led to a considerable increase in the rates of many. The change will lead to great changes in the regional patterns of business rates. The grant system is also to be radically changed and simplified.

The method of capital expenditure control is to be changed from a system of capital allocations to a system of credit approvals and credit limits. Local authorities are to be required to use capital receipts from council house and other sales largely to redeem debt, and the method of debt repayment is to be changed. More use of charging for local services is to be encouraged and in some cases required. All of these changes will reduce the financial autonomy and flexibility

of the local authority. Again, 1989 has been a year of preparation for the changes
in local finance as authorities prepare the community charge register and develop
new computer systems.

Competition

The Local Government Planning and Land Act 1980 introduced competitive
tendering for highways and building construction and maintenance. The Local
Government Act 1988 has extended this competitive approach to a number of other
local authority services – known as 'defined activities'. If the local authority wishes
to carry out a defined activity by the employment of its own labour force, then it
is required to win the right to do so in a specified tender process, with private sector
companies being allowed to compete for the work. The defined activities are refuse
collection, cleaning of streets and buildings, catering, vehicle and grounds
maintenance and the management of sports leisure facilities. Authorities are
required not to act in such a way as to restrict competition, for example, by creating
contracts that are so big that no firms can compete for them. The tender process is
specified and if the local authority wins the tender then it must keep a separate
internal trading account for the relevant service. The first round of tenders were
held in August 1989 and were largely won by the local authorities. Further rounds
of competition will be held every six months. The impact on the management of
local authorities, particularly shire district councils has been considerable, for
example, with the establishment of internal client–contractor systems.

The Conduct of Local Authority Business

The Widdicombe Report proposed changes in the way that the business of the local
authority was conducted and particularly in the relation between officers and
members and the operation of committees. Many of these recommendations, with
some adjustment and reinterpretation, are now implemented in the Local
Government and Housing Act. Each authority is required to designate a head of
the paid service, who must report annually on the management of the authority.
The authority must designate a monitoring officer who must check the legal
propriety of actions taken by the authority. The Secretary of State is to set rules on
the appointment, discipline and dismissal of officers. Places on committees are to
be required to be allocated in accordance with the relative size of political groups
on the Council. Officers of a relatively senior level are to be disqualified from being
elected members of other authorities and from playing an active part in politics.
There are also likely to be changes in the way that members' allowances will
operate in future.

The Inner City

The government's stated commitment to the development of the inner cities has had limited effect. A number of programmes have been introduced, for example, the extension of Urban Development Corporations and the establishment of City Action Teams. But no clear unified policy has emerged and the Audit Commission has condemned the government's approach as a 'patchwork quilt of complexity and idiosyncrasy'. Much of the problem follows from the lack of co-ordination between departments in central government.

The Nature of the Change

The changes that have been introduced by the government are based upon a number of concepts, at the base of which is the attempt to reduce the self-sufficient power of the local authority. This is to be done through the introduction of a combination of central control, the establishment of specialist agencies, the enhancing of citizen choice and the development of market processes. The extreme vision is of the local authority as an enabling body, itself providing only the minimum of service and acting to ensure that other bodies are able to develop and deliver services through a combination of contracting, grant-aiding, hiving-off and co-operative working. The vision is of a much more dispersed pattern of provision at the local level, integrated through market-type processes rather than through planning and local authority control. The management of the public service is seen as requiring an increasingly commercial approach.

Central Control

The growth of central control has been a consistent feature of government action since 1979, as can be seen in the considerable number of powers that have been taken by ministers in the various statutes that have been introduced on local government matters. Ministers, with their powers to make subsidiary legislation, are able to make rapid changes in the way that local authorities shall operate. It can be argued that central controls have been increased only so that the centre can give greater power to the citizen, but, whatever the reason, the increase in central power has led to an increase in the tension between the two levels of government, often ending in the courts. The large number of statutes and the level of change that they embody are bound to lead to a continuation of contests between central and local government in the courts. Co-operative working between the two levels of government is difficult.

Market Mechanisms

The introduction of market mechanisms is central to many aspects of the government's policy towards local authorities. Even if services are not to be provided by the private sector it is still possible to create such mechanisms. The most obvious example is the requirement that local authorities compete for the right to provide certain services after winning a tender. Even if they win they must operate on an internal trading basis. But, more generally, many of the changes that have been introduced are based upon the separation of the roles of provision and production and the development of internal markets. The concept of the enabling authority, as it has been propounded by Nicholas Ridley, is largely based upon the idea that those who are responsible for ensuring that services are provided need not actually provide those services themselves. Their job is to specify what is required, let contracts and monitor performance.

The attempt to develop the enabling approach has led a small number of authorities to consider how they can rid themselves of the direct responsibility for provision, for example, through management buyouts, the use of the voluntary sector or other authorities actually to produced services or the wholesale privatization of activities. In the long term it may be that some authorities will reduce their direct service delivery provision considerably but there is no evidence that this will be a rapid process, and the vast majority of authorities see themselves as continuing to be major producers of services through directly employed labour.

The more common process is the separation of client and contractor roles within the authority. The introduction of competitive tendering almost inevitably means more internal separation of client and contractor if the authority is not to be seen as having behaved anti-competitively. The reorganization of the education service is based partly on the separation of client and contractor relations, with the school being free to use certain of the authority's services as a client. The concept is developing more widely as each service within the authority begins to see itself as having an internal or external client to whom it must market its services. A number of authorities are establishing central services such as law and personnel on a trading basis within the authority, with other departments, as clients, contracting for specific levels of service at a given price.

Managerial Changes

Patterns of management are changing in response to the legislative and other changes that local authorities face. The main developments are the delegation of financial responsibility, service decentralization and the search for more accountable and performance-based management. The separation of client and contractor roles and the requirement to compete are leading authorities to create a cost- and profit-centre based form of management. The managers of cost and profit centres are given greater responsiblity for their budgets than has traditionally been the case. In one or two cases there have even been management buyouts of local authority services, for example, refuse collection in Westminster. Financial delegation is not only being required by central government, as in the case of schools, but actively developed by a number of local authorities.

Service decentralization has been a strong theme in some authorities and some services. A very small number of authorities have organized themselves predominantly on a decentralized basis, most notably Tower Hamlets. More commonly the principles of decentralization have been applied to specific services, particularly housing and social services. Housing departments have been establishing neighbourhood and estate offices and social services departments developing patch teams and local management. Along with decentralization goes an emphasis on more accountable management and performance. Senior managers are increasingly being appointed on fixed term contracts, and paid according to performance.

The Consumer Emphasis

Local government has traditionally been dominated by professionals. The present changes are leading to a new focus on those who receive the services that are produced. In part this development is the result of self-interest and a desire for self-preservation, with local authorities concerned to ensure that their housing tenants or schools do not desert them. But there is also a recognition that people can begin to see alternatives to the provision of local services by local government. Local authorities are decentralizing services in order to bring them closer to those who need them. They are introducing changes that are intended to make services more easily accessible to those who use them. Westminster City Council, for example, has introduced a 'one-stop shop' so that people do not have to find their way to a number of different and scattered offices in the authority. Others are introducing complaints systems and, in one case, a citizens' charter. Many authorities have introduced marketing officers and approaches to try to improve the way that their services are delivered. Consumer surveys have become popular as authorities have become concerned to discover what those who use their services think of what they get and what it is that they want.

Politics

The changes that are being introduced in local government focus on the way in which services are to be managed. Indeed the way in which management is to operate (for example, the degree to which internal trading or markets are appropriate), has itself become a political matter. The emphasis on management brings into question the role that the elected members will play for example, in the monitoring of services that are subject to competitive tendering. In some authorities new mechanisms such as management boards which operate rather differently from traditional committees have been introduced. But many elected members find themselves unclear about how they fit into the new systems, and new emphases, such as those on strategy and enabling, will take a great deal of working through. Many of the changes that have been introduced take too little account of the political nature of local government, which goes beyond the provision of services to a concern for the overall nature and development of the local community.

There was little formal political change in local authorities in 1989. There were elections in the shire county councils. The main result was a move away from 'hung' authorities in which no single party had overall control, with both Labour and Conservative parties gaining control of a number of counties. The vote for the Alliance declined, though not by as much as might have been expected on the basis of opinion polls. Local politics are likely to be of great significance in coming years since many of the major changes being introduced by the government affect the local authority so directly. The increase in the importance of local government as a political arena, which has been apparent in the 1980s, is likely to continue.

Conclusion

Local government is changing quickly in the face of new problems, changes in the statutory framework within which it must operate and new ideas about appropriate forms of the management and delivery of service. Externally local authorities face new problems, for instance, as the concern for the environment develops. A number of authorities are coming to see themselves as having a total responsibility for the character and well-being of the local area in which they operate, which has been heightened by recent public health worries and disasters. Increasing attention is being paid to the regulatory role of the local authority. Local authorities, faced with the limitations on their powers to provide individual services, are widening their view of the way that their influence can be used.

Internally local authorities will face problems in the 1990s as the shortage of staff which is already affecting a number of authorities, particularly in the South-East of England, becomes more acute. These problems and anxieties are likely to enhance trends that are already apparent. A broader concern for health and the environment will require authorities to work with other agencies. Shortage of staff will force authorities to look for new ways of working.

The year 1989 has been one of massive change for local government. Authorities have had to prepare for new legislation in housing, finance, education, the conduct of business, economic development and competitive tendering. But the changes that are happening do not result only from the pressure of legislation; they also reflect changed views about how local authorities should be managed. There is a growing concern for the quality of service and for developing services that are less remote and more responsive. Though much of the pressure for change has come from outside the authority, many authorities have themselves recognized that new approaches to the development and delivery of services are necessary.

Chronology

2 Feb: Local Government and Housing Bill published. It aims to limit local authorities' powers to spend capital receipts from the sale of council houses on council building. Its most controversial aspect is a restriction on the political activities of senior local government officers. It also strengthens the power of local government ombudsmen and introduces tighter controls on local government expenditure.

14 Feb: Order to prevent councils from using receipts from council house sales to pre-fund projects for future years issued. Any temptation to use share-dealing to lessen the impact of the compulsion to redeem council debt is also removed.

15 Feb: Government announces that businesses are to be cushioned against steep increases in rates when the national business rate is introduced in 1990.

28 Feb: Government refuses to come to the aid of Hammersmith and Fulham Council which faces potential losses of up to £60 million on elaborate interest rate swap dealings on the money markets over the past two years. The auditor's report suggests that some of these were possibly illegal.

2 Mar: It is revealed that Haringey Council has also made losses on interest rate swap deals.

3 Mar: Full account of the chain of events that led to the crisis at Hammersmith and Fulham released.

7 Mar: Bradford budget cuts and zero rate increase set on the casting vote of the Tory Lord Mayor.

22 Mar: Default notices against two of the local authorities involved in interest rate swap deals, Hammersmith and Fulham and Blackburn, issued by Saloman Brothers.

29 Mar: British Bankers' Association lobbies for an amendment clarifying the position on interest rate swap deals to be inserted into the Local Government and Housing Bill.

31 Mar: Audit Commission suggests tighter controls to prevent councils over-committing themselves to the financial markets.

21 Apr: In Stockdale v Haringey Council the Court of Appeal rules that ratecapped councils could not use their loans funds to meet expenditure.

24 Apr: Leading international banks announce decision to go ahead with legal action to recover funds from Ogwr council owing on interest-rate swap deals.

9 May: Government forced to halt the distribution of an explanatory leaflet on the poll tax in England and Wales after a High Court judge ruled that it was potentially misleading.

10 May: Hard-left candidate committed to confrontation with the government ousts the moderate leader of Labour- controlled Lambeth Council.

16 May: Attempt to halt £1 million publicity campaign for the poll tax fails in the High Court.

23 May: Legal challenge to Bradford's Lord Mayor's use of the casting vote to put through controversial Tory measures dismissed in the Court of Appeal.

22 June: Queen's Bench rules that Greenwich Council was entitled to remove two councillors who had resigned from the ruling Labour group from committees in order to ensure that it could carry out its policy.

27 June: Writs served on a number of interest rate swap councils by Midland Bank and Citicorp.

28 June: Nicholas Ridley refuses to use the Local Government and Housing Bill to clarify the law on interest-rate swaps.

12 July: It is confirmed that at least 16 councils have asked questions on poll tax registration forms which are illegal under the Data Protection Act.

19 July: BBC television programme, 'Panorama', accuses the Conservative-controlled Westminster Council of gerrymandering by pumping money into services in key marginal wards in order to retain control.

The government changes its poll tax safety net designed to ease transition to the system for the first four or five years.

25 July: Revelation that Westminster Council hired far-right activists to boost its flagging electoral fortunes.

Regulations on poll tax rebates in England and Wales approved in the Commons.

3 Aug: Plans for economic development powers for local authorities published.

14 Aug: London Fire Brigade announce plans for 26 high-technology resuscitation units spread through the capital.

4 Sept: Order issued for Bristol and Hillingdon to answer allegations of anti-competitive practice under the Local Government Act 1988.

5 Sept: New powers for the Fire and Civil Defence authorities to co-ordinate responses to disasters in metropolitan areas announced.

8 Sept: Competition for building and highways maintenance work extended.

26 Sept: Plans for changing the approach to the management of waste disposal announced.

2 Oct: Consultation paper on political activity by local government officers published.

Hammersmith and Fulham admit in the High Court on the first day of the case brought by Anthony Hazell, the District Auditor, that £6 billion worth of deals it undertook on the money markets were illegal.

9 Oct: Government announces changes to poll tax rules giving local authorities discretion to set lower or no charges for second homes and exempting about 50,000 young people in schools and further education.

11 Oct: Government to spend more than £1 billion before the next general election to smooth the introduction of the poll tax in England and Wales by subsidies rather than safety net funded by lower charge paying areas.

18 Oct: Ministers accept Opposition amendments to the Local Government and Housing Bill limiting the curbs on the political activities of senior local government officers.

1 Nov: £6 billion interest-rate swap deals by Hammersmith and Fulham Council ruled unlawful in the High Court.

6 Nov: Assumed figures for the poll tax charges in each local authority in England announced by the government.

27 Nov: *The Price of Winning Services to Community Action and Trade Unions*, a study for Manchester City Council, shows that local councils have won 81 per cent of compulsorily tendered contracts but at the cost of substantial job losses among lower paid workers and for an estimated saving of £50 million.

Britain and the European Community

STEPHEN GEORGE

During 1989 the issue of Britain's role in the European Community (EC) became central to domestic political debate, helped by the elections to the European Parliament that took place in June and by the pressure for rapid progress towards closer European unity that came from Brussels. The parameters for the debate had been set in September of 1988 in a speech by the Prime Minister to students of the College of Europe in Bruges.

The Bruges Speech

In her speech Mrs Thatcher outlined the policy of the British government towards Europe. Although she emphasized Britain's commitment to the EC, the passage that received the most publicity was that in which she rejected the idea of increased centralization of power in Brussels, and supported instead the idea of 'willing and active cooperation between independent sovereign states.'[1]

The speech caused quite a stir because it was seen as a challenge to several aspects of the '1992' programme. The EC aims by 1992 to have abolished all remaining barriers to the free movement of goods, labour and capital between its member states, and thereby to have created a single European market. This freeing of the internal market is fully supported by the British government, but the European Commission and most of the other member states believe that it is necessary for the freeing of the market to be accompanied by certain other measures with which the British government does not agree. Of these other measures the most significant are the introduction of a monetary union that would involve a single European currency either existing alongside or replacing national currencies, and of a 'social charter' that would guarantee certain minimum rights to workers throughout the EC.

Within a few weeks of the Bruges speech the President of the European Commission, Jacques Delors, and the prime ministers of most of the other member states, had made public their disagreement with Mrs Thatcher's view of the future of Europe. But the speech also led to the formation of groups in Britain, France and other member states which supported her rejection of centralized regulation and

her celebration of national identity. Although the Bruges speech really said nothing
new, it became a focal point for debate about the future of the EC.

Corruption and Fraud

During the first three months of 1989 the opponents of more supranational control
were apparently offered a perfect opportunity to press their case. In January the
European Parliament opened public hearings into the use of fraud to obtain
payments from the budget of the EC. The initial evidence indicated that fraud,
particularly to obtain money from the fund that covers the Common Agricultural
Policy, was widespread and on a large scale.

When in February the Secretary of State for Agriculture publicly called for
urgent action to curb such fraud, it looked as though the government was about to
use these revelations to make political capital in its dispute with the Commission.
That impression was reinforced when Sir John Hoskyns, who was thought to be
close to the Prime Minister, used the occasion of his farewell speech as Director
General of the Institute of Directors, to launch a fierce attack on the EC, accusing
the Brussels machine of being 'corrupted both intellectually and financially'. He
spoke of 'growing evidence of confused objectives, protectionism, cynical
disregard of Community rules, dreams of sixties-style social engineering,
administrative incompetence, bureaucratic dishonesty and fraud', thereby linking
a restatement of Mrs Thatcher's objections to some aspects of the Commission's
programme for 1992 with the fraud issue.[2]

However, any idea that Sir John was acting as a mouthpiece for the Prime
Minister or the government was soon dispelled. Peter Jenkins reported in *The
Independent*[3] that Mrs Thatcher sent a 'hot-line message' to Jacques Delors
disassociating herself from the sentiments expressed, and Lord Young of Graffham,
the Secretary of State for Trade and Industry, publicly criticized the speech for
raising unnecessary fears. Despite a report from the House of Lords' highly
respected Select Committee on the EC, which criticized the failure to deal with
fraud,[4] the government allowed the issue to drop from public view, while
continuing to press for action behind the scenes.

The significance of this episode is that the Prime Minister seems to have realized
that reaction to her Bruges speech had made the government appear to be anti-EC,
an impression that had to be dispelled if Britain were to succeed in its diplomatic
objective of moving the EC towards being a free market with minimum regulation
and open to trade with the rest of the world. The Bruges speech almost certainly
made a more negative impression than intended, and to have treated the problem
of fraud as a condemnation of the Commission would have strained relations with
the rest of the EC even further.

Monetary Union and the Social Charter

Central to the disagreement between Britain and the rest of the EC was the issue of whether the freeing of the internal market should be accompanied by moves towards a monetary union and by the introduction of a social charter of workers' rights.

Monetary union was a particular concern of President Mitterrand of France, backed by Chancellor Kohl of West Germany. Both wanted to see the strengthening of the exchange rate mechanism (ERM) of the European Monetary System (EMS), which formally tied together the values of the currencies of participating states. Their aim was that the EC should in effect have a single currency after 1992, with some form of European central bank to administer the single currency.

Mrs Thatcher spoke out strongly against the creation of a European central bank at the Hanover meeting of the European Council in July 1988, and this was interpreted by the media as opposition to any form of monetary union, especially as she had repeatedly declined to take sterling into the ERM. However, the Prime Minister did agree at Hanover to the creation of a committee of governors of national central banks under the chairmanship of Jacques Delors, to consider the steps needed to achieve monetary union.

That committee reported in April 1989. It proposed a three-stage process of movement to monetary union, culminating in a single currency administered by a committee of national central banks working together with a European institution that looked very like the European central bank that Mrs Thatcher had said she could not accept.[5] The report was agreed unanimously, and signed by the Governor of the Bank of England, Sir Robin Leigh-Pemberton. However, it was rejected by Nigel Lawson the Chancellor of the Exchequer, who said that Britain would be producing its own counter-proposals. (These were eventually unveiled at a meeting of Finance Ministers in September 1989 and involved member states agreeing to accept the currencies of other member states as legal tender; but they were largely ignored by the other members.)

In May, the Commission unveiled its draft proposals for a 'social charter' to guarantee workers within the EC a minimum protection on working hours, freedom of movement and fair pay, freedom of association and collective bargaining, the right to professional training, the right to information about the future plans of the company for which they worked, the right to be consulted on decisions that affected their future, the right to have their health and safety at work protected, and equal pay and opportunity for women.[6]

Lord Young had already attacked the proposals before they were published. During a debate in the House of Lords on 3 May he said that Britain had 'far too much experience of well-intentioned social legislation which had the opposite effect to that planned', and had restated the government's belief that deregulation was the way forward.[7] Immediately after the production of the draft charter,

Norman Fowler, the Secretary of State for Employment, pledged his opposition to a number of key aspects.

On these two issues the scene appeared to be set for a confrontation between Mrs Thatcher and her fellow heads of government at the forthcoming Madrid meeting of the European Council. Before that, though, elections to the European Parliament took place throughout the EC.

The European Election

In Britain the European election campaign was marked by serious divisions within the Conservative Party and by an apparent conversion of the Labour Party to being the more 'European' of the two major parties.

Divisions within the Conservative Party over Mrs Thatcher's seeming hostility to developments in the EC had been apparent for some time, but came to the surface most dramatically following an interview which the former Prime Minister, Edward Heath, gave to the BBC television programme 'On the Record' on 14 May and a speech which he made in Brussels a fortnight later. Mr Heath, who had taken Britain into the EC in 1973, strongly attacked Mrs Thatcher for misleading the British people about the risk of the EC turning into a 'socialist superstate', and in the television interview he went on to warn of the danger that if Britain tried to hold up the development of the EC the other 11 member states would go on alone, leaving Britain as a second-class member.

This same warning was given by Michael Heseltine in a book published also in May.[8] Mr Heseltine, who had resigned as Secretary of State for Defence over the Westland affair, was widely seen as a prospective future leader of the Conservative Party. He argued for full British participation in developments within the EC, and stated his belief that British Ministers knew that the country's future lay in the EC, but were reluctant to reveal the full extent of British involvement because British voters were thought to be not too keen on membership.

These sentiments were far from being reflected in the Conservative Party's campaign for the election, which was widely believed to have been approved by the Prime Minister personally. This emphasized the negative side of EC developments, suggesting that there was a real threat of British life being controlled by the Commission if it were not for the stolid opposition of the Conservative government.

In contrast the Labour Party presented itself as being more 'European' than the Conservatives, and in particular gave its support to the social charter. This was a marked change from the previous image of Labour as being the more hostile of the two major parties to the EC. The election result, which was a resounding victory for Labour over the Conservatives, appeared to vindicate the arguments of Mr Heseltine, and somewhat undermined Mrs Thatcher's own position of authority on this issue.

The Madrid European Council

At the Madrid meeting of the European Council the Prime Minister surprised many people by adopting a much more conciliatory tone towards the idea of monetary union. She accepted implementation of the first phase of the Delors Report, involving closer co-ordination of national economic and monetary policies, while restating that Britain would not be happy to go all the way along the route to monetary union that the Report mapped out. She also accepted that an inter-governmental conference should be convened to consider what changes to the governing treaties of the EC would be needed in order to proceed further. And for the first time she abandoned the vague formula that sterling would join the exchange rate mechanism 'when the time is right', specifying instead four conditions which, when met, would allow membership to occur. These concessions were interpreted by some commentators as evidence that the European election results had forced Mrs Thatcher to take a more accommodating approach towards the EC.

Before the end of the meeting, though, the limits of that more accommodating approach had been reached, with the British Prime Minister in her not unfamiliar role of being a minority of one, on the question of the social charter. She was not prepared to accept what she considered to be a serious departure from the fundamental principle of free market economics. What remained in doubt was how much of the social charter could be implemented by majority voting under the rules of the Single European Act of 1987, and would therefore be forced on Britain, and how much was subject to the rule of unanimity and could therefore be vetoed by Britain.

Vigilance and Scrutiny

Shortly before Madrid, Mrs Lynda Chalker, the Foreign Office Minister with special responsibility for EC affairs, told the House of Commons Select Committee on Foreign Affairs that the government was convinced that the provisions of the social charter would require unanimity.[9] Mrs Chalker also told the Committee that the Prime Minister was concerned about attempts by the Commission to extend its competence, and wanted to ensure 'proper scrutiny of everything that comes up …to see whether it should be a matter of Community competence'.[10]

The process of scrutiny led Britain to threaten to veto a Commission programme ('Lingua') to promote foreign language teaching in schools, and to oppose a proposal for a standard EC health warning on cigarette packets. Critics in Britain who attacked these moves on the grounds that the measures were inherently desirable missed the point that a principle was at stake, that the EC should only be able to extend its competence with the explicit agreement of the member states.

Mrs Thatcher's concern for close scrutiny of EC proposals for legislation did not appear to extend, however, to wanting to increase the powers of scrutiny of the House of Commons. In 1987 the Select Committee on the European Communities had asked that its terms of reference be widened to allow it to monitor EC developments better. The request was refused, but strong pressure from the chairmen of other Commons' Committees, and from backbenchers on all sides of the House, forced the government to make concessions, and in July 1989 the Leader of the House agreed with the Chairman of the EC Committee that it would be supplied with a wider range of documents than just those covered in its terms of reference, thereby extending its scope *de facto.*[11]

Dirty Water and Floating Money

In September a controversial Cabinet reshuffle removed Sir Geoffrey Howe from the Foreign Office, amidst suggestions in the press that this was partly due to disagreements with the Prime Minister over her approach to the EC. John Major, the new Foreign Secretary, made Britain's relationship with the EC the subject of his first significant public statement on policy, in a speech in Washington. Although publicized in advance as a new statement, this marked no discernible change from previous official policy.

The saliency of the EC as a domestic political issue was increased in October when the European Commission announced that it was taking the government to the Court of Justice over its failure to ensure that Britain's drinking water met EC standards of purity. Environmental concern was high on the policy agenda, and this move was another blow to the government's image. But what made matters worse was that the water supply industry was scheduled for privatization, a move that had already proved unpopular even with Conservative voters. The Commission's move on water purity made the prospects for a successful sale to the private sector less likely, and undermined the advertising campaign aimed at convincing the public of the merits of the water authorities as potential recipients of their investment funds.

Then in October the pound came under intense speculative pressure on the foreign exchanges in the face of persistently high deficits on the balance of payments and rising inflation. This produced renewed calls for sterling to be taken into the ERM as soon as feasible. The government resisted these calls, but the Labour Party announced its conversion to membership, and political pressure began to build up after the Chancellor responded to the crisis by raising interest rates, which were already at levels that were damaging the interests of both industry and home-owners.

Nigel Lawson's position was made more difficult by rumours that he was in favour of taking sterling into the ERM, but that he was being blocked by the Prime Minister, who was responding to the hostility to the EMS of her personal economics adviser, Sir Alan Walters. When advance copies began to circulate of an article by Sir Alan that was about to appear in an academic journal, and in which he fiercely attacked the EMS, Mr Lawson resigned as Chancellor, causing the Prime Minister severe embarrassment. The EC had thus become the focal point for the most dramatic development in British politics in 1989.

The Strasbourg European Council

In the subsequent Cabinet reshuffle John Major became Chancellor, and Douglas Hurd took his place at the Foreign Office. This did not alter significantly the pressure on the Prime Minister to continue with her new more accommodating line towards the EC, as Hurd was widely believed to be on the same wavelength on the EC as the Deputy Prime Minister, Sir Geoffrey Howe, and Major soon indicated that like his predecessor he was in favour of early entry to the ERM.

The combination of pressures on Mrs Thatcher produced a continuation in Strasbourg in December of the more conciliatory line that she had adopted in Madrid. Although she voted against adoption of the social charter, and against early convening of the inter-governmental conference, she indicated that Britain would play its full part in the EC despite differences of opinion. This attitude was applauded by all the national delegations.

Conclusion

By the end of 1989 the European Community had become central to domestic political debate in Britain. Mrs Thatcher's resistance to developments was coming under increasing challenge, and public opinion polls showing a small but consistent majority of the electorate in favour of a central European government by 1992, taken together with the European election results, indicated that perhaps her nationalistic attacks were no longer gaining her the domestic political popularity that they once had. After a decade in office, Mrs Thatcher was being accused of losing touch with the mood of the country, and the issue of Britain's relationship with the EC seemed to be an example of this. The feeling was growing in Brussels that the government would have to start to backtrack on its opposition to the Commission's programme, and that in the post-Thatcher era, which her difficulties with the EC might hasten, Britain could cease to be the quite the awkward partner that it had consistently been since joining in 1973.

Notes

1. Margaret Thatcher, *Britain and Europe. Text of the speech delivered in Bruges by the Prime Minister on 20 September 1988*, Conservative Political Centre, London, October 1988.

2. Sir John Hoskyns, 'Why the Single Market programme is in trouble', *Director*, 31, 13 March, 1989, pp. 64–9.

3. Peter Jenkins, 'How Britain can avert a two-tier Europe', *The Independent*, 7 March 1989.

4. House of Lords, Select Committee on the European Communities, *Fraud Against the Community, 5th Report, Session 1988–89*, HL Paper 27, HMSO, London, 21 February 1989.

5. Committee for the Study of Economic and Monetary Union, *Report on Economic and Monetary Union in the European Community*, European Community, Brussels, April 1989.

6. European Commission, *Social Dimension of the Internal Market*, COM(89) 248 final, Brussels, May 1989.

7. House of Lords, *Parliamentary Debates* (Hansard), 5th Series, sixth volume of session 1988–89, HMSO, London, 3 May 1989, col.158.

8. Michael Heseltine, *The Challenge of Europe*, Weidenfeld and Nicolson, London, 1989.

9. House of Commons, Foreign Affairs Committee, *The Single European Act: Minutes of Evidence*, HMSO, London, 21 June 1989, 446–i, p. 12.

10. Ibid, p. 8.

11. House of Commons, Select Committee on European Legislation, *First Special Report for the Session 1988–89*, HMSO, London, 19 July 1989, HC533.

Chronology

5 Jan: Lord Cockfield steps down as Vice-President of the European Commission.

23 Jan: EC public hearing into fraud against the EC budget opens.

8 Feb: Bruges Group, inspired by Mrs Thatcher's Bruges speech of the previous September, formed to campaign for Thatcherite free-market policies in the EC.

13 Feb: John MacGregor calls for urgent action to curb fraud against the EC farm budget.

28 Feb: Critical attack on corruption at Brussels and the unpreparedness for 1992 by Sir John Hoskyns, Director General of the Institute of Directors.

1 Mar: Furious response to Hoskyns' speech from Jacques Delors, the President of the EC Commission, and from Euro-MPs.

9 Mar: Report of the Lords select committee on the European Communities criticizes the EC failure to deal with fraud against the Community budget.

12 Apr: The Delors Report on prospects for economic and monetary union in the EC agreed by central bank governors meeting in Basle.

17 Apr: Delors Report, proposing a three-stage movement towards a common economic policy and a single currency, published. It is rejected by Nigel Lawson.

10 May: Britain opposes an attempt by the EC Commission to introduce a common identity card for pensioners.

14 May: Edward Heath accuses Mrs Thatcher of deliberately misleading the British public about the threat of a European 'socialist superstate.'

16 May: Lord Plumb, the President of the European Parliament, in a speech to the Royal Institute of International Affairs, distances himself from Mrs Thatcher and criticizes most aspects of her Bruges campaign.

17 May: The Social Charter proposals are presented by the EC Commission. Norman Fowler pledges his opposition to a number of key aspects.

EC Commission backs down in its battle with Thatcher over her determination to retain zero-rate VAT on food and children's clothes.

17 May: SLD manifesto on the Euro-elections launched.

18 May: Green manifesto on the Euro-elections launched.

New EC Commission guidelines on VAT and excise duty rates presented.

22 May: Conservative manifesto on the Euro-elections launched.

23 May: Labour manifesto on the Euro-elections launched.

29 May: Mr Heath attacks Mrs Thatcher and accuses her of trying to break up the EC.

15 June: European elections.

26 June: A more conciliatory attitude on the EMS is taken by Mrs Thatcher at the start of the EC Summit in Madrid.

27 June: Madrid Summit ends. Mrs Thatcher is isolated in her opposition to the Social Charter.

13 July: Sir Leon Brittan urges radical review of procedures for monitoring the EC at Westminster.

25 July: Government resists pressure to give wider remit to the European Legislation committee of the Commons.

6 Sept: EC report on progress towards 1992 in member countries shows Britain and Denmark, often criticized for their 'anti-European' behaviour, are amongst those which have made the most progress.

9 Sept: Meeting of European finance ministers in Antibes to discuss the Delors Report. At it Nigel Lawson suggests his alternative of a system of competing currencies acceptable anywhere in the EC. This was largely ignored by his counterparts.

27 Sept: The Social Charter, only slightly amended from the draft presented earlier in the year, is published.

30 Oct: Britain is isolated in its opposition to the final draft of the Social Charter.

2 Nov: Major scheme for system of competing currencies in EC announced.

7 Nov: Sir Leon Brittan, in his Granada lecture at the Guildhall on 'Europe: Our Sort of Community' called for a change from the government's generally obstructive attitude and a rapid entry of the ERM to further Britain's interests and to enable Britain properly to influence coming events in Europe.

18 Nov: EC summit on events in Eastern Europe held in Paris.

20 Nov: Brittan at the CBI conference attacks Britain's 'semi-detached' attitude to the EC.

22 Nov: Plans for a new economic and trade organization embracing EC and EFTA members are unveiled by the Foreign Affairs Commissioner Frans Andriessen, who hinted at the same time that if Britain found it impossible to stomach political union she could return to EFTA.

1 Dec: M Delors in London for talks with Mrs Thatcher.

5 Dec: Lords Select Committee on the European Communities, *The Delors Committee Report*, HMSO calls for an immediate commitment to join the ERM before July 1990.

9–10 Dec: EC summit in Strasbourg.

The Media

COLIN SEYMOUR-URE

Newspapers in 1989 were still responding to the changes in technology, costs, and industrial practices symbolized in the word 'Wapping'. Since Rupert Murdoch's successful defiance of the trade unions after the overnight transfer of his publications to a new plant in Wapping in 1986, publishers and would-be publishers had probably had a greater scope to innovate than at any time since the early years of the century. The broadcasters, in contrast, were bracing for change but not yet hit by it. For them, 1989 was a year of lobbying and hand-wringing (especially by the ITV companies) about the government's White Paper published late in 1988. This proposed the biggest upheaval in broadcasting since the creation of the BBC in 1926.

The media were also under a variety of pressures about their contents. Changes were made or threatened in the laws on secrecy and privacy. Broadcasters had to work with the government ban on spoken words by Irish extremists. The new Broadcasting Standards Council was promised statutory powers to set and back up standards of taste and decency. Such developments amounted to the most substantial challenge to media news values and public accountability since 1945. Moreover, they raised the entirely distinct question, since some of them came from the government, of the capacity of media to hold the government itself publicly accountable. In the confrontation of government and media, which is David, which Goliath?

In a generally declining market for national newspapers, the new economic conditions provided several openings. New titles, firstly, might now have a realistic chance of breaking into one of the existing segments of the market. *The Independent*, which had done this at the end of 1986, continued to gain circulation among the broadsheet papers. In the shrinking middle market dominated by the *Daily Mail* and *Daily Express*, *Today* (founded a little earlier than *The Independent* and not owned by Rupert Murdoch) had had a harder time but was not getting established. In November 1988 Eddie Shah, *Today*'s founder, tried again with the *Post,* hoping to find a niche for a mass market tabloid; but the paper closed after one month.

The Independent announced a Sunday version for early 1990 and launched a junior weekly, *The Indy.* The Sunday paper was beaten to the market by the *Sunday Correspondent,* first published on 15 September and aiming at the same readership.

Before publication, the *Sunday Correspondent*'s management tried without success to interest *The Independent* in a joint venture.

The new conditions, secondly, gave existing papers greater flexibility to make themselves competitive – and a greater need to do so. To cut costs and arm the *Sunday Telegraph* against the growing competition, the two Telegraph papers were reorganized on unified lines, with the Sunday staff much slimmed down. *The Observer*, too, looked vulnerable, since it lacked a weekday partner. Among the tabloids, the *Sun* and *Daily Mirror* battled as before, with the *Star* providing scant opposition and the *Mirror* benefiting from the introduction of colour.

Broadcasting Legislation

The Broadcasting White Paper was the outcome of lively disagreements within Whitehall. It reflected the oblique nature of British media policy and the historic pretence that none exists – hence the non-existence too of a Minister for Communications. Although the Home Secretary is responsible for broadcasting, Departments such as Trade and Industry have a strong interest.

The White Paper sought a balance between market values (the language of audience 'choice') and controls to protect quality (the language of 'public service' broadcasting). Thus, the Independent Broadcasting Authority (IBA) was to be replaced by an Independent Television Commission (ITC) – with a lighter touch and fewer powers over franchise awards, company takeovers and programme contents. Franchises, including for a new Channel 5, would be allocated by auction. The BBC, on the other hand, was to remain the cornerstone of public service broadcasting and would shift gradually from finance by compulsory licence fee to voluntary subscription. ITV would have 'positive programming obligations', such as impartial, high quality news and adequate regional programmes.

The proposals caused an outcry. Supporters of the existing system saw them spelling doom for the benign duopoly of BBC and ITV, which combined the virtues of competition for audiences with those of separate, non-competitive sources of finance – the licence fee for the BBC and advertising revenue for ITV. By sheltering the BBC from competition for revenue at the introduction of ITV in 1955, programme standards had been safeguarded; but under the new proposals, the argument went, neither BBC or ITV would be able to afford the risk of making either expensive blockbusting series (such as 'Brideshead Revisited') or specialized minority programmes. Nor was there relevant experience abroad to show whether a subscription channel could work on a scale needed to maintain the BBC's standard of service.

From the ITV companies – and the Chairman-elect of the ITC, George Russell (who is Chairman of the IBA) – came dismay at the possible implications of a 'light touch' and, especially, at the impoverished programme quality that would follow if the balance between the auction principle and the 'quality' threshold imposed on applicants were struck in the wrong place, or if it simply failed in practice.

Some aspects of the White Paper, of course, were widely welcomed. These included the Fifth Channel, and details such as improved quotas for independent producers.

It became clear that the government would accept some of these criticisms. The Bill published in November went some way towards reinventing the powers of the IBA and watering down the auction principle.

Not all broadcasting development waited on the Bill. Rupert Murdoch's Sky satellite channel was launched; and it made heavy losses, said to be running at £2 million a week by the Autumn. In this, it followed the historic pattern of broadcasting launches; ITV, BBC2, LWT, LBC, Channel 4 and TV-AM were all initial disasters. Murdoch said in October that he would keep the channel going at least for five years. His main domestic satellite competitor, the British Satellite Broadcasting (BSB) consortium, was badly delayed by technical difficulties and postponed its launch into 1990. For the network companies it was a profitable year – including TV-AM, which settled a long-running strike over manning levels in the summer. Independent Local Radio continued to expand, following a government decision to let existing stations split their frequencies and offer different services on AM and FM.

Official Secrecy

The main change in the law affecting what media publish was the reform of the Official Secrets Act. Nearly everyone agreed that Section 2, in particular, which most affected journalists, was ready to be 'pensioned off' (in the words of a Judge in 1970); but views differed greatly on how it should be replaced. A Conservative Bill in 1979 was defeated by hostility in the House of Lords, and several liberalizing Private Members' Bills had been squashed by the government.

The 1989 Act was very far from the Freedom of Information measure most news media wanted, and its passage required a three-line whip. The old Act had made the receipt and publication of any unauthorized official information an offence. The new one narrowed the scope to just six areas (following the 1979 Bill and the Franks Report of 1972). These are defence; security and intelligence; international relations; confidential government-to-government information; matters useful to a criminal; and official interception of mail and telephone calls. In all but the last, where disclosure is *ipso facto* an offence, the prosecution now has to prove there has been harm to the public interest or the work of the security services. Harm is regarded as having automatically happened when disclosure is made by members of the security services themselves (*Spycatcher* would thus be covered). Offences will carry a maximum two-year prison sentence and/or a fine.

The government claimed it would be no trivial task for the prosecution to prove harm; and it can be a defence to claim that one had no reason to know harm would be caused. But reformers were particularly disappointed that it will be no defence to claim (like the civil servant Clive Ponting about his *Belgrano* leaks) that disclosure is in the public interest; nor that prior publication has taken place. Freedom of Information supporters pointed out, too, that civil service disciplinary procedures cover what the criminal law no longer covers, and that other laws, such as that of 'confidence' (under which *Spycatcher* was prosecuted) remain in place. They argued that the new Act tidies up and tightens the controls on official information and does nothing to diminish unnecessary secrecy.

Other Pressures on Broadcasting

Throughout the year, broadcasters had to get used to a different kind of restriction on publicity – the unique ban on the broadcast of words spoken by representatives of organizations proscribed by the Prevention of Terrorism Act and Northern Ireland Emergency Legislation, or by Sinn Fein, Republican Sinn Fein and the Protestant Ulster Defence Association.

Ministers have always had the power to make or prevent the BBC and ITV broadcasting a particular programme. They have almost never used it, preferring informal methods of persuasion. Douglas Hurd, Home Secretary, imposed the ban in October 1988, after eight soldiers died in a bomb explosion. Nothing prevents banned persons' words being read verbatim 'voice-over' by someone else or reported in summary. But broadcasters dislike this. The result was therefore that Sinn Fein claimed media enquiries were down by 75 per cent over the year. Their leader Gerry Adams appeared twice on BBC network news (via a reader), in contrast to twelve appearances in the previous year.

Broadcasters naturally hated the ban. They tended to view it, for instance, as making them agents, no longer just observers, of the government's Northern Irish policy. It cramped radio phone-in shows; and it created anomalies during local and European elections, when it was temporarily lifted. BBC Chairman Marmaduke Hussey (a Thatcher appointee) feared it was a 'dangerous precedent'.

A further example of the government's attitude to programmes on Northern Ireland was its reaction in January to the independent inquiry into 'Death on the Rock', a Thames TV documentary on the SAS shooting of three unarmed terrorists in Gibraltar. Headed by a Conservative former Home Office and Northern Ireland Minister, Lord Windlesham, the three and a half months inquiry rejected allegations that the programme was 'trial by television' and had prejudiced the Gibraltar inquest. Despite its evenhandedness – criticizing the programme's one-sidedness and acknowledging the Foreign Secretary's right to try and halt it before transmission – the report was rubbished out of hand by Downing Street and the original criticisms were repeated. Thames TV's subsequent caution, bearing in mind too the renewal of franchises starting in 1991, was reflected in the Company's decision in October to drop production of a play about Irish nationalists imprisoned in the UK.

The government took an interest, too, in general broadcasting standards of taste and decency. In part at least this was to remedy the lack of control over, say, pornographic programmes that soon might be beamed into British homes by overseas satellites. But the powers of the government's chosen instrument, the Broadcasting Standards Council chaired by the former *Times* editor, Lord Rees-Mogg, covered domestic broadcasting too and were to be put on a statutory basis. Even though the powers amounted to little more than a code of practice, with broadcasters obliged to publish the Council's findings about breaches, the BBC and the IBA felt that their own existing codes and complaints procedures (including the Broadcasting Complaints Commission, which would now be abolished) made them unnecessary.

News Management and News Values

In addition to censoriousness, the government continued to be accused (as are most governments) of news management. The recent arguments about lobby journalism rumbled on; the main complaint being that the traditional practice of non-attributable group briefings by the Downing Street Press Secretary gave the government too much scope to determine the news agenda and fly kites. This was implicitly a compliment, albeit backhanded, to Bernard Ingham – Press Secretary for all but the first six months of Mrs Thatcher's term and exceptionally close to her. *The Scotsman* joined *The Independent* and *The Guardian* in absenting itself from collective briefings, but the system did not crumble.

A newer type of criticism was prompted by the rapidly increased scale of government advertising, which had approximately doubled in the last three years. It was attacked by the Opposition as party political, with privatization the main target. An expensive TV advertising campaign was undertaken, for example, in order to prepare the public for the aptly named flotation of shares in the water industry.

The government, of course, was not alone in criticizing the media and trying to use them to advantage. Two backbench MPs introduced anti-press Bills: one would have given a right to privacy, the other a 'right to reply'. They were popular enough to make the government set up a Home Office Committee (under David Calcutt, QC) to review the law on privacy. Most hostility was felt towards the mass market tabloids, which arguably carried harassment and intrusion to excess in the competition for sales. That such methods could backfire (after the Hillsborough football disaster, for instance) was conceded when the *Sun* appointed an 'Ombudsman' to deal with readers' complaints. (Central TV made a similar appointment.)

The same concern with news values and standards led the Press Council to make a review of its constitution and procedures under its new Chairman, Louis Blom-Cooper, QC. The readiness of juries to award six-figure libel damages was sometimes explained on the same grounds. Nothing in 1989 matched the recent £1 million payout to Elton John by the *Sun*, but £600,000 was awarded against the magazine *Private Eye* to Sonia Sutcliffe, wife of the 'Yorkshire Ripper', for allegations that she had profited by her husband's notoriety, a sum subsequently much reduced in an out of court settlement. At the end of the year, the astonishing sum of £1.5 million was awarded against Count Nikolai Tolstoy for allegations – in a privately circulated pamphlet, not even a published article – that the former Minister Lord Aldington was a war criminal.

A unique and bewildering case of pressure on media was the 'death sentence' on the author Salman Rushdie for his novel *The Satanic Verses*. Pronounced by the Ayatollah Khomenei in February 1989, this kept him in hiding throughout 1989. It posed dilemmas of conscience and commerce alike for booksellers and for its publishers, Viking Penguin (not the least being whether or not a paperback edition should be published – a dilemma that still had not been resolved by the end of the year); and its religious dimension made it turn out to be rather more complex than a simple liberal issue of free speech.

Media Concentration and Conglomerates

Taking the press, television and radio together, the events of 1989 confirmed the extent to which mass media continue to develop as part of a complex international structure of interlocking finance, ownership, organizations and technologies. Some enterprises, such as Rupert Murdoch's, remain chiefly concerned with mass media, world wide. (Spain, late in 1989, was the latest country in whose papers he took a stake.) Others, such as Pearson, Associated Newspapers, or the Canadian newcomer, Conrad Black's, have major interest in other fields such as banking and property.

The groups interlock not least in cross-ownership: Murdoch has a stake in Pearson, Lonrho (*The Observer*) in the Australian Bond Group, Bond and Pearson in the BSB Satellite, Black in United Newspapers (the *Express* group). The concentration of different media within one group was perhaps best illustrated in 1989 by the fate of independent book publishers: in January Collins failed to fight off a takeover bid by Murdoch, and in July Century Hutchinson, the last of the large independents, was sold to Random House. The possible implications of media concentration were the subject of an inquiry initiated by the Office of Fair Trading. This was prompted by the ostentatious way in which Murdoch's newspapers promoted his sky TV channels.

With the different media technologies developing as they are, and with control often resting in the hands of multi-national conglomerates, it is increasingly difficult to define the common denominator of mass media. But it is small wonder that governments and pressure groups continued to credit them in 1989 with a power sometimes comparable (though imprecise and intangible) to that of government itself.

Chronology

3 Jan: Announcement that the *Illustrated London News* is to become a quarterly rather than a monthly, a move forced by losses.

6 Jan: Lord Chalfont to be the new deputy chairman of the Independent Broadcasting Authority, a widely attacked appointment.

Rupert Murdoch's News International acquires Collins, the Scottish publishers.

10 Jan: *The Scotsman* withdraws from the Westminster lobby system of unattributable briefings.

18 Jan: Douglas Hurd announces tougher controls to prevent broadcasting being dominated by 'a handful of tycoons or international conglomerates'.

19 Jan: Two private bills designed to ensure privacy against press intrusion published.

25 Jan: Louis Blom-Cooper, Chairman of the Press Council, proposes major changes in its organization, including a press ombudsman.

26 Jan: Windlesham report on the Thames TV documentary *Death on the Rock* clearing it of bias and of prejudicing the inquest into the shooting of three IRA terrorists in Gibraltar by the SAS in 1988 is published. It is dismissed by the government.

New censorship rating '12' is proposed to the film and video industry by the British Board of Film Classification.

27 Jan: John Browne's Privacy Bill fails to win enough support to move to a Second Reading.

3 Feb: A backbench Right of Reply Bill, which would give a right of reply to media distortions, is given an unopposed Second Reading.

5 Feb: Sky TV launches the first four of its planned six channels, bringing satellite television to Britain.

6 Feb: ITV scrapes all agreements with the trade unions and serves notice that it will end national pay bargaining in July.

British Telecom responds to the outcry about its chatlines and suspends them.

14 Feb: Skyphone, the world's first satellite telephone service, launched on a British Airways flight to New York.

16 Feb: Office of Fair Trading launches an inquiry into the ownership of broadcasting and the press after complaints that the Murdoch press was being unfairly used to promote his Sky satellite television.

The ombudsman for *The Sun*, appointed in January, makes his first adjudication, against the newspaper.

22 Feb: United Newspapers set to move from Fleet Street.

24 Feb: New Broadcasting Standards Council code restricts some offensive scenes until after 9.00pm.

5 Mar: Thomson Organization launches *Wales on Sunday*.

23 Mar: Penguin sells Sphere Books to Maxwell Communications Corporation for £13.75 million.

24 Mar: The new censorship rating '12' introduced.

Reorganization of the *The Daily Telegraph* and *Sunday Telegraph*.

3 Apr: Channel 4 begins a breakfast television service.

5 Apr: International Federation of Journalists report condemns the government for attacking press freedoms in Britain which, it says, has damaged Britain's standing abroad and bolstered the case for a written constitution.

7 Apr: Final edition of the *Daily Express* in Fleet Street before moving to new offices in Battersea.

Peter Galliner, director of the International Press Institute says Britain is 'the only black spot on Western Europe when it comes to freedom of the press'.

14 Apr: Campaign against Pornography and Censorship launched.

17 Apr: In the annual report of the Press Council Louis Blom-Cooper calls on the press to put its house in order before parliament does it for them.

Broadcasting Standards Council finds more concern about bad language than about explicit sex on its fact-finding tour.

21 Apr: Tony Worthington's Right of Reply Bill talked out in the Commons. However the Home Office pledges to review law and practice governing standards of press reporting. The review is welcomed by the Press Council.

24 Apr: Successful applicants for new commercial radio franchises announced.

2 May: *Freedom in Broadcasting* published by the Institute of Economic Affairs draws attention to the dichotomy in Mrs Thatcher's policy between an emphasis on deregulation and consumer choice and increased censoriousness over what people see and hear.

5 May: John Browne's Invasion of Privacy Bill withdrawn.

8 May: *The Independent*, *The Sunday Times* and the now defunct *News on Sunday* each fined £50,000 for contempt of court in publishing material from Peter Wright's *Spycatcher* in April to August 1987.

14 May: Four new franchises for commercial radio announced.

15 May: Government appeals to the Lords after the Scottish Court of Sessions refused a temporary injunction to prevent *The Scotsman*, the *Glasgow Herald* and Scottish TV publishing extracts from *Inside Intelligence*, the memoirs of former MI6 officer Anthony Cavendish.

Inenco Group claim there is widespread overcharging by British Telecom.

19 May: Tighter controls on media ownership announced.

22 May: Central TV sets up its own ombudsman to handle complaints.

23 May: Greater competition for British Telecom outlined in Oftel's annual report.

24 May: Peter Brooke, Chairman of the Conservative Party, accuses the BBC of breaking the rules on the coverage of elections.

Record libel damages of £600,000 awarded to Sonia Sutcliffe, the estranged wife of the Yorkshire Ripper, against *Private Eye*.

26 May: High Court challenge to the government's ban on broadcasts involving Sinn Fein or other supporters of terrorism dismissed.

7 June: US publisher, Random House, pays £64 million for the last large independent British publisher, Century Hutchinson.

13 June: Government announces toughening of the broadcasting White Paper proposals on franchise auctions, standards and ownership.

15 June: British Satellite Broadcasting obtains a monopoly of all the UK television channels using direct broadcasting by satellite.

28 June: Sir Leon Brittan indicates he intends to force the deregulation of national telecommunications markets in the EC.

3 July: Post Office announce plans to reintroduce Sunday collections in 1990.

4 July: Douglas Hurd announces a package of measures to force terrestial pirate radio stations off the air.

10 July: *Quality on Television* John Libbey, the result of a six year survey, argues that bad language, violence and sex are the most common causes of complaints from television viewers.

21 July: Commons select committee on foreign affairs suggests that the BBC world service should be given an exceptional grant to met unexpected additional costs.

27 July: Guy Cumberbatch and Dennis Howitt, *A Measure of Uncertainty – The Effects of the Mass Media* Broadcasting Standards Council published. This major review of research into the effect of television on people's behaviour finds that most of it casts little light on the subject.

30 July: Kelvin Mackenzie, the editor of *The Sun*, apologises for his newspaper's coverage of the Hillsborough disaster in the wake of Press Council criticism.

31 July: Oftel report points out the need for a new telephone numbering system in the next few years.

1 Aug: A new law to modernize copyright protection, establish a new industrial design right and combat privacy comes into force under the Copyright, Designs and Patents Act 1989.

23 Aug: Method of squeezing cinema quality pictures onto television frequencies unveiled by the BBC research department.

25 Aug: Rupert Murdoch delivers the McTaggert lecture at the Edinburgh television festival in which he criticized British television for being 'obsessed with class, dominated by anti-commercial attitudes and with a tendency to hark back to the past'.

26 Aug: Concern at the danger of the introduction of cable-distributed soft pornography on television in Britain in the next few years voiced at Edinburgh.

27 Aug: Telepoint, a mass pocket telephone network organized by a consortium led by British Telecom, is launched in Britain.

1 Sept: New Irish commercial pop radio station, Atlantic 252 starts. It also intends to cover most of mainland Britain.

3 Sept: Ending of the Royal Mail's monopoly put back on the political agenda.

4 Sept: Thirty-four year ban on advertising by registered charities on radio and television is lifted. A watchdog is established to regulate this.

7 Sept: Report by the Consumers Association argues that the quality of the first class post has declined over the past four years.

11 Sept: Britain's first sponsored peak-time television programme is the ITV weather forecast.

12 Sept: Newspaper Publishing, the publishers of *The Independent*, announce that a sister Sunday newspaper is to be launched in January 1990.

17 Sept: New Sunday newspaper, *The Sunday Correspondent*, is launched.

21 Sept: *The Indy*, a weekly offshoot of *The Independent* for teenagers, is launched.

4 Oct: Ian Chapman, former head of Collins, sets up his own publishing company, Chapmans.

9 Oct: *The Daily Telegraph* announce move to 7 day a week publishing operations. This prompts a 36 hour protest strike against these new arrangements by staff.

19 Oct: Court of Appeal overturns £600,000 libel damages award to Sonia Sutcliffe against *Private Eye*.

6 Nov: *Private Eye* settles the Sutcliffe libel action out of court for £60,000 plus £100,000 for a separate action.

8 Nov: Associated Newspapers announce the abandonment of collective bargaining.

17 Nov: Publishers Faber and Faber restructure to avoid takeover.

19 Nov: Sunday mail collections restart in selected areas.

20 Nov: Wendy Henry sacked as editor of *The People* by Robert Maxwell for publishing 'distressing photographs'.

20 Nov: Mr Justice Scott in the case of *BBC Enterprises* v *Hi-Tech Xtravision Ltd* in the Chancery Division rules that proprietors do not have exclusive rights over the supply of decoders of programmes broadcast by satellite.

21 Nov: In the Queen's speech legislation to introduce a fifth, commercial, television channel, to replace the IBA with an Independent Television Authority and to introduce more competition in independent broadcasting is announced.

Lord Donaldson, Master of the Rolls, denounces the government's restrictions on broadcasting of interviews with members of organizations supporting terrorism in Northern Ireland as 'half-baked' at a hearing on the legality of the restrictions in the Court of Appeal.

22 Nov: Ruling by Mr Justice Hoffmann that a journalist on *The Engineer* magazine must reveal the source of leaked details of a company's financial standing.

Sir Bryan Carsberg, Director-General of Oftel, warns that complaints about British Telecom will reach a record 32,000 in 1989, showing the need for more competition in the telecommunications field.

28 Nov: The committee of the editors of the national press chaired by Andreas Whittam Smith of *The Independent* announce a Code of Practice and the establishment of a system of readers' representatives to screen reporting.

30 Nov: *Trade and Industry Committee: Report on the Post Office* HC 559, HMSO, condemns the deplorable performance of the first class mail service.

6 Dec: Legal challenge to the government's ban on direct-speech broadcast interviews with members of Northern Ireland terrorist groups decisively rejected in the Court of Appeal.

7 Dec: Broadcasting Bill published.

Strict code of practice and conduct introduced for telephone chatline services.

12 Dec: Appeal by Morgan-Grampian, the publishers of *The Engineer* against the Hoffmann ruling is turned down in the Court of Appeal. The refusal of a journalist to disclose his sources was a threat to the rule of law declared Lord Donaldson.

Code of practice reforming the procedures of the Press Council is published.

14 Dec: Government inquiry into the way media companies promote their own interests is set up under John Sadler.

18 Dec: Broadcasting Bill passes its second reading in the Commons by 310 to 238.

29 Dec: Robert Maxwell announces that Richard Stott is to become editor of *The People* and prepare it for a management buyout whilst his editorial chair at the *Daily Mirror* is filled by Roy Greenslade.

The Legal System

CAROL HARLOW

This was the year that the legal profession nearly foundered on the rock of a reforming Lord Chancellor; or once more wriggled off the hook of thoroughgoing reform – whichever way you like to look at it.

The Green Paper: A 'Sinister Document'?

On 25 January 1989, the Lord Chancellor published three Green Papers: the first concerned the way in which the two branches of the profession would be organized and work; the second attacked the thorny question of contingency fees; the third dealt with conveyancing, for more than a century a monopoly for solicitors and the bread-and-butter of small practices.[1] The government described its overall objective as the provision of a free and efficient market in legal services which were cost-effective and expert. Whether these aims were consistent with each other, let alone compatible with the contents of the papers, was to become a matter of considerable dispute. After so many abortive attempts to reform the profession or persuade it to reform itself,[2] everyone could have seen the proposals coming. Nevertheless, they contained enough surprises for the Bar to appeal for a fighting fund to brief Saatchi and Saatchi; it is said that nearly £1 million was raised, some of it from solicitors.

On one central point there was unanimous opposition from all sectors of the legal profession and many outside it.[3] The metamorphosis of the worthy but toothless Lord Chancellor's Advisory Committee into a 'vigorous and active standing committee' responsible for formulating policy on matters including professional conduct and standards; criteria for certification of advocates; and last, but by no means least, legal education, rang alarm bells. That the final decision would rest with the Lord Chancellor and his Department whose novel powers to implement their policies in delegated legislation would be subject (the Lord Chancellor assured us) to the doctrine of ministerial responsibility, comforted nobody. In an unwritten constitution without constitutional guarantees, the proposal seemed to stretch beyond the profession to touch the independence of the judiciary. A torrent of insults flowed from senior judges including Mrs Thatcher's first Lord Chancellor, Lord Hailsham, and the Lord Chief Justice, Lord Lane, who not only described the Green Paper as 'one of the most sinister documents ever to emanate from government' but even threatened to close the Royal Courts of Justice one Monday for the judges to discuss their response. (The parallel with the dockers' strike was not missed but happily for all concerned, this storm in a teacup was averted by the tact of the Lord Chancellor MacKay before some mischief-maker could apply to the Lord Chief Justice for an injunction.) Solicitors and academic lawyers scrambled to assert their potential for appointment to the bench. It was left to the Legal Action Group to hang on to these demands for a less inbred judiciary, proposals for a more proficient and better trained judiciary – ultimately perhaps a career judiciary.[4]

Bar and Bench were more concerned with the decision to grant rights of audience in the higher courts to solicitors, supposedly opening the way for the decline of the Bar and ultimate fusion of the professions. Describing itself as 'the most competitive business going' and standing on its duty to 'represent fearlessly any client without regard to the character, reputation or cause of the client' (the so-called 'cab-rank' rule), the Bar ferociously defended all its existing privileges. Thus it was willing to see court doors opened to 'other lawyers' but only if barristers were not handicapped; only 'independent sole practitioners' who acted 'as consultants', respected the 'cab-rank' rule and had been 'recognized' by the judges, should be granted rights of audience in the higher courts.[5]

The Law Society, generally favourable to the proposals and aware that it had already lost the battle on conveyancing, smugly described restrictions on solicitors' rights of audience as a 'quirk of history' and supported their removal, subject only to post-qualification training and experience.[6] It did, however, warn that, in the absence of effective safeguards against possible abuse, 'lending institutions' and high-street 'one-stop property agencies' oper ated by estate agents, might in the end prove as monopolistic and less accountable than a well-disciplined profession. The ending of both restrictions was duly welcomed by the powerful consumers' lobby.[7]

The White Paper: 'Sparkling Footwork'

It could be said of the White Paper[8] that nobody was allowed to lose too much face. A huge, collective sigh of relief greeted the U-turn over the Advisory Committee which would now fill a purely advisory role. Chaired by a judge, it would be composed of six professionals and eight lay members, all to be appointed by the Lord Chancellor after consultation. Solicitors gained a right of audience subject only to recognition by the Law Society, whose powers would be embodied in legislation. But judges gained a toehold in the process, as both professional bodies would have to satisfy the Lord Chancellor and senior judges on their competence to evaluate their own members and uphold professional standards. That 'senior judges' were not won over by the concession became obvious when the Master of the Rolls, Sir John Donaldson, threatened to use these rule-making powers to block extensions to solicitors' rights of audience.[9] But a respite had been granted for the profession to put its house in order, as responsibility for both the structure of the profession and the content of legal education was left effectively in its own hands. The Bar's proposals – for example, to increase the numbers of practising barristers by modifying the rules about 'chambers' and adopting the Scottish 'library system', and to organize a less inadequate Free Representation Unit – had been put forward in their *Response* and were already under way. Finally, the conveyancing monopoly would be ended but subject to safeguards concerning 'fair competition', conflicts of interest and proper provision for complaints. The public was left to wonder who had won what; even as Austin Mitchell was calling the White Paper 'a humiliating climbdown for the government', a legal weekly was congratulating the Lord Chancellor on his 'sparkling footwork'.[10]

Legal Aid: A Hidden Agenda?

The hole in the heart of both Green and White Papers lay in the fact that, although explicitly aimed at improving access to 'good quality legal services', they catered only for the top segments of the market.[11] And although the Green Paper described access to legal services as 'fundamental to the rule of law', in the next line it was guilty of the paradox that 'such access does not mean access to a lawyer'. The advice agencies now entered the fray to warn that they too were seriously underfunded and overextended; without more funding they could not take on the extended role implicit in the Green Paper's proposals. Not that the profession wanted them to; they were more concerned over the declining eligibility for legal aid.

Criminal legal aid had, since 1986, been substantially eroded by the need to make contributions. London solicitor Cyril Glasser was the first to show the extent to which eligibility for civil legal aid had also dropped from a 1983 threshold of 70 per cent.[12] Soon after, a study done at the London School of Economics showed that 14 million people who would have qualified in 1979 no longer did so and that this was due not (as the government insisted) to greater prosperity but to failure to uprate the eligibility levels in line with inflation.[13] The 'Green Form Scheme' (which, briefly, provides for a fixed amount of legal advice prior to or outside the context of litigation) was also threatened. In the teeth of a survey from the Lord Chancellor's Department which showed it to be working well,[14] the Legal Aid Board was charged to consider retrenchment. The Law Society showed that there had already been retrenchment in the shape of an 8 per cent drop during 1989. Into the bargain, practitioners pointed out, the level of legal aid had slipped to a point that legal aid solicitors could scarcely survive; law centres, for the most part dependent for funding on financially distressed local authorities, were closing their doors while small high street solicitors, whose financial stability was threatened by the ending of their conveyancing monopoly, might also cease to exist. This could hardly be described as easier access.

To the profession the answer was simple: increased funding. The government, which pretended to have dealt with the problem in 1988 simply by passing a Legal Aid Act, now passed the parcel to its new Legal Aid Board to provide the answers. The tenor of the Board's consultation paper[15] was that the Green Form Scheme would, in the interests of 'cost-effectiveness' have to be pared down. Some areas (for example, welfare benefits), could be excluded altogether; others would be covered by a new method of 'franchising' firms either to do all legal aid work if they had a £40,000 turnover of legal aid work or in some special ized areas. Whether the franchises would be exclusive or not was not made clear. This solution, respondents pointed out, would do nothing to enhance consumer choice for the poor.[16] But perhaps this had never been the government's intention?

Pay-if-you-win: Contingency Fees

During 1987, a protracted and unsuccessful piece of litigation by victims of the arthritis drug Opren[17] had revealed a serious problem over legal aid in group actions when the Court of Appeal ruled that all litigants must contribute to the costs. There was public concern that elderly and impecunious litigants were only able to proceed through the personal generosity of millionaire Geoffrey Bradman. An unprecedented series of calamities – the Kings Cross underground fire, the Clapham train crash, the Alpha Piper oil rig explosion, the Lockerbie air crash, the sinking of the *Marchioness* – fuelled the fire of public resentment at the inability of the legal system to compensate accident victims swiftly and sufficiently. Bitterness over the level of compensation was expressed after the death of small children in the *Herald of Free Enterprise*, revealed to the general public for the first time that compensation for sorrow caused by bereavement was pegged at the notional sum of £3,500.[18] The award by a jury of £600,000 damages in a notorious libel case against *Private Eye* later in the year, fanned the flames and the strength of public opinion moved the Court of Appeal to redress the balance by issuing new guidelines which would result in lower awards in defamation awards.[19]

The logical solution to the problem posed by disasters is a state-funded compensation scheme but this is clearly unacceptable to the present government and perhaps also to the public at large, disillusioned by the parsimonious level of welfare bene fits and lured by skilful propaganda into thinking that there is more money to be gained in class (or group) actions financed by American-style lawyers on a contingency basis. A new pressure group, Citcom, was formed to press for reform and got as far this year as sponsoring a Private Member's Bill. The Green Paper, however, expressed doubts about 'pay-if-you-win' fees and the White Paper borrowed the more appropriate Scottish 'speculative fee' model, in which payment of fees can be made contingent on winning but which does not allow the lawyer to reimburse himself from his client's damages. In the meantime, the Legal Aid Board was asking for power to nominate and pay for a single legal aid solicitor in group or multi-party claims.[20] These peripheral proposals, as the National Consumer Council (NCC) noticed, left the kernel of the problem – namely, the need to prove negligence and the proper level of damages in personal injury claims – unresolved. Making common cause with the British Medical Association and the Civil Justice Review,[21] the NCC urged the government to return the question of accident compensation to the political agenda.[22]

Criminal Justice

The criminal justice system may have been less in the news but it has had its bad moments. Complaints over the low standards of the Crown Prosecution Service (CPS) had been endemic since its inauguration; this year they proliferated.[23] In fact, poor recruitment was such a problem throughout government legal services, that Sir Robert Andrew was asked to review it; he found it to be particularly grave in the CPS.[24] This necessitated pay awards plus a special recruitment campaign and, in an attempt to make the service more attractive, the Green Paper proposed giving CPS members full rights of audience in all courts.

Magistrates' courts were also suffering an exodus of court staff which was helping to build delays, estimated to be nine months or more in simple cases. Numbers of persons committed for trial had been rising fast: from 67,000 in 1982 to 105,000 in 1988. All this had put pressure on the already overcrowded remand system (as many as one in every ten prisoners today may be awaiting trial). Hastily the government published proposals to clear the cluttered magistrates' courts by streamlining old-fashioned committal proceedings. Judge Owen Stable QC grew choleric over solicitors who encouraged their clients to elect jury trial in minor cases, a right already cut by a series of Criminal Justice Acts; it could, he opined with advantage be cut once more.[25] The ancient right to 'trial by one's peers' took another knock when the Court of Appeal held that the Criminal Justice Act 1988, which had drastically cut defence rights to object to jurors, left no residual judicial discretion to ensure a racially or sexually mixed jury.[26] The year ended with a new and reput edly hardline Home Secretary (David Waddington) announcing his commitment to substantial reforms to be placed before the next Parliament. This measure is likely to dispose of another ancient safeguard, the 'right to silence', a change inaugurated, like so many repressive measures, in Northern Ireland and now under consideration by a Home Office Working Party. The change has been resisted by a wide coalition of the Criminal Bar and civil liberties group.[27]

This leads logically to the low point of the year which came in November, when the Director of Public Prosecution (DPP) had pub licly to admit that he could no longer support the conviction of the 'Guildford Four', imprisoned for a bomb outrage in a controversial trial in 1976. Two days later, they were freed by the Court of Appeal. For once the Home Office did not quibble and generous interim compensation awards of £50,000 were announced almost immediately. The public was left to argue over the exact implications for the criminal justice system. Did the fault lie with the repressive terrorism laws which allow suspects to be detained too long and which Parliament, in defiance of the European Court of Human Rights, has just put on to a permanent basis? Does the Police and Criminal Evidence Act 1984 provide safeguards to prevent such miscarriages of justice? What of other doubtful convictions; the Maguires, the 'Birmingham Six' and Winston Silcott were all dragged into the argument. Arguably, as *Justice* has always maintained, such cases ought to be referred to a special tribunal whose lay members would have less interest in maintaining the status quo.[28]

The prosecution had better success in the Court of Appeal. This year, the first appeals by the Attorney-General against sentence, using his new statutory powers, reached the Court of Appeal. The first concerned sentencing in sexual abuse cases, the second in cases of motor manslaughter. In both, the Court of Appeal increased the sentences substantially, taking the opportunity to lay down general guidelines.

Justice at Risk?

Like every public service, legal services are under pressure. Lack of resources and low morale are draining the system; government cannot begin to compete with the big City firms and the commercial sector in terms of pay. Both civil and criminal courts are bulging at the seams. The high cost and inordinate delays of litigation which had led to the Civil Justice Review, led to the announcement in April of a five-year action plan. But the temptation is always to delegate: from Crown Courts to magistrates, from the High Court to County Courts; from County Courts to tribunals; from trained advocates to solicitors to lay advisors and representatives. This process cannot continue indefinitely. The already overcrowded institutions at the bottom can no longer deal with the overflow while more positive reforms such as the Family Court are pigeonholed for lack of money. Who can say that the quality of justice is not being strained?

Notes
1. *The Work and Organization of the Legal Profession*, Cm.570; *Contingency Fees*, Cm.571; *(Conveyancing by Authorized Practitioners*, Cm.572. The conveyancing monopoly was finally ended by the Building Societies Act 1986 but this has not been brought into force. For the reasons, see statement by Lord Mackay in *New Law Journal*, 10 March 1989, p. 318.
2. See particularly, *Report of the Royal Commission on Legal Services* (The Benson Report), Cmnd.7648 1979; *A Time for Change*, The Marre Report on the future of the legal profession, 1988.

3. See Hugo Young, 'Purple posse against the Green Paper', in *The Guardian*, 13 March 1989.

4. *Response to the Lord Chancellors's Green Papers*, Legal Action Group, 1989.

5. *Quality of Justice, The Bar's Response*, General Council of the Bar, 1989.

6. *Striking the Balance*, Law Society, 1989.

7. See *Ordinary Justice, Legal services and the Courts in England and Wales: a Consumer View*, HMSO, 1989.

8. *Legal Services: A Framework for the Future*, Cm.740, 1989.

9. In a speech to the annual Bar Conference, *The Lawyer*, 10 October 1989, p. 1.

10. *The Independent*, 10 July 1989; *New Law Journal*, 21 July 1989.

11. Roger Smith, 'The Green Papers and legal services', 1989, 52, *Modern Law Review*, 527.

12. 'Legal services and the Green Papers', in *Law Society Gazette*, 5 April 1989.

13. *Legal Action*, October 1989, pp. 7–8.

14. John Baldwin and Sheila Hill, *The Operation of the Green Form Scheme in England and Wales*, Lord Chancellor's Department 1988.

15. *Second Stage Consultation on the Future of the Green Form Scheme*, Legal Aid Board, May 1989.

16. See, *Reponse to the Legal Aid Board's Second Consulta tion Paper on the Green Form Scheme*, Legal Action Group, September 1989; 'Franchising' in *Legal Action*, January 1988, p. 5.

17. Reported as *Davies v Eli Lilly*, 1987 1 Weekly Law Reports 1136.

18. Although this was actually a reform introduced by section 3 (1) of the Administration of Justice Act 1982, the common law did not award damages for sorrow or in respect of the death of a third party.

19. *Sutcliffe* v *Pressdram, The Guardian*, 20 October 1989. The damages were later reduced from £600,000 to £60,000 in an out-of-court settlement.

20. *Consultation Paper on Multi-Party Actions*, Legal Aid Board, May 1989.

21. *Civil Justice Review*, Cm.394, 1988.

22. *Ordinary Justice*, National Consumer Council, HMSO, 1989.

23. Anne Grosskurth, 'The CPS: a service in crisis', in *Legal Action*, July 1989, pp. 8–9.

24. *Review of Government Legal Services* (The Andrew Report), HMSO, 1989.

25. See 'Crown court trials', in *New Law Journal*, 1 September 1989.

26. *R. v Ford* (Royston), 1989, 3 Weekly Law Re ports 762.

27. Gabriel Black, 'The right defence', in *Legal Action*, January 1989, p. 9; 'Silence and safeguards', in *New Law Journal*, 13 January 1989.

28. 'Miscarriages of Justice', *Justice*, 1988.

Chronology

3 Jan: Recruitment campaign announced to combat shortages of lawyers in the Crown Prosecution Service.

4 Jan: Law Society submission on safeguarding the suspect's right to silence in the light of recent changes in Northern Ireland.

9 Jan: The National Council for Civil Liberties is relaunched as 'Liberty', campaigning for a Bill of Rights, freedom of information and the repeal of the Prevention of Terrorism Act.

25 Jan: Publication of three Green Papers on the legal profession, conveyancing and the introduction of 'no wins, no fees' briefs. The Law Society welcomes the proposals to

end the Bar's monopoly of advocacy before the higher courts and of judicial recruitment. The Bar Council is bitterly critical.

26 Jan: *Legal Aid,* the annual report by the Law Society/Lord Chancellor's Advisory Committee suggests that the government could make big savings on the service by stream lining magistrates' courts procedure and by introducing a family court.

3 Feb: Court of Appeal approves the sterilization of a 36-year-old mentally handicapped woman without her consent.

14 Feb: Lord Chief Justice denounces the legal profession Green Paper as 'one of the most sinister documents ever to emanate from Government'.

17 Feb: Bar Council launches its critical response to the legal profession Green Paper.

20 Feb: Private member's Bill to enable accident victims to win more generous compensation published.

3 Mar: Scottish judge, Lord Mayfield, rules that a husband can be charged with raping his wife even though they were still living together.

10 Mar: Michelle Renshaw gaoled for seven days for contempt of court by Judge James Pickles at Leeds Crown Court after she refused to give evidence against a man accused of attacking her.

13 Mar: Consultative Paper on reform of the Scottish legal system published. The most controversial proposals give solicitors the right of evidence in Scottish supreme courts, allow advocates to form partnerships and establish a legal ombudsman.

15 Mar: Mayfield judgment upheld in Scottish Court of Appeal.

22 Mar: Court of Appeal rules that a UK statute is valid in cases where it is apparently inconsistent with European law until a ruling by a European court.

30 Mar: *The Families of Murder Victims Project: First Year Report 1988* published. It argues that the criminal justice system often shows little regard for the feelings of families of murder victims.

6 Apr: Lord Mackay outlines a five-year programme to provide faster and cheaper civil justice, with a shift of cases between the High Court and the lower county courts.

13 Apr: Senior judges scrap plans to meet in court time to consider the Green Papers.

17 Apr: Anti-abortion MPs urge the Attorney-General to investigate a High Court ruling that doctors could abandon procedures to prolong the life of a brain-damaged baby girl (Baby C).

18 Apr: Law Commission suggests a criminal code covering more than 90 per cent of serious crimes be enacted.

20 Apr: In the Baby C case the Court of Appeal ruled that the baby should be allowed to die with dignity.

1 Apr: New Legal Aid Act comes into force.

21 Apr: Damages of £1,002,799 awarded to a girl brain-damaged by the administration of the wrong treatment by Newham Health Authority.

24 Apr: Legal history made in Scotland when a woman accuses her husband of raping her. Two days later he was cleared of the offence.

25 Apr: Survey in *Lawyer* shows a growing shortage of high street solicitors.

28 Apr: UN Human Rights Commission found that the Law Lords, sitting as the Privy Council, breached the international convention on human rights when they decided not to order a retrial in a Jamaican murder appeal, raising questions in the Commonwealth over the authority of the Privy Council as a final court of appeal.

1–2 May: Law Society and Bar Council send their responses to the Green Papers to the Lord Chancellor.

2 May: Lords give consent to the sterilization of a 36-year-old mentally handicapped woman, despite the fact that she was incapable of giving her consent for the operation.

4 May: Consumers' Association supports the Green Papers.

11 May: National Audit Office report points to the failings of the Crown Prosecution Service, beset by staff shortages and low morale prompted by low pay and poor career prospects. White Paper outlining powers to curb fraud, mismanagement, dishonesty and inefficiency in Britain's £13 billion per annum charities is unveiled.

22 May: Bar Council working party produces *Televising the Courts* and calls for televising of cases to enhance confidence and educate the public in the workings of the legal system.

23 May: Critical response to the Green Papers from the Judges Council.

24 May: Record libel damages of £600,000 awarded to Sonia Sutcliffe, estranged wife of the Yorkshire Ripper, against *Private Eye*.

25 May: The Sutcliffe case prompts the announcement of a review of the libel law.

25 May: A new training scheme for the Crown Prosecution Service to fill its staff shortages, announced.
Lords rules that doctors can sterilize mentally ill or handicapped people who are incapable of giving their consent but that in practice court approval should always be sought.

5 June: Law Commission's *Right to Goods in Bulk*, HMSO, suggests changes to sale of goods and bills of lading legislation.

5 July: Government backs down on plans to allow partnerships between solicitors and barristers.

18 July: Attorney-General asks Court of Appeal to increase three-year gaol sentence for incest, the first test of powers granted by the Criminal Justice Act 1988 for review of sentences considered to be unduly lenient.

19 July: Lord Mackay's White Paper on the legal professions envisages new rights of audience for solicitors, and will allow building societies and banks to do conveyancing.

25 July: Home Office working party suggests some cautious moves towards undermining a suspect's right to silence.

31 July: New system allowing appeals against a judge's decision that a criminal case should be heard in camera comes into force under section 159 of the 1988 Criminal Justice Act.

2 Aug: Continuing delays and staff shortages pointed to in the annual report of the Crown Prosecution Service.

1 Sept: Legal precedent set as Mr Justice Popplewell is granted a High Court order appointing a receiver to seize the assets of a drug trafficker after he refused to pay money confiscated by a court, acting under the 1986 Drug Trafficking Offences Act.

11 Sept: National Association for the Care and Rehabilitation of Offenders report argues sentencing by the courts is out of control and that offenders are often dealt with ineffectively, haphazardly and inhumanely.

19 Sept: Investigation into who should make decisions for mentally handicapped adults launched.

23 Sept: Lord Justice Butler-Sloss, who chaired the Cleveland child sex abuse inquiry in 1988, launches an education programme for judges on the sentencing and treatment of child sex abusers.

9 Oct: The number of people entitled to legal aid has fallen by 14 million since 1979 according to Legal Action.

10 Oct: Scottish solicitors monopoly over conveyancing is to be ended and their rights of audience extended to Scotland's supreme courts.

Law Commission calls for three new criminal offences to curb computer hacking.

13 Oct: Lord McCluskey puts off sentencing a sex attacker in order to give the victim an opportunity to express her view on what the sentence should be, a decision unprecedented in Scottish law. This decision was overturned in the Scottish Court of Appeal on 19 Oct.

17 Oct: The Director of Public Prosecutions asks for the convictions of the Guildford four to be quashed and initiates criminal proceedings against some of the police officers involved in their conviction for the bombing of a pub in Guildford in 1974.

19 Oct: Court of Appeal overturns the £600,000 libel damages awarded to Sonia Sutcliffe against *Private Eye* and Lord Donaldson rules that juries should receive guidance on awards.

Merlyn Rees points out that the Guildford four, just released having been wrongfully convicted of the Guildford pub bombing in 1974, would have been executed had capital punishment been then in force and hopes that this case will bring to an end attempts to reintroduce the death penalty.

23 Oct: *Charities in Scotland: A Framework for Supervision*, Scottish Office, suggests improvements in the supervision of Scottish charities by empowering the Inland Revenue to maintain a public index of names and addresses.

6 Nov: *Private Eye* settles the Sutcliffe libel action out of court for £60,000 plus £100,000 for a separate action.

7 Nov: Church leaders in Birmingham call for a review of the case of the Birmingham Six.

8 Nov: Lord Donaldson calls for new powers for the Court of Appeal to reassess damages in a libel case.

10 Nov: Test case on judge's decisions to hear cases in camera is rejected in the Court of Appeal.

13 Nov: £5 million reform package to extend legal aid to more children, pensioners and personal injury claimants announced.

21 Nov: Wide-ranging changes to the legal profession and legal system are to be brought about by the Courts and Legal Services Bill announced in the Queen's speech.

Also in the Queen's speech was the announcement of a miscellaneous package of law reforms for Scotland, including means-tested fines, the opening of conveyancing to financial institutions and entitling solicitors to plead before the Scottish supreme courts.

23 Nov: European Parliament votes to set up an inquiry into the case of the Birmingham Six.

29 Nov: Duty Solicitor Scheme criticized in a report by Birmingham University for the Lord Chancellor's Department.

30 Nov: Jury awards Lord Aldington record libel damages of £1.5 million in his claim against Count Tolstoy and Nigel Watts.

White Paper, *Charities: A Framework for the Future* published. It aimed to increase accountability and trustees' responsibilities.

1 Dec: First convictions for corporate manslaughter on the directors of David Holt Plastics Ltd in Preston Crown Court.

4 Dec: Inquiry under Sir John May into the case of the Guildford Four opens.

7 Dec: Courts and Legal Services Bill published.

Damages for various categories of victims raised by the Home Office.

12 Dec: Reclassification of the Birmingham Six as category 'B' instead of category 'A' prisoners.

Police and Public Order

ROBERT REINER

During 1989 it became clear that the British public's remarkable love-affair with the police had come to an end. The way that the police acquired a sacred status as a symbol of national pride, especially in the post-war, *Dixon of Dock Green* era, has always seemed odd to foreigners. To them it would appear natural that the police, the body charged with the function of maintaining order, if necessary by force, should be viewed at best with ambivalence and scepticism. Controversy about many aspects of policing had been growing in Britain for two decades, but it was only in 1989 that this really began to register in polls of general public opinion. Throughout the 1980s, surveys had shown that there was considerable suspicion of the police amongst specific groups in the population (young, male, economically marginal, ethnic minority, inner-city residents in particular), and that growing proportions of all groups recognized some problems (such as corruption and discrimination) existed. But the overall standing of the police seemed to remain robustly high.

During 1989, however, a series of prominent polls documented that public trust in the police was plummeting. The clearest evidence of long term decline was a Market and Opinion Research International (MORI) poll for *Newsnight*, published in November, which showed that while in the 1959 survey for the Royal Commission on the Police, 83 per cent of a national sample expressed 'a great deal of respect' for the police, only 43 per cent now did. Today, 41 per cent have 'mixed feelings' compared with 16 per cent in 1959, and 14 per cent have 'little respect', by contrast with a 1959 figure of less than 1 per cent. As recently as August 1981, 75 per cent said they were 'satisfied' with how their area was policed, but in 1989 polls by MORI this had declined to between 58-64 per cent. Several other polls during 1989 echoed MORI's results.

To an extent the police are sharing in a more widespread decline in the standing of all public institutions. Although falling, the proportion of the public perceiving the police as 'well-run' stood up well compared with other institutions, according to several 1989 studies (including the fifth *British Social Attitudes Survey*, and a Consumers' Association study published in July 1989, as well as the MORI polls themselves).

Nevertheless, greater questioning of the police is more than just a reflection of declining respect for public institutions in general. It is a reaction to numerous controversial trends in policing. All of these go back for many years, but their legacy lives on, and indeed in crucial respects came to a head in 1989. The issues which have contributed to this crisis of public confidence in the police crystallize around five basic themes: abuse of powers, corruption, effectiveness, the militarization of public order methods, and the control and accountability of the police with respect to all these controversial areas.

Abuse of Powers

No other single case did more to shake the foundations of trust in the police than the Court of Appeal's decision in October 1989 to release the 'Guildford Four', the three men and a woman sentenced to life imprisonment in 1974 for the Guildford and Woolwich pub bombings. The reverberations shook not only the police but all parts of the criminal justice system, in particular the Director of Public Prosecutions (DPP) office and the Court of Appeals. But particular attention was focused on the police, as the decision to release the four was based on evidence (gathered by the Avon and Somerset Constabulary) showing that some of the Surrey police officers involved in the 1974 case 'must have lied' (in the Lord Chief Justice, Lord Lane's, words). The comment of *Police Review* that 'the service is facing the greatest attack on its credibility since the allegations in Operation Countryman', is a massive understatement. Political and press attack reached as high as the Metropolitan Commissioner, Sir Peter Imbert, who had been involved in the case at various tangential points. Twenty-five backbench Labour MPs called for his resignation. The release of the Guildford Four also re-invigorated campaigns for the release of the Birmingham Six (convicted for the 1974 Birmingham pub bombings), and other celebrated cases. The controversies surrounding these cases are timebombs waiting to go off.

The Guildford Four was the most dramatic of a series of sensational revelations of police malpractice in the gathering and presentation of evidence which erupted in 1989. At the end of June the whole of the West Midlands Serious Crimes Squad was disbanded by the Chief Constable, Geoffrey Dear. This followed a series of allegations about 'serious and widespread malpractice in the handling of evidence, which had been made by, amongst others, Clare Short, the MP for Birmingham Ladywood. This was the most dramatic personal intervention by a Chief Constable since Sir Robert Mark's days as a crusader against corruption at Scotland Yard in the early 1970s. Whether Dear's decisive action will suffice to stem the apparent sapping of trust in police evidence remains doubtful. In November 1989, following the Guildford Four release, connections were made between the recent Serious Crimes Squad scandal and the Birmingham Six, who had been convicted in 1974 on evidence largely assembled by the Squad. Early in December this was raised at a meeting of the West Midlands Policy Authority, at which Mr Dear claimed there was no link between the cases. The controversy is undoubtedly going to continue into 1990.

Record damages of £100,000 were awarded in December by a High Court jury to a black lay-preacher who had cannabis planted on him by a Metropolitan policeman. The sum was the highest ever awarded against the police. The case was one of more than ten which originated from a series of incidents involving the same constable at Notting Hill. In one of these cases in late November, another black man was awarded £3,000 after a jury held he had been beaten and had cannabis planted on him by the same constable and his associates.

There were numerous other episodes in which police abuse of power was alleged during 1989, some new, some continuations of earlier sagas. In February, disciplinary hearings were announced against twenty Royal Ulster Constabulary Officers, arising out of the inquiry begun by John Stalker and completed by Colin Sampson, which had probed allegations of a shoot-to-kill policy and high-level cover-ups.

In March 1989, a man shot in the heart in 1985 by police officers who mistook him for an armed robber sued the Met. for damages. He was eventually awarded £59,000. In April a black man received £7,000 for false imprisonment and malicious prosecution after a drink-drive charge, and a 70-year-old black man won £5,000 on similar grounds. Both claimed they had been subjected to racist abuse.

There were several cases during the year of people dying after high speed police chases. Concern about the issue led to new guidelines being promulgated by the Association of Chief Police Officers (ACPO) in June, in which responsibility for decisions in police pursuits was moved to Force control rooms.

In January, thirteen Metropolitan Police officers were suspended following the investigation of allegations of violence by police at the picket lines outside News International's plant in Wapping in 1987. They were returned to duty later in the year, following successful Police Federation pressure. But the Wapping controversy continued to simmer. In July a cameraman sued the Metropolitan Police for injuries sustained at Wapping. At the end of October the DPP initiated a challenge in the High Court against an earlier ruling in May by a magis trate that proceedings against the police officers arising out of the Wapping dispute should be halted because of the delay in bringing the prosecution.

In September the investigation into allegations made in 1986 by a Kent Police Constable that crime figures were being rigged in order to boost detection rates, led to one Detective Sergeant being sacked, and five other officers being fined. Ironically, Constable Ron Walker, who was praised by the Chief Constable for his courage in making the original allegations, also faced disci plinary action for refusing to report for duty. He claimed he had done this because of fear of persecution due to his colleagues' animosity.

In July a North Wales Police Constable was jailed for a month after an incident in which he had violently attacked a speeding motorist in August 1988. Unfortunately for him, a cameraman happened to be testing a video camera at the spot, and TV viewers, as well as the trial jury, were able to witness the assault for themselves. Throughout the year campaigning continued around allegations of malpractice in the investigation into the murder of PC Keith Blakelock during the 1985 Broadwater Farm rioting. This reached the headlines in May when the London School of Economics (LSE) students' union voted in Winston Silcott (who had been convicted of the murder) as their 'president. Silcott turned down the post after some controversy, but a campaign was begun by the governing body of Oxford students' union to follow the LSE example, though this was unsuccessful. However, in September the Police Complaints Authority directed that disciplinary charges should be brought against a Detective Chief Superintendent who had been in the forefront of the investigation into Blakelock's murder. Broadwater Farm was again in the news in October when a drugs raid, which had been revealed in advance to some journal ists who were allowed to accompany it, led to accusations that dealers had been tipped-off. The involvement of the Press was in accordance with Sir Peter Imbert's much-praised policy of 'Glasnost' at the Yard, and the controversy surrounding the raid could lead cynics to feel that the police cannot win.

Altogether 1989 was a singularly bad year for scandals concerning police abuse of power, and no doubt this was a major element in denting their public standing. No wonder MORI found 63 per cent of its November sample agreed with the view that the police 'sometimes "bend the rules" in order to get a conviction'.

Police Corruption

The main police scandals in 1989 concerned abuse of power for organizational purposes rather than purely personal corruption for individual reward. However, there were some prominent cases of straightforward corruption allegations. Early in the year press allegations were made about the involvement of a former Detective Superin tendent, Tony Lundy, in corrupt leaking of information about a major cocaine-importing case. These were the basis of a Granada TV *World in Action* documentary in April, which led a group of MPs to seek Parliamentary debate on corruption in the Metro politan Police. The allegations were consistently denied by Lundy, but the case kept alive memories of the 1970s corruption scandals.

During the year there were several cases in which police officers were accused of rape or sexual assault, and in a few cases the allegations were officially confirmed. In August a Nigerian woman was awarded £8,000 damages against a Metropolitan Police Constable (who had since left the force) who had sex with her after threatening action to deport her unless she submitted. In October another Metropolitan Constable was jailed for raping a teenager while on duty. The same week a woman Police Sergeant from the Metropolitan Police accused a Hampshire Inspector of raping her while they were attending courses at Bramshill Police Staff College. In November a Warwickshire Police Constable was cleared for the second time on a rape charge. (Magistrates had earlier dismissed the case for lack of evidence, but the Crown Prosecution Service (CPS) obtained leave from the High Court to re-open it.)

In October a former Regional Crime Squad detective was charged with a £1.25 million blackmail demand, said to have been made while he was in the police force, involving alleged contaminated tins of baby food and other products. All these cases received lurid publicity, and no doubt contributed to the fall in the polices public standing over 1989.

Public Order Policing

During the 1980s police tactics for dealing with public disorder became increasingly militaristic, utilizing defensive and offensive riot control equipment, and more tightly co-ordinated methods for assembling and deploying highly trained manpower. Concern about this was crystallized in a much discussed book by BBC journalist Gerry Northan, *Shooting in the Dark*, which appeared at the end of 1988 and revealed details of the secret ACPO manual on public order tactics. Another highly publicized journalistic account of the police, Roger Graef's *Talking Blues*, appeared in 1989 and described the public order conflicts of the 1980s, especially the 1984-5 miners' stike, as the police Vietnam, a major trauma which shook confidence inside and outside the force.

Echoes of these disputes, and the militarization of police public order strategy, continued in 1989, although there were no major new confrontations.

The suspension and trial of officers accused of violence against picket-lines in Wapping was mentioned above. In November the Court of Appeal freed three Chelsea supporters who had been convicted of football hooliganism. This followed the similar collapse in 1988 of several cases in which evidence had been gathered by infiltration of organized hooligan gangs. In June ACPO announced the formation of a new national intelligence unit to combat soccer hooliganism.

In April 1989 the Hillsborough tragedy occurred in which 95 football fans died and 173 were injured at the Sheffield Wednesday ground. The inquiry by Lord Justice Taylor, which published an interim report in August, claimed that 'the main reason for the disaster was the failure of police control'. The Chief Constable of South Yorkshire, Peter Wright, offered his resignation but the police authority voted unanimously to reject it, and Mr Wright stayed on.

Many disorders which occurred were echoes of events of previous years. In May rioting broke out in Wolverhampton following a raid by drug squad officers on a pub. In St Paul's, Bristol, where nine years earlier a raid had sparked off the first of the major urban disorders of the 1980s, police in riot gear were deployed after a crowd stoned some plain-clothes officers making an arrest.

In June a High Court judge granted an injunction banning 25 alleged hippie leaders from going within three miles of Stonehenge, on the grounds that public disorder was feared after the experience of previous years. Later that month, 200 people were arrested as they tried to reach Stonehenge for the midsummer solstice.

The annual Notting Hill Carnival in London at the end of August once more saw the deployment of some 5,000 police, many in riot gear or on horseback. Disturbances occurred when some youths stoned the police, and the Home Secretary asked for a police report on the violence.

A new occasion for disorder was the series of protests by Muslims over Salman Rushdie's book, *The Satanic Verses*. There were major clashes in Bedford and Dewsbury during June. In August the West Yorkshire police proposal to buy an armoured car provoked Muslim protests, as they feared its use against them in anti-Rushdie demonstrations.

In 1988 an ACPO report had sparked off a moral panic about a supposedly new phenomenon, rural violence committed by mobs of affluent 'lager louts'. In April, the Home Office Research Unit published a study which refuted much of the basis for panic. It showed that such disorder was not a new phenomenon, occurred mainly in towns and predominantly involved unemployed or low-waged youths. It recommended some practical steps to facilitate police control, such as encouraging the sale of low-alcohol beers and staggering pub closing hours. The study's findings were dismissed as 'codswallop' by the Police Federation, but received widespread attention.

While the moral panic of 1988 was being scotched, a new one appeared to replace it: acid house parties. Numerous incidents of disorder and violence at such parties were reported. In late September, for example, 26 police in riot gear were deployed in Surrey to deal with one party, and came under attack from security men guarding the party who deployed CS gas and Rottweiler dogs. In October seven forces in the south of England announced the formation of a special intelligence unit to combat such parties.

The extent of toughening of police riot control tactics was ironically underlined during the year by the rate at which officers sustained injuries during riot training. In January, a Cheshire Police Constable received £3,375 damages for injuries sustained in riot training, while in October the Police Federation announced that 150 London officers had been injured during riot training in the previous three months, 14 by the use of petrol bombs.

Police Effectiveness and 'Value for Money'

Concern about 'value for money' from policing, as from all public services, has been a major theme of the Thatcher government throughout the 1980s. Home Office Circular 114 of 1983 signalled the government's intention to make additional resources conditional on evidence that existing resources were being used as efficiently, effectively and economically (the dreaded three 'E's') as possible. The tougher Circular 106, which was issued at the end of 1988, cast a chill over police managers and staff associations which continued throughout 1989. Under its guidelines, which require Chief Constables to specify the objectives which are to be met by each new post asked for, police forces throughout the country fared disappointingly in their bids for increased strength in 1989. In November it was announced that the Home Office had approved only 957 out of 2,349 extra posts requested.

The harder line the government was taking to police expenditure was also indicated by the long-running and complicated dispute between the government and the Police Federation over rent allowances and the implications of poll tax for the rates element of it. By the end of 1989 there were clear signs of a return to the police militancy of the late 1970s which culminated in the Edmund-Davies inquiry. At the end of November, the Federation declared 'out and out war' with the government over rent allowance issue, and an article in its magazine saw 'this law and order government's honeymoon with the police as over'.

Underlying police fears was a perception that the government was tacitly pursuing a policy of privatization of policing by holding back expenditure on public forces and implicitly encouraging the growth of private security and volunteer forces as substitutes. In this context there was particular resentment among the police about their use to fill the places of other striking public sector workers, during the prison officers' dispute in early 1989, and the ambulance drivers' action at the end of the year.

Throughout the year police representatives were active in highlighting the trends towards creeping privatization. For example, a *Police Review* survey published in January found over 500 non-police patrols in public places in twenty forces throughout Britain. This coincided with the announcement of Circular 106, and the two were evidently linked. The ACPO joined the Federation in condemning the government for effectively encouraging private security as 'a cheap option' by restricting policy manpower. In February these arguments were strengthened when it was announced that British Transport Police were being replaced by private security guards at Sealink terminals, and this was also happening to Ministry of Defence police at some establishments. This became acutely controversial after the September bombing of Deal barracks by the IRA, as it had been guarded by private security.

The dangers for effectiveness of economizing were highlighted at various points in the year. The potential negative implications of the policy of civilianization were underlined by police associations when police civilian employees went on strike in July. In May the Metropolitan Commissioner, Sir Peter Imbert, criticized attempts to measure police effectiveness and efficiency by methods derived from commercial organizations, implicitly questioning the Home Office's 'value for money' thrust. In an unprecedented joint initiative ACPO, the Police Federation and the Superintendents' Association began a review of the effects of the new financial management policies and whether they were detrimental to traditional policing. The new Police Federation Parliamentary adviser, Michael Shersby, attacked proposals to finance forensic laboratory services by charging individual force users. The Federation Annual Conference generally condemned the trend to wards policing 'for profit, not people'.

The growth of volunteer initiatives in policing, notably the much publicized import from New York of the Guardian Angels (who began patrols on the London Underground), stimulated police efforts to find official alternatives for this fervour of citizenship. In February the Metropolitan Police urged members of the Guardian Angels to join the Special Constabulary, and in March the government argued similarly for Neighbourhood Watch participants. In April, the idea of a volunteer force to help police, under police control, was floated by John Dellow, Deputy Commissioner of the Metropolitan Police and now President of ACPO. In December a group of young volunteers to help the police, the 'Blue Angels', was formed by the Metropolitan Police.

All these trends were stimulated by a growing public awareness of the declining extent to which the police were able to clear-up crimes reported to them. The third British Crime Survey was published in August and showed an increase in the proportion of people who did not report crimes because they felt the police could or would have done nothing (32 per cent of victims said this, compared with 23 per cent in 1984). One source of this declining public confidence was the controversial 'case-screening' system which the Met. had introduced as a way of ensuring optimum concentra tion of resources. In November it was announced that 'case-screening' would be dropped as a part of a reorganization of detective procedures, the Crime Investigation Priority Project. This was intended to make victims' needs paramount in criminal investigation, and implemented an internal report published in April. Whatever the success of these efforts may prove to be, they are a response to the damaging undermining of public confi dence which had become apparent.

Control and Accountability of Policing

For most of the 1980s the policing debate focused largely on the issue of accountability, in particular the question of relations between Chief Constables and local police authorities. This controversy did not surface in 1989, but a number of developments signified its other face, the trend towards greater centralization of policing and its control. The tendency to establish centralized units to deal with specific problems was illustrated by new units set up to provide intelligence on football hooliganism and acid house parties. These sorts of unit are not new, the football hooligan one explicitly following the earlier model of the Drugs Intelligence Unit. But they are a pattern likely to be adopted more often in the future.

The increased role of Her Majesty's Inspectorate of Constabulary as a body for co-ordinating standards was indicated in January by the appointment of Colin Sampson, formerly Chief Constable of West Yorkshire, as the first HMI for the

Met. The *de facto* role of ACPO as a body for harmonizing policies between forces was encouraged by the then Home Secretary, Douglas Hurd, at ACPO's autumn conference. He called on them 'to deliver effectively co-ordinated operational action'. Failing this, he implied, the present structure of local policing might be replaced by either regional forces or a single national force. ACPO's higher profile role was also emphasized by their decision in October to appoint a firm of specialists in 'headhunting' senior managers to find a suitable candidate for the post of general secretary.

Mr Hurd's speech at ACPO was the most prominent example of a series of interventions during the year raising the case for a regional or national structure for more centralized policing. The professional police journals have been filled with articles advocating various alternative models for achieving centralized control. In April, for example, the Chief Constable of Leicestershire, Michael Hirst, outlined a scheme for ten regional 'super forces' to replace the present local structure, while in November, Steve Males, Assistant Chief Constable in Wiltshire argued the case for a possible national structure (both in *Police Review*). In March the Adam Smith Institute published a report on Scotland in which they proposed a two-tier structure of a national force combined with the provision of basic neighbourhood services 'at a very local level'.

In April, the Chairman of the Commons Home Affairs Committee (HAC), John Wheeler, advocated the formation of six regional forces with an enhanced control from the centre, to replace the present tripartite structure of control involving local authorities. Like the other exponents of centralization he emphasized the need for this in the light of the advent of greater European integration after 1992. Later in April, the HAC was critical of the inconsistent format of Chief Constables' Annual Reports and urged greater co-ordination. In May the HAC reported on the training of senior police officers. It concluded that all senior officers should be appointed by the Home Office, removing one of the few remaining powers of local authorities. It recommended that the Home Office should be more closely and explicitly involved in all aspects of training and selecting senior officers.

During the year a number of important police voices called for the establishment of specialist units at national level. In April, Roger Birch, Chief Constable of Sussex (and past President of ACPO) pressed for a Europe-wide group for police co-operations. Douglas Hurd proposed a European drugs unit. In July Sir Peter Imbert advocated the establishment of a national FBI-style force to combat major crime. Speaking at the Superintendents' Association in September, Douglas Hurd appointed a modified version of this idea, a national criminal intelligence unit to combat organized crime. In November, the Home Office suggested setting up a National Air Support Unit for police.

Other developments in this direction included the Police Federation's appointment in July of an MEP as their first European consultant. In May, Parliament passed the Police Officers (Central Services) Bill, which gave police, seconded to central services (such as HMI or the staff college), the powers of constable which they previously only enjoyed in their 'home' forces. It is clear that the trend is set towards much greater central control, although the precise structure of the future is yet to be decided.

The other element of accountability which has remained controversial during the year is the system for handling complaints against the police. Survey evidence suggests clearly that the fact that a system rests primarily on police investigation of complaints against themselves is an important source of distrust. One practical consequence of this is the increasing trend for people with grievances to pursue civil actions (such as the ones mentioned in the section on abuse of powers rather than formal complaints).

On the other hand, the Police Federation, despite its support in recent years for a completely independent system, has been locked into conflict with the Police Complaints Authority (PCA), which represents at least half a loaf of independence. In its May Annual Conference the Federation unanimously passed a vote of no confidence in the PCA, with delegates describing it as cancerous and amateurish. The Federation was particularly angered by the PCA's 1989 Annual Report, published in the previous month, which advocated a system of administrative dismissal of incompetent officers (a proposal which gained ACPO support). In October the Federation lost a High Court case in which it had sought a ruling that PCS members should be barred from attending interviews with officers suspected of disciplinary or criminal offences.

In November it was reported that Sir Peter Imbert was considering a radical plan to publish the names of officers found guilty of misbehaviour in *The Job* (the Metropolitan Police newspaper). He was also considering a number of other radial reforms, including changing the burden of proof from beyond reasonable doubt (the criminal standard) to the civil standard, the balance of probabilities. He was also looking at introducing a new offence to cover officers acting as a group. Under the pressure of falling public confidence, the impact of the cases of abuse which have been publicized during the year, it appears that quite dramatic changes in the complaints and discipline systems are on the horizon.

Conclusion

One could forgive many police officers for feeling intensely frustrated about the present crisis of confidence in them. As Robert Chesshyre's excellent recent study of the Metropolitan Police, *The Force*, indicates, in many ways the standards of recruitment, training and managerial professionalism are higher than ever before. Yet there are more sensational scandals (some time-bombs from the past) and less evidence of results, with predictable effects in falling public trust. Most senior officers recognize the problem. Sir Peter Imbert's recent 'Plus Programme' to revamp the Metro politan Police image is a reflection of this, and it seems he may be prepared to grasp some very prickly nettles to ensure control of malpractices.

Whatever the long term prospects, the immediate future is likely to bring more of the controversies and *causes célèbres* which have made the last year a particularly bad vintage for the police. As an editorial in the Police Federation Magazine aptly expressed it: 'These are dark days for our service, and we would all be glad to see the back of 1989 were it not for our foreboding as to what 1990 and 1991 may have waiting for us.'

Table 1. Police manpower (England and Wales excluding the Metropolitan Police)

Year	Authorized	Actual
1979	91,733	89,226
1980	92,353	92,310
1981	93,431	93,006
1982	93,510	93,181
1983	93,532	92,785
1984	93,564	92,337
1985	93,768	92,468
1986	94,270	92,905
1987	94,833	94,910
1988	95,436	94,982

Source: Report of H.M.Inspector of Constabulary 1988 HC 449, HMSO, Norwich, 1989

Chronology

12 Jan: Thirteen Metropolitan police officers suspended after an investigation into violence on the picket lines outside News International's Wapping plant in January 1987.

25 Jan: Members of the New York Guardian Angels arrive in London aiming to set up a similar vigilante organization on the London underground.

30 Jan: Government to spend an extra £290 million on increasing police manpower by 1,100.

27 Feb: Commons Home Affairs Select Committee criticizes under-funding leading to low morale in the forensic science service.

14 Mar: Controversy over accidents during high-speed police chases begins after a woman is killed by a police car on its way to an investigation. In all eight people are killed and three police officers injured in accidents involving police cars in March.

3 Apr: Allegations of police corruption in connection with a recent £100 million drugs smuggling case are aired on Granada TV's *World in Action*.

5 Apr: Home Office study into rural violence, *Drinking and Disorder: A Study of Non-Metropolitan Violence*, is published. It suggests cheaper low- and non-alcoholic beers should be available, altering the image of public houses, staggering their closing hours and encouraging the presence of young women.

7 Apr: John Dallow, the deputy commissioner of the Metropolitan police, reveals that the police are contemplating recruiting civilians into a volunteer force.

14 Apr: An 11-year-old girl mauled to death by two Rottweilers. Start of public concern about a number of savage attacks by this breed of dog.

15 Apr: Plain clothes policeman murdered whilst investigating an illegal drinking club in Birmingham.

24 Apr: An internal inquiry by the Metropolitan police, *The Investigation of Crime in Territorial Operations: Priority Project*, calls for radical changes in the way the police handle crime and its victims and indicts current practice.

1 May: Call for tougher gun laws in the wake of the carnage left by a gunman on the rampage at Monkseaton rejected by Douglas Hogg, Minister of State at the Home Office.

3 May: Charges against 13 officers in connection with violence at Wapping in 1987 thrown out at the first commital hearing.

16 May: Guardian Angels launch their first patrol on the London underground.
Police Federation calls for a national police reserve.

17 May: Police Federation conference passes a vote of no confidence in the Police Complaints Authority.
Douglas Hurd, the Home Secretary, rejects police calls for the regulation of the private security industry.

19 May: Commons Home Affairs Select Committee urges the re-vamping of the police appointments system, to be controlled from Whitehall.

23 May: Plan for a national register of the DNA profiles of convicted criminals announced.
Drugs raid in Wolverhampton followed by street fighting and looting.

2 June: Nicholas Ridley rules out a national dog register to control dangerous breeds despite growing concern at a series of savage attacks by Rottweilers.

15 June: Backbench Tory attempts to introduce a national dog registration scheme are defeated in the Commons by 159 to 146.

16 June: Guidelines on high-speed police pursuits issued.

17 June: Disturbances over the Rushdie affair in Bradford.

21 June: 250 people arrested as police strove to prevent hippies from celebrating the summer solstice at Stonehenge.

23 June: Accusations of falsifying of evidence lead to the disbanding of the Serious Crimes Squad in West Midlands.

27 June: Procedures for police authorities for hearing complaints against senior police officers to be tightened.

1 July: Police crack down on acid house parties in the Home Counties.

4 July: Confidential guidelines to Metropolitan Police stations advise that only about 15 per cent of crimes reported are likely to justify the effort involved in investigation.

6 July: Sir Peter Imbert, the Metropolitan Police Commissioner, calls for a national detective agency, based on the American FBI, to meet the challenges posed by 1992.

7 July: Dangerous Dog Bill, enacting tougher controls, goes through all stages in the Commons.

2 Aug: Police Review reveals that there were almost 20,000 assaults on officers in 1988, a 15 per cent increase on 1987, resulting in the loss of 42,000 working days.

10 Aug: Government consultation paper, *Action on Dogs*, on how to deal with stray dogs is denounced by animal charities.

14 Aug: Home Office paper on police powers and criminal investigation published.
Resignation of Peter Wright, Chief Constable of South Yorkshire, over the Hillsborough disaster is unanimously rejected by South Yorkshire Police Authority.

24 Aug: Call in the Police Federation's *Police Journal* for radical changes in the selection and training of senior police officers.

28 Aug: Notting Hill carnival ends in violence.

29 Aug: Douglas Hurd orders a report into the violence at Notting Hill.

1 Sept: Police empowered to seize terrorist funds in Britain as well as Northern Ireland.

13 Sept: Lawyer calls for a ban on Rottweilers at an inquest into the death of the girl killed by them earlier in the year.

14 Sept: Announcement of a 50 per cent increase in the demand for Rottweilers in the wake of recent publicity about their savagery.

19 Sept: Investigation into police corruption in Kent leads to disciplinary action against 33 detectives and the dismissal of one officer.

25 Sept: International Police Exhibition and Conference opens in London.

26 Sept: Inquiry launched into allegations of bribery amongst No.5 squad of the CID. Senior police officers call for powers to take DNA fingerprints.

28 Sept: Two people are killed during police high- speed chases.

29 Sept: Big police drugs raid at the Broadwater Farm estate in North London.

1 Oct: Over 100 people arrested and 16 police officers injured as police tried to deal with public order and drugs offences at acid house parties.

12 Oct: Policeman gaoled for seven years for raping an 18-year-old woman. He was in his marked patrol car, on duty and in uniform at the time of the incident in April 1988.

17 Oct: Criminal proceedings against some of the officers involved in the conviction of the four accused of the Guildford pub bombing in 1974 are initiated by the DPP.

6 Nov: The Metropolitan Police abandons its much criticized crime screening system as part of a package of measures designed to improve crime investigation in London.

10 Nov: Metropolitan Police cleared of using excessive force in dispersing a student demonstration outside Parliament in 1988 in the report of the inquiry conducted by Ian Kane, Chief Constable of Cambridgeshire.

14 Nov: Tighter rules on gun club membership announced.

16 Nov: Three Chelsea football supporters gaoled in 1987 for plotting violence are cleared and freed by the Court of Appeal after the court heard that the police had probably falsified evidence.

30 Nov: Nationwide review of police training urged by the Audit Commission.

1 Dec: First joint investigation unit involving police and customs to combat the drug crack is announced.

5 Dec: Record damages of £100,000 awarded against the Metropolitan Police after a High Court jury decided that the police had planted drugs on a young man. Home Office suggests legislation to regulate acid house parties.

6 Dec: Announcement of a new central fund of £1 million to help the government to meet the additional costs incurred in combating international drugs dealing.

7 Dec: Sir John Woodcock appointed HM Chief Inspector of Constabulary in place of Sir Richard Barratt.

19 Dec: High Court upholds the magistrates' decision to dismiss charges against six officers accused of brutality on the Wapping picket line in 1986.

29 Dec: Public order disturbances in Southwood estate, Bristol.

Crime and Penal Policy

TERENCE MORRIS

Cataclysmic Events in Criminal Justice

There seems little doubt that the year 1989 will be remembered for a set of events that were set in train in January and reached an astounding climax in mid-October with the release from prison of three young Irishmen and one woman who had been convicted in 1975 of responsibility for the detonation of bombs in two pubs in Guildford and another in Woolwich in October and November 1974. The deaths and injuries in these two outrages had been horrific as were those when 21 people died and many others were injured in a similar bombing in Birmingham in November 1974. Six Irishmen were arrested and subsequently convicted of this offence.

For more than two years, from early 1973, the IRA mounted a campaign of sustained terror against both military and civilian targets in England. Bombs packed with heavy nails had effects not dissimilar to the fragmentation anti-personnel devices used in conventional warfare; explosives were placed under cars and letter bombs sent to particular 'targets'. Public and political reaction after the Birmingham bombing had been so strong that the Wilson government introduced the Prevention of Terrorism Bill only eight days later. When both the Guildford and Birmingham bombers came to trial serious allegations were made by the defence that their clients had been subjected to beatings and psychological intimidation and that their confession statements were wholly unreliable. Neither of the juries, who could not possibly have been unaffected in some degree by the strong current of public anger then flowing against the IRA – which also resulted in hostility and suspicion towards almost all ordinary Irish people living in England at the time – accepted any evidence other than that of the police and all the accused were sentenced to life imprisonment. But for the fact that Parliament had abolished capital punishment for murder in 1969, only Carole Richardson, who was 17 at the time, would have escaped the gallows.

The stories of the Guildford Four and the Birmingham Six, although similar in many respects, are not directly related; that of the Maguire Seven, in contrast, is closely intertwined in that the father of one of the Guildford defendants, Guiseppe Conlon, was arrested and charged with the Maguires, one of whom, Mrs Annie Maguire, was Gerard Conlon's aunt. The Maguire Seven were convicted of operating a bomb factory and received sentences of up to 14 years. All have since been released except Guiseppe Conlon, who died in the course of his 12-year sentence. In another dimension, all three cases are related in that each has, and continues to have, a high profile in the context of Anglo-Irish relations in general and the Anglo-Irish Agreement in particular. In Ireland there is a deep suspicion about the objectivity of the British criminal justice system as far as Irish suspects are concerned and on the British side there has been anger at the difficulties experienced in obtaining the extradition of suspects from the Republic who are wanted for questioning in Britain.

Nor does the complexity of the matter rest here. For yet another group, known as the Balcombe Street Gang on account of their having been holed up under seige for a week by the Metropolitan Police in December 1975, are important members of the *dramatis personae*. When arrested, the four members of the gang admitted to having carried out both the Guildford and Woolwich bombings in co-operation with two other men and a woman who have, to this day, never been caught. This evidence was unknown to the jury in the Guildford case and when the Guildford Four appealed in 1977 it was rejected on the grounds that the Balcombe Street Gang were capable of lying at no cost to themselves to assist the appellants. Unlike the Balcombe Street Gang, the Guildford Four, the Maguire Seven and the Birmingham Six were, from the outset, all most unlikely people to be members of any IRA active service unit; most were ordinary Irish working people, one at least was a petty thief and one a drifter who was still a drug abuser at the time of her arrest, and all stoutly protested their innocence. Their claims to innocence began to be increasingly articulated after the statement by members of the Balcombe Street Gang that the Guildford Four were definitely *not* bombers was dismissed by the Court of Appeal. A number of MPs of all parties including the late Sir John Biggs-Davidson, Gerry (now Lord) Fitt and Chris Mullin, took up the case. Yorkshire Television devoted broadcasts of its *First Tuesday* to the issue in March 1984, July 1986 and March 1987. A book on the subject was published and after the release of Ann Maguire in 1985 Granada TV's *World in Action* produced a programme, followed by another in 1986. Robert Kee also took up the issue and following a Channel Four programme in 1986, published *Trial and Error* on the Guild ford and Maguire cases. A second Channel Four programme that year devoted no less than a 90-minute slot to the issue.

By now a number of very influential figures in the political, legal and ecclesiastical establishments were voicing serious doubts about some or all of the cases including the former Law Lords, Lord Scarman and Lord Devlin, to former Home Secretaries, Roy (now Lord) Jenkins and Merlyn Rees, Cardinal O'Fiaich of Armagh, Cardinal Hume of Westminster and the Archbishop of Canterbury, Dr Runcie. As a result of investigations by the Avon and Somerset Police, after the Home Secretary referred the case to the Court of Appeal in January 1989, the case for the Crown against the Guildford Four collapsed as the appeal was about to be heard in October. Alibi evidence that had never been available at the trial and evidence that Richardson, a drug abuser, had made a confession statement under the influence of a drug, produced irreparable cracks in the prosecution case. Following a new inquiry by the Avon and Somerset Police into the conduct of the 1974 investigation, the Director of Public Prosecutions suddenly announced, as the matter was to come before the courts again in October, that the convictions of the Guildford Four 'could no longer be sustained'.

After October events moved swiftly. Douglas Hurd, shortly before he was transferred to the Foreign Office, announced the estab lishment of an inquiry under a retired Judge of Appeal, Sir John May. After their release, the Guildford Four all described inter rogation by techniques that could in no way be justified; prison ers were said to have been stripped, threatened and abused. Figures in the political and legal establishment have attempted to play down the significance of the whole business while radical critics of the criminal justice system have expressed fears that the May Inquiry will eventually turn out to be no more than a whitewash, scapegoating minor figures in the *dramatis personae* and leaving those in higher positions unscathed. A powerful argument has been presented by Ludovic Kennedy, a veteran cam paigner against wrongful convictions since the time of the Evans case in 1950, that the English system of criminal justice ought now to adopt the inquisitorial system of mainland Europe in place of the centuries old adversarial arrangement and that there ought now to be a Court of Last Resort, above the existing appellate courts, comprised of both legal and lay members. At the Anglo-Irish level, although matters have been expressed in a muted fashion, the Prime Minister of the Republic has made no secret of the fact that Irish opinion expects the United Kingdom government to investigate the cases of the Birmingham Six in a similar fashion. On 12 December it was announced that the Home Office had recategorized the Birmingham Six from Category 'A' to Category 'B' prisoners, with the disclaimer that this was no more than a routine administrative arrangement, but as any experienced Home Office watcher would know, such 'reclassification' is frequently an early step in the process of executive intervention.

The State of Prisons

The year 1989 saw a Report of Her Majesty's Chief Inspector of Prisons probably more comprehensive than at any time since the modern inspectorate was set up. The burden of his report was that the way in which inmates are treated is characterized by great inconsistency, the quality of life for an inmate often being 'random, haphazard and dependent upon the accidents of geography and allocation'. Local prisons remained severely overcrowded, appallingly insanitary and providing little by way of useful occupations or diversions for inmates. What emerges from the report is that even in institutions which might be expected to offer something better, namely open prisons and establishments for young offenders, the

Inspector found regimes characterized by idleness, a lack of purpose and inactive staff in seedy and unkempt accommodation.

However, 1989 saw a fall in both the number of young offenders sentenced to custody and the number of prisoners held on remand. In November, the Home Office deferred the final stage of its £1 billion prison building programme on the grounds that so much accommodation will not be needed in the next three years. The fall in numbers, both actual and expected, can be attributed to two causes. In the first place, strong pressures have been put upon the courts, especially magistrate's courts, to reduce where possible the numbers sent to prison on sentence or remand. Secondly, over the next few years, the demographic changes that have already occurred will reduce the number in the 15–25 age group which is the peak age for criminal conviction. David Waddington, who became Home Secretary at the end of the year, addressed a prison governors' conference in Bournemouth in November in terms that were decidedly optimistic. No doubt recalling the discomfiture of his predecessor, Leon Brittan, who predicted in 1983 that we were on course for ending prison overcrowding by the end of the decade, Mr Waddington will have been reasonably sure of the basis of the forecast. Clearly, the demographic element is certain, as is the trend in the courts away from the use of custody. But there remain problems. One is the margin of the surplus of places over demand, especially since it is in the short term prison sector that both demand and overcrowding are at their worst; another is the extent to which bail hostels and other residential provisions outside the prison system will be able to deal with some of the more intractable problems of remand prisoners, especially those in the younger age group.

Prison Suicides

In this context the subject of suicides among young remand prisoners became the focus of attention in 1989. In November during a Commons debate, David Mellor, Minister of State at the Home Office, gave the figure of 46 suicides so far in 1989. This was a total for all age groups, mainly of men held in remand facilities. At Brixton prison the suicide figure was approximately one death every eight weeks during 1989. In February Brian Emes, the deputy director of the Prison Service was sent to Leeds prison by Douglas Hogg, the junior minister responsible for prisons, to inves tigate the suicide problem after the death of 18-year-old Phillip Beckett, the fifth youth to die since May 1988, the youngest being 17 and the oldest 19. In the same period there were, according to the Prison Officers' Association, 22 suicide attempts. The Howard League requested that the minister order a public inquiry but this was declined and in April, Mr Hogg informed the League that the Emes Report would not be published. In May the minister announced a new Circular Instruction on suicide prevention and the Howard League decided to set up its own inquiry under Mrs Helen Grindrod QC, a Recorder on the Northern circuit. The reaction of the minister was negative and he both declined to meet the Howard League team and refused it access to Leeds pris on. Although individual staff were informed that they could contribute to the inquiry, they received no encouragement to do so. The Grindrod Report was published in September and details the many shortcomings in the arrangements for vulnerable young offenders whilst remanded in custody besides evidence of some insensitivity on the part of the prison authorities after sui cides had occurred.

Remand Facilities

Remand facilities in general were the focus of problems and criticisms throughout the year. That at Risley in Cheshire dated only from 1965. It was, however, described by the Chief Inspector of Prisons as 'poorly designed' with 'barbarous and squalid' conditions in which inmates were kept in 'appalling and totally unacceptable' circumstances. Designed for 514 men and 92 women, by mid-1988 its numbers had grown to 823 and 124. Its reputation for inmate suicide was among the earliest to be established. In May 1989 there was a four day riot in which the staff lost control. There had been another riot in April and between them hundreds of thousands of pounds worth of damage was done. Young offenders had been removed following the Chief Inspector's earlier report, but during refurbishment severe overcrowding occurred. In July, the then Home Secretary, Douglas Hurd, announced that following a report by Ian Dunbar, the South-West Regional Director of the Prison Service who recommended that the remand facility be closed 'at the earliest possible moment', Risley would cease to be a male remand centre by mid-1990. Known popularly as 'grisly Risley' its forthcoming closure was generally welcomed. Other remand centres continued to give cause for anxiety. At Hull prison the especially bleak conditions of the young offenders' remand block were the subject of a television documentary in December. There, numbers of youths, some still within the juvenile court age range, are contained in a depressing block of cells in which the windows are permanently broken and which overlooks a yard into which urine, faeces and other waste matter is continually hurled while the inmates shout to each other and catcall abuse and obscenities.

Conclusion

In the space available it is not, of course, possible to do more than to highlight some important issues. In this respect 1989 must stand out in two respects. The first relates to the cataclysmic effect of the abandonment of the Crown case against the Guildford Four which severely dented confidence, not merely in the conduct of the police but the shortcomings of the appellate system. Coming as it did in the same year that the Chief Constable of the West Midlands, Geoffrey Dear, disbanded its

Serious Crimes Squad after allegations of corrupt practices, its consequential effects are likely to be felt for some considerable time to come. The second, less popularly newsworthy issue, was that of the continued deterioration of conditions within the prison system notwithstanding a slight fall in the numbers of some categories of inmate. The prison system continues to be inextricably linked to questions of government policy with regard to both finance and the deployment of resources, the sentencing practices of the courts and levels of staff morale which do not seen noticeably to have improved during the year.

Table 1. Notifiable offences (thousands) in England and Wales

Offence group	1984	1985	1986	1987	1988
Violence against the person	114.2	121.7	125.5	141.0	158.2
Sexual offences	20.2	21.5	22.7	25.2	26.5
Robbery	24.9	27.5	30.0	32.6	31.4
Burglary	892.9	866.7	931.6	900.1	817.8
Theft and handling stolen goods	1808.0	1884.1	2003.9	2052.0	1931.3
Fraud and forgery	126.1	134.8	133.4	133.0	133.9
Criminal damage	497.8	539.0	583.6	589.0	593.9
Other notifiable offences	15.0	16.7	16.7	19.3	22.7
Of which:					
trafficking in controlled drugs	6.6	8.0	7.3	7.1	7.8

Source: *Criminal Statistics: England and Wales* CM847, HMSO, Norwich, 1989

Chronology

9 Jan: Riot in Northeye Prison, East Sussex.

30 Jan: Prison officers walk-out in Wandsworth over shift arrangements. Police sent in to man the prison.

7 Feb: Prison officers at Wandsworth vote to return to work.

10 Feb: Home Office confirms there will be a six-month trial of electronic tagging as an alternative to custody in Nottingham and North Tyneside.

20 Feb: Plan to end slopping out within seven years published as *Prison Sanitation: Proposals for the End of Slopping Out* by Stephen Tumin, the Chief Inspector of Prisons.

Letter by 11 paediatricians to *The Guardian* in defence of Dr Marietta Higgs, the paediatrician at the centre of the Cleveland child abuse crisis reopens the issue.

1 Mar: Publication of a report on private sector involvement in the remand system by Deloitte, Haskins and Sell. Douglas Hurd gives the go-ahead for privately built and managed remand centres.

8 Mar: Agreement between Britain and Switzerland under which the Swiss agree to help to trace and freeze assets held in its banks by suspected drug traffickers and to confiscate the assets of drug traffickers convicted in Britain (in the wake of similar agreements with the USA, Australia and the Bahamas).

11 Mar: *Police Fear of Crime Survey* by Peter Last and Stephen Jackson alleges most people have an exaggerated fear of crime fed by media reporting.

23 Mar: Britain's largest ever drugs trial ends.

Parole and Related Issues in Scotland, the report of the committee chaired by Lord Kincraig, is published. It urges that there should be a longer wait for parole in the most fundamental review of the Scottish parole system since it was set up in 1968.

A study in Birmingham concludes that the reflex anal dilation test used in the Cleveland affair of 1987 to detect child abuse is a poor diagnostic tool.

19 Apr: Channel 4 programme draws attention to obscene telephone calls and alleges that the authorities and British Telecom do not take this seriously enough.

30 Apr: A man goes on the rampage with a shotgun in Monkseaton, Tyneside, killing one man and injuring thirteen.

1–2 May: Demonstrations at Risley remand centre during which two wings of the prison are destroyed.

3 May: Demonstrations at Risley end. A full inquiry into conditions at Risley is ordered.

11 May: Plans to introduce electronic tagging are deferred, although three pilot schemes will go ahead.

Measures to tackle the rising number of suicides in prison announced.

15 May: National Association for the Care and Rehabilitation of Offenders (NACRO) report concludes that the intermediate treatment schemes, introduced in 1983, are a successful alternative to custody for many young offenders.

19 May: Thirty inmates on Kirklevington Young Offenders Institution go on an overnight rampage.

25 May: A survey reveals the extent of the problem of child abuse.

29 May: Report complains that women in the only top security wing for women, in Durham, live in 'unacceptable conditions'.

10 June: NACRO report shows there is an increasing likelihood of female offenders being gaoled.

14 June: Police survey of crime in Cheshire shows that many crimes are not reported for fear of retaliation from neighbours.

26 June: Agreement between Britain and Spain signed to stop British drug traffickers using the Costa del Sol as a base for their operations.

3 July: Report by *Justice* argues that innocent people are being imprisoned because mistakes by the police and the courts are not being corrected by the appeals system.

25 July: Risley is to no longer be used as a remand centre.

Report by the Chief Inspector of Prisons says that many of Britain's prisoners are kept in inhuman, filthy, overcrowded and insanitary conditions.

Police and Customs set up a task force to investigate the spread of the drug 'Crack' in Britain.

27 July: Commons Home Affairs Select Committee calls urgently for public awareness campaign aimed at reducing demand for 'Crack'.

2 Aug: Scotland Yard claims to have smashed an Asian international crime ring based in Southall.

3 Aug: Douglas Hurd rejects calls for a national campaign to fight 'Crack'.

14 Aug: Pilot schemes of electronic tagging begin.

NACRO report *Crown Immunity and the Prison Service* calls for an end to crown immunity from prosecution for insanitary conditions.

The 1988 British Crime Survey Home Office Research Study 111 published. There are some differences with police figures.

26 Aug: Lynda Chalker, Minister for Overseas Development, promises to step up financial support for worldwide anti-narcotics efforts.

7–8 Sept: Leaders in *The Independent* and the *Economist* advocate the decriminalization of drugs.

8 Sept: Customs officers claim they have smashed a substantial drug smuggling ring with the seizure of £7 million worth of cannabis.

Douglas Hurd attacks the minority view that legaliza tion and regulation of drugs is the only way to deal with the problems they present.

12 Sept: Special unit for sex offenders at Wormwood Scrubs is in chaos according to the prison's probation staff.

13 Sept: A consultant psychologist at Wormwood Scrubs says he believes that the special unit offering psychotherapy to sex offenders will not stop them reoffending.

14 Sept: Anthony Hughes, with a record of violent crime, kills a police inspector at a motorway service station in Yorkshire and later commits suicide. This leads to renewed calls for the restoration of the death penalty from the Police Federation, certain newspapers and some Tory MPs.

David Thornton of the Young Offenders Psychology Unit at the Home Office tells the BAAS annual meeting that spending money on nursery schools and screening of potential offenders at schools is a better and cheaper way to reduce crime than employing more policemen.

21 Sept: New system of vehicle numbering and registration to cut theft of construction plant introduced.

25 Sept: Police survey shows that more than half the banks and institutions in the City have been subject to fraud worth hundreds of millions of pounds. The true extent of the swindling remains in doubt because about 17 per cent of firms fail to notify the police for fear of adverse publicity. Fraud, particularly computer fraud has increased dramatically in the last ten years.

29 Sept: Independent inquiry under Helen Grindrod QC into teenage suicides in the remand wing of Leeds prison makes its recommendations.

11 Oct: Douglas Hurd announces new police squads to deal with 'Crack'.

18 Oct: *Report of the Select Committee on Murder and Life Imprisonment* HL 78, HMSO recommends that there should be a statutory definition of murder and mandatory life sentences.

19 Oct: Report by Stephen Tumin, Chief Inspector of Prisons, argues that Wandsworth prison fails to meet basic standards of humanity and propriety and makes 153 recommendations for change.

25 Oct: Revelations that witness statements by victims in sex offences cases have been circulating in prisons for decades as a form of gaol pornography.

7 Nov: *Criminal Statistics* HMSO reveal decline in total offences reported but rises in violent crime and sexual offences.

21 Nov: Bill to deal with cross-border crime announced in the Queen's speech.

3 Dec: Penal Affairs Consortium report *Juveniles on Remand* recommends that they should be sent to community homes instead of to the bullying they too often face in remand prisons.

7 Dec: Home Affairs Select Committee, *Drug Trafficking and Related Serious Crime*, HMSO calls for urgent action to prevent the laundering of drugs profits in Britain.

11 Dec: *Report of the Working Group on the Fear of Crime*, HMSO chaired by Michael Grade argues that fear of crime in Britain is higher, as a result of media attention, than in Europe, with less justification.

12 Dec: Commons votes 348 to 123 endorsing the need for legislation to allow war criminals now living in Britain to be tried in British courts.

15 Dec: Announcement that a review of links between pornography and sex crimes is to set up in January during an adjournment debate on the subject in the Commons.

18 Dec: National Association of Probation Officers calls for systematic ethnic monitoring of the entire criminal justice system, anti-racist training and amendments to the Bail Act.

19 Dec: Oftel says the number of obscene calls to women could be more than 10 million per year.

Foreign Policy

CHRISTOPHER HILL

We may be living in an era of Britain's declining international influence, but foreign policy still has the capacity to throw up major challenges for the British government and to spill over significantly into major issues of domestic policy. Over recent years foreign policy has lost its protective screen of bipartisan consensus, and has moved nearer the eye of the storm of public political debate. The last year has continued this trend, while adding new issues to the list of major foreign policy dilemmas confronting the Thatcher government.

Ten years into Thatcherism, the Prime Minister's claim to have raised Britain's profile and reputation in the world – or at least, to have prevented it from falling further – seems not to be without substance, if we are to judge by the number of meetings which take place with foreign leaders. In 1989 the Prime Minister made a five-country African tour, visited Japan (with a Moscow stop-over on the way back), Malaysia (for the 49-nation Commonwealth Heads of Government meeting), and the United States, quite apart from the many intra-European hops which nowadays virtually count as domestic. Moreover, she has acted as host in London to the heads of state or government of the two superpowers, Israel, Nicaragua, Poland, Jamaica, Australia, Pakistan, Nigeria, Uganda, and South Korea, not to mention the aforesaid Europeans and the various foreign ministers who have also come to London for consultations.

Such diplomatic movements are important, but they can easily disguise the realities of foreign policy. For example, it is often just as important to note where visits are not made, or who does not come to the United Kingdom. After the massacre in Tiananmen Square in June, it proved impossible for the Prince and Princess of Wales to visit China as planned (although they did insist on going to Hong Kong), while the fall-out from the Falklands War continues (among other factors) to stand in the way of a Prime Ministerial visit to Latin America. As it happened, China and the Falklands represented two opposite trends for Britain in 1989, the one bringing sombre new problems, and the other at last proving susceptible to some diplomatic movement.

Colonial Legacies

The 1984 Joint Declaration by Britain and China over Hong Kong had always contained within it the haunting possibility for Britain that things might go wrong, that China might seek to renege on the agreement to maintain Hong Kong's way of life until at least 2047, and that its overwhelming predominance of power on the ground would be brought into play. But until 1989 anxieties had been restricted to the problem of how to reassure the inhabitants of the colony about their future without granting unrestricted rights of immigration to the UK, and without alienating Beijing by introducing too many new elements of western-style democracy before the Chinese take over in 1997. In 1989, however, a most serious new element was added to British calculations by the Chinese repression of the pro-democracy movement in the first week of June. For the first time it seemed possible that the regime in Beijing might prove capable of breaking its word at some time in the future by in sisting on Hong Kong's conformity to its renewed communist ascet icism. Equally important, the citizens of Hong Kong, for whom Britain is still responsible, believed this to be the case, and understandably began to panic, raising the temperature in the debate about immigration, and putting pressure on their own relations with China, as well as on Sino-British relations.

The Hong Kong problem has been seriously complicated by the fact that the colony contains actual as well as potential refugees, in the shape of 44,000 Vietnamese boat-people, living in squalid camps but still representing a standing invitation to others to follow them on their risky journey across the South China Sea. Thus the moral dilemmas of foreign policy are for once sharply evident for Britain in Hong Kong, and in multiple form: should – as the government has finally decided – the boat people be sent home? Should the citizens of Hong Kong be granted (as Paddy Ashdown, the Leader of the Liberal Democrats has suggested) right of abode in Britain in the hope that this will assuage their concerns without leading to a mass exodus? Should Britain itself risk being seen as reneging on the 1984 agreement in an attempt to protect its citizens against the kind of repression which might befall them after 1997? These issues have certainly had practical consequences, such as a British attempt to improve relations with Vietnam, and the undermining of the government's natural preference for keeping the political temperature low in Hong Kong.

The other major colonial legacy still to be causing problems (Spanish entry into the European Community having reduced the difficulties over Gibraltar), is the Falklands. In 1989 there were some distinct signs of progress over this issue, after several damaging failures in the years since Britain retook the islands in June 1982. The election of a new Argentine government under Carlos Menem, although at first a worrying development for Britain, given Señor Menem's strong language about continuing to strive to establish Argentinian sovereignty, turned out to have a thawing effect on bilateral relations. As so often, it proved easier for the ideologues than for the moderates to execute a *volte-face* in policy, and Menem's sympathetic approach to the disgraced military gave him the freedom of manoeuvre to put the sovereignty issue on one side and begin talks with Britain on the technical questions of fish ing, tourism and trade.

In this case, Britain's membership of the EC was undoubtedly a strong bargaining-card, with 1992 on the horizon and Argentina concerned about her trading access. The first round of talks took place in New York in August at the level of United Nation representatives, and seems likely to lead, in due course, to a relative normalization of relations, so long as domestic developments on either side do not lead to further attempts to put the sovereignty question on the agenda. For past wars carry a great deal of emotional baggage into the future - as shown by the row in January over whether the Duke of Edinburgh and the Foreign Secretary should attend Emperor Hirohito's funeral in Japan – and can all too easily flare up to sour what seem to be good relations established on a rational basis.

The Commonwealth is also naturally associated with the colonial past, even if these days it is more of a broad forum for North-South diplomacy. In 1989 it once more came into sharp focus through its biennial Heads of Government meeting, held in October in Kuala Lumpur. Although the environment and other functional issues took up a good deal of Commonwealth leaders' time, South Africa once again dominated the headlines, with Mrs Thatcher determined not to be trapped into sanctions or even strong condemnation of South Africa, at a time when she perceived the de Klerk government to be making rapid progress towards democratization, and indeed when British exports to that country had risen again, to nearly three times those to Nigeria. In this she was assisted by the announce ment from Pretoria at the start of the conference that South Africa had successfully concluded an agreement with its bankers to reschedule its debts. The final agreed communiqué on the subject therefore included several 'footnotes' by which Britain disassociated itself from various measures hostile to South Africa. This was followed by the Prime Minister unexpectedly issuing a separate statement explaining Britain's position, and holding a press conference in which she made it clear that being in a minority of 48 to 1 caused her not the slightest discomfort. This was to lead to a furious public row with, in particular, Brian Mulroney of Canada.

Literature and Foreign Policy

British foreign policy suffered another *cause célèbre* in 1989 in the Salman Rushdie affair, whereby the publication of Rushdie's novel giving offence to Moslems brought forth a sentence of death from the Ayatollah Khomeini, and an eventual breach of diplomatic relations between London and Tehran. This was a considerable blow to the Foreign Office, which had painstakingly begun to rebuild relations with Iran, with some promise of success. The hopes for the freeing of the British hostages in the Lebanon, together with expectations of renewed commercial activity, therefore once more crashed to the ground. The incident also demonstrated how foreign policy can reverberate domestically, not only with Rushdie having to go into hiding at high cost to the Exchequer, but with tensions rising between sections of the Islamic and other communities in Britain. Nor did it help British policy in the Middle East, which, based as it is on an agreed European Community position increasingly critical of Israel, has been gradually taking a higher profile, with William Waldegrave becoming the first minister to meet Yasser Arafat, and then reminding members of the Israeli government of their own past terrorist activities. The Rushdie affair served only to reinforce the position of the radical elements already deeply suspicious of these shifts in policy. Britain is thus now in a condition of ruptured diplomatic relations with all three of the radical states of Libya, Syria, and Iran.

Special Relationships, East and West

One of the pillars of British foreign policy since the war, and of the Thatcher years in particular, has been the 'special relationship' with the United States. In 1989, however, even this came in for a new degree of questioning. In the first instance this was because of the retirement of Ronald Reagan, and the coming to power of President George Bush, with whom Margaret Thatcher does not have anything like so comfortable a relationship. With no pause for breath, the State Department announced that Bush would be attending Hirohito's funeral, and that the US tie with Japan was its 'most important bilateral relationship in the world'. Subsequent events tended to play up the sense of a change; the unexpected quickening of the pace towards economic and monetary union inside the European Community, and the domestic difficulties that the Prime Minister had fallen into due to her robust opposition to the trend, both helped to cast her in Washington's eyes as, for once, a real conservative who may have lost her instinct for necessary change. The dramatic unravelling of the existing order in Eastern Europe, towards the end of the year, served to confirm this image in the popular eye at least, as Mrs Thatcher preached caution and refused to advocate European unity as the solution to putative moves towards German reunification.

In the grey area where foreign policy meets defence policy, Britain had also been highly circumspect over the last twelve months. The concern shown over the Reykjavik summit of 1986, that the superpowers might negotiate away strategic nuclear weapons like Trident without any British veto, inevitably began to resurface, albeit in a minor key. The prospect of real build-down negotiations between Moscow and Washington, perhaps given life by the summit-at-sea off Malta, has serious implications for both Britain and France, just as the withdrawal of American troops from West Germany – or even the failure to modernize short-range nuclear weapons – would have implications for European spending on conventional defences. It is, perhaps, not surprising that Britain tended to emphasize the status quo for fear of something more expensive and possibly more insecure.

At the same time, a more constructive note has continued to be struck on the fundamental issue of the source of the threat to British security which requires such expensive insurance policies. Britain has been revitalizing its stagnant biliteral relations with the Soviet Union and the states of eastern Europe since just before Mikhail Gorbachev came to power. The events of 1989, therefore, although their pace and scale have caused some alarms, have represented something of a triumph for a forward-looking foreign policy, and there has been no sign of wavering in the support, personal and official, which the Prime Minister has offered to President Gorbachev as he continues his courageous, risky, programme of structural change. Brief visits have been exchanged this year between the British and Soviet leaders, together with warm compliments. There were, however, difficulties during May, a month after Gorbachev's visit to Britain, when Whitehall initiated a round of tit-for-tat expulsions over alleged spying activities. In this Gorbachev demonstrated that a superpower was not be treated lightly, and refused to be bounced by Britain into what would have been a public disavowal of the KGB. In the end, both sides seemed to have decided to limit the damage to their reputations and mutual relations, which seem not to have been seriously disturbed.

Three Wise Men

One of the most dramatically changing dimensions of British foreign policy in 1989 has been the policy-making process itself. It has been an exceptional year simply in terms of the fact that it has seen three different individuals serving as Foreign Secretary. This was due in large proportion to the dynamics of foreign policy itself, in that the Prime Minister clearly felt the need to transfer Sir Geoffrey Howe in July because of her unhappiness at his sympathy for the trends towards European integration, evident at the Madrid summit just finished, at which she had been forced to compromise. At the same time the Thatcherite Francis Maude was transferred to the Foreign Office to handle, *inter alia*, aspects of European policy. The second round of change was part of the same process, if more indirectly connected to it. Nigel Lawson's resignation as Chancellor of the Exchequer in October was the result of a clash over the proper channels of advice, but more fundamentally it related to a disagreement with the Prime Minister over whether Britain should join the Exchange Rate Mechanism of the European Monetary System, a matter over which Sir Geoffrey Howe and Nigel Lawson may have had something of an informal alliance. Lawson's departure meant that the newly ar rived Foreign Secretary, John Major, was moved back into the Treasury, while Douglas Hurd took over his job as Foreign Secretary.

There is a certain irony in the outcome of this game of musical chairs, as the Foreign Office is now run by an ex-professional diplomat, and someone from the liberal wing of the Tory party to boot, who is known for a more positive attitude towards European co-opera tion than the Prime Minister herself. Given the need to avoid further damaging upheavals in the run-up to an election, Hurd is virtually immovable, and there have already been signs that he and Howe, now Deputy Prime Minister, intend to rein in Mrs Thatcher's increasing tendency to act as her own Foreign Secre tary. The professionals in the Foreign Office are probably also delighted not to have to train Mr Major – no doubt a quick learner but still likely to need a year or two to gain weight in the job, if Sir Geoffrey Howe's experience is anything to go by – since that would weaken their bargaining position with No. 10 and other government departments.

The events of this year have shown, if it needed to be shown, that foreign policy now has to be conducted with constant reference to often unpredictable domestic inputs. Who, for example, would have predicted that the issue of Cambodia, a remote country with no tangible British interests at stake, would have provoked (after John Pilger's challenging television programme) a wave of popular protest at Britain's continued association with the Khmer Rouge's claim to participate in the government of the country. The protests rapidly brought changes in at least Britain's public posture on the issue. More frequent difficulties, however, are likely to be visited on the British government in those areas where the actual distinction between foreign and domestic policy is becoming increasingly less clear, and where Britain is locked into certain collaborative arrangements. The European Community represents both kinds of trend, and as now the major single framework for the formulation of British foreign as well as economic policy, it will continue to have a substantial effect upon it.

Ambassadors
Austria – R. J. O'Neill CMG, B. L. Crowe CMG
Belgium – Sir Peter Petrie Bt CMG, R. L. O' Neill CMG
Brazil – M. J. Newington CMG
China – Sir Alan Donald KCMG
Cuba – A. D. Brighty CMG CVO
Czechoslovakia – P. L. O'Keefe, CMG CVO
Denmark – N. C. R. Williams CMG
Egypt – W. J. Adams CMG
Finland – H. A. J. Staples CMG, G. N. Smith CMG
France – Sir Ewen Fergusson KCMG
FDR – Sir Christopher Mallaby KCMG
GDR – N. H. R. A. Broomfield CMG
Greece – Sir Jeremy Thomas KCMG, Sir David Miers KBE CMG
Holy See – J. K. E. Broadley CMG
Hungary – L. V. Appleyard CMG
Ireland – Sir Nicholas Fenn KCMG
Israel – M. Elliott CMG
Italy – Sir Derek Thomas KCMG, Sir Stephen Egerton KCMG
Japan – Sir John Whitehead KCMG, CVO

Kuwait – P. R. M. Hinchcliffe, CMG CVO
Luxembourg – Mrs J. J. d'A Campbell CMG
Netherlands – M. R. H. Jenkins CMG
Norway – J. A. Robson CMG
Poland – S. J. Barrett CMG
Portugal – M. K. O'Simpson-Orleber CMG, H. J. Arbuthnott CMG
Saudi Arabia – Sir Stephen Egerton KCMG, A. G. Munro CMG
South Africa – Sir Robin Renwick KCMG
Soviet Union – Sir Rodric Braithwaite KCMG
Spain – Lord Nicholas Gordon Lennox KCMG KCVO, P. R. Fearn CMG
Sweden – Sir John Ure KCMG LVO
Switzerland – C. W. Long CMG
Turkey – Sir T. L. A. Daunt KCMG
United States – Sir Anthony Acland GCMG KCVO
Yugoslavia – A. M. Wood CMG, P. E. Hall CMG

Governors of selected Dependent Territories
Bermuda – Sir Desmond Langley KCVO MBE
Falkland Islands – W. H. Fullerton
Gibraltar – Air Chief Marshal Sir Peter Terry GCB AFC, Adm Sir Derek Reffell KCB
Hong Kong – Sir David C. Wilson KCMG
St Helena – R. F. Stimson

High Commissioners to selected Commonwealth Countries
Australia – Sir John Coles KCMG
Canada – Sir Alan Urwick KCVO CMG, B. J. P. Fall CMG
India – Sir David Goodall KCMG
Malaysia – J. N. T. Spreckley CMG
New Zealand – R. A. C. Byatt CMG
Nigeria – B. L. Barder
Pakistan – N. J. Barrington CMG CVO (Ambassador 1 October 1989)

Chronology

2–11 Jan: Tour of the Middle East by Sir Geoffrey Howe. In the course of this he visited Kuwait, Saudi Arabia, Abu Dhabi, Dubai, Muscat, and Dhijbouti.

3 Jan: Czechoslovakia accuses British intelligence of kidnapping a Czech diplomat who disappeared in New Delhi in December. The Foreign Office would only say that the diplomat, Vlastimil Ludvik, had been granted asylum in Britain.

9 Jan: Government decides to send the Duke of Edinburgh and Sir Geoffrey Howe to the funeral of Emperor Hirohito of Japan despite strong opposition from ex-servicemen associations.

13 Jan: Foreign Office minister William Waldegrave meets Yasser Arafat in the first ever high-level talks between Britain and the Palestine Liberation Organisation (PLO). Mr Waldegrave's subsequent efforts to encourage the Israelis to talk to the PLO receive a frosty response.

27 Jan: Britain closes its Kabul embassy in the light of the deteriorating situation in Afghanistan.

4 Feb: British diplomats fly out from Kabul.

7 Feb: Spain suggests a change in the status of Gibraltar as a way of solving the long-running Anglo-Spanish dispute.

20 Feb: Two-day Anglo-German summit begins in Frankfurt. Differences over the modernization of NATO's short- range nuclear weapons are the main feature.

Britain withdraws its diplomats from Iran over the Rushdie affair but maintains diplomatic relations through Sweden as the protecting power. EC foreign ministers issue joint statement on the Rushdie affair recalling their ambassadors and freezing high level contacts with Iran.

21 Feb: Britain expels the Iranian Charge d'Affaires and demands a full retraction of Ayatollah Khomeini's death sentence on Rushdie. This is followed in the succeeding days by further expulsions.

27 Feb: Anglo-French Summit in Paris.

28 Feb: Iranian parliament votes to break off diplomatic relations with Britain within seven days unless Rushdie is denounced by the British government.

William Waldegrave embarks on a tour of Israel and Jordan and the occupied territories.

2 Mar: Britain rejects a talks offer on the Rushdie affair from Iran.

6 Mar: Mrs Thatcher cancels proposed visit to Sudan.

7 Mar: Iran unilaterally breaks off diplomatic relations with Britain.

10 Mar: Chinese repression in Tibet provokes wave of concern in Hong Kong.

15 Mar: Hostile response from Singapore government to criticism from the British government of recent changes to the legal system and of the decision to bar Anthony Lester QC from defending political detainees in Singaporean courts.

16 Mar: Islamic Conference Organization conference ends with a call for the withdrawal of Salman Rushdie's *The Satanic Verses* and a boycott of its publisher. However the Iranian death threat to Rushdie was not supported.

18 Mar: End of the Prince of Wales' visit to the Gulf.

20 Mar: EC countries (except Britain) to allow their ambassadors back to Iran.

22 Mar: Total of Iranians expelled since Rushdie affair began rises to 18 with the expulsion of a further nine.

23 Mar: Sir Geoffrey Howe tells the Commons foreign affairs committee that there will be no amendment of the immigration laws to allow Hong Kong Chinese to settle in Britain.

27 Mar: Start of a 24-hour visit by Sir Geoffrey Howe to Pakistan.

Start of six-day tour of Africa by Mrs Thatcher, beginning in Morocco.

28 Mar: Mrs Thatcher makes stop-over visit to Nigeria.

29 Mar: Mrs Thatcher in Zimbabwe, where she also has talks with President Chissano of Mozambique.

30 Mar: Mrs Thatcher in Malawi.

1 Apr: Mrs Thatcher in Namibia.

British troops are part of the UN force which officially takes over the South African military bases in the run-up to independence in Namibia.

2 Apr: Bomb attacks on British embassy car and British Council building in Turkey over the Rushdie affair.

5 Apr: Mikhail Gorbachev begins a two-day visit to Britain.

7 Apr: Gorbachev's visit culminates with an invite to the Queen to visit the Soviet Union.

9 Apr: Controversy over the alleged sale by the German company MBB of ballistic missile technology to Argentina, which could be used against the Falklands.

Lord Glenarthur, Minister of State at the Foreign Office, begins a five-day visit to Vietnam where he discussed Cambodia, economic reform and the boat refugees in Hong Kong.

17 Apr: Hong Kong presses for as many Hong Kong people as possible with British passports to be given the right to live in Britain before Hong Kong returns to China in 1997.

25 Apr: Iran expels 18 Britons.

5 May: Britain expels three South African diplomats over the arms deal with the Protestant paramilitary in Northern Ireland.

8 May: President Daniel Ortega of Nicaragua visits London.

9 May: President Ibrahim Babangida of Nigeria begins a three-day state visit to Britain.

11 May: Alhaji Umaru Dikko, the former Nigerian minister wanted in Nigeria for corruption has his right of residence in Britain withdrawn.

15 May: Sir Geoffrey Howe voices concern over the incendiary rhetoric of the new Argentine President, Carlos Menem, over the Falklands.

19 May: Eight Soviet diplomats and three journalists are expelled for spying.

21 May: Soviet tit-for-tat expulsion of the same proportions of British diplomats and journalists.

Yitzhak Shamir, the Israeli Prime Minister, arrives in London for three days of talks.

22 May: Russians threaten to slash the number of Britons allowed in the Soviet Union from 375 to 205 to bring them into line with the size of the Russian establishment in Britain.

25 May: Four Czech diplomats expelled for spying.

Hong Kong Legislative Council votes that 50 per cent of its members should be popularly elected by 1997 and all by 2003. This decision followed on demonstrations in Hong Kong in support of the pro-Democracy students' movement in Peking.

26 May: Tit-for-tat expulsions of British diplomats from Czechoslovakia.

30 May: Compromise in the dispute with the Soviet Union in sight.

1 June: President George Bush in London at the end of his week-long trip to Europe.

3 June: Despite the death of Ayatollah Khomeini the Fatwa against Salman Rushdie remains.

3–4 June: Massacre of pro-Democracy students in Tiananmen Square in Peking. There are sympathetic demonstrations in Hong Kong where concern about 1997 escalates.

5 June: Hang Seng index on the Hong Kong stock exchange falls by 22 per cent in the wake of Tiananmen Square. Hong Kong Chinese are critical of the tepid condemnation by the Governor, Sir David Wilson, and by the British government.

Britain calls off planned official visits to China but rules out sanctions.

6 June: No change to British immigration rules to allow Hong Kong Chinese into Britain reiterated.

10 June: General Jaruzelski, the Polish President, arrives in London for two days of talks.

13 June: UN conference on the refugees from Indo-China opens in Geneva. Britain and Hong Kong seek the forced repatriation of the Vietnamese boat people.

14 June: Three-day visit by Michael Manley, Prime Minister of Jamaica, begins.

16 June: Three more Iranians expelled.

20 June: Bob Hawke, Prime Minister of Australia, begins a four-day visit to Britain.

28 June: Vietnamese foreign minister in London for talks.

29 June: Commons Foreign Affairs Select Committee report on Hong Kong advocates international guarantees for Hong Kong but rejects the right of abode in Britain as an insurance policy.

2 July: Sir Geoffrey Howe receives a hostile reception at the beginning of a visit to Hong Kong.

5 July: Benazir Bhutto, Prime Minister of Pakistan, arrives for a week-long visit.

Report of the Commons Foreign Affairs Select Committee on Hong Kong derided by Hong Kong legis lators.

10 July: President Yoweri Museveni of Uganda in London for talks.

Announcement that Pakistan is to rejoin the Commonwealth in October.

14 July: Three day summit of the Group of Seven begins in Paris.

21 July: Commons Foreign Affairs Committee report on the Foreign Office and the Overseas Development Administra tion.

28 July: Israeli kidnapping of a leading figure in Hizbollah renews concern about the plight of the hostages in the Lebanon.

Government blocks the sale of 50 Hawk training jets to Iraq.

30 July: US Secretary of State, James Baker, warns Britain against the forcible repatriation of the Vietnamese boat people from Hong Kong.

Riots in the camps of the Vietnamese refugees in Hong Kong against British policy begin. These lead to increasing hostility towards the Vietnamese from the people of the colony.

2 Aug: Argentina lifts the restrictions on trade with Britain which have been in force since the Falklands War.

16 Aug: Anglo-Argentine talks in New York.

20 Aug: China reacts angrily to British suggestions that it should review its plans to station troops in Hong Kong after 1997.

27 Aug: Riot in Vietnamese detention centre in Hong Kong.

30 Aug: Sir David Wilson warns the new Foreign Secretary, John Major, of the danger of a mass exodus from Hong Kong and increasing antagonism towards the Vietnamese in the colony.

3 Sept: Mrs Thatcher meets President Gorbachev in Moscow.

5 Sept: Mrs Thatcher writes to leaders of the USA, France and West Germany asking for more aid for Poland and Hungary to ease their progress away from Eastern bloc communism.

10 Sept: Paddy Ashdown reaffirms his advocacy of a right of abode for the Hong Kong Chinese in Britain at an SLD conference rally.

11 Sept: John Major begins a visit to the USA.

14 Sept: The government is accused of hypocrisy over the sale of fighter systems to China after arms sales were banned in the wake of Tiananmen Square.

17 Sept: Francis Maude, Minister of State at the Foreign Office, begins a visit to Hong Kong.

19 Sept: Mrs Thatcher begins a visit to Japan.

20 Sept: John Major visits Bonn.

23 Sept: Mrs Thatcher has talks with President Gorbachev in Moscow on her way back from Tokyo.

27 Sept: John Major announces in his maiden speech to the UN General Assembly that a RN frigate and a small number of British soldiers are to be sent to Columbia as part of a 'substantial package of assistance' for that country in its war with the drug barons.

Talks between John Major and the Argentine Foreign Secretary, Domingo Cavello, the first between a British Foreign Secretary and his Argentine opposite number since the Falklands War.

27–29 Sept: First Sino-British talks on Hong Kong since Tiananmen Square.

1 Oct: Pakistan rejoins the Commonwealth.

11 Oct: The Queen begins a three-day visit to Singapore. This is followed by a visit to Malaysia where she opens the Commonwealth Heads of Government meeting in Kuala Lumpur on 18 Oct.

17–19 Oct: Anglo-Argentine talks in Madrid which end with an agreement to formally end the hostilities over the Falklands.

18 Oct: Nigerian Chief Emeka Anyaoku is elected to succeed Sir Shridath Ramphal as Commonwealth Secretary-General.

22 Oct: Britain issues a separate communiqué on South Africa at the Commonwealth meeting clarifying its reserva tions about the official communiqué on South Africa in which it was in a minority of 48 to 1 on the issue of sanctions.

25 Oct: Britain is to send Vietnamese boat people back from Hong Kong and give each resettlement aid worth £380.

4 Nov: The Prince of Wales begins visits to Indonesia and Hong Kong.

8 Nov: Government distances itself from the Khmer Rouge which it has been accused of recognizing and supporting.

23 Nov: Mrs Thatcher in pre-East–West summit talks with President Bush at Camp David.

25 Nov: Rioting in Vietnamese detention centres in Hong Kong.

28 Nov: South Korean leader, Roh Tae Woo, arrives in London for a three day visit.

29 Nov: West German Foreign Minister, Hans-Dietrich Genscher in London for talks.

Lech Walesa, leader of Poland's Solidarity, in London for talks.

5–6 Dec: Anglo-Argentine talks in Montevideo.

7 Dec: First British envoys to Cambodia for 14 years.

11 Dec: Forcible repatriation of 51 Vietnamese refugees from Hong Kong. Demonstrations against this in the detention centres begin.

12 Dec: Hungarian Prime Minister, Miklos Nemeth in London to discuss economic aid.

14 Dec: 1922 committee of Conservative backbenchers rejects the government's plans to allow about 150,000 Hong Kong Chinese to emigrate to Britain.

19 Dec: Two Iranians to be deported under the Prevention of Terrorism Act.

20 Dec: Douglas Hurd announces that the government proposes to grant full British citizenship to 50,000 key people and their dependants in Hong Kong to increase their confidence in the colony's future and reduce emigration.

29 Dec: Thousands of Vietnamese boat people riot in Hong Kong.

Defence Policy

JOHN BAYLIS

Future historians will probably point to 1989 as being a key date in the post-Second World War era. During the past two or three years the system of European security based on the two hostile, armed camps facing each other across a divided Germany has increasingly been challenged by the momentous events taking place in the Soviet Union and Eastern Europe. In 1989 the pace of change quickened considerably. For British defence planners these events have created a security situation which in some important respects is more favourable than at any time since 1945. The dramatic political changes in Eastern Europe and the unilateral reductions in Soviet and East European defence expenditures has meant that the traditional NATO fear of a surprise Warsaw Pact invasion has all but disappeared. The vastly improved political climate between East and West over the continuing progress in arms control negotiations has opened up the prospect of a fundamental reordering of the European security system which has prevailed since the early Cold War days of the late 1940s.

At the same time, despite the unilateral cuts and far-reaching changes which have taken place, the Soviet Union has retained an impressive array of military capabilities. The growing turmoil in the Soviet Union associated with economic crisis, ethnic clashes and nationalist aspirations raises doubts about President Gorbachev's long term future. Rapidly changing events in Eastern Europe and reawakening dormant nationalist disputes have also created uncertainty about whether the process of change can be managed peacefully.

In this context the British government has pursued somewhat ambivalent policies during 1989. On the one hand Mrs Thatcher has welcomed the changes taking place in the Soviet Union and praised the courage of the Soviet leader. Her visit to Moscow in September highlighted the Prime Minister's determination to retain the close relationship with Mr Gorbachev established in recent years. At the same time, however, she has continued to argue forcefully within the Western alliance that the West must not lower its guard at this time of uncertainty and transition. The essence of the Prime Minister's approach was summed up in her statement in the House of Commons in December 1988 when she argued that Britain's 'task is to make certain we always have sure defences while at the same time trying to extend the hand of friendship across the European divide.'[1]

What has been intended as a subtle and pragmatic dual approach, however, has often appeared to some observers to be rather contradictory and overly cautious as the government has tried to come to terms with the unprecedented developments taking place on the world stage. Defence planners appear to have found it far from easy during 1989 to cope with the contemporary uncertainty. Their hesitant attempts to adjust to the new and constantly changing security agenda is revealed in four main areas: arms control and alliance relations; weapons procurement; defence expenditure; and the ongoing debates over the need for a defence review.

Arms Control and Alliance Relations

In 1987 Britain played a key role in persuading a reluctant West German government not to stand in the way of an Intermediate Nuclear Force (INF) agreement between the United States and the Soviet Union. In December 1987 the so-called 'Double Zero' agreement was signed which eliminated all US and Soviet land-based missiles in Europe with a range in access of 500 kilometres. During 1988, as the focus of arms control attention shifted to shorter-range missiles, the positions adopted by the British and West German governments underwent a significant change. For the Thatcher government further European nuclear disarmament would undermine alliance security. It was argued that existing short-range weapons, like Lance missiles, should be modernized and the negotiations with the Soviet Union should concentrate on conventional and chemical weapons. The Kohl government, however, prompted by its Foreign Secretary, Herr Genscher, felt singularly threatened by the remaining short-range nuclear forces (SNF) and argued that the time was ripe for early negotiations with the Soviet Union on these weapons. From the West German point of view it was inappropriate to make decisions on modernizing nuclear weapons, like Lance, when East-West relations were improving so quickly. As a result of these differing perspectives, by the early months of 1989 a bitter dispute had broken out between the two governments which threatened to undermine the NATO summit to be held in May to celebrate the fortieth anniversary of the alliance.

Initially Britain's hard-line position was supported by the new Bush administration in the United States. By the time of the summit meeting, however, it was clear that domestic public opinion in West Germany would not allow any retreat by the Kohl government. At the last moment President Bush engineered a compromise which postponed a decision on Lance modernization until 1992 and called for negotiations to begin with the Soviet Union on short-range missiles once a conventional arms control agreement had been signed and implementation was underway. Mrs Thatcher declared herself 'very satisfied' with the compromise concluded at the May summit and pointed to the section in the communiqué which insisted that the SNF negotiations, when they eventually took place, would only involve 'partial' reductions and not their total elimination.[2]

For many observers, however, Britain had suffered a significant defeat. After its early support for Britain the Bush administration had softened its position to take account of West German sensitivities – thus signalling a shift away from the intimate Reagan-Thatcher 'special relationship' of recent years. Mrs Thatcher had also been forced to accept the principle of SNF negotiations when previously these had been adamantly opposed on the grounds that they would be likely to lead to a third zero. Despite the communiqué's insistence that a spectrum of nuclear weapons would remain necessary 'for the forseeable future' and 'while present circumstances prevailed', West German officials quickly let it be known that a third zero was still possible because of the rapidly changing nature of 'present circumstances'. Even worse for the British government, Mrs Thatcher had also failed to achieve an early decision on the modernization of Lance which British officials had constantly argued was so important to maintain the credibility of alliance strategy.

The compromise agreement had averted a major crisis within the alliance between Britain and West Germany but the episode had left Britain isolated with the United States, France and the other smaller Western European states responding with greater sensitivity to the exigencies of West German public opinion. The compromise also stored up difficulties for the future. Britain continued to argue that the modernization of Lance missiles would be essential in 1992 while the West German government emphasized that the nature of East-West relations would probably render such a decision inappropriate. The battle therefore remains to be refought in the early 1990s.

Weapons Procurement

The Gorbachev challenge has been felt in another important area of British defence policy: the procurement of Trident missiles to replace Polaris as Britain's strategic nuclear deterrent in the 1990s. Following warnings in May by the House of Commons All-Party Defence Committee that staff shortages at Aldermaston threatened the delivery of new warheads, a new crisis emerged in October following events in the United States.[3] In the new improved atmosphere in East-West relations (and faced with a major budget deficit) the Senate Appropriations Committee passed a Bill in September designed to cut funding for the production of the Trident missile by $1.8 billion (£1.1 billion). This was followed in November 1989 by the announcement by the US Secretary of State for Defence, Richard Cheney, that substantial cuts would be introduced in American defence spending over the next five years. These proposed cuts could mean significant delays in the 1990 production of the D-5 missile just as the first missiles are supposed to be delivered to Britain. Apart from delay, the Senate Committee decision, if implemented, is likely to impose time and cost penalties on the British programme.[4]

Procurement difficulties with the United States have arisen in another area as well during the year. Following the disastrous experience of the go-it-alone attempt to build Nimrod, Britain signed a deal with the United States company Boeing in 1986 to purchase AWACS early warning aircraft. As part of this deal Boeing pledged to spend an extra $1.5 billion over eight years in the United Kingdom. It was estimated at the time that this 'off-set' arrangement would create around 40,000 new jobs in Britain.[5] By November 1988 Boeing claimed to have placed contracts worth more than $625 million with British companies. Disagreements arose, however, in early 1989 when the Defence Export Services Organization (DESO) disputed a significant proportion of these claims on behalf of the Ministry of Defence (MOD).[6] When it looked into these claims in June the House of Commons Defence Committee highlighted the intrinsic difficulties in establishing the real benefits of 'offset' agreements and criticized the MOD for failing to set up effective monitoring arrangments to determine the number of new jobs created. According to the Committee, the employment argument had been an important element in the government's case to purchase AWACS but no arrangements were made to substantiate its claims.[7]

The momentous events in Eastern Europe and the cooling of the Anglo-American 'special relationship' has produced uncertainty in another area of procurement policy. In 1988 talks began between Britain and France on the joint development of a new air-launched nuclear missile. It appeared that despite Mrs Thatcher's reservations about Europe, changing events might cause Britain to make a different choice from the past and opt for greater European nuclear co-operation at the expense of the special nuclear relationship with the United States which has prevailed since the 1950s.

In March 1989, however, when the Defence Secretary, George Younger, met his French counterpart, Jean-Pierre Chevenement, in Paris it appeared that Mrs Thatcher's determination to include the United States in the research and development of the new weapon had effectively destroyed the prospect of an Anglo–French deal. For the French, nuclear co-operation with Britain would allow Europe 'to build up its own nuclear weapons technology and alter the balance of its lopsided defence relationship with the US'.[8] The British government, however, was concerned with more pragmatic military considerations. Britain needed an air-launched missile with a longer range, greater accuracy and more technically advanced specifications than the French envisaged. Despite the flirtation with France the answer seemed to lie once again with the purchase of an American missile. The Americans were working on a new generation of their Short Range Attack Missile (SRAM) which in terms of specifications and costs was more in line with British requirements. As in the past, political considerations were pulling Britain towards greater European co-operation but military logic and finance still suggested that a decision would be made in favour of an American deal.

By November 1989, however, opinion had shifted once more. Instead of the expected announcement of an Anglo–American deal, the government decided to postpone the decision and spend more time reconsidering the possibility of collaboration with France.

Defence Expenditure

The concern and dilemmas associated with the costs of procurement were highlighted in the government's *Statement on the Defence Estimates* published in May.[9] The White Paper revealed a steep rise in the price of new equipment facing the MOD with 32 major defence projects costing £2.9 billion more than the previous year. Despite the efforts of the MOD in recent years to get better value-for-money from its suppliers, it was clear that defence equipment costs were still increasing more quickly than the rate of inflation in the economy as a whole.

The problem was made worse, however, by a continuing fall in spending on equipment as a proportion of the defence budget. In 1985-6 procurement accounted for nearly 46 per cent of the total. By 1988 this had fallen to around 43 per cent and in the 1989 estimates the figure was 41 per cent. While weapons costs soared the proportion of the defence budget devoted to equipment was reduced for the fourth successive year.

The government's response to criticism of this decreasing allocation of resources to procurement was to point to an overall increase in the defence budget which had taken place during the past year. It was argued that the 1989–90 defence budget of £20,143 million was £928 million more than the original estimates for 1988–9 and £175 million more than was planned for 1989–90 in the 1988 Public Expenditure Paper. The planned figure for 1990–1 at £21,190 million was also £610 million more than the figure announced in the 1988 Public Expenditure Paper. The government argued that these cash increases over previous plans were 'the biggest for any three year period since the first cash planning survey in 1981 (Falklands additions aside)'.[10] In the context therefore of what it argued would be real growth in the defence budget between 1988–9 and 1991–2, together with its value-for-money measures, the government saw no significant difficulties in fulfilling its procurement plans.

This explanation, however, did not satisfy the critics of the government's handling of defence policy, who in recent years have pointed to a 'funding gap' between what was needed to sustain defence commitments and the money which would actually be available. In 1988 David Greenwood, one of Britain's leading independent defence economists, estimated that the defence budget in 1990–1 needed to be £25 billion rather than the planned £21.18 billion.[11] Even though that planned figure has now been increased to £22.1 billion the gap would appear only to have been narrowed rather than closed, if Greenwood's estimates are correct.

Some support is given to the Greenwood critique by the fact that when George Younger announced the main increases in defence spending in November 1988 the figures were based on an inflation rate of around 3.5 per cent for 1990–1 and three per cent for 1991–2.[12] Since then, however, the inflation rate has risen to nearly 8 per cent by the end of 1989 suggesting that unless there are further significant increases defence spending will be likely to decline in real terms rather than increase over the next few years. In a period when East-West relations are improving dramatically, and the government will be facing a general election in 1992, it seems highly unlikely that major increases in defence spending will be possible. Pressure to spend more on education, health and ameliorating the effects of the poll tax are likely to keep defence spending, at best, at level funding levels. In practice, unless inflation falls quickly the chances are that the allocation of resources to defence will decline in real terms.

The Question of a Defence Review

In the light of the changes in the international climate and the growing pressures on the defence budget, the question whether or not there ought to be a defence review has continued to dominate the security agenda in Britain during the past year.

In 1985 the House of Commons Defence Committee undertook a review of Britain's current and future defence commitments and resources following the government's decision to end the 3 per cent per annum real increase in defence spending which had begun in 1978. In their report the Defence Committee concluded that future defence budgets were likely to fall 'substantially short of the resources required to maintain capability to meet commitments'. It was feared that the result would be a 'defence review by stealth' as incremental cuts were made in a range of defence capabilities.[13]

In their evidence to the Defence Committee, defence officials stressed that improved efficiency, competition, increased collaboration and flexible planning would see the Ministry through. A greater emphasis on value-for-money techniques and normal adjustments to the programme eliminated the requirement for a defence review, it was argued.

The government's objection to a defence review continued through to 1989. The 1989 Defence Estimates argued that the existing budgetary plans 'provide a firm framework for the next three years'. It was emphasized that the plans provide 'valuable certainty and confidence to forward planning', and, as a result, there need be no talk of a defence review.[14] This determination by the government not to have a defence review was supported in public by strategic arguments and in private by rather more political arguments.

Defence officials argue that there is a strong case for 'strategic pluralism', keeping one's options open through the provision of the wide-range of military capabilities. This is true, they argue, even in normal circumstances but the present unprecedented changes create such uncertainty about the future that making strategic choices about priorities and thereby narrowing the base of defence capabilities could well be a major error. Those who support this argument point to the 1981 Defence Review which decided on major cuts in spending on the surface fleet. Shortly afterwards the Falklands War erupted in which the surface fleet played an indispensible role. The 'incrementalist' or 'managerialist' approach, therefore, was regarded as preferable because when cuts in capability have to be made they are spread across the board allowing the government to maintain a balanced defence effort to deal with a range of unpredictable events which might occur in an uncertain world.

In private, defence officials also point to the political costs of defence reviews for the government of the day. All the major defence reviews of the post-war period in 1953–4, 1964–8, 1974 and 1981 created political difficulties for the government in terms of criticism, either from the Opposition parties or from within the government's own party (or both). For a Conservative government which has benefited politically since 1979 from targeting the Labour Party's inadequacies on defence, there is a positive disincentive to raise difficulties for itself by engaging in a bruising public defence review.

Critics of the government's position in recent years have included Sir John Nott, a former Conservative Defence Secretary and Sir Leon Brittan, a former Conservative Minister of Trade and Industry. In a series of articles in *The Times* in October 1987, Sir John Nott highlighted the structural problems which militated against a major review. In his view the Ministry of Defence was like a 'huge super-tanker, well-captained, well-engineered, well-crewed, its systems continuously updated – but no one ever asking where the hell it was going'.[15] There was, however, he argued, a strong case to be made for a review like the one he had himself undertaken in 1981 to provide new strategic direction for British defence policy into the 1990s.

This case was reinforced by Sir Leon Brittan in June 1988 when he wrote a pamphlet (shortly after leaving office) urging his former colleagues to meet the new challenges facing them by taking a fresh look at the pattern of British commitments and the ability to meet them effectively. In his opinion a defence review was a rational step which needed to be taken to meet changing political, strategic and financial circumstances. 'It cannot be right,' he argued, 'to muddle through when there are legitimate grounds for a review.'[16]

The critics would seem to have a point. Apart from the growing financial pressures, the 'managerialist' approach, despite its pragmatic virtues, fails to provide clear strategic direction, at a time when such direction is desperately needed. It also fails to deal adequately with the need to identify priorities in defence capabilities as pressures on the defence budget build up once again. 'Salami-slicing' creates the danger that the whole of the defence effort will sooner or later be weakened.

The need for a defence review became more pressing towards the end of 1989 as the threat from the Warsaw Pact was significantly eroded by the rapid changes taking place in Eastern Europe. Reports appeared in the press in November that the government had finally conceded the case for a review.[17] It was suggested that as the military threat on the central front had all but disappeared the Ministry of Defence was planning to shift resources away from the army and give greater priority to the Royal Navy. Despite the government's categorical denial that such a review was taking place, the unexpected decision in December to order three Type 23 destroyers indicated that a shift in defence priorities might already be underway.[18] It was not clear, however, whether this was part of an incremental adjustment or part of a broader radical review.

The key question by the end of the year was not so much whether a defence review was inevitable at a time of potentially dramatic change in East–West relations. There was little doubt that the government could, if it wished, muddle along in the traditional way using a 'managerialist' approach to conduct its defence policy. A much more important question was whether it was desirable to conduct a major review of defence commitments and capabilities.[19] In the context of the economic, political and technological challenges facing defence planners, British defence policy had reached a cross-roads. A growing consensus seemed to be emerging that a radical defence review, which forced defence officials and government ministers to raise their heads from the minutiae of day-to-day problem-solving and provide longer-term strategic direction to defence policy, was a major priority for the year ahead.

Notes

1. *The Independent*, 9 December 1989.
2. *The Independent*, 31 May 1989.
3. *The Independent*, 12 May 1989.
4. *The Independent*, 4 October 1989.
5. *The Independent*, 27 March 1989.
6. *The Independent*, 13 June 1989.
7. Ibid.
8. *The Independent*, 1 March 1989.
9. *Statement on the Defence Estimates*, Vol.1, 1989, London, HMSO, 1989.
10. Ibid.
11. David Greenwood, 'Defence', in P. Cockles (ed.), *Public Expenditure Policy*, London, Macmillan, 1985.
12. *The Independent*, 2 November 1988.
13. *The Third Report from the Defence Committee, Defence Commitments and Resources and the Defence Estimates, 1985/6*, Vol. 1, London, HMSO, 1985.
14. *Statement on the Defence Estimates*, 1989, HMSO.
15. See *The Times*, 5 and 6 October 1987.
16. Leon Brittan, *Defence and Arms Control in a Changing Era*, Policy Studies Discussion Paper 21, London, Pinter, 1988, p. 20.
17. *The Sunday Times*, 19 November 1989.
18. *The Independent*, 20 December 1989.
19. See John Baylis, *British Defence Policy: Striking the Right Balance*, London, Macmillan, 1989.

Chronology

3 Jan: Ministry of Defence report concluding that a defensive anti-missile umbrella could be established around Britain is published. George Younger makes it clear that no such thing is contemplated in Britain.

13 Jan: Labour calls for a select committee to monitor MI5.

16 Jan: Call for a select committee on MI5 defeated in the Commons by 232 to 163, despite support from four rebel Tory MPs.

30 Jan: Sir Geoffrey Howe discusses with Joe Bossano, Gibraltar's Chief Minister, and confirms leaked reports that Britain plans to more than halve the size of the garrison on the Rock.

Spending on defence in 1989/90 up by £150 million.

3 Feb: National Audit Office report *Ministry of Defence: Reliability and Maintainability of Defence Equipment* argues that nearly £1 billion per year could be saved if maintenance procedures were tightened up.

27 Feb: Britain's three minesweepers are withdrawn from the Gulf. The armilla patrol remains.

Security Service Bill, which puts MI5 on a statutory basis for the first time, gives power to the Home Secretary to issue warrants for entry or interference with property and allows for review of such warrants by a commissioner and investigation of public complaints by a tribunal, is given its second reading in the Commons.

3 Mar: Man accuses of spying for the Czechs is gaoled for ten years.

7 Mar: Lord Bethell reveals that Hurd has told him that disclosures by former members of the Secret Service might be authorized if they caused no damage to national security.

9 Mar: Second reading of the Official Secrets Bill, which replaces Section 2 of the Official Secrets Act 1911. It provides protection over a more limited range of official information, ends the public interest defence for those who disclose proscribed information and makes it an absolute offence for any member or former member of the security and intelligence services to disclose information relating to the services.

17 Mar: HMS *Sandown*, first of a new generation of advanced mine hunting ships, commissioned.

18 Mar: Britain shelves plans to develop an air launched nuclear missile with France because of Mrs Thatcher's strong desire to involve the Americans.

3 Apr: A move to provide a public interest defence in the committee stage of the Official Secrets Bill in the Lords is defeated by 157 to 101.

Brigadier Michael Willcocks, *The British Army and the Operational Level of War*, Tir Service Press, argues that the potential of battlefield helicopters is being neglected by Britain in the same way that the tank was in the inter-war years.

5 Apr: New command bunker for Britain's air defences opened at High Wycombe.

10 Apr: Plans for satellite communications facilities (Ship at Anchor) announced by the Ministry of Defence.

19 Apr: Britain offers to take the lead in deploying the new NATO air launched short-range nuclear weapons to smooth problems over this issue, particularly with West Germany.

21 Apr: West Germans decide to seek early talks on short-range missiles in Europe, prompting critical responses from Britain and the USA.

27 Apr: Security Service Bill receives royal assent.

2 May: Statement on the Defence Estimates reveals a steep rise in the cost of new equipment.

3 May: Security review at Shorts and at Northern Ireland Territorial Army bases following loyalist attempts to pass top secret missile equipment to South Africa.

11 May: Anglo-German talks in London on short-range nuclear missiles make little progress. The Official Secrets Act receives royal assent.

Staff shortages at Aldermaston mean possible delays in the Trident programme.

22 May: Brigade of Gurkhas to be reduced by up to 50 per cent as part of the British withdrawal from Hong Kong.

24 May: Ministry of Defence admits that the first of the new Type 23 frigates may be armed with missile systems incapable of distinguishing between friendly and hostile aircraft.

29 May: NATO summit begins. President Bush offers significant cuts in troops, tanks and aircraft.

30 May: *The Politics of British Defence Procurement*, Market Access International, criticizes the procurement process and argues for buying equipment off the shelf rather than supporting British and collaborative projects.

Agreement on short-range nuclear weapons seals the success of the NATO summit. It also marks a victory for the West Germans and a defeat for the British.

12 June: *The Working of the AWACS Off-Set Agreement: Third Report* of the House of Commons Defence Committee published. It is very critical of the Ministry of Defence's handling of the agreement.

22 June: Secrecy of the Ministry over weapons procurement criticized by the Commons defence committee.

3 July: Report by the Commons Defence Committee on *The Progress of the Trident Programme* argues that the shortage of expert staff jeopardizes plans to arm the Royal Navy with Trident missiles by 1994.

4 July: Commons Defence Committee reports on *The Royal Navy's Surface Fleet: Current Issues* expressing concern about the rate of warship orders and manpower.

6 July: Government attempts to expand the law banning the reporting of the memoirs of security service officers are unanimously rejected by the Law Lords.

20 July: Women to be allowed to fly unarmed aircraft in the RAF for the first time.

1 Aug: The first Cruise missiles are sent back from Greenham Common to the USA as the first phase of decommissioning NATO's intermediate nuclear forces begins.

9 Aug: £150 million spending by the Navy on new battle computers announced.

17 Aug: Commons defence committee report criticizes the inability of the weapons systems on Type 23 frigates to distinguish between friendly and hostile aircraft.

19 Aug: Jerome Ellig, *Set Fair: A Gradualist Proposal for Privatizing Weather Forecasting*, Research Report 13, Social Affairs Unit, makes a case for privatizing the Meteorological Office, part of the Ministry of Defence.

26 Aug: Allegations of fraud at the atomic weapons establishment at Llanishen, near Cardiff. A senior official is suspended.

31 Aug: Fall in armed forces manpower by nearly 8,000 is announced.

13 Sept: Soviet spymaster, Yuri Modin, the controller of Philby *et al*, reveals that there was a fifth man but declines to disclose his name.

24 Sept: Tom King defends the use of private security firms to guard military establishments in the wake of the Deal bombing.

25 Sept: Review of security at army bases established.

It is announced that the army is to recruit many more women and open more trades to them.

4–5 Dec: NATO summit at which Bush briefed his allies on the results of the Malta East-West summit. Thatcher appears more cautious on Eastern Europe than her colleagues.

5 Dec: Announcement that the management of all the Atomic Weapons Establishment research and production sites is to handed to private contractors.

Announcement that the permanent army presence on Gibraltar will end in March 1991.

14 Dec: Public Accounts Committee, *Ministry of Defence: Control and Use of Manpower*, HMSO, published.

Economic Policy and Macro-Economic Developments

ALAN BUDD and ALAN DAVIES

A Troubled Year

The questions about the economy that were being asked at the beginning of 1989 seemed little closer to resolution at the end of 1989. In particular, would the government's policies succeed in bringing down inflation? If they did, what would the cost have to be in terms of a slower growth of output? In the actual conduct of policy, what part, if any, should be played by exchange rate policy?

That final question was eventually to be singled out as the immediate cause of Nigel Lawson's dramatic resignation. However, since John Major's conduct of policy seemed, so far as one could tell, to be indistinguishable from that of Mr Lawson's, it was difficult to understand the fuss. Behind it all, one must assume, lies the far deeper question of Britain's relationship with Europe. That question goes way beyond the seemingly technical issue of when the UK would join the exchange rate mechanism (ERM) of the European Monetary System (EMS).

An Overview

After five years of economic growth, averaging 3 per cent per annum, production moved up a gear in 1987 and 1988. The increase in output was 5 per cent and 4.6 per cent respectively, and rather more for the non-oil economy. This performance can rightly be labelled an economic boom and represented the fastest *sustained* period of growth in the post-war period. However, during the course of 1988, problems emerged. The level of capacity utilization reached an all-time high while skilled labour shortages were also a factor in the inflation pressures that were building up. At the same time, domestic demand was rising at an even more rapid pace than output. The increase in consumers' expenditure accelerated to 7 per cent in 1988, fuelled by a strong growth in real incomes and a rapid rise in borrowing, especially by means of mortgages. House prices soared by over 30 per cent, further contributing to the strength of borrowing and spending, and the personal sector's saving ratio was down to 4 per cent, the lowest for some 30 years. The strength of consumers' expenditure was joined by a sharp upturn in business investment which meant that, despite a burgeoning public sector surplus, the economy as a whole was experiencing a widening gap between domestic saving and investment. As a result, the United Kingdom's balance of payments current account deficit rose to over £14 billion, or 3 per cent of GDP in 1988.

The government first began reacting to the 1987–8 economic boom in the early summer of 1988. After reaching a low point of 7.5 per cent in May 1988, monetary policy was steadily tightened and bank base rates were raised no fewer than nine times and reached 13 per cent in November. In part, the reversal of earlier interest rate reductions reflected the abandonment of an exchange rate policy directed at holding sterling's value stable against the Deutschmark; but domestic economic considerations came increasingly to the fore and by the autumn the Chancellor was asserting that it was possible to have too much of a good thing. The Chancellor was relatively sanguine about external deficits *per se*, except to the extent that they were symptomatic of excess demand and inadequate saving, rather than temporarily high investment. However, whatever the interpretation, it was the record balance of payments for October 1988 which provoked what seemed to many to be the final turning of the monetary screw when base rates rose to 13 per cent on November 25, taking mortgage interest rates to around 13.5 per cent compared with a low of 9.5 per cent in the spring of 1988.

Expectations about 1989 at the turn of the year can be measured reasonably by the average of a number of independent forecasts published by the Treasury in January. Growth was set to decelerate from the 4.6 per cent recorded in 1988 to 2.8 per cent in 1989; the retail price inflation rate, which had risen from 3.3 per cent in early 1988 to 6.5 per cent by the fourth quarter, was forecast to ease to 5.3 per cent by the fourth quarter of 1989; while the balance of payments deficit was expected to decline a little. At the same time, interest rates were projected to fall – to around 11 per cent by the end of the year; as was the exchange rate – by an overall 6 per cent during the course of the year.

When the Treasury forecasts were published at the time of the Budget in March, the key macro-economic forecasts were very similar to those of the independent forecasters. Gross Domestic Product (GDP) growth was set to slow to 2.5 per cent, with a much sharper slowdown in domestic demand growth in general and consumers' expenditure in particular. Growth was to be sustained by an increasing contribution from (net) exports, although the balance of payments current account was expected to do no more than stabilize in 1989 at £14.5 billion, which was the latest estimated out-turn for 1988. The retail inflation rate was projected to rise from the 7.5 per cent figure prevailing at the time to about 8 per cent, before falling back to 5.5 per cent in the fourth quarter of the year and then further to 4.5 per cent in the second quarter of 1990.

As for the Budget measures and fiscal policy, the Chancellor was faced with an embarrassment of riches. A year earlier, the Chancellor had expected to be able to repay £3 billion of public sector debt in the 1988–9 financial year. In the event, the

Public Sector Debt Repayment (PSDR) turned out to be some £14 billion, or 3 per cent of GDP. The Chancellor reaffirmed a balanced budget as a guiding principle for the longer term. However, since the immediate priority was to restrain demand, the main Budget measures were confined to a modest (in relation to the fiscal surplus) reduction in National Insurance contributions along with the non-valorization of the main excise duties (a measure designed directly to hold down the 'headline' inflation rate by 0.3 percentage points). Given an increase in public expenditure of around 1 per cent which, as is usual, had been set the previous autumn, the Chancellor was able to project a further public sector debt repayment of £14 billion for the 1989–90 fiscal year.

From the Budget on, the key issue was the appropriateness of the stance of monetary policy, a debate which intensified, as interest rates were raised, first to 14 per cent in May and then by a further 1 per cent to 15 per cent in September. On each occasion, the exchange rate had been a key factor. In May, it was a sharp general weakening of sterling against all currencies that caused the authorities to conclude that: 'in order to prevent their monetary policy from being undermined by a lower exchange rate, a rise in interest rates was warranted'.[1] In September, it was the release of the balance of payments statistics showing a near record of £2 billion current account deficit followed by a 1 per cent increase in German interest rates that resulted in sharp downward pressure on the exchange rate and the decision to raise UK interest rates again, to 15 per cent. The resignation of Nigel Lawson as Chancellor of the Exchequer on October 26 threatened to turn economic difficulties into a political crisis. Mr Lawson's stated reason for resigning concerned the open criticism by Sir Alan Walters, the Prime Minister's economic adviser, of Mr Lawson's handling of the exchange rate in general and his attitude towards Britain's entry into the exchange rate mechanism of the European Monetary System in particular. How much deeper differences of opinion went between the Chancellor and the Prime Minister concerning Britain's future role in Europe is difficult to say. In any event, the new Chancellor, John Major, was immediately faced with the question of how vigorously the exchange rate should be defended; for the political turmoil itself resulted in further downward pressure on sterling at a time when many commentators were arguing that domestic monetary conditions were already sufficiently tight to threaten outright recession. Although the financial market's response to Mr Lawson's resignation was contained, the policy dilemma seemed set to be a recurrent feature of the economy over the winter months.

Some Comments on the Policy Debate

The government no doubt hoped that the raising of interest rates to 13 per cent by the end of 1988 would be sufficient to slow down demand and reverse the acceleration of inflation. In the event, it made two further increases, to 15 per cent. These moves raise two related questions about the conduct of policy. The first was whether domestic conditions justified these increases: the second was whether the government was, wrongly, switching its attention away from monetary indications towards the exchange rate.

Whatever the merits of responding to exchange rate movements, it can be argued that domestic conditions themselves justified the further tightening of policy. Despite the evident weakening of the housing market, particularly in the South East, the economy continued to show sustained strength through much of the year. Total consumer spending continued to rise until mid-year and capital spending remained buoyant. Further evidence for the pressure on resources was provided by the balance of payments. The rise in the current account deficit to an estimated £20 billion was driven by surging import volumes rather than a weak export performance (the increase in non-oil export volume was, in fact, the strongest for 13 years). Similarly, the labour market offered little comfort to those who argued that the medicine was too strong. The fall in unemployment continued at a strong pace and by the autumn was, at 1.7 million, some 350,000 lower than at the start of the year, the lowest figure since October 1980 and lower than the average for the European Community. At the same time, wage settlements moved up to a 7.5–9 per cent range compared with the 5–6.5 per cent seen a year earlier; and, although it is normal for wage costs to lag behind the economic cycle reflecting *past* inflation experience, the inflation story in 1989 was not reassuring. For although the retail price inflation rate peaked in May at 8.3 per cent, the rate stayed above 7 per cent in the second half of the year, compared with the Chancellor's Budget forecast of 5.5 per cent by the fourth quarter, which was itself an upward revision to the 5 per cent which had been projected by the Treasury the previous autumn. It is true that excluding mortage interest charges the underlying rate stayed close to 6 per cent (a figure which was, it will be recalled, depressed a little by the decision not to raise excise duties); but it is clear that the inflation problem proved far more intractable than seemed likely when it was referred to as a 'blip' earlier in the year. Moreover, the failure to see how entrenched the inflation problem might be was not just a government error. As we have seen, nearly all independent forecasters expected lower inflation and an easing of monetary policy at the start of the year. In the circumstances, the monetary authorities can be held to have acted with reasonable pragmatism (although one would have to question whether those circumstances could have been prevented). In particular, the argument that the authorities paid undue attention to holding up the exchange rate hardly squares with the 9 per cent depreciation which took place even before the difficulties caused by Mr Lawson's resignation.

The evidence therefore suggests that a further tightening of policy was necessary in the light of domestic developments during 1989. However, the conduct of policy should be directed at the future, rather than at responding to the past. This is particularly true of counter-inflationary policy since there are long delays between the causes and the effects. Those who favour monetarist policies claim that monetary indicators do provide advance warning of future problems and that therefore policy should concentrate on monetary targets. In fact the monetary authorities continued to set a money supply target – for the narrow monetary aggregate, MO, which consists overwhelmingly of notes and coin. The target range for 1989–90 was set at 1–5 per cent and in his Budget speech, the Chancellor noted that, although MO growth was above the target range, 'its very low growth over the past six months suggests that it will fairly soon come back within the range'. Six months later, however, MO growth was still outside its target range following an increase of 9 per cent per annum in the intervening period, despite the raising of interest rates. Similarly, the broad measures of the money supply provided little cause for comfort. Lending to individuals, especially in the case of mortgages, decelerated sharply; but overall borrowing and broad money aggregates continued to increase by approaching 20 per cent. Given these developments it was somewhat surprising that monetarists were among those who criticized the raising of interest the rate in October.

Other criticisms of policy concerned the balance of policy and the perceived excessive reliance on high interest rates. One view was that credit controls would have been preferable to the high interest rate policy. However, not only was there the objection that such controls could be circumvented in a world free of exchange controls, but it would also have been a case of locking the stable door after the horse had bolted. Consumer credit, the usual focus of attention, accounts for only 15 per cent of total personal borrowing (the rest is mortages, where nobody suggests a return to rationing) and in the case of credit cards, lending growth had actually been decelerating sharply throughout the consumer boom.

Some argued that the pain of high interest rates could have been avoided if greater reliance had been placed on fiscal policy, by raising taxes or cutting public expenditure. However, since 1980, fiscal policy had been placed within a medium-term strategy designed progressively to lower public expenditure (as a share of GDP) in order to facilitate both lower government borrowing and lower tax rates. This policy was primarily concerned with providing a fiscal environment and tax regime in which private enterprise could flourish. It was not directed at short term demand management and it is difficult to envisage such a fundamental policy reversal at a time when the government had arrived at the position of running a budget surplus unmatched by any other industrialized country. However, as we have already seen, the government did behave flexibly in this area, by budgeting for a continued large fiscal surplus.

Finally, there is the question of whether economic conditions would have been less painful if we had joined the ERM of the EMS. There are many dimensions to this issue but on the basis of short term macro-economic judgement, joining the ERM would have been no panacea. If Britain had joined the ERM, say at the start of 1989, there are two possibilities. First, if Britain had joined with total credibility in the sense that the perception was that sterling's exchange rate would remain virtually stable for the foreseeable future, then UK interest rates would surely have fallen towards, say, German rates. It is hard to believe that this would have been appropriate to an economy seeking to cool excess demand pressures. Conversely, if on entry to the ERM the feeling was that sterling's position in the EMS was unsustainable and that we would have to devalue sooner or later, then UK interest rates would probably have had to rise even further than was the case for, despite 15 per cent interest rates, sterling still depreciated by some 10 per cent against the Deutschmark. The government therefore concluded that Britain would not join the EMS until, *inter alia*, Britain's inflation rate had moved back down to the European average. (The other conditions for EMS membership established at the Madrid EC summit in June 1989 were that exchange controls should be abolished in the main EC countries, and that significant further progress should be made towards completing the single market.)

In short, there was no obvious alternative to a major policy tightening over 1988–9 in order that the inflation pressures that had developed in the 1987–8 boom were reversed. Given the scale of that boom, it was inevitable that the cooling-off period would not be painless.

Conclusion

For some, 1989 was the year which proved that Britain's apparent economic miracle in the 1980s was a mirage. However, such a conclusion cannot be maintained on the basis of short term fluctuations in the business cycle, however painful the troughs (or enjoyable the peaks). For Britain, five years of output growth of 3 per cent per annum were followed by output growth in the non-oil economy of over 5 per cent in 1987 and 1988. These boom conditions exaggerated Britain's underlying economic strength, just as a period of below-trend growth will understate it. But there is nothing so far which seriously undermines the view that Britain in the 1980s has raised its sustainable growth rate. The importance of the short term economic cycle is reinforced by the international perspective. For it is not just Britain that has been going through a period of unsustainably rapid growth which requires a policy tightening. All major economies experienced unexpectedly rapid growth during 1987 and 1988 (the 1987 stock market crash notwithstanding) and most countries have been forced to tighten monetary policy in the face of rising inflation, which by 1989 had reached a three-year high in the other major industrialized economies. Indeed, excluding mortgage charges, the rise in Britain's inflation rate to 6 per cent from around 4.0 per cent in 1987 is comparable to the rise in, say, German inflation. It is true that Britain's boom was that much more pronounced but, whilst there is no cause for complacency, it should be remembered that Britain's inflation will have peaked way below the levels of over 20 per cent reached in the aftermath of the two previous major post-war booms, in the early and late 1970s. Moreover, in Europe at least, the strength of the upswing is continuing which suggests that, as the British economy slows down both inflation differentials and the balance of payments deficit should narrow. The narrowing of

Table 1. The UK Economy

	1982–86 average	1987 outturn	1988 outturn	1989 estimates
Year average				
% change over previous year:				
GDP (Output measure)	3.0	5.0	4.6	1.5
Non-oil GDP	2.6	5.4	5.5	2.8
Manufacturing production	2.1	5.5	6.8	4.0
Consumers' expenditure	3.3	5.4	6.9	3.75
Government consumption	1.2	1.2	0.4	−0.25
Fixed investment	4.9	8.8	13.1	5.25
Export volumes (goods and services)	3.9	5.1	0.7	4.75
Import volumes (goods and services)	6.1	7.6	12.2	9.25
Average earnings	8.0	7.8	8.7	9.0
Real personal disposable income	2.3	3.6	4.9	4.2
Retail prices	5.5	4.1	4.9	7.9
End year				
% change over previous year:				
Current account (£ bn.)	2.7	−3.7	−14.6	−20.0
Retail prices		3.7	6.8	7.5
MO		4.2	8.5	5.0
M4		16.3	17.6	16.0
Unemployment (million adults)		2.57	2.04	1.6
Short-term interest rates (%)		8.9	13.1	15.0
Sterling exchange rate index (1985 = 100)		93.6	97.4	87.1[a]
Dollar/sterling		1.87	1.80	1.56[a]
D.Mark/sterling		2.96	3.21	2.84[a]

[a] As at 23 November 1989.
Source: HM Treasury Autumn Statement; and Barclays Bank Economics Department

inflation differentials will satisfy one of the conditions for Britain joining the EMS. Whether that will be sufficient is a matter for 1990.

Note
1. *Bank of England Quarterly Bulletin*, August 1989.

Chronology
2 Jan: Mr Lawson says high UK interest rates will combat inflation.
16 Jan: A fall in retail sales leads to speculation that interest rates have peaked at 13 per cent.
25 Jan: Mrs Thatcher rules out joining the EMS in the current Parliament.
    Mr Lawson's Chatham House speech rejects full economic and monetary union in the EC and calls for a free-market Europe.
30 Jan: Government announces public spending plans for the coming financial year unchanged at £167.1 billion.
17 Feb: Retail inflation rate in January rises to 7.5 per cent.

20 Feb: Sterling comes under pressure, partly in response to prospects of higher interest rates abroad.

22 Feb: EC Commission's annual report on members' economies draws attention to British inflation and the balance of payments deficit.

11 Mar: Brady plan to reschedule Third World debt launched by Nicholas Brady, US Treasury Secretary.

14 Mar: Cautious budget designed to reduce inflation introduced by Nigel Lawson. The main features include changes to national insurance, pensions and capital gains tax. Projections include a public sector surplus of £14 billion, 5.5 per cent inflation at the end of the year and a balance of payments deficit of £14.5 billion.

29 Mar: Sterling weakens following the announcement of a £1.7 billion current account deficit in February.

2–3 Apr: Group of Seven meeting in Washington on the Brady plan.

6 Apr: Life insurance tax cut.

10 Apr: Mr Lawson rejects devaluation and says interest rates will be raised again if necessary.

14 Apr: Retail inflation rate rises to 7.9 per cent.

17 Apr: Delors Report, proposing a three-stage movement towards a common economic policy and a single currency in the EC, published. It is rejected by Mr Lawson.

24 Apr: Commons Treasury and Civil Service Select Committee criticizes the management of the economy.

26 Apr: A lower current account deficit of £1.2 billion in March eases interest rate pressures.

27 Apr: John Major tells the American Chamber of Commerce that 'the government will not permit the depreciation of sterling as a way of artificially improving competitiveness'.

2 May: Sir Alan Walters returns as Mrs Thatcher's personal economic adviser.

19 May: Annual retail inflation rate for April rises to 8 per cent.

20 May: Pay award of 9.2 per cent for power workers fuels fears of inflationary wage pressures, periodically reawakened by other settlements of over 9 per cent for other groups of workers throughout the summer.

Mr Lawson denies rumours of a rift with Mrs Thatcher over exchange and interest rate.

23 May: Sterling continues to weaken, partly because of the strong dollar, but also more generally. A remark by the Prime Minister in the Commons is misinterpreted by the financial markets as implying that interest rates would not be raised to support sterling.

24 May: Interest rates put up to 14 per cent.

12 June: Nigel Lawson declares to the Commons Treasury and Civil Service Select Committee that Britain will not join the EMS until late 1990 at the earliest in an attempt to heal a renewed rift between the Prime Minister and himself on the issue.

Announcement of a 2.5 per cent rise in retail sales in May fuels fears that the economy is not slowing sufficiently. Sterling continues to weaken.

14 June: Agreement in the EC to phase out the ounce, the pound, the gill, the fathom and the therm, but no such decision on miles, acres, or pints of beer and milk.

21 June: CBI calls for Britain to become a full member of the EMS.

26–27 June: At Madrid summit Mrs Thatcher rejects stages 2 and 3 of the Delors Report.

27 June: Green Paper launches consultation on the extension of Britain's summer time.

2 July: Announcement of a record fall of £2.2 billion in Britain's foreign currency and exchange reserves in June.

10 July: Retail sales fall by 1.8 per cent in June.

14 July: Retail inflation rate unchanged at 8.3 per cent in June.

26 July: Commons Trade and Industry Select Committee call for membership of the exchange rate mechanism of the EMS as soon as possible in its report *Financial Services and the Single Market.*

11 Aug: OECD report points to the strengths of the UK economy but calls for a tighter fiscal policy.

Ministers warn that high pay awards are increasing inflationary pressures.

18 Aug: Annual rate of retail price inflation dips to 8.2 per cent in July.

21 Aug: *Consumer Trends: Marketing Implications on the 1990s* Key Note Publications, predicts fall in self- employed and rise in unemployment.

A Return to Trade Surplus? The Impact of Japanese Investment on the UK published by the Japanese stockbroker Nomura predicts continued high investment by the Japanese in Britain leading to a return to trade surpluses and other economic improvements.

23 Aug: July current account deficit posted. At £2.1 billion it was the second highest ever.

8 Sept: Treasury statement denies market rumour that Mr Lawson had resigned.

9 Sept: Lawson scheme of competing currencies acceptable anywhere in the EC put forward.

13 Sept: *Blue Book* published. It shows GDP up by 4.5 per cent in 1988 and manufacturing output up by 7 per cent.

18 Sept: CBI forecast stagnant output over the next quarter.

24 Sept: Group of Seven agrees to attempt to lower the dollar after its recent rise.

27 Sept: The pound slides on the foreign exchanges after a £2 billion trade deficit in August is announced.

5 Oct: Base interest rates are raised to 15 per cent in the wake of a 1 per cent rise in rates in West Germany.

9 Oct: Sterling weakens further, falling through the DM 3.0 level.

11 Oct: CBI presses for Britain to join the ERM.

19 Oct: Mr Lawson defends his conduct of monetary policy in his Mansion House speech, emphasizing particularly that interest rates will remain high.

26 Oct: Mr Lawson resigns as Chancellor of the Exchequer and is replaced by John Major. Sir Alan Walters also resigns.

2 Nov: Mr Major announces proposals for a system of competing currencies in the EC, elaborated in the Treasury document, *An Evolutionary Approach to Economic and Monetary Union.*

15 Nov: Mr Major's Autumn Statement includes a £5.5 billion increase in government expenditure, principally on health and transport. Slow growth of 1.25 per cent in 1990 is predicted, with the balance of payments deficit falling to £15 billion and retail inflation declining from 7.5 per cent to 5.75 per cent.

20 Nov: Sterling again under pressure because of the strength of the DM and nervousness over the balance of payments figures.

23 Nov: Sterling stabilizes after an improved current account deficit of £1.5 billion in October is announced.

5 Dec: Lords Select Committee on the European Communities calls for commitment to join the ERM before July 1990.

28 Dec: Sterling at new low against the DM.

The City

MARGARET REID

For the City of London, in its broad sense as Britain's financial community, 1989 has been a year of mixed trends, one of the brightest of which has been a fresh upsurge in the stock market. By the end of the year, share prices stood 32 per cent higher than at its beginning, having finally recouped the last of the losses sustained in the sharp crash of October 1987. This rise mirrored movements in world markets generally but took place against the background of a slowdown in Britain's economic growth to less than half the previous year's at just 2 per cent and the prediction of a fresh slackening to only 1.25 per cent in 1990. The latter and other forecasts highly relevant for the financial community were given in November by the new Chancellor of the Exchequer, John Major. Mr Major also anticipated that Britain's current balance of payments gap would narrow to a still very wide £15 billion in 1990 from a record £20 billion in 1989; that inflation in the twelve months to the last 1990 quarter would ease to 5.75 per cent from 7.50 per cent a year earlier; and that 1990 consumer spending would rise only 1.25 per cent, against an increase of 3.75 per cent in 1989.

It was clear that the new Chancellor looked to continued high interest rates to squeeze demand and inflation. Yet the market soon sensed that Mr Major was perhaps more reluctant than his predecessor would have been to raise interest rates above the politically very unpopular level of 15 per cent (double their 1988 low) which they had reached in the autumn. Instead, he appeared readily to tolerate some fresh fall in the pound and, indeed, sterling was, by the end of December, 11.7 per cent lower than at the start of 1989 after a sharp drop since the change of Chancellor. This decline, boosting the sterling worth of exports by numerous companies, was one factor giving stock markets an end-year boost. Another was the generally favourable trend on world bourses, helped by signs of the Cold War's ending.

The chequered context of investment optimism but steep interest rates and a decelerating economy called for carefully weighed responses from leading sectors of City activity. The securities market has had to face up to the fact that its multi-billion pound investment for the future in the Big Bang restructuring three and a half years ago has almost certainly left it with over-capacity. For their part, the banks are also confronting the challenge of a more harshly competitive climate as the highly profitable credit boom subsides. Various financial institutions, including banks, building societies and insurance companies, which branched out

Table 1. Market data: world equity market capitalization

	Market capitalization 29 Sept. 1989	
	US $bn.	%
USA	3002.1	31.0
Canada	275.5	2.8
North America	**3277.6**	**33.9**
UK	790.0	8.2
W.Germany	279.4	2.9
Switzerland	173.1	1.8
France	286.2	3.0
Netherlands	103.4	1.1
Italy	155.7	1.6
Sweden	112.1	1.2
Spain	111.8	1.2
Belgium	67.7	0.7
Denmark	34.0	0.4
Norway	22.1	0.2
Austria	17.4	0.2
Europe	**2173.1**	**22.5**
Japan	3915.0	40.5
Australia	138.5	1.4
Singapore	57.3	0.6
Hong Kong	74.9	0.8
Far East	**4185.7**	**43.3**
World	**9671.4**	**100.0**

Source: Morgan Stanley Capital International SA, Geneva

by amassing chains of estate agents are also feeling the backwash of the housing market's slowdown in losses on these new interests.

Securities Markets

For London's stock market industry, mostly spread among a number of wide-ranging, bank-owned groups shaped to their present form before Big Bang, 1989 developments posed persistent problems. Although investment business through the market – the world's third largest, with an 8 per cent share, after Japan's and the USA's (table 1) – picked up from the depressed post-crash 1988 levels, it has not revived enough to sustain profitable operation at many houses. High costs and under-use of capacity, even in the boomlets of January, the summer and the year-end, left various groups running at substantial losses. Andrew Hugh Smith, who had recently taken over as chairman of London's International Stock Exchange (ISE) from Sir Nicholas Goodison, an architect of Big Bang, in February 1989 described estimates of an aggregate annual loss rate of £500 million among securities' houses as not looking exaggerated.

Share market business with customers picked up to 50 per cent above the depressed level a year earlier by the third quarter of 1989 but later fell away again. Commission income for the year was estimated at £665 million, 25 per cent up on 1988 but still down on the buoyant 1987. All this meant that, while overall loss rates have probably declined, even the best-placed players are failing to make the profits hoped for, while many continue to incur losses. Uncertainties over how far share prices, and with them turnover, will revive further have postponed radical action at various of the larger houses. But there are still too many stock market firms chasing too little business.

Responses to the situation have been threefold: a reduction of capacity in some cases; a holding on in the hope of better times at others; and finally, at the ISE, reviews and adjustments of post-Big Bang trading rules to produce, for some at least, a better trading environment.

In February, two major changes were brought in following recommendations from an ISE committee chaired by Nigel Elwes. Market-makers (successors of the old jobbers as 'wholesalers' of shares) were absolved from the obligation to do business with other market-makers, as distinct from brokers and big clients, at the share prices they advertised on the Exchange's screen market. Also, details of large (£100,000-plus) deals became disclosable only the following day, instead of immediately. The first change was in answer to complaints from major market-makers that their smaller brethren had been too easily able to off-load on to them their own unwanted 'positions', so avoiding the need to commit capital to carry the risks themselves. The second was addressed to worries that instant revelation of a big transaction made it too simple for rivals to guess and take advantage of a competitor's position.

It is unclear how far these alterations have eased previous problems. But they have reversed the previous situation under which some large houses had ceased in late 1988 to quote screen prices in more than the trifling obligatory minimum of 5,000 shares, instead fixing deals directly with big institutional clients. The previous trend had, in the degree to which it existed at one stage, caused fears that the market was fragmenting and ceasing to be a central, visible one.

The Elwes committee produced further proposals, including ones for testing market-makers' performance to check they were fulfilling their duty to be continuous, not just 'fair weather', dealers; possibly raising minimum quote levels; and obliging agency brokers to offer the business to a market-maker before doing a matching deal between two of their own clients. These ideas are shelved for the moment but others may be taken up later, while there could also be a further review of the rule changes to date. In essence, there is a clash of views between, on the one hand, agency brokers and smaller market-makers, who worry about restriction

Table 2. Capitalization of gilt-edged market makers (in £m)

GEMMS' capital as at 27 October 1986[a]	595
Changes as companies joined or withdrew[b]	− 70
Net injections or withdrawals of capital	+ 85
Operating losses[c]	−190
GEMMs' capital as at end-1988	420

[a]Capital base. Note that 27 Oct. 1986 was Big Bang day.
[b]Hoare Govett withdrew from the market on 4 Jan. 1989, but its withdrawal is included in this table (which otherwise records changes up to 30 Dec. 1988).
[c]Net profits/losses after overheads.
Source: *Bank of England Quarterly Bulletin*, Feb. 1989, p. 51

of competition and having their style cramped, and, on the other, the big market-makers, who fear that, unless trading conditions are adequately favourable to them, the whole prosperity and future of the London market could be at risk. It should be noted that the Office of Fair Trading, with a watching brief to ensure adequate competition, is observing developments closely.

Meanwhile, during the year, some firms withdrew from major sectors of activity in the face of adverse conditions, following the merchant bank Morgan Grenfell's closure of its main securities business, with 450 job losses, in November 1988. In January 1989, the large US bank Chase Manhattan ceased market-making in UK equities and later also pulled out of dealing in gilts. Near the year's end, several further firms, including the Australia and New Zealand Bank group, cut back their operations, which left 29 concerns making markets in UK equities, compared with 35 three years previously.

In the gilt-edged market in UK government bonds, the shakeout of dealers has been sharper, not least because the government's policy of running a Budget surplus, with consequent repayment of some National Debt, caused the nominal value of quoted gilts to fall by 10 per cent in the year to September 1989 to £127 billion. Additionally, competitive pressures among the greatly increased crowd of gilt market-makers which, at Big Bang, succeeded a previous handful of jobbers, has led to a steady stream of firms quitting after making losses. By late 1989, ten concerns had withdrawn, although two, the Japanese groups Nomura and Daiwa, had joined, leaving a total of nineteen. Early in the year the Bank of England revealed that losses to the end of 1988 among gilt market-makers had reached £190 million. Allowing for injections and withdrawals of capital, this meant that the £595 million committed to this market by 27 firms at Big Bang had, by the start of 1989, shrunk to £420 million, spread among fewer groups (table 2).

In addition to the losses and withdrawals in the market, there is no doubt that a persistent trends towards concentration has taken place. For some time now the eight largest market-makers among the 29 dealing in UK equities have, between them, done as much as four-fifths of the total business. At the close of 1989 it was still unclear how far further cuts in capacity would be needed to adjust to future levels of turnover and exactly which firms would be the survivors of any further contraction.

Settlement – Seeking the Paperless Solution

One of the chief problems continuing to face the stock market is its antiquated paper-based settlement system which is much more prone to delays than more modern foreign structures. After prolonged discussions, slowed by complications including cost, the investing public's attachment to share certificates, the interests of banks now acting as registrars, and companies' need for access to lists of their shareholders, a solution appeared by the year-end to be in sight in the shape of a new computerized scheme named TAURUS. The chosen version of TAURUS would replace the paper system by an all-electronic one, operated on a nominee basis but with particulars about individual shareholders held in sub-registers maintained by brokers, registrars and others serving as TAURUS Account Controllers (TACs). During 1989 the Bank of England, fearing that settlement delays, which can magnify chances of default, could hurt London's standing as an international market, pressed for quick progress on this issue. The influential international bank body 'The Group of Thirty' has also called for the different nations' bourses to have 'a Central Securities Depository in place by 1992 to . . . provide participants with an efficient, low-risk method for achieving early and secure transaction settlement'. Meanwhile, in 1989 the ISE introduced a Securities Automated Execution Facility (SAEF) for the easy transaction of small share deals. SAEF is, however, rivalled by two commercial competitors within the market.

On a different matter, the Stock Exchange is proposing to end, after a shortish experiment, its junior Third Market in small and young companies. This will leave the Exchange's companies divided between the majority in the main market, with a full listing, and those in the popular Unlisted Securities Market (USM). At the same time, the minimum trading record for admission to the former will be reduced from five to three years and for the latter from three to two, though with certain special provisions for very new firms. There will be a one-year phasing-out period for the Third Market. These arrangements are designed to bring the ISE's practice into line with that elsewhere in Europe, ahead of the application in 1990 of the European Community's Mutual Recognition of Listing Particulars law. This provides that a company having a listing in one EC country can seek to get its shares listed in another, using the same particulars.

A new chief executive, Peter Rawlins, took over during the year as the ISE's chief executive, succeeding Jeffrey Knight, who left after seven years in the post.

Table 3. Big-four UK banks' Third World loan exposure and provisions after 1989 first-half statements

	LDC[a] exposure £m	Provisions £m	% cover
Barclays	1988	960	48.3
Lloyds	4185	1988	47.5
Midland	4785	2414	50.4
NatWest	2800	1346	48.0
Total	13,758	6708	

[a]LDC = less developed countries

Banking Business

For the big banks, grappling as they are with fresh pressures in their lucrative home market, the year's outstanding event was, nonetheless, their fresh action to surmount the last ravages of their vast Third World debt problem. Having previously put aside provisions equalling some 30 per cent of their near-£14 billion loan exposure in this field, the Big Four groups earmarked £2 billion more in mid-year to increase this cushion to almost 50 per cent (table 3). Then some months later, two banks, Lloyds and National Westminster, set apart further large sums to lift to around 70 per cent or more their cover against risks of non-payment by the troubled borrowers of Latin America and elsewhere. If other banks emulate them (and this cannot be assumed since provisions are already high) the sector would be very well protected against all future risks in this context. Thus, the banks would at last have conjured away a shadow that has hung over them, and their international counterparts, since 1982. It was in that year that Mexico's financial emergency triggered the banking industry's largest-ever debt crisis, as some 30 developing states faced problems over servicing hundreds of billions of dollars worth of bank loans. Deteriorating economies in the Third World, some non-payment even of interest due, and the plan of the US Treasury Secretary, Nicholas Brady, to foster long term help to debtor nations have all contributed to the banks' more sombre assessment of the debt outlook.

It is as well that the banks are near to overcoming their overseas debt burden, since they are now facing tougher times in the UK market. Their new drive into the mortgage market and their large expansion of consumer lending (partly through credit cards) in the 1980s deregulated UK financial climate have produced a buoyant and most lucrative domestic business for most of the past decade. At the start of 1989, the loans outstanding in these fields from the eight largest high street banks, £64 billion, were 41 per cent of all their sterling lending. But now steep interest rates are squeezing credit demand. And although for years past the net interest margin on the banks' UK lending business has been a generous 5 per cent-plus – generating profits highly useful in offsetting Third World problems – this figure has been falling under the recent pressures. Higher funding costs now that savers expect better returns, an abatement in the rush to borrow, and more competition are making profits rather harder to earn. High interest rates are motivating borrowers on credit card accounts (the big ones were mainly charging a 29.8 per cent real rate in late-1989) to trim their balances. And increased competition by new card-issuers in cutting interest rates has also threatened the big bank's credit card profits. From February 1990, Lloyds Bank, in introducing a £12 a year credit card fee, is cutting interest from 29.8 per cent to 26.8 per cent, effectively ending the subsidization of non-borrower by borrowing customers.

In all these circumstances, the expenses side of the banks' businesses has come under renewed scrutiny, particularly at groups with the relatively dearest operations. In November, TSB, the sixth largest high street bank, developed from separate savings banks and merged in a new group before its shares were floated in 1986, mounted a major economy drive to improve its above-average cost-income ratios. Three thousand jobs are to go in the current year, with 2,000 more to follow, while important operations will be shifted from London to cheaper regional centres. Other clearing banks have been more modestly trimming expenses.

Additional action to adjust strategies towards concentration on mainstream activities and to cut back others has involved reductions in some overseas interests, notably outside Europe. For instance, Barclays Bank sold its US consumer lending and instalment credit arm, BarclaysAmerican, late in 1989 in a move following similar retrenchment in North America by other clearers.

The banks are, however, paying increasing attention to Europe as the 1992 single market looms nearer. Through selective expansion, Barclays has already become the UK bank with the biggest European presence, while it also ranks as the largest foreign bank in France and Spain. National Westminster, for its part, bought control of Banco NatWest March in Spain during 1989 and could make further moves, by way of acquisition, strategic alliance or joint venture, to enlarge its European business.

Banks – Organization

The shake-up in the financial industry's organization already seen, during the Thatcher government's years, in the securities market became more evident in the banking world itself in 1989. Abbey National, previously the country's second largest building society, took advantage of the possibilities opened up by the Building Societies Act 1986 to transform itself into a commercial bank. After this conversion, shares of the new Abbey National plc were launched on the stock market in July through a flotation valuing them at some £2 billion. Abbey National, now the UK's fifth largest bank, has said it will continue to emphasize personal banking services, while pursuing moderate diversification. No other building society followed suit in 1989 but competitive pressures encouraged mergers within the sector, as in Cheltenham and Gloucester's deal to absorb Guardian through a merger on terms giving saver members of the latter, smaller, society a cash bonus. Another symptom both of the breaking down of sector barriers and of privatization policy is the plan for the state-owned Girobank to be bought by the Alliance & Leicester Building Society.

One instance of the big banks' desire to part with interests peripheral to their main operations (often in the interests of boosting their capital) was the sale early in 1990 of Yorkshire Bank, the profitable retail banking group until then jointly owned by four other, larger, clearers for £977 million. The purchaser was National Australia Bank, which in 1986 had bought banking chains in Scotland, Northern Ireland and The Republic of Ireland from Midland Bank.

Foreign predators' eyes have lately focused increasingly on Britain's merchant banks, whose advisory and investment management skills, often more highly rated than their Continental rivals', are in demand in the run-up to the post-1992 single EC banking market. The latest move of this kind came in November when Deutsche Bank, Germany's largest, extended its European expansion by securing Morgan Grenfell for £950 million. The latter, which had also been in the sights of the French bank Indo-Suez, is among London's largest traditional names and is prominent in corporate finance and fund management. Earlier, a sequence of European purchases of British fund managers had occurred, a notable one having been the French Société Générale bank's acquisition of Touche Remnant.

The City – General and Other Aspects

One City market which has continued to grow rapidly is that in foreign exchange, the trading of one currency for another. London, long the leader in this field, has retained its premier place, according to Bank of England and other central bank surveys in 1989. These showed that $187 billion of turnover is transacted daily through London, more than twice the 1986 figure of $90 billion. New York and Tokyo respectively trade $129 billion and $115 billion a day, while the figures for Switzerland, Singapore and Hong Kong, the next most active markets, are $57 billion, $55 billion and $49 billion respectively. This means that a daily total of $592 billion, without allowing for smaller centres' business, washes through the world's money markets daily. And that implies a yearly figure, for all business days together, of over $154 trillion – or some 50 times yearly international trade in goods – eloquent testimony indeed to the effects of deregulation.

Just how much the British financial community has grown in recent years is shown by figures putting employment in Great Britain in banking, finance,

Table 4. Employment in the financial sector (numbers of employees in thousands)

	Sept. 1981		Sept. 1984			Sept. 1987			Mar. 1989		
	numbers	%	numbers	%	Change	numbers	%	Change	numbers	%	Change
Banking and finance[a]											
Great Britain	465	2	507	2	+42	574	3	+67	618	3	+44
Greater London	162	5	167	5	+5	198	6	+31	–		–
Insurance											
Great Britain	224	1	223	1	–1	240	1	+17	272	1	+32
Greater London	60	2	59	2	–1	55	2	–4	–		–
Business services[b]											
Great Britain	849	4	1037	5	+188	1271	6	+234	1473	7	+202
Greater London	302	8	354	10	+52	450	13	+96	–		–
Others[c]											
Great Britain	191	1	221	1	+30	224	1	+3	266	1	+42
Greater London	45	1	52	2	+7	51	1	–1	–		–
Total											
Great Britain	1729	8	1988	10	+259	2309	12	+321	2630	12	+321
Greater London	569	16	632	18	+63	753	21	+121	784	22	+31
All industries and services											
Great Britain	21,309		20,846		–463	21,271		+425	22,233		+962
Greater London	3567		3463		–104	3505		+42	3590		+85

[a]There may of course have been second-order employment gains in other sectors (such as the legal profession).
[b]Estimates by the London Chamber of Commerce suggest that employment by foreign banks and securities houses rose by 20,000 over 1984–87, before falling by 2000 in 1988 to stand at 53,000.
[c]Renting of movables and owning and dealing in real estate.
Source: Bank of England Quarterly Bulletin, Nov. 1989, p. 517

Table 5. 'Output' of the financial sector (GDP at factor cost; £s in billions)

	1975	1985	1987	1988
Banking, finance, insurance, business services and leasing (BFIBsL) (including net interest receipts)	10.0	48.5	65.6	76.9
Rest of economy	88.1	273.4	309.3	339.9
Total of above	**98.1**	**321.9**	**374.9**	**416.8**
Total after adjusting for net interest in financial services = GDP	94.7	305.9	355.7	394.6
BFIBsL (including net interest receipts) as a percentage of GDP	10.6	15.9	18.4	19.5
BFIBsL (excluding net interest receipts) as a percentage of GDP	7.2	10.6	13.0	13.9

Source: *Bank of England Quarterly Bulletin*, Nov. 1989, p. 517

insurance, business services and leasing at 2.63 million in March 1989. This was 22 per cent of the working population and represented a 52 per cent increase in numbers since 1981. The figures for Greater London was 784,000, up 30 per cent over eight years, reflecting much additional staffing for Big Bang (table 4). These statistics make it clear that, despite some recent City job losses, employment in finance has grown greatly in the 1980s. The 'output' of the sector has also risen strongly (table 5). By 1988 overseas earnings of the UK financial industry came to £7.4 billion, down from £8.7 billion in 1987 but up on the £6.8 billion of 1985 and only £1 billion in 1975.

One effect of high interest rates has been to diminish the flow of cash-raising stock market issues, compared with the peaks in the 1987 boom when high share prices and modest interest rates allowed companies to issue both shares and bonds on favourable terms. Bank borrowing has played a relatively larger role lately in meeting industrial and commercial companies' external funding needs. For while physical capital investment has remained high, companies' net market issues in 1989 were £7.16 billion, little changed from the £7.18 billion in 1988 and less than half the £15.44 billion in 1987.

The merger trend, seen in other parts of the financial world, has continued to spread in the accountancy world. But this movement in an important professional sector has not been without its problems, partly due to the very international character of the biggest groups concerned. While Ernst & Whinney teamed up in 1989 with Arthur Young to form Ernst & Young, a projected merger of Price Waterhouse and Arthur Andersen was abandoned. And plans for Deloitte Haskins

& Sells to join forces with Touche Ross were superseded when the UK side of Deloitte opted instead to get together with Coopers & Lybrand.

The Watchdog Function – Supervision and Regulation

The stress on regulation which has been notable for some time past in the interests of fairplay for investors and safety for bank depositors remained to the fore in 1989, despite shortcomings revealed in occasional scandals. Britain's own watchdog system has been tightened in the Thatcher years partly to compensate for the extra risks in deregulated markets. Furthermore, international coordination of regulation has lately increased, so that developments in this field increasingly need to be viewed in an international setting.

In banking, where the Bank of England's supervision of banks under the Banking Acts of 1979 and 1987 is now well established, progress was made towards implementation of new international standards aimed at creating a competitive 'level playing field' among banks worldwide. Already, by the end of 1989, the capital adequacy rules of the world agreement in this field, the 'Basle pact' – which among other things requires banks to keep at least minimum capital of 8 per cent assets – were in force for UK-supervised banks. Important progress was also made during the year in the finalization of the European Community's Second Banking Directive, aimed at creating a single open market in banking in the Community after 1992. Under its provisions, banks, once authorized by their home supervisors, will in effect have a 'passport' to operate throughout the 12-nation Community.

The newer and separate, though related, system by which UK investment businesses are surveilled under the Financial Services Act (FSA) 1986 on a basis partly legally-backed and partly self-regulatory evolved further in 1989. The main development was a move towards some easement in the rigour and complications of the watchdog system launched to protect investors in 1988 and operated via the Securities and Investments Board (SIB), a City body to which government powers have been devolved, and its five associated Self-Regulating Organizations (SROs).

This change, worked out under SIB's relatively new chairman, David Walker, a Bank of England director, involves the replacement of controversially complex rulebooks by a new three-tier system of regulation. The top tier will consist of ten general principles, known as 'the Ten Commandments' – including a requirement that financial firms shall 'act with due skill, care and diligence' – which all will be expected to observe. The second tier will consist of 46 more detailed 'designated (or core) rules', which will be legally enforceable. The structure is to be rounded off with a third tier of more detailed guidance from the relevant SRO, partly by way of enforceable rules and partly through a more informal 'highway' code of conduct. Recent legal changes to the FSA, introduced in the Companies Act 1989, leave only certain of the requirements legally enforceable and somewhat restrict investors' powers to sue investment firms.

Meanwhile, sharp criticisms, in a DTI inspectors' report on a cash-raising deal for the Blue Arrow employment services company, of actions by persons within County NatWest, the securities side of National Westminster Bank, and UBS-Phillips & Drew, the securities group owned by Union Bank of Switzerland, led in 1989 to departures from both groups and to subsequent charges against a number of people. The affair concerned the allegedly inadequate disclosure in the autumn of 1987 of certain shareholdings following the rights issue by Blue Arrow in which both companies were involved.

An interim report was also delivered to the DTI, near the end of 1989, by inspectors investigating events at Guinness in connection with that company's takeover of Distillers. A number of people have been charged and were, at the year end, still awaiting trial in connection with this affair.

Chronology

4 Jan: Hoare Govett pulls out of the gilts market and dismisses 135 staff.

6 Jan: Chase Manhattan closes share-dealing in London.

9 Jan: Special sub-committee of the ISE's UK equity market committee reports with recommendations to protect market-makers from further heavy losses and redundancies.

8 Feb: The Queen at a luncheon to celebrate the 800th anniversary of Lord Mayoralty of London emphasizes the need for ethics in the City.

13 Feb: ISE abolishes the obligation on market-makers to deal with each other at the share prices they quote on Seaq.

23 Feb: ISE ends publication of big share deals on Seaq.

6 Mar: Companies involved in the Third Market call for its restructuring.

10 Mar: E.J. Collins, the stockbroking firm, is closed down by the Securities Association.

14 Mar: Significant boost to unit trusts in budget.

17 Mar: National Westminster Bank announces it is to more than double the range of shares available on its instant share dealing service at 260 branches.

3 Apr: ISE recommendations on computerized trading mean the likely disappearance of share certificates in the next three years.

11 Apr: Abbey National shareholders vote to turn the building society into a bank and float it on the stock exchange.

14 Apr: ISE policy document released, heralding a shake-up in trading methods.

19 Apr: Cheque card limits of £100 and £250 to be permitted under new limits. The banking industry is unenthusiastic.

20 Apr: Alliance and Leicester building society to buy National Girobank, privatized by the government, for £130 million.

10 May: ISE opens moves to play a leading role in the setting up of a centralized European equity market.

16 May: Anglo-American agreement over commodity regulations between the US Commodity Futures Trading Commission and the Securities Investment Board.

19 May: Plan for merger between Arthur Young and Ernst & Whinney, which would create the largest professional services/accountancy firm in the world, announced.

22 May: ISE Green Paper sent to security firms outlining proposals, based on the report of the committee chaired by Nigel Elwes, for the reform of the ISE rules. A rival blueprint produced by Touche Ross is also published.

25 May: Bank of Yokohama becomes the first Japanese institution to acquire a British bank when it secures Guinness Mahon, the London merchant bankers.

6 June: Proposed merger between the Institution of Chartered Accountants of England and Wales and its Scottish counterpart is rejected by Scottish accountants.

25 June: Partners in Ernst & Whinney and Arthur Young vote for merger.

26 June: Takeover Panel amends rules on hostile takeover bids.

30 June: James Capel sacks 100 employees.

3 July: All Seaq international market-makers forced to report details of share bargains to ISE.

6 July: Accountancy firms Price Waterhouse and Arthur Andersen announce a proposed merger.
Accountancy firms Deloitte, Haskins & Sells and Touche Ross announce a proposed merger.

7 July: Link-up between the London International Financial Futures Exchange (Liffe) and the London Traded Options Market begins with the sharing of trade-matching systems.

12 July: Abbey National, formerly the second largest building society, makes its stock exchange debut as Britain's fifth biggest bank.

20 July: Damning DTI report into the conduct of County NatWest during the Blue Arrow takeover of Manpower in 1987 published. The Serious Fraud Office and the City of London police launch criminal investigations.

25 July: Lord Boardman, the Chairman of National Westminster Bank, heads the resignations in the wake of the report into the Blue Arrow affair.
Lloyds Bank announce first-half loss of £88 million after making £483 million provision against Third World debt.

1 Aug: Interim profits at National Westminster Bank slide to £352 million after provision against third world debt of £395 million.

2 Aug: Barclays Bank announce interim profits of £590 million after £233 million provision for Third World debt.

3 Aug: Midland Bank announces an interim loss of £531 million after making a £846 million debt provision. At the same time its Chairman, Sir Kit McMahon, attacks the Brady plan to reduce Third World debt which has led to all these massive debt provisions.

4 Aug: Brian Pitman of Lloyds Bank also criticizes the Brady plan.

7 Aug: It is revealed that the Abbey National flotation was more botched than at first appeared and that some 300,000 to 400,000 share certificates worth £50 million were deliberately incinerated.

8 Aug: New draft rulebook of the Securities and Investments Board published.

9 Aug: Bank of England outlines plans to modernize the archaic system of settlements in the sterling money markets.

16 Aug: Standard Chartered Bank report a £48 million first-half loss after a £208 million provision against Third World debt.

17 Aug: Lloyds underwriter Ian Posgate and his colleagues are finally cleared of conspiracy charges.

19 Aug: It is revealed that 500,000 Abbey National share certificates failed to reach investors.

7 Sept: A record 1,760 members quit Lloyds in the previous year, a net outflow.

11 Sept: Accountancy firms Spicer & Oppenheim and Horwath & Horwath announce talks on a possible merger.

Liffe announces the first European Currency Unit interest rate futures contract, to be launched on 26 Oct.

Six months after it was abolished the queueing system for new sterling bond and share issues is restored, differing mainly in now being voluntary rather than compulsory.

13 Sept: Survey by leading central banks shows that the foreign exchange market in London remains easily the biggest in the world.

15 Sept: European exchanges agree to set up the Pipe, a system for storing information on quoted companies, volume of trading and prices.

25 Sept: Police survey shows that more than half the banks and institutions in the City have been subject to fraud worth hundreds of millions of pounds. The true extent of the swindling remains in doubt because about 17 per cent of firms fail to notify the police for fear of adverse publicity. Fraud, particularly computer fraud has increased dramatically in the last ten years.

26 Sept: Price Waterhouse and Arthur Andersen call off their proposed merger.

2 Oct: Australian Mutual Provident launch a £1.1 billion takeover bid for the Pearl Group. Progress report from the ISE committee on the domestic equity markets chaired by Nigel Elwes suggests a revision of market times, a new basis for classifying stocks and the introduction of a facility to enable clients to execute transactions automatically at pre-set prices.

3 Oct: Deloitte, Haskins & Sells call off merger talks with Touche Ross.

4 Oct: Coopers & Lybrand and Deloitte, Haskins & Sells confirm that they are to merge their UK practices to create the UK's largest accountancy firm.

17 Oct: Fears of another October crash averted but the FT-SE index falls 70.5.

24 Oct: New measures designed to stamp out growing abuse in the Lloyds insurance market are introduced.

31 Oct: ISE proposes to abolish the Third Market.

2 Nov: £50 million compensation scheme to help victims of fraud on the Lloyds insurance market to be introduced in 1990.

9 Nov: Bank of England study on the City's success as an international financial centre appears in the *Bank of England Quarterly Bulletin*.

Eleven arrested by the Serious Fraud Office over the 1987 Blue Arrow affair.

Lloyds Bank set aside £1.2 billion and National Westminster £575 million against Third World debts.

21 Nov: TSB announce job cuts of 5,000 over the next five years, with 3,000 to go in the next twelve months.

27 Nov: Deutsche Bank launches a £950 million agreed bid for Morgan Grenfell.

28 Nov: Australian Mutual Provident claims victory in its hostile £1.24 billion takeover bid for Pearl.

Survey by Weatherall, Green and Smith shows city firms expect to increase the number of employees by up to a quarter in the next decade.

30 Nov: Royal Bank of Scotland raises its provisions against Third World bad debt to 97 per cent of medium and long term lending, reducing pre-tax profits by £108.3 million to £228.2 million.

5 Dec: Lloyds Bank announce issue of £100 cheque guarantee cards for selected customers from April 1990.

19 Dec: Government agrees to pay £150 million in compensation to 18,000 investors in the Barlow Clowes investment empire after being accused of mishandling the affair in June 1988 by the Parliamentary Commissioner for Administration, Sir Anthony Barraclough.

22 Dec: EC directive to liberalize insurance industry announced.

28 Dec: GAN of France launches £290 million bid for the insurance company General Portfolio.

Industry's View of the Economic Background

BRENNAN HIORNS

For the men who manage British industry 1989 will be remembered as the year budgets were missed for the first time in many years. It was the year in which politicians' aspirations outran the capacities of both plants and managers in the UK. The costs of the world stock market crash of October 1987 were finally to be reckoned. The response of the G5 politicians to the market crash was to encourage a further expansion of demand especially in the United States. The shock of the market correction, which had probably stemmed from a momentary hesitation in Japanese willingness to continue to buy American debt, engendered fears of recession in the US and thus in the world. In a move to restore confidence interest rates were lowered and money supply loosened. In the UK the Chancellor added to an already buoyant level of demand by making substantial tax cuts in the Budget of 1988. The steady growth in UK economic activity now accelerated in response to the enhanced demand. The ability of UK industry to respond to the heightened and probably unexpected growth in demand was limited and imports rose, export growth fell, and the first signs of a deficit problem appeared. Markets had already started to lose confidence and the demand-led growth in inflation was showing the first signs of translating into a cost push, and more specifically, wage push inflation. In May 1988 the first upward move in base rate occurred, from 7.5 per cent and as currency markets became unstable rates rose to 15 per cent by October 1989. Throughout the summer of 1988 consumers had shown no willingness to cease buying; house prices had, for example, continued to rise and the growth in interest rates was obviously necessary to bring demand under control. Thus, 1989 opened on the paradoxical note that the brakes had plainly been applied to the economy and yet industrialists were expecting record results to come.

There was much optimism at the beginning of 1989 that the slowing of both US and UK economies would be achieved with a 'soft landing', that inflation would be brought under control and exchange rate stability achieved without engendering recession, so that corporate profits would continue to show healthy nominal growth, and that growth would also be real because inflation would be contained. In the US there were signs that problems of capacity constraint and inflation were indeed contained relatively quickly, reflecting the natural resilience and responsiveness of the US economy. For the UK the result was not so happy. The manufacturing component of the economy was only in its first phase of regeneration after the traumatic but necessary closure of so much obsolete and inherently unprofitable capacity in the late 1970s and early 1980s. Productivity had indeed shown major improvement but the surge in demand was too great to be readily satisfied by growth in domestic capacity. The deterioration in the balance of trade had set in 1988 but it was in mid-1989 that financial markets became obsessed with deteriorating revisions by City commentators (the 'teenage scribblers' of Chancellor Lawson's private demonology). Another base rate rise to 15 per cent was necessary and that, together with liberal use of the reserves, ensured that no sterling crisis blighted 1989. The hoped for decline in interest rates, expected in the latter half of 1989 was postponed to 1990. The mid-year obsession with the trade deficit and the consequent extension of the high base rate period lessened the chances of a soft landing but as 1989 turned the year into 1990, the period now thought to be the trough of the economic cycle, the general level of economic activity, unmeasured as yet by the statisticians, had on the basis of an anecdotal report from industry appeared to be generally mixed. Some industries are undoubtedly suffering from lower demand and higher costs but the pattern is by no means universal and current conditions do not amount to recession.

For the industrialist 1989 should have been a year of steady growth, slower than in 1988 but at least offering the prospect of further stable growth in 1990. The interest rate rises of 1988 were probably sufficient to control the level of demand in the economy and to balance demand in line with UK capacity. The balance of trade problems, as they were defined and envisaged by exchange markets in mid-1989 have placed at risk the prospect of stable growth in 1990. In mid-1989 a realistic future view would have implied that the developing trade deficit was an inevitability and that exchange markets should have been aware of that and should have not been unduly obsessed with the matter. Such would have been the probable outcome had not the Prime Minister and Chancellor indulged in a long public debate which neatly focused the thoughts of exchange dealers on the vulnerability of sterling at precisely the wrong moment. The resignation of the Chancellor and the appointment of Mr Major, if only because unanimity then reigned, reduced market emphasis on sterling. The new Chancellor's apparent policy of allowing some weakening in sterling coincided well with the encouraging decline in import growth and increase in exports which was already occurring in response to the high interest rate regime. So to the industrialist, having suffered a year of tribulation from the economic point at least, a modicum of hope appeared in the balance of trade statistics.

1989, Testing the Thatcher Revolution

The year 1989 was the first for some time in which the short term economic influences upon companies have not been universally benign and we do not yet know how well industry has performed during the testing months because companies report their results at a minimum of three months beyond the end of the year. If profit is the main criterion used to judge performance the startling rates of growth shown in the late 1980s will not be repeated, and on previous experience quite severe declines in reported profit should now be expected. But such severe declines in profit are not expected, at least not for the major companies which have stock market quotations. The extent to which the major corporations within the economy do not suffer because of our difficult domestic conditions will be an excellent measure and test of whether the Thatcher years have really resulted in improvement in the underlying performance of the corporate sector. This question can be described in a different way. Economists analysing and forecasting the profit performance for the corporate sector as a whole believe that in 1990 the corporate sector will show no growth at all. Company analysts, whose *raison d'être* is forecasting the profits of companies as individual units, still expect, when their estimates are summed for all large companies, that profits will grow by 10 per cent in 1990. The difference in expectation between the analysts and the economists is also a measure of the efficiency with which British industry has redeployed its assets to protect itself from the economic shortcomings of the UK as a corporate home.

The significance of this can only be understood by reviewing the history of the corporate sector since the coming to power of the first Thatcher government. Prior to that the corporate sector was impoverished by heavy taxation and invested in technically obsolete and dramatically inefficient UK based assets. Protection of one kind or another discouraged investment which, if desired by companies, could not be implemented because of the power of trade unionism. The existence of the investment premium pool prevented free international investment comparison and choice for the managers of companies. Traditional attitudes, the accident of imperial history and belated entry to the Common Market had compounded the internal limitations to ensure that what British investment had been made overseas was in the low growth economies of the Commonwealth.

The high interest rates imposed by the first Thatcher administration cleared up a whole batch of symptoms of the British disease. The closure of inefficient manufacturing plants released large amounts of capital. The control of public spending growth allowed reduction in onerous corporate taxation. The removal of perverting investment allowances improved the process of project evaluation and, of course, changes in labour legislation finally allowed managers to concentrate on competing with foreign companies rather than union oligarchs. The dramatically improved cashflows of the larger companies were directed predominantly overseas to build up local investment in key target markets such as the United States and Europe. The US attracted the lion's share of investment as the biggest and most liberal capitalist market open to UK investors. This process attracted considerable political obloquy but with hindsight it can be seen that the domestic UK economy, for reasons which are not entirely clear, cannot yet sustain a growth rate sufficient to allow the corporate sector to grow at rates comparable to its international competitors. On the ground, presence in the major world economies is essential not simply for corporate survival, but for healthy export growth from the UK to those markets, as well. Any analysis of domestic industrial performance and any prospect of future domestic economic success depend strongly on the skill of British corporate management in making overseas investment.

It is already clear that the financial performance of British companies in 1989 strongly reflects the extent to which they operate overseas. At this stage of the economic cycle in previous downturns those companies involved in basic manufacture would be showing much greater declines in output and profit than is the case. It is those companies involved in servicing domestic demand, the house builders and the retailers who are bearing the brunt of the current downturn.

A preliminary answer to the question posed as to the benefit or not of the Thatcher revolution must be that, although only the early stages of the downturn can yet be observed, for the larger companies in the economy the changes are of benefit.

Hard Times for the Small Man

The option to decide whether to invest in the United States or Germany is hardly open to all companies in the economy. Decisions of that kind are only practically available to the large corporations. A highly satisfying element in the Thatcher revolution has been the renewed development of small companies. Industrial regeneration in the UK cannot come simply from improving the competitiveness of existing large companies, it must also stem from the growth of small companies. After a hesitant start in the early 1980s the small company sector has grown well. But, while the larger corporations have successfully evolved a degree of isolation from the problems of the UK economy, their smaller colleagues have not. It is in this part of the industrial sector that the traditional Darwinian process will exert its sad harvest. The year 1989 has also been a record one for bankruptcies. The smaller company must, by its very nature, concentrate its early development of markets upon the domestic economy and the early years of growth are inevitably extremely demanding in requiring capital. The vulnerability to downturn is thus great.

One of the factors which disturbed equity markets in the course of the year was a *Bank of England Quarterly Bulletin* which reported on the worrying rise in corporate sector deficit. Having moved into surplus during the early 1980s, the sustained period of economic growth which characterized the 1980s has resulted in the development of a substantial corporate deficit as active policies of investment and acquisition have been followed. While the equity market has been used to some extent to finance such operations the main source of capital has been loan stock and, especially if overseas acquisitions have been made, locally denominated loan. This has resulted in very high gearing development and concern is indeed growing in equity markets that even some major companies may overreach themselves and be forced into rights issues. There are good reasons why liquidity crises of the kind which occurred in the 1970s and early 1980s may not develop. The most prominent one must be that companies have become more aware of balance sheet control and extreme gearings have not been generated. Cashflow control has become much more significant as a management tool and companies have placed much greater emphasis on maintaining high interest covers to protect themselves against interest rate and revenue variation. While concern about the liquidity of the big companies has been exaggerated the worrying overall corporate sector liquidity figures reported by the Bank of England describe a real crisis for the small company sector, whether these companies are public or private. The year 1989 showed an increase in bankruptcies, 1990 will probably show even greater failure in this sector.

Industry Experience in 1989 by Industrial Sector

If, as has been argued earlier, 1989 and 1990 taken together will stand as a test of whether British industry is in the early stages of a healthy adaptation, then the various industrial sectors which make up the economy should be showing a diversity of response to the current downturn. That is indeed the experience as it stands at the end of 1989.

Two sectors stand out as suffering the classical symptoms of heavy dependence upon demand levels within the UK economy. The housebuilding cycle responded quickly to the 1988 mortgage rate rise and by 1989 housing starts were 40 per cent down. The companies were able to disguise the downturn by using property profits to bolster 1989 profits but 1990 will not escape and significant profit declines will be reported. The observer of particular sector cycles should note that once again the stock market has acted as a much better guide to reality than the companies themselves and started to discount the building cycle decline in 1988. It is also worth noting that the interest rate mechanism operates upon the general level of demand through the mortgage rate. Mortgage borrowers are perceived as having a greater propensity to spend and mortgage rate increases are thought to be the most efficient means of controlling spending. The building materials companies, where exposed to housebuilding, have suffered the same decline while those material suppliers which are more exposed to infrastructure expenditure, the cement and aggregates suppliers, continue to prosper. Once again those UK companies in the sector which have diversified overseas have weathered the year better than their stay-at-home colleagues.

The other major casualty of the domestic downturn has been the retailing sector. Once the interest mechanism was invoked there was an inevitability that 1989 would be disastrous for retailers but there are interesting elements which compound their problems. The long period of prosperity in the consumer sector has been accompanied by a rearrangement of the major companies under the management of several charismatic retailers but by the late 1980s the shine was tarnishing. The confidence of years of sustained growth has resulted in a measure of over-expansion of capacity. Profits growth had also benefited from strong contribution from realization of property profits, accruing as a result of the active realignment of retailing outlets. All of these elements combined to give the retailing sector a very poor year. At the moment retailing is the only sector where the problems now encountered may have implications for the structure of the industry running well beyond the current cyclical downturn.

There is a middle ground of sectors where the companies cannot escape the problems of the domestic cycle but where the apparently modest nature of the downturn seems not to be causing severe damage. Food retailing and food manufacturing, hotels, and breweries all seem to fall in this category. For all of these, if there are significant matters, they lie outside the immediate domestic economic cycle. The TV industry was beginning to suffer a sharp downturn in advertising revenue towards the end of the year, when growth was static. Normally, advertising revenue runs at double the rate of inflation. The industry also suffered a 40 per cent increase in Exchequer Levy during the year. Their franchises will come up for the competitive reapplication in 1992 and so the corporate struc ture of the industry is hardly a stable one.

The brewers have had a remarkably good year and this is nothing to do with the state of demand. The *Monopolies and Mergers Report* published in March contained recommendations which, if implemented, would have radically changed the industry. The major brewers would have had to divest themselves of their tied houses and hence lost the element of price control which they possess. It has been impressive to see the display of lobbying power and influence which has substantially muted the recommendations so that the essentially powerful position of the big brewers has been preserved. Although the brewers have won a famous victory it has still encouraged them to evaluate long term corporate strategies, and active policies of either acquisition or investment are under way. Trading was good in 1989 and the traditional relationship of brewing prosperity to the domestic cycle, so savagely illustrated in the 1970s and early 1980s may now have been broken down, illustrating the success of their managements' strategic decisions then taken. An important sub- sector, whisky distilling, has also shown remarkable recovery from the disasters of ten years ago and, it too, appears to have traded well through the year.

The pharmaceutical industry illustrates almost perfectly the point that to perform well the UK must have only a minimal role as the market for a company's products. Eighty per cent of the sector's profits continue to be derived from overseas and profit has grown, and is expected to continue to grow well in excess of inflation. With strong cashflow and a continuing record of scientific discovery which is turned into product and sales, pharmaceuticals is a model for the rest of industry. The Beechams Smith Kline merger represents a major change in the structure of the UK industry.

The chemical industry is also one which traditionally has suffered major reverse on a domestic decline. Our sole true multinational bulk chemical producer, ICI, recognized its extreme vulnerability 20 years ago and has been diversifying both by product and market ever since. As the industrial cycles have passed by so the relative volatility of ICI's profits has reduced. The year 1989 illustates the problems which a geographically well diversified company will encounter. Having escaped the strait-jacket of the UK, the international slowdown was developing and so after an impressive first-half performance, the international chemical cycle is causing problems in spite of the years of careful diversification.

For defence contractors, and this includes much of the electronics industry, 1989 will be remembered as the year of perestroika. The sudden change in political and military confrontation in central Europe came as the unpleasant culmination to a period in which defence spending in the UK had been growing less rapidly anyway so that profit performance in 1989 was already suffering. A period of radical change is under-way as conglomerization of European companies takes place to reflect the imbalance of European capacity against European demand, for the extreme cost of defence projects has overcome some of the nationalistic attitude to defence expenditure. Plessy was taken over by GEC and Siemens; Thomson CSF acquired the defence operations of Phillips and Ferranti ended the year a potential bid victim, weakened by the disastrous acquisition it had made in America. The electronics sector more than any other shows that the development of pan-European companies is already occurring and that British companies do not necessarily compare well with their European comparatives. We must then expect that many traditional names will disappear within anonymous European conglomerates.

The reduction in European military confrontation, whilst unlikely to result in extremely rapid force reduction, is now seen as a process which will genuinely reduce demand for weapons in the long term. This represents a quite distinct change in outlook for the defence contractors and will hasten the development of European conglomerates.

The telephone networks sector, essentially British Telecom (BT) and Cable and Wireless, performed well in 1989. BT itself acquired a major holding in McCaw, a North American company and so began the process of diversification away from the home base. Cable and Wireless is reversing the process and just starting to gain return from its major investment in Mercury. If the privatization process is ever questioned then the development of these two great corporations exemplifies its benefits.

It is in the engineering sector that a microcosm of the United Kingdom's opportunities is observed. The fortunes of any individual company depend on exposure to the various elements of the engineering cycle. Not surprisingly domestically orientated companies supplying the building sector picked up the effects of the interest rate rise in early 1989. The initial reports were of cost pressure rather than volume problems but by the end of the year both were influencing profit. The automobile cycle has now become a European rather than a domestic one and it held up well until late in 1989 when a general downturn appeared. The UK automotive industry is now starting to benefit from the presence of Japanese investment. Nissan's plant is approaching significant levels of output, Toyota commence construction of their plant in 1990 and Honda are also close to beginning construction. The aerospace sector will seemingly avoid any weakness because of the heavy demand from world airline fleets and 1989 will have been a strong year for them. Those manufacturers supplying capital goods for the investment cycle have also experienced a rewarding year and they can look forward with more than usual confidence because the privatization of the water supply and electricity distribution and supply industries will extend the normal life of the cycle. The water industry alone will need to spend £20 billion at current prices over a ten-year time span.

The engineering sector has made considerable gains in productivity, though the improved record for labour relations was marred in 1989 with the claim by the workforce for a 35-hour week. The international competitiveness of our basic manufacturing industries must ultimately improve to sustain a viable economy when the massive balance of trade benefits of North Sea oil run out. There remain massive productivity benefits to be gained but the industry will not grow within the UK if the gains made are pre-empted by the workforce. The outcome to this particular pay and conditions negotiation is crucial.

For the oil industry 1989 saw several accidents with the Brent System which supplies about 25 per cent of the UK's oil, and it was shut down for a period early in the year after an explosion. The Piper tragedy of 1988 had already set in train a safety review. Fulmar and Clyde were among other oil fields which suffered accidents. North Sea output reached the lowest levels of output since 1979 during the summer. This occurred at a damaging time from the balance of trade point of view. But as output recovered towards the end of the year the rise in world crude oil price aided the trade figures.

The series of accidents which affected the UK industry were repeated worldwide and the cost of this was added to the cost of increased interest in environmental protection so that petrol prices surged for UK customers towards the end of 1989. In the UK, changes in the tax regime resulted in unleaded petrol rising from a market share of 20 per cent to nearly 25 per cent by the year end.

For the companies and sectors which compose British industry, 1989 has been a generally successful, if very uncertain, year. It was the first year for a long time in which out-turn was not necessarily better than budget and it was a year in which few companies escaped a serious problem in at least one operation. Most boards will feel that the work done and the risk acquired in making acquisitions and overseas investments has improved corporate stability and the slowing in UK activity confirms the need to continue to invest overseas.

The high level of demand in the economy will not necessarily have been a blessing and foreign exporters of goods to the UK have been the main beneficiaries. The year 1990 will bring the price to be paid for Nigel Lawson's miscalculation.

Longer Term Influences which Appeared During the Year

Having already returned British Telecom, British Petroleum and British Gas to the private sector, the government added the water industry to the stock market in November 1989. The flotation was much more successful than most commentators would have thought even weeks before the flotation. The issue was floated on a valuation based powerfully on yield and the issue was undoubtedly a pathfinder in front of the enormous electricity industry flotation scheduled for commencement in 1990. The issue was strongly influenced in the early weeks of the stock market trading by the appearance of French water companies as acquirers of strategic stakes, repeating the pattern of acquisition which they had already shown in buying strong stakes in the old water companies.

The privatization of the electricity industry could well have a radical effect on British industry. The development of British industry has, for a generation, suffered severely from the high degree of intervention by government in the pricing of energy. Coal prices have been kept at artificially high levels and the coal mining industry has been preserved in an uncompetitive and obsolete form. It has the potential to compete if its markets are subject to competitive pressure. The generation sector has also pursued technical options which, under conditions of competition, would be revealed rapidly as misguided. The withdrawal of nuclear power generation from flotation was a revelation not only to the public but to government itself as to the true cost of nuclear power. To create an electrical energy supply industry which provides electricity prices based on market competition was revealed in 1989 as extremely complex. If government can achieve this then British industry will possess a firm basis for long term confidence even if the initial years of change will be difficult ones for those companies that have, in effect, received subsidized power.

'Greenism' received major political support when Mrs Thatcher adopted it as a political tenet. The cost base of industry will rise significantly in future years as a result of public concern with the variety of issues which will emerge. Already power generation will be severely affected as flue gas desulphurization becomes a requirement. The cost of water investment has probably been doubled by the EC directives covering clean and waste water. The real change which has emerged for industry in the past few years is that not only must it respond to the opinion of its national public but to public opinion across whole continents.

Never have the forces upon British companies been so great to build their futures outside the domestic economy. The '1992' legislation is, in reality, only an emphasis by the EC authorities to bring home to European companies that major processes of trans-European conglomerization are underway. British and European companies continued to make acquisitions in the other's territory in 1989, all part of the course of European integration. Were it not for the active use of stock markets as part of this it is likely that the value of companies would be lower. The liberal nature of the UK stock market makes British companies particularly vulnerable as targets.

This is especially so since many industrialists feel that British companies which have market quotations suffer from the 'short term' attitudes of British investors. In essence the emphasis placed by investors on profits to be reported in the next six or twelve months, with the inference that shares will be bought or sold upon this basis, means that British companies cannot confidently invest in projects which require four or five years to reach profitable maturity. A continental company, and especially a German or Japanese company would, because of the different capital structure, receive the support of its investors with greater certainty through this difficult period. This debate has yet to be satisfactorily resolved, and its resolution must encompass answers which determine the long term progress of industry in the UK.

Chronology

3 Jan: Announcement that the Loan Guarantee Scheme (which helps entrepreneurs to borrow money), due to expire in March, is to be extended and the maximum guaranteed loan to be raised from £75,000 to £100,000.

BP announce the sale of BP Minerals to RTZ for £2.4 billion in the largest ever deal between two British companies.

12 Jan: MMC and the competition authorities in Brussels announce investigation into the GEC/Siemens bid for Plessey.

19 Jan: Attempt by the Metsun consortium to launch a bid for GEC fails.

2 Feb: MMC clears Minorco's bid for Consolidated Gold Fields.

20 Feb: Minorco renew bid for Cons. Gold. The bid of £3.2 billion was then the biggest ever for a UK company.

27 Feb: Government writes off £390 million of debt at Shorts, the Northern Ireland arms and aerospace firm, in preparation for privatization.

6 Mar: Government launches £1.3 million research programme to investigate Britain's failure to exploit its science and technology base for competitive advantage.

8 Mar: MMC report *Elders IXL Ltd and Scottish and Newcastle Breweries PLC: A Report on the Merger Situations* published.

9 Mar: Lord Young rejects the recommendations of the Commons trade and industry select committee's December report calling for a coherent policy on information technology. In a new White Paper he instead argues that 'the emphasis must be on market forces'.

10 Mar: Fifteen per cent foreign shareholding in British Aerospace breached, presenting the government with the choice of either forcing share selling or raising the limit.

13 Mar: Thorn-EMI announce the sale of Inmos, the manufacturer of the revolutionary transputer, to the Franco-Italian SGS Thomson.

15 Mar: Government confirms there will be no launch aid for Rolls Royce's RB211-524L engine.

16 Mar: NEDO report criticizes the government's lack of direction in technology policy.

Sir Leon Brittan, European Commissioner for competition policy, launches an investigation into the European beer industry.

21 Mar: MMC report labels the Big Six brewers as monopolistic and anti-competition. It recommends that no brewery should own more than 2,000 tied public houses and insists

on a greater choice of brews.

Lord Young on the recommendations of the MMC, blocks the bid from the Australian brewer, Elders IXL, for Scottish and Newcastle and orders it to reduce its shareholding.

22 Mar: US court victories for Cons. Gold set back Minorco's bid prospects.

Government support worth £500 million for a management and employee buy-out at Harland & Woolf's Belfast shipyards announced.

23 Mar: Commons trade and industry committee on information technology demands explanation from the government for its recent 'negative' White Paper.

1 Apr: Announcement that Beecham and the US company Smith Kline Beckman are discussing a merger which would create one of the largest pharmaceutical companies in the world.

6 Apr: Inmos is to be at the heart of the Jessi programme to develop a European family of microprocessors SGS Thomson announce.

10 Apr: Minorco increases its offer for Cons. Gold.

12 Apr: Beecham/Smith Kline Beckman merger unveiled.

13 Apr: GEC and US company General Electric announce that they have completed arrangements to merge their European interests.

18 Apr: Toyota announce plans for a £700 million car plant in Burnaston, near Derby.

19 Apr: GEC/Siemens bid for Plessey cleared by the EC Commission.

20 Apr: A record number of Queen's Awards to Industry (116 for export and 40 for technology) are distributed.

21 Apr: GEC/Siemens bid for Plessey cleared by MMC.

22 Apr: Study shows that foreign brewers are waiting to carve up the British industry in the wake of the MMC report.

24 Apr: Rank Hovis MacDougall launches a £1.34 billion bid for the Australian Goodman Fielder Wattie.

26 Apr: Minorco secures 54.8 per cent of the shares in Cons. Gold.

Announcement that the government is to spend £22 million on information technology initiatives fails to satify the Commons trade and industry committee who remain very concerned about Young's non-committal White Paper and Britain's £2.5 billion deficit in IT.

Intrum, Europe's biggest commercial debt-recovery group claims that British businesses lose as much as £20 billion of business each year because of sloppy debt-recovery procedures.

1 May: WPP launches bid for Ogilvy in an attempt to become the second largest advertising agency in the world.

12 May: Tootal agrees to a £395 million bid from Coats Viyella.

16 May: Minorco withdraws from its £3.5 billion bid for Cons. Gold after a New York judge upheld an injunction blocking the takeover.

19 May: Ogilvy agrees to a takeover by WPP.

24 May: RHM bid for Goodman Fielder Wattie lapses.

30 May: Courtaulds win first annual Design Effectiveness Award.

Oxford Economic Forecasting predicts manufacturing growth will outstrip that of services in the 1990s.

31 May: CBI conference highlights lack of British preparedness for the rise of the Green consumer.

9 June: Joint European Submicron Silicon Project (JESSI) gets the support of the EC Commission.

12 June: Hanson launches a £3.1 billion bid for Cons. Gold.

14 June: Lord Young begins to back down in his confrontation with the brewers.

27 June: Coats Viyella's £395 million bid for Tootal referred to the MMC.

4 July: Cons. Gold accepts revised offer from Hanson.

Report says British firms lag behind major overseas rivals in attitudes to research and development and to high technology.

10 July: Lord Young further complicates situation in the brewing industry by announcing a review of the licensing system.

Merger planned between Cambridge Instruments and Wild Leitz of Switzerland, to make the world's largest optical equipment group.

11 July: Sir James Goldsmith's Hoylake Investments makes £13.4 billion takeover bid for BAT industries.

13 July: Honda announces it is to take a 20 per cent stake in Rover and build a £300 million plant at Swindon.

Announcement that the Co-operative Development Agency is to be wound up in 1990/91.

Unilever revives bid for Elizabeth Arden and Faberge which was allowed to lapse on 28 April.

18 July: Government announces fresh legislation to outlaw cartels and anti-competitive agreements throughout business and the professions.

22 July: Mrs Thatcher criticizes huge increases in salaries for leading figures in industry.

27 July: Newly merged Smith Kline Beecham makes its stock market debut.

31 July: Sir Leon Brittan says he aims to set up one-stop merger control in the EEC in 1990.

1 Aug: A new law to modernize copyright protection, establish a new industrial design right and combat privacy comes into force under the Copyright, Designs and Patents Act 1989.

3 Aug: Lifting of restrictions on foreign shareholding in Rolls Royce and British Aerospace from 15–29.5 per cent.

GEC/Siemens relaunch £2 billion bid for Plessey.

7 Aug: Hanson claims victory in the battle for Cons. Gold.

14 Aug: Reports of a confidential dossier by the Health and Safety Executive which condemns 'inappropriately low' fines imposed by magistrates on firms breaking safety regulations.

21 Aug: CBI launches new survey into research and development efforts by British companies.

25 Aug: Serious Fraud Office begins an inquiry into the troubled industrial holdings group Eagle Trust.

30 Aug: British Aerospace becomes the first non-American firm to supply the Japan air self-defence force.

13 Sept: Fears of a takeover bid at Jaguar as interim profits slashed to £1.4 million are announced.

4 Sept: European group of chemical companies set up an advisory group headed by Peter Doyle of ICI to fight EC proposals for approving drugs and other chemicals.

7 Sept: Survey of heads of company research departments points to Britain's poor record in supporting or financing technological innovation.

8 Sept: GEC/Siemens finally clinch their bid for Plessey.

11 Sept: BP withdraws its 49 per cent in the huge Olympic Dam mine in South Australia from its sale of BP Minerals to RTZ.

Trading in Ferranti shares suspended over an inquiry into its accounts.

15 Sept: Independent accountants called in to investigate 'significant irregularities' in overseas contracts at Ferranti.

BAT Industries appeals against the Takeover Panel's decision to allow Hoylake's £13.5 billion bid to lapse.

16 Sept: Ferranti says it was a victim of a major fraud when it took over the US company ISC two years ago.

19 Sept: Ford applies for leave to acquire 15 per cent of troubled car maker, Jaguar.

20 Sept: RTZ sells its chemicals division to the French company Rhone-Poulenc for £568 million.

21 Sept: Lines of credit for Ferranti agreed, offering it some respite.

Mrs Thatcher gives her backing to Ford taking 15 per cent stake in Jaguar.

Nicholas Ridley decides not to refer the Hoylake bid for BATs to the MMC.

26 Sept: Announcement of restructuring at BATs fails to end Hoylake's predatory attentions.

16 Oct: British Aerospace is to merge its missiles business with that of CSF-Thomson, forming Europe's largest guided missiles weapons contractor. The new company, jointly owned by its parents, is to be called Eurodynamics.

19 Oct: Admission in the Commons that nearly one- fifth of factories and places of work have not been inspected for five years or more.

20 Oct: Fraud investigations launched into Ferranti's takeover of ISC in 1987.

27 Oct: Polly Peck becomes the first foreign company to take control of a Japanese listed company after rescuing troubled hi-fi manufacturer Sansui through taking a 51 per cent stake in a £68.7 million deal.

30 Oct: Courtaulds announce plans to demerge its chemicals and textiles operations into two separately quoted companies.

31 Oct: Government drops its veto on bids for Jaguar, clearing the way for a takeover battle between the American giants Ford and General Motors.

2 Nov: Ford acquire Jaguar in a £1.6 billion deal.

24 Nov: *Barriers to Takeovers in the EC*, HMSO, a report for the DTI by Coopers and Lybrand, draws attention to widespread variations in company law and to differences in corporate culture in the rest of the EC as barriers to attempts by British companies to expand by continental takeovers. It also points to the relative vulnerability of UK companies.

28 Nov: National Audit Office report on the sale of Rover to British Aerospace in 1988 condemns the government's conduct of the sale.

30 Nov: Government admits withholding details of the £38 million inducement package used to clinch the sale of Rover to British Aerospace.

Ferranti issue writs for fraud totalling £126 million over the ISC takeover in 1987.

1 Dec: Landlord and Tenant Bill, the first part of the reform of the brewing industry, introduced in Parliament.

5 Dec: Sir Leon Brittan confirms that there is to be an EC Commission investigation into the government's deal with British Aerospace over Rover.

6 Dec: EC strategy for the European car market after 1992 is unveiled.

13 Dec: Mr Ridley describes golden shares as undesirable to the Commons trade and industry select committee.

18 Dec: Fisons pay £272 million for BATs industries' controlling stake in VG Instruments.

20 Dec: Tootal and Coats Viyella merger called off.

21 Dec: EC Commission to be given exclusive responsibility for vetting mergers with EC-wide implications between corporations with world turnover of at least £3.5 billion.

22 Dec: Allied-Lyons pays £545 million for Whitbread's wines and spirits operation.

Blue Circle pays £197.5 million for Myson, which had just been cleared for takeover by the MMC on 21 Dec.

British Steel's £330 million bid for C. Walker and Sons referred to the Monopolies Commission.

Energy Policy

NEIL WALDEN

Britain has no energy policy. Government actions in this field have been the result of other policies, for example, the preference for privately owned industries, the desire to reduce public expenditure, and the determination to reduce the power of the coal miners. These explain the attempted privatization of electricity supply, the reduction in energy efficiency budgets and the determination to ensure a future for nuclear power.

During the Second World War, the energy industries came under close public control. The immediate post-war Labour government saw the coal, electricity and gas industries as the 'commanding heights' of the economy that it was essential to nationalize. Unfortunately, this was seen as a sufficient solution in itself, and left many of the industries' problems unresolved. Massive expansion of energy consumption and production occurred: the nuclear power programme being publicly announced by the Conservative government in 1955 and expanded as a result of the 1956 Suez crisis. The 1960s 'white hot heat of the technological revolution' Labour government continued this expansion, and the role of the nuclear industry was enhanced further as a result of the 1973 oil crisis.

Mrs Thatcher therefore inherited an expensive and expanding nuclear industry, and saw it as her main weapon against the power of coal-mining trade unionists. Since the defeat of the miners' strike of 1984–5, government energy plans have been dominated by nuclear power, despite wide and increasing opposition. Now, simply by exposing the nuclear industry to the private market, the government has been forced to recognize at last the real costs.

Throughout the post-war period, excessive resources have been focused on energy supply, and frequently the management of these resources has been poor. Now there is the opportunity to focus policy on the real needs of consumers, ensuring energy is used efficiently and produced with acceptable environmental impact. The events of 1989, however, were mainly irrelevant to this.

The Privatization of the Electricity Industry

The year 1989 saw many changes on the energy scene, and much government activity – particularly with regard to the processes involved in privatizing the electricity industry. Privatization of the whole industry proved impossible, as many commentators had forecast, and the last day of Parliament before the summer recess saw Cecil Parkinson, in one of his last duties as Energy Secretary, announce that the oldest nuclear reactors (the Magnox stations) would be excluded from the sale and remain in the public sector. In November, his successor, John Wakeham, announced that the remaining nuclear stations (the AGRs and the still incomplete Sizewell B PWR) would also not be sold. These two announcements removed the whole basis of the design of the privatization package, turning what had been highly contentious legislation into farce.

By November, Walter Patterson, a long-standing and effective critic of policies, was referring to the electricity privatization package as 'a misshapen clump of incoherent notions masquerading as a policy'.

The current electricity privatization proposal has no clear objectives. At the end of 1989, it was clearly neither going to get rid of the whole industry to the private sector nor solve the nuclear sector's financial problems. It is the most complicated piece of privatization the government has yet attempted, and apart from the water industry, probably the least sensible. Electricity, unlike water, cannot be stored in large quantities, and has to be supplied instantly. Security of supply is therefore essential, and it is not clear how this can be guaranteed by private suppliers. It is interesting to note that the consumer, who is supposed to be the person benefiting from all this, was never consulted.

The privatization legislation introduced the concept of a non-fossil fuel obligation (N-FFO), specifically framed to protect nuclear power. This was originally set at a level which meant that both Sizewell B and Hinckley C would be required. However, at the year end, with both the projects in doubt, the N-FFO was itself under revision.

What will happen to the British nuclear power station is, at the time of writing, anyone's guess. In the United States, conversion of nuclear power stations to other fuels has already happened. The Consumers Power Company plant in Michigan has been converted to gas firing, and the Zimmer plant near Cincinatti to coal. Left to market forces, we should see such conversions taking place in Britain, with resulting lower generation costs and higher energy efficiencies. However, we have yet to see what decisions are made by government on the British nuclear stations.

On a lighter note, but showing how the unexpected can affect energy policy, the dry hot summer led to problems with both nuclear and coal stations – lack of water for cooling resulted in a cut in the supply of French electricity to Britain and the Drax station cooling towers emitting vapour contaminated with sewage.

The Nuclear Component

There was very little good news on the nuclear front in 1989. The high point was probably in March, when Professors Pons and Fleischmann announced 'cold fusion' to the world. A vision of cheap, limitless energy opened up – a quicker way of replicating the power of the sun than the energy-intensive TORUS technology of the European JET fusion project, which after expenditure of hundreds of millions and over 20 years is still at least that far away from commercial energy production. At least one university vice-chancellor thought cold fusion would revolutionize energy supply, but a team from the United Kingdom Atomic Energy Authority Harwell laboratories spent three months and £0.33 million pounds trying to replicate the results, and found nothing.

Bad news during the year included the continuing restrictions on lamb production as a result of the Chernobyl accident, more than three years after the event. This compares with the government statement four days after the cloud of radioactive fallout reached the UK, that levels were nowhere near those at which there was any health hazard, and that it was perfectly safe to drink tap water and milk. Since then, it has been estimated that over 150 people in the UK will die of cancer as a result of Chernobyl, and that half of the radiation dose was from contaminated milk.

A number of families living in the Sellafield area began proceedings against British Nuclear Fuels in June over the abnormally high incidence of childhood leukaemia. In the same month, it was confirmed that about 500 of the workers at Sellafield are still being exposed to radiation doses above the recommended limit, in spite of new evidence that this is three times more likely to cause cancer than previously thought.

Sellafield is one of the few major employers in rural Cumbria, and the same is true of Dounreay in Caithness. In October, Malcolm Rifkind, the Scottish Secretary, gave permission for a plutonium reprocessing plant to be built at Dounreay, sweeping aside half of the conditions recommended by the public inquiry reporter. However, although permission was given, funding was not. This plant is tied in with the proposals for a European demonstration fast breeder reactor, which many commentators now see as unlikely to be built. So far £3.2 billion has been spent on British fast breeder reactor research. Whether the Dounreay plant will ever be built, and if so whether it will ever be needed, are unclear.

What is needed is some sensible plan for dealing with nuclear waste; this remains the achilles heel of the nuclear industry. In Caithness also proposals for a waste storage site were rejected decisively by local people in the autumn, much to the concern of NIREX, the government body in charge of waste disposal. This left only the reactor sites themselves as possible locations, and these may not be geologically acceptable.

Energy Efficiency

Recent evidence of global climate changes and ozone depletion over the Antarctic and Arctic clearly indicate the need to move away from our current wasteful and messy use of energy. As the first industrialized nation, Britain has a particular responsibility and still uses many long-out-of-date technologies.

The Prime Minister claims to be concerned about these issues, and to be leading the world, but the evidence – despite high-profile statements such as her address to the United Nations – is, in fact, that she is holding back international efforts to address the situation.

If one compares government action to save energy in 1989 with the 'Save It' campaign of the mid-1970s, itself criticized as half-hearted, it can be seen how low a priority this issue is given. Increasingly, however, there is evidence that the technologies exist to reduce energy consumption dramatically without decreasing comfort or the quality of life. In fact many of the new energy-efficient technologies offer other advantages. Recent developments have been spectacular. As Amory Lovins, a US energy specialist puts it 'You can save twice as much electricity as five years ago, at one third of the cost: it has rocketed sixfold in cost effectiveness.'

Intelligent office buildings like the DCI group's Northgate building in Cowcaddens, Glasgow can achieve phenomenal savings – up to 80 per cent on lighting and around 50 per cent on heating and ventilation - though, of course, building costs are on average a third higher. Such buildings use both simple design concepts, such as restricting width to ensure the building is mainly lit by natural light, and advanced technology, for example, glass tech nology to prevent excessive solar gain and infrared movement sensors to sense when rooms are occupied.

There are other examples which show what can be achieved. Sainsbury's supermarket stores use only 60 per cent of the energy of those built 10 years ago; Safeway halved the number of lighting tubes and installed energy efficient lamps saving £360,000 per annum; the Co-op reduced head office electricity consumption by 21 per cent. Proctor and Gamble reduced energy use by 38 per cent between 1976 and 1986 as production volume rose by 50 per cent. Currently available technologies could enable other firms and householders to achieve similarly dramatic savings.

The problem so far in Britain has been a lack of initial demand sufficient to bring about the mass availability of such energy-efficient devices, particularly to the domestic market. One example is the 11-watt light bulb giving the equivalent output of a 60-watt bulb and lasting 13 times as long. These were introduced to the Brit ish market at a high price, had low sales, and are now often difficult to find. The result is that sensible technologies are not being adopted. This will only be overcome, in the short term, by government action to encourage people to switch.

The situation can be compared to that of unleaded petrol – for which there was said to be virtually no demand before the government reduced the tax level relative to leaded petrol and which thereafter accounted for more than a quarter of the market within a matter of months. This clearly demonstrates how sensible policies can encourage consumers to make more efficient purchases that benefit us all.

Energy saving needs to be seen to be as important as the removal of lead from the atmosphere, and will similarly require government action. At the end of 1989 there was no sign that it was yet on the government's agenda, even though John Wakeham, the Energy Secretary, himself described energy conservation as the single most effective way of cutting carbon dioxide emissions. In April 1989 the funding available for promoting energy efficiency was reduced from the 1987 figure of £26 million to £15 million for 1989 and £12 million for 1990.

What is required is political will at Cabinet level. The issues are well understood by energy specialists and the relevant civil servants, as this example will make clear. In the first issue of the restyled *Energy Management*, the Department of Energy's journal, April 1988, the most comprehensive 'energy audit' of any region of the UK was reported, showing that a likely 24 per cent increase in energy demand in North West England could be limited to 3 per cent, despite the anticipated growth of 30 per cent in Gross Domestic Product over the period. Robert Bailey of March Consulting Group pointed out that 'over and over again the message is the same, we are still wasting energy on a prodigious scale. It may not be very glamorous to conclude that implementing existing technologies more widely should remain a priority but it underlines the opportunities we have been missing. The study proves that the savings are indisputable, the return on invest ment assured and that action is already long overdue.'

Regrettably, little had changed at the end of 1989. On 20 November, Friends of the Earth published a study using the Energy Efficiency Office's own figures to demonstrate that the use of energy could be cut by 20 per cent a year if a £3.8 billion programme was undertaken. This contrasts with the government's predictions of what is likely to happen otherwise: a 73 per cent increase in carbon dioxide emissions in the next 30 years given a continuation of present policies. It will be interesting to see whether serious action on improving energy efficiency is taken during 1990.

Hopeful Pointers

Against this background, there were a few hopeful signs of movement towards more sensible policies: they came not from the government, but from individual utilities. In April, British Coal announced that 'the first of a new generation of Britain's privately-owned, coal-fired, mini-power stations' had been commissioned by Slough Estates, the country's largest industrial estate operator. It will use a fluidized bed combustion system that produces fewer pollutants and less carbon dioxide than conventional coal-burning technology, and will have an overall efficiency of 85 per cent as a result of using waste steam to heat local premises. While this is welcome news, it must be remembered that there have been calls for the introduction of such technology for at least a decade, and that countries such as Denmark have had such combined-heat-and-power installations for many years.

The four northern electricity boards in England, NORWEB, MANWEB, NEEB and Yorkshire Electricity have been examining the economic potential of renewable sources of energy. Some small-scale local schemes have already been implemented, and there is clearly much potential, probably initially in the extraction of energy from waste, but in the longer term also from wind, wave and tidal power. Solar energy can also contribute, even in the northern parts of Brit ain. British Telecom is using solar panels to provide power for some of its rural telephone boxes, and in November the University of Strathclyde opened its first halls of residence heated by solar energy, designed to provide comfortable conditions in the Glasgow climate yet require additional energy input on only four days a year.

What is clear is that sensible technologies can be developed, given the political will. A major question for 1990 will be whether the government gives the required attention to setting and achieving appropriate targets for reducing energy consumption and increasing energy efficiency. The Consumers Association calculated that if everyone bought the most efficient appliance rather than the worst, in the year 2001 (now only 11 years away) the difference would account for all electricity produced by our two largest power stations. Of course, to make such informed choices, consumers require accurate labelling of products' energy consumption. This we may begin to see in 1990, possibly because of the run-up to the 1992 harmonization of European community markets, if not for reasons of domestic energy policy.

Least Cost Planning

In July, the government rejected a House of Lords amendment to the Electricity Bill that would have given the post-privatization regulatory body the power to force companies to conserve energy. The amendment was an attempt to introduce least cost energy planning to the UK, and although not yet adopted in this country, this technique has proved its worth overseas and is likely to be implemented here sooner or later. Least cost planning involves viewing demand not as given, but as a variable which can be reduced by investment in energy management programmes. The most sensible mix of demand and supply technologies is then determined by assessing the relative costs of each, and going for the least cost solution. Such an approach has proved its worth in Scandinavia and the USA – Oslo City Light have succeeded in improving energy efficiency exactly in line with their predictions, and according to Commissioner Duda of the Public Utility of California, 'It has saved billions of dollars for California and increased competition in electricity generation.' Least cost planning ought, therefore, to be attractive to the current British government, which itself now admits energy efficient technologies are cheaper than PWR nuclear power stations. Time will tell whether we move to such a rational method of determining the optimal mix of generating capacity and conservation for a given level of energy service.

Energy in Transport

Attention to the 'greenhouse effect' of global warming increased as the year progressed, with environmentalists criticizing the government's lack of concern over the role played by road transport – the 'car' in carbon dioxide, as Walter Patterson labelled it. A quarter of the energy used in Britain is for transport, and on current trends car mileage is expected to increase dramatically over the next decade. In November Chris Patten, the Environment Secretary, responded in a speech to the CBI conference. Referring to forthcoming European Community standards for reduced car emissions, he acknowledged that these benefits would be lost if, at the same time, there was a great increase of vehicles on the roads, 'so we are obviously going to have to look at the future of transport'.

In the Autumn statement, however, John Major, the Chancellor of the Exchequer, had announced a massive increase in funds for road building. How transport policy develops in 1990 with respect to energy implications will be worth watching. It is likely that there will have to be major changes in either the design of car engines or the way in which cars are used.

The Way Forward

As 1989 drew to a close, it appeared that the construction of Sizewell B would continue, and that permission for construction of Hinkley C would still be sought. This despite estimates that electricity from such PWR stations would cost more than three times the alternatives, and would reduce carbon dioxide emissions only a third as much as energy efficiency measures. Sizewell B, it was claimed, would cost the taxpayer £1 million for every day of its 35 year planned life. The *Observer* called for its abandonment, saying 'Had the truth been told long ago, Britain's energy policy would not now lie in ruins . . . The country should construct an energy policy based on the real world, rather than a nuclear fantasy.' What is needed is an integrated policy across all fuels. The Commons Select Committee on Energy rightly called for a 'vital' separate Department of State where the sole concern is energy policy: 'However important issues like the privatization of the gas and electricity industry, or the support for the coal industry have been, they are dwarfed by the crucial importance that we have a coherent policy applied across all sectors to deal with problems which almost certainly lie ahead.'

As the industries turn from being product-led to focusing on the real needs of their consumers, the changes are likely to be profound. British Gas has taken some tentative steps in this direction, mailing a questionnaire to all its 17 million

Table 1. Inland consumption of primary fuels and equivalents for energy use (in millions tonnes of coal or coal equivalent)

	1984	1985	1986	1987	1988
Coal	79.0	105.3	113.5	116.2	112.0
Petroleum	135.2	115.0	112.6	109.3	116.1
Natural gas	76.5	82.3	83.6	85.9	81.5
Nuclear electricity	19.5	22.1	21.3	19.8	22.9
Hydro electricity	2.1	2.1	2.4	2.1	2.4
Net electricity imports	–	–	1.7	4.7	5.2
Total	312.2	326.9	335.2	338.1	340.1

Source: *Digest of United Kingdom Energy Statistics 1989* HMSO, Norwich, 1989

customers. There has, however, been much disappointment at the very limited interpretation British Gas has made of the requirement in its privatization legislation secured by the House of Lords to 'advise and inform' consumers about energy saving. British Gas also needs to examine the truth of its statements in the light of the very real environmental impact of the energy industries – an extremely expensive promotional campaign during 1989 focused on the company's initials B G in a variety of ways, including 'Beautiful Globe . . . no smoke, no dust, and no ash' with no reference whatever to the carbon dioxide produced with every therm.

Thirteen years ago the Energy Policy Review of 1977 pointed the way forward: 'The objective of energy policy is to secure that the nation's energy needs are met at the lowest cost in real resources, consistently with achieving adequate security and continuity of supply, and consistently with social, environmental and other policy objectives.' These remain the relevant criteria. Regrettably, the many events on the energy scene during 1989 moved us little nearer to achieving sensible policies.

The problems will not go away, and the urgency for solutions is increasing. Let us hope that in 1990 real progress is made towards more efficient energy technologies.

Chronology

3 Jan: BP agree to buy back more than half the Kuwaiti stake in the company in a £2.4 billion deal.

16 Jan: Ofgas criticizes the high cost of the gas supplied by British Gas.

17 Jan: Furore over a leaked draft speech in which John Baker, Chief Executive designate of National Power, states that profits will come before security of electricity supply after privatization and cast doubt on the viability of new nuclear plant unless heavily subsidized by the government.

18 Jan: Piper Alpha disaster public inquiry, chaired by Lord Cullen, begins in Aberdeen.

23 Jan: British Coal suggests the establishment of pithead power stations run in co-operation with the privatized electricity industry, in which thousands of miners would be offered shares in return for signing what would amount to no- strike agreements.

25 Jan: John Baker's speech delivered in toned-down form.

31 Jan: CEGB announces that it wants to build a second PWR at Sizewell.
Four hundred and fifty pit jobs axed in the Nottinghamshire coalfield.

7 Feb: Lords Science and Technology Committee warns that Britain is in danger of losing its world leadership in the field of nuclear power because of a lack of coherent policy on long term research.

8 Feb: Five hundred and fifty jobs go in the Nottinghamshire coalfield.

14 Feb: The Finnish company, Ahlstrom Corporation, finance continued research by British Coal in a programme to develop low-pollution, high-efficiency coal-burning power stations.

3 Mar: Axing of more than 7,400 jobs in the Yorkshire and South Wales coalfields announced.

24 Mar: Explosion at Marathon Oil's Brae B oil platform in the North Sea.

31 Mar: Berkeley nuclear power station shut down.

5 Apr: CBI calls on the government to retain the nuclear power industry in state control when the electricity generation industry is privatized.

10 Apr: Third reading of the Electricity Bill, to privatize the industry, is passed in the Commons by 251 to 193.

17 Apr: Ofgas criticizes gas price levels in Britain.

18 Apr: Explosion on Shell's Cormorant Alpha rig in the North Sea slashes oil production by a quarter and leads to soaring prices.
CEGB applies to the Secretary of State for Energy for permission to build a PWR at Wylfa Head, Anglesey.

26 Apr: Cracks on Shell Expo's St Fergus gas plant in North East Scotland severely disrupts gas supplies from the North Sea.

27 Apr: Plans unveiled for a 'clean coal' power station to be built in Berkshire, coming on stream in 1991.

2 May: National Utility Service warns that electricity prices are rising more steeply in the UK than in competitor economies, putting industry and commerce at a disadvantage.

22 May: Professor Stephen Littlechild appointed director general of electricity supply with responsibility for the regulation of the privatized industry.

12 June: Deal between British Coal and the Union of Democratic Mineworkers at the proposed Margam superpit in South Wales announced.

12 June: New safety rules for North Sea oil workers announced.

16 June: Coal Information and Consultancy Services, *Whose Coal in the Power Stations?* warns of the danger of the undercutting of British coal by foreign imports and the massive pit closures that could result.

5 July: North West Electricity Board suggests that the area could get more than 10 per cent of its power needs from renewable energy sources by the turn of the century.

11 July: Watt committee on energy stresses that Britain is falling behind in the search for alternatives to natural gas for when North Sea reserves run out.
Shell and Esso announce £700 million North Sea oil development in Gannet field.

24 July: Government announces that all nine Magnox reactors are to remain in public ownership when the rest of the electricity industry is privatized.

31 July: Report in *Nuclear Engineering International* points to the relative inefficiency of Britain's nuclear reactors.

1 Aug: National Audit Office report *National Energy Efficiency* calls on the government to set demanding energy saving targets.

2 Aug: Chairman of the UK Atomic Energy Authority, John Collier, condemns the government's plans to privatize the electricity industry as 'terribly, terribly messy'.

17 Aug: New oil rush in North Sea predicted.

25 Aug: Last Kent coalpit closes with loss of 600 jobs. Two Nottinghamshire pits also close.

29 Aug: Announcement by Occidental Petroleum that its new East Piper field contains an estimated 100 million barrels of high quality oil.

3 Sept: BP announces it is to spend £1.5 billion in the largest undeveloped gas field in the North Sea, the Bruce field.

7 Sept: The heads of the electricity industry argue in a letter to the government that its privatization is at risk unless they retain a monopoly over 70 per cent of the power market for up to 15 years.

14 Sept: BP announces a reorganization of its oil exploration business involving the sale of $1.3 billion of assets and redundancies for 1,700 workers, mostly in Scotland.

Monitoring and Control of British Nuclear Fuels PLC 33rd report of the public accounts committee published. A critical report which demands an independent inquiry.

24 Oct: Commons Energy Select Committee report suggests that the government should give more help to UK energy- related industries which want to export to the USSR.

25 Oct: Malcolm Rifkind approves a £350 million nuclear reprocessing plant to be built at Dounreay in Caithness.

8 Nov: North Sea exploration rig Interocean II sinks in high winds.

9 Nov: Nuclear power stations pulled out of the electricity privatization.

16 Nov: Leaked government energy forecast predicts that by 2020 nuclear power will be a largely spent force and that emissions of carbon dioxide will be 75 per cent if present trends continue.

21 Nov: Coal Industry Bill announced in the Queen's speech will wipe out £5 billion of British Coal debt, end subsidies and provide for the expansion of the private coal industry.

4 Dec: British Coal agrees to freeze the cost of supply of coal to power stations between 1990 and 1993 but ensures that its coal quota is not drastically reduced in the process.

18 Dec: Lord Marshall resigns as Chairman of the CEGB.

21 Dec: Commons Select Committee on Energy publish es a critical report on the sale of Britoil to BP.

Transport

P. B. GOODWIN

Introduction

Transport in the modern world has lost much of the romance of Victorian exploration, and neither the power of steam and electricity nor the promised freedoms of internal combustion have quite the resonance they used to command. For much of the time journeys range from uncomfortable and stressful to a relatively neutral pause for thought between home and destination, interspersed with too frequent moments of pain and too rare occasions of pleasure and achievement.

Something of this gap between hope and reality emerged to make transport one of the recurrent sources of 'big' news stories in 1989, as well as providing a continuous undercurrent of complaints – and new thinking – among professionals and the public.

It is the new thinking, rather than the events, which may have the biggest effects in the near future: in my view a remarkable sea-change happened during the year, which was more fundamental and more rapid than anybody expected, but has not yet been fully recognized. It is marked by dissatisfaction with accidents and congestion, an emerging perception of the short and long term responsibilities of individuals, corporations, social institutions and the market, and an increasing recognition of the important links between transport, the economy and the environment.

Public Transport Accidents

Images of public transport disasters do not fade quickly, and events of recent years – Zeebrugge, Kings Cross, Lockerbie, Clapham – were reinforced by a few, but horrifying, air and train accidents including the 737 which crashed on the M1, and train crashes in Purley and Glasgow.

Investigations into the immediate cause of the accidents in most cases identified the specific events which enabled them to occur, and made recommendations – such as chains of command, working practices – to prevent them. Public debate, however, tended to focus on two additional questions: was there some general *pattern* in these accidents which signified some probably rather unpleasant feature of the organizations themselves? And, arising out of that, should there be allocation of responsibility at management or political, rather than operational, level?

The question of 'pattern' is a difficult one because the search for it may itself, in such circumstances, tend to find links where they do not really exist. Cecil Parkinson indicated that comparisons of Clapham, Purley and Bellgrove rail crashes 'did not suggest there was any single underlying cause' – Clapham for example was attributed to a series of operational errors. Nevertheless media and political debate did point to a possibly dangerous *combination* of features which are unquestionably a hallmark of the 1980s, namely (a) rapidly growing traffic without capacity increasing in proportion; (b) increased pressure on transport managements to act commercially, cut costs, and reduce staffing levels with consequent reliance on fewer, or less well qualified staff, or excessive overtime; (c) reduced government interference or control in operations. *Prima facie*, it would be odd if this combination did *not* increase the risk of accidents, either directly or by exaggerating the consequences of individual human error or component failure. The question, now raised, is unlikely to go away.

Senior responsibility is a logical consequence. If government policies or management strategies are part of the cause of an accident, it would feel unjust to visit all the force of punishment or criticism on the individual train driver, mechanic or pilot who was the immediate agent. This argument has been particularly strongly put in Parliament, for example, by the Opposition transport spokesman John Prescott in debate with then Secretary of State, Paul Channon. To date the strongest application of the principle was the resignation of the two most senior London Transport executives following the report on the Kings Cross fire. The inquiry report on the Clapham Junction crash of December 1988, reporting in November, emphasized a 'collective responsibility' of British Rail, and a senior engineer in the signals department immediately resigned, taking early retirement. In other contexts the phrase 'corporate manslaughter' has been introduced into discussion of major public transport accidents and it is yet to be seen what comes of this.

Meanwhile, it is fair to say that senior managements in public transport organizations have become much more sensitive about the need to improve safety procedures. The problem of *how* to incorporate safety expenditure in the formal objectives of commercial companies remains unclear.

One other public transport safety question emerged during the year – as a straw in the wind rather than as (yet) a serious problem. The 1985 Transport Act deregulated bus operations outside London. The immediate transitionary period was marked by disruption and uncertainty, but clearer developments are now emerging including a rapid growth in the use of minibuses, and downward pressure on bus drivers' wages, expenditure on maintenance, and some conditions of service (including in particular changes in the wages structure that encourage drivers to continue working during short periods of illness). There has not been a great increase in bus accidents – nothing mirroring, for example, the one-third *reduction* in fatal accidents that followed the introduction of regulation in 1930 – but similarities to the 'pattern' mentioned above may be signs of problems to come.

Traffic Accidents

Peter Bottomley, Minister for Roads until reshuffled to Northern Ireland, consistently and creditably used the occasion of major public transport accidents as a reminder of the far greater accident toll from traffic accidents. Deaths continue at over 5,000 a year, over 60,000 seriously injured, and over 300,000 casualties altogether. Cars remain between 10 and 20 times more dangerous, for journeys of an equivalent distance, than air, rail or bus. (Pedal and motor cycles are even more dangerous per journey, but are used by a smaller proportion of the population so the actual number of casualties are less.)

Accident figures for the whole of 1989 are not yet available, but there are some signs that the fall – not altogether under stood – since 1986 has not been continuing. Pedestrian acci dents in particular remain high, and one worrying theory is that motorists, feeling more secure themselves, drive in a way which increases danger to others. There has been some encouraging research on the effectiveness of rather low-cost accident preven tion schemes using traffic management techniques. Perhaps the most important change has been the continued change in accept ability of more stringent breath testing regulations. This is usually called 'random' breath testing (though most usefully applies to non-random checks in times and areas of greatest offending, for example, outside pubs at closing time). The White Paper, *Road User and the Law*, following many of the recom mendations of the North Committee, foreshadowed a shift in empha sis away from the personal freedom of the motorist towards his responsibility to other road users and the community in general.

Traffic Growth

The Department of Transport *National Road Traffic Forecasts (Great Britain) 1989* provided the first revised long term forecasts since 1984.

These forecasts are of central importance in British road planning, being used to assess the need for and benefits from trunk road building, as well as the timing of major schemes. They span a period of 30 years, and are based on statistical analysis of earlier trends, as well as surveys of, for example, relationships of car ownership with income, household size, and petrol prices. The earlier forecasts had been much criticized: at a national level traffic growth had exceeded the upper end of the forecast since 1986, and locally traffic on major roads such as the M25 had reached capacity levels much earlier than anticipated. (The thirtieth anniversary of the opening of the M1 in October provided a media reminder of how quickly the optimism of opening speeches had been dispelled.)

The forecasts were published at a time when public and media awareness was already sensitive to the effects of a 44 per cent increase in traffic levels in the previous ten years, and most recently three consecutive years of increases of about 6 per cent.

Using 1988 as a base of 100, the forecasts offered a range from a 'low' of 183 by 2025, to a 'high' of 242 (and still increasing at 1–2 per cent a year). There would be an increase of between 27 per cent and 46 per cent by the year 2000. The Department of Transport commented: 'The new forecasts are considerably higher than the 1984 NRTF, which forecast growth from 1988[1] to 2000 of between 11 and 25 per cent. The main reason for the upward revision of the forecasts is more optimistic expectations of future economic growth.'

Within the totals, private car use would grow fastest to 2000, and lorry (especially heavy lorry) growth would be faster in the later period. Buses and coaches would not grow at all. It was implied, but not quantified, that most of the growth would be in off-peak times, suburbs and rural areas, since peak periods in towns and the major motorways clearly could not support anything like the anticipated growth.

Forecasting methodology has come up against increasing criticism in recent years, both because of its ex-post accuracy and its internal assumptions. The former criticism often observes that the forecasts have been underestimates, the latter suggests that forecasts will be overestimates (or, more precisely, 'self-fulfilling' estimates). The two criticisms can be reconciled by a recently developed theory that 'roads tend to generate their own traffic'. In the official method there is no calculation either of the extra traffic that might be created by improvements in travel conditions, or of any 'damping' effect on traffic of deteriorations in travel conditions. Thus, the criticism goes 'the extra traffic will only be there if new roads are built – but their justification is mainly based on the need to provide for the forecast traffic'.

In the past, this argument has been somewhat arcane, and confined to small groups of specialists. Now it has become a central research issue in transport policy, with studies being launched both by the Department of Transport and by other agencies.

The Argument about Policy

There is a view that traffic is a self-correcting problem requiring little external intervention – people will find their own solutions to congestion, and 'policy' means letting things alone. The view enjoys periodic revivals (and still has a little support) but is now rarely advocated officially. Leaving this aside, there are five main streams of techniques designed to tackle the evident and increasing imbalance between the demand for movement and the supply of transport facilities. These are (i) building more roads; (ii) expanding public transport; (iii) traffic engineering measures to improve efficient movement; (iv) traffic 'calming', i.e. reducing the amount of movement and making it more environment friendly; (v) road pricing.

All streams are seriously supported, but there has been a quite distinct movement in public and professional opinion down this list during the year.

Building more roads

The focus of government policy has been a long term trunk road construction policy of £12 billion, with considerable interest in its sustenance against Treasury pressures, currently a preoccupation of Secretary of State Cecil Parkinson. Lobbies such as the British Road Federation, and industrial interests, especially the CBI, have supported the general approach (though with some difference of emphasis on specific schemes). Opposition parties have distanced themselves from the strategic view of road building as a central solution to transport problems. All specific schemes going to public enquiry now expect local opposition. Although the amount of money seems large, the schemes are mainly filling in 'gaps' in the motorway network, by-passes, and widening or upgrading the most congested sections of trunk road – they are not (and could not be) directed at providing a doubling of road capacity to match the forecast doubling of traffic levels.

New major urban road schemes are no longer accorded the same key importance that they had in the 1960s, because of the great opposition they generate and their dubious success. Nevertheless they have not been formally abandoned as some of their opponents have demanded. In London, consultants had been working since 1984 on selected options in specific corridors. They reported in December, with four very large reports packed with useful and interesting suggestions that, nevertheless, failed to convey a clarity of strategic thinking. The Department of Transport issued a response in the same words to each of the reports:

The Department accepts the consultants' findings that:
- if nothing more is done beyond existing transport programmes for the study area, conditions will get much worse;
- immediate improvements should be sought through tougher parking restrictions with better enforcement, and more traffic management schemes;
- better parking enforcement and traffic management will not provide sufficient relief for the long term;
- some problems would be relieved by improvements to the public transport system;
- improving public transport cannot by itself solve the traffic and associated environmental and economic problems;
- some improvements to the main road network are needed;
- new road capacity provides the opportunity for traffic calming measures on adjacent local roads;
- road improvements will significantly reduce accidents and enhance safety.

Some specific major new road schemes were rejected. One of the outstanding problems is that each of the consultants stressed that their recommendations were a 'package' of road and public transport improvements and traffic calming, and should be assessed in total. But the responsibilities are separate: at the time of writing both government and British Rail are disclaiming financial responsibilities for the public transport components. At the same time, a new set of tough parking restrictions on selected 'Red Routes' into London were announced.

The other main strand of road building policy was launched in a consultation paper 'New Roads by New Means – bringing in private finance' in May 1989. Channon announced: 'I believe that still more of our roads and bridges can be financed privately. The Dartford-Thurrock Bridge – the first private road scheme this century – is our starting point.' However, the consultation paper argued both that: 'Such roads . . . will add to and complement the existing and proposed public network' and that 'the annual level of expenditure on the road programme is determined by the government in the light of the economy generally . . . a different method of financing it does not make more resources available.'

A number of quite difficult questions remain about the attractiveness to the private sector of such schemes: there has developed little of the momentum which would make privatization in this sphere analogous to the upheavals in other sectors of the economy.

Public transport expansion

British Rail in May drew together their proposals for solutions to London congestion in the short term (more capacity on Network South East, expanding use of a through link from Kings Cross to Blackfriars, more rail car parks, more and higher capacity trains) and the long term (substantial new rail infrastructure development across central London, and to Stansted, Heathrow and Kent). They concluded:

London will stagnate unless positive solutions are implemented to relieve its transport congestion.

There is no road solution for this congestion crisis. The roads and car parks are already at saturation and they cannot offer any significant improvement.

The solutions for London's congestion have to lie with rail and the five short term solutions will increase capacity by 30 per cent.

The long term solutions for the turn of the century can only lie in a major increase in Rail's infrastructure. This must include two £1.3 billion Cross Rail tunnels in partnership with London Underground.

British Rail privatization does not now seem on the cards, having been gently relegated to some unspecified future date by Cecil Parkinson in his speech to the Conservative Party Conference in October. However, part or full private sector funding is a government target for virtually all the major possibilities for both rail and bus expansion.

On rail, the extension to the Docklands Light Railway and the new link to Heathrow have some private funding. New light rail systems (sometimes called trams, though they are usually more like small street-level trains than the sort of 'bus on rails' that people think of as a tram) emerged as serious projects in Manchester, Sheffield, Bristol, Birmingham, Southampton and Leeds, with interest in most other cities and even some medium size towns.

A rather small amount of public expenditure has been made available for these schemes, but on very strict conditions which can only be justified (a) when there is a significant benefit to other road users and (b) when it is not possible to recover the cash directly from the users. The prescribed methods of calculation make it much more difficult to justify public expenditure on these schemes than would be the case for a road scheme, and private sector funding is expected to be the main source if the systems are to happen at all, which is doubtful for some of them. At the time of writing, Manchester is likely to go ahead.

It is, however, a matter of increasing consensus among transport planners that when infrastructure development is justified at all, some form of modern, light, computer controlled, high capacity rail system is exactly what towns and cities need. Such systems are very widely in place in Europe, and much of the argument in the UK is not whether, but how. Labour authorities in many of the big cities have been reasonably comfortably sitting down with merchant bankers to try and get a light rail system for their areas, and if this fails to deliver I should expect Conservative authorities equally comfortably to advocate public expenditure on the same systems.

The other major issue of private funding in rail transport has been the unsuccessful attempt to support a fast link from London to the Channel Tunnel, culminating in a decision by British Rail in November to put off for one year the private Bill in Parliament that would be necessary. Here the problems seem more deep rooted, with several apparently irreconcilable conflicts. Angry opposition from residents along the planned route persuaded the government to insist on design changes, including tunnelling, to reduce environmental impact. This increased the cost to a level which could not be recovered from eventual fares without the tunnel being uncompetitive with air and ferry alternatives. The tunnel itself, meanwhile, was faced with construction delays and substantial increases in its own costs, needing additional finance from its bankers. A degree of prospective air deregulation in Europe, and the promised but ignored developments in ferry technology, increase pressure on Eurotunnel's traffic and profit margins.

The government has maintained throughout that both the tunnel and the rail link must be constructed without public funds: it became more and more difficult to see a solution capable of commanding a consensus. At one point, there were even serious suggestions that the French Railways, SNCF, would help to fund the British Rail link. The year closed, as it opened, in uncertainty.

While all the news has been on rail questions, Britain's main method of public transport has remained the bus, now deregulated, and largely private. A combination of increasing use of small buses, local authorities spending their reducing subsidy allocation on filling in gaps in the commercial network, and competition on some of the most popular corridors, had resulted in an increase in overall vehicle miles run, though this was very patchy. Fares continued to increase, and overall there was a decline in demand rather greater than transport planners had expected, or could explain. The importance of bus transport was, in fact, rather neglected during the year.

Traffic control

As traffic demand outstrips supply, there has been increasing interest in the use of traffic management procedures to get the best use out of existing infrastructure. Two new themes have been particularly important – the potential of advanced information technology, and the changing psychology of road users.

'Autoguide' is a system for giving automatic in-vehicle guidance to drivers on the route to be taken for a journey, a sort of automatic navigator with (in theory) perfect information on where the jams are and how to avoid them. It is one of many systems now in the development phase making use of a range of communication technologies – satellites, microwave, infrared and telephone – to give better advice to drivers. The European communities launched a £30 million international research and development project ('Drive') with the aim of ensuring that European companies were in the forefront of the technical developments, and British researchers (but not, by-and-large, British industry) took a major part in this.

At the other extreme, there was increasing recognition that simple enforcement of existing traffic regulations might have more to offer than the most advanced of new technologies. Research published by the Department of Transport indicated that public opinion was much more in favour of a 'tough' line with offenders than had been realized, and this was reinforced by several opinion polls by market research agencies.

Traffic calming

Germany, Holland and some other European countries have for some years been quietly pursuing a selective policy of 'traffic calming', variously described as making traffic more environment-friendly, shifting the 'balance of power' against cars and in favour of pedestrians and cyclists, or adopting urban plans which reduce the need for some excessive movement (for example, by the location of facilities). Although pedestrian shopping precincts have been applied in Britain, the strategy as a whole had not been considered a mainstream transport policy, being viewed as cranky, exaggerated, unrealistic or (more often) ignored.

In some ways, the analysis mirrored public and professional views on the much bigger environmental questions – global warming, the ozone layer and so on – and the increase in awareness of both has been parallel. The techniques of applying traffic calming – formerly a skill developed in this country mainly by two or three small private consulting companies with a partly educational function – became an established part of the professional scene. Many of the big transport planning and engineering consultancies are starting to develop their skills, because there is a market mainly at local authority level for rather small towns, though it should be said that this is still an approach in its infancy.

Road pricing

Perhaps the most startling development during the year has been an 'invisible explosion' of professional interest in road pricing – invisible (at the time of writing) because it has not yet been widely realized how extensive and rapid the development has been. At the current rate, however, I would expect it to become a major issue of public debate before this chapter is published.

Road pricing is not a new idea: a government report in 1964 had described it as technically feasible and economically desirable, though nothing much happened as a result. Basically, the idea is that each vehicle would have some sort of taxi-meter or other device, by which the driver would pay for the use of the road. The important point is that the *amount* of payment would vary according to the amount of usage, and according to the costs the driver imposed on other drivers in terms of delays. Therefore, congested areas or times would be charged more than when traffic was light.

The theory is that each journey will then only be made if the benefits gained by the driver exceed the costs – a necessary condition for market efficiency. The result in practice would be some reduction in the total volume of traffic, by deterring the least 'valuable' trips; an increase in speed; a substantial amount of revenue available for some combination of road building, compensating public transport improvements, tax reductions or other social expenditure. Growth in support may be seen in the following survey of opinion.

Professional institutes

The Institute of Civil Engineers issued a major report, *Congestion*, from its Infrastructure Policy Group. This stated:

In support of road pricing there are four fundamental points.
(i) Very high traffic growth is a reflection of increasing social and economic activity and as such is an indicator of a thriving nation. This had led to severe congestion on all forms of transport.
(ii) Mitigation of congestion will require substantial additional physical facilities to be constructed if activities are to continue to thrive.
(iii)Physical facilities alone will be insufficient, ineffective and/or uneconomic in mitigating congestion. The time taken for construction will mean that significant relief even where available by that method will, except in very limited instances, be many years in becoming effective.

(iv) Other measures are therefore required in addition to produce timely relief to congestion. The Institution believes it is now necessary to include road pricing as part of any plan to deal with London and other areas of widespread congestion.

At the Chartered Institute of Transport Conference in May, a working party was set up. Its report, launched in early 1990, argued: 'The main advantages of road pricing will be to give better speeds to essential traffic which does not meet its full cost and to generate sufficient income to pay for road, public transport and environmenal improvements.' It was recommended that a scheme for London should cover the whole area up to and including the M25, and was expected to pay for itself within months.

The Royal Institute of Chartered Surveyors commissioned a report for its conference in October. Its author Bendixson argued: 'As businesses become increasingly aware of the rising cost of congestion, opposition to using price to regulate roads is diminishing. Road users pay heavily to make use of the highways, but . . . they pay at the wrong place, at the wrong time and in the wrong way.'

Local government bodies

The London Planning Advisory Committee (a post-GLC co-ordinating body of London Boroughs), commissioned a study from consultants MVA; this found that road pricing in Central London was not only beneficial in its own right, but would increase the benefits from a wide range of other policies. (The same consultants later advised close monitoring of potential application in Birmingham also.)

The Association of London Authorities, comprising mainly Labour boroughs, issued its transport strategy, 'Keeping London Moving' stating:

There is now wide support for restraint based on electronic road pricing, with the revenue being used to improve public transport, and the road space freed reallocated to improving pedestrian and cycle facilities, the environment, and catering for essential traffic. This would be efficient, flexible and fair. Because most poorer people, especially women, cannot afford a car and rely on buses, which a road pricing system would really help, it would not have the inequitable effects that many people fear.

Industry

The industrial sector has been more cautious in its response. For example, the Freight Transport Association had in November 1988 stated (in the context of possible pan-European vehicle taxation after 1992): 'In principle the concept that lorries should pay their way is one which FTA members go along with . . .' But this was confined to road wear considerations, not congestion costs. Because the majority of freight operators would not have the operational flexibility to avoid the times and areas of highest charging, 'road pricing for them would just increase costs and would be a retrograde step'.

But there was a possible shift of emphasis by May 1989, when FTA Director General, Garry Turvey, pointed out that many private motorists' journeys were unnecessary, and interfered with the major productivity gains achieved by lorries.

So, 'one day they (private motorists) might be able to match the productivity and efficiency gains of road freight but until then any thought of restraint through road pricing or any similar arrangement most surely fall exclusively upon the non-essential journey'. The idea of road pricing as a tool to benefit high productivity vehicles (lorries) or high efficiency vehicles (buses) is emerging as an important theme. The Confederation of British Industry, in a policy statement 'Trade Routes to the Future', also touched on road pricing, saying: 'Public transport facilities should be greatly improved to help overcome existing congestion and prepare the way for introducing road pricing.'

Government views

Mr Channon, addressing transport professionals at the CIT Annual Conference in May, made a very clear statement:

The first problem with road pricing is that it means different things to different people. For some, the goal is to set an economically efficient price for roads, so that the true cost of using them is paid at the point of use. They see this as a goal in its own right - the application of market forces to roads. It is uncertain what the effect would be on congestion. This brings me to the second school of thought, which sees eliminating congestion as the goal and would, presumably, argue that we must go on raising the price for entering a city centre until we reduce congestion to the desired level, whatever that may be.

Both approaches have a host of practical problems associated with them. As transport professionals, these will be obvious enough to you, so I shall just mention briefly some of the key points. The cost of installing the necessary technology. The problem of policing. The geographical coverage. The impact on traffic flow just beyond the boundary line. The case for exemptions. But the idea of using road pricing to suppress demand raises some bigger issues. The main advantages are that inner cities would become more pleasant places to live and work in, and that essential road users, such as the emergency services, would be able to move about much more easily. The key advantages are the element of unfairness – the rich in their cars and the rest on the trains – and the fact that any demand-suppression measure, however well- intentioned, has a distorting and very uncertain effect on the economy – on jobs and land values, at large and locally.

So, what is the government's position on the use of road pricing to combat congestion? Are we for it or against it? That's rather like asking whether we're for or against war. We're against it if it can be avoided. But if it cannot be avoided, then it has to happen. This government has shown in the past that it is willing to grasp nettles that others have shied away from. And I've no doubt we shall grasp this one if we have to. But the first step, as the CIT have themselves suggested, is more research into the mechanics of road pricing and into its likely consequences.

This slightly open door was subsequently (apparently) closed, Parkinson formally rejecting road pricing 'for the foreseeable future'. It should be said that many professionals are interpreting that phrase to mean a fairly short space of time.

Perhaps the most important government initiative was the Department of the Environment's publication of the Pearce Report on *Sustainable Development*. This spells out the 'polluter pays' principle applied to the services provided by natural environments. 'Environmental goods and services . . . are not bought and sold in the market place. Thus if we leave the allocation of resources to the unfettered market, it will tend to *over-use* the services . . .' The Report advocated a comprehensive system of actual or notional prices to be applied to the environmental costs of pollution, use of finite resources, loss of amenity, disappearance of species. Road pricing would fit very comfortably within this framework and could indeed be one of its most important applications.

Other studies

Other initiatives during the year include a wide- ranging interest by research organizations. The Institute for Public Policy Research (sometimes described as a 'left-wing think tank') issued its first Green Paper on *A Cleaner, Faster London: Road Pricing, Transport Policy and the Environment* by Patricia Hewitt. This gave an extensive discussion on road pricing emphasizing especially

It is the absence of road pricing, not its introduction, which is unfair . . . car drivers on congested roads are imposing costs on other people for which they are not charged themselves. In other words, the drivers are being subsidized . . . The subsidy is going to the better-off members of the community . . . Because road pricing removes this unfair subsidy to car drivers, it would in fact be fairer than the present situation.

This argument was thought to be influential in persuading the Labour Party to say cautiously that they would look at 'the feasibility (in some circumstances) of road pricing, and using the money raised to fund improvements in public transport', in its new transport policy statement 'Moving Britain into the 1990s' issued after its Annual Conference in October.

Internationally, road pricing was the subject of a European Conference of Ministers of Transport seminar in February, and a key theme in EC discussions on international lorry taxation (called 'territoriality') and also in the international 'Drive' research programme. The Round Table of European Industrialists, a body of leading companies, decided to commission a study of the case for using road pricing as a source of infrastructure funds. The Dutch government resigned and fought an election on their environmental plan which included a form of road pricing, and is now being actively prepared. Specific schemes were launched in Norway, Singapore and elsewhere.

Academics and researchers also published extensively on the topic (including the present author, with an argument that the apparent unanimity of support was fragile, because each interested party saw road pricing as being applied to its own favoured general transport strategy: only a *sharing* of the released road space and revenue benefits by environmental, industrial, public transport and motoring interests would enable a consensus to be reached in practice).

Conclusion

The symbol of the development of transport thinking in 1989 was perhaps a small conference in London in November. This was hosted by the organizations of both Conservative and Labour boroughs, who presented a joint draft policy statement based not on road building but on public transport improvements and traffic restraint and a long term view of integration of these with land use planning, a greater regard for the environment and a reduction in the amount of unessential traffic. Such an approach expressed a degree of cross-party consensus that has not applied in recent history. (A 'consensus of everybody except the Department of Transport' was one quite inaccurate, though understandable, comment.)

The user of Britain's transport systems in 1989 was probably preoccupied mainly by the observation that queues, congestion, delays, discomfort and safety were all – or seemed – worse. There was a perception of a slow deterioration, not fulfilling dire predictions of traffic 'grinding to a halt', but certainly not being seen as progress. But the process of rethinking that took place justifies calling 1989 a watershed in transport policy development.

Note

1. The forecast 1988 figure itself being considerably lower than the actual outcome.

Chronology

6 Jan: Tighter security introduced at British airports in the wake of the Lockerbie disaster.

9 Jan: Major fare increases for BR passengers, especially long distance commuters.

British Midland Boeing 737 crashes on the M1 with the loss of 44 lives.

11 Jan: Urgent checks on Boeing 737s ordered by the Civil Aviation Authority (CAA).

22 Jan: Large demonstrations against the Channel Tunnel high-speed rail link in Maidstone.

26 Jan: Channon unveils plans to build two new rail tunnels under London as part of a £3.5 billion programme to ease congestion on London's rail and tube networks.

30 Jan: Spending on transport up £240 million in 1989/90.

6 Feb: Paul Channon announces that legislation to clear the way for toll roads will be introduced in the next session.

The National Freight Corporation is successfully floated on the stock exchange.

A package of measures designed to improve safety on London underground announced.

7 Feb: White Paper *The Road User and the Law* outlines proposals to improve and better enforce road safety.

20 Feb: Public inquiry into the Clapham rail disaster of December 1988 begins, chaired by Anthony Hidden QC.

21 Feb: Before the Hidden inquiry BR accept responsibility for the Clapham crash.

26 Feb: 15,000 protesters against the Channel Tunnel link march through London.

4 Mar: Two trains crash in Purley. Five people are killed.

6 Mar: British Rail indicates £800 million more is available to make the tunnel link more acceptable.

Head-on crash of two suburban trains in Glasgow kills two.

7 Mar: The preferred route for the link between London and the Channel Tunnel is unveiled by British Rail.

Mrs Thatcher rules out a government subsidy for the rail link.

Internal inquiry into the Glasgow crash concludes that it was due to driver error.

13 Mar: The long-awaited report on the Manchester air disaster of 1985 is published. It calls for intensive research into water sprinkler systems and other safety features.

14 Mar: Paul Channon is accused of lying over his handling of an American security bulletin which warned of terrorist threats to Pan Am flights two weeks before the Lockerbie disaster.

Government efforts to keep the 38-tonne axle weight limit up to the end of 1998 are opposed by the EC, which wants a 40-tonne limit from the end of 1996.

21 Mar: Commons Transport Committee says responsibility for air traffic control should be stripped from the CAA and that the government should construct a second runway at Gatwick in a report which is generally very critical of the air industry's safety record.

23 Mar: New rules on the marking and training of drivers of vehicles with explosive cargoes to be introduced in the wake of the fire and explosion at Peterborough the previous day. They came into force in July.

27 Mar: Alastair Morton, the Chairman of Eurotunnel, says BR should consider two further links across Kent if the whole of Britain is to benefit from the tunnel. Saying that Eurotunnel may consider building these lines itself, he deplored the lack of clear strategy and funding for the whole policy area from the government.

29 Mar: CBI report puts the cost to the British economy of the shortcomings of road, rail and air transport in London at £15 billion per year and targets 30 long term projects to prevent London becoming even more congested.

BR tells the inquiry into the Purley crash that it was caused by driver error.

3 Apr: RIBA report warns that Kent could be swamped by heavy lorries if adequate provision for freight movement to the Channel Tunnel is not made by BR.

11 Apr: Six-year campaign to save the Settle–Carlisle railway ends in victory when the government announces that the line is to remain open and in the hands of BR.

19 Apr: Moves to improve pedestrian safety are announced.

3 May: Parliamentary Advisory Council for Transport Safety proposes the introduction of random breath tests.

5 May: Backbench Labour MP's Bill to introduce random breath tests killed in the Commons.

12 May: International Federation of Air Traffic Control Associations criticizes long term planning for control of air traffic over Europe as threatening to institutionalize congestion rather than relieve it.

18 May: White Paper, *Roads for Prosperity*, unveils plans for a £12 billion road building programme, mainly consisting of the widening of motorways and trunk roads.

Public Accounts Committee publishes a report highly critical of the Department of Transport's forecasting in the past, particularly in its estimated traffic flows on the highly congested M25.

20 May: US bank, Manufacturers Hannover, promotes an alternative Channel Tunnel link.

22 May: Transport Green Paper outlines scheme for private toll roads.

23 May: Scathing attack on London underground's safety procedures and management system made in a report by the Railway Inspectorate.

26 May: Tiphook and the Swedish company Stena launch a $824 million joint bid for Sea Containers.

30 May: DPP criticized for not bringing charges of corporate manslaughter against London Transport over the Kings Cross fire disaster.

5 June: 40-tonne lorries to be allowed in Britain from 1999.

10 June: BR offer a new mid-Kent station on the Channel Tunnel link in an effort to mollify Kent protesters.

22 June: Summons for manslaughter issued over the Zeebrugge ferry disaster of March 1987. £250 million urban road and motorway scheme in Glasgow unveiled by Strathclyde Regional Council.

4 July: European transport ministers agree to establish a single agency in Brussels for the flow management of European civil flights.

12 July: New £10 million approach control centre opened at Heathrow.

19 July: EC reveal plans to deregulate European airlines.

20 July: Commons Transport Committee *Report on Airport Security* suggests spot checks by inspectors posing as terrorists, and a £2 a head security tax in the wake of the Lockerbie disaster.

21 July: Plans to introduce a pilot test of Autoguide, an electronic system warning of traffic jams and advising on better routes, by the end of 1993, are announced.

30 July: Two men killed in a train crash in West London.

2 Aug: Approval for a £240 million plan to extend the Docklands Light Railway five miles to the east to Beckton.

3 Aug: Environmentalists' response to the London Road Assessment Studies, threatening some 10,000 homes in four swathes across the capital, is published.

6 Aug: Vandals derail the Oxford–Paddington express.

8 Aug: BR announces a joint venture with French and Belgian railways to spend £500 million on a fleet of 30 TGV-style trains to link the regions with the Channel Tunnel.

9 Aug: BR amends the Channel Tunnel link route to a more environmentally friendly alignment.

Commons Environment Select Committee recommends that the British Waterways Board should encourage canal boats to change to cleaner and quieter electrically powered engines.

19 Aug: Airport security inspectors are given tougher powers.

20 Aug: Thames pleasure cruiser, the *Marchioness*, sinks after being struck by a dredger under Southwark bridge. An immediate inquiry is ordered. Fifty-one people lost their lives.

21 Aug: Tougher safety rules for passenger vessels on the Thames announced.

London Underground's plan to reduce overcrowding by imposing fare increases above the rate of inflation should, according to the Consumers' Association, be referred to the MMC.

22 Aug: Commons select committee on transport deplores congestion on the transport systems and the resulting detrimental effect on the economy, highlights the fall in expenditure on public transport in recent years and calls for more spending on roads and rail. The overall cost of delays caused by the transport system to the British economy is estimated at billions of pounds.

23 Aug: Work is begun on the £65 million second terminal at Birmingham airport.

24 Aug: Transport Users' Consultative Committee for Southern England annual report complains of vandalism and overcrowding on rail and the underfunding of the rail service.

25 Aug: Details of new fire safety precautions on underground systems announced.
New computerized traffic control system for East London announced.

30 Aug: Report on a near disaster at Gatwick in February 1988 published.

31 Aug: New safety rules for vessels on the Thames announced in the wake of the interim report into the *Marchioness* disaster.
BR is to spend £257 million on 400 new coaches for Network South East.

6 Sept: 21 leading European airlines call for a continent-wide air traffic control system to ease congestion.

8 Sept: The government issues new proposals to liberalize European air transport.

11 Sept: Air Europe is to challenge British Airways on transcontinental routes.

12 Sept: Transport 2000 report warns that privatizing BR could lead to higher fares, worse standards of service and safety and line closures.

13 Sept: Review of Scottish airport policy announced.

14 Sept: Announcement that £1 billion needs to be raised on the Channel Tunnel project to cope with escalating costs and delays.
Fire safety precautions at the proposed Channel Tunnel terminal at Kings Cross are criticized in a report by Gerald Clarkson, London's chief fire officer.
The final route of the Channel Tunnel link is announced.

18 Sept: New fire regulations on the London underground are announced.
Tougher safety rules for boats on the Thames introduced.

19 Sept: Penalties on utilities whose road excavations cause avoidable delays announced.

20 Sept: BR unveils its new Inter-City 225 express train.

21 Sept: *A Cleaner, Faster London: Road Pricing, Transport Policy and the Environment*, Institute for Public Policy Research, published. The first report of the new left-wing think-tank advocates a road pricing scheme to cut traffic in central London.

23 Sept: Government rules out help from public funds for the Channel Tunnel link.
Environmental groups' *Roads to Ruin* condemns the roads *White Paper*.

26 Sept: Call for random breath tests from the Police Superintendents Association.

27 Sept: The contract for the first phase of Greater Manchester Metrolink (a new tram system) and plans for a second phase are announced.

2 Oct: Proposals for a £100 million privately- financed dual carriageway linking the M8 and M74 motorways in Scotland are announced.

9 Oct: Terence Bendixson, *Transport in the Nineties: The Shaping of Europe*, Royal Institute of Chartered Surveyors, published. It predicts the development of a European megalopolis based on high-speed rail networks.

9 Oct: A Department of Transport report argues that wheelclamping in London has significantly cut illegal parking offences.

24 Oct: Approval for Manchester's new Metrolink light railway given.

1 Nov: SNCF offers to increase BR's share of revenues from the Channel Tunnel in order to try and revive plans for a speedy commencement of work on the Channel Tunnel link.

3 Nov: BR formally shelves plans to build a high- speed Channel Tunnel link for at least a year because of the government's refusal to help finance the £3.5 billion project or to support the necessary enabling Bill. It also indicates that plans for extensive tunnelling on the route, not least under London, may now have to be replaced by overground lines because of the cost.

5 Nov: Thousands of demonstrators against the Channel Tunnel march in London.

7 Nov: Report by Sir Anthony Hidden QC on the Clapham rail disaster of Dec 1988 criticizes poor administration, working practices and quality of work and calls for major improvements in these areas and in the design of trains amongst its 93 recommendations.

8 Nov: *Trade Routes to the Future* CBI argues £21 billion must be spent on improving the road, rail and air network.

15 Nov: An extra £3 billion allocation for improvements in the transport system announced.

16 Nov: Announcement of a 10-mile extension to the Jubilee line to East London in which private developers will share 40 per cent of costs.

20 Nov: Sir Christopher Foster of Coopers and Lybrand suggests privatization of the motorways to the CBI conference as a way of generating the money necessary for the upgrading of the roads network.

21 Nov: New measure to deal with terrorism at sea and at ports and airports announced in the Queen's speech.

23 Nov: *Accident Prevention – A Social Responsibility*, Royal College of Surgeons, argues that cyclists should be required to wear crash helmets and that the blood alcohol levels of all people involved in accidents should be checked.

28 Nov: Gallup poll shows that Londoners would prefer improved public transport and curbs on cars rather than the government's plans for more roads into the capital.

30 Nov: *Road Accidents Great Britain 1988 – The Casualty Report*, HMSO, shows the death toll on the roads to be the lowest since 1954.

5 Dec: EC agreement reached on air transport deregulation package.

World Wildlife Fund report claims that the government's transport policies are working against its stated aim of reducing emissions of greenhouse gases.

6 Dec: Appointment of Bob Reid to replace Sir Robert Reid as Chairman of BR announced. Liberal Democrat scheme of day licences to drive into cities to deal with traffic congestion is unveiled.

7 Dec: *Quality of Control of Road and Bridge Construction*, National Audit Office, argues that poor workmanship and inadequate supervision of construction is costing millions of pounds per annum in avoidable repairs.

8 Dec: Tiphook and Stena raise their bid for Sea Containers to $1.04 billion.

13 Dec: Deal between British Airways, KLM and Sabena announced.

14 Dec: New road network scheme for London announced.

15 Dec: Accident inquiry into the Lockerbie disaster of Dec 1988 announced.

Aviation Safety Bill published.

18 Dec: £635 million allocated for road and parking development by local highway authorities in England.

19 Dec: Regulations to combat air fatigue among pilots issued by the CAA.

20 Dec: Plans for a link-up of ferry services between Sealink and P&O are blocked by the MMC.

21 Dec: The government response to the Commons Transport Committee outlines improvements to airport security.

Acknowledgement

This analysis is influenced by research carried out in the 'Transport and Society' project supported by the Rees Jeffreys Road Fund.

Retailing

GARY DAVIES

An Historical Context

The sale of goods by an intermediary to a consumer, rather than by a maker directly to a consumer, distinguishes retailing as a broad sector from other commercial activity. While retailing as such has been a major feature of the economy since ancient times, the nature of retailing has arguably changed more in the twentieth century than in the rest of history. Reflecting a wider move in focus from production industries to the service sector in the aptly described post-Fordian economy of the late 1980s, power in distribution has moved from the manufacturer and wholesaler towards the retailer. The dominant feature of this shift in control has been the rise of the large multiple retailer and the consequent growth in concentration in the retail sector. In 1900 independent retailers dominated retailing. By 1989 multiples held over 50 per cent of retail sales. The market share of both the independent and co-operative subsectors had declined.

A more precise and detailed analysis of the structure of retailing by 1989 would depend upon the definition selected for retailing. Most national statistics, for example, tend to include mail order but to exclude car sales, to include some service retailers but to exclude travel and estate agents, fast food, banks, building societies and public houses, all of whom have regarded themselves at one time or another as 'retailers'. Retailing within its narrow, high street and product definition continued to lose market share of consumer expenditure, but the more broadly defined retail sector continued to expand its share of Gross National Product (GNP).

Whether one ignores the problem of definition or not, the effect on all retail sectors of increased concentration remains the dominant factor and its effect on retailing has been profound. Larger, more proactive retailers have become more centralized. Control within the typical business has shifted from the store and to a widening strata of specialists at head office. Buying has been centralized, systems are defined centrally, corporate image is developed centrally to be manifest in redesigned stores, own label products, customer care programmes and advertising. The discretion delegated to store management on matters such as buying, merchandizing and layout has declined, leaving store management as implementors and people managers.

Education and Training

Retailing has traditionally been regarded as the job of last resort rather than the career of first choice. In some ways as a response, 1989 saw two developments that reflected the increased demand for more sophisticated management in retailing and the need to develop the typical retail employee better. In 1989 the first graduates in retailing were taking up their appointments. Their course, BA (Hons) Retailing Marketing at Manchester Polytechnic, was followed by three similar retail programmes being announced in that same year at Surrey, Dorset and Ulster. MBAs in retailing were available at Stirling and Sheffield Polytechnic. Chairs in retailing had been funded by House of Fraser, MFI, the Body Shop and Asda.

Initiatives in higher education were matched in retail training through an active support of the National Vocational Qualification (NVQ) by retailers, led by the newly formed National Retail Training Council. The four-level NVQ differed from a traditional qualification in its emphasis on the assessment of competence rather than knowledge, although some knowledge and understanding was acknowledged to be essential for the scheme. Levels I and II in NVQ for retailing were formally launched in 1989. In January some £260,000 was raised to develop a distance learning course based on the Manchester degree for Level IV.

Mergers and Acquisitions

Retailer concentration had often been effected by merger and acquisition. The process appeared to accelerate in the late 1980s through the device of the leveraged buyout, where one company would be purchased by another, or by its own management, using a balance of short term loans and equity finance. The leveraged buyout principle was arguably particularly attractive in retailing where return on capital was often very high and where businesses often included a number of self-contained subsidiaries that could be sold for a good deal more than any valuation inferred from the stock market quotation of the parent company. Unfortunately, retail takeovers financed substantially by borrowing, fell doubly foul of the steady rise in interest rates during 1989. Companies such as MFI and Magnet, both bought by their management, found demand for their high ticket lines static, while the interest to be paid on their borrowing rose. Rumours of other takeovers and buyouts, so rife earlier in the year, subsided by October. Even so Boots acquired Ward White, and Isosceles succeeded in buying Gateway, promptly selling their larger stores to Asda. On the sidelines accusation and counter-accusation continued to surround the takeover by the Al- Fayed brothers of House of Fraser.

Issues in the Law and Government Policy

The prospect of 1992 continued to provide a focus for discussion in all economic sectors as to the nature and extent of harmonization of trading law and practices and no less so in retailing. However, in terms of specific retail developments, the issue of Sunday trading dominated the popular and trade press. During the year, local authorities had felt unable to enforce the Sunday trading law following what appeared initially to be a successful appeal to the European Court by B&Q, that to ban Sunday trading was a denial of free trade. USDAW, the shopworkers' union, the religious lobby and many retailers, continued to argue against seven-day trading, but as 1989 drew to a close, England and Wales seemed certain to follow Scotland sooner rather than later.

Government at local and national level is closely involved with retailers in appraising planning applications for new sites both for individual stores and for shopping centres. By the end of 1988 Britain had only two large out-of-town shopping centres (where large meant occupying more than 500,000 square feet), the Gateshead Metro Centre and Brent Cross in North London. Such centres were, by comparison, commonplace in North America and increasing in France and Germany.

By 1989 the total volume of new shopping schemes that had been given planning consent had reached 50 million square feet. Planning applications totalled nearly 80 million square feet and with 31 million square feet already under construction, this implied the equivalent of 300 new regional shopping centres somewhere in the pipeline. While some of this capacity would be denied planning, and some would replace existing footage, it was clear that a substantial increase in retail floorspace could be expected.

Worries over the effects of a boom in out-of-town locations were being voiced by the residents of suburbia (concerned about the green belt) and the inner city councils (concerned about the so- called doughnut effect, where nothing taxable is left in the middle of a city).

The British government was faced with an interesting dilemma. On the one hand there were the pressures of the environmental lobby in largely Conservative constituencies and a genuine concern for the likely social impact upon urban areas. On the other hand, there were the pressures from developers pointing out the employment benefits of constructing and manning new centres, let alone the benefits of a free retail market unconstrained by barriers to entry created by wholesale denials of planning permission.

Products and Consumers

The year 1989 saw the emergence of the environmentally conscious shopper, the so-called 'green' consumer. Fears about the consequences of holes in the ozone layer saw a wholesale switch away from aerosols containing cholorofluoro hydrocarbons (CFCs). The likely effects of pollution from car exhausts and a reduction in tax on lead-free petrol saw a similar switch to unleaded petrol. Supermarkets vied to compete for the title of the greenest retailer, a prize eventually awarded by one writer to Safeway.

Scares on what is safe or unsafe to eat are not infrequent in history, but the crisis caused by junior Health Minister Edwina Currie's comments on eggs in 1988 was nearly repeated in 1989 over cheese and chilled foods, both susceptible to contamination by the bacteria listeria, an organism that is resistant to cooking. However, sales in convenience foods continued to increase, with Marks and Spencer to the fore having been credited with having made the TV dinner respectable.

Fur sales were damaged by the publicity given to allegations about the cruel treatment of animals kept or trapped for their skins. A number of products were affected by totally different actions, the deliberate contamination of products by blackmailers threatening to damage the business of both retailers and manufacturers.

Mainstream product matters were dominated by a continued growth in own-label products, sold under the retailers' own name rather than those of manufacturers. Individual retailers such as the Co-op, Marks and Spencer and Sainsbury had always relied heavily upon own-label products. Other retailers had followed. While it was difficult to conceive of many own-label toys, where the brand name was identical to the product, there were even predictions for an own-label car.

Some retailers controlled the supply of own-label products by ownership of the manufacturer. While there were examples of vertical integration in 1989 (Benetton, MFI with Hygena and Schrieber, British Shoe Corporation) retailers had tended to divest their manufacturing interest and control their suppliers by controlling the marketplace. Own-label was increasingly sold on quality rather than just on price, using the retailer's presence in the high street to promote the product rather than the more expensive route of mass advertising that remained the main method of market control for most manufacturers.

Retail Image

The changing status of retailing in society was reflected in the way retailers chose to present themselves to customers. Gone were the days of piling it high and selling it cheap as the norm. Value for money was still important but value included a desire for pleasant surroundings. Retailers in turn turned to non-price methods of competition, methods encapsulated by the term 'image'. Image in turn was created by store design, products and their price points, and the people in the store, be they customers or staff.

Expenditure on store design apparently slackened in 1989, if judged by the incomes of design companies, due probably to doubts on the returns that were possible on any investment in refurbishment. Attention appeared to shift instead to customer service, or customer care as it was termed. Conditioned responses from company training sessions such as 'Have a Nice Day' were being superseded by attempts to introduce better human relations policies promoting an environment where staff would find it easier to be pleasant to customers. There were signs of trends away from a long term reduction in staffing levels and away from a reliance on part-time staff hours, trends that had dominated employee policy in retailing since the war.

The more cynical pointed to a similar emphasis on service in the 1920s, another era of high unemployment amongst the semi-skilled. But an emphasis on service appeared towards the end of 1989 to permeate more than just interpersonal relations in retailing. Money back guarantees, in-store banks, lit car parking, creches, facilities for the disabled, long opening hours and many more implied a genuine attempt by retailing to lead rather than follow the mainsteam service sector in serving the customer.

Chronology

1 Jan: New ruling that goods no longer have to be marked by their country of origin comes into effect.

17 Jan: High Court ruling that Lord Young must refer the House of Fraser takeover to the MMC and publish the department's report on the takeover. The government appeals.

20 Jan: Court of Appeal overturns High Court's decision on House of Fraser. Lonrho appeals to the House of Lords.

21 Feb: Backbench Bill to end the Net Book Agreement introduced in the Commons.
Barclays Bank launch their new Assent credit card.

22 Feb: Nicholas Ridley turns down plans for a major shopping and leisure complex in Hertfordshire and awards the inquiry costs to St Albans City Council against the developers, Town and City Properties (Development) Ltd, thus signalling his preparedness to defend the Green Belt against major shopping developments.

1 Mar: Midland Bank launch their new credit card, Indigo Visa.

30 Mar: Special midweek edition of *The Observer* leaks details of the DTI's report on the House of Fraser takeover.

10 Apr: Law Lords turn down Lonrho's appeal seeking to force the DTI to publish its report on House of Fraser.

18 Apr: The supermarket chain Gateway receives a hostile £1.74 billion bid from the Isoceles consortium led by SG Warburg.

20 Apr: William Low, the Dundee-based supermarket chain, launches a £136 million agreed bid for Budgen.
Two Scotland Yard Fraud Squad detectives return from an unsuccessful trip to Egypt to inquire into the Al-Fayed brothers and the House of Fraser affair.

25 Apr: MMC inquiry into Grand Metropolitan's acquisition of the William Hill chain of betting shops announced.

28 Apr: Office of Fair Trading launches an inquiry into the Net Book Agreement.

12 May: Low pulls out of its bid for Budgen.

15 May: Retail Credit Group, which represents retailers as credit granters and issuers of credit cards launches an attack on the conduct and conclusions of the Jack Committee on banking services law.

18 May: Lords reject Lonrho appeal on House of Fraser.

1 June: *Which* survey finds poor hygiene in sandwich shops in the London area.

12 June: Publication of a survey carried out by Mintel/NOP in April which demonstrated the growth of green consumerism.

19 June: All American £2 billion leveraged buyout bid for Gateway agreed by the latter's board.

29 June: European Court setback for B&Q in the first stage of their battle to change the Sunday trading laws.

30 June: Call by a group of Tory MPs for the imprisonment of Sir Terence Conran because of the flouting of the 1950 Shops Act provisions governing Sunday trading by his Storehouse group.

3 July: Boots make an £800 million hostile bid for Ward White.

13 July: Isoceles claims victory in the battle for Gateway.

3 Aug: Office of Fair Trading decides not to refer the Net Book Agreement to the Restrictive Practices Court despite pressure from Pentos.

4 Aug: Boots raises its offer for Ward White to £900 million.

Thorn EMI announces it is to restructure Rumblelows, its loss-making electrical goods chain.

7 Aug: The government announces it will press for the rapid introduction of an EC scheme to give green labels to products that do minimal harm to the environment. This is in the face of an increasing number of these green labels being attached to products by the manufacturers, not always with ample justification.

8 Aug: Stiff fines for DIY stores before Coventry magistrates for illegal Sunday trading.

Grand Metropolitan buys United Biscuits restaurants division, which includes Wimpy and Pizzaland, for £180 million.

14 Aug: Shares in Lowndes Queensway suspended as a rescue package is put together.

22 Aug: MMC report suggests that credit card shoppers should be charged more than cash customers.

Lloyds Bank announce that its Access holders will be charged a £12 annual fee from next year and that its interest rates will meanwhile drop by three per cent.

Boots claims victory in its bid for Ward White.

23 Aug: MMC gives Grand Metropolitan the green light to acquire the William Hill chain of betting shops.

24 Aug: The British brewer, Bass, becomes the largest hotel group in the world with the acquisition of the Holiday Inn label in a £1.25 billion deal.

4 Sept: European food retailing liaison between Argyll, Koninklijke Ahold of the Netherlands and Groupe Casino of France takes shape in the form of the European Retail Alliance.

5 Sept: Brent Walker buys Grand Metropolitan's betting shops.

11 Sept: TSB becomes the first bank to offer a £100 cheque guarantee card to all its customers.

18 Sept: DTI rejects call from the Retail Commission for an inquiry into two practices not covered in the MMC report on credit cards.

25 Sept: *Retail and the Shopper 1989*, Mintel International, points to retailers' failings in the areas of customer services, staff training and after sales service.

2 Oct: Midland Bank launch a £250 cheque guarantee card – but only for its wealthy Meridian account holders.

8 Nov: In votes on Sunday drinking in 14 districts of Wales, 12 vote to remain wet, Ceredigion goes wet and only Dwyfor remains dry.

22 Nov: A Bill to give tenanted landlords greater freedom to extend their range of beers is announced by Nicholas Ridley.

23 Nov: A Food Safety Bill introducing tough new regulations and fines for food retailers is published.

Both sides claim victory after the European Court of Justice ruling in Torfaen Borough Council v B&Q plc on whether or not the ban on Sunday trading in Britain breaks EC rules.

27 Nov: Rochdale Borough Council wins victory on Sunday trading over Texas Homecare at Leeds High Court.

5 Dec: Lord Sainsbury, the head of the supermarket chain, strongly supports government plans to introduce food irradiation during the second reading debate on the Food Safety Bill in the Lords.

6 Dec: Kingfisher launches hostile £568 million takeover bid for Dixons.

13 Dec: Survey by the London Food Commission shows that most retailers oppose irradiated food.

15 Dec: Dr Roy Spencer, head of scientific services at Sainsburys, defends the stores group's decision to sell irradiated food.

21 Dec: Retailers are to be allowed to charge more to shoppers paying with credit cards.

22 Dec: EC food labelling directive issued.

Tourism

DAVID HARDMAN and GRAHAM STONE

Tourism and the UK Economy

As an economic activity, tourism contributes approximately 3.5 per cent to the Gross Domestic Product of the UK and constitutes between 5 and 6 per cent of all consumer spending. In foreign exchange terms, tourism represents more than 25 per cent of all service industry exports (greater than the earnings of financial institutions, sea transport and civil aviation), and more than 9 per cent of all visible earnings (exceeding earnings from electrical machinery and textiles). The industry is estimated to employ more than 1.3 million people in Great Britain. Set against this is the growing imbalance between tourism earnings and expenditure which in 1988 reached a £2 billion deficit. Although the tourism balance is a crude measure, which does not seek to quantify secondary and tertiary effects, it contributes significantly to the UK balance of payments deficit.

Visits Abroad by UK Residents

Since 1980, visits abroad have increased by nearly 65 per cent whilst expenditure in constant terms has risen by 57 per cent (see table 1A). This growth has been stimulated by increases in real disposable income, the relative strength of sterling, the competitive prices of the tourism product abroad, including air fares, and the changing demographic profile of the UK. Even during the period 1981–3, with high levels of unemployment in the UK economy, the propensity of the British to travel abroad was maintained, reaching a peak growth in 1986. This continued until 1989, when the growth rate declined with the effects of high interest rates on disposable incomes, an effect which is likely to continue into 1990. To an extent, this effect has now been offset by the relative costs of package holidays, 65 per cent in 1988 of all holidays abroad, and the price wars of the tour operators.

In 1988, the most popular destinations abroad were countries in the European Community (over 78 per cent of visits) and the rest of Western Europe (15 per cent). In 1987 and 1988 a growth in visitor numbers to North America as a consequence of the weakening of the dollar, a trend which is likely to reverse in

Table 1A.   Tourism flows from Great Britain

	Visits (millions)	Current expenditure		Constant expenditure (1985)	
		£ bn.	% change	£ bn.	% change
1980	17.5	2.7	+29.8	4.2	+27.3
1981	19.0	3.3	+19.5	4.5	+ 7.0
1982	20.6	3.6	+11.2	4.5	− 1.0
1983	21.0	4.1	+12.4	4.6	+ 3.9
1984	22.0	4.7	+14.0	4.8	+ 2.7
1985	21.6	4.9	+ 4.5	4.9	+ 2.5
1986	24.9	6.1	+24.9	5.5	+12.2
1987	27.4	7.3	+19.7	6.3	+15.9
1988	28.8 (P)	8.1(P)	+10.9	6.6(P)	+ 4.8(P)

All figures rounded   (P) = provisional estimates
Source: *International Passenger Survey*, HMSO

1989 and 1990, was experienced. The major purpose for visits abroad was holiday making (more than 70 per cent of the total) with two-thirds taking inclusive/package tours. The most popular destinations in 1988 were Spain (34 per cent), France (11 per cent), Greece (10 per cent) and Italy (five per cent). The popularity of Spain as a destination has been maintained only by very competitive pricing with a consequent effect upon quality, an increasing cause for complaints and adverse publicity in 1989. France continues to be a popular destination in 1989, although the number of recorded visitors is inflated as France is a major entry-point to Europe by car-based touring holiday makers. There are increasing indications that package holidays are changing in relative importance both in the form of holiday (for example, seats only) and destinations (the growing popularity of the Eastern Mediterranean, particularly Turkey, and the growth in the long haul market, i.e. Australia and the Caribbean). Non-holiday visits constitute approximately 28 per cent of the total, although these may include a holiday element, with business travel (13 per cent of total) and visiting friends and relatives (11 per cent). This element, in addition to the varied destinations and purpose of visit, has reduced the seasonality impact of outbound tourism: for example, first quarter visits at 15.6 per cent of total, second quarter at 25.4 per cent, third quarter at 38.3 per cent and fourth quarter at 20.7 per cent.

There were many difficulties for outgoing tourists in 1989, with delays through strikes by air-traffic controllers, an increase in adverse publicity at airports and some European destinations, complaints about the quality of provision in some hotels and the good summer weather in the UK. These short term effects complicate the general picture in terms of existing trends and the extent to which newer trends are emerging.

Table 1B.   Tourism flows into Great Britain

	Visits (millions)	Current expenditure		Constant extenditure (1985)	
		£ bn.	% change	£ bn.	% change
1980	12.4	2.9	+ 5.9	4.4	− 10.5
1981	11.5	3.0	+ 0.3	3.9	− 11.2
1982	11.6	3.2	+ 7.3	3.9	− 1.6
1983	12.5	4.0	+25.6	4.6	+18.1
1984	13.6	4.6	+15.3	5.0	+ 8.0
1985	14.4	5.4	+17.9	5.4	+ 9.9
1986	13.9	5.6	+ 2.0	5.2	− 4.6
1987	15.6	6.3	+12.7	5.5	+ 5.7
1988	15.8 (P)	6.1(P)	− 1.6 (P)	5.2(P)	− 3.9(P)

All figures rounded   (P) = provisional estimates
Source: *International Passenger Survey*, HMSO

Overseas Visitors to Great Britain

Since 1980, overseas visitors to Britain have increased by 27 per cent, with expenditure in constant terms rising by 18 per cent (see table 1B). However, within this period there have been important changes. The market remained fairly stagnant between 1977 and 1982, between 1983 and 1985 there was a slow growth of approximately 7 per cent, whilst between 1986 and 1988 a growth in Western European visitors compensated for a decline in numbers from North America. The most important segment of visitors from overseas remains the North American market, contributing 20 per cent in numbers and 25 per cent in expenditure. This segment is heavily influenced by exchange rates and with the strengthening dollar is expected to increase from 1989. Visitors from Western Europe (60 per cent of the total) have shown a steady growth, with France, West Germany and the Irish Republic accounting for more than 50 per cent of all Western European arrivals. Nearly one-quarter of all arrivals constitute business visits, significantly higher than most major tourist destinations, which contributes to a higher than average spend. These inward flows are linked with general levels of economic/business activities in generating countries. Holiday arrivals constitute about two-fifths of total numbers with a relatively small proportion of inclusive/package tours. This is an indication of the relatively underdeveloped concept of inclusive tours in the generating countries compared with Britain. The proportion of visits to friends and relatives (20 per cent of the total) reflect historic, cultural and business links with Great Britain in that 35 per cent of visitors come from English-speaking countries. The proportion of excursionists (those remaining for less than 24 hours) is low for geographic reasons. Presently over 60 per cent of arrivals in Great Britain are by air, the vast majority arriving at or departing from Heathrow either by national airlines or British Airways. This factor tends to a concentration of visitors to London (which accounts for more than half of all bed nights by foreigners) and to the South-East. Thus, despite heavy marketing activities by the British Tourist Authority, the major impact and benefits of incoming visitors tend to be concentrated in the South-East. The pattern of these visits is not excessively seasonal (first quarter 17.6 per cent; second quarter 25.4 per cent; third quarter 35.1 per cent; fourth quarter 21.9 per cent); this not only allows a more efficient use of tourist resources, but is a reflection of the importance of the business travel element (which has grown by nearly 40 per cent since 1980), the availability in Britain of tourist products which are not weather-dependent and the promotional activities of the British Tourist Authority.

The years 1989 and 1990 are likely to show important growth in incoming visitor numbers with the weakening of sterling, particularly against the West German and American currencies. This may be offset to a degree by the high levels of inflation with Great Britain and the extent to which the UK economy experiences a downturn which will, in turn, affect the level of business visits.

The Tourist Industry in Great Britain

The complexity of the tourist product is reflected in the industry which is concerned with the provision of transport, food, drink, accommodation, finance, entertainment amongst other things. For most people, the visible manifestation of the industry is through tour operators and travel agents, particularly if an overseas visit is contemplated. These organizations are becoming increasingly integrated in order to benefit from high utilization of the fixed assets and economies of scale of operation. Measures of market share vary according to criteria used, but in the tour operating sector, two organizations predominate. Thomson Travel Group (which includes Orion and Britannia Airlines, Horizon and Portland Holidays) with 40 per cent of the market, dominates the inclusive tour holiday market. This concentration considerably enhances their negotiating position *vis-à-vis* overseas destinations (they are responsible for more than 60 per cent of inclusive tour visits to the Balearic Islands and 51 per cent to mainland Spain) and is reflected in low priced packages and thus increased demand.

The other major operator is International Leisure Group (incorporating Intasun, Global Holidays, Club 18-30 and Air Europe) with a market share of nearly 20 per cent. This predominance has resulted in price discounting for many years which, in the shortrun, has been of benefit to the customer, but given the very low level of profitability of package holidays (in 1987 the net profit margin of the top 30 air travel organizations was -0.9 per cent) has often been at the expense of product quality. Announcements for 1990 prices presage the end of the price-war when anticipated price rises of at least 10 per cent should assuage the situation. The fact that the top four tour operators (Thomson, International Leisure, Redwin and Airtours) have more than 50 per cent of the market for inclusive tours is of concern to the customer and resulted in the reference of the Thomson–Horizon merger to the Monopolies and Mergers Commission in 1988. Travel agency operations show similar trends in integration and market domination, with the top four agencies (Lunn Poly, including Pickfords and Ellerman, with a 24 per cent share; Thomas Cook, including Frames and Blue Sky, with 15 per cent; Hogg-Robinson including Exchange and Blue Star Travel, with 4 per cent; and A.T. Mays, including Nairn Travel, with 4 per cent) sharing almost half of the market for inclusive holidays and they are using price discounting to maintain and enhance market shares. Such scale of operations has improved the speed and efficiency of bookings through the acquisition of expensive computer technology. It has also resulted in more co-operation and direct links with tour operators which may require increasing governmental regulations in the future if the interests of the customers are to be safeguarded.

As a reaction to these structural changes, the smaller organizations have sought to develop more specialist tourist products for specific market segments, for example, direct sales (Tjaereborg); age groups (Saga); self-catering (Eurocamp); coach tours (Wallace Arnold) and long haul (Kuoni) which increasingly reflect the requirements of a more sophisticated traveller. If these segments develop, future growth will be with groups that market a range of tourist products under different brand names within fewer corporate structures, with the consequent implications of oligopolistic exploitation. The other major change in this area will centre upon the development and acceptability of user-friendly information technology systems which will allow enquiries and bookings within the home using sophisticated interactive technology.

Domestic Tourism

Events at home and abroad have led to an increase in domestic tourism in 1989. Frustrations at airport delays and strikes and the burden of higher mortgage payments have affected the growth in 'sun, sea and sand' package holidays abroad although after record-breaking visitor figures for Easter those for the summer peak at some British resorts were perhaps lower than anticipated. However, provisional figures suggest that 33 million people took holidays of four nights or more in Britain in 1989 (a 20 per cent increase in the past two years) with a total spend of approximately £8 billion. Add to this the importance of day trippers and the short-break markets and the direct and indirect benefits of tourism via wealth and job creation can be clearly seen in coastal, rural and urban areas.

The British coast is coming under increasing pressure with the West Country the favourite destination for holidaymakers. Traditional resorts (Blackpool, Bournemouth, Torbay) remain important but are having to adapt and invest in order to retain markets. Blackpool still remains the most significant resort with 16 million visitors per annum and a total tourist revenue of £306 million. The Pleasure Beach with its 6.5 million visitors (spending £25 million) is also Britain's largest single attraction. Continued investment by First Leisure Corporation (for example, Winter Gardens), the attraction of the Sandcastle as a wet-weather facility and the general upgrading of facilities are typical of the changing face of the British seaside resort. The duration of the Illuminations, attracting eight million visitors (total spend £80 million), was increased by a further week in 1988 and 1989 and is a classic example of the value of an extended tourist season.

Nationally, however, there is a problem of beach quality and 136 (34 per cent) of the 403 officially recognized beaches in Britain still breach EC regulations. An investment programme of £1.1 billion should bring 95 per cent of British coastal bathing waters up to EC standards by the mid-1990s. It is also hoped that the creation of the new Broads Authority will go some way towards solving the water quality and tourist-related problems of an increasingly sensitive rural environment.

The development of leisure complexes continues: exemplified by Tower Park Leisure at Poole, and Peter de Savary's plans to build a waterfront village at Hayle which will include a covered entertainments park and a wild-life sanctuary. The continued success and exceptionally high occupancy rates (over 95 per cent) of Centre Parcs' Sherwood Forest operation point to an increasing demand for high-quality leisure facilities while elsewhere theme parks (for example, Frontierland, Morecambe) show promising results.

On a much larger scale the planned Zeri Wonderworld Project on the site of a disused power station at Accrington aims to become the largest and most comprehensive all-weather development in Britain. Two thematic covered areas (Summerworld, Winterworld) will recreate Caribbean, Italian and Swiss environments together with a glass-domed stadium, overhead rail link and a variety of accommodation types. An investment of £300 million will create 3,500 jobs thus indicating the employment potential of such large-scale site attractions. However, both here and at Battersea Power Station, where there are similar plans for a leisure complex, obtaining planning permission is a necessary hurdle.

In areas of attractive landscape, proposals to develop leisure complexes can divide public opinion. An Glynrhonwy near Llanberis there are plans to convert an abandoned slate mine into a £50 million leisure centre which will include dry ski facilities, hotel and cottage accommodation, sports facilities and a simulated tropical rain forest. The partnership between the public sector (Arfon Borough Council) and a private developer (Leading Leisure) is typical of such developments. The need for permanent jobs in the area (600 are envisaged) and the A55 improvements which will result in a catchment area of 6.5 million potential visitors within a two-hour drive, add support to the proposal, but environmental impact has to be considered in such close proximity to the Snowdonia National Park. In 1989 Scotland's first gondola system at Aonach Mor near Fort William was developed; this represents an important addition to Scotland's winter sports facilities.

In urban areas an increasing realization of the benefits of tourism had led to its recognition as a catalyst in generating both wealth and jobs as well as benefiting from and contributing to environmental improvements; as such it has a vital role to play in integrated land-use development strategies. At the national level the opportunities for urban-based tourism have been recognized by the English Tourist Board (ETB) via its Inner City Challenge which seeks to direct tourism-led regeneration in five areas (London, Manchester, Black Country, Sheffield, Cleveland). Within Manchester the ETB-led Strategic Development Initiative brings together the Manchester, Salford and Trafford District Councils and the Central Manchester and Trafford Park Development Corporations to plan tourism initiatives. The Central Manchester Development Corporation's Development Strategy includes a Tourist Development Zone, Tourist Accommodation Quarter, Holiday World and other facilities within a mix of commercial, residential, retailing and leisure developments. Salford Quays' Strategy Review emphasizes water-based tourism opportunities while in adjacent Trafford the Wharfside proposals have a similar focus. Manchester's bid to host the 1996 Olympics is also worthy of note as success would generate new tourism resources and new markets.

Urban areas can also benefit from business tourism, nowhere more so than at Birmingham where it accounts for over 80 per cent of a total visitor spend of over £390 million. Tourism-dependent jobs in the area exceed 73,000. Further developments are planned, notably the new convention centre to complement the National Exhibition Centre by 1991. The planned restoration of 260 miles of canals will constitute a further tourist resource. Birmingham is also one of the 18 cities which have joined together to form the Great British Cities Marketing Group that offers a range of urban-based, short-break holidays.

Docklands, too, continue to demonstrate their tourism potential, examples of proposals and/or on-going development in 1989 including Barry, Cardiff, Hartlepool, Newcastle Quay and Southampton's Ocean Village. Liverpool's Albert Dock is one of the most successful initiatives, typically representing a partnership between central government's Merseyside Development Corporation and the private sector's Arrowcroft Group. Its four million visitors per annum place it in the forefront of British attractions and helped to earn a share of the 'Come to Britain' Trophy for 1989.

At the site level, several attractions completed their first year in 1989. In Manchester Granada Studio Tours attracted nearly 600,000 visitors to their £9 million investment and during the year won three national awards for marketing and five for the product. At Canterbury, the Pilgrim's Way Centre drew in 151,000 visitors, reflecting the growing interest in such heritage attractions. The objectives and historical accuracy of such developments is, however, open to debate, offering as they frequently do, cosy and bowdlerized views of the past. A question of priorities may also have to be faced, not least at Chester where the Deva-Roman

Table 2. Domestic tourism in Britain 1980 – 1988

	All tourism (millions)			Holiday tourism (millions)		
	trips	nights	spending (£)	trips	nights	spending (£)
1980	130	550	4550	75	415	3025
1981	126	520	4600	72	385	3075
1982	123	505	4500	72	375	3100
1983	131	545	5350	78	410	3625
1984[a]	140	565	6975	79	405	3800
1985	126	500	6325	70	355	3900
1986	128	510	7125	71	360	4250
1987	132	495	6775	73	340	4300
1988	130	505	7850	73	355	4975

[a]New base
Source: *British Tourism Survey Monthly*

Chester planned development will require the destruction of a Georgian Grade 2 Listed Building. At Portsmouth the Sealife Centre (250,000 visitors) is one of a number of similar new attractions appealing to the educational, wildlife and conservation-orientated markets. Industrial archaeology was represented by the first stage of the George Stephenson-related railway developments in North Tyneside, while the largest science museum to be built in Britain in the last 30 years was begun on the site of an abandoned coal pit at Coalville. Nationally there is an increasing demand for 'hands-on' opportunities (from children of all ages!) and many tourist attractions have responded, examples including Jodrell Bank, Blackpool Tower and 'Xperiment' at Manchester's Museum of Science and Industry.

In London two visitor-related developments are worthy of mention. At the Natural History Museum the 'Creepy Crawlies' exhibit showed the value of modern display techniques in presenting a potentially complex subject (anthropods) in simple terms to the general public. On the South Bank the Museum of Moving Image (MOMI) completed a very successful first year with 540,000 visitors. Built without government subsidy at a cost of £12 million, MOMI is a division of the British Film Institute and has been called 'the world's most exciting cinema and television museum' and 'probably the most exciting museum in Europe'. It incorporates modern laser technology and won eleven awards in 1989 including the BTA's 'Come to Britain' Trophy (joint winner) and the ETB's 'Development Award for Visitor Attraction'. Its markets include Greater London (45 per cent), other UK (32 per cent) and overseas (23 per cent).

Finally, it is pertinent to draw attention to some of the possible constraints on the development of tourism. Certain focal points for tourism, both foreign and domestic, lack sufficient accommodation especially in the lower price bracket. This is true of York, Cambridge, Manchester and especially London where it is estimated that a further 19,000 bedrooms will be needed over the next ten years to cope with the likely demand that the Channel Tunnel will create. At the more local level changes in the funding of day visits by schoolchildren to heritage and other sites is likely to reduce the market for such educational groups. In general the off-season closure of too many hotels, guest houses and site attractions does not help to extend the season and tourism also continues to suffer from an archaic national policy of restricted Sunday trading.

Chronology

11 Jan: The takeover by the largest tour operator, Thomson Travel, of the third largest tour operator, Horizon, is given the go-ahead by the MMC.

30 Jan: The government ends the grant scheme operated for nearly 20 years to attract investment to tourism projects.

28 Mar: British Tourism Authority report shows increasing numbers of Britons holidaying in Britain with the West Country remaining the favourite destination. A record 24 per cent of the population took more than one long holiday.

6 Apr: Two tour operators, Ventura Holidays and Arrow Holidays, collapse. Concern that there could be other collapses is expressed with bookings down 5 per cent on the previous year.

12 June: Announcement of an investigation into the promotion of timeshare deals to be undertaken by Sir Gordon Borrie, the director general of the Office of Fair Trading. There was a record £2.1 billion deficit in tourism in 1988 according to a survey by Mintel.

16 July: The Secretary of State for Wales temporarily halts plans for a £50 million leisure complex to be built just four-and-a-half miles from the summit of Snowden.

30 July: French air traffic control engineers dispute leads to airport chaos.

8 Aug: Plans of a Manchester millionaire to create a Venice-style theme park at Accrington are announced.
Failure of Paramount, the Bristol-based charter airline.

9 Aug: Seven-day strike by French air traffic control technicians begins, disrupting holiday flights.

22 Aug: Thomson Travel reports a first half loss of £13.3 million.

30 Aug: Thomson Travel cuts half a million holidays from its 1990 summer programme and increases prices by 10–15 per cent in response to the continuing crisis in the package holiday business.

6 Sept: Harry Goodman, the head of Intasun, says that the travel industry's price war is at an end as his firm follows Thomson Travel and Horizon in cutting holidays and increasing prices.

9 Sept: London Transport says that the capital will need at least 19,000 more hotel bedrooms by 2000 to cope with the growing demand that the Channel Tunnel will create.

19 Sept: Sunseeker Holidays collapses leaving more than 700 holidaymakers stranded.

28 Sept: The government welcomes the signing of an agreement between the Countryside Commission and the English Tourist Board which sets out guidelines for the development of green tourism in the National Parks and the Norfolk Broads.

12 Oct: The foundation stone for the largest science museum to be built in Britain for 30 years is laid at Coalville, Leicestershire.

20 Oct: Details of a £1.1 billion investment programme to clean up British coastal bathing waters are announced.

25 Oct: Further reductions of overseas holidays for 1990 announced by leading tour operators.

15 Nov: Thomson Travel cuts 500,000 holidays from its 1990 programme and announces the closure of eight regional offices.

22 Dec: EC-wide rules on package holidays announced.

Agriculture

B. A. HOLDERNESS

The last few years have not been good for British agriculture. As a historian brought up among farmers and conversant with the profession, I am oppressed by their foreboding, by the sense that the industry has lost it way between the thickets of Common Agricultural Policy (CAP) bureaucracy and the quicksands of popular revulsion against their methods of producing what the public still wants, but wants with flickering attention – cheap and palatable food. These doubts are perhaps misdirected, but they are substantial and cannot be conjured away by the snap of Oberon's fingers. Several problems have converged in recent years. There is at present a financial crisis in agriculture *and* a failure of confidence in the industry's ability to restore its fortunes by using methods with which agriculturists had for a generation become familiar.

Financial Difficulties

The financial difficulties of farmers owe much, but not all, to the first substantive attempt at reforming the CAP. British agriculture reached a recent peak in entrepreneurial terms in 1984 when net farm income and the cash flow of farmers and their spouses touched a height not seen since the late 1970s. Thus the indices of farm net income which had averaged 222 in 1971–6 (278 in 1973) only achieved 105 in 1983–8 (136 in 1984) [1986 prices = 100]. For the 1980s in general, the only farmers who have felt reasonably satisfied with events have been those specializing in wheat and oilseeds, although even they have suffered from the combination of economies in the price support and poor seasons in 1985–8. Input prices have tended to rise modestly in real terms throughout the 1980s, whereas product prices have declined by about 15 per cent between 1981–4 and 1985–8 (by about 50 per cent since the mid 1970s). Even effective self-sufficiency declined from 1984 to 1988. The same fall has occurred in gross capital formation from a decadal high point in 1984. Two ominous statistics further illustrate the financial constriction of many farmers. Net rent continued to rise through the economic reces sion, virtually doubling in the six years 1981–6 and then resting on a plateau. Bank debt also nearly doubled in the same years. By 1986, interest charges equalled almost half of farmers' aggregate incomes, and conditions have not improved since. Land prices have fallen since their peak in 1983 but not in a ratio equal to the decline of net income in agriculture.[1] The 1989 figures are not yet available, but do not promise very much relief even though the haemorrhage may have been staunched. The year has been more favourable than farmers at first expected. There was a time early in the growing season when farmers in South East England, looking upon their barley, sugar beet and potatoes, feared a dearth. It did not happen; even the milk supply, always vulnerable to protracted drought, was maintained. Warm summers, even without rain, do not often impair production, for a shortage in volume is usually compensated by an improvement in quality. Farmers in East Anglia have found the excellence of this year's crops a thankful relief from the rain-soaked, unserviceable abundance of the past three years. In some parts of the pasture districts, the experience has been less gratifying, but the drought has caused few profound difficulties in land management. Apart from the outbreak of rhizomania in sugar beet there has even been little infestation sufficient to repress yields. We do not know what the final production figures may be, but farmers have little reason to feel despondent simply on that score. They will probably have reaped a harvest unequalled for quality since 1983.

Agricultural Policy

The malaise is more than merely financial. The overriding difficulty confronting farmers is over-abundance. The 1980s have seen, besides a deteriorating financial position, a record in the production of foodstuffs which amounts to an oversupply of the market. The spectre of dearth has been laid since 1972–3 and increasing affluence in the developed world has not only made consumers more selective in the foods they purchase but has also reduced significantly the relative proportion of disposable income expended on foodstuffs. Agriculture by its efficiency in producing ample, cheap food has hit against the principle of diminishing returns. The CAP more even than the national policy of protecting the industry disguised this disequilibrium for many years by supporting producers' prices and encouraging agricultural productivity. In the context of the CAP, 'cheap' food is a relative expression. Food is inexpensive in terms of income; it is made artificially dear by European Community (EC) intervention in comparison with the prices ruling in Chicago. The difference, together with other transfer payments, accounts largely for the prosperity of the agricultural sector in western Europe from 1960 to 1984.[2] This could hardly be expected to last idefinitely, even though the EC remains committed to supporting the essential structure of the continental rural social order. Production schedules in a period of rapid technological change are difficult to control. Farmers throughout the core region of western Europe have made increments of productivity that owe less to planning and more to the application of scientific innovations in the industry. Britain, for instance, had almost achieved self-sufficiency in temperate food crops by 1983 at the same time as the pressure to export food in neighbouring member-states was never greater. The market in this country is supplied not merely with abundance but also with unprecedented variety, in which, however, the opportunities for domestic producers of food to diversify and to capitalize upon the more eclectic tastes of consumers are neither expanding nor expansible. There are, of course, niches to be occupied by special interests, especially in the production of organic, additive-free commodities, but British agriculture at large is ill-equipped to seize these opportunities, because of its organization around great, capital-intensive farms. If agricultural policy, in Brussels as in London, signally changes direction, the exposure of agriculture in this country to an indicative monoculture will bring about its starvation. In agricultural recessions factory farms are usually worse affected than family holdings; and added to the capitalist farmers' operational problems is their overborrowing, which here has been impelled as much by conspicuous investment as by reproducible capital formation.

The general crisis has not yet arrived. It may indeed be averted since there is no political predisposition within the EC as a whole to sabotage the agrarian order in the interests of suprastate bookkeeping, but the underlying problem has in some way still to be resolved. The last Community initiative to tackle agricultural plenty, the once fearsome milk quotas, has proved less than terrifying to farmers still in dairying. When the profit margins of agriculture have elsewhere plumbed immemorial depths since 1986, dairy producers have enjoyed an unexpectedly prosperous eighteen months, thanks to the effects of the milk quotas in reducing surplus production.

Dealing with Over-Production

The Ministry of Agriculture, Fisheries and Food (MAFF), accustomed before 1973 often to restrain the farmers' will to produce, is once again thinking out ways of squaring the circle. Since the price mechanism is neither under British control nor accessible to the disciplinary effects of free trade the options that mitigate but do not flout the rules of the CAP are few. The difficulty with any attempt to compensate landholders for not using their whole area for agriculture is that enforcement is haphazard and evasion easy to achieve. There is little doubt that much British agricultural land is marginal for cultivation, that there is little point in producing poor crops on infertile land or that the post-war craze for ploughing up much ancient grassland impaired a valuable asset. But taking land out of cultivation, except to be built upon, and reconverting arable to pasture are questionable proceedings. In the first place, the alternatives to tillage are less attractive than growing wheat, barley, sugar beet, coleseed, and other crops since the products of pastoral farming have generally suffered a greater decline than those of arable farming. Who needs more beef or lamb, milk, butter or cheese? Secondly, farmers have been inclined in the past to take grants-in-aid to reduce output and then to raise overall productivity with the proceeds. Thirdly, the profitable alternatives to agriculture, residential building, coniferous afforestation, facilities for organized leisure have encountered public (local) disapproval. The 'set-aside' scheme finally devised by the Ministry in 1987 has been slow to win acceptance. The calculations to be made by farmers in opting for the scheme are not complicated but there is a certain emotional resistance to the idea of disusing even part of a factor of production which had attracted so much previous investment. Whether a set-aside scheme is appropriate to the long term problems of agricultural over-production remains in doubt. With a view to the future, most agronomists appear to believe that the technological miracle will continue to work its magic upon agriculture in the developed world. Even less, probably much less, land will be required to produce the same quantity of foodstuffs in a generation or two, if no disasters befall. Thus, there are proposals in active discussion to remake the 'waste', to create new broadleaved forests even in the South East and to set up nature reserves. Yet, the pressure upon 'ecologically sensitive' areas, upon the surviving marshlands, water meadows and ancient woods, has not diminished.

It is, however, from a different quarter that relief may come, less from farming than from development, housing and road building especially, since the taste of the times is for 'green field' sites, for ruri-urban amenities rather than inner-city reconstruction. For several generations 12,000–20,000 hectares were lost each year to urban use. In the past 15 years the tempo has tended to increase. In 1988 about 30,000 hectares were taken out of agricultural use, a figure which does not include temporary conversions. The public is told repeatedly that there is a chronic shortage of land for development in the regions of Britain which are best suited to agriculture. In the South East especially, agriculture is under real stress from the incoherence of planning policies. Landowners are often frustrated in their attempts either to dispose of land for building or, paradoxically, to prevent suburban sprawl and fragmentation of their businesses. The ending of the boom in the district may have brought relief but, given the competing demands upon land use, the problem will not be resolved without a strategy for converting surplus agricultural land to new purposes. So far, all the decisions have been tactical or even illogical, which has merely increased confusion.

The Quality of Food

It would be a maladroit reporter who omitted to investigate the public disquiet with agriculture that agitated the media at the end of 1988 and has since remained intermittently hectic like tertian fever. Public awareness of agriculture is seldom manifest; it floats beneath the current breaking surface only when excited by strong feelings, of displeasure or of gratitude as may be, and lasting only so long as the emotion is exploitable. Agriculture generally has a good 'image', but the defects of agricultural practice are resented the more for their scouting of illusion. This is especially true of the increasingly sentimental response to animal keeping. The issue of salmonella infestation in poultry intersected with so many prejudices and anxieties that it was destined soon as it was disclosed to become a *cause célèbre* of the ecologists. It is difficult to tell from reading the press reports whether people were more vexed by the disillusioning reminder of battery farming or by the evidence, contestable and contested as it was, of the risks to the food supply that mass production by factory methods had not eliminated. If livestock and their products were infected as the result of authentic production methods and not merely through carelessness or fraud, the edifice of modern agriculture might fall, since its walls, like the second pig's house of sticks, would not withstand the breath of public scrutiny. Only if good practice were to be speedily restored and the causes of disaffection eradicated, that is to say only if the problems were not structural but superficial, would the line hold. Many in farming were not optimistic and talked of relief rather than reform. And yet there was no real evidence of an incurable disorder of the intensive livestock industry. Farmers naturally desire to make profits and the returns upon intensive poultry keeping are not substantial. Since the essence of the business is to obtain the greatest production of eggs or broiler meat that is possible, feed is critical. For long the supply of protein-rich materials, essential for rapid growth, was taken as fish-meal; when that became expensive in terms of expected profits, the industry, millers as well as farmers, turned instead to cheaper additives including proteins derived from dead chicks. This induced cannibalism is not only repugnant, but also hazardous since salmonella is enzootic in fowls and infestation is both rapidly spread and difficult to eradicate. Prohibition of high- risk protein ingredients in compound feeds will not solve the problem, but it will remove the worst contaminant out of the system.

The solution has been compromised, however, by the reluctance of the industry to admit any shortcomings. When it is easy for microbiologists to confute claims that food from the EC is pure and unadulterated, something more than a defensive closing of ranks is necessary. The storm, which was partly created by the wind machine of publicity, could have been ridden out, had it not been for the discovery of listeria in many other products. Expectation of risk-free foodstuffs, even perhaps to the point where faulty refrigeration or inept microwave cookery carry no dangers, has become the consumer's birthright. That is the farmer's real problem, for since he stands at the beginning of a complex chain of production, he is vulnerable to oscillations of popular demand for nutriments that satisfy emotional as much as physiological needs. Faddism, or to be fair, the preference for extending as much as for preserving life, is now a vector in the agro-industrial calculus.

Agriculture and the Environment

The problems besetting agriculture may be ecological and may indeed evoke an emotional response out of proportion to their solution, but they are woven so tightly in the tissue of agricultural progress that disentanglement of the strands in order to eliminate defective material could well result in the unravelling of the industry's nerve system. Eventually perhaps a synthesis will emerge resolving or subsuming the contradictions between the prowess necessary to achieve cheap food and the suspicion of gratuitous technical efficiency, but at present it is possible only to apprehend the antithesis to scientific agriculture. We can be sure that the course chosen will not lead far towards natural regimina of production, not least because few, if any, farmers are now equipped mentally or materially to attend to the different disciplines imposed by organic production schedules. A farmer of my acquaintance, an expert in the revival of old techniques, who cultivates one-tenth of his ground 'organically,' is of the opinion that he can convert little more because he, like others of his kind, has forgotten the art of rotations and interlocking mixed husbandry. Moreover, the gains for the producer of such change are elusive. His yields of wheat grown organically often may not exceed one-third of the yield obtained from the fields strewn with organo-mineral fertilizers or pesticides, whereas the price for such a crop is never more than twice that of the mass-produced commodity. Allowing for the fact that organic produce is as yet a scarce commodity in the market, the economics of back-pedalling does not seem very attractive. Even if there were any savings to be made upon machinery, the notably increased demand for labour in a prospectively tight market would annul them. Agriculture may be in a dilemma but it is not of the farmers' making. The crux of the matter is resolvable only by consumers in alliance with government regulatory agencies. There may be evidence, touchingly reinforced during the recent food crisis, that consumers will pay more for ecologically benign produce (if any exists), but this remains an untried proposition. It is one thing to offer buyers the choice between organic and 'inorganic' production, quite another to eliminate choice altogether. Reinventing the dung-cart in the interests of protecting the environment in itself will serve no useful purpose. Intensive mixed husbandry sufficiently widespread to produce 'organic' commodities to provide for the whole population would, in effect, desecrate the earth's living envelope no less than factory farming. In the Netherlands, for example, one of the principal environmental grievances against agriculture is the high level of methane emissions from decayed organic matter.

Conclusion

The years 1988–9 are not an epoch of agricultural history. The weeds which spoiled the harvest of consumer satisfaction were sown long before. Some, like poppies, lay dormant in the earth only to spring up when disturbed; others have grown interspersed with the corn every year, accepted through familiarity until their noxious effect was pointed out by over-candid friends. The super-structure of progressive, scientific agriculture has been under bombardment for years but the guerrilla forces opposed to the landed interest were too disunited and their ranging salvoes too eratic to raze the fortress. The metaphors of infestation or siege may seem highly coloured for use in describing so prosaic a problem as the deflation of agricultural expectations. They are justified only because I wish to raise the consciousness of the reader, to turn what is flat and even tedious into something more graphically vivid. The prospects for a true understanding of the ecological disequilibria affecting the advanced parts of the world depend upon exact science and accurate history. The recent problems of agriculture reflect the problems confronting society in its choice of a way through the post-industrial landscape. The message is that there are no simple solutions.

Notes
  1. Most of these statistics are derived from the Ministry of Agriculture, Fisheries and Food annual series, which have been compressed in a manageable form by Hilary Marks in, *A Hundred Years of British Food and Farming: A Statistical Survey*, D. K. Britton (ed.), London, 1989. For 1988 onwards the Ministry compendium *Agriculture in the UK*, HMSO, 1989, supplements Marks' data which end in 1986–7.
  2. The EC position is set out statistically in *The Agricultural Situation in the Community 1987* (the 1988 edition is not yet to hand), which compares the national data of all twelve countries.

Chronology
3 Jan: Farmworkers call for 60 per cent increase in their basic wage and a cut in their working week from 40 to 35 hours.
11 Jan: Sir Donald Acheson, Chief Medical Officer of Health, agrees that salmonella in eggs is a serious public health problem but that Edwina Currie was wrong to say most of Britain's production was infected.
12 Jan: Coypu capture campaign pronounced a success and wound up.
24 Jan: Ministry of Agriculture, Fisheries and Food criticized by the Lords Select Committee on Science and Technology for cutting back spending on research into food poisoning.
10 Feb: Government announces an inquiry into all aspects of food poisoning in the wake of the scare about salmonella in eggs.
21 Feb: Debate on food standards in the Commons. Labour's motion of censure over the government's handling of the food poisoning scare is defeated by 289 to 199.
27 Feb: Announcement of a pilot scheme of subsidies to encourage beef farmers to revert to more traditional methods with a scheme for arable farmers to follow in 1990.
3 Mar: Commons agriculture committee report on the eggs scare, *Salmonella in Eggs*, HC 108 is published.
14 Mar: National Consumer Council report declares many consumers believe much of the food they buy is unfit to eat and feel ill-informed about safety standards.
21 Mar: Closure of five agricultural research stations announced.

5 Apr: Richard Ryder, Parliamentary Secretary at the Ministry of Agriculture, Fisheries and Food denounces the reluctance of magistrates to impose heavy fines on farmers who pollute rivers after a record number of cases were recorded.

24 Apr: Sabotage of Heinz baby food revealed, the first of a number of such incidents throughout the year.

2 May: Announcement that a UK Register of Organic Food Standards is to be set up.

4 May: Countryside Commission proposes plans to encourage farmers to undertake ecologically sound activities. This involves the setting up of Environmentally Sensitive Areas where farmers will be given money to preserve traditional farming practices.

5 May: Three-day festival of British Food and Farming in Hyde Park begins.

22 May: Government refuses to ban use of cattle brains in meat products, despite growing concern over bovine spongiform encephalopathy.

12 June: Warning to avoid all brands of hazelnut yoghurt after an outbreak of botulism.

13 June: Total ban on the use of some types of cattle offal in meat pies and other foods announced in an effort to curb fears of the spread of bovine spongiform encephalopathy to people.

19 June: Trial begins whereby farmers in East Anglia are paid to restore wildlife to land damaged by intensive farming methods.

26 June: Ban on the sale of hazelnut yoghurt lifted.

12 July: Department of Health warns pregnant women not to eat pâté until further notice and orders a survey of all types of pâté on sale in Britain.

25 July: Salmonella outbreak in North Wales.

27 July: All food premises must be registered under new legislation proposed in the White Paper *Food Safety: Protecting the Consumer*. This document was condemned as inadequate by food consultants and other bodies.

9 Aug: New outbreak of salmonella in Cheshire and Lancashire.

Lords select committee on the European Communities report *Nitrates in Water* warns that the proposed EC target for cutting the use of nitrates could put farmers out of business in areas where the levels of nitrates in groundwater are considered too high.

18 Aug: Government announces the type of salmonella which contaminates eggs is rampant in a high proportion of chicken flocks.

19 Aug: Steve Tompkins' *Forestry in Crisis* attacks forestry policy and especially the environmental effect of the spread of conifers.

22 Aug: Inquiry into the performance of microwave ovens and their contribution to food poisoning ordered. BSI is also asked to review its performance tests for the ovens.

24 Aug: One in ten portions of Belgian pâté sold in Britain contain listeria according to Acheson.

Consumers' Association calls for an independent food watchdog.

26 Aug: Review of straw and stubble burning announced.

7 Sept: Polly Peck buys the fresh fruit businesses of the American company Del Monte for £557 million.

21 Sept: Lord Lewis, Chairman of the Royal Commission on Environmental Pollution, calls for a ban on stubble burning.

22 Sept: Survey by the Public Health Laboratory Service Communicable Disease Surveillance Centre in the *British Medical Journal* says that eggs, egg products and chickens are the prime sources of salmonella and not poor kitchen hygiene.

26 Sept: Dr Richard Gilbert, Director of the Public Health Laboratory Services food hygiene laboratory, warns that food low in salt and sugar, aimed at the health-conscious consumer, could be high in bacteria.

3 Oct: Announcement that egg hatcheries are to be monitored for salmonella.

10 Oct: Britain is ordered by the European Court of Justice immediately to suspend key provisions of the 1988 Merchant Shipping Act which were designed to repel a 100-strong Spanish fishing fleet.

25 Oct: Government cuts in food safety research are criticized by the Food Safety Advisory Centre which represents the major food retailers.

2 Nov: Plans for a new Food Safety Directorate announced.

8 Nov: Restrictions on farms selling beef or milk because of lead contamination begin.

9 Nov: Public Accounts Committee *Sale of the National Seed Development Organization and Part of the Assets of the Plant Breeding Institute*, HMSO, is sharply critical of the sale of these to Unilever by the government in 1987.

13 Nov: Use of cattle brains and certain other types of cattle offal in food is banned.

21 Nov: New powers to regulate and control food production are to be introduced in the Food Safety Bill announced in the Queen's speech.

23 Nov: Food Safety Bill introducing tough new safety regulations and penalties and ending crown immunities on most government buildings is published.

30 Nov: Announcement that stubble burning is to banned from autumn 1992.

5 Dec: Survey of microwave ovens by the Agriculture and Food Research Council finds several failed to kill food poisoning bacteria, leading to the withdrawal of several models from sale.

19 Dec: EC quota for North Sea fishing announced.

21 Dec: Three elderly people die in a salmonella outbreak in Oldham.

Britain's Foreign Trade, Payments and Exchange Rates

PETER SINCLAIR

The geography composition of a country's foreign trade analyses the shares in its exports and imports attributable to different countries or geopolitical blocs. Slightly more than half Britain's overseas trade in goods is not conducted with its eleven partners in the European Communities (EC). The United Kingdom is the only EC country which exports at least as much to the rest of the world as to the other EC countries. The United States is at present Britain's largest single export market, absorbing one-eighth of British exports. The second largest share of UK exports goes to West Germany (11.4 per cent), and the third to France (10 per cent). The only other markets to receive 5 per cent or more of UK exports are the Netherlands, Belgium (including Luxembourg), Ireland and Italy. Nearly 8 per cent of British exports are destined for Commonwealth countries, among which Canada (2.6 per cent), Australia (1.8 per cent) and India (1.6 per cent) stand out. Japan receives a modest 2.7 per cent of the UK's exports. These data, and those in the three paragraphs that follow, all relate to the first four months of 1989. They have been computed from statistics contained in European Commission trade statistics publications.

The EC share of UK imports is nearly 52 per cent. West Germany accounts for the largest slice (16 per cent of total British imports), with France, the Netherlands and Italy providing 8.9 per cent, 7.2 per cent and 5.4 per cent respectively. The second largest source of UK imports is the United States (11.6 per cent). Japan is also a leading exporter to the UK, and accounts for 5.7 per cent of Britain's import bill, more than double her share of UK exports. The Commonwealth supplies a bare 5 per cent of Britain's imports, of which Canada accounts for nearly half. Outside the EC, Sweden is the source of 4.8 per cent of British imports (more than Belgium or Ireland).

Within the EC, Britain is the dominant trading partner for Ireland. The UK accounts for nearly two-thirds of EC exports to Ireland, and almost half her exports to the EC. Geographical proximity is a major influence on trading patterns, largely for reasons of transport costs. Thus, almost three-fifths of the Netherlands' exports to the EC go to West Germany or Belgium. Spain is Portugal's largest source of imports, although curiously Portugal exports more to France, West Germany and the UK than to Spain. France and West Germany are easily each others' leading trading partners. Britain accounts for nearly 20 per cent of Norway's imports from EC countries, but only 3 per cent of Austria's. Historical links also play a role. Britain accounts for more than half EC exports to Barbados, Botswana and Zambia, for example, as does France to several of her former colonies. Britain provides one-third of the Commonwealth's imports from the EC. The persistence of these historical trade links testifies to the force of inertia, and the big problems of establishing trust and surmounting switching costs that trading firms face when they start to sell in a new foreign market. Politics provide a further influence. Seven years after the Falklands War, Argentina continues to import very little from the UK: Britain's share of EC exports to the Argentine is barely 3 per cent. Greece accounts for less than 1 per cent of Turkish imports from the EC.

There is no reason why goods trade between individual pairs of countries should be balanced. Britain today has a trade surplus with Saudi Arabia, and a big deficit with West Germany; and West Germany has a deficit on its bilateral trade with Saudi Arabia. Germany's imports of Saudi oil help to generate electricity, a key input into the steel and machine tools she sells to Britain, for example, and Britain can turn those products into drilling equipment and armaments she sells to Saudi Arabia, with which she can develop and defend her oilfields. And Britain's wide visible trade deficits with Germany and Japan are partly offset by bilateral surpluses on invisibles such as financial services.

For much of the nineteenth century, Britain traded more outside Europe than within it. This pattern persisted until the early 1950s. The post-war decades have seen the UK reorient its trade increasingly towards Europe. The trend began long before Britain's accession to the EC in 1973, but the subsequent removal of tariffs on trade with its EC partners has accelerated it. The major changes that the 1980s have brought to the geography composition of UK trade are illustrated in the piegrams in chart 1. In January 1980, West Germany was the UK's largest export market (9.7 per cent), with the US a close second (9.3 per cent). But the US provided the UK with its largest source of imports (12.6 per cent), with Germany in second place here (9.8 per cent). As we have seen, this order had been reversed by 1989. Japan's shares of Britain's exports and imports were barely half their 1989 levels in 1980. The growth in North Sea oil production has all but eliminated imports from Saudi Arabia, which had been high in 1980 (3.4 per cent), while UK exports there have risen. UK trade with France, Ireland, Italy, the Netherlands and Spain has grown in importance in the 1980s, while that with Austria, Belgium, Sweden and Switzerland – three of them erstwhile partners in the European Free Trade Association – has slipped back.

EXPORTS

IMPORTS

1980

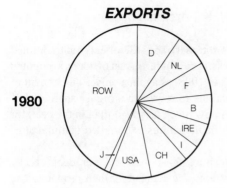
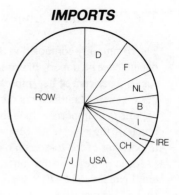

1989

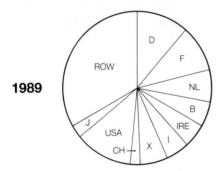
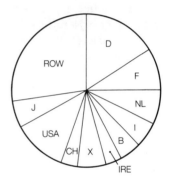

Code: D : West Germany   X : Other members of EC–12
      F : France   (Denmark, Greece, Portugal, Spain)
   NL : Netherlands   CH : Switzerland
      B : Belgium (including Luxembourg)   USA : United States
       I : Italy   J : Japan
  IRE : Ireland   ROW : Rest of World

Sources: EUROSTAT Statistical Publications

*Chart 1   Piegrams for the export destinations and import
sources for UK trade*

The Commodity Composition of UK Foreign Trade

The commodity composition of Britain's external trade still reflects her traditional dependence on imports of primary products. As a whole, this set of goods accounted for 19.2 per cent of her imports of goods in 1988, as against only 15.8 per cent of her exports. Manufactures therefore continue to represent a higher share of UK exports than imports, although the gap is now much narrower than in the past: for much of the nineteenth century, British manufactures exports led manufactures imports by a four-to-one margin.

Agriculture, forestry and fishing account for barely 2.3 per cent of UK employment and GDP today, well below domestic demand for their products. The shortfall is made up, as it has been for centuries, by imports. Foodstuffs represent 8.2 per cent of UK imports of goods, but only four per cent of UK exports. This imbalance is partly redressed by beverage and tobacco products. These account for 2.5 per cent of UK exports, as against a mere 1.4 per cent of her imports. Raw materials claim a five per cent share of goods imports, but just 2.3 per cent of imports, reflecting Britain's narrow resource base. But the discovery and exploitation of North Sea oil in the 1970s has made Britain a substantial net exporter of fuel products in the 1980s: these accounted for nearly 7 per cent of exports, yet just 4.3 per cent of imports. The varied requirements for different oil and petroleum products, and the particular characteristics of British oil, create room for two- way international trade in this set of goods. Primary products also embrace the tiny category of oils, fats and waxes – SITC classification 4 – where imports predominated.

Machinery and transport equipment is responsible for nearly half Britain's total exports and imports of manufactures. The share of exports led the share of imports for these products in 1988, as it has done since the industrial revolution. But the exceptionally large overall visible trade deficit meant that Britain actually spent considerably more on imports of transport equipment and machinery than it earned from exports of them in that year. The ratio of export earnings to import payments was barely 80 per cent in 1988. Britain first registered a deficit in this category of goods in 1983. Britain is not the only EC net importer of machinery and transport equipment: Denmark, France, Greece, the Netherlands, Portugal and Spain were also in this position in 1988, but curiously enough not Ireland.

Britain also displays deficits in 1988 for other groups of manufactures: miscellaneous manufactures, and manufactures classified by material. These two categories accounted for 13.3 per cent and 17.8 per cent of imports of goods, and 12.7 per cent and 15.3 per cent of exports. Chemicals, on the other hand, yielded a surplus, and represented 11.7 per cent of exports as against only 7.7 per cent of imports. Goods not specified elsewhere provided 6 per cent of both exports and imports.

By and large, countries tend to export those goods which, in the absence of trade, would have been relatively cheap. They sell them to other countries where they would otherwise be relatively scarce. Britain's net imports of foodstuffs are best explained by her pattern of endowments of factors of production. She has a large workforce and stock of capital relative to her land surface area. Agriculture is intensive in land. So, in the absence of trade, food would be very expensive in the UK in comparison, say, with manufactures. Precisely the opposite is true for New Zealand. So Britain imports lamb and dairy products from New Zealand, and exports machinery there in return.

The influence of factor endowments on trade patterns may be qualified or reinforced by other considerations, such as technology and tastes. Britain's exports of whisky must owe something to the high productivity and state of technical know-how in her Scottish distilleries, for example, as well as to the relative abundance of suitable natural resources. And although the expiry of patents, opportunities for copy-catting and reverse engineering, and technology transfer by multinational firms all tend to spread technology across international borders, the phenomenon of learning by doing may recreate a productivity advantage for experienced firms as fast as this process undermines it. Demand also matters for trade. And trading patterns are also affected by government intervention.[1] The rules of the EC Common Agricultural Policy (CAP) prevent Britain from importing as much as she would – and did before 1973 – under free trade from Canada and New Zealand. Levies imposed on non-EC food imports cause her to buy much high-priced grain and butter from EC sources instead.

Perhaps the most striking characteristic of manufactures is their diversity. Heterogeneity has increased as products have become more sophisticated and specialized. Countries export and import cars between each other, for example, because indivisibilities in plant and product development narrow the range of products that a vehicle assembler can sensibly produce. But tastes are diverse. So some Frenchmen's ideal set of characteristics embodied in a motor car may be approximated better by a German or Italian product than a home made one, and vice versa. Variety is not confined to manufactures, either: many Britons and Frenchmen eat both camembert and stilton cheese, for instance. They like to ring the changes. So there is two-way Anglo-French trade in cheese.

Oligopoly can be an additional factor making for two-way international trade, even in homogenized goods. One or two domestic firms that enjoyed exclusive access to their domestic market would tend to set high prices. Foreign firms would find it profitable to sell into that market if international trade were permitted – and the home country's firms should also find it profitable to do the same in foreign markets. Monopolistic competition (the market form where many different, imperfect substitutes are available, each from a single producer) and oligopoly (few firms) are two overlapping types of imperfect competition. Imperfect competition is the rule rather than the exception in manufacturing industry. Imperfect competition provides additional reasons for thinking that international trade is socially beneficial, although it also supplies some subtle arguments in favour of some form of government intervention.[2] Although Britain may now have a deficit in much of its trade in manufactures, this does not mean that her exports of manufactures are unimportant – still less that she would stand to gain by curtailing her imports of manufactures.

In sum, Britain enters the 1990s as a net importer of most categories of manufactures, in addition to food and raw materials in which she has always registered a trade deficit. In partial compensation, she remains a net exporter of beverages and tobacco, and of chemicals. In the 1980s, she has also been a net exporter of fuel products, but this may not persist for long as current North Sea oilfields are gradually being exhausted. Britain's overall visible trade balance is negative. Indeed, it has been negative for all but a handful of years this century. Usually the visible deficit is more or less offset by a surplus on invisibles. The years 1988 and 1989 are rather exceptional in this respect. There is a large current account deficit because the deficit on visibles has widened so much that the invisibles surplus can only pay for about one-third of it.

In 1978, Britain ran a small current account surplus of 0.6 per cent of national income – 1978 was a much more typical year in this respect than 1988. Visible trade was as usual in deficit, but only slightly (0.2 per cent of national income). It is instructive to contrast Britain's commodity composition of trade at that time with the statistics for 1988. Chart 2 presents piegrams for the fourth quarter of 1978, alongside those for 1988. In 1978, Britain enjoyed a healthy surplus on trade in machinery and transport equipment, which accounted for 35 per cent of her exports and only a quarter of her imports. There was a small deficit on trade in miscellaneous manufactures (9.9 per cent of exports but 10.1 per cent of imports) but a surplus of manufactures classified by material (24.9 per cent of exports and 22 per cent of imports) and, as in 1988, also on chemicals (11 per cent and 7.1 per cent). Manufactures as a whole displayed a trade surplus, and represented nearly 83 per cent of exports and only two-thirds of imports. In sharp contrast with 1988, there was a large deficit on trade in fuel products, which accounted for 11.3 per cent of imports and just 6.5 per cent of exports.

The emergence of trade deficit on manufactures in the mid-1980s caused grave disquiet in many quarters. It contrasted painfully with Britain's historical record as the first industrial nation. The rising penetration of imports in Britain's car market (up from 10 per cent in the 1950s to over 55 per cent by 1985) was plain for everyone to see. Imports led exports for many products that had been invented in Britain in the previous half century or so (jet aircraft, television sets, computers). Perhaps the saddest spectacle was the slow demise of Britain's shipbuilding industry. Within living memory, at the end of the nineteenth century, Britain had accounted for some 70 per cent of world exports of ships. By the late 1980s, her share had slumped to under 1 per cent.

Many of British manufacturing industries had been bedevilled by a vicious circle that ran from poor profits, to faltering investment, failures to raise productivity and innovate, and thence to increasing uncompetitiveness, falling orders and a further slide in profits. The situation was aggravated by fierce overseas competition,

EXPORTS

IMPORTS

1978

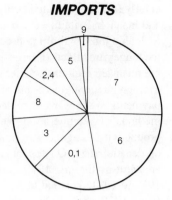

1988

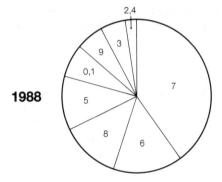

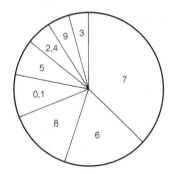

Code: 0,1: Food, Drink and Tobacco
     2,4: Raw Materials
       3: Fuel Products
       5: Chemicals

6: Manufacturers Classified by Material
7: Machinery and Transport Equipment
8: Miscellaneous Manufacturers
9: Other Manufacturers

Sources: EUROSTAT Statistical Publications

Chart 2   Commodity composition of UK trade

chiefly from the defeated belligerents in the Second World War – Germany, Italy and Japan. In Britain, weak management succumbed to myopic unions which tried to defend jobs by limiting productivity and resisting innovation, and failed to see the longer run effects of large wage claims. Firms were bribed by well-intentioned but mistaken regional policies into constructing high-cost plants in areas of above average unemployment, far removed from their major markets. Incentive-based payments systems were replaced by 'measured day work' and other flat-rate methods of remuneration which bought fairness at a high cost in terms of productivity foregone. Key industries were disrupted by proposals to nationalize or denationalize. On top of all these structural weaknesses, which were fully apparent by the mid 1970s, came the massive appreciation of sterling from late 1977 to 1981. This led to a collapse of manufacturing output (down 15 per cent from 1979 to 1981), a rash of bankruptcies and plant closures, and the disappearance of one-third of the manufacturing sector's jobs.

The deindustrialization of the early 1980s, and the jump in sterling that precipitated it, were both traceable in part to oil developments. 'Dutch disease' is the unlovely term coined to describe the weakness of the Netherlands' non-energy traded sectors in the 1970s. The Dutch exported large amounts of North Sea gas to Germany. The gas export boom led to monetary expansion and wage inflation in the Netherlands (it would have led to exchange rate appreciation of the Dutch florin had the rate not been tied closely to the German mark). That in turn undermined the international competitiveness of other Dutch industries. These events were to repeat themselves in the UK when North Sea oil production began in earnest in the late 1970s. But for Britain, there was an added twist. The world price of oil doubled in 1979-80. This made sterling look still more attractive. The implication, well told by Corden,[3] is that if one traded sector in an economy booms because of technical or geological discoveries, or favourable world price movements, the others have to run faster to keep up with the adverse pressures this induces.

In the event, many of Britain's non-oil traded sectors did run faster to keep up. Labour productivity jumped by nearly 40 per cent between 1982 and 1985 in three important industries, all threatened by cheaper imports: steel, vehicle assembly and coal mining. In 1988, manufacturing labour productivity as a whole stood more than 50 per cent above its 1980 level. This contrasts sharply with the record of stagnating productivity observed between 1973 and 1980. The firms and industries that had survived the competitiveness crisis of the early 1980s saw a welcome recovery in profits, as well as productivity growth. But often productivity rose more from the shedding of labour than from increases in output. And the excessively rapid demand boom of the late 1980s was to lead to capacity shortages, and a huge jump in imports.

North Sea oil probably made some decline in UK manufacturing inevitable. It certainly hastened some structural changes that would have occurred anyway. Despite its seriously adverse, if transient, effects on unemployment, deindustrialization has had some compensations. Many service sector jobs are widely thought to be more challenging and satisfying than the manufacturing jobs they succeeded. Service jobs seem to be less inimical to the environment. And if Britain had lost its comparative advantage in several manufacturing industries, many argue that it would have been romantic folly to perpetuate what had become an unsustainable and wasteful allocation of resources. Furthermore, deindustrialization has only been partial. Total manufacturing production and exports were no lower at the end of the 1980s than they were at the start. The improved productivity and profit performance of the firms and industries that remain suggest that they are well placed to prevent further erosion of this sector in the decade to come. And the negative trade balance in manufactures, which has in any case been bloated by the exceptionally high level of domestic demand in 1987–9, should not blind one to one interesting fact: Britain's exports of manufactures still account for more than twice the share of national income we observe in Japan.

British Trade and the European Communities

The Single European Act

The Single European Act specifies that by 1 January 1993, internal economic borders within the European Communities shall have been removed. Its principal provisions, and associated proposals, include:

i   capital and labour shall be free to move across these borders without restriction (although Greece, Portugal and Spain have been given periods of grace before they have to remove present restrictions on outward capital movements). This is in fact merely a restatement of one of the terms of the original 1957 Treaty of Rome;

ii   procurement by public authorities in each EC country shall be opened up to competition by firms in all other EC countries;

iii   technical standards applied for a particular product or trade shall be recognized by all other EC countries (the 'mutual recognition' principle) and minimum standards are to be agreed upon and enshrined by statute. This effectively means an end to the non-tariff barriers applied by several EC countries on imports from their EC partners, and requires EC-wide agreement on what restrictions to place, if any, on imports from outside the EC;

iv   some progress towards harmonization – but not (yet) equalization – of rates of indirect tax on goods, such as VAT and excise duties, to the point where scrutiny of flows of goods across internal boundaries can all but cease.

The European Commission called for an official report on the likely economic consequences of the Single European Act, under the chairmanship of Professor Cecchini. The ten-volume report, and its brief summary were published in 1988.[4] Cecchini predicts a positive impact on Europe's real national income of the order of 5 per cent, spread over several years, and a fall in unemployment of about two million. It also attempts to quantify the micro-economic gains held to result from the various measures, which aggregate up to the separate 'macro-economic' prediction of a 5 per cent or so real national income gain.

Removing restrictions on the intra-European movement of capital and labour is held to generate income gains on the argument that if factors migrate from where they are paid less to where they are paid more, aggregate output can only go up. The logic behind this analysis is irreproachable in a world of perfect information and competition, complete markets, compensatory lump sum taxes and harmonized tax rates. Since these conditions are sadly not fulfilled in practice, some commentators have been more qualified in their discussion of the likely consequences of the measure. But there are no compelling reasons to think that a more general and realistic analysis would necessarily lead to lower estimates of output gains. One difficulty, however, is that factor migration does not benefit everyone. German workers, for example, could find their pay or jobs threatened by an influx of workers from elsewhere. The demand for labour, furthermore, is generally going to fall in countries from which capital migrates.

The opening up of public procurement is held to be beneficial on the following argument. Contract and tender prices – in areas such as highway construction or electricity generating equipment – will be brought down, it is assumed, to something close to the average of prices currently observed in the cheapest four countries in the EC. Domestic firms now selling to their national authorities or state agencies behind closed doors at higher prices will be forced to cut their costs in line, releasing resources for more gainful employment elsewhere in the economy. And finally, the existence of scale economies – often pronounced – will lead to the rationalization of plants and firms, and thence to still lower prices. The major problem here is the question of implementation and enforceability. Links between state governments and agencies, and the local firms supplying them, are apt to be close and secretive. It will be hard for firms in other countries to discover if they have been unfairly treated, and still harder to prove it.

Technical standards harmonization has proceeded quite rapidly. A majority of the 300 or so directives have already been agreed upon. The central difficulty is what to do about non-tariff barriers on imports from outside the EC. At present Denmark and the Netherlands have no barriers of this sort against car imports from Japan, for example. But the UK limits Japanese vehicle imports to 11 per cent of its car market, France to 3 per cent of hers, and Italy to less than 1 per cent. Once the Single European Act is in force, a car brought into Rotterdam can be sold without let or hindrance in Paris or Milan. There is a clear conflict of interest between north European consumers (who would like cheap good cars, whatever their provenance) and French and Italian employees and shareholders in automotive companies (who want to protect their livelihoods). This conflict has yet to be resolved. There are other flashpoints too. Should vehicles assembled in the UK plants of Japanese companies (Nissan in Sunderland, Toyota near Derby) be treated as EC products or Japanese exports? French complaints on this score were resolved in the UK's favour in 1989. In its dealing with non-EC imports, the European Commission has emphasized the significance of 'reciprocity'. That means treating imports from country X in the way X treats exports from the EC. But would that imply setting up a byzantine structure of regional restrictions on the European operations of US banks to reflect the complex state rules that govern interstate banking in the United States? Or can the EC try to insist that the US monetary authorities treat EC banks more generously than their own? Answers to these intriguing questions will emerge in the next year or two. Yet a further problem, this time relating to intra-EC trade, is the disparities, often large, in standards currently imposed by different EC countries. Greece, for example, may be more tolerant than West Germany about pollution controls or product safety. Do the West Germans have to accept Greek goods that contravene their own stricter regulations? Are they not handicapping their own domestic firms unfairly? Or are the Greeks to be denied access to the German market, in direct contravention of the Single European Act?

How much Western Europe as a whole gains or loses from standards harmonization, clearly depends on the view one takes about whether the particular standards are too tight or too loose. Furthermore, there will be some efficiency gains from liberalizing the intra-EC movement of goods, but if barriers against non-EC imports remain, trade will be diverted (a welfare cost) and not just created (a gain).

The simplification and elimination of customs formalities at internal borders will allow for numerous if modest efficiency gains. These include such things as the value of time saved in queuing at frontiers, some bonus from increased intra-EC trade, and the redeployment of officials to socially more valuable activities than checking trucks and forms. The British authorities maintain, however, that complete removal of border formalities could threaten the UK with an influx of criminals, terrorists, rabid animals, illegal immigrants and other assorted unwelcome guests. The disputes on this subject await resolution. Indirect tax harmonization will bring welfare and real income gains under certain conditions: for instance, if governments' objectives, consumers' preferences, and producers' technologies are sufficiently similar across the EC, and the new average rates of tax represent an optimal tradeoff between the different factors material to the determination of tax rates (chiefly, economic efficiency and equity considerations). But there are numerous problems. North Europeans appear more willing to pay income tax than Mediterraneans. So Italy, for example, relies heavily on indirect taxes on gasoline and consumer products to redress the balance. Her public finances are already beset with a budget deficit of some 15 per cent of national income. If fiscal harmonization requires her to cut her indirect taxes, serious implications could follow. North European governments are alarmed at the prospect of having to cut duty on alcohol and tobacco products. The UK government has a well-known aversion to imposing VAT – even at the modest rate of 3 per cent – on food and children's clothes. All these contentious issues remain under debate.

Many observers consider that the Cecchini Report's predictions of the benefits of the Single European Market are somewhat exaggerated. Smith and Venables, for example, present a fascinating account of the likely effects of the programme on imperfectly competitive industries, backed up by highly sophisticated reasoning and attempts at quantification.[4] The inferences they draw from their analysis incline one to pessimism. There are others, however, who consider that Cecchini understates the gain. Foremost among them is Baldwin who argues that increasing returns may generate a continuing positive impact of the programme on Western Europe's rate of economic growth.[5] But most of those who commented on this contribution to the important Economic Policy symposium on this issue expressed some scepticism.[6]

Agriculture

Over two-thirds of the European Commission's £35 billion annual budget at present goes to the price support programmes of its Common Agricultural Policy, which does two things. First, it sets internal prices for foodstuffs at levels often well above, sometimes hugely in excess of, those prevailing in international markets. Secondly, it stabilizes internal prices at these preset levels, which are not allowed to move in response to fluctuations in world prices.

The point at which internal prices are set is often so high that, despite its obvious lack of comparative advantage in agriculture in comparison with, say, North America, European demand actually falls short of European supply. When that happens, the gap is made up by intervention buying. Sometimes the surpluses are stored, at considerable cost, in the hope that there will be a shortage next year. Sometimes they are dumped abroad at very low prices (often to Eastern Europe), and sometimes they are simply destroyed. The annual financial cost of these policies is of the order of £20 billion – enough to give each of the EC's seven million farmers a free gift of £3,000 a year. There are typically welfare costs over and above these financial costs: resources are expensively retained in agriculture when they could earn more (at international prices) in other uses. And consumers, particularly low income consumers, are induced to buy less than they would at international prices.

From the British standpoint, the common agricultural policy (CAP) piles insult on injury. Its generous system of producer income support sends most of its payments towards economies with much larger agricultural sectors. The revenues from the tariffs the British authorities are forced to apply on imports of foodstuffs of non-EC origin are diverted in full to Brussels, along with a large slice of VAT receipts, to help defray the massive losses sustained on intervention buying. All that can be said in favour of present arrangements is that Japan and the United States appear to have equally wasteful systems of agricultural support (the reader is referred to a splendid comparison of all these policies by Winters,[7] and that some of the UK's EC partners – principally West Germany – have generously agreed to give the UK some relief against the exorbitant net contributions she would otherwise have to pay.

Britain abolished tariffs on imported food when it repealed the Corn Laws over 150 years ago. That act hurt landowners and agricultural workers, especially in the 1870s when food prices tumbled. But it brought much larger income gains to industrial labour and capital. France and Germany, on the other hand, reacted to falling world prices of grain and other foodstuffs by imposing large tariffs on imports. It was argued that social stability required a thriving peasantry, and, sotto voce, fat rent rolls. The CAP today is the lineal descendant of that ultimately mistaken decision.

The price stabilization role of the CAP brings some benefits to consumers and producers, to the extent that they are averse to the risk that goes with uncertain food prices. But it also induces efficiency losses as well, over and above those implied by imposing tariffs on imports. These arise because producers would gain more than consumers lose by letting domestic prices climb – to encourage exports – when world prices are very high, and because consumers would gain more than producers lose if prices were allowed to drift down – encouraging imports – at times when world prices are low.[8]

The world is sufficiently complex that it is usually hard to tell whether a particular phenomenon or policy is good or bad, let alone gain a reasonably precise numerical estimate of the gains and losses it yields. The CAP is a glorious exception to this rule. It is an unmitigated disaster. The real challenge is to devise a way of getting rid of it that makes all parties, even the farmers it is designed to support, better off than they are with it – and persuading the Council of Ministers to adopt the strategy.

Invisibles

Invisibles refer to those elements in the current account of the balance of payments other than trade in goods. They embrace three particular categories: international trade in services; payments of interest, profits and dividends across the exchanges, and; international transfers paid or received by domestic residents and government authorities.

Table 1 presents the latest official estimates, published in *Financial Statistics*, for UK invisibles in 1988, and comparisons with 1980. International services fall under four major headings: sea transport, civil aviation, travel and tourism, and financial and other services. In 1988, the UK is estimated to have earned some £27 billion on exports of these four groups, and spent nearly £22 billion on imports. So there is a substantial overall surplus. But this masks the fact that there were deficits on the first three of these four categories. By contrast, all four were in surplus in

Table 1. Balance on invisible trade, 1980 and 1988 (in £m.)

	1980	1988
Services		
Sea transport	14	-576
Civil aviation	383	-862
Travel	223	-2042
Financial and other	3883	9478
Interest, profit and dividends	-205	5619
Private sector transfers	-204	-306
General Government transfers		
Total	-1780	-3269
Of which with EC institutions	-825	-1437

Source: Financial Statistics, CSO

1980 (in the case of sea transport, by the slenderest of margins). The export/import ratio for financial and other services was nearly three in both years. This testifies to the international importance of Britain's banking, portfolio management and insurance industries. In 1988 they earned more than twice as much foreign currency as the UK obtained from exports of oil.

Interest profits and dividends (IPD) showed small negative balance in 1980. This was a major departure from the typical historical pattern, for Britain has traditionally always had a surplus on this item (in 1913, the surplus here amounted to nearly 10 per cent of national income, an enormous figure). But by 1988, IPD was in surplus, equivalent to the more modest figure of 1.1 per cent of national income. The real reason for this transformation during the 1980s is the massive export of capital that occurred in these years. The UK built up a net overseas asset position that peaked in 1986 at some £105 billion. In a sense, Britain was exporting a large slice of its net revenues from North Sea oil. This was allowed to happen, because the UK authorities had decided, in 1979, to abolish restrictions against the export of capital by domestic residents. Rates of return on capital in the UK had fallen, by 1980, to levels well below those evident in many other countries. So there was a natural pull to invest overseas, reinforced by considerations of the benefits from international portfolio diversification to reduce risk.

The 1979 policy changes were controversial. The trade unions and many Labour politicians argued that emigration of capital would be inimical to the interests of labour – wage rates would be cut, or employment levels instead if wages were sticky – and that aggregate demand would suffer, in the meantime, because of lower levels of domestic investment. But advocates of the change, such as Forsyth and Kay,[9] argued that discovering and exploiting North Sea oil was rather like winning the football pools – the prudent man would recognize that this was an unrepeatable windfall gain most of which should be saved, and made to earn as much as it could, to generate a sustainable flow of income which could continue to finance higher consumption long after the oil had gone. And if the rate of return on capital at home was lower than abroad, capital exports made sense.

The resulting net export of capital is largely responsible for restoring the positive balance on IPD. But the large current account deficits in 1988 and 1989 have had to be financed, in the main, by net imports of capital. If they persist for long, at or close to current levels of 3 per cent of national income, the IPD surplus will be trimmed back toward balance. It should also be stressed that these official IPD estimates are subject to much more uncertainty than the relatively 'hard' statistics, for instance, for visible trade. The IPD estimates are derived from identified estimates of international capital exports and imports in past years. For much of the 1980s, the balance of payments accounts have shown an embarrassingly large positive entry termed the 'balancing item'. This can be thought of, in the main, as unrecorded capital imports. The interest payments due on these liabilities, if this supposition is correct, are therefore a negative item to be subtracted from the official published IPD estimates.

The balance of transfers is negative for the private sector, and has run at about £250 million or more for most of the 1980s. It consists chiefly of remittances by expatriate Britons working abroad, net of overseas remittances by foreigners working in the UK. The public sector has a large negative balance on transfers, nearly half of it in the form of UK government net transfers to the European Communities. The lion's share of that, of course, is connected with the CAP, but there are also inflows and outflows associated with other EC activities, such as the Regional Development and Social Funds.

When the services, IPD and transfers accounts are aggregated together, the resulting figure is the total net surplus on invisibles. This was positive in both 1980 and 1988, and much higher in the latter year. In 1988, the surplus on invisibles went nearly a third of the way towards financing the massive £21 billion visible trade deficit, bringing the current account deficit (the sum of visible and invisible balances) down to under £15 billion. It is to the analysis of the current account deficit that we next turn.

Britain's Current Account Balance of Payments Position

Britain's current account balance has always undulated between surplus and deficit. Deficits are usually greatest in wartime, and in booms. In the later stages of a trade cycle upswing, domestic demand outstrips productive potential in sector after sector. The rising tide of excess demand is met by burgeoning imports. Domestic producers may also be induced to divert some of their production from exports to the lucrative home market in such conditions. Surpluses on the current account of the balance of payments tend to be high when UK demand is weak, as in trade cycle

Contemporary Britain

troughs. They can also arise when major overseas markets are booming, and when exchange rate and unit labour cost changes have given British export firms a strong competitive edge over their overseas rivals.

Every year from 1980 to 1985, Britain ran a surplus on her current account. Much of it could be put down to net exports of (then) high-priced oil. The period also saw a very sharp climb in British unemployment, both absolutely and in comparison with nearly all other developed countries. That testified to the relatively weak state of domestic demand, which held imports down. But the surplus slipped after 1981, the year that marked the trough of the UK business cycle, and by 1986 it had gone. From 1986 to 1988 the current account swung into very large deficit. By 1988 the deficit had reached almost 3.5 per cent of national income, a historically very high figure. Only a slight improvement has been revealed for 1989. Developments from 1986 to 1989 invite comparison with those from 1972 to 1974. In those two years, the current account deteriorated from a surplus of 0.3 per cent to a deficit of nearly 4 per cent of national income.

Some of the massive deficit in 1974 can be put down to the huge jump in the prices of primary products that occurred in the early 1970s, above all in oil. The nominal US dollar price of oil rose fourfold between 1973 and 1974. At this stage, Britain was a net importer of oil. The rise in oil and other primary product prices – prices of goods that Britain imported – led to a deterioration in her terms of trade of nearly 25 per cent between 1971 and 1974. A country's terms of trade are the ratio of a price index of its exports to an index of its import prices. But the Organization of Petroleum Exporting Countries oil price hike and the terms of trade changes do not tell the full story. Germany and Japan suffered these same shocks, but their current account balances deteriorated much less. What marked the UK out from these other countries was the exceptionally expansionary domestic monetary and fiscal policies that she pursued, almost uninterruptedly, from late 1971 to late 1973. Credit liberalization, rapid growth in monetary aggregates, and large cuts in income tax combined to give a huge injection into private sector demand. This propelled imports up sharply. The ratio of imports to national income jumped by nearly half from mid-1971 to end-1973. Rather over half this rise represented an increase in the volume of imports, which in 1973 stood a full 25 per cent above their 1971 level.

The current account deterioration from 1986 to 1988–9 is almost as rapid, in relation to national income, as that from 1972 to 1974. Once again, import volumes shot up in the face of measures to liberalize credit, rapid growth in most definitions of the money supply, and a sequence of large cuts in income tax. Just as in 1972, these took the form of reductions in tax rates and large increases in exemption limits. The parallels are not quite exact. The government's budgetary position improved in the late 1980s, swinging into surplus even after allowance for privatization sales which, since they are one-off portfolio swaps of equity for debt, should never be allowed to contaminate proper definitions of deficits. From 1972 to 1974, it registered rapid deterioration. Britain's terms of trade displayed little change in the second period, but worsened in the first. In the first period, sterling depreciated heavily and government spending rose in relation to national income; exchange rates and government spending were quite flat in the second. But other similarities are striking. Unemployment fell quickly in both periods. Inflation climbed in both periods which saw large rises in interest rates as the authorities intervened to steady the exchange rate, curb private spending and regain control over ballooning wider definitions of the money supply. Both periods saw a hectic real estate boom that ended in tears, and some sharp drops in equity prices.

The conventional explanation of the behaviour of a country's current account balance starts with two national accounting identities:

national income = private sector consumption and investment
+ public sector spending + exports
− imports   (1)

national income = private sector consumption
+ private sector savings
+ taxes   (2)

Subtraction of (2) from (1) and rearrangement gives:

exports − imports = private sector savings net of investment
+ public sector surplus   (3)

The left hand side of (3) is the surplus on the current account of the balance of payments. It also follows that:

deterioration in the   fall in private sector savings
current account   =   + rise in private sector investment
balance   + rise in public sector deficit   (4)

There was clearly no rise in the public sector deficit – in fact exactly the opposite happened between 1986 and 1989. These years did witness a considerable increase in private sector investment, as firms responded to the output boom and to rising profits by adding strongly to plant and equipment. But in terms of equation (4) the really big change was in the private sector's savings. Household savings collapsed in the second half of the 1980s, having already slipped back considerably from their peak in 1980.[10] Muellbauer and Murphy's study identify a number of factors, the most important of which appears to have been the great rise in house prices. Houseowners were persuaded to spend some of the enhanced equity value of their houses, and found it much easier to do so than it would have been in previous periods as a result of the liberalization of credit conditions after 1985. My only major reservation about this impressive study is that one needs to ask why house

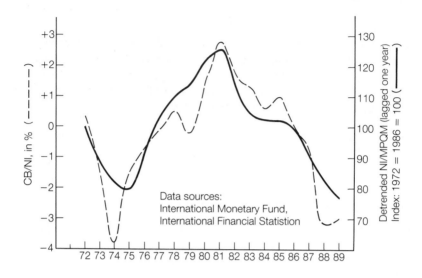

Chart 3 *The close association between the current balance/national income ratio and the income-velocity of broad money*

prices were going up so fast. The same factors that could explain why savings fell – such as greater optimism about future real incomes, tax changes, easier credit terms, and rapid monetary expansion to a name a few – must surely have impacted on housing markets too. So it is not so clear that rising house prices give a satisfactory independent explanation of falling savings. And if one thinks carefully about the status of equations (1) to (4), one realizes that they are just definitions that tell us nothing about what caused what. So exactly the same factors that could have been squeezing savings and driving up house prics might well have been exercising direct influences on the balance of payments current account, too.

The oldest explanations of the balance of payments and why it can change, go back to the eighteenth century philosopher, David Hume.[11] Hume argued that a fall in the money supply would lead to a surplus in trade, and that a rise in the money supply would cause a deficit. Monetary expansion would put upwards pressure on domestic costs and prices; international competitiveness would suffer; imports would rise and exports fall as domestic and foreign residents responded to changes in relative prices. So it is worth looking at whether the evidence bears out the Humean story.

Some impression of the role of monetary policy in shaping the current account balance can be gleaned from chart 3. The lower curve, defined on the left hand axis, depicts the evolution of the current surplus or defict as a proportion of national income from 1972 to 1989. The upper curve illustrates the income-velocity of what the International Monetary Fund terms 'money plus quasi money' (MPQM). MPQM is a wide definition of the UK money supply, corresponding approximately to the recently discontinued series called sterling M3. The income velocity of a monetary aggregate is the ratio of national income (NI) to that aggregate. Roughly speaking, it tells us how quickly bank deposits, as a whole, change hands over a year. The NI/MPQM ratio is defined on the right-hand axis, with an index of 100 in 1985. The downward timetrend in the ratio (nearly 2 per cent per year, over the period as a whole) has been removed to make the two curves as commensurate to the eye as possible. Each year's figures for NI/MPQM have been brought forward by one year for the same reason. So one year's current account balance/national income ratio can be compared visually with the previous year's detrended NI/MPQM ratio.

Chart 3 shows that the two curves look rather similar. Closer statistical analysis confirms this impression. A simple bivariate ordinary least squares (OLS) regression of the CB/NI ratio (CB – current balance) on lagged NI/MPQM reveals a highly significant positive association. Two-thirds of the variance in CB/NI is explained by its covariance with the previous year's NI/MPQM ratio. A 10 per cent fall in NI/MPQM in one year corresponds with a one per cent deterioration in CB/NI in the next. So in 1989, a 10 per cent rise in broad money, relative to national income, seems to lead to a £4,500 million deterioration in the current balance.

David Hume's theory may well, therefore, have something useful to say about why the UK's current balance has worsened so much in the late 1980s. But we have to be cautious, the correlation could be an accident. NI/MPQM is affected by all manner of variables, such as interest rates, expected inflation and the structure of the banking system, which have no obvious bearing on savings, spending or trade. The CB/NI ratio is also affected by North Sea oil, by oil price changes, and by changes in competitiveness and exchange rates which may not necessarily be linked to NI/MPQM (although they could be). And perhaps most important of all, NI/MPQM could have dropped simply because the demand for bank deposits or bank loans or both went up – caused maybe by some of the elusive factors that we saw could have underlain the co-movements of house prices, savings and the trade balance. It is well worth noting that the British authorities had moved increasingly away from watching broad money to looking at narrow money in the later 1980s (and regressions of CB/NI on various narrow money variables do not fit the evidence well); and they had also moved away to some degree from attempting to target or control any monetary aggregate directly in favour of setting interest rates and exchange rates.

The monetary explanation therefore looks promising, but as yet unproved. It also fails to tell the full story. The fiscal explanation – income tax cuts – has plausibility too, and there is of course not the slightest reason to doubt that they both played a role. There is also the effect of the big slide in oil prices after 1985, which lowered Britain's net surplus on trade in oil by at least £4 billion ignoring feedback effects. And a final contributor to the deterioration in the current balance will surely have been the worsening competitiveness position (the exchange rate appreciated in 1988 as a result of interest rate hikes in London, engineered to attract the inflows of capital needed to finance the current account deficit, and wage rates were rising faster in the UK than abroad at this time). If forced, this author would hazard the conjecture that approximately half the current account deterioration was due to excessive broad money growth and credit liberalization, 25 per cent to income tax cuts, 15 per cent to the direct and indirect effects of falling oil prices after 1985, and 10 per cent or so to the worsening competitiveness position.

So much for why the current account has deteriorated so fast in the late 1980s. Does it matter? The answer here is that it should matter. One away of looking at a current account deficit is to treat it as an index of suppressed or potential inflation – inflation that has been triggered, perhaps, by excessive monetary expansion, but prevented from running its natural course, thus far, by measures to stop the exchange rate from falling. This is a fashionable interpretation. Another view would treat it as a real, not a monetary phenomenon. Running a current account deficit means selling net overseas assets. That in turn implies buying more jam today at the cost of reduced consumption of jam tomorrow. There is no reason in principle why residents of different countries should not wish to conduct this kind of inter-temporal trade, perhaps because income expectations or preferences are not the same. But you cannot go on running a current account deficit for ever. Sooner or later the bailiffs arrive. And the fact that a deficit on this massive scale is unsustainable means that measures must be taken to reduce it. Indeed, several measures have already been taken with this end in view, above all the policy of interest rate increases.

Interest rates were raised sharply in 1988 and 1989. There is little doubt that this policy should succeed, eventually, in reducing the rates of monetary growth (they have already fallen sharply). It is squeezing consumer spending on durable goods, and house prices. But non-durable consumption is not very sensitive to interest rates. And there are some distinctly unwelcome side effects: capital flows in from abroad, but that pushes up the exchange rate in the short run, weakening competitiveness, and cuts IPD net inflows in the long run; and it squeezes investment spending, with adverse implications for tomorrow's jam as well as today's. It is to be regretted that the government's political commitments ruled out the possibility of tax increases in 1989. Tax rises would have enabled the authorities to avoid raising interest rates so much. Tax increases are far from innocuous either, but if the root of the problem is that the private sector is saving too little, the clinching argument is that the government should try to compensate for this by saving more itself.

The Exchange Rates for Sterling

The 'nominal' exchange rate for a currency is its price in terms of another: the number of US dollars or German marks that one pound sterling can buy, for instance. The 'effective' exchange rate for sterling expresses its value against a weighted average of different currencies, the weights reflecting the various countries' relative importance in UK trade. The 'real' exchange rate gauges one country's competitiveness, on some definition, against another (or set of others). An appreciation in Britain's real exchange rate against France, for example, tells us that some index of UK prices (such as export prices, wholesale or retail prices, or unit labour costs) have risen relative to their French counterpart, when expressed in a common currency.

At one extreme, the nominal exchange rate between two currencies may be fixed for a long period. At the other, it may float freely, governed solely by the forces of market demand and supply. Between these two polar cases lie many other possible arrangements: managed floating; frequent changes in exchange rate parities; bands, secret or published, wide or narrow, conditional or invariant, temporary or longlasting, between which the rate can float. For 25 years after World War II, sterling was pegged to most other currencies through a set of parities with the US dollar. There were just two parity changes for sterling – devaluations in 1949 and 1967. For most of the period since August 1971 it has floated, often quite freely. There were just two important exceptions: a three-month experiment with tightly fixed rates against other major European currencies, which ended in a massive capital outflow from sterling in June 1972, and heavy depreciation; and an informal two-year attempt to keep sterling close to three German marks, abandoned in 1988.

The last 30 years have seen sterling lose about three-quarters of its value against the Japanese yen, the German mark, the Swiss franc and the Dutch florin. Its value against the US dollar has almost halved over that period. But there has been little long term trend, and in some cases even appreciation, against Scandinavian, European Mediterranean and Australasian currencies. These long run changes in nominal exchange rates approximately match differences in inflation rates (and, to a reduced extent, differences in monetary growth rates). So real exchange rates show little long term trend, however violently they swing about on a monthly or even annual basis.

Sterling fell most in the four and a half years after June 1972. With the advent of North Sea oil, and increasing reliance on promises of tight monetary policy in the UK, it recovered much of this lost ground in the four years from August 1977. Consensus opinion blamed the depreciation of sterling for much of the jump in Britain's inflation in the mid-1970s (though both were partly caused by expansionary monetary policy in 1971–3) and sterling's subsequent appreciation for much of the jump in unemployment after 1979. After these sharp changes, the years from 1981 on have witnessed much gentler movements in the effective exchange rate for sterling. There have been three principal interludes of depreciation (1981–3, 1986 and late 1989).

Since 1981, British policy has often been directed to charting a middle course for sterling between the German mark and the US dollar. This was achieved by periodic manipulation of UK interest rates and direct Bank of England intervention in the foreign exchange markets to buy or sell sterling. The Prime Minister, and her chief economic adviser from 1981–3 and 1989, Sir Alan Walters, continued to favour British monetary independence from the rest of Europe. They stressed the need for strict financial policies at home and the risks that went with exchange market intervention. Nigel Lawson, Chancellor of the Exchequer from 1983 to 1989, came to support Britain's full participation in the EC Exchange Rate Mechanism (ERM).

In the short run, joining the ERM would involve a return to fixed exchange rates with its key currency, the German mark. By 1988, the ERM was seen as heralding closer harmonization of financial policies with the Deutsche Bundesbank, and other European Central Banks, and eventually, perhaps, a European monetary union. At the European summit in June 1989 in Madrid, Mrs Thatcher committed Britain to ERM participation, but with no date, and subject to certain conditions. Britain's inflation rate, then nearly 8 per cent per annum, would have to have fallen back towards the EC average, and France, Italy and Spain would have to have followed Britain's 1979 decision to remove controls over international capital movements. In doing this, she conceded qualified agreement to the first stage of the EC Commission's Delors Plan, but remained opposed to its second and third stages. Those involved a social charter governing workers' rights, and steps towards a common European currency, and a European Central Bank to administer it. The British Labour Party supported the social charter, and, with some misgivings, British entry into the ERM. At least the first stage of the Delors Plan was viewed sympathetically by many Treasury and Bank of England officials, and several cabinet ministers, most notably Chancellor Lawson.

Proponents of Britain's participation in the ERM argued that trade was disrupted by unforeseen exchange rate fluctuations. They pointed to the excellent inflation record in Germany, and the reasonably painless and rapid disinflation her EC partners had experienced after linking their currencies to the mark. They questioned whether Britain's monetary autonomy had really brought her any benefits. They emphasized the role that sterling's large real appreciation from 1977 to 1981 seemed to have had in the trebling of unemployment after 1979. Many fewer jobs would have been lost, it was claimed, had Britain not stayed aloof from the ERM at its inception in March 1979. They maintained that a European monetary union without Britain could establish rules that operated against her – as had happened with the CAP – rules that Britain would be in a position to influence as an initial participant, but not as outsider or latecomer.

Opponents claimed that Britain could, if it liked, achieve greater effective exchange rate stability outside the ERM than inside it. Greater stability against the

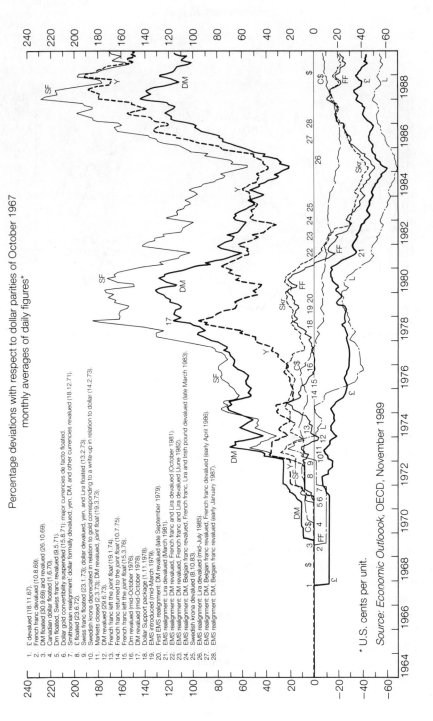

Percentage deviations with respect to dollar parities of October 1967
monthly averages of daily figures*

1. £ devalued (18.11.67).
2. French franc devalued (10.8.69).
3. DM floated (30.9.69) and revalued (26.10.69).
4. Canadian dollar floated (1.6.70).
5. Dm floated, Swiss franc revalued (9.5.71).
6. Dollar gold convertibility suspended (15.8.71); major currencies de facto floated.
7. Smithsonian realignment: dollar formally devalued; yen, DM, and other currencies revalued (18.12.71).
8. £ floated (23.6.72).
9. Swiss franc floated (23.1.73); dollar devalued, yen, and Lira floated (13.2.73).
10. Swedish krona depreciated in relation to gold corresponding to a write-up in relation to dollar (14.2.73).
11. Markets closed (2.3.73); DM revalued, joint float (19.3.73).
12. DM revalued (29.6.73).
13. French franc left the joint float (19.1.74).
14. French franc returned to the joint float (10.7.75).
15. French franc left the joint float (15.3.76).
16. Dm revalued (mid-October 1976).
17. DM revalued (mid-October 1978).
18. Dollar Support package (1.11.1978).
19. EMS introduced (mid-March 1979).
20. First EMS realignment: DM revalued (late September 1979).
21. EMS realignment: Lira devalued (March 1981).
22. EMS realignment: DM revalued, French franc and Lira devalued (October 1981).
23. EMS realignment: DM revalued, French franc and Lira devalued (June 1982).
24. EMS realignment: DM, Belgian franc revalued, French franc, Lira and Irish pound devalued (late March 1983).
25. Swedish krona devalued (8.10.83).
26. EMS realignment: Lira devalued (mid-July 1985).
27. EMS realignment: DM, Belgian franc revalued, French franc devalued (early April 1986).
28. EMS realignment: DM, Belgian franc revalued (early January 1987).

* U.S. cents per unit.

Source: Economic Outloook, OECD, November 1989

Chart 4   Nominal exchange rates of major currencies against the dollar

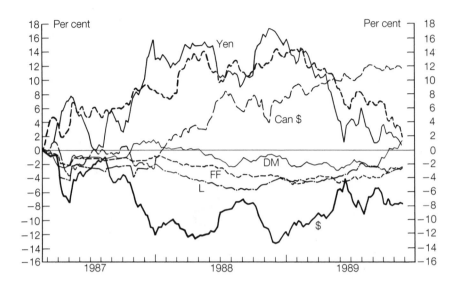

Chart 5   Effective exchange rate changes since Louvre Accord(1)

mark inside the ERM might entail less stability against the dollar. Some of them argued that stabilizing exchange rates was undesirable anyway, and could involve violent swings in interest rates. They stressed traders' opportunities for forward exchange rate cover, which could insulate them quite cheaply against almost any foreign exchange risk. They pointed to the volatility of world oil prices, which could make fixed parities between oil-exporting Britain and oil-importing EC countries unworkable. They recalled the events of June 1972, mentioned earlier, when Britain had found herself forced out of a European exchange rate system much like the current ERM. It was also claimed that there are still too many barriers to trade and factor movements within the EC for it to qualify as an optimum currency area.

This section concludes with a brief summary of how sterling fared in 1989, and some charts that chronicle the movement of sterling exchange rates – nominal, effective and real – over a longer time span. In the course of 1989, the effective exchange rate for sterling fell by one-tenth. Its nominal rate against the US dollar registered a 10.8 per cent decline over the year, while that against the German mark posted a 7.7 per cent drip. Each of the first three-quarters saw the effective exchange rate fall by about 2 per cent, and the heaviest fall occurred in the fourth quarter

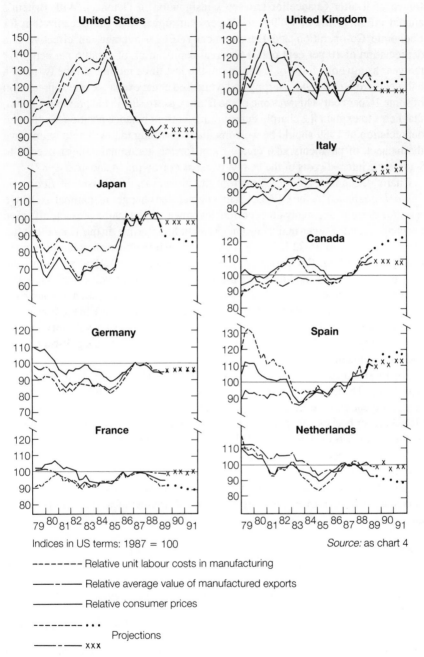

Fall indicates improvement in competitive position

United States

United Kingdom

Japan

Italy

Canada

Germany

Spain

France

Netherlands

Indices in US terms: 1987 = 100

Source: as chart 4

- - - - - - - Relative unit labour costs in manufacturing

————·—— Relative average value of manufactured exports

——————— Relative consumer prices

- - - - - - - •••
——————— xxx Projections

Chart 6   Real exchange rates, 1979–89

(much of it after Chancellor Lawson's resignation in October). With Britain's annual inflation rate in 1989 some 4 per cent higher than the Organization for Economic Co-operation and Development (OECD) average, an effective rate depreciation of 10 per cent points to a real depreciation of about 6 per cent over the year as a whole, most of it coming in the last three months. In the two and a half years from mid-1986, sterling had witnessed a real exchange rate appreciation of some 16 per cent. This was one of the factors, as we saw in the previous section, that helps to explain the sharply deteriorating current balance position. So the real depreciation of 1989 should be welcomed as something that will help to improve the balance of payments, and create room for the additional exports needed to service the interest costs of the heavy overseas borrowing in and after 1987.

Charts 4, 5 and 6 are all taken from the November 1989 issue of *Economic Outlook*, published by the OECD. Chart 4 depicts the changes in nominal exchange rates for sterling, and many other currencies, since 1967. Chart 5 presents effective exchange rates for seven major currencies, including sterling, in the 33 months after the Louvre Accord on 22 February 1987 (by which these seven countries agreed to intervene to limit fluctuations in the key exchange rates). Real exchange rate data are illustrated in chart 6 for sterling and eight other currencies since 1979. For all the turbulence visible in chart 5, chart 6 shows that real exchange rates have been much steadier in the second half of the 1980s than they were in the first. Chart 6 also reveals that the UK and the US have seen rather greater volatility in their real exchange rates than most of the other countries (including significantly, the ERM participants).

For 1990 and 1991, chart 6 presents OECD forecasts of how real exchange rates will move. These are illustrated by the circles and stars. A rise means a fall in competitiveness, either because prices and costs rise faster in that country than elsewhere, or because of appreciation of the nominal (effective) exchange rate. So on these forecasts the UK is expected to become more competitive up to mid-1990; after that, competitiveness is predicted to improve a little on an export price definition (further exchange rate depreciation?) but deteriorate on a labour cost definition (slower relative productivity growth?). Japan is predicted to display the opposite pattern of movement. Only time will tell whether these forecasts are borne out.

Notes

1. S. A. Heffernan and P. J. N. Sinclair, *Modern International Economics*, Basil Blackwell, Oxford, 1990.
2. W. M. Corden, 'Booming sector and Dutch disease economics: a survey', *Oxford Economic Papers*, 36, 1984, pp. 359–380.
3. P. Cecchini, *The European Challenge 1992: The Benefits of a Single Market*, Aldershot, Wildwood House.
4. A. Smith and A. J. Venables, 'Completing the internal market in the European Community', *European Economic Review*, July 1988, pp. 1501–25.
5. R. Baldwin, The growth effects of 1992', *Economic Policy*, 9, October 1989, pp. 247–70.

6. Economic Policy, *Symposium on Europe 1992*, 9, October 1989, Cambridge University Press.

7. L. A. Winters, 'The economic consequences of agricultural support: a survey', *OECD Economic Studies*, 9, Autumn 1987, pp. 7–54.

8. D. Newbery, 'The theory of food price stabilization', *Economic Journal*, 99, December 1989, pp. 1065–82.

9. P. Forsyth and J. A. Kay, 'The economic consequences of North Sea oil', *Fiscal Studies*, 1, pp. 1–28.

10. J. Muellbauer and A. Murphy, 'Why has UK personal saving collapsed?', *Credit Suisse*, First Boston Economics Research, July 1989.

11. D. Hume (1752), 'Of the balance of trade', in *International Finance: Selected Readings*, (ed.), R. N. Cooper, Penguin, Harmondsworth, 1969, pp. 25–37.

Chronology

1 Mar: January current account deficit of £1.6 billion announced.

6 Mar: Trade deal signed with USSR during Anglo-Soviet summit, potentially worth £1.6 billion.

8 Mar: Dispute with France over whether Nissan cars imported from Sunderland should count as British or Japanese cars starts. This eventually results in a British victory.

23 Mar: Jordan cancels a £500 million order for Tornadoes because of an economic recession.

29 Mar: Current account deficit in February of £1.7 billion announced.

26 Apr: Current account deficit in March of £1.19 billion announced.

29 Apr: Corruption during the £15 billion sale of Tornadoes to Saudi Arabia disclosed at the official inquiry.

11 May: Trade deal potentially worth £3 billion signed between Britain and China.

12 May: Relaxations in the procedures governing the sale of high technology goods to friendly countries announced.

25 May: Current account deficit in April of £1.66 billion announced.

30 May: Declaration by President Bush of an end to the 'no exceptions' rule covering transfers of technology to the USSR is expected to boost UK high-technology trade with the East.

6 June: Britain bans arms sales to China in the wake of Tiananmen Square massacre.

27 June: Current account deficit in May of £1.32 billion announced.

17 July: A British businessman accuses the US authorities of hounding him to reveal information on people who export high-technology goods to the USSR and its allies.

26 July: Current account deficit in June of £1.52 billion announced.

23 Aug: Current account deficit in July rises to £2.06 billion.

26 Sept: Current account deficit in August of £2 billion announced.

24 Oct: Current account deficit in September of £1.64 billion announced.

23 Nov: Current account deficit in October of £1.54 billion announced.

29 Dec: Current account deficit in November of £1.41 billion announced.

Trade Unions and Industrial Relations

RICHARD HYMAN

Industrial relations in the 1980s have presented a radical contrast to the situation in the 1970s. In 1989 there have been increasing signs that further changes are in process, so that the pattern in the 1990s may be different again. There are indications that a decade of drastic – and often traumatic – restructuring of employment relations is giving way to greater stability, and that management approaches are changing accordingly; that trade unions have stemmed the decline in their membership, and are developing new policies; and that many groups of employees are becoming more assertive as conditions in the labour market turn in their favour.

What should be the focus of an annual survey of trade unions and industrial relations? Unions have both a public and a private face. The debates and decisions of conferences, the elections of chief officers and their official pronouncements, the conduct of prominent national negotiations and disputes, all commonly make the headlines. But the main work of trade unions is far more mundane: advice and assistance to members, representation of individuals with employment grievances, a multiplicity of small-scale negotiations conducted largely by shop stewards and other 'lay' officials. An account which solely chronicles the former can provide a distorted picture.

The same is true of industrial relations more generally. Press and TV coverage normally concentrates on strikes, particularly in services which directly affect the public; whereas most industrial relations activity is far less dramatic, and directed to the avoidance of conflict. Moreover, when industrial conflict does occur it is likely that the preceding initiatives – in many cases those of management – are as significant as the strike or lockout which follows.

Most students of industrial relations would insist that a focus on discrete events obstructs understanding of the underlying processes at work. Others would add that the traditional identification of industrial relations with the actions of trade unions is far less valid today than in the past. The changing structure of employment – from manufacturing to the service sector, from large plants to smaller units, from old industrial centres to greenfield sites, from traditional full-time contracts to 'non-standard' forms of employment – has moved the centre of gravity away from strongly unionized environments. Privatization has removed many groups of workers from the previously entrenched mechanisms of public-sector collective bargaining. Managements, even where they recognize trade unions, have increasingly developed new procedures of their own for communication and consultation with employees as part of a strategy of 'human resource management'. Arguably, such developments must be seen as central to the agenda of industrial relations. While the following discussion covers more conventional themes, these cautions need to be remembered.

Trade Union Membership and Organization

The decline in British trade union membership which has occurred throughout the 1980s seemed to have come almost to a halt in 1989. At the start of the decade the number of union members – 13,447,000 – was the highest ever recorded, both absolutely and relatively (over 55 per cent of those in work). The Certification Officer's report, published in February 1989, showed total membership at the start of 1988 as 10,480,000 – little more than 100,000 down on the previous year. The Trades Union Congress (TUC), traditionally strongest in industries which have contracted sharply, having lost some 3.5 million members seems also to have stabilized; total affiliated membership at the start of 1989 was 8,652,000; the bulk of the decline since a year before was caused by the expulsion of the Electricians (EETPU) at the 1988 Congress. Out of 78 affiliated unions, 27 registered an increase in membership.

Organizationally, 1989 saw continued moves towards trade union mergers and amalgamations. The white-collar union APEX became part of the General, Municipal and Boilermakers (GMB) in March. The Transport and General Workers' Union (TGWU) began merger discussions in 1988, still continuing, with the National Union of Mineworkers (NUM); and in 1989 commenced amalgamation talks with the white-collar conglomerate Manufacturing, Science and Finance (MSF). In the public sector, detailed plans to merge the National and Local Government Officers (NALGO) with the National Union of Public Employees (NUPE) are being developed, and the Confederation of Health Service Employees (COHSE) has also joined the talks; while the two largest civil service unions are also discussing merger. Other moves towards unity involve the main unions in postal and telecommunication services, in printing, in railway and sea transport, and in film and broadcasting. Talks between the EETPU and the Amalgamated Engineering Union broke down in 1989, but it was subsequently suggested that the Electricians might approach the TGWU for merger.

These moves reflect in part the pursuit of economies of scale as unions seek to recruit and retain members by offering an enhanced range of services. In part also, they indicate a growing awareness that inter-union rivalries can no longer be afforded when the economic and political environment is far less favourable than in the past. A consequence has been the growing *concentration* of unions: the Certification Officer's report showed that of a total of 334 trade unions, 24 with over 100,000 members accounted for over 80 per cent of aggregate membership; while the ten largest organizations made up almost 60 per cent of total membership. The trends towards a handful of super-unions is not necessarily bringing a simpler structure to the movement: most of the largest bodies are conglomerates which straddle a range of industries and occupations, in most of these competing for members with other giants.

The TUC has sought to encourage closer co-operation between unions in response to the more difficult environment for recruiting and retaining members. A detailed report by its Special Review Body outlining a strategy for the 1990s was approved by the annual Congress in September. Congress also reflected a conscious effort to project an image of unions as caring, socially sensitive organizations: women's representation on the TUC governing body, the General Council, was substantially increased; and major policy documents were adopted on health, education, and equal rights. One non-event of 1989 also deserves mention: the inter-union battle which many predicted when the EETPU was expelled from the TUC. Neither the Electricians, nor their rivals within the TUC, have seemed anxious to intensify their competition for members; and the TUC has given only token support to the left-wing breakaway from the EETPU, the Electrical and Plumbing Industries Union.

The year 1989 has seen the acceptance by a growing body of key union leaders of a changed relationship with the Labour Party. The policy document published in May – *Meet the Challenge, Make the Change* – may be seen as a shift towards the traditions of continental social democracy and a rejection of the policies (for example on nuclear disarmament, public ownership and industrial relations legislation) to which many leading unions and the TUC itself have been formally committed. Accompanying this shift has been an attempt to distance the party symbolically and organizationally from the unions. If Neil Kinnock's project for the party has some affinities with that of Gaitskell three decades earlier, it is notable that the response from within the unions has been very different. Even from the trade union left, opposition to the policy changes has been restrained; and the goal of moving from the dominance of the trade union block vote towards the principle of 'one member, one vote' has been strongly advocated by such union leaders as John Edmonds of the GMB.

Pay Bargaining and Industrial Disputes

The pattern of pay agreements changed markedly in 1989. During the previous two years, the 'going rate' remained steady at 5–6 per cent; for most of this period, this figure was sufficient to ensure real pay increases. But by the beginning of 1989, the retail price index had risen above the median level of pay settlements; and throughout the year, wage bargaining was marked by efforts to keep up with inflation. By August, the median settlement level of 8 per cent appeared to have stabilized real wages; but the sharp increase in mortgage interest rates provided a fresh stimulus, and in the last quarter of the year 9 per cent appeared to have become the norm. Some groups did significantly better in negotiations: for example, a 13 per cent settlement was agreed at the end of the year for workers in the (privatized) railway workshops.

Predictably, the rise in average settlement levels was associated with an increased dispersion between different negotiating groups. Many public sector unions with negotiations in the early part of the year fared relatively badly. It is also noteworthy that the average earnings index in 1989 moved some 2 per cent above the median rate of pay agreements: a reflection of increased overtime working, of production- and performance-related bonus payments, and of various discretionary rises above those formally negotiated. Such 'earnings drift' probably increased the relative advantage of private sector employees.

The sharp increase in prices helps explain the growth of wage militancy during 1989, while strikes and strike threats may be seen as contributing to the higher rates of settlement. In 1989, many commentators spoke of a 'summer of discontent'. This catchphrase (like the 'winter of discontent' in the last year of the Callaghan government) is misleading. The number of officially recorded stoppages in 1989 is likely to be below that of 1988 – which was the lowest for over half a century. The numbers of workers involved, and of days lost, will almost certainly be well below the average for the 1980s.

What *was* distinctive about 1989 was the public visibility of a number of important disputes, and the degree of success achieved by the workers and unions involved. Both features were evident in the overlapping series of one-day strikes in British Rail (BR) and the London underground. Pay was a major issue in both cases; but conflict was exacerbated by BR's attempt to impose radical changes in the machinery of representation and negotiation, and by disagreements over work arrangements and staffing levels on the tubes. Despite the disruption resulting from these disputes, the unions were remarkably successful in maintaining public sympathy for their position. The outcome in BR was a pay rise of 8.8 per cent, and an agreement to resume negotiation over procedures; the settlement on London underground was similar. Analogous issues lay behind the dispute between NALGO and the local authorities; one-day stoppages by almost half a million staff in July brought salary increases ranging from 8.6 to 9.5 per cent. Earlier in the year, the action by academic and related staff in universities brought a significantly improved pay settlement (though still below the 'going rate'). Less successful were the dockers in the TGWU, faced by the hurried abolition of the National Dock Labour Scheme and the employment protections provided. Because of the employers' use of the law (described below) their strike took place only after the scheme had been abolished, making strikers liable to dismissal without redundancy payments; and national unity soon disintegrated. Another dispute which achieved no immediate success was that of the ambulance drivers, which began in September after a 'final' offer of only 6.5 per cent. While the unions' stand (which included holding back from full strike action) won widespread public sympathy, no significant concessions had been achieved by the end of the year.

Most strikes could be regarded as defensive: a response to management attempts to enforce new forms of work organization or alterations to bargaining machinery. In some cases the trade unionists involved (such as the prison officers at Wandsworth at the beginning of the year) considered themselves locked out rather than on strike. Even in the case of pay disputes, most claims represented efforts to keep wages in line with inflation rather than to win real improvements. One important exception was the action of the engineering unions in support of a shorter working week. In reviving their 35-hour campaign after a decade of quiescence, the unions seem to have drawn on the experience of their German counterparts (who are also about to resume pressure on this issue). Strike action commenced at the end of October in a selected number of profitable companies, with a levy on other union members permitting strike pay far higher than normal. Some employers quickly agreed to introduce a 37-hour week, but the dispute was still in progress at the end of the year. The outcome of this conflict may be significant in influencing the confidence of other groups of trade unionists in 1990.

The Law and Industrial Relations

The government's programme of industrial relations legislation – often summarized as 'regulating the unions, deregulating the employers' – maintained its impetus in 1989. The major initiative was the passage through Parliament of the Employment Bill. This removes most legal restrictions on the conditions of female employment (including underground working in mines), and also eliminates protective regulation of the working hours of young people. Provisions in earlier legislation for time off for trade union duties are reduced, and a £150 deposit is specified in order to discourage complaints to industrial tribunals. As a separate initiative, the government was also actively considering abolition of the remaining Wages Councils, which set minimum rates in certain low-paid industries. The extent to which the labour market activities of employers have now been deregulated in Britain helps explain the government's near-hysterical opposition, throughout 1989, to the modest employment rights proposed in the European Community Social Charter.

Previous moves to control trade unions received an authoritative rebuff in April, when the Committee of Experts of the International Labour Organization (ILO) ruled that provisions in the 1980 and 1988 Employment Acts, and the banning of trade union membership at GCHQ Cheltenham, breached ILO Conventions. Nevertheless, the government proceeded with additional curbs on unions. A Code of Practice was issued covering ballots on industrial action; though not legally binding, this can be taken into account in cases before the courts. This move was generally regarded as a response to trade unions' success in most of the strike ballots held under the 1984 Trade Union Act, and to the consequential strengthening of their hand in bargaining with employers. Two Green Papers were also published during the year. The first, in March, proposed to prohibit the pre-entry closed shop and a variety of measures tightening the legislation of previous years. The second, in October, proposed to make unions responsible for industrial action organized unofficially by lay representatives or officers, unless strenuous measures were taken to repudiate the action; selective dismissal of unofficial strikers would also be permitted. This proposal was perhaps stimulated by the London underground dispute earlier in the year, which was initially co-ordinated by an unofficial committee of branch representatives. A Bill covering both subjects was published at the end of the year.

There was evidence in 1989 of a significant increase in employers' use of the law in order to frustrate industrial action. The port employers obtained in June an injunction against the TGWU, on the novel grounds that dockers were under a statutory duty to work and that the 'public interest' made the intended strike unlawful. The House of Lords reversed this decision, but only after the 28-day validity of the union's ballot had expired; and by the time a new ballot could be completed, the government's deregulation of the industry had been accomplished. London Underground Ltd gained an injunction against the NUR on the grounds that its strike ballot conflated several separate issues; rather than proceed to appeal, the union successfully held a new ballot. British Rail also challenged the NUR ballot, alleging that it was invalid because certain members had not received papers; but on this occasion the judges held in favour of the union. The same was true in the first case brought by the new Commissioner for the Rights of Trade Union Members, also over the NUR ballot. In October, a similar effort by British Aerospace – the main firm targeted by the engineering unions – had mixed results: it successfully challenged the validity of the MSF ballot, but failed in the case of the AEU.

Despite the prominence of such cases, involvement of the courts in industrial relations remained exceptional. Most employers, it would seem, still feel that use of the law is costly and uncertain, and may sour relations with their workforce. It is significant that employers' organizations such as the Confederation of British Industry and the Institute of Personnel Management expressed only lukewarm support, and in some cases active opposition, towards the government's new initiatives in labour law. If trade union power and industrial disputes were once seen by employers as a central problem, this is now far less obviously the case.

Employers and the Labour Market

As suggested at the outset, industrial relations as traditionally understood is far less central than in past decades to the concerns of employers. In many new areas of employment, trade union influence is weak. Even when unionism remains firmly established, collective action is rarely a major worry. Far more prominent in employers' discussion in 1989 was the growing problem of recruitment and retention of scarce categories of labour. Despite the reduction in officially recorded unemployment (in part a statistical artefact, produced by tightening the basis of registration), the aggregate level at over 6 per cent remained high by European standards throughout 1989. For professionals, technicians and skilled manual workers, however, employers reported growing difficulties in attracting suitable labour. Many of the developments in 'human resource management' – personalized payment schemes, fringe benefits, job redesign, flexible working arrangements – can be seen in part as efforts to compete for an insufficient pool of qualifications.

For some commentators, these problems were a predictable consequence of the traditional neglect of vocational training in Britain. The government's most recent initiatives – abolishing the Training (formerly Manpower Services) Commission and creating a network of committees dominated by local business interests – were seen by critics as an inadequate response to a developing skills crisis. The TUC, in its policy statement, *Skills 2000*, clearly identified this as an issue on which to make a political and social impact, and also as a basis for common action with more enlightened employers.

The 1980s were a decade in which the position of trade unions was significantly weakened, and the character of British industrial relations was reshaped in a variety of ways. Another turning point was represented by 1989. In the 1990s, new changes seem increasingly probable; their nature is however far from clear.

Chronology

3 Jan: British Airline Stewards' and Stewardesses' Association (a section of the TGWU) discuss transferring to the British Airline Pilots' Association.
Overtime ban by manual workers at Rolls Royce factories in support of a pay claim.

9 Jan: The beginning of the university teachers' dispute, and a threatened boycott of students' exams.

12 Jan: Voting changes increase the power of the Yorkshire miners in the National Union of Mineworkers.

24 Jan: GMB launches a financial services package.

28 Jan: GCHQ protest march and rally.

30 Jan–7 Feb: Prison officers walk-out in Wandsworth over shift arrangements.

31 Jan: The Post Office announces a major loyalty bonus deal with the Union of Communication Workers.

6 Feb: ITV scraps all agreements with the trade unions and serves notice that it will end national pay bargaining in July.

7 Feb: The TUC publishes *Review of Working Time in Britain and West Europe*.
Labour Research Department survey shows employment rights in Britain lag behind those on the Continent.

21 Feb: Survey of responses to the proposed abolition of wages councils shows only the Institute of Directors in favour.

22 Feb: Over 900 miners strike at Frickly colliery, West Yorkshire, over working conditions.

1 Mar: APEX/GMB merger becomes effective.

2 Mar: Last union member at GCHQ sacked for defying the ban on unions.

7 Mar: Draft balloting code criticized by ACAS, the Institute of Personnel Management and the CBI.

13 Mar: A survey shows that provision of workplace nurseries is very limited, especially in the private sector.

20 Mar: Action to end the closed shop outlined in a Green Paper. It also threatens to legislate on secondary action.

23 Mar: British Airways threaten to withdraw from national bargaining machinery if the unions refuse to recognize the breakaway from the TGWU, now known as Cabin Crew '89.

James Curran, *Employment and Employment Relations in the Small Firm*, Kingston Business School, explodes some myths about industrial relations in small firms.

3 Apr: Sam McCluskie, General Secretary of the National Union of Seamen calls for the EETPU to be reinstated in the TUC.

4 Apr: TUC issues 1992 checklist for negotiators.

British Coal applies UDM pay agreement to all miners, despite the non-agreement of the NUM.

7 Apr: Abolition of the National Dock Labour Scheme announced. This is followed by an unofficial walkout and disclosures of the extent of preparations to face the expected national dock strike.

13 Apr: MMC report on labour practices in the film and television industries published which exonerates current working practices.

20 Apr: Unofficial tube strikes begin.

Whitley Councils HC 109–I and *Midwives Regrading* HC 289 published by the Commons social services committee. The first draws attention to the fact that the proposed introduction of flexible pay in the NHS may increase the wages bill.

24 Apr: First of a series of 24-hour stoppages at the BBC.

27 Apr: International Labour Office argues that the government's trade union legislation has breached international employment conventions.

8 May: Overtime ban on BR in support of a 8.8 per cent pay claim.

15 May: 24-hour tube and bus strike in London over pay.

17 May: The Social Charter proposals are presented by the EC Commission. They include better working hours and conditions, freedom of movement and fair pay, freedom of association and collective bargaining, the right of professional training, equal pay and opportunity for men and women, the right of information, consultation and worker participation, and the right to health protection and safety at work. Norman Fowler pledges his opposition to a number of key aspects.

19 May: Dockers vote for an indefinite strike over the end of the dock labour scheme, pending court decisions.

22 May–6 July: Unofficial stoppages by North Sea construction workers.

1 June: University lecturers accept a 6 per cent pay offer, ending a 5-month dispute.

7 June: The Court of Appeal grants an injunction banning an official national dock strike.

8 June: League Watch set up to expose and end secret blacklisting of political and trade union activists by employers (and especially by the Economic League).

Unofficial dock strikes in protest at the Court of Appeal decision.

9 June: Norman Fowler threatens legislation against wildcat unofficial stoppages.

Seamen's 16-month dispute with P&O finally ends.

13 June: TUC Special Review Body issues Warwick Report on single bargaining table arrangements.

AEU abandons merger talks with the EETPU.

CPSA conference instructs its executive to end merger talks with the GMB and AEU.

20 June: BR attempts to obtain an injunction to prevent a one-day strike called for 21 June rejected by the Court of Appeal.

21 June: Twenty-four hour strike on rail, London tube and buses.

27 June: NALGO calls a series of one-day strikes in support of a pay claim.

TGWU and MSF discuss merger.

3 July: The Dock Work Act gets royal assent effective from 6 July.

7 July: Dockers vote for a national strike which begins on 10 July.

10 July: Overtime ban by ASLEF begins.

11 July: TUC issues report on six local labour market studies with pilot effort to co-ordinate union recruitment.

26 July: NALGO begins a series of indefinite stoppages.

27 July: Rail union leaders call off their series of one-day strikes.

1 Aug: TGWU ends dock strike after many dockers had already returned to work.

2 Aug: More than 2,300 dockers defy the call to return to work.

8 Aug: Last dockers in Liverpool return to work.

9 Aug: Acceptance of an ACAS formula heralds the end (on 14 Aug.) of the London underground dispute.

10 Aug: NALGO pay dispute ends.

18 Aug: 24 hour strike by British Airways cabin crews over the dismissal of a stewardess accused of a drinks fiddle (she was vindicated before an industrial tribunal on 6 Nov. and offered her job back and lost wages).

31 Aug: TUC turns down an application to rejoin from the EETPU.

3 Sept: Institution of Professional and Civil Servants renamed as the Institution of Professionals, Managers and Specialists and calls for the creation of a white-collar group of politically neutral unions in the TUC.

Ambulance staff overtime ban begins in support of a pay claim.

Two-year dispute on staffing at TV-AM finally ends.

Journalists on the *Daily Telegraph* and the *Sunday Telegraph* begin a work-to- rule.

4 Sept: The number of seats reserved for women on the General Council of the TUC increased from 6 to 12.

5 Sept: TUC conference opposes the NHS reorganization, calls for comprehensive disability income, endorses the TUC environmental charter, urges trade unions not to handle toxic waste, calls for tougher action against racist activity in the trade unions, for financial incentives for employers to provide childcare facilities, and for trade unions to press child care claims during collective bargaining.

Left-wing trade union leaders demand an inquiry into the activities of Mainstream, the right-wing trade union organization chaired by Bill Jordan of the AEU.

6 Sept: TUC conference calls for more resources for teacher training and investment in school building repairs, demands a national minimum wage and increased child benefit, calls for legislation against takeovers by asset-strippers, stresses commitment to the public ownership of oil, gas, electricity, rail, and coal, calls for a campaign against the poll tax and a shorter working week.

TUC publishes reports on organizing in the 1990s and Europe 1992.

7 Sept: TUC Congress supports a multilateral defence policy, votes to phase out nuclear power within 15 years, demands stronger powers for environmental health officers over food production and sale, calls for tough sanctions against South Africa, condemns government opposition to the EC Social Charter, and the removal of bargaining rights from teacher unions.

8 Sept: TUC Congress presses affiliated trade unions to devote up to 0.5 per cent of subscription income to sponsorship of the arts, calls for the repeal of the Prevention of Terrorism Act and the withdrawal of the broadcasting ban on supporters of terrorism in Northern Ireland, accuses government of underfunding the emergency services, and reaffirmed its support for public service broadcasting.

21 Sept: Electrical workers at the atomic weapons establishment at Aldermaston go on strike.

27 Sept: BR cap the pay disputes of the summer by giving pay rises to its managers of up to 19 per cent (the average was 11.8 per cent).

2 Oct: *Management Salary Survey September 1989* Reward Group, shows that pay rises for managers are averaging 11 per cent, almost double the figure of a year before.

9 Oct: *The Daily Telegraph* staff begin a 36-hour strike over plans to introduce a flexible working week.

10 Oct: The Green Paper on curbing wildcat strikes is presented.

30 Oct: Indefinite stoppages begin at British Aerospace's plants at Chester and Preston and at Rolls Royce's plant in Glasgow in an attempt by the engineering unions to further their campaign to cut the working week in the industry from 39 to 35 hours.
Britain is isolated in its opposition to the final draft of the Social Charter.

7 Nov: Kenneth Clarke announces that the army and police are to be called in to help run London' ambulance services after management suspended staff and closed the capital's 71 ambulance stations.

8 Nov: Police Federation put pressure on the government to concede the claim of the ambulancemen for an automatic pay award system such as that which operates for the other emergency services.
Associated Newspapers announce the abandonment of collective bargaining.

19 Nov: CBI warns the government not to interfere and try to restrain private sector pay settlements at the start of its annual conference.

21 Nov: Employment Bill to deal with unofficial strikes is announced in the Queen's speech.

22 Nov: *Management Remuneration in Europe* Monks Partnership, shows that British top managers came 11th out of 12 by gross earnings.

30 Nov: *Director's Rewards 1989–1990* Reward Group published.

4 Dec: Report by the Industrial Relations Research Unit, University of Warwick claims government pressure to decentralize the management of public enterprises has led to local disputes, wage inflation and financial constraints all of which have contributed to deteriorating services.

6 Dec: Lords Select Committee on the European Communities *A Community Social Charter*, HMSO, urges the government to abandon its hostility to the Social Charter.

7 Dec: Mark Hollingsworth and Charles Tremayne *The Economic League: The Silent McCarthyism*, Liberty, calls for legal curbs on the Economic League.
Leadership of the breakaway Association of Professional Ambulance Personnel recommend acceptance of the 9 per cent offer over 18 months. This is rejected by their membership.

8 Dec: The final draft of the Social Charter is published.

13 Dec: NATFHE begin exam boycott in support of a pay claim.

15 Dec: A petition with 4.5 million signatures in support of the ambulancemen is presented to the Commons.

17 Dec: Labour's Shadow Employment Secretary, Tony Blair, renounces the closed shop, since the Labour Party conference approved the principle of the Social Charter, the final draft of which enshrined the right of non-membership of unions.

18 Dec: Certification Officer, Matthew Wake, refuses to recognize the staff association set up at GCHQ as a trade union because it is subject to the approval of GCHQ's director.

21 Dec: Employment Bill outlining measures to outlaw the closed shop and curb unofficial actions is published.

Health

KEN JUDGE

'Twas in truth an hour
Of universal ferment; mildest men
Were agitated; and commotions, strife
Of passion and opinion, filled the walls
Of peaceful houses with unquiet sounds.

Wordsworth, *The Prelude*, IX

In the bicentenary year of the storming of the Bastille, Wordsworth's poetry as aptly describes popular reaction to the government's proposed reforms of the National Health Service (NHS) as it did the French Revolution. The White Paper, *Working for Patients*,[1] dominated the health agenda throughout the year in a quite unprecedented way. It would, therefore, be quite possible to justify focusing attention exclusively on this topic. But to do so would be a mistake. A wider set of concerns remained important, even if somewhat overshadowed, and they merit some consideration.

Three issues have dominated debates about British health policy in the 1980s. First, there have been continuing attempts to improve the management of health services so as to obtain better value for money. Second, there has been repeated concern about the adequacy of spending on the NHS. Finally, the publication of the Black Report[2] at the beginning of the decade stimulated persistent extra-governmental concern about the wider aspects of public health issues.

In 1989 the publication of *Working for Patients* and the British Medical Association's (BMA) opposition to both the new contract for General Practitioners (GPs) and the more general aspects of the government's proposed reforms of the NHS dominated the health agenda. In the last quarter of the year, however, the other two recurrent issues of the 1980s surfaced again. First, the Chancellor of the Exchequer's autumn statement, which announced a massive cash injection for the NHS, reopened the debate about the adequacy or otherwise of public spending on health care. Second, the publication of Edwina Currie's *Life Lines*, reminiscences about her tenure as a minister of health, which followed closely on the heels of Margaret Whitehead's critique of health education policy, *Swimming Upstream: Trends and Prospects in Education for Health*, meant that public health was less neglected than had previously been the case.

The aim of this review is to examine aspects of the key health issues of the 1980s by focusing on four particular themes. First and foremost, the general tenor of the proposals outlined in *Working for Patients* has to be considered. Second, a related but distinct issue which warrants examination is the imposition of a new contract for GPs despite fierce opposition from the profession. Third, the adequacy of the additional funds made available to lubricate the NHS reforms needs to be assessed. Finally, it is worth paying some attention to health education because it focuses attention on the role of personal responsiblity as a central tenet of Conservative social policy in the Thatcher era.

Towards Managed Competition

Working for Patients, which was published in January 1989, signalled the most far-reaching programme of change for the NHS since its foundation in 1948. The principal intention is to increase efficiency in the use of resources by making hospitals compete for contracts from health authorities and GP budget holders. At the same time, the reforms aim to make services better managed, more responsive to patients, and to improve the quality of care provided.

Tax relief on private health insurance is to be made available to those aged over 60 who want to take advantage of it, but for the majority of the population access to health services will be based on need and not ability to pay. The NHS will continue to be funded mainly out of general taxation and there are no new plans to extend user charges.

Potentially, a number of the White Paper's proposals could help to improve the use of resources, and stimulate greater responsiveness to patients. On the other hand, the use of incentives to change the behaviour of doctors and hospitals could result in greater inequities and a reduced access to some services. Nearly everything depends on the way in which the White Paper is implemented and the safeguards that are built in to the new arrangements. In view of the magnitude of the changes proposed, and the corresponding uncertainty about their impact, it will be important to monitor carefully the operation of these arrangements to ensure that equity and access do not suffer in the quest for efficiency.

The most radical element of the White Paper is the introduction of *managed competition*.[3] By separating responsibility for funding services from their provision, the government hopes that providers will compete for contracts from health authorities, GP practice budget holders and private insurers. The aim is to turn health authorities into discriminating purchasing agencies, seeking the best deal for their residents by buying services from a range of public, private and voluntary providers. GPs who volunteer to hold practice budgets will act in a similar way for those services which they provide or purchase.

There is no reason in principle why the separation of responsibility for funding and provision should undermine the values on which the NHS is based. Indeed, by redistributing purchasing power, and by creating an arm's length relationship between purchasers and providers of care, it may be possible for health authorities and GPs to offer better services to their patients. At the same time, there is legitimate concern that the strategy of competition may distort priorities. This could happen if hospitals concentrate on providing services that are in demand by purchasers of care from outside their locality, such as elective surgery, at the expense of services that are needed by local people. There may also be a greater divergence in standards of care. For example, those GPs who are well organized and provide a good service to their patients may be able to develop their practices by becoming budget holders while smaller practices and single-handed GPs fall behind. A further concern is that it may be difficult to ensure an integrated approach to service delivery if responsibility for hospital services, community health services and primary care becomes increasingly fragmented.

There can be no doubt that the government has embarked on an ambitious, high risk strategy which could bring about real improvements to health services but also carries significant dangers. As the task of implementing change falls to the NHS itself, a heavy responsibility rests on regional health authorities and district health authorities, as regulators and purchasers of care respectively, to manage competition in a way which minimizes these dangers.

The GP Contract

One of the most important aims of the government's reforms of the NHS is to increase the accountability of the medical profession. Discontent about this aspect of the changes focused principally on the proposals for a new contract for family doctors. The first draft of the new GP contract was published in February 1989 following the publication of a White Paper, *Promoting Better Health*,[4] which had emphasized *inter alia* the need for new contractual arrangements to promote preventive medicine, to introduce performance related pay and to make GPs more responsive to the needs of their patients.

Discussions about a new contract had been taking place between the Department of Health (DOH) and the General Medical Services Committee (GMSC) of the BMA throughout 1988. These had proceeded at a snail's pace on a confidential basis until *Working for Patients* was published. Thereafter, partly as a direct consequence of the BMA's fury at the wider aspects of the government's proposals for the NHS, megaphone diplomacy became the order of the day.

The proposed new contract was leaked to the profession by the GMSC, and opposition to the proposals grew in intensity. A compromise was negotiated between the DOH and the GMSC, but this was disowned by the BMA's members. Kenneth Clarke, the Secretary of State for Health, then decided to impose the revised contract against the wishes of the BMA. Eventually, despite much blustering, campaigning and personal vilification of the Secretary of State, the

BMA capitulated and the DOH luanched their own campaign to sell the new changes to a bemused public. The sequence of some of the critical events during 1989 is shown in the following table:

Sequence of Events

31 Jan:	*Working for Patients* published
4 Feb:	Clarke sends details of the new contract to GPs: negotiations continue
6 Feb:	GMSC negotiators believe that this effectively shifts the level of debate away from *Promoting Better Health* and decide to break confidentiality on the negotiations with the DOH
6 Mar:	GMSC meeting reports widespread 'grassroots' opposition
7 Apr:	Conference of Local Medical Committees' (LMC) representatives vote unanimously to reject the contract, but not for resig nation
4 May:	GMSC negotiators and the department agree a compromise
1 Jun:	A second LMC conference rejects the compromise contract by 166 votes to 150 and asks for talks to be reopened. Clarke threatens to impose a contract. The GMSC agrees to conduct a ballot
20 Jul:	A GMSC meeting announces that a ballot of GPs shows a major ity of 75.9 per cent are opposed to the contract. Further discussions with Clarke sought
3 Aug:	Clarke announces that he is to impose a contract 'based on agreements reached with the GPs leaders earlier this year'
9 Oct:	GMSC decides against mass resignation or working-to-rule
8 Nov:	DOH launches 'You and Your GP' advertising campaign

These changes are of enormous significance because they are an important landmark in the twentieth-century history of negotiations between government and the medical profession. In a very important sense, the outcome of the negotiations about the new GP contract demonstrates that the assumed veto power of doctors in relation to changes in the NHS is a form of emperor's clothing. The bluff of the BMA has been called and this could have profound implications for the future development of health care in Britain.

Spending on the NHS

The announcement by the Chancellor of the Exchequer, John Major, in November 1989 of a massive injection of additional resources into the NHS was seen as an important step in the process of convincing the electorate that the Conservative administration is a 'caring' one. At first sight, the extra £2.6 billion promised for health care in 1990 is an impressive sum, but it needs to be assessed in a wider perspective.

Table 1. Spending on the NHS in England: the Thatcher years (£m. at 1988/9 volume prices)

Year	HCHS current	HCHS capital	FPS	Total NHS[a]
1978/9	12,050	764	4000	17,201
1988/9	13,007	1112	4917	19,639
% increase 1978/9 – 1988/9	7.9	45.5	22.9	14.2
% per annum	0.8	3.8	2.1	1.4

[a]*Miscellaneous central expenditure is not shown separately.*

Throughout the 1980s Mrs Thatcher's government has been vulnerable to the claim that it has starved the NHS of finance. Faced with demands for new resources – associated with demographic and technological change and essential service developments – running at an average rate of 2 per cent per annum in the hospital and community health services (HCHS), it is a simple exercise to demonstrate that the record of the government is, at best, a mixed one. It is important to note that there is room for dispute about the size of the increased demands placed on the HCHS during the 1980s, but there is a substantial consensus amongst informed commentators that this was of the order of 20 per cent.

Table 1 illustrates the Conservative record: compared with the level of demand, the volume of new resources made available for the HCHS – less than 8 per cent since Mrs Thatcher came to power – leaves much to be desired. The growth of capital spending appears to be much more satisfactory, but investment was at a nadir in the late 1970s and substantial improvement was almost inevitable. The record of the family practitioner services (FPS) – where the volume of resources increased by almost one quarter during the decade – is much more impressive, although it is worthy of note that this has been one of the most significant areas of governmental expenditure not subjected to cash limits.

It is the HCHS, though, which has been Mrs Thatcher's achilles heel, and strenuous efforts have been made over the years to put the government's record in a more favourable light. The most enduring way of doing this has been to emphasize the steadily increasing value of cash-releasing cost improvement programmes (CIPs). Table 2 illustrates their relative importance by 1988–9; almost doubling the volume of new resources made available, and significantly reducing the gap between the flow of new resource inputs and the demands placed on them.

Serious reservations about the accuracy of these estimates, however, are commonplace. For example, a study conducted by the Institute of Health Services

Table 2. Spending on the HCHS in England: the Thatcher years (£m. at 1988/9 volume prices)

Year	Spending	CIPS[a]	Total
1978/9	12,050	–	12,050
1988/9	13,007	786	13,793
% increase 1978/9–1988/9	7.9		14.5
% per annum	0.8		1.4

[a]Recurrent value

Management, the National Association of Health Authorities and the King's Fund Institute reached the following conclusion.

Cost improvement programmes have been a major source of health authority finance for service development since 1984–5. A National Audit Office investigation carried out in 1986 raised some fundamental questions about the way savings are recorded, their impact on service levels and the way in which monitoring and audit are carried out. Our study suggests that these questions remain unresolved. The imprecision surrounding CIP savings makes the certainty with which they are quoted at the national level a source of concern. If the figures quoted do not reflect genuine additional sources of finance, they must provide part of the explanation for the severe funding problems faced by many health authorities in recent years.[5]

Against this background, how much difference will the extra resources promised for the NHS in 1990 make to the overall picture? Everything depends on future rates of inflation. If increases in pay and prices can be held to 5 per cent as the government hopes, then the growth in real resources available for the HCHS in 1990–1 will be 3.4 per cent. This would represent a significant improvement for a single year, but on its own it would do little to offset the cumulative starvation of the 1980s. In fact, the government's forecasts of future inflation are invariably over-optimistic. An authoritative survey of the financial position of health authorities by their national association suggests an inflation rate of 7.4 per cent for 1990–1.[6] If this proves to be correct, the growth in real resources available to the HCHS will be reduced to 1.09 per cent; hardly sufficient to meet the extra demands placed on them. The financial predicament may be ameliorated by new cash-releasing CIPs, but these are subject to the caveats outlined above. Continuing demands for more resources, therefore, are unlikely to diminish.

Public Health and Health Education

Public health issues burst on to the political agenda at the end of 1988 in a controversy about eggs and salmonella, but disappeared just as quickly after Mrs Currie resigned as a health minister in 1989. The topic resurfaced in the autumn, however, with the publication of Edwina Currie's book, *Life Lines*, which provides an interesting insight into Conservative public health policy.

Public health is a wide-ranging concept which embraces disease prevention and health promotion not only in relation to individual human beings but also the social and economic environment in which they are situated. The Thatcher government, however, has focused on the education of individuals through the use of the mass media. The danger of this rather blinkered perspective is that, 'to place primary emphasis on individual behaviour not only will be ineffective in reducing levels of disease, but also serves only to draw attention away from those social, economic and environmental conditions which create vulnerability to disease and illness in the first place'.[7]

So why has the government adopted such a limited approach? One clue lies in Conservative political philosophy: individual responsibility and choice are of primary importance, and the exercise of free choice is thought to be constrained by lack of knowledge and not by cultural or social circumstances. According to Edwina Currie, 'The problem very often for people is just ignorance – failing to realize that they do have some control over their lives. I honestly don't think that the problem has anything to do with poverty . . . some of these problems are things we can tackle by impressing on people the need to look after themselves better.'[8]

Conservative public health policy, therefore, emphasizes the need to encourage individuals to change their own lifestyles. Mass media advertising is the way to disseminate such messages and wider action on the socio-economic front is anathema, 'To me this ministerial effort was the antithesis of the nanny-state. In other countries the law was changed, products were banned, compulsion and enforcement were the rule. In this country . . . we have tried mostly to proceed by persuasion . . . If the public won't act on it [the information], then at least we have done our bit.'[9]

What emerges from Mrs Currie's account is that there have been two principal strands to public health policy in the 1980s. First, there is an explicit assumption that the key to promoting better health is to seek to change individuals' lifestyles through the provision of education. Second, mass media campaigns are thought to be the most effective way of achieving this and changes in public awareness are seen as the most important measures of success.

This 'official' approach to health education has been criticized on two main counts. First, that it is far too narrowly based. Margaret Whitehead's review of trends and prospects in health education provides evidence of the growing 'realization that education rarely works without being linked to complementary social and public policy. Education for health stands most chance of success when backed-up by fiscal, legal and other regulatory measures.'[10] Second, that it can be ineffective and even counter-productive. In the specific area of mass media work there is now a very considerable amount of sophisticated research and experience available to improve the impact of advertising. But too few government programmes in this area have taken sufficient notice of the development of good and effective practice in the advertising industry. Knowledge about how to increase the readability and impact of mass communication messages so that they produce the required effect has steadily increased. There are many instances – AIDS and drug abuse campaigns, for example – where government action has produced inconsistent messages which have confused the public and professionals. At the same time, limited resources have been squandered on expensive campaigns of limited effectiveness at the expense of other 'legal drug problems, such as alcohol, tobacco and prescribed medicines which deserved a higher claim for national action'.[11]

Mrs Currie's meteoric rise and fall certainly put health onto the political agenda and raised its visibility in 1989, but the narrowness of the approach by the government she served may have done more harm than good. A comprehensive public health policy which addresses the health care needs of the whole population is still required to put alongside the demonstrable commitment to improving the management of sickness services.

Conclusion

Any overall assessment of health policy in Britain in 1989 must return to the dominant theme of the availability of resources and their most efficient use. The Prime Minister's review of the NHS, which resulted in *Working for Patients*, was set up in 1988 in response to a funding 'crisis' experienced by health authorities. This crisis was manifested in widespread service cuts and ward closures as authorities sought to maintain expenditure within cash limits. Despite the extra funds allocated to the NHS during the 1989 public expenditure negotiations, alleged underfunding of the NHS during the 1980s, in particular in the hospital and community health services, has not been satisfactorily resolved.

Evidence suggests that public expenditure on health services in the UK is lower than might be expected, both in relation to other developed countries and in terms of the government's own estimates of the cash required to meet the needs generated by new technology, the ageing population and service development.[12] Specific requirements are a major investment in the capital stock, improvements in health services' wages and salaries to overcome labour shortages, and extra expenditure to tackle unmet need in areas such as waiting lists and community care. Moreover, additional transaction costs associated with recording and billing will arise in a system of managed competition. There is also a need for funding to support medical audit, resource management and other key elements in the government's programme. Unless more resources are provided for these purposes, there will be less money available for patient care.

Such claims are not meant to imply that there is no scope for using existing resources more efficiently. In view of the tight pressure put on support services' expenditure during the 1980s, the most promising areas for action are clinical practices, given well-established variations in performance between doctors and hospitals. Many of the White Paper's proposals should enable progress to be made in these areas. The size of the savings that can be obtained from greater efficiency in clinical practices is difficult to estimate, but is unlikely to be sufficient – certainly in the short term – to overcome the funding shortfall that currently exists.

For this reason, extra resources are still needed. The minimum requirement is that the volume of resource inputs per head of the population available for patient care be maintained. If this cannot be achieved then it will be difficult to implement the reform programme, and the government will be vulnerable to the claim that accountants, lawyers and computer specialists are benefiting at the expense of patients.

Notes

1. Cm.555, *Working for Patients*, London, HMSO, 1989.
2. P. Townsend and N. Davidson, *Inequalities in Health*, Harmondsworth, Penguin, 1982.
3. King's Fund Institute, *Managed Competition: A New Approach to Health Care in Britain*, London, King's Fund, 1989.
4. Cm.249, *Promoting Better Health: The Government's Programme for Improving Primary Health Care*, London, HMSO, 1987.
5. Institute of Health Services Management, National Association of Health Authorities, and the King's Fund Institute, Efficiency in the NHS, King's Fund, 1989, London.
6. National Association of Health Authorities, *Health Service Costs: autumn survey of the financial position of district health authorities 1989*, Birmingham, NAHA, 1989.
7. Research Unit in Health and Behavioural Change, *Changing the Public Health*, Chichester, John Wiley, 1989.
8. Edwina Currie, *Life Lines*, London, Sidgwick and Jackson, 1989.
9. Ibid.
10. Margaret Whitehead, *Swimming Upstream: Trends and Prospects in Education for Health*, London, King's Fund, 1989.
11. Ibid.
12. King's Fund Institute, *Health Finance: Assessing the Options*, London, King's Fund, 1988.

Chronology

4 Jan: BMA gives unanimous support for the junior doctors' campaign for a 72-hour working week.

22 Jan: Department of Health orders an investigation into claims that two Turkish men had sold one of their kidneys at a West London private hospital.

25 Jan: Lord Rea moves the second reading of his Bill in the Lords to set 72-hour working week for junior doctors.

30 Jan: Spending on health for 1989–90 up by £1.46 billion.

31 Jan: NHS White Paper *Working for Patients* published. Its main points envisaged self-governing hospitals, a new Policy Board, GPs managing their own budgets, individual appointments for patients, tax relief on private health insurance for those over 60 and a 100 extra consultants.

6 Feb: Special Aids information campaign launched in the gay press.

20 Feb: Further eight working papers on the White Paper and how it will be implemented are published.

14 Mar: Tax relief on private health insurance for the over-60s to be introduced from 6 Apr 1990.

16 Mar: MMC report *Services of Medical Practitioners* says that prohibitions against advertising by GPs are against the public interest and should be scrapped.

27 Mar: Dr Chris Johnston serves a writ on Bloomsbury Health Authority after working a 112-hour week for failing to safeguard his health and thus endangering his patients. The action has the backing of the junior doctors committee of the BMA.

28 Mar: Office of Health Economics *The Impact of New Medicines on Health Care Costs* proposes new drugs budgets.

1 Apr: Prescription charges raised 20p to £2.80.

Free eye tests end.

4 Apr: Royal College of Nurses follow the BMA in campaigning against the NHS White Paper.

11 Apr: Major reorganization of Birmingham's health services announced.

13 Apr: £50 million extra funds announced in an effort to recruit 100 extra consultants over the next three years.

15 Apr: Royal College of General Practitioners becomes the last of the medical institutions to reject the NHS White Paper decisively.

20 Apr: Government publishes its Bill making it a criminal offence to make or receive payment for organs for transplants.

21 Apr: Survey in London shows that the threat of Aids has made little difference to the behaviour of drug addicts.

28 Apr: Hearing Aid Council (Amendment) Bill, to protect deaf people from the unscrupulous activities of certain hearing aid companies, passes the Commons without a division.

2 May: Report by the National Kidney Research Fund says 1 in 10 kidney failures could be prevented if family doctors made routine checks on high blood pressure patients.

4 May: Deals on new contracts for GPs agreed.

£7 million co-ordinated programmes for teaching schoolchildren about the risks of drugs, alcohol and Aids launched.

5 May: Report links the pill with greater risk of breast cancer.

8 May: Campaign against health fraud launched, seeking legislation to protect the public from the unsubstantiated claims of alternative medicine and to encourage alternative practitioners to submit their methods to scientific scrutiny.

11 May: Two new hospitals in Scotland announced.

17 May: BMA votes not to co-operate in the implementation of NHS reform but urges Kenneth Clarke to discuss sensible experiments in one NHS region.

22 May: Composition of the new nine member NHS policy board announced.

27 June: *The Peckham Report* by Action Research for the Crippled Child calls for legal requirements for children to be immunized from a range of childhood diseases.

6 July: Human Organ Transplant Bill (outlawing the trade in organs) completes its passage of the Commons.

13 July: Announcement that the government is planning to use private money to hasten the closure of long-stay mental health institutions.

16 July: Survey in Edinburgh published in the *British Medical Journal* argues for the need to eroticize condoms in the face of Aids and to encourage prostitutes to have regular medical checks.

20 July: GPs reject by 3 to 1 Kenneth Clarke's new contracts but he says he will impose them anyway.

30 July: Doctors are still prescribing too many tranquillizers despite official advice to limit their use according to the Association of Community Health Councils.

31 July: Human Organs Transplant Act receives the Royal Assent.

2 Aug: Department of Health study (*Economic Aspects of Hospital-Acquired Infections* Centre for Health Economics, University of York) estimates that hospitals could save £36 million a year if hospital-acquired infections were controlled more effectively.

3 Aug: Government announces its decision to publish ozone levels daily for the benefit of asthmatics and sufferers from bronchial complaints.

7 Aug: Report in the *British Journal of Obstetrics and Gynaecology* argues oral contraceptives have reduced deaths from cancer of the ovaries.

8 Aug: Government launches a £4 million drive to recruit nurses to a wave of criticisms from the Royal College of Nursing.

9 Aug: Val Mason, *Women's Experience of Maternity Care – A Survey Manual*, HMSO, urges health authorities to improve maternity services, which were found to be too impersonal.

10 Aug: Mr Clarke's NHS plans are criticized as a leap in the dark by the Commons Social Services Select Committee.
Resourcing the NHS: The Government's Plans for the Future of the NHS, the report of the Commons Social Services Select Committee, argues for a slow-down in the re-shaping of the NHS.

14 Aug: Cash increases of 1.5 per cent for the NHS after allowing for inflation planned for the next year.

15 Aug: National Audit Office reports that the NHS lacks the level of financial expertise to implement the government's planned reforms.

23 Aug: Package of measures designed to improve the quality of care in out-patient departments announced.

24 Aug: Institution of Environmental Health Officers warns of the danger to health posed by a 20 per cent increase in the rat population in England and Wales in the last year.
Report by a working party chaired by Desmond Julian for the British Heart Foundation calls for major changes in the way and speed with which heart attack victims are treated.

30 Aug: Announcement that NHS consultants are to be sent to business schools for management training.

5 Sept: *Epidemiological and Statistical Aspects of the Aids Epidemic*, Royal Society, published, suggesting that the current Aids epidemic amongst male homosexuals may be nearing its peak.
Report on Efficiency in the NHS argues that the government has seriously overestimated the amount saved by cost-improvement programmes.

6 Sept: Researchers from the West Midlands Regional Children's Registry note a tenfold increase in a rare form of childhood cancer in the Dudley area.

7 Sept: Christine Godfrey, Geoffrey Hardman and Alan Maynard, *Priorities for Health Promotion: An Economic Approach*, Health Education Authority/Centre for Health Economics, University of York published. An analysis of health promotion campaigns.

11 Sept: It is revealed that Mrs Thatcher has vetoed a study on sexual behaviour designed to cast light on the spread of Aids.

14 Sept: Report by Dr Michael Goldacre in the *British Medical Journal* shows that emergency readmissions to hospitals have risen by 75 per cent, suggesting that patients are being discharged too early.

11 Oct: Committee on the Safety of Medicines are to review their advice to diabetics after the deaths of patients taking insulin derived from human rather than animal sources.

16 Oct: New contracts are imposed on GPs.

Wellcome Trust is to provide £900,000 so that the sex survey vetoed by the government can go ahead.

30 Oct: All-party campaign to give patients the legal right to see their medical records is launched.

3 Nov: Mr Clarke announces the 79 NHS units which are applying to opt out.

6 Nov: New helicopter ambulance service, Careflight, launched for the rapid transit of patients to specialist units.

7 Nov: Army and police called in to run London ambulance service after management suspends ambulancemen.

£300,000 publicity campaign promoting changes in the family doctor service launched. *Efficiency of Theatre Services*, College of Anaesthetists argues that 20,000 extra operations per year could be carried out if hospital theatres were properly managed to eliminate wastage of time and resources largely caused by cancellations.

8 Nov: Report of the Chief Medical Officer published.

15 Nov: Spending on health raised in the autumn statement for 1989–90 by £2.6 billion over the previous year's figure.

21 Nov: A Bill to introduce an internal market in the NHS is announced in the Queen's speech.

22 Nov: National Health Service and Community Care Bill published.

23 Nov: The government is to pay a lump sum of £20,000 to the estimated 1,100 haemophiliacs who contracted HIV from infected blood products supplied by the NHS and to the families of about 100 victims who have died as a result.

24 Nov: Mass anonymous testing of blood for HIV is to begin in January it is announced.

29 Nov: First long term health education programme is launched by the Health Education Authority.

30 Nov: Aids epidemic will hit the heterosexual population in the next five to ten years according to Professor Roy Anderson, an adviser to the Department of Health.

5 Dec: *Charities and the National Health*, Directory of Social Change, criticizes the use of charitable fundraising by the NHS to make up for shortfalls in government funding as unfair competition with charities and also possibly unlawful.

8 Dec: Influenza epidemic confirmed by Department of Health.

11 Dec: £10 million anti-smoking campaign aimed at teenagers launched by the Health Education Authority.

National Health Service and Community Care Bill passes second reading in Commons by 323 to 247.

12 Dec: Department of Health report urges various ways in which cuts in sugar consumption could be encouraged.

14 Dec: Cash allocations to regional health authorities announced.

15 Dec: *Mental Health Act Commission Third Biennial Report*, HMSO, recommends that district health authorities should have to buy in secure care for severely mentally disordered patients.

29 Dec: Federation of Opthalmic and Dispensing Opticians survey shows a fall of a third in the number of eye tests since charges were introduced in April.

Social Security Policy

KATHY SUTTON

'For the 1990s we must have a social security system which helps, not hinders, the country's growing prosperity.'[1]

Throughout a decade of Conservative rule, social security policy has been dominated by a mixture of radical ideology, responsive pragmatism and an overriding commitment to reduce public expenditure. In that sense, 1989 represented no departure from what had gone on before.

The gap between the rich and poor continued to grow apace as the government pushed ahead with yet more proposals to push the unemployed into low paid labour and as the hidden welfare state of tax cuts, tax reliefs and occupational perks and benefits continued under a Chancellor who had promised much for the low paid and delivered little in his budget of 1989. In the middle of the year one minister had the audacity to suggest that poverty no longer existed in the country. This was too much even for the government. He was soon to disappear from the scene leaving the unprecedented number of people living on low pay and low incomes behind him.

The government's radical ideology has moulded social security in this country into a new shape with new values and a new style. No longer are social security policies consistent with the one- nation philosophy espoused by some members of the Conservative Party. The purpose of social security is no longer social integration but social control; the social security system must help the economy by indirectly subsidising employers through in-work benefits to families.

This ideology tells us that the social security system fosters a craving dependence upon it and nurtures attitudes amongst its recipients which are an anathema to economic progress. In the government's view the positive values of individualism, a return to 'family values', self-help and the promotion of independence from the state are impeded by the social security system established by Beveridge.

The key 'buzzwords' of social security in the 1980s are terms such as economic efficiency, simplification and targeting. For the government they symbolize all that is progressive about their new social security system; for the claimant and the critic all that is wrong. Increasingly, the government distinguishes an ever-decreasing group of deserving poor from an ever-increasing group of undeserving poor.

Simplifying the System – The Social Security Act 1988

According to the government, the 1986 Social Security Act simplified the benefits system. This act was heralded as the most significant reform of the social security system since Beveridge. To some extent 1989 has represented a consolidation of the government's radical policies towards social security. It has been a year when the real impact of the changes subsequently introduced in April 1988 have begun to bite.

The 1986 changes strengthened means-testing. But it was not easy for claimants to see just how the benefits system had been simplified. In housing benefits and in-work benefits such as Family Credit, new capital rules were introduced. Claimants were required to answer more and more questions which intruded ever further into the personal and private areas of their lives.

For many thousands of claimants this Act quite simply meant cuts in benefit and to their rights to benefit. Although claimants who had claimed benefits before April 1988 received transitional protection so that they did not suffer actual financial loss as a result of the direct cuts in benefits, more and more claimants in 1989 suffered even greater levels of hardship, deprivation, debt and poverty particularly when interest rates rose throughout the year.

Throughout 1989 the impact of the government's simplification of the benefits system was brought to public attention by such organizations as the National Association of Citizens Advice Bureaux (NACAB) and Shelter. The benefits reforms intensified the growing divide between rich and poor in the country.

The year 1989 was the year of benefit losers. Pensioners, women, black people, people with disabilities, widows – many groups reliant on state support suffered as a result of the 1988 changes. The Social Services Committee of the House of Commons concluded that the social security changes had left hardly any gainers, apart from the most severely disabled. The changes had deprived hundreds and thousands of claimants.[2]

Four groups in particular continued to suffer badly.

Young people

The Social Security Act 1986 removed the right of 16–17 year olds to claim Income Support and introduced lower benefits rates for people under 25. Throughout the year there were vigorous campaigns led on behalf of young people to restore their lost benefits. For most young people under the age of 18 the ultimate safety net had been removed as of right and only discretionary hardship payments were available.

Partial relaxations in the benefit rules for young people under the age of 18 were introduced following a vigorous press and publicity campaigning on behalf of young people by such organizations as Shelter and NACAB. A report by NACAB highlighted the many cases of hardship being experienced by young people and Shelter launched a 'Give Us a Break' campaign to fight for the same benefit levels as those of 25 and over. These highlighted the awesome plight of young people whose entry into near-adult life was a seamy and squalid affair. Losing the right to state subsistence led to increasing homelessness and hardship for thousands of young people throughout the country. The government failed to restore fully the benefits lost by young people.[3] Nor did the amendments quell criticisms that the social security system was taxing on youth and creating tension and division within poor households, leaving young people reliant on family assistance.

To make matters worse, changes in the way that income support was calculated for boarders and hostel dwellers created special problems for young people between the ages of 18–24.[4]

The homeless

As means-tested benefits for personal needs and housing support were reduced in real terms, 1989 saw an increasing number of homeless living in cardboard cities, particularly in inner-city areas. Things were made worse by the fact that the Department of Social Security (DSS) appeared to have bungled the transitional protection for such people.[5] A large proportion of these were young people and single-parent families who are more likely to have to rely on means-tested benefits than other families. Shelter estimated that more than 150,000 16–25 year olds were homeless in Britain.

One-parent families

At a national level a review of the position of lone parents was carried out. The government promised that this would not be a cost cutting exercise. At a local level single-parent families felt the impact not only of benefit cuts, but also of stricter administration concerning maintenance payments for their children. The social security changes of 1988 paradoxically placed a larger number of one-parent families on to greater reliance on the state. This was because childcare costs could no longer be disregarded for Income Support purposes. Because of a chronic shortage in childcare provision amongst other things, single parents are more likely to live in poverty than other families. The average income of single parents is 40 per cent of two parent families and they are almost four times as likely as any other group to be living on an income below the poverty line.[6]

People with disabilities

The Conservative Party manifesto of 1979 had said 'our aim is to introduce a coherent system of cash benefits to meet the costs of disability so that more disabled people can support themselves and lead normal lives. We shall work towards this as swiftly as the strength of the economy allows.' In 1984 the Conservative Party commissioned the Office of Population, Censuses and Surveys to research into the extent and nature of disabilities in the country, promising that a comprehensive review would be carried out once these had been completed. In July 1989 the last of the six reports on the extent of disability had been published but in December the review had yet to be announced.

Disability Alliance calculated that at least one million people lost out as a result of the 1988 changes.[7] Although a number of welcome changes were announced throughout the year, for example, changes in the six-month rule for attendance allowance, the extension of attendance allowance for young children under the age of two and the extension of mobility allowance to the blind deaf, the failure to announce a comprehensive review has done nothing to ameliorate the growing poverty of people with disabilities.

While the November upratings provided extra money for people with disabilities it did so at the cost of cutting Statutory Sick Pay (SSP).[8] Disability Alliance criticized the fact that this extra money had also come as a result of freezing child benefit. It said, 'it is not acceptable to transfer money from one group of claimants to another.'

Pragmatism

Few governments, however great their convictions, are entirely resistant to public pressure. The present government is no different. Social security policy in 1989 has been characterized by a mixture of ideological conviction and responsive pragmatism. Certain retreats from the 1988 benefit changes were witnessed in 1989, including those for young people, widows and asylum seekers.[9] These were either forced on the government by public pressure or successful test cases.

Although the government successfully fought off attempts by the House of Lords to strengthen child benefit, its pragmatism came to the fore in December 1989. A vigorous parliamentary campaign, with cross-party support, on behalf of war widows bereaved before 1973, ended in success when the government announced a flat rate increase of £40 per week for such widows. The campaign had started during the Social Security Bill which dominated the parliamentary scene for much of 1989. Many of the campaigners said the government had done too little, too late. With the war widows dying at the rate of ten a day, there would be some who would hear the announcement but never receive the extra money.

On 3 March Nicholas Scott announced that the deadline for applications for Housing Benefit transitional payment would be continued to be received for three more months following a low number of applications. Later on in the year the National Audit Office severely criticized the government for the slipshod way in which the scheme had come into operation.

Social Security and Public Expenditure

The 1989 Budget

Nigel Lawson's champagne budget of 1988 was followed by a budget which made small change to the position of the poor.[10] The Chancellor had done nothing to alter the unplanned result of the interaction of the benefits and tax systems better known as the poverty trap. The failure to uprate Child Benefit for the third year in succession meant that the poverty trap would intensify.[11]

As a result of the Budget, the Low Pay Unit calculated that an extra 150,000 would be caught by the poverty trap. It was calculated that 635,000 workers would now be trapped by marginal tax rates of 70 per cent or more.[12] As means-tested benefits grow, more and more people are drawn into the cruel effects of the poverty trap.

In 1979 the overall burden of taxation as a proportion of national income was 34 per cent; after the 1989 Budget it was 37 per cent. People on half average earnings in 1989 paid more in direct deductions from their wages than in 1979.

The November upratings

In November 1989, Tony Newton, the new Secetary of State for Social Security, announced that for the first time ever social security spending would, from 1990, reach £1 billion per week.[13] Although Mr Newton believed that the 1989 government upratings 'underline our commitment to ensure that our country's greater prosperity is widely shared', the facts told a different story.

Firstly, the announcements made in the Autumn Statement disguised the fact that social security spending had, in real terms, been cut by over £1,000 million over the period from 1988. The Low Pay Unit calculated that the announcements by Tony Newton disguised a real cut of another £1,000 million for the year from 1990. Social Security claimants had actually experienced a real cut of 3.3 per cent in social security spending.[14]

Increased unemployment, larger numbers of elderly people, one-parent families, disabled people and an ever-increasing number of people living in poverty or on its margins, were the main factors underlying this growth in social security spending. Between 1979–80 and 1988–9 there was an unprecedented growth in means-tested benefits. It was not that the poor were getting better benefits, but that more people were claiming inadequate benefits.

In supplementary benefit, the numbers grew from 2.9 million to almost five million. In housing benefit the numbers more than trebled from just over 1.25 million to nearly 4.5 million. In 1989, the government announced that 11 million people would be eligible for its newly created means-test – poll tax rebate – over 40 per cent of the country's employee workforce. The scale of reliance on means-tested benefits is unprecedented.

The Social Fund

The Social Fund, introduced by the Social Security Act 1986, was a clear example of how much public spending dominated government thinking about social security. It was a cash-limited fund replacing the system of single and urgent needs payments which had been available for supplementary benefit claimants. The year 1989 saw the completion of the first full year of the Social Fund. The Fund consists of three elements: budgeting loans, crisis loans and community care grants. Each has a fixed annual budget which cannot be overspent. Public spending constraints are placed in higher priority to the urgent needs of individuals. If a claim is disputed there is no right to independent appeal.

In the first year of operation the Social Fund was able to remain in budget. This was partly due to the fact that 600,000 claimants had their claims refused.[15] In 1989–90, however, demand grew considerably with an increasing rise in the rate of refusal. In the November upratings the government announced that it was going to freeze the Fund for a second year running.[16]

The Widening Divide

In the middle of the year John Moore, Secretary of State for Social Security, told the country in a well-publicized speech that poverty no longer existed. When the poverty lobby argued that one-third of Britain's people were living in poverty they were, he argued, really talking about inequality. He claimed that capitalism had 'wiped out the stark want of Dickensian Britain'.[17] His words caused an uproar. The Bishop of Stepney immediately issued him with an invitation to visit the East End of London to see the poverty of 'despair – of discouragement, of scraping by Giro to Giro'. Mr Moore's speech was ill-timed and ill-judged. Pragmatist politics won the day – Mr Moore was removed in the autumn reshuffle and Tony Newton took his place.

Even according to the government's own statistics on low income which they had discontinued the previous year, there were, argued critics, 9.4 million people living on or below the supplementary benefit level in 1985 – a rise of 55 per cent since 1979.

Critics said that the Chancellor of the Exchequer's economic miracle was really a mirage. The increase in living standards during the 1980s had averaged 1.9 per cent a year during the 1980s – exactly the same as the 1970s.

While the Chancellor had pursued a tax policy designed to encourage incentives for the rich in the hope that the effects would trickle down to the rest of the economy, Britain faced record levels of poverty, homelessness and unemployment. The poor, far from benefiting from trickle-down, paid for tax cuts in higher prices and higher interest rates.

Table 1. Benefit rates from April 1989 (Social Security Benefits Up-rating Order 1989 SI No. 43)

Benefit	Amount (£s)	Benefit	Amount (£s)	Amount (£s)
Contributory benefits		**Housing benefit**		
Invalidity benefit		Non-dependant deductions	rent	rates
Invalidity pension	43.60	boarder or adult working		
Invalidity allowance		24 hours or more per week		
higher rate	9.20	earning lat least £52.10	9.15	3.35
middle rate	5.80	Other adults in work		
lower rate	2.90	aged 25 or over on IS	3.85	3.35
Maternity allowance	33.20	aged 18–24 on IS	nil	3.35
Statutory maternity pay		Amenity deductions		
lower rate	36.25	Heating		7.00
Retirement pension		Hot water		0.85
Category A	43.60	Cooking		0.85
Category B for widow/er	43.60	Lighting		0.55
Category B for married woman	26.50	Premiums		
Category C for married woman	15.65	As for IS, except		
Category C for others	26.20	Lone parent premium		8.60*
Category D	26.20	Capital cut-off		6000.00*
Statutory sick pay		Capital disregarded		3000.00*
Earnings £84.00 p.w. or more	52.10			
Earnings less than £84.00 p.w.	36.25	**Income support**		
Sickness benefit		Personal allowances		
Over pension age	41.80	Single person aged		
Under pension age	33.20	less than 18		20.80
Unemployment benefit		18–24		27.40
Over pension age	43.60	25 or over		34.90
Under pension age	34.70	Lone parent aged		
Widow's benefits		less than 18		20.80
Widow's allowance	57.65*	18 or over		34.90
Widow's payment (lump sum)	1000.00*	Couple		
Widowed mother's allowance	43.60	both under 18		41.60
Widow's pension		one or both 18 or over		54.80
standard rate (age 55)	43.60	Child or young person aged		
Addition for spouse or person looking after children		0–10		11.75
Claimant receiving		11–15		17.35
retirement pension, invalidity pension,		16–17		20.80
unemployment benefit if claimaint of		18		27.40
pensionable age	26.20	Premiums		
		Family premium		6.50

	£
unemployment benefit	21.40
sickness benefit if claimant of pensionable age	25.10
sickness benefit	20.55
Dependency additions for children	
For each child of claimant receiving retirement pension, widow's benefit, invalidity benefit, invalid care allowance, severe disablement allowance, and (if claimant over pensionable age) sickness or unemployment benefit	8.95

Non-contributory benefits

	£
Attendance allowance	
higher rate	34.90
lower rate	23.30
Child benefit	7.25*
Guardian's allowance	8.95
Industrial disablement benefit	
18+ and 100% disabled	71.20
Under 18 and 100% disabled	43.60
Invalid care allowance	26.20
Mobility allowance	24.40
One parent benefit	5.20
Severe disablement allowance	26.20

Social fund

	£
Maternity payment	85.00*

Family credit

	£
Applicable amount	54.80*
Maximum family credit	
Adult (couple or lone parent)	33.60
Child or young person aged	
0–10	7.30
11–15	12.90
16–17	16.35
18	23.30
Capital cut-off	6000,00*
Capital disregarded	3000.00*

	£
Disability premium	
single person	13.70
couple	19.50
Pensioner premium	
single person	11.20
couple	17.05
Higher pensioner premium	
single person	13.70
couple	19.50
Severe disability premium	
single person	26.20
couple (lower rate)	26.20
couple (higher rate)	52.40
Hostel dwellers	
(is no longer available for boarders, see 1988 SI 1445)	
Personal expenses	
single person (lower rate)	11.95
single person (higher rate)	13.25
couple (lower rate)	23.90
couple (higher rate)	26.50
Dependent child aged	
0–10	4.10
11–15	6.05
16–17	7.00
18	11.95
Meals	
breakfast	1.10*
midday/evening	1.55*
Limit	70.00*
Extension	
lower rate	17.50*
higher rate	35.00*
Capital cut-off	6000.00*
Capital disregarded	3000.00*

* denotes no increase from last year's rate
Source: Legal Action, April 1989

Estimates produced by the London School of Economics showed that the real living standards of the poorest fifth of households had falled by 6 per cent between 1979 and 1988 while those of the richest fifth increased by 38 per cent.

The hidden system of tax benefits for the rich, the alternative welfare state for the rich, had led to a widening division between rich and poor.[18] Low pay remained a major cause of poverty. The Low Pay Unit calculated that 9.9 million workers were earning less than the Council of Europe's Decency threshold.[19] The poorest tenth of male manual workers earned less, relative to the average, than in 1986 when figures were first collected.

Economic Efficiency

'Those who remain unemployed when there are jobs ready and waiting for them do themselves no service, put an unnecessary burden on the taxpayer, and create a barrier to employment growth.'[20]

For many claimants economic efficiency has become synonymous with the creation of a low wage-low productivity economy in which the benefits system has a crucial role to play. Not only does the benefits system subsidize the lowest paying employers (and, often, the least efficient) but it also acts as a socio-economic mechanism for keeping wages levels depressed at the lower end of the wages scale. Claimants are trapped in a spiral of ever lower wages and even lower benefits.

Increasingly, the government sees the unemployed as the main part of the undeserving poor. A substantial minority of them are voluntarily unemployed refusing to price themselves into the labour market. It is they who should share the responsibility for unemployment since they have priced themselves out of the market.

Low pay is not, in the government's view, a problem or a cause of poverty but a solution to the problem of unemployment. Low pay is a necessary stepping stone to better paid jobs and to economic recovery not only for the individual, but for the country as a whole. It is the benefits system which has been used to encourage or to compel people to take low paid jobs.

The Social Security Act 1989

'It will help to open up labour markets and encourage people to take up the growing number of jobs on offer.' The Social Security Bill, which was introduced at the end of 1988 and received Royal Assent in July 1989, strengthened the role of the social security system within the labour market. Although parts of the Bill were concerned with equality in employer-related benefits, the major clauses were concerned with establishing greater control of the unemployed and their re-entry into the labour market.

The main provisions of the Act were the introduction of an actively seeking work test for unemployed claimants. Further changes were made so that claimants could no longer refuse jobs on the grounds that they were not suitable or because of the levels of pay. The Act was based on the government's convictions that a significant minority of the unemployed lacked motivation and were not actively seeking work. It resurrected a 1920's rule which required claimants to show that they were 'genuinely seeking' work. Widespread complaints had led to the repeal of this rule in the 1930s.

In the committee stage, the Opposition won a qualified victory when the government agreed that the unemployed would not have to take

jobs of less than 24-hours duration a week. Their travel expenses could also be taken into account. However, the government refused to accept that the unemployed should be able to refuse a job on the basis that they would be better off out of work. In 1989 government ministers calculated that 15,000 workers were better off out of work.[21]

Regulations published later on in the year showed the steps that claimants were expected to take to show that they were actively seeking work.[22] The key principle, according to staff instructions, was that 'claimants must look in those places where the work that they are seeking is likely to be found; and if opportunities exist they must apply for the job.'[23] At any time claimants may be required to show the Department of Employment what efforts they have made to find work.

In total, the government calculated that 50,000 workers should be removed from the unemployment benefit count. In October the government published further regulations which introduced a new test for unemployment benefit.[24]

Undermining Contributory Benefits

The contributory system of benefits runs alongside the means-tested benefits system. In 1989 the tripartite system in which the employer, employee and government made financial contributions was ended. The Social Security Act 1989 finally ended the Exchequer contribution to the fund.

This followed a government policy which has sought to weaken the state insurance scheme of benefits for unemployment, sickness and retirement and to strengthen and provide incentives for private insurance schemes. Not only had the qualifying conditions for the main contributory benefits been made more stringent but the earnings related component of such benefit had almost entirely been abolished.

Contributions

National insurance contributions have been used as a tax on the poor. There has been a gradual erosion of the social insurance principle and an increased reliance of individuals on means-tested benefits. A rising proportion of national insurance contributions have started to finance general expenditure because the Fund contributes to spending on the National Health Service. The link between rates of benefits and the contributions people paid had been removed. Increasingly, people who have a right to contributory benefits have to claim means-tested benefits in order to survive as the real value of contributory benefits has fallen.

Qualifying for unemployment benefit

The Social Security Act 1989 made it more difficult for people to requalify for unemployment. In order to requalify for unemployment benefit a recent work test was introduced. Prior to making a claim a person must have worked in the 13 weeks before the claim. The government calculated that 3,000 people would lose their rights to benefit.

Testing unemployment

Thousands more claimants lost their right to unemployment benefit as a result of the new unemployment regulations introduced in spite of resistance by the CBI, the Low Pay Unit and the Social Security Advisory Committee. Claimants earning the equivalent to the amount at which National Insurance Contributions become payable in any one week, lost their right to unemployment benefit. In 1989 the amount was £43. The government calculated that 30,000 workers would be removed from the unemployment benefit count at any one time.

This was the new test for unemployment. Prior to this the right to benefit had always been assessed on a daily basis – claimants who earned no more than £2 in any day could claim unemployment benefit on the days on which they did no work. Unemployment benefit was linked to the notion of full-time employment. This new test broke the links between benefit and full-time work linking the payment of benefit to a new earnings rule. These regulations imposed unacceptable means-testing of a contributory benefit. The sum of £43 represented less than the average earnings for a day's work let alone one week's.[25] The Social Security Advisory Committee, the official watchdog on social security, advised the government from introducing such rules. It argued that a reasonable onlooker would not view somebody earning £43 a week as unemployed.

The Low Pay Unit calculated that more than 50,000 short-time and part-time workers, at any one time, would be affected by the new rule. It said that it was likely that this rule change could lead to more unemployed workers being forced to take part-time work of £43 or more in any one week, and linked these changes to new availability rules.[26]

Cutting sick pay

In the November upratings the government also made cuts in SSP, the state scheme administered by employers. Over the years the value of state sickness benefits has fallen through the removal of the earnings related supplement and by taxing the benefit. SSP is currently paid on two levels according to the amount an individual earns. By raising the threshold for the higher rate of SSP £35 above the rate of inflation, nearly two million workers lost their right to the higher rate of SSP – three quarters of these are women.

Means-Testing the Poor

One of the most significant aspects of the Conservative government's social security policies in the 1980s was that it gained a reputation for promoting independence and lack of reliance on state benefits. In reality, however, the picture could hardly be different. As the government has weakened people's benefits as of right, it has strengthened the position of means-tested benefits. As the government, through indirect and direct subsidies to employers has created unprecedented levels of low pay in Britain, so too has the reliance on means-tested benefits grown to support families and pay housing costs. It has attacked the state insurance principle to produce increasing numbers of people reliant on state means-tested benefits with fewer rights and greater controls. By increasing discretion in the means-tested system of benefit it has made claimants more reliant on the servants of the state.

Means-testing helps to isolate claimants from the rest of society which has no material interest in this part of the welfare state. Not only this but as means-testing has taken place within the strict limits of overall spending on social security, it has helped to play off claimant against claimant; for example, the disabled have been played off against those who are sick. So not only are claimants isolated from the rest of society they may be isolated from themselves.

Far from viewing means testing as unacceptable and intrusive, the government argues that the social security system provides a more efficient means of giving people a minimum income than a minimum wage.[27]

Family Credit v Child Benefit

The jewel in the crown of the government's new reformed benefits system was Family Credit. This tax-free benefit replaced Family Income Supplement and was calculated on net earnings. It is paid on top of new earnings to people who work for 24 hours or more a week and have dependent children. The advantages of Child Benefit are that it is simple, easy to administer and is paid to the mother. It is a crucial part of the independent income of women. Even though income support recipients are no better off because child benefit is taken into account as earnings, it is still of primary importance because of this fact. In 97 per cent of cases where income support is claimed by a couple, it goes to the man.

The tenth anniversary of the full implementation of Child Benefit was marked by two notable events: in April, for the second year running, Child Benefit was frozen and, in the same month, the DSS launched a £5 million advertising bid to persuade families to take up Family Credit.[28]

Although its election manifesto of 1987 said that, 'Child Benefit will continue to be paid as now, and direct to the mother', the government supports Family Credit as an alternative to Child Benefit. Child Benefit is a universal benefit which replaced child tax allowances. It is taken up by 98 per cent of its eligible recipients. Unlike Child Benefit which reaches 98 per cent of the eligible recipients, Family Credit bears the same characteristics as other means-tested benefits. It has a low take-up, is costly to administer, complicated and weakens people's individual efforts through the poverty trap.

The government had originally estimated that Family Credit would go to nearly half a million low paid families. Despite the campaign, take-up of Family Credit had only risen from 254,000 families in March 1989 to 320,000 in July 1989. Later on in the year the Public Accounts Committee viewed the campaign as a failure. Despite an amendment in the House of Lords, and opposition within its own ranks, Child Benefit was frozen for the year 1990–1 (for the third year running) a fall of 19 per cent in the real value of the benefit. This saved the government £250 million in net terms in 1990–1.

In the November upratings, Mr Newton said that these funds would be redistributed to the poorest families. His plan included shifting even more resources into Family Credit at the expense of Child Benefit. Mr Newton was making families with children pay for the poorest. Each time Child Benefit is frozen more people fall into the poverty trap.

Conclusion

The year 1989 was hardly good news for the millions of claimants lunging into ever increasing depths of poverty. As low pay and poverty increased the government continued to pursue its policies of targeting and economic efficiency; to manipulate the social security system increasingly into a police force of the poor.

What Beveridge had intended as a safety net, in 1989 had become a poverty trap forcing people into unsuitable low paid work and subsidizing the worst employers to undercut the bad.

Notes
1. John Moore, DSS Press Release, 88/465, 16 December 1988.
2. 9th *Report of Social Services Committee 1988–9*, House of Commons paper 437–I, HMSO, 1989.

3. DSS Press Release, 98/107 Extra help for 16 and 17-year olds. Nicholas Scott in a parliamentary question told Jim Lester MP that 'our policy is the correct one for the vast majority of 16 and 17-year olds; it would be irresponsible to provide a perverse incentive for people of this age to leave home needlessly' (see footnote 2).
4. Income Support (General) Amendment Regulations, 1989.
5. This quotes David Amery, of a Bloomsbury homeless family centre as saying: 'Families say they are only eating one meal a day now because they can't afford any more. They are also borrowing money without any idea how they are going to pay it back', *Observer*, 4 June 1989.
6. For essential reading on the position of single parents in this country see, *Assisting Lone Parents: Gingerbread's Response to the DSS Lone Parent Review*, October 1989.
7. *Disability Alliance, Parliamentary Briefing Paper 9. Disability Benefits: Current Issues and Background Information.*
8. Ibid. A memorandum to the SSAC from the DSS indicated that the increases in disability benefits had come from savings in SSP.
9. On 28 February John Moore announced that he was extending widows benefit to those women who were widowed before 11 April 1988. Over 20,000 women would be affected. This followed anoma lies for widows benefits following the benefit changes of 1988 and a successful legal challenge. The government continued to insist that 'the measures taken to change Widows' Benefit were right'.
10. The principle change in the Budget claimed by the Chancellor for the low paid was the reform of the National Insurance Contri butions (NICs). As a result of the changing structure of NICs most tax payers gained £3 per week with the exception of workers at the lower end of the wages scales. A worker who earned £115 a week gained £3.01 but a worker earning £71 gained a mere 21 pence. The Chancellor also removed the earnings rule for pension ers. This meant that pensioners no longer had their pensions reduced if they had earnings over £75.
11. A major problem with means-tested benefits is the poverty trap. The most common poverty trap occurs when low paid workers, reliant on means-tested benefits, experience a sharp withdrawal of benefit when they gain extra money in wages. A low paid worker can lose as much as 96 pence in the pound through this withdrawal of benefits.
12. *Low Pay Review*, 36, Low Pay Unit, spring, 1989.
13. DSS Press Release, 25 October 1989, 89/454.
14. *A Major Disappointment for the Poor*, Low Pay Unit, 1989.
15. 'Budget pressures threaten benefits', *Observer*, 31 July 1989. Civil service unions reported that there were wide ranging cuts in grants and loans, such as homeless families moving to unfurnished accommodation, getting a cooker but no cash for carpets or cooking utensils or removal costs. Women fleeing violent partners were denied help unless they had exceptional circumstances.
16. 'Social Fund hit by further squeeze', *Guardian*, 15 November 1989.
17. *The Daily Telegraph*, 15 May 1989.
18. 'Rich-poor gap is wider says Low Pay Unit', *Financial Times*, 15 May 1989.
19. *Ten Years On: The Poor Decade*, Low Pay Unit, 1989.
20. *Employment for the 1990s*, Cm.540, December 1988, p. 58.
21. The main in-work benefit for families on low wages is Family Credit. Families on Family Credit lose 85 per cent of their housing benefit since it is taken into account as income. Under the old benefit, Family Income Supplement, low paid families got free school meals. Under Family Credit they do not. Since housing benefit does not help people with

mortgage costs, low paid fami lies, particularly home owners, can be worse off under Family Credit than out of work.

22. Social Security (Unemployment, Sickness and Invaldity Bene fit) Amendment No.2 Regulations. The best guide available to the regulations is *Signing On and Actively Seeking Work*, Unemployment Unit, 1989.

23. DE Circ., 161/1/p. 241.

24. 'Creating a conscript army of cheap labour: the government's new unemployment regulations', Low Pay Unit, December 1989.

25. See Tony Lynes, 'Welfare Watch', *New Statesman and Society*, 18 August 1989.

26. Briefing on the Social Security (Unemployment, Sickness and Invalidity Benefit) Amendment No.3 Regulations, 1989, Low Pay Unit, 1989.

27. For an introduction to Conservative philosophies, see 'Manifesto for the poor', in *The New Review*, Low Pay Unit, December 1989/January 1990, pp. 6–10.

28. For a more detailed discussion of this, see *Low Pay Review* 36, Low Pay Unit, 1989.

Chronology

10 Jan: The Social Security Bill receives a second reading in the Commons by 292 to 230. It tightens the legislation requiring people on unemployment benefit to demonstrate that they are 'actively seeking work', stops unemployed persons turning down a job because of low pay after a maximum of thirteen weeks, removes income support for most 16–17 year olds (in connection with a guarantee of a YTS place) and allows benefits for injured persons to be recouped from their insurance companies.

18 Jan: A Labour motion censuring the freezing of child benefit for the second successive year is defeated in the Commons by 297 to 231.

30 Jan: A drive against social security fraud is announced, with the focus being on employers who condone such frauds as well as the employees themselves.

28 Feb: The Social Security Commissioner rules that the Department of Social Security was wrong to withhold payments to widows whose husbands died in the six months before the 1986 Social Security Act, which decreed that only widows aged 45 or more at the time of their husband's death were entitled to pensions (the age limit was previously 40), came into force in April 1988.

7 Mar: Backbench attempts to amend the Social Security Bill so that war widows whose husbands completed their service before April 1973 are paid at the level of post-1973 war widows, who receive more than twice as much, fail in committee.

13 Mar: Government announces that from July those young people who qualify for income support and are exempt from the requirement to be either at school, in work or on YTS will get £27.40 rather than £20.80 per week plus housing benefit. Other minor changes are also announced.

5 Apr: Deadline for special incentive for people to take out personal pensions and opt out of the State Earnings Related Pensions Scheme.

10 Apr: Removal of the benefit payments towards the costs of meals of homeless families temporarily housed in bed and breakfast hostels announced. This is a consequence of the transfer of responsibility for this from the Department of Social Security to the local authorities.

24 Apr: Conservative backbench attempt to restore the index-linking of child benefit defeated in the Commons by 294 to 194.

1 May: Low Pay Unit report, *Ten Years On: The Poor Decade* argues that nearly half of Britain's employees are earning wages below the European decency threshold.

11 May: Anger over the attempts by John Moore to redefine poverty in a speech in London.

5 June: Mr Moore says pensioners are healthier and wealthier than ever before.

15 June: Lords select committee on the European Communities report *Equal Treatment for Men and Women in Pensions and Other Benefits* is published. This suggests that retirement for both sexes should be allowed at any age between 60 and 70.

28 June: Measures to ensure that fathers pay for the upkeep of their children are discussed by Mr Moore before the Commons Social Services Select Committee.

12 Sept: Report by MIL Research argues that up to 65 per cent of the people entitled to Family Credit, the state benefit targeted at poor working families, are still failing to receive the payment.

17 Sept: Changes to benefits since 1985 have hit the availability of hostels and bed and breakfast accommodation for the homeless according to the Central London Social Security Advisers' Forum.

20 Sept: Frank Field, *Losing Out: The Emergence of Britain's Underclass*, Basil Blackwell, published.

5 Oct: Reforms of national insurance outlined in the budget are introduced.

9 Oct: New regulations come into force requiring people out of work for more than 13 weeks to accept low-paid jobs or lose their benefits.

25 Oct: Announcement that child benefit is to be frozen for the third year running.

8 Nov: Commons Social Services Select Committee Report (HC 437) suggests that teenagers sleeping rough should qualify for state benefits and that other changes to the amended system set up in April 1988 should be made.

15 Nov: Chris Patten announces relaxation of social security rules affecting the homeless.

21 Nov: Major changes in the rights of employees in company pension schemes are announced in the Queen's speech.

22 Nov: Government rejects demands for a raise in the pensions of widows of servicemen killed before 1973 to equal that of those killed afterwards.

6 Dec: Government agrees to review war widows' pensions.

7 Dec: Report for the EC Commission prepared by the Child Poverty Action Group shows a rise in the number in Britain living in poverty rose from 3.6 million to 6.6 million in 1975–85.

10 Dec: Change in benefit rules which mean that any unemployed person who earns more than £43 in a week loses a week's benefit come into effect.

11 Dec: £40 per week flat-rate increase in pensions of widows of servicemen killed before 1973 announced.

19 Dec: Low Pay Unit and Labour Party studies show widening gap between rich and poor and North and South since 1979.

28 Dec: Report by Action Trust argues that the long term unemployed are being driven into the black economy by a combination of financial hardship and boredom.

Employment Policy

KATHY SUTTON

'We must increase the flexibility with which industry, commerce and individuals respond, and break down the barriers which inhibit progress and which hold back employment growth.'[1] At the end of 1988 the government sought to persuade us that 1989 was the year in which we should move gracefully into the 1990s. If the 1980s had been a decade of despair and the dole for millions of people in Britain, the Department of Employment's well-oiled publicity machine aimed to convince us that we must all adapt to the new world of the 1990s and the Single European Market of 1992. This new modern world of expanding employment and equal opportunities required us to be increasingly flexible and industry to break down the remaining barriers that stood between Britain and further employment growth.

In 1989 the government's employment policy was dominated by four 'D's: demography and the workforce, deregulation, decentralization of training and downwards equalization. The scene was set when the government published its White Paper *Employment in the 1990s* in December 1988. This laid the basis for the framework of the government's employment policy throughout the 1990s.[2]

The year 1989 was significant for another reason. This was the year which marked the commencement of a growing and unresolved battle between the government and the European Commission over the role of the European Community in the provision of social legislation to protect European workers in employment. If, at the beginning of the year the government could confidently put forward its employment policy with little mention of Europe, there were signs throughout the year that the government's confidence was weakening and that policy was increasingly being shaped with an eye to Europe.

The presence of Europe acted as a block to some of the more regressive policy intentions of the government. This does not mean that the prospect of a Single European Market or its accompanying Social Charter is inherently progressive. For many millions of migrant and black workers within the community, the prospects of 1992 were daunting: imposing stricter immigration controls and excluding the principle of racial equality so that Europe was a fortress keeping black workers out.

Declining Standards

For many, government employment policy was not leading us confidently to the 1990s but despondently back to the nineteenth century. Unprecedented numbers of workers were employed in exploitative conditions and on low levels of pay. While the number of those on the official government unemployment count continued to decline throughout the year, many believed that such reductions were being created at the long term cost of the economy. Unemployment was being reduced through the creation of low paid, casual and part-time work and by forcing young people and others on to low quality and poorly managed government training schemes.

Part-time working

As Britain's manufacturing sector continued to decline, employment growth was concentrated in the service sector where part-time working had always been more common. Secondly, as employers chose to reduce labour costs to respond to fluctuating demand, substitution of full-time workers with part-time workers employed on poorer terms and conditions became more common.[3]

Figures revealed to Parliament showed that while the number of full-time jobs fell between 1980–8, part-time working rose by one fifth.[4] Four out of five part-time workers were low paid and the overwhelming majority of part-time workers were women.[5]

Flexibility

All too often, flexibility – which sounded quite attractive – led to low pay, loss of employment benefits, insecurity of employment and none of the legal rights enjoyed by the ever decreasing numbers of full-time permanent employees.[6]

Breaking down the barriers

For millions of people the term 'breaking down the barriers' was synonymous with an attack on collective bargaining rights and the sponsoring of an individualistic ideal which runs counter to the philosophy of collective action. Nor could individuals expect this individualistic ideal to be mirrored in employment legislation as individual employment protection rights had been weakened throughout the 1980s.

Setting the Context: The Government's White Paper

The White Paper on employment set the context for the continuation and development of employment policy for 1989.[7] According to the White Paper, industry must take various measures to cope with the changing demographic trends. These trends were leading to a major reduction in the numbers of young workers entering into the labour market.

The White Paper said that employers must become more flexible and be more prepared to take a positive view on the employment of groups of workers, sometimes ignored by them: older workers, women workers, workers with disabilities and black workers. There was also a major task for both government and industry to ensure that 'outdated attitudes and behaviours in industrial relations' were countered. The White Paper argued that these hindered productivity and inhibited change. In 1989 further assaults were made on trade union powers.[8]

Not only this, but 'inflexible pay arrangements and excessive pay increases' continued to threaten jobs and growth. By the end of the year the government had failed to keep pay increases down below the rate of inflation (the underlying increase being 9.25 per cent) and was embroiled in a bitter dispute with ambulance workers in the public sector who had overwhelming public support for their calls for higher pay.

According to the government, another major barrier to employment growth was the attitudes of the employed. The government argued that unemployment could be considerably reduced and many vacant jobs filled if the unemployed would just change their general attitudes. They needed to look more intensively and effectively for work. As unemployment figures declined, the doctrine grew that the unemployed were responsible for their situation. Reasons put forward were the effects of the dependency culture encouraged by the over-generous welfare state, lack of initiative on the part of the unemployed and the fact that the unemployed were not engaged in actively seeking work.

Above all else, the White Paper urged that: 'we must invest in the skills and knowledge of our people and build up industry's skillbase, through a strategy of training through life.' Few people could disagree with such sentiments. By the end of 1989, however, the government's role in training was well on the wane as it chose to divert training responsibilities to the private sector whose accountability was primarily to its shareholders.

The White Paper outlined a series of measures to meet these broad objectives. Most were contained in the Employment Bill 1988/9 which dominated the parliamentary session and which finally received Royal Assent in November 1989.

The main provisions of the Employment Act were concerned with discrimination, health and safety protection, rights at work, industrial tribunals and training.

European Intervention and the Employment Bill

Ironically, the original motivation for the Employment Bill came not from the government from but from Europe. In October 1986 the European Commission issued a 'reasoned 'opinion that section 51 of the Sex Discrimination Act 1975 was in breach of the European Equal Treatment Directive. This states that there should be no sex discrimination in access to employment, training, working conditions, promotion and dismissal. Section 51 of the Act provided for all statutes predating the Act to be excluded from the requirements of the Act. This opinion meant that the government was forced to amend the current equality legislation to comply with Europe's requirements. It also had to review other potentially discriminatory legislation passed prior to the Sex Discrimination Act 1975. This paved the way for the government to tread further down the road of deregulation.

Health and safety deregulation

In 1986 the government had commenced deregulation of health and safety protection for women on the pretext that it was necessary to remove discrimination as well as outmoded barriers to women's employment.[9]

Similar tactics were used again in 1989 to remove large chunks of protective legislation from women and young people. In its analysis of discriminatory legislation passed prior to the Act, the government focused on health and safety laws and regulations. It gave little or no consideration to the option of removing discrimination by extending protective legislation to men. Indeed, an earlier consultative document issued in 1988 had argued that it was the maintenance of such protective laws that had to be justified. Although the government was right to say that some legislation was archaic, critics believed that the government should have considered reviewing and standardizing the existing legislation so that all workers had proper protection at work.

The Employment Act 1989 concentrated on two groups of people crucial to the labour market – women and young people. Of major concern was the sweeping away of protective legislation concerned with young people's working hours. All restrictions on the working hours of young people in shops, factories and mines and quarries were removed. These gave young workers the right to meal breaks, holidays, maximum work periods, maximum working days and weeks and starting and ending times for work. Critics argued that these changes would give the green light to employers to substitute cheap youth labour for more experienced adult workers.[10]

The government argued that protective legislation acted as a barrier to the employment of women. Although both domestic and European legislation ensured that special protective measures could be retained for women to protect them because of pregnancy and childbirth, the Employment Act provided for the removal of a wide number of laws cutting across a variety of industries and occupations.

These included protective legislation concerning work with certain specified dangerous substances, the lifting of heavy loads, the cleaning and maintenance and operation of dangerous machinery and the removal of restrictions on the employment of women from certain industries such as productive mining.

The National Council for Civil Liberties pointed out that there was a growing body of opinion which pointed out that the reproductive health of men may be more vulnerable to industrial processes than that of women.[11]

This part of the Employment Act was symptomatic of the government's approach to European intervention. Because it was bound to implement European equality legislation, it found it impossible to resist making changes to its laws to ensure compliance. However, this process was normally characterized by downwards equalization which acted to the detriment of women so that the original aims and intentions of equality laws were perverted.

Deregulation – the weakening of employment protection law

'The government believe that a sustained programme of deregulation in the labour market is necessary if we are to secure the flexibility we need for further economic growth.'[12]

Over the years of Conservative rule, employment protection legislation has been considerably weakened as the government saw it as a barrier to employment growth. For example, in 1980 women in small firms lost their automatic right to return to work after the birth of a child and the qualifying period for protection against unfair dismissal had been extended from six months to one year and then to two years. The Employment Act continued this process of the weakening of employment protection.

The Act provided that workers who are employed in firms with less than 20 employees would no longer have the right to a written statement of disciplinary procedure. In addition to qualify for the right to a written statement of the reasons for dismissal, workers would have to have been employed by their employer for two years continuous service as opposed to six months.

Of equal concern was the proposal to introduce a deposit of up to £150 for workers at industrial tribunals to deter 'ill-founded applications'. In an earlier White Paper, the government had proposed the introduction of a fee for tribunals of £25 which had been condemned as cheque book justice or a tax on justice.[13]

What was interesting about these provisions were that they drew back from the earlier proposals in the government's White Paper, *Building Businesses . . . Not Barriers* (1986). Here, major proposals had included further restrictions on the maternity rights of women and the raising of the hours threshold at which individual workers would qualify for full employment rights – a measure which would have had the greatest impact on part-time women workers. While the UK government had consistently blocked attempts in Europe to implement a part-time workers' directive and parental leave directive, these earlier proposals were dropped in the face of likely European resistance and the development of the social dimension of the single market.

Downwards equalization

There were, however, more positive aspects to the Employment Act which provided for the equalization of redundancy payments for men and women. This measure followed the successful case that Mrs Cato had taken against her employers. Here it was held that age differentiation for collectively agreed redundancy payments which precisely mirrored the statutory scheme contravened Article 119 of the Treaty of Rome which guaranteed equal pay for work of equal value. So the government had been forced to introduce this change.

For adherents of equal opportunities the provision enabling women to work down the mines was also a positive one; supported by the Equal Opportunities Commission and rejected by both unions and employers.

Overall, however, the Employment Act continued a process of equalization downwards for women with effective protective legislation being stripped away and further deregulation taking place in the labour market. The weakening of individual employment protection rights particularly affected women who were less likely to be protected by collective bargaining and more reliant on employment protection legislation. The maintenance of special health and safety provisions for women would still enable employers to discriminate against women.

Deregulating Wages

Just as poor industrial relations were a barrier to future employment growth, so too, according to the government were excessive pay increases and inflexible pay arrangements.

The government argued that the going rate was outmoded and should play no part in the 1990s. In order to break down the role of national agreements in determining pay the government continued its measure of privatization, deregulation and the contracting out of public services through compulsory competitive tendering.

Private sector wages – getting rid of wages councils

The government issued a consultation document urging the abolition of wages councils.[14] Wages councils set minimum pay and overtime rates in some of Britain's lowest paying industries: shops, hotel and catering, pubs and clubs and clothing manufacturing. Three-quarters of those who would be affected by abolition were women. Over two million women stood to lose their rights to minimum pay protection if the government went ahead. Abolition would leave the

UK alone in the European Community in not providing any minimum wages protection at all.

The government had already taken a number of measures designed to eliminate the principle of statutory pay rights. In 1980 it abolished the rights of workers under Section 11 of the Employment Protection (Consolidation) Act 1978 to apply to an industrial tribunal if they believed that they were not being paid the going rate for the job. In 1983 it abolished the Fair Wages Resolution created to ensure that workers on public contract should receive fair wages. Finally, in 1986 the Wages Act substantially weakened the wages councils, set up by Winston Churchill to protect workers in 'sweated' trades.

The Wages Act 1986 removed young workers under the age of 21 from the scope of wages councils, abolished the rights of wages councils to set differentiated rates within the industries and to set other terms and conditions such as holiday pay. As a result of the Act, wages councils could only set one minimum hourly rate and an overtime rate.

The government's main argument against the wages councils was that they priced people out of work. Little evidence was produced by them to support these statements and many agreed with the response given by the Northern Ireland Equal Opportunities Commission that: 'the proposals [to abolish wages councils] are neither coherently nor cogently argued and rely heavily on factually unsubstantiated assumptions about the concept of wages councils and the workings of the economy.'[15]

The government also put forward a number of other justifications for their proposals including the fact that many workers who would be affected were part-timers providing income for the home, that it was unlikely that wages would fall if protection was removed and that, in any case, there were substantial in-work benefits for people.

A report showed that not even employers were necessarily sympathetic to such views.[16] It showed that there was no clear majority favouring abolition amongst employer organizations. Not a single workers' organization supported abolition. Many employers believed that wages councils actually improved industrial relations and assisted the process of wages determination. Employers argued that wages councils actively helped small firms by preventing competitive wage undercutting and providing stability in the market. Some employers, also, were rightly concerned that workers should not be exploited: 'We do not believe that wage rates should be regulated by how desperate a person may be to find work, but should be based on a fair return for a day's labour.'[17]

Over 2.25 million workers in wages council industries were left guessing about the government's intentions throughout the year. It was not until after Christmas 1989 that a newspaper report in *The Times* on 26 December indicated that the government had, at least for the immediate future, decided against introducing legislation to abolish wages councils. But it was still not clear whether the government had dropped or merely delayed its plans.

Even so, the government's resolution to abolish wages councils had faltered at a crucial point in the development of the country's employment policy. In December the UK has been isolated in the Madrid summit conference on the European Social Charter. The UK had been the only country to vote against it. In the years before 1992 the government could expect much European pressure to accept regulatory measures to protect European workers.[18] Faced with such pressure and the likelihood of its increasing, the resignation of the Secretary of State for Employment for personal reasons, and increasing problems on the domestic front due to inflation and the poll tax, the government, at least for the time being, was prepared to drop these plans which would have led to a further deterioration in the wages levels of workers in the country.

The low pay economy

Nevertheless, despite this partial victory for wages council supporters, in 1989 there were unprecedented numbers of workers in the country earning low pay. An analysis of official government figures showed that 10 million workers earned less than the Council of Europe's decency threshold for wages. The low paid earned less relative to the average in 1989 than in 1886 when statistics were first collected.[19]

Decentralizing Training

'It is at the local level that jobs and the need for particular skills arise. It is at the local level that people live and work and would wish to be trained for new or changing jobs.'[20]

Training and enterprise councils

The centrepiece of the government's stated economic policy was the decentralization of training and the formation of training and enterprise councils (TECs). Decentralization divested responsibility for training and the development of small and medium sized businesses to the private sector. Private sector employers were given the key role in the development of TECs which would plan and deliver training (through sub-contracted trainers) throughout the country: 'Employers are very conscious of skills shortages. These are the people who face the problems and they are keen to help solve them. We are providing the mechanism for them to do so.'[21]

The TECs will control the government's training and business programmes such as Employment Training (ET), the Youth Training Scheme (YTS) and the Business Growth Training (launched in April 1989) as well as developing their own local strategy. The government envisaged that about 100 TECs would be established. At least two-thirds of their memberships were to be employed at top management level in the private sector. Employer-led groups were invited to apply to operate TECs from February 1989 and the scheme was officially launched in March 1989. Development funding of £2 million was announced in July 1989 for 19 areas and the first TECs are planned to be fully operational early in 1990.

These measures not only undermined the central role of the state in providing an adequately skilled and trained workforce but, also, the role of trade unions and community groups in training provision. These groups have been given no representation on TECs and can merely put forward individuals to sit on TECs. The exclusion of such groups raised concerns that with training solely in the hands of employers the essential safeguards controlling quality of training, job substitution and terms and conditions for trainees could be effectively removed.

This is not the only problem with TECs. In essence, the TECs are both self-appointing and self-policing with no lines of accountability to the local community which they will apparently serve. Additionally employers have a poor record of investing in training on a voluntary basis leading one lobby group to call the government's actions as 'a dangerous and reckless gamble'.[22]

Privatizing training

At a national level, the government sought to diminish the role of the state in training through the privatization of training bodies such as the Skills Training Agency in March 1989 and the establishment of the Training Agency which replaced the Training Commission. The latter was identified as a civil service department which would ultimately be privatized through the government's Next Steps programme and unlike its predecessor, gave no representation to the TUC. The Training Agency had responsibility for developing national training strategies. In addition, a National Training Task Force was established to advise the government and to assist in the establishment of TECs – two-thirds of its twelve members were to be employers.

Finally, the government sought to remove the statutory constraints on employers to invest in training through the abolition of the remaining Industrial Training Boards. They would lose their rights to raise levies on employers and were expected to become independent, non-statutory training organizations.

This strategy of the government's rested heavily on removing existing legislative requirements on employers and replacing them with financial inducements through the transfer of billions of pounds of public resources to the private sector to encourage a more active participation by employers in the provision of training. It also reflected the fact that the government's training programmes had not been a huge success.

Employment training

As numbers on YTS declined, in September 1989 ET had completed its first full year. All the signs were that the government's much hyped scheme had failed for a number of reasons. Revised estimates by the government suggested that just over half a million places on ET would be filled. By August 1989 the government was able to announce that only 200,000 people were in training.[23] Underfunding of training and its consequent effects on the quality of training were largely blamed. A nationwide survey put the drop-rate as high as 66 per cent.[24] The payment of benefit plus to unemployed people was condemned in principle by some employers and many claimant groups and the low level of training allowances was linked to the problem of recruitment and retention for ET.[25]

For many, central government's investment in training programmes had less to do with providing high quality training packages which would deal with current skills shortage but more with undermining wages levels, providing subsidies for low paying employers and managing unemployment. As stricter rules governing the availability of benefits for the unemployed were introduced so refusal of government training schemes became more difficult. As training allowances lost their relative value this acted further to undermine wages. The signs were that these schemes skimmed the surface of the structural problems facing the country. Lack of quality control, accountability and effective planning to identify skills shortages and to match training to requirements in any centralized and planned way, did not augur well for the unemployed or the country as a whole.

Defusing the Demographic Timebomb

As part of the government's attempts to defuse the demographic timebomb it sought to encourage employers voluntarily to widen their recruitment and retention policies. The government argued that with one million fewer young people in 1993 than in 1983 employers were spending too much time trying to recruit young workers. Some employers, such as Tesco, were responding to the changing supply in the labour market by wages increases.[26] The government sought to reduce employers' dependence on young workers which would lead to further wages increases for this group and to widen employers' recruitment horizons to 'include older workers, unemployed people, women returners, people with disabilities and members of ethnic communities'.[27]

Older workers

One of the key themes of the government's demographic policies was to encourge employers to make use of older workers. Two key developments took place in 1989. In October the government abolished the earnings rule for state pensions. Prior to this, women aged 60–64 and men aged 65–69 had their pension reduced if they had earnings over £75 a week.

The Fifty-Plus Jobstart scheme was launched in July 1989. It provided a subsidy to employers to pay and to encourage workers to accept a very low level of earnings. Its predecessor, Jobstart, tops up the wages of people who take low paid work (up to £90 for a 39-hour week) for a maximum period of six months. Fifty-Plus Jobstart seeks to encourage older workers to take up part-time work. To qualify for the allowance you must be over 50, unemployed for at least a year and earn less than £2.57 per hour. Quite simply, Fifty-Plus Jobstart acts as a short term subsidy for low paying employers.

Norman Fowler, Secretary of State for Employment, argued that it would 'allow us the opportunity to harness the skills and experience of older workers and help them get re-established into the labour market'. By the end of the year, however, fewer than a hundred places had been taken. In one London office chosen to pilot the programme, only one place had been taken up with average earnings of £2.20.

The unemployed

The official unemployment figures continued to decline throughout the year. But the reduction of the official count did not necessarily imply job creation. The independent Unemployment Unit outlined 29 changes that had taken place in calculating the count including benefit changes.[28] The Social Security Act 1989 removed the rights of unemployed workers to refuse jobs on the basis of low pay or unsuitability and imposed a new actively seeking working test on benefits claimants. Government estimates calculated that 50,000 would be removed from the register as a result of these changes. In December new unemployment regulations removed the rights of thousands of part-time, temporary and short-time workers to claim benefit for days on which they did not work if they earned £43 or more in any part of the week.

The government also introduced a new pilot programme called Action Credit. This was designed for the long term unemployed who had completed ET. This offered those who were on benefit the right to work in temporary and part-time employment for earnings of up to £43 per week for up to six months. Action Credit agencies keep the worker's earnings until they have earned up to £500 or until they have worked six months whichever was the sooner. If a worker gets a job they can get the earnings as a bonus. If, however, they remain on benefit after their time on the scheme is completed, the amount earned is taken off their benefit. The scheme did not prove to be attractive to employers or the unemployed and like Jobstart and ET, take-up was poor. Concerns were expressed that such a scheme would be used by employers to make short term use of the long term unemployed on extremely low rates of pay.

Black workers

Just as the government was prepared to give lip service to equality for women, it had a similar position towards black workers who continued to suffer inequalities and discrimination in the labour market and to have suffered from higher levels of unemployment than other sectors of the population.

Michael Day, the head of the Commission for Racial Equality (CRE), argued that the role of the CRE was hindered through lack of funds and that people were being denied legal representation by the CRE because of this.[29] The financial weakness of the CRE was mirrored by legislation which failed to challenge the institutional racism that effectively exists in the UK. Michael Day identified three key changes requiring race relations legislation in the country: a statutory requirement for ethnic monitoring, the right of the CRE to bring actions on a collective basis and the redefinition of indirect discrimination.

Workers with disabilities

In July 1989 the government published the final of its reports on disability conducted by the Office of Population, Censuses and Surveys (OPCS). Of the 6.5 million people with disabilities in the country the survey showed that only 31 per cent of those were in paid employment (compared to 69 per cent of the population). A person with disabilities was twice as likely to be unemployed as people in general and the level of pay likely to be lower. By the end of the year, however, no announcement of a review had been made.

Women

In 1989 the Low Pay Unit published a report which indicated that women lost a staggering £17 billion a year as a result of sex bias in employment.[30] Earlier in the year the Equal Opportunities Commission published its strategy for the 1990s. Like government policy this document relied heavily on working to make employers voluntarily comply with equal opportunities legislation without major additional regulatory legislation being introduced. Later on, the EOC published its formal consultation document on equal pay. In March 1988 the EOC had put forward formal proposals to the government calling for new and revised legislation for sex equality in the form of a new simplified Equal Treatment Act. By the end of 1989 the government had failed to respond despite its apparent call for equality.

Just as it ignored these proposals, so too did it do little to help the EOC which suffered from a chronic shortage of funds and powers. While it called for employers to make use of women returners it did little to deal with a major issue facing women returners – that of childcare responsibilities. A report in 1988 to the European Commission by the European Childcare Network on childcare throughout Europe showed just how far the UK lagged behind other countries having the lowest level of childcare provision for the under-fives.[31] Nor was the government ready to support the calls of both lobby groups, employers and a national newspaper to remove the tax on workplace nurseries despite the fact that a study by the Institute of Manpower Studies calculated that an extra million women would participate in the labour market if there were better childcare facilities.[32]

Many improvements that women gained in 1989 were not by government intent. They were gained either through the impact of European equality legislation or through women taking successful test cases through the courts.

Europe and its Social Charter

The development of the European Social Charter dominated EC affairs throughout 1989. It had a growing influence on employment policy in this country. Both the TUC and the CBI became firm supporters of the Social Charter. The development of the government's employment policy now faced this new and unique combination of alliances. As the single market approached and the European Commission prompted discussion and debate about the social dimension the government's forward looking language seemed oddly out of kilter with its stance on the European Social Charter.

The European Community's proposed Social Charter was anathema to the British government. It included articles on the employment and remuneration (most notably and controversially on the right to fair remuneration), working and living conditions, the right to social protection, freedom of association and collective bargaining, the right to equal treatment, health and safety in the workplace, the right to social protection, vocational training and freedom of movement. In addition, special articles concerned children and adolescents, the elderly and the disabled. Government ministers repeatedly warned against it. Far from accepting the need for regulation as a means of controlling competition between the European communities and preventing social dumping, the government argued that further regulations would not create jobs which should be the social priority of Europe.

The European Commission and the other member states were not convinced of such arguments. Just as the original intention of European equality legislation, incorporated into the Treaty of Rome, had been the protection of French industry (which already had equal pay laws) from other countries, so the idea of a Social Charter arose not only from practical concerns about the implications of the single European market but also from the desire of the more economically and socially advanced countries to ensure that competition was fair through upholding a floor of minimum standards and the harmonization upwards of social legislation.

Drawing on similar European conventions such as the Council of Europe's Social and Economic charter, the first draft Social Charter was released in June 1989 and a revised version appeared in October. According to the European Commission, the aim of the Charter is to establish the major principles on which the European pattern of labour law, the role of labour and the European concept of society are based. The Charter was finally adopted by the European Commission on 8 December 1989 with only one dissenting voice, that of Mrs Thatcher.

If the Charter was a statement of principle, the Action programme published by the Commission in November was a detailed guide to the legislative proposals needed to enact the Charter. The action programme contained 47 separate proposals of which 17 were directives.[33]

In order to attempt to get British approval, the European Commission watered down some provisions within the Action Programme, most notably on minimum wages. Rather than calling for a directive on minimum wages the Charter merely proposed to make a recommendation. However, the Action Programme contains certain proposals which would have a profound impact on UK legislation. These include a directive on atypical working which would strengthen the rights of part-time and temporary workers; a directive on working time which would set minimum requirements in relation to the maximum duration of the work, rest periods, holidays, night work, week-end work and systematic overtime and a directive on written contracts of employment ensuring that all workers would have rights to a written statement.

The European Commission's gamble did not pay off. The UK government voted against the Charter in December. However, the fact that the UK government rejected the Charter did not mean that the battle was in any way over. Qualified majority voting is available on health and safety matters and it is arguable that most of the proposals could be implemented by a majority vote on the basis that they relate to the welfare of workers.[34]

The government's resistance to the Charter reflected the fact that employment rights in Britain lag far behind some of the European competitors. Despite the fact that the Charter was a disappointment for minimum wage supporters the changes it proposed would have an impact on the employment conditions of millions of workers in this country. It was a bold and forward looking document in comparison with Britain's regressive domestic employment policies.[35]

Conclusion

By the end of the year, we were no further forward in establishing whether the government would be successful in making Britain one of the social dumping grounds of Europe. There were ominous signs that the government may be successful. There were unprecedented numbers of low paid workers accompanied by the increasing casualization of the labour market. There were training schemes that consistently failed to provide high quality training matched to skills shortages and had gained a reputation of being cheap labour schemes used by the smaller employers and ignored by the larger ones.

It was clear by the end of 1989 that the government was not entirely the director of its own employment policy. It looked as if the real horse trading would take place in Europe. The European Commission was pledged to ensuring that the widest number of measures concerned with the social dimension would be considered under qualified majority voting. If the government was to have its way, one thing was clear, the veto that it had so often used before to prevent progress and greater equality in Europe was absolutely essential to it. The answer would unfold in the following year.

Notes

1. *Employment in the 1990s*, Department of Employment, December 1988.
2. Ibid.
3. Discrimination against part-time workers is not, in itself, unlawful under domestic legislation. It may, however, constitute indirect discrimination under the Sex Discrimination Act and Equal Pay Acts.
4. *Hansard*, 28 February 1989, cols. 171–4.
5. Figures calculated by the Low Pay Unit in 1989 showed that 4.8 million part-time workers were earning below the Council of Europe's Decency threshold of £163 in 1988. Of these, 3.5 million were women. See *Low Pay Review*, 37, Summer 1989.
6. *What Price Flexibility, the Casualization of Women's Employment*, Ursula Huws, Jennifer Hurstfield and Riki Hotmaat, Low Pay Unit, 1989.
7. *Employment in the 1990s*, Department of Employment, December 1988.
8. Cross reference to piece on trade unions.
9. The Sex Discrimination Act 1986 repealed all protective legislation concerned with restrictions on adult women's working hours.
10. *Newsbrief*, Summer 1989, Low Pay Unit Wages Rights Office, pp. 10–11. See also *Newsbrief* No.2, February 1990 for a timetable of when the main provisions of the Employer Act 1989 came into effect.
11. 'Equal rights for women', Newsletter of the National Council for Civil Liberties Women's Rights Unit, Spring, 1989, p. 1.
12. *Employment for the 1990s*, Department of Employment, December 1988, p. 21.
13. 'Equal rights for women', *Newsletter of the National Council for Civil Liberties Women's Rights Unit*, Spring, 1989, p. 1.
14. Wages Councils, 1988 Consultation Document, Department of Employment.
15. Northern Ireland Equal Opportunites Commission response to DE Consultation paper on wages councils, January 1989.
16. *Undervalued, Underpaid and Undercut: the Future of Wages Councils*, Alex Bryson, Low Pay Unit, May 1989.
17. Letter of the National Federation of Fish Friers to the Department of Employment, 12 January 1989.
18. See discussion on the European Social Charter below.
19. The Council of Europe's Social and Economic Charter defines its decency threshold for earnings at 68 per cent of average earnings (£163 1989/90); the Low Pay Unit's definition is two- thirds of male median earnings (£157 1989/90) and the TUC defini tion is two-thirds of mean male manual earnings (£145.20 1989/90). For a fuller discussion of the problems of low pay in 1989, see *The New Review*, No.1, Low Pay Unit, December 1989/January 1990.
20. *Employment for the 1990s*, Department of Employment, December 1988, p.29.
21. Department of Employment Press Release, 9 January 1989.

22. *Unemployment Bulletin*, Spring 1989, Unemployment Unit.
23. Department of Employment Press Release, 2 August 1989.
24. *Employment Training*, National Association of Educa tional Services for Adults, 1989.
25. Trainees receive benefit plus £10–£12 per week. They are able to claim travel costs and childcare costs of up to £50, these are available for single parents. During the year, Kay Jackson successfully took a case under the Sex Discrimination Act, arguing that lack of provision for married women constituted discrimination on the grounds of marital status. An amendment was accordingly added to the Employment Bill.
26. Tesco awarded their young workers substantial pay increases in 1989: 17-year olds received a 20 per cent increase and 16-year olds, a 22 per cent increase. This compared with an overall increase of 8 per cent for Tesco workers.
27. Department of Employment Press Release, 24 October 1989.
28. *Unemployment Bulletin*, December 1989.
29. *Annual Report*, Commission for Racial Equality, 1989.
30. 'Equal Pay: What can it do for women?' in *Low Pay Review*, 37, Summer, 1989.
31. *Childcare and Equality of Opportunity*, Consolidated report to the European Commission, Peter Moss, April 1988.
32. *The Under-utilization of Women in the Labour Market*, IMS, 1989.
33. Directives are legally binding on member states. They state what ends are to be achieved and leave member states to decide how those are to be achieved.
34. 'Charting progress', *Legal Action Bulletin*, November 1989.
35. The UK government had had more European judgments made against it than any other government in the field of equality legislation. It had consistently blocked directives on part-time working, temporary working and parental leave granting either parent the right to three months paid leave following the birth of a child.

Chronology

11 Jan: Employment Bill, lifting the ban on women working in mines, sweeping away restrictions on the working hours of young people, exempting small firms from having to provide reasons for dismissal and limiting the range of trade union activities for which officials are entitled to paid time off, increasing the age limit on women's entitlement to statutory redundancy payments to 65 and formally replacing the Training Commission with the Training Agency, introduced.

24 Jan: £55 million training programme aimed at small and medium sized companies, called the Business Growth Training Scheme, launched.
Members of the National Training Task Force announced.

27 Jan: The Jobclub network, which seeks to ease the unemployed back into the labour market, is to be cut from 1,200 to 1,000 centres.

8 Mar: Commons public accounts committee says nearly 43 per cent of the small businesses started under the Enterprise Allowance Scheme failed within three years. More than 300,000 have joined the scheme since 1982.

10 Mar: Mrs Thatcher launches £3 billion training scheme involving the setting up of 100 training and enterprise councils over the next 3–4 years.

13 Mar: Announcement that the loss-making Skill Training Agency is to be privatized. The Opposition accuses the government of serious underutilization of the Agency's centres.

14 Mar: Teenagers on the Youth Training Scheme are informed that they are no longer entitled to a set of minimum working conditions.

10 Apr: Survey published by Blue Arrow Personal Services shows that managers are refusing to change their recruitment policies and methods despite an increasing lack of skilled labour and an expected shortfall of school leavers in the mid-1990s.

11 Apr: Safety regime for the YTS to be tightened up.

12 Apr: Cash boosts announced for Employment Training, the scheme for the long term unemployed launched in September 1988.

2 May: Unemployment Unit shows that two-thirds of the unemployed referred to Employment Training rejected a place.

9 May: Richard Pearson and Geoffrey Pike, *The Graduate Labour Market in the 1990s*, Institute of Manpower Studies, warns that Britain could face a new graduate brain drain to Europe in the 1990s.

22 May: *The Next Rung Up – Training, Enterprise and Unskilled Workers* Full Employment UK proposes a programme to encourage unskilled workers in dead-end jobs to seek training.

23 May: The Council for Social Aid, the Manchester-based diocesan charity and one of the largest employment training scheme managers in the North West goes into receivership.

26 May: Government intends to axe disability allowances for handicapped people on the Employment Training scheme.

21 June: Chris King, chairman of BP's further and higher education board tells a conference on skills of his concern at the lack of literate and numerate skills amongst many graduates.

28 June: NEDO report *Work in the Countryside* suggests up to a quarter of the jobs on the land, about 90,000, might go in the next ten years.

4 July: CBI task force in its report *Towards a Skills Revolution* warns that the gap between Britain and its competitors in the field of training is still increasing and calls for national attainment targets to be set and for young people, adults and companies to be given financial credits with buying powers in a new educational and training market.

5 July: Nearly two-thirds of employers are having difficulty recruiting graduates according to the Association of Graduate Recruiters.

13 July: Announcement that Britain is to get £418 million from the EC social fund, more than any other country, towards employment and training schemes.

14 July: Survey of 1,013 students carried out by Research Surveys finds only 7 per cent of students would seriously consider a career in service or manufacturing industry, which was placed lowest of all occupations.

26 July: *Report on Literacy and Numeracy in YTS* indicates that over a quarter of trainees on the Youth Training Scheme need help with numeracy and 17 per cent with literacy.

30 July: Latest monthly survey suggests that nine out of ten leave the Employment Training Scheme and only four out of ten actually start the Scheme.

7 Aug: TUC strategy document, *Skills 2000*, calls for a statutory right to training to boost Britain's skills base.

8 Aug: CBI survey shows that half of their member firms are facing skill shortages.

9 Aug: *One Parent Families: Benefits and Work*, NACAB, says single-parent families are often worse off if they take employment and therefore have little incentive to seek work.

22 Aug: Call for tighter financial control of training programmes in the National Audit Office's *Provision of Training through Managing Agents*.

31 Aug: Mike Dicks and Neal Hatch *Discussion paper 39: The Relationship between Employment and Unemployment*, Bank of England, attributes much of the steep fall in

unemployment over the last three years to government training schemes rather than growth in jobs.

4 Sept: Survey of companies by Full Employment UK finds dissatisfaction with the Employment Training programme which they see as low level training for no-hopers which fails to produce the skilled staff industry needs.

11 Sept: *Recruitment and Retention: Tackling the Universal Problem*, Industrial Relations Services, published. This argues recruitment and retention has reached crisis proportions, with particular problems finding computer staff, skilled manual staff and engineers.

18 Sept: Hilary Metcalf and Patricia Leighton, *The Under-Utilization of Women in the Labour Market*, Institute of Manpower Studies, argues that more than one million women could be coaxed back into the labour market by better childcare and career prospects.

27 Sept: Labour promises to double the number of 16–18 year olds in full time training or education under a future Labour government.

24 Oct: *Defusing the Demographic Timebomb*, NEDO points to the need for companies to adjust their recruitment so as to tap not just the shrinking number of school leavers but also women who have had children, the unemployed and the disabled, and argues that few companies have thus far begun to pursue these more radical recruitment policies.

1 Nov: *How many Graduates in the 21st Century? The Choice is Yours*, Institute of Manpower Studies, calls for a dramatic increase in the number of children staying at school after 16, especially among the children of manual workers.

16 Nov: *Training in Britain*, HMSO (survey and series of research reports) published.

21 Nov: Initiatives to boost youth training announced at the CBI conference by Fowler, including the widening of the inner city compact scheme.

30 Nov: Survey by Jeff Hyman and Karen Bell of Strathclyde University argues that the government's Employment Training scheme is being virtually ignored by companies in Scotland.

David Kraithman and Al Kainnie, *Recruitment in Crisis?* Hatfield Polytechnic, argues that employers in the South East are 'hopelessly prepared for the future'.

18 Dec: Richard Waite and Geoffrey Pike, *School Leaver Decline and Effective Solutions*, Institute of Manpower Studies, examines the regional dimensions of this problem.

26 Dec: TGWU warns that the jobs of 300,000 workers in the defence industries are at risk.

Personal Social Services

ADRIAN WEBB

From the very first days in office the Thatcher administrations have been seen as harbingers of radical and possibly permanent change in the 'welfare state'. Yet, in one sense, the upheaval has been surprisingly unhurried in its unfolding. The pace and drama of ideological and intellectual change has been undeniable, but the inherited structure of state social service provision was transformed selectively rather than comprehensively during the first half of the 1980s. Supply side policies (expenditure cuts) and taxation changes drastically redistributed life chances to the detriment of poorer people and eroded rights and expectations (most especially in the housing and income maintenance fields). Yet the main systems of service provision remained intact. Privatization within the state services had focused on peripheral support services (for example, 'domestic' services in hospitals) rather than on core professional activities.

By the late 1980s, however, policy had begun to catch up with political rhetoric: questions about the role of the state in social policy and the legitimacy of the state services as 'monopoly' suppliers had come to the fore. Perhaps surprisingly, the Personal Social Services (PSS) were suddenly spotlighted at the very centre of this debate. Community care services for elderly, mentally handicapped, mentally ill and physically handicapped people became the test-case for the proper role of the state in social provision. In the process both the cutting edge and the intellectual corruption of partisan political analysis were revealed to the full.

The PSS are not normally at the forefront of major social and political change. In the course of a year, on past form, they would deliver social work services and domiciliary, day and residential care to millions of elderly, handicapped and sick people; support some – but too few – of their carers; and intervene in the lives of thousands of children and their parents.[1] This work would take place in over a hundred local authority social services departments, and countless voluntary organizations. One major event might seize national public attention, almost certainly the death of an abused child, but for the most part the existence of the PSS would go unremarked. These services are not generally the stuff of which stirring events are made.

A case could be made for seeing the Children Bill,[2] which wended its way through parliamentary processes in 1988–9, as a major development of considerable significance – and an exception to the rule. It is certainly important.

It represents a substantial consolidation, replacing seven separate pieces of legislation with a single legal framework covering child care. More fundamentally it marks yet another shift in the relationship between the state, children at risk, and their parents. Attitudes about the balance to be struck between these interests inevitably shift periodically. For many years there has been a gradual acceptance that children and their parents should be more fully involved in decisions made for them and about them by Social Services staff and by the courts.[3] The Children Bill was designed to enshrine that principle in law and to entrench new rights for children and their parents *vis- à-vis* the state. The growing concern about the power of the state had been dramatically highlighted by the large-scale removal of children into care in Cleveland in 1987.[4] Although the contents and likely conse quences of the Children Bill were subject to lively debate and contention, there was no doubt that the balance of rights and responsibilities binding the state and citizens were being changed in significant ways. In the process, the role of the state as the detailed scrutineer of professional practice and guardian of individual rights was highlighted.

However, it was an eminent businessman addressing an apparently mundane though massive muddle who placed the PSS at the centre of a much larger and more fundamental debate about the role of the state – and generated an entirely contrasting set of demands on Social Services departments and their staffs. Sir Roy Griffiths produced a report on community care in 1988 which ministers finally accepted in large measure in 1989.[5] Moreover, his prescription for change in the PSS was subsequently reflected, in modified form, in the even more important White Paper on the National Health Service (NHS).[6] Taken together, these two developments have transformed the assumptions embedded in the post-war consensus about social policy. For good or ill, they will also affect the lives of millions of potentially very dependent people for years to come.

Community Care: The Problem

Community care can be seen as an object lesson in policy failure. For 30 years, at minimum, there has been a clearly stated intention of enabling many of the most vulnerable people in our society – the frail and confused elderly, people with mental illness, the physically disabled and chronically sick and people with learning difficulties (mental handicap) – to live as independently as possible in the community. The corollary has been a commitment to reduce the number of such people living in hospitals and other institutional environments. However, this policy has been an incipient political scandal for decades: risible achievements have repeatedly been overlaid by vaunting rhetoric. There has been progress but it has been patchy, episodic and insufficient.[7]

Having previously advised the government on the introduction of managerial structures and processes in the NHS, Sir Roy Griffiths was again called upon when a way forward was sought in respect of community care. His report, published in the spring of 1988, was an official response – albeit semi-detached and very belated – to Titmuss's question of 1968: 'Community Care: Fact or Fiction?[8] Sir Roy Griffiths made no attempt to deny the scale of the fiction, but he wasted little time on the history of shortcomings and disillusionments.

The Griffiths Report was very much a product of our times: a short, sparse substitute for what in a previous era would have been the weighty report of a Royal Commission. As Sir Roy himself noted, he was able largely to take for granted the Audit Commission's prior analysis[9] of problems and to concentrate on practical solutions. Nonetheless, his report was a distinctly personal document and the proposed solutions were set against a lightly etched – but fundamentally important – background of values, goals and criticisms of existing arrangements.

Because he relied heavily upon it, the Audit Commission's analysis of where we have gone wrong has to be read into Sir Roy's own report. The Commission took a strategic, top-down viewpoint.[10] Failures of co-ordination were a central theme. Government policies contradict one another: the logic of community care places a major burden of service development on local authorities and yet the weight of expenditure constraint imposed on local government inhibits such development; the need for alternatives to residential care has been the credo of community care for 30 years and yet, in the 1980s, social security policies have facilitated run-away growth in private residential care (at a cost of nearly £900 million by 1988). These failures of policy co-ordination in central government have exacerbated the already powerful structural and cultural barriers to co-ordination between sectors (statutory, voluntary, private and informal care) and between the health, housing, education and personal social services – and their professional staffs. At root, therefore, our present ills were seen by the Audit Commission to arise from policy fragmentation, organizational fragmentation, and a system of financial incentives and disincentives which is often perverse.

This analysis was not the unique or original product of the Audit Commission's work. Indeed, it was almost wholly prefigured in the literature.[11] The Audit Commission's function was that of legitimating with ministers and practitioners the conclusions of otherwise suspect academics; its authoritative synthesis made action seem all but inevitable. But, as a coda to its strong analytical theme, it offered rather weakly argued suggestions as to the form that action might take. In so doing, it deserted its central and contemporary concern for processes and for incentives to individual and group behaviour, and took an atavistic step. It placed almost all its eggs in the basket of structural change: prime responsibility for mentally handicapped people might, for example, be vested in local government while that for the mentally ill might go to the NHS. The non-structural barriers to effective policy implementation were underplayed and the often empty charms of organizational simplicity were relied upon.

It was thought that Sir Roy might follow this lead which first prompted widespread anticipation of radical change. A substantial redrawing of the

Table 1. Gross expenditure on care services for community care (£m.)

Domiciliary care	1979/80	1987/8	Residential care	1979/80	1987/88
Local Authority			**Local Authority**		
Home helps	209	535	Elderly	458	914
Meals on wheels	27	59	Young people	30	44
Aids and adaptations	15	49	MH children	16	52
Elderly day care	27	77	MH adults	44	144
Other day care	35	78	Mental illness	12	29
Social work	88	202			
Total	464	1167	*Total*	560	1183
Community health (domiciliary)			**Community health (residential)**		
District nursing	109	261	Income support for		
Health visiting	7	15	residential nursing		
Chiropody	19	44	home care	10	744
Total	135	320			
Total domiciliary	599	1487	*Total residential*	570	1957
Total Community Care	1169	3444			

Source: *Caring for People: Care in the Next Decade and Beyond* CM 849, HMSO, Norwich, 1989

boundaries between local government and the NHS seemed a real possibility. Indeed, given the clear managerial lines of the NHS since Sir Roy's intervention in that arena, and given his own roots in the commercial sector, a dramatic loss of functions by local government – to the health services and the private sector – seemed likely. In the event, the appropriateness of local government responsibility for community care was firmly endorsed. Local determination of structural arrangements was also preferred to central prescription of a uniform pattern. The respective roles of health and local authorities were to be established in the light of local circumstances. Yet Sir Roy's approach proved to be a truly radical one precisely because he avoided the option of structural change.

The Griffiths Report: A Blue Print for Radical Change

'Nothing could be more radical in the public sector than to spell out responsibilities, insist on performance and accountability and to evidence that action is being taken; and even more radical, to match policy with appropriate resources and agreed timescales.' Despite this *cri de coeur*, the report masqueraded as an essentially down-to-earth checklist of practical proposals, and it was widely received in that vein. The basic suggestions were simple enough:

- local authorities should be unambiguously accountable for community care;
- diverse patterns of funding should give way to a single flow of community care resources into local government (via a specific grant which would include a transfer of monies previously spent on community care through the social security system);
- local authorities should have overall responsibility for planning, but not for delivering, local services;
- service production and delivery should be achieved by the creation of 'managed markets' with suppliers competing for local authority contracts on the basis of specification, price (and quality?);
- local authorities as the managers of these 'markets' should ensure that services 'are provided within appropriate budgets but the public or private (including non-profit) sector according to where they can be provided most economically and efficiently';
- a clear system of planning, monitoring and accountability should link local authorities to a new minister with responsibility for community care in the Department of Health;
- resources and expectations should be brought into some reasonable balance.

These proposals might be viewed as those of a business manager imbued with the government's own distaste for state monopolies and for the entrenched position of public service professions. But this would be to obscure the more complex and challenging values and objectives which underpin the report. It reflected long-standing academic and political criticisms of state social services by no means all of which come from the right. It also, albeit implicitly in some instances, laid down challenges to some of the government's core prejudices: such a large role for local social services departments sat uneasily alongside the continuing marginalization of local government; the proposed line of accountability to a minister for community care would place a clear responsibility on government to ensure plans were realistic and goals were attainable; but, above all, the proposed specific grant and the call for a reasonable balance between expectations and resources raised fundamental questions about the government's continuing approach to public sector management.

Capitalism is not an undifferentiated monolith: there is no obvious reason why business values should wholly and simply coincide with those of government, even a government bent on driving down public expenditure and on adopting 'market solutions'. That Griffiths had presented the government with a bitter pill as well as an ideological sweetener was apparent; the fate of community care – and the personal social services – would depend upon the government's willingness to swallow the prescription as a whole. Griffiths began his task by viewing 'the position at the two extremes, of policy at the centre and of consumer satisfaction'. The latter viewpoint yielded a mixed bag of suggestions. The first was that the PSS should be personal. Family practitioner services, for all their imperfections, provide some likelihood of continuous personal service from a named professional; social care services do not. People undergoing traumatic experiences and transitions should be the responsibility, as far as possible, of a named individual – a key worker. It is an approach to practice and interprofessional collaboration which has gained currency, in principle, in recent years; Sir Roy sought a clearer translation of the principle into reality.

However, consumer choice and satisfaction, quality assurance and cost effectiveness were primarily seen to flow from an end to 'state monopoly' in service provision. The assumption that any involvement of the state in meeting social need should automatically involve monopolistic state provision has rightly been criticized in recent decades. The multiple roles of the state need to be disentangled and in the process it is useful to focus attention on what the state alone can or should do. Under the Griffiths formula the actual provision of services became the least essential role of the state, with private and voluntary providers vying with each other and with statutory services to produce social care. But the state, central and local, was seen to be the primary source of funding, the sole locus for strategic planning and management, and the principle guarantor of standards and quality. Local authorities were quite literally charged with the responsibility of ensuring that community care happens. As a result, responsibilities redolent of a by-gone era of public service were re-exhumed: the measurement of local needs, the development of strategic plans, the assessment of individual need, and the evaluation of services and outcomes. They were allied to the new tasks of taking full account of personal preferences, assembling packages of care, and acting as 'designers, organisers and purchasers of non-health care services, and not primarily as direct providers'.

The importance attached to a multiplicity of services providers was driven home by placing the onus upon the local authority to make 'the maximum possible use of voluntary and private sector bodies to widen consumer choice, stimulate innovation and encourage efficiency'. In its purest form, a Griffiths Social Services Department would bifurcate: one part would design, purchase and monitor all social care provision while the other would act as but one of the providing agencies bidding competitively for contracts. To this end, the notion of financial neutrality also came to the fore. Local authorities must not stand to lose or to gain by using one service provider rather than another. Consequently, for example, Griffiths argued that social security support for people in residential homes should be much lower than at present and that local authorities should subsidize everyone whom they judged to be in need of residential care (but unable to afford it) whether they receive that care in the public, voluntary or private sectors. The object in residential care, as in all other aspects of community care, was to expose the *providers* of welfare to a competitive market without exposing needy people themselves to the tender mercies of the market place.

State social services have been excoriated for their paternalism by the libertarian left and right. The 'radical centre' has also made its mark with a trenchant advocacy of pluralism – of a 'mixed economy of welfare'[12]. A narrow preoccupation with what the state has on offer has been seen to crowd out a wider view of how people perceive their own problems and devise ways of mobilizing their own skills and resources, including their informal networks. Professional insularity has been identified as one barrier to a more responsive approach in which state services and welfare professionals work closely with other agencies to supplement rather than supplant people's own ways of coping. A realignment has gradually been sought between the local state, non-statutory agencies and the fine structure of society (families, neighbourhoods and communities of interest).

For the right, the monopoly power of the state has provided sufficient explanation of these defects of our social service system. But values and cultural inheritance may be as important as structures. The tendency to treat people as recipients rather than as sentient problem solvers, and to take over their problem rather than support them in tackling it, lurks in the long shadow of the Poor Law and the tradition of institutional care on which it rested. Community care has therefore involved a slow but fundamental transformation of core assumptions about the way in which the state should relate to vulnerable people: what it should seek to achieve on their behalf, and in co-operation with them, and how. It was easy, in the 1940s and 1950s, to desire an end to institutions. It has taken time to explore what a positive alternative, which supports and empowers people in their own homes and communities, might mean. But that process of generating a new philosophy – and of prescribing new roles for state services and their professionals – has been yielding results. The philosophy of *normalization*, of creating opportunities for an ordinary way of life, has reinforced the need to see the state as a facilitator and partner rather than as the dominant and rather non-responsive provider of essentially standardized services.

One powerful response, pioneered by Bleddyn Davies and his colleagues, has been to recast the role of front-line workers as *case managers* by giving them a notional budget per case to 'spend' on developing opportune packages of help.[13] This approach may have been driven forward by considerations of efficiency, but the research evidence suggests that case managers can create community based care for frail elderly people which is also more effective than residential care. Consumer choice has been extended by making community care a practical and affordable alternative to residential care, but also by encouraging case managers to arrange support and care in what ever ways seem most appropriate and not merely by relying on the services provided by their own statutory agency.[14] Griffiths approved of case managers; a new role definition has certainly been born. But whether normalization, case managers, price-conscious contracts and a 'managed market' fit easily together is not an issue which Griffiths even began to explore.

However, he did try to come to terms, to a surprising degree, with another defect intrinsic to the existing state social services which needs to be resolved with great care as well as determination. A founding principle of the British social services system was that professionals (most obviously, but not only, doctors) should serve the best interests of their clients unencumbered by cost constraints. This principle was compromised from the beginning by an imbalance of supply and demand; rationing and the setting of priorities has always been the order of the day. To waste resources, or to meet need in any one instance without regard to cost, is to limit the help available to those waiting in the queue. To use resources in the best possible way should be a matter of equity and social justice rather than a purblind exercise in managerial penny- pinching.[15] The corollary is that cost awareness, overt rationing procedures and a concern for resource allocation should be a central part of professional practice and of the professional value system – not an unwelcome adjunct.

Research and scholarship have given prominence to scarcity and rationing for many years.[16] A combination of scarce resources and *ad hoc* processes for allocating them cannot be long defended; neither can the ignorance of costs within which professionals have traditionally made their decisions. But the separation of decisions about resource allocation and service goals is endemic: professional staff cannot be expected to bear all, or even most, of the blame. In particular, relationships between central and local government are complex and fragmented;[17] they are also characterized by functional disaggregation and incoherence.[18] The centre subjects localities to semi-autonomous, often highly contradictory, streams of policy about objectives and output targets on the one hand and resource constraints on the other.[19] There is no 'invisible hand' of public administration to guarantee that what a government wills in terms of policy it pays for in terms of resources.

Griffiths implicitly recognized this by calling for a systematic planning process linking central and local government, but he went further. In his cautious, courtier's way, Sir Roy made it plain to ministers that local social services departments and their professional staff could not be expected to shoulder the burden of change unless government faced up to its own responsibilities by bringing supply and demand into some kind of harmony: 'To talk of policy in matters of care except in the context of available resources and timescales for action owes more to ideology than to the purposeful delivery of a caring service.' This was a strong and welcome call for political honesty. Despite a remit which emphasized better use of existing expenditure, Sir Roy clearly underlined his concerns on this score. 'Many social services departments and voluntary groups grappling with the problems at local level certainly felt that the Israelites faced with the requirements to make bricks without straw had a comparatively routine and possible task.' Officially Griffiths took no position on whether resources should increase or expectations fall, but his report left little doubt that local authorities needed more funds to do the job and implied that local authorities dependent on the community charge and the traditional financial system would be unable to cope.

The Griffiths Report therefore contained an intriguing mixture of commitments: to the market, to state subsidy and financing, and to strategic planning and public sector management. It potentially moved beyond sterile posturing in defence of the market, the state or the voluntary sector and directed some welcome attention to *ends* rather than means. It implicitly recognized that any available shortfall in efficiency or effectiveness diminishes social justice by squandering resources, without making 'efficiency' a synonym for cuts and penny pinching. It emphasized a commitment to the consumers, rather than the producers, of care. Above all, it gave local authorities a major and demanding task while hinting that central government should put its own house in order. But the effects of any road paved with some good intentions are suspect. What, in practice, might be the consequences of treading the path signposted by Sir Roy?

The future of community care depends in large measure upon two considerations: the merits of the Griffiths approach itself and the government's response to it. The Griffiths formula was widely, though cautiously, welcomed in local government, not least because it promised an end to debilitating uncertainty. Yet its defences are manifold. In particular it followed the now well trodden path which leads directly, without pause for thought or empirical evidence, from a diagnosis of apparent ills in state services to a quasi market solution.

The epitaph of Thatcherism must include the words 'intellectual sloth and dishonesty'. As a political movement it is far from being alone in this respect, but the flight from rigour, rationality and systematic policy analysis has been profound and may have inflicted enduring damage to our political culture as well as our institutions. Sadly, Griffiths contributed to this legacy, as so many others have done, by juxtaposing known and closely attested shortcomings of state services and the hypothetical virtues of free and effective competition. One profound objection to this intellectual sleight of hand is that it simply ignores or discards the experience of other countries which have signally failed to create and control competitive markets in social welfare.[20] Another is that it demonstrates a profound ignorance of the actual process of helping socially vulnerable people. As was noted earlier, the emergent philosophy of community care emphasizes *normalization* – the creation of opportunities for people to lead as ordinary a way of life as possible. Such opportunities cannot simply be designed and prescribed by one group of people, produced by another, and offered as discrete 'choices' to be selected from the supermarket shelf by 'consumers'. As research on community services for mentally handicapped people in Nottinghamshire has demonstrated,[21] there can be no simple dividing line between assessing a person's need and providing the help required.

Enabling an adult person with learning difficulties to gain in independence, and enabling parents to 'let go' of an adult who has assumed the role of a permanently dependent 'child', is a long term process of advising, supporting, and of testing out new possibilities such as day care, respite care and independent living. The planners (care managers) and field workers (case managers) have to be closely involved in creating and continuously recreating environments which meet the changing needs, capacities and expectations of both the individual and his or her parents and carers. Normalization involves helping people to enrich, even transform, their lives; the 'product' is in fact a *process* – an exploration and acceptance of change mediated through social relationships – not a standardized item of service. Albeit implicit, the consumer goods market is a misleading analogy, despite – if not because of –

its cultural dominance. A market in consumer goods 'works' because it offers a wide variety of standardized products which can be consumed seriatim or in varying combinations. But in the case of social care the 'consumer' cannot be moved on from one day centre or group home to another each time there is a change in needs or realizable potential: each type of service, not merely the array of services, must be capable of adaptation and change. Yet price sensitive competition engenders standardization and could inhibit such responsiveness. To change the market analogy, effective and responsive social care is not amenable to 'portion control'. Sir Roy Griffiths may fully appreciate these essential differences, but if the logic of market competition by price takes root standardization and 'portion control' are endemic and the safeguards of quality are under pressure.

It is paradoxical indeed that the Kent Community Care Project[22] has served as such an important source of inspiration and legitimation for the kinds of change advocated by Griffiths. Whereas the former unites decisions about care and cost in the person of the case manager, the latter – in his insistence on competition and tendering – threatens to divorce the processes of designing and purchasing care on the one hand and providing it on the other. The very idea of dividing responsibility for these processes is an unduly theoretical one derived from the market analogy. In its operation the model could be dangerously close to the Poor Law model: it could lead to people being treated as passive recipients of efficiently produced services rather than as partners with the state and professional helpers in solving problems.

Implementing Griffiths: The Government's Response

Throughout the mid-1980s ministers urged local authority social services departments to see themselves as 'enablers' rather than as providers of services. That a report which offered a means of turning this rhetoric into reality should attract no governmental response for eighteen months underlined the depth of political mistrust of local government, and the priority accorded to the concurrent review of the NHS. Both the Secretary of State's statement in June 1989 and the subsequent White Paper[23] eventually confirmed that local government was to be entrusted with the major role for community care, though neither went so far as Griffiths' unequivocal endorsement of local government's pivotal responsibility.

The government's proposals, according to the minister, are '80 per cent Griffiths'. The missing 20 per cent could be crucial – in different ways. The White Paper proved to be a curiously unspecific and disappointing document. Few of Griffiths' certainties emerged undiluted. One result is that local authorities are free, in principle at least, to transform their traditional roles and styles of operation in a spasm of radical change or to approach change cautiously and with circumspection. They must satisfy the Department of Health that they are taking voluntary and private forms of provision into account and pursuing cost-effectiveness, but –

depending on bureaucratic interpretation – this need not necessarily mean a sharp move away from statutory provision or a wholesale shift towards tendering and contracting out.

The fact that the White Paper[24] is not sharply prescriptive may prove beneficial. A simplistic faith in the efficacy of markets is dangerous enough, but Griffiths proposed a leap in the dark. Neither local authorities nor the public sector in general has substantial and prolonged experience of running a quasi-market (or managed pluralism) involving competition between statutory, voluntary and private-for-profit producers. But the tone of the White Paper does not preclude rapid change. Most local authorities – and many voluntary and private agencies – had begun to adjust to the Griffiths doctrine in advance. Some local authorities are enthusiastically planning to divest themselves of residential homes as quickly as possible, with other departments to follow. The 'consumer' can only benefit if the end result is a market which is both closely policed in terms of quality and yet competitive by price. However, residential care remains riven by perverse financial incentives: local authorities have every reason to move out of direct statutory provision but no real reason to create competitive, well policed markets. The preconditions of genuinely competitive, consumer responsive markets are exacting, and the potential for 'regulatory capture' is great if the paymaster/monitor lacks alternative suppliers – and sanctions.[25] In practice some authorities may create new voluntary agency monopolies or lose control of private-for-profit producers. But, overall, the range of local responses is likely to create diversity and generate empirical evidence about the implications of different ways of organizing social care. Whether lessons can be systematically learned from such experience is a different matter.

Perhaps the most predictable slip between Griffiths cup and White Paper lip concerns accountability. Griffiths was keen on accountability, but he was even handed: both local and central government needed to do better. The recipe for central government was to establish a clear planning and monitoring link from locality to centre and to match resources to responsibilities – not least by means of the proposed community care specific grant. The planning processes may come into place despite the White Paper's lack of precision and depth. The Social Services Inspectorate (SSI) is the natural locus for these processes: it is the regionally based arm of the Department of Health and it has begun to make the transition from the 'micro-inspection' of professional standards to the larger tasks of monitoring policies and the effectiveness of management and service systems.[26] But it has a long way to go in developing the required breadth and expertise.

However successfully the SSI may develop its role, however, it cannot offset the failure of the government to buttress planning processes with a specific community care grant. With the limited exception of mental health, the government has declined to acknowledge Griffiths' coded but clear argument. It has refused to accept its own responsibility to match rhetoric with guaranteed resources, to fulfil its own part of the accountability contract. A specific grant combined with a strong planning structure was always a two-edged sword: it could easily degenerate into detailed central intervention and control. But a weak line of accountability to central government could be even more portentous: central government may be more inclined to decentralize blame for future failures than to throw its weight behind success.

The real test of government's intentions will come long after the community care policy has ceased to be newsworthy. It will emerge gradually and belatedly in the 1990 public expenditure negotiations as the financial strategy becomes clear. Some resources will certainly be transferred to local authorities but in the absence of a specific grant the central government subvention is far more likely to be a static, one-off boost rather than a dynamic flow of resources. The pressure will be on local government to meet the growing cost of caring for an ageing population, of a more positive and responsive concept of care in the community, and of those existing residents of private and voluntary ones who will need financial help when their personal savings are exhausted. The only way forward for local authorities will be to squeeze greater efficiency out of the system if supply fails to grow with demand. It is therefore hardly surprising that there are already fears for future standards of care.

There is room for greater efficiency at the level of systems and the level of case management.[27] But the stark facts are that home help provision, for instance, fell by 11 per cent compared with the number of old people aged 75 and over between 1976 and 1981 alone[28] and that local authorities presently help only 35 per cent of those old people with needs above the threshold established by their own policies and practices.[29] At the same time, social services departments sink deeper into the mire of child care and family support. They inevitably pour much of the available resources into this area. Their priorities are determined by the political risks attaching to child care and by the impact of a polarized society on low income families.[30] Without a full and honest recognition of the resource problem, local government will be tarnished yet further, vulnerable people will be at risk, and the urgent need to locate professional decision-making within a proper awareness of costs and opportunity costs will be jeopardized.

The government's proposals could provide a tumultuous but real opportunity to breath some new life into community care – and into thinking about the relationship of the state to some of its most hard pressed citizens. Alternatively, they could signal a gradual turning off of the life support machine on which those people and a large part of local government depends. Sir Roy's warning shots about the need to match resources to policy aims were indeed welcome, but they can give little ground for optimism when government consistently seeks to isolate specific social issues and policies from the wider maldistribution of incomes and economic opportunities within which they are located.

Notes

1. A. L. Webb and G. Wistow, *Social Work, Social Care and Social Planning: The Personal Social Services since Seebohm*, London, Longmans, 1987.
2. Children Bill, London, HMSO, 1988.
3. DHSS, *The Law on Child Care and Family Services*, Cm.62, London, HMSO, 1987.
4. *Report of the enquiry into Child Abuse in Cleveland in 1987*, Cm.412, London, HMSO, 1988.
5. *Community Care: Agenda for Action, A Report by Sir Roy Griffiths*, London, HMSO, 1986.
6. Department of Health, *Working for Patients*, London, HMSO, 1989.
7. See, for example, A. L. Webb and G. Wistow, *Social Work, Social Care and Social Planning*; A. L. Webb and G. Wistow, *Planning, Need and Scarcity: Essays on the Personal Social Services*, London, Allen and Unwin, 1986; A. Walker (ed.), *Community Care*, Oxford, Basil Blackwell and Martin Robertson, 1982; N. Martin (ed.), *Reassessing Community Care*, London, Croom Helm, 1987; S. Baldwin, G. Parker and R. Walker (eds), *Social Security and Community Care*, Aldershot, Gower, 1988.
8. R. M. Titmuss, *Commitment to Welfare*, London, Allen and Unwin, 1968.
9. Audit Commission, *Making a Reality of Community Care*, London, HMSO, 1986.
10. B. Davies, 'Making a reality of community', in *British Journal of Social Work*, Vol.18, Supplement, 1988, pp. 173–87.
11. Audit Commission, *Making a Reality of Community Care*, London, HMSO, 1986.
12. S. Hatch, *Outside the State*, London, Croom Helm, 1980; R. Hadley and S. Hatch, *Social Welfare and the Failure of the State*, London, Allen and Unwin, 1981; and see M. Brenton, *The Voluntary Sector in British Social Services*, London, Longman, 1985; N. Johnson, *The Welfare State in Transition*, Sussex, Wheatsheaf, 1987.
13. D. Challis and B. Davies, *Case Management in Community Care*, Aldershot, Gower, 1986.
14. Ibid.
15. A. L. Webb, 'Alternative futures for social policy and state welfare', in R. Berthoud, *Challenges to Social Policy*, London, Gower, 1985.
16. See P. Foster, *Access to Welfare*, London, Macmillan, 1983.
17. R. Rhodes, *Beyond Westminster and Whitehall: The Sub- Central Government of Britain*, London, Unwin Hyman, 1988.
18. A. L. Webb and G. Wistow, 'The social services', in S. Ranson, G. Jones and K. Walsh (eds), *Between Centre and Locality*, London, Allen and Unwin, 1985; A. L. Webb and G. Wistow, *Social Work, Social Care and Social Planning*, 1987.
19. Ibid.
20. R. A. Parker, *The Elderly and Residential Care: Australian Lessons for Britain*, Aldershot, Gower, 1987.
21. Webb and Wistow, forthcoming.
22. D. Challis and B. Davies, *Case Management in Community Care*, Aldershot, Gower, 1986.
23. *Caring for People*, Cm.849, London, HMSO, 1989.
24. Ibid.
25. A. L. Webb, 'Alternative futures for social policy and state welfare', in R. Berthoud, *Challenges to Social Policy*, London, Gower, 1985.
26. A. L. Webb, 'The Social Services Inspectorate', *Health Care UK 1989*, Newbury, Policy Journals, 1990.

27. B. Davies and D. Challis, *Matching Resources to Needs in Community Care*, Aldershot, Gower, 1986.
28. A. L. Webb and G. Wistow, *Planning, Need and Scarcity: Essays on the Personal Social Services*, London, Allen and Unwin, 1986, Chapter 3.
29. D. Challis and B. Davies, *Case Management in Community Care*, Aldershot, Gower, 1986, p. 179.
30. A. H. Halsey, 'Social polarization, the inner city and community', in M. Bulmer, J. Lewis and D. Pichaud, *The Goals of Social Policy*, London, Unwin Hyman, 1989.

Chronology

2 Jan: Dr Norman Vetter of the special research unit at the University of Wales publishes a report attacking current provision for the elderly as wasteful and paternalistic and calls for a three-tier care system centred on comprehensive community care centres.

13 Mar: The Association of Directors of Social Services argues that services are being blighted by the government's failure to decide on its response to the 1988 Griffiths Report.

25 Mar: Cabinet committee set up to review comminity care.

27 Apr: The Children's Bill, which overhauls child care law and establishes a new framework of rights and responsibilities for parents, children and local authorities (largely based on the Butler-Sloss Report on the Cleveland affair) is given an unopposed second reading.

10 May: *Abuse of Elderly People: An Unnecessary and Preventable Problem*, British Geriatrics Society draws attention to abuse of the elderly in institutions and by carers and calls for legislation to solve this.

22 May: *Social Work in Crisis* for NALGO shows that essential services have suffered as social workers concentrated on child abuse. It also covers stress in the social services.

12 July: The government gives its response to the Griffiths Report of 1988 on community care, broadly accepting its recommendations.

23 Aug: Appeal Court ruling upholds the decision of Croydon's social services to take a child away from a white mother and place it with a black family in the light of the council's policy that every child should be brought up by families of the same ethnic group.

25 Aug: A report on the implications of the Croydon case is called for by David Mellor, Minister of State at the Department of Health, who also hints that the Children's Bill might be amended in the light of the case.

18 Sept: Plans to encourage child abusers to leave home, avoiding the need to remove the children, drawn up.

22 Sept: David Mellor threatens to close the British Agencies for Adoption and Fostering unless its guidelines on transracial fostering and adoption are changed.

27 Sept: Wirral council becomes the first to privatize all its old people's homes.

28 Sept: Concern is expressed about abuse of mentally ill people in Bristol hostels for homeless people.

23 Oct: *Is Community Care Working?* Westminster Association for Mental Health claims that one in four psychiatric patients formerly in central London hospitals, far from being cared for in the community, are now homeless.

26 Oct: Audit Commission's report, *Developing Community Care for Adults with a Mental Handicap*, HMSO, on the implications of setting up 'care managers' to run services for the mentally handicapped is published.

1 Nov: Coroner's verdict that Beverley Lewis, a deaf, blind and mentally handicapped woman, died from natural causes rather than because of the lack of care by her mentally ill mother and the local welfare authorities is condemned as a disaster for handicapped people.

6 Nov: *Charitable Trends*, Volunteer Centre UK, shows a fall in government and corporate charitable donations.

16 Nov: White Paper, *Caring for People*, Cmd.849, incorporating many of the proposals of the Griffiths Report, is published.

Care of Elderly People: Market Survey 1989–90, Lang and Buisson argues that a two-tier system of care for old people in independent homes is developing with publicly funded patients getting the worse deal.

24 Nov: Inquiry into the child abuse case of a boy killed in December 1987, *Liam Johnson Review*, is published by the London Borough of Islington.

12 Dec: New methods of financing community care for the mentally ill announced.

15 Dec: Inquiry under Mark Evans finds many serious mistakes by South Glamorgan social services caused by understaffing and overwork.

22 Dec: nquiry into child care practice in Humberside under Robert Harris criticizes practices but emphasizes that child abuse cannot be reliably predicted.

Housing

ALAN MURIE

Most accounts of the development of housing in Britain emphasize continuity. The encouragement of home ownership has been maintained over the last three decades in spite of changes in government. The decline of the private landlord and the improvement in house conditions have been continuing features. And rather than housing policy being the key determinant of change, it is the taxation treatment of housing and broad patterns of demographic, social and economic change which have had most impact on housing. Nevertheless, most commentators would accept that the advent of a Conservative government in 1979 speeded the process of change and added some new policy elements designed to achieve this. The introduction of the Right to Buy, under legislation in 1980, and the continuing squeeze on local authority capital expenditure, combined to erode the size and share of council housing in the market.

The Policy Background

At the end of 1988, approaching ten years of Conservative housing policy, the number of houses sold under the Right to Buy and the buoyancy of the home ownership market were regarded as a success by the government. A new strategy of demunicipalization and privatization was being embarked upon. The measures proposed during the general election of 1987 had been split into two pieces of legislation. The Housing Act 1988 had already been placed on the statute book and the Local Government and Housing Bill was in preparation. Taken together, this legislation was intended to deregulate the private rented sector, provide new impetus to the voluntary (now to be termed independent) housing association sector and introduce greater choice and direct accountability for council tenants. A new regime for rents, subsidy and management of council housing would lead tenants to look again at the Right to Buy and at the services their landlord offered and to consider making use of new statutory procedures for transferring to a new landlord (Tenants Choice). The initial hiatus around Tenants Choice, the proposals for Housing Action Trusts (HATs) (private trusts to take over selected council estates) and the development of ideas for large scale voluntary transfers of housing from local authorities to independent landlords, created the impression of a beleaguered council sector coming to the end of its life. Even before the new subsidy scheme with its implications for higher rents was in place, the uncertainties surrounding council housing had contributed to a higher level of council house sales (rising in Great Britain from 113,503 in 1986 to 192,368 in 1988). This increased uptake was also influenced by higher unemployment, rising incomes and awareness of the increase in house prices. The boom in house prices which had commenced in 1986 was affected by income and employment growth. General changes in taxation and declining mortgage rates fuelled this growth as did the effect of the decision to restrict the £30,000 mortgage interest tax relief limit to the residence rather than the individual from 1 August 1988. This meant that many purchases, which would probably have otherwise taken place in 1989, were brought forward to the period between April and July 1988. The spectacular increase in house prices up to August 1988 had encouraged private speculative building. The number of private sector housing starts rose from 180,000 in Great Britain in 1986 to 216,000 in 1988. What was occurring was a speculative boom in housing creating rapid inflation of house prices – and fuelling a more general inflation and pushing up interest rates.

This picture of a buoyant housing market and the success of a switch to greater dependence on the private sector was, even in 1988, only part of the picture. Alongside booming home ownership was rising homelessness. Rising house prices involved increasing affordability problems. Social polarization and changes to housing benefits resulted in a widening gap between those in buoyant parts of the market and those outside or trying to get in. And the continuing reduction of public sector building programmes meant that there were declining oppportunities to find housing in many local authorities – even if you were homeless.

After the House Price Boom

Since the beginning of August 1988, the private housing market has faltered. By early 1989 the boom was clearly over. In the first five months of 1989, building societies approved 374,000 new loans, about a third fewer than the 562,000 approvals in the corresponding period of 1988. The number of housebuilding starts also fell. A major contributory factor to this change in 1989 was rising interest rates. Mortgage rates had fallen to around 9.5 per cent in May 1988, the lowest level for ten years. However, by October 1989, mortgage rates had risen to some 14.75 per cent. Four rises in less than twelve months had lifted rates by as much as 5 per cent and taken them back to a level last seen in 1981. Rising interest rates created increased problems (and increased arrears) for those with mortgages. Some households decided against trading up. Other households could not afford the asking prices emerging from booming expectations and the mismatch between what people had been hoping to sell for and what people could afford or could borrow, contributed to a lower level of activity. Longer chains, longer delays, problems of selling and actual losses on sales became more common. Newspaper accounts of home owners in difficulties replaced earlier accounts of a home ownership bonanza.

These changes brought home ownership into the centre of the political and economic stage. It was home owners who were seen as bearing the brunt of the Chancellor of the Exchequer's reliance on interest rates to deal with inflation. The changing costs of home ownership were the result of economic, rather than housing policy and home owners as voters could not be assumed to overlook what was happening to them.

Housing Policy in 1989

Thus far, what happened to housing in 1989 seems to have had little to do with housing policy. The housing policy agenda set in 1987 was swamped by a Treasury tide. By the end of 1989 some of the major planks of housing policy were hardly visible any longer. Most notably the reduction in funding for HATs was a tacit admission that they had very limited appeal to tenants. Activity connected with the Tenants Choice measures in the Housing Act 1988 had died down and scenarios for dramatic demunicipalization seemed increasingly unlikely. The Chancellor backed up the intention to give housing associations the dominant role in rented housing provision by increasing funds available to the Housing Corporation. But housing associations generally were obviously not able to fill the gap left by declining council and private building. The new framework for their operation was still being adjusted to. The reduction in private sector building and the lower level of transactions involved one major builder (Kentish Homes) going out of business, and other builders and exchange professionals laying off staff and closing offices. Amid all of this, it is not clear what has happened to private renting. New investment under the Business Expansion Scheme has occurred but has not been a runaway success. It would seem likely that just as some landlords will have been encouraged by very high house prices to sell in 1988, others will have decided to let houses in 1989 because of difficulties in selling.

And what of council housing? The major inroads from the 1988 legislation failed to materialize. The changing circumstances of the private sector made it less easy to imagine a world without it and more easy to imagine that arguments for increased investment would begin to succeed. The Conservative controlled Association of District Councils continued to express concerns about affordability problems, especially for first-time buyers in the South of England, and continued to press for increased investment in council housing. Reports of research commissioned by the Department of the Environment and the Welsh Office made it clear that local authorities could not generally be assumed to be less economic, efficient and effective landlords than housing associations. Whether the additional cost of housing association provision was justified by the difference in performance was open to question. In this sense the view that local authorities were inherently inefficient and bad landlords or that their role in housing was no longer necessary, was under severe attack. The Chancellor's Autumn Statement included a £250 million package to help homeless people. This involved a two-year programme aimed at London and the South East with about a third of the money channelled through housing associations and the rest through local authorities. However belated a response this was to earlier calls for emergency action, it did represent a recognition of the severity of the problem and the role of rented and council housing in the market. Some commentators would associate the change with the general softening of the approach to policy following the replacement of Nicholas Ridley by Chris Patten as Secretary of State for the Environment. However, in 1989 this was only a slight softening. Housing associations rather than local authorities were generally favoured and the same Autumn Statement involved speeding the rate of growth of funds for housing associations. Planned levels of expenditure implied that by 1992–3 central government support for housing associations would exceed the amounts spent by local authorities for the first time. While HATs were clearly failing and the private sector was in disarray, there was still an alternative to municipal socialism.

The Local Government and Housing Act

The plans for reform of council housing centred on the Local Government and Housing Act 1989. This was designed to operate in conjunction with the Housing Act 1988. The Act involved a variety of measures relating to issues other than housing. For housing the most important elements of the Bill were new financial arrangements to deal with the 'muddled and inconsistent' arrangements, establish a new 'Housing Revenue Account Subsidy' and establish new arrangements for dealing with capital expenditure and receipts.

The government proposed that from April 1990 there should be a new housing revenue account (HRA) subsidy to replace the existing Exchequer housing subsidy, rate fund contributions (to HRAs) supported by rate support grant and the rent rebate element of housing benefit subsidy. Transitional arrangements were proposed to avoid any sharp change in the level of rents or spending in any individual authority. HRA subsidy would meet the notional deficit on the account irrespective of actual decisions on rents, maintenance or managerial efficiency. Because it would not be possible to make transfers to the HRA from the rates, the new arrangement would put pressure on rents and on maintenance or spending on other aspects of the service. The new system in general represented a modification to the existing incremental deficit housing subsidy system. It restored central government leverage on rents, particularly by incorporating rent rebate subsidy. It further limited local autonomy in determining overall rent levels.

The Secretary of State for the Environment was reported to have stated that the new system would give Whitehall control of all subsidies going into the council house sector, and inefficient housing departments would no longer be able to conceal poor management standards or extravagant costs behind subsidies from rate-payers to their housing revenue accounts. He was quoted as saying, '... tenants will be able to take better-informed decisions about the alternatives the government's housing policy is placing before them, and to decide whether to exercise the options the government is giving them through the Right to Buy and Tenants Choice'. The arrangements appear to involve a change in national accounting conventions by taking rent rebate subsidy out of the social security budget and putting it (back) into the housing budget. Whether the remainder of the housing benefit budget will follow remains to be seen.

The elimination of mandatory and discretionary rate fund contributions to the HRA has received most attention. Ring- fencing of the HRA is expected to result in substantial rent increases. However, the proposed transitional subsidy arrangements and the community charge safety net are designed to prevent major changes. In view of this, the most important effect of the new system is not that associated with ring-fencing but is the incorporation of rent rebate subsidy and the leverage this provides on rents. Rents would not be based on historic costing or a locally determined calculation designed to balance the HRA in the light of other costs. They will be centrally determined based on ministerial formulae and judgements about affordability and value.

In September 1989 some further details of what is likely to emerge became available. In particular, ministers outlined a new rent guideline method. The rent guideline method is designed to allow geographical variations to be assumed in subsidy 'reflecting the variations in demand for housing'. The proposals for doing this involved reference to variations in prices of dwellings sold under the right to buy. The exemplifications produced by the Department of the Environment applied two different damping mechanisms. They involved rent increases of up to 29.9 per cent. The outcome of all this will involve significant rent increases and this is part of a strategy to encourage tenants to exercise the right to buy and tenants choice – and for local authorities to contemplate voluntary transfers of stock.

Because the HRA subsidy will include the rent rebate element of housing benefit subsidy, the immediate impact of new arrangements will be a transfer of housing benefit costs associated with council housing to other council tenants. The Exchequer will pick up the deficit left after rents and other income has been taken into account. Thus, for example, where local authorities are currently in surplus on their HRA, that surplus will effectively subsidize housing benefit. Under the old subsidy system, all the then subsidy had been withdrawn and the government's capacity to lever rents upwards was minimal in such authorities. By incorporating a new subsidy it has recreated leverage – there is a subsidy to withdraw and local authorities will again be obliged to increase rents (and rents alone under new arrangements) in order to balance their budget. Local authorities will have less room to manoeuvre; central government will have more capacity to implement a rents policy and to reduce the housing benefit Bill; the tenant will be more likely to find rents rising and issues of housing benefit eligibility or right to buy purchase will become more immediate.

Overall, these proposals amounted to a new assault on the role of local authorities as the major providers of rented housing and a further pressure towards residualization. They also represent a much more determined and wide ranging effort to re-establish a private rental market.

Proposals for the reform of home improvement policy were also included in the Local Government and Housing Act. The Act included major reforms to the current system of renovation grants and improvement areas. There will be a new minimum fitness standard. Properties falling below this will be eligible for mandatory grant, but the applicant will be subject to a test of means. This is not detailed in the Act, but has been set out in a separate Department of the Environment consultation paper. In addition, local authorities will have discretion to provide grants for works up to a new higher target standard, together with small works grants up to a maximum of £1,000 for works to properties occupied by elderly people. In relation to area improvement, the existing housing action areas (HAAs) and general improvement areas (GIAs) are to be replaced by housing renewal areas. Finally, local authorities are given explicit powers to set up and run, or find other organizations to run, any services of any description aimed at helping owner occupiers to improve their housing. These proposals are intended to achieve better targeting of home improvement grants. However, the details of means testing and the abolition of tax relief for home improvements may mean that some sectors of the private housing market are likely to experience greater repair and maintenance problems.

Conclusions

By 1989 the housing policies of the previous ten years were coming to fruition. But providing the climate in which the private sector could develop had not produced a stable situation in which housing needs were met. Instead, there was growing evidence of problems. Key factors in this were the volatility of the market and rising interest rates. This volatility has been argued to be a predictable quality of the way the private sector operates. Other problems relating to homelessness and shortages of rented housing were anticipated. In housing there are significant time lags between some policy interventions and changes in outputs and opportunities. As with the loss of relets from council house sales, there is a cumulative effect which was having an impact by 1989 and will continue to have an effect. The problems of 1989 are in some contrast to earlier years, but have not led to a significant rethink in policy. Council housing is still out of favour and the strategy for demunicipalization is still being built. The rented sector is still undergoing radical reorganization and housing associations, private landlords and council housing are continuing to change. At the same time, increased competition is continuing to affect the private sector. Rationalization and integration of mortgage lending, estate agency and other services has probably been speeded up by the volatility of the market. Only the Abbey National Building Society opted for stock market flotation (and its unhappy experience may reinforce the hesitation of others) but other societies embarked on amalgamations and established links with estate agency and insurance companies. These changes in the organization of housing are the outcome of financial deregulation and competition and are not orchestrated by housing policy or government. Some of the outcomes in terms of differentiation within home ownership and the increased lending to reschedule loans, remortgage or consolidate other consumer debt, change the role of housing and home ownership. These are developments which do not lead to housebuilding or provision for the homeless. Falling private sector starts, alongside low public sector building, does not offer much comfort to those on the margins of the housing market. Continuing high interest rates and the reaction of the home owner with a mortgage may, however, provide a more powerful political influence.

Chronology

6 Jan: Halifax and Abbey National building societies raise their mortgage rates to 13.5 per cent.

7 Feb: Local and central government criticized in the Audit Commission's report *Housing the Homeless: The Local Authority Role* for failing to tackle the growing problem of homelessness.

18 Feb: The Bow Group calls for the abolition of mortgage tax relief.

23 Mar: Association of County Council's report urges the government to take urgent action over soaring house prices in rural areas, in order to preserve country life. *Homes We Can Afford* points out that the use of rural housing as second, retirement and commuter homes has led to a decline of village life and amenities.

28 Mar: *One Day I'll have My Own Place to Stay*, compiled by Shelter and the Central London Social Security Advisers Forum, published. Based on diaries kept by homeless young people it shows them drifting into begging, crime and prostitution.

12 Apr: *A Practical Guide to Providing Affordable Village Housing*, National Agricultural Centre Rural Trust, published. It calls for the building of low cost rural homes, arguing that more than 50,000 houses are required.

20 Apr: Lords rules that surveyors are responsible when housebuyers lose money as a result of negligent mortgage valuations, a decision which could lead to higher valuation fees.

27 Apr: Birmingham University report shows mortgage default is the fastest growing cause of homelessness, accounting for 1 in 10 cases in the South of England.

8 May: Shelter argues that Scottish landlords are not cutting rent bills even though, with the introduction of the poll tax, rents no longer include the rates contribution. It also complains that attempts by Scottish authorities to prevent landlords profiteering by reducing the housing benefit tenants receive has been frustrated by a Department of Social Security circular.

25 May: National Housing Forum report *Housing Needs in the 1990s* draws attention to growing homelessness, alleges that one million homes are unfit for habitation, and that two million extra homes are urgently needed to meet these problems and that an extra 3.2–4 million affordable houses are necessary by 2001.

12 June: RIBA policy document *Housing in Crisis: A Policy Statement* laments the demise of Parker Morris housing standards at the start of the 1980s and the current state of housing policy.

21 June: Announcement that the Office of Fair Trading is to draw up a code of practice for estate agents.

24 July: Royal Institute of Chartered Surveyors reports falling house prices across the country.

27 July: Report by the Department of Pyschology, University of Surrey, claims that there are up to 75,000 homeless people in London living in squats, hostels or on the streets.

4 Aug: Report *Raising the Roof on Housing Myths*, Shelter, criticizes housing policy and points to the widening gap between the rich and the poor in the housing market.

7 Aug: Association of District Councils says that the problem of the inability of first time buyers to afford homes continues despite a slump in prices and calls for more council housing to be built.

13 Sept: The UK's largest estate agency chain, Prudential Property Services, announces interim losses of almost £25 million.

24 Sept: IMF calls for the abolition of mortgage tax relief in the UK.

9 Oct: Britain's largest building society, the Halifax, announces a 1 per cent rise in interest rates to 14.5 per cent in the wake of the rise in base rates. It is followed by the other building societies.

Young Runaways . . . Findings from Britain's First Safe House, Church of England's Childrens' Society, published. A report on the fate of young homeless people in London.

30 Oct: Pilot scheme to allow tenants of Scottish new towns to buy their own homes by converting their rent into mortgage repayments is launched.

15 Nov: An extra £250 million to tackle homelessness and cut the number of families in temporary bed and breakfast accommodation announced.

22 Nov: Local authority rent arrears have jumped by a third to more than £450 million following cuts in housing benefit in 1988 according to the Audit Commission's survey of just under 250 local authorities, *Survey of Local Authority Housing Rent Arrears*, HMSO.

4 Dec: MPs and lawyers press for repeal of the 1824 Vagrancy Act under which at least 60 people a week in London are fined or gaoled for being homeless.

21 Dec: Increases in council housing rent averaging 10 per cent announced.

Education

STUART MACLURE

Public education in 1989 was dominated by the Education Reform Act which had received the Royal Assent on 29 July 1988. Different parts of the Act were due to come into operation at different dates in the ensuing years, and throughout 1989 the Department of Education and Science (DES) was initiating parliamentary orders, introducing regulations and issuing circulars, to implement particular chapters and sections of the Act.

The National Curriculum

Work went ahead on the national curriculum, the first stage of which came into force for children entering the primary schools at the age of five, in September. Orders, laying down the attainment targets and programmes of study, for mathematics and science, had been laid before Parliament in December 1988; the order for English was introduced in April 1989.[1]

From September 1989, also, all maintained schools were obliged to provide a balanced curriculum covering all the subjects prescribed in the Education Reform Act without waiting for the parliamentary orders or the publication of attainment targets and programmes of study for all subjects. In-service training at local level was intended to prepare the schools for the introduction of the new course, but it was acknowledged that the first months would depend on hectic improvisation, particularly in subjects like science where the national curriculum made large additional demands.[2] Extending high quality coverage was hampered by the lack of teachers in the primary school with more than an elementary standard of formal science education.

During the year a working group continued to formulate curriculum proposals for technology. Others were set up to work on history and modern languages. The interim report on history appeared in August, putting forward detailed programmes of study for all levels from the beginning of the primary stage to the end of the compulsory period. The choice of prescribed and elective topics was intended to embrace a 'historical knowledge and understanding' with a skills approach and was, on the whole, well received, but in his comments the Secretary of State, John MacGregor, called for more emphasis on facts and the ability to recapitulate historical knowledge. A start was made in July on the preparation of a modern language curriculum with the appointment of a working group under the chairmanship of Professor Martin Harris, Vice-Chancellor of Essex University. An interim report was expected early in 1990.

Work advanced on the development of Standardized Assessment Tests (SATs), and materials for the in-service training of teachers, needed to carry out the Education Reform Act's requirements for assessment and testing at ages 7, 11, 14 and 16. Contracts for research and development on materials for testing at age 14 (the end of 'key stage 3') to the value of £14 million were placed in July, 1989. Assessment remained the most controversial aspect of the national curriculum. In August it was made clear that SATs would take precedence over teachers' professional assessments in the formal testing of pupils. The Report of the Task Group on Assessment and Testing (1988) had given the two forms of teachers' assessments parity with the standardized tests and had proposed a moderation process to sort out differences. It was also announced (September) that Level 10, the top level of the national assessments, would be set at a higher level than a Grade A in the General Certificate of Secondary Education (GCSE), thereby paving the way for some sort of Distinction Grade to be introduced for GCSE. About the same time there were suggestions (mainly from independent school sources) that GCSE was failing to stretch the cleverest students, which brought assurances from Alan Howarth, the recently appointed Parliamentary Under Secretary of State at the DES that if necessary, the new examination would be made more stringent. Her Majesty's Inspectors remained convinced that the introduction of the GCSE and the changes in teaching methods associated with it had made an important contribution to the increase in the number of pupils staying on at school beyond 16, and the expected continuing increase in the number going to A levels. A parliamentary answer, shortly before Parliament rose for the summer recess, showed that the proportion of 16-year-olds staying on in full-time education – in maintained schools, independent schools and further education colleges – reached 48.4 per cent in 1988–9. This was the largest proportion so far achieved, narrowly exceeding the levels at the beginning of the 1980s. Unpublished figures circulating in the autumn indicated that in September 1989, there had been a further increase in staying on, the number of 16-year-olds returning after the summer vacation amounting to more than 52 per cent of the age group. The number of A level successes also increased sharply, causing universities and polytechnics and other higher education colleges to raise their intake by about 6 per cent.

The development of the national curriculum took place against the background of continuing reports of a shortage of specialized teachers in mathematics, science and languages (see below) and of the money with which to buy the new books and teaching materials to teach new syllabuses. In September a survey by the Publishers Association found that spending on school books had fallen by £6 million (4 per cent) in 12 months or £19 million after allowing for inflation. A study by the Book Trust estimated that new spending ought to be £15.27 per primary pupil, and £24.97

per secondary pupil. Later DES figures were £9.06 (primary) and £14.92 (secondary).

Other Aspects of the Reform Act

Local Management of Schools, the name by which the process of delegation of control over finance and staffing to the level of the individual school had come to be known, remained a preoccupation in every local authority, and in many schools. During the year the schemes submitted by the local authorities to the DES were haggled over and amended and the first batch, led by Norfolk, was approved in August. Meanwhile, surveys carried out by teachers unions showed that the operation of the formula would mean that some schools would lose income (just as others would gain) and that this would apply with particular force to schools which had a high proportion of staff members who were at the top of their respective scales.[3]

DES guidance required authorities to devise formulae for the distribution of their aggregated schools budget mainly based on the ages and stages of the pupils. This threw into relief the historic difference in funding between primary and secondary schools and generated strong demands from the primary schools for a more even balance. It was clear that one of the aims behind the 'finance and staffing' sections of the Act was being achieved: historical anomalies were being swept away by the introduction of formula-funding. Unfortunately new anomalies were also being created. In response to widespread anxiety, Angela Rumbold (Minister of State at the Department of Education) announced in August that the safety net arrangements were being extended, and that no school would lose more than 1 per cent of budgetary income in any one year as a result of the introduction of local school management.

The grant-maintained school sections of the Act had, by September, produced 62 ballots, of which 47 had been in favour of opting out, and 15 against. Eighteen grant-maintained schools opened in September, with another eight in the pipe-line for 1990. Five schools where a majority voted to opt-out had their proposals turned down by the Secretary of State. The most common reason for seeking grant-maintained status was to avoid closure or merger in a local reorganization scheme. As a consequence, many local authorities shelved proposals for reorganization.

In the case of Cardinal Vaughan in West London (a Roman Catholic aided school), Cardinal Hume, the Archbishop of Westminster in which diocese the school was located, sought to dismiss governors appointed by him in his capacity as trustee because they had voted, against his wishes, for grant-maintained status. Litigation followed, and eventually the Cardinal lost in the Court of Appeal in July. The effect of the judgment was to oblige him (against his own judgement as trustee) to appoint pro-opting out governors to the transitional governing body to help draft the scheme which the school will put to the Secretary of State to apply for grant maintained status.

A case which raised not altogether dissimilar points, involving the ILEA and its nominees on the governing body of another voluntary school, Haberdashers' Askes (Hatcham), went to the House of Lords which also denied the authority the powers to dismiss its nominated governors because they departed from party policy.

The Cardinal Vaughan episode confirmed the fears voiced by the Roman Catholic hierarchy when the Education Reform Bill was on its way through Parliament.

Two new city technology colleges – at Nottingham and at Middlesborough – opened in September, to join the first CTC, Kingshurst, which had opened at Solihull, a year earlier. Seven more were at an advanced planning stage – due to open in September 1990, were colleges at Bradford, Dartford, Gateshead, Telford, Walsall, and two in Croydon, one of them a college sponsored by the electronic music industry and specializing in the technology of the performing arts. It was also confirmed that the government had no plans to extend the network of city technology colleges after the 20 originally planned have been established. This was greeted in the press as a government retreat, but simply confirmed the limits which the Treasury had already set, from which the euphoric marketing techniques adopted by the city technology trust had served to divert attention.

Much concern, during the year, was focused on the supply of teachers and shortages, present or expected. Hard evidence was not always easy to come by. When eventually the 1989–90 educational year began, the DES announced that vacancies numbered 3,600 – less than 1 per cent of the national complement of teachers and little different from any normal year. Against this, there was evidence of shortages in the South East, particularly in London and the Home Counties, and wherever house prices were particularly high. London attempted to relieve a shortage of primary school teachers by recruiting abroad, sending teams to the Netherlands and Denmark in search of qualified teachers. It was reported that 80 were recruited from Holland and four from Denmark. Even so London began the year 160 teachers short. As usual, schools in Tower Hamlets, with its large ethnic minority population, were hardest hit.

In the government reshuffle in the summer, John MacGregor succeeded Kenneth Baker as Secretary of State. The change indicated no change in policy. It fell to Mr MacGregor to implement changes in the arrangements for the training and certification of teachers which were at an advanced stage of preparation when the ministerial changes took place. Two new paths to teaching qualifications were introduced in addition to the traditional B.Ed and PGCE routes; two new types of trainees were created – articled teachers and licensed teachers.

Articled teacher status was for would-be teachers setting out with preliminary qualifications which did not fully meet those hitherto demanded. These would include many overseas candidates whose university degrees failed to satisfy the rules applied by the DES. They could gain qualified teacher status after a period of teaching in a school, under suitable supervision.

Licensed teacher status, on the other hand, was intended to smooth the path for any one over 25 with two or more years of higher education, who chose to enter teaching and follow a course of training, part-time, while on the job. Both schemes aroused hostility from the teachers' unions, and from the leading members of the teacher education establishment in the universities and colleges, but plans were being pushed forward for a start in 1990.

School teachers' pay was increased from 1 April in accordance with the recommendation of the Interim Advisory Committee chaired by Lord Chilver. The resulting settlement gave heads 7.5 per cent, and assistant teachers 6.0 per cent. In addition there was an increase in the number and value of incentive allowances.

A dispute between the university teachers and their employers concluded at the end of May with a settlement worth 6.7 per cent. The dispute had arisen from a deliberately fudged settlement in 1986 which the employers maintained was meant to cover 1987–8 as well (though the staff side never accepted this).

The result was a settlement at below the inflation rate. What had happened to teachers' salaries in 1989 meant that once again there had been an erosion of the real value of the incomes of most teachers in primary, secondary, further and higher education. At professorial level, the government pressed for more flexible pay arrangements which were widely resisted on collegial grounds, notably by dons at Cambridge. In the autumn, a new remit to the Interim Advisory Committee for school teachers' pay instructed Lord Chilver and his colleagues to work within a 7.5 per cent ceiling for 1990–1.

Also in the autumn, Mr MacGregor shelved plans for teacher appraisal – one of the issues on which Sir Keith Joseph had campaigned most assiduously when he was Secretary of State (1981–6). He gave as his reason the danger of overloading teachers and local authorities – already they were snowed under with work on the national curriculum and local school management. (The advice from the pilot projects in teacher appraisal which his predecessor had set up, was that a properly-resourced appraisal scheme would cost £36–40 million.) He also dropped the idea of introducing a national records of achievement scheme to give each pupil a record of what he or she had done in school and out-of-school activities to augment the record of academic achievement. The Secretary of State took the view that the formal assessment built into the national curriculum – taken together with the external examinations – would serve adequately.

Higher Education

On 1 April, the University Grants Committee gave way to the new University Funding Council (UFC), and the Polytechnics and Colleges Funding Council took over from the National Advisory Body. Both bodies then began to look for ways of distributing money on the basis of bids from institutions competing for funds. Another exercise in the evaluation of the quality and quantity of research carried out by university departments, produced a familiar league table headed by Cambridge, Oxford and London. The gap between the 'best' and the 'worst' appeared to have widened since the 1986 survey (which was said not to be strictly comparable, but was nevertheless compared avidly). Earlier in the year (April) the government issued a consultative paper on 'Shifting the balance of public finding of higher education to fees', which outlined the policy of raising the notional fees charged to home students – 'notional' because in most cases fees are paid automatically by local education authorities – so that a university's income should be more closely dependent on how many students it admitted. By raising the fee of £607 a year to £1,600 in 1990–1, the universities would have every incentive to take in more marginal students wherever there was room to do so economically, thereby, in theory at least, making them more market-orientated and more responsive to demand. The consultative document implied that if more students were admitted no cash limit would be placed on the amount of money paid out in fees. But it was also made clear that the Treasury would monitor the situation and adjust UFC grants over a time in line with public spending plans. In other words there was no guarantee that what was given with one hand might not be taken away with the other. Nor could there be, given the normal budgeting constraints of public finance. The vice-chancellors tried to get firmer guarantees, but had to make do with paraphrases of the terms already set out.

There were also moves, vigorously supported by Mr Robert Jackson, the Junior DES Minister responsible for higher education, from some universities to introduce their own premium fees to be charged directly to students, over and above the normal official fee. Vice-chancellors were deeply divided on the issue at their meeting at Leeds in October, with a few, like Sir Graham Hill (Strathclyde) and Sir John Kingman (Bristol) strongly in favour, and others like Dr Clark Brundin (Warwick) and Lord Flowers (London) strongly opposed.

Arguments about university finance and fees merged into the continuing debate on the matter of student loans – another topic on which vice-chancellors and principals differed. Many who were prepared to accept a loan scheme in principle saw little attraction in the cumbersome scheme outlined in the DES White Paper issued at the end of 1988 on which consultations took place during the first half of 1989. The case for loans was argued on grounds of equity – it was unfair that tax-payers, most of whom did not go to higher education, should have to pay collectively for the maintenance of the privileged few who did, seeing that graduates could expect (on average) to earn good salaries. It was also regarded as a necessary part of any programme of extended access that some of the cost should be raised from those who benefited directly. And ministers held that students who were personally committed, financially, would approach their studies in a more responsible frame of mind. But it still remained to devise a workable scheme. The government objected in principle to allowing loan repayments to be collected through income tax or National Insurance mechanisms. This effectively ruled out any simple and economic scheme. In a speech at Lancaster in January, Kenneth Baker held out a vision of the higher education population doubling over the next 25 years, but nowhere spelled out how this might be brought about or how student loans could be made into an incentive for marginal first generation candidates for university or polytechnic.

Notes
1. *Science in the National Curriculum; English in the National Curriculum; Mathematics in the National Curriculum*, Department of Education and Science/Welsh Office.
2. See *Teaching and Learning in Science* in HMI series, Aspects of Primary Education, October 1989.
3. NASUWT survey, October.

Chronology
6 Jan: More bursaries for trainee teachers, schemes to pay some teachers more in shortage subjects and areas and recruitment of older people are all announced.

9 Jan: The beginning of the university teachers' dispute, and a threatened boycott of students' exams.

18 Jan: Angela Rumbold is appointed to chair a group of experts to review nursery school provision.

27 Jan: Kenneth Baker announces the licensed teachers scheme. He also announces tax-free bursaries for chemistry teachers (in addition to those already on offer to maths, physics and technology trainees).

29 Jan: The university vice-chancellors ask Mr Baker for an extra £183 million over the next two years to help with difficulties in retaining and recruiting top quality academic and technical staff.

30 Jan: Education spending is increased by 6.3 per cent in 1989–90.

14 Feb: Concern about the decline in the number of philosophers in universities is voiced in a UGC working party report.

15 Feb: Kenneth Baker argues that Britain should move towards universal education up to 19.

20 Feb: Institute of Fiscal Studies report calls for child benefit to be paid directly to 16-year olds to encourage them to stay at school.

23 Feb: A confidential and detailed plan is put before the university vice-chancellors on charging fees to students.

The Lords rule that Birmingham Council was acting unlawfully in providing more grammar school places for boys that girls.

28 Feb: *Standards in Education 1987–8*, HMI annual report, is issued. It warns of a shortage of qualified teachers.

9 Mar: Polytechnics and colleges should compete against each other and bid for funds according to how many students they can attract according to *Funding Choices: Methods of Funding Higher Education in Polytechnics and Colleges* Polytechnics and Colleges Funding Council.

10 Mar: More money is made available for university teachers, but it is contingent on the calling-off of the boycott of exams.

13 Mar: *Discipline in Schools: Report of the Committee of Enquiry chaired by Lord Elton*, HMSO, plays down violence in schools to the fury of the teachers' unions.

14 Mar: The first orders enforcing a national curriculum for schools are laid before Parliament.

16 Mar: The education committee of the Labour controlled Association of Metropolitan Authorities unanimously passes a resolution that no more voluntary aided schools of any religious body should be set up.

17 Mar: The AUT leaders reject a 6 per cent pay offer.

Mr Baker is to seek support to strengthen the role of grammar in schools against the recommendations of his advisers.

22 Mar: UMIST announces the launch of a study sponsorship scheme.

30 Mar: *The Elton Report* is criticized at the NAS/UWT conference as not coming near reflecting the level of violence in schools.

1 Apr: Polytechnics and colleges become independent of local authorities and self-managing under a new central body.

The Universities Grants Committee is replaced by the Universities Funding Council, which is directly responsible to Parliament.

6 Apr: A report is published into education in Newham, one of the lowest achieving authorities, in terms of exam results in England, based on interviews with pupils. It points to a need to raise pupil expectations, insist on punctuality and clamp down on bullying. It also points out that anti-racism has done little to raise educational achievements.

25 Apr: Mr Baker proposes a trebling of tuition fees to shift funding from central grants to the ability to attract students. A banding scheme would mean that universities receive more for students in medicine and engineering than for arts and humanities students. (*Shifting the Balance of Public Funding of Higher Education to Fees*, HMSO).

27 Apr: Controversy begins over the election of Winston Silcott, gaoled for murdering Police Constable Blakelock during the 1985 Broadwater Farm riots, as honorary president of the London School of Economics students' union.

2 May: The government pulls out of the EC Commission's Lingua programme launched to promote foreign language teaching and due to start in 1991.

Plans to overhaul teacher training are announced by Kenneth Baker.

3 May: Proposals that classroom discipline is to be a compulsory part of teacher training are released.

8 May: DES draft circular proposes 25 hours contact time in a teaching week.

11 May: The launch of Nicholas Barr's *Student Loans: The Next Steps* which says that the proposed student loans could be repaid by an extra penny in the pound on National Insurance contributions.

23 May: *Aspects of Primary Education: The Education of Children Under Five*, report by HMI Inspectors, is published favouring nursery education.

'Try Teaching' initiative launched by the Independent Schools Joint Council. This gives students a month's paid teaching in public schools in an attempt to encourage them to fill their own teacher shortage.

British attempts to prevent the Lingua programme being extended from higher/vocational education to secondary levels fails as the EC Social Affairs Commissioner claims competence on the issue has passed to Brussels.

24 May: The NUT warns that school trips are being phased out in a number of areas because of some of the provisions of the 1988 Education Reform Act.

29 May: A Gallup poll reveals that nearly a third of teachers are considering leaving the profession.

1 June: The NAHT conference pass unanimously a motion asserting that the requirement under the 1988 Act to have a daily act of broadly Christian worship is potentially divisive and damaging.

University lecturers' dispute ends.

9 June: Attempts by Havering council to recruit teachers in Germany to overcome staff shortages are revealed.

19 June: Mr Baker announces how the government's top-up loan scheme for students should work.

22 June: *English for Ages 5–16*, National Curriculum Council, is published.

5 July: The booklet *Safety in Outdoor Education* outlines guidelines in wake of accidents in recent years.

6 July: Robert Jackson, the Minister of Higher Education, says that student loans would cost £8 per week over ten years by the time the scheme reaches maturity in 2007.

12 July: The UFC proposes that universities will have to bid to provide courses in future.

20 July: Local authorities ask for extra cash to help recruit and retain teachers.

24 July: An HMI report calls for an improvement from the present poor quality of maths teaching in primary schools.

27 July: A private employment agency for temporary teachers begins trading in London.

29 July: Vice-Chancellors warn that the government must provide the extra money that it promised or thousands of students will have to be refused places at universities this autumn.

31 July: The UFC confirms that money for teaching will be on the basis of competitive bidding for funds. Furthermore universities are to be given incentives to devise two year rather than three year courses (three rather than four in Scotland) to increase the throughput of students.

8 Aug: Announcement of fundamental changes to the rules governing GCSE exams, including the abolition of exams based entirely on course-work.

10 Aug: The interim report of the national curriculum *Working Party on History* (chaired by Michael Saunders Wilson) is published.

16 Aug: Examination boards say that poor results in the new AS levels are because schools had not prepared pupils for the exams in the way the government had intended.

22 Aug: Government admits failure of AS levels.

23 Aug: Replacing O Levels with GCSE has led to a 15 per cent rise in equivalent passes in the two years of the scheme according to the GCSE Joint Council.

25 Aug: UFC publishes an audit of quality of research in British universities in the last five years.

Report by the Book Trust shows cut in spending on new books by public libraries of up to 50 per cent over the past decade.

26 Aug: Labour Party survey estimates that there is a shortage of 15,000 teachers and argues that there are too few specialist teachers to implement the national curriculum.

29 Aug: Government denies that there will classes without teachers in the new academic year.

5 Sept: Children sent home from some London schools because of the teacher shortage.

6 Sept: Sir Sam Edwards, retiring President of the British Association for the Advancement of Science (BAAS) and head of the Cavendish Laboratory at Cambridge, calls for the lowering of university standards for science degrees if a national shortage of technically trained manpower is to be solved. He also called for less specialization and more flexibility in science training.

11 Sept: Survey by the Committee of Vice-Chancellors and Principals and the AUT finds that 28 per cent of vacant professorial and 18 per cent of lecturers posts remain unfilled (especially in engineering, business studies and computing).

12 Sept: Gerry Fowler, Chairman of the Committee of Polytechnic Directors, calls for an end to the 'outmoded' differentiation of titles between universities and polytechnics.

14 Sept: David Thornton of the Young Offenders Psychology Unit at the Home Office tells the BAAS annual meeting that spending money on nursery schools and screening of potential offenders at schools is a better and cheaper way to reduce crime than employing more policemen.

15 Sept: Sir Claus Moser, President of the BAAS, closes its annual meeting by warning that Britain will become 'one of the least educated countries in the world' unless the government changes its priorities.

18 Sept: £100,000 campaign to entice teachers back to the classroom launched.

19 Sept: Warning from Martin Marriott, the Chairman of the Headmasters' Conference, that private schools are starting to face teacher shortages.

Survey of School Governors published by the National Foundation for Educational Research.

21 Sept: Government admits shortage of 3,600 teachers at the start of the new school year.

25 Sept: HMI's report on the inadequacies of *The Lower Attaining Pupils' Programme 1982–88* is published.

26 Sept: Confidential paper by Sir John Kingman, the vice-chancellor of Bristol University, which argues that students should be charged fees covering the full cost of their courses and that higher education funding should be overhauled to allow the introduction of a state scholarship scheme based on merit, is discussed at the annual meeting of the Committee of Vice-Chancellors and Principals at Leeds.

The Recruitment, Retention, Motivation and Morale of Senior Staff in Schools, National Foundation for Educational Research, is published.

27 Sept: Government drops plans to legislate on students' unions as a survey on their activities has revealed that the problem of political donations was less than ministers had thought.

David Lane, Director of the Professional Development Foundation Research Trust, publishes *Bullying: An International Perspective*. He argues that British schoolchildren are up to three times as likely to be bullied as their European counterparts.

28 Sept: Committee of Vice-Chancellors and Principals announce that they are now intending to pursue the option of charging students the full costs of their courses.

4 Oct: *Assuring Quality in Education: The Role of Local Education Authority Inspectors and Advisers*, HMSO, published for the Audit Commission. It argues that school inspectors are poorly equipped for their future role of monitoring the national curriculum.

5 Oct: *The English Polytechnics: An HMI Commentary*, HMSO, points out that there has been a 47 per cent rise in the number of students in polytechnics over the last eight

years without a reduction in the quality of teaching. This rise has however put pressures on facilities which are compounded by underfunding.

9 Oct: HMI report *Aspects of Primary Education: The Teaching and Learning of Science*, HMSO, points to improvement in primary science education over the past decade but argues that it still suffers from poorly-trained teachers, inadequate space and equipment and poor organization.

10 Oct: Southampton University announces plans to more than double student numbers to 15,000 over the next 35 years by building an additional campus.

13 Oct: Report for BP by Professor Alan Smithers and Pamela Robinson of Manchester University suggests that loans should be offered to sixth formers and further and higher students to encourage more young people to stay in education at 16.

19 Oct: HMI report *The Teaching and Learning of History and Geography*, HMSO, condemns the standards of history and geography teaching in primary schools.

24 Oct: UFC drops a scheme to close or merge more than 30 small physics and chemistry departments.

1 Nov: *How Many Graduates in the 21st Century? The Choice is Yours*, Institute of Manpower Studies, calls for a dramatic increase in the number of children staying at school after 16, especially among the children of manual workers.

6 Nov: Survey of teacher shortages by the teachers' unions *AMMA, NAHT, NAS/UWT, NUT, PAT, SHA: Report of the Joint Union Survey of Teacher Shortages* suggests that there are twice as many as the government have admitted, with particularly high vacancy rates in schools for children with special needs and in primary schools.

8 Nov: Report commissioned by Islington council shows widespread dissatisfaction with the lack of discipline and the lack of emphasis on basic skills in local schools amongst ethnic minority parents. They are also unhappy with the low expectations teachers seem to have for their children.

10 Nov: Plans by Greenwich council to give local children preference in the allocation of school places are ruled invalid in the High Court. This decision was upheld in the Court of Appeal on 19 Dec.

16 Nov: The final report of the working party on English in the national curriculum (chaired by Professor Brian Cox) is published.

20 Nov: First report of the geography working group on the national curriculum (chaired by Sir Leslie Fielding) is published.

21 Nov: Education (Student Loans) Bill announced in the Queen's speech.

22 Nov: Education (Student Loans) Bill published.

Nationwide appeal to raise £4 million for playgroups for the under-fives launched by John Patten, Minister of State at the Home Office.

24 Nov: Survey for the Polytechnics and Colleges Funding Council finds that urgent repairs costing £74.5 million are needed simply to comply with health, safety and fire regulations.

27 Nov: *The Supply of Teachers: A National Model of the 1990s*, Institute of Manpower Studies, University of Brighton, predicts that England and Wales could be short of 50,000 secondary and nearly 10,000 primary schoolteachers by 1997.

4 Dec: Survey by Public Attitudes Survey Ltd for the government shows widespread concern among parents about educational standards and discipline and a large measure of support for the aims of the national curriculum.

National Union of Students survey, *Opportunity Lost*, argues one in six of those intending to study in higher education will change their minds if a loan scheme is introduced, increasing to one in four among those from manual working class backgrounds.

5 Dec: Education (Student Loans) Bill gets its second reading in the Commons by 301 to 220. Four Conservatives rebelled against the government.

13 Dec: NATFHE begin exam boycott in support of pay claim.

18 Dec: Study of children in South Yorkshire shows nearly 20 per cent suffer from bullying at school.

20 Dec: The high street banks who indicated willingness to operate student loans schemes, Barclays, National Westminster, Midland, TSB and Royal Bank of Scotland, withdraw from it.

A Survey of the Quality of Education for Four Year Olds in Primary Classes, DES, finds much of this teaching unsatisfactory.

28 Dec: Alan Smithers and Pamela Robinson, *A Study of Teacher Loss*, University of Manchester, argues government statistics grossly underestimate the scale of the problem.

Population and Society

A. H. HALSEY

The New Demographic Order

Britain in 1989 still floated on the edge of Europe. Geographically this is an ineluctable commonplace. Religiously and historically it is a misleading modernism. Economically and politically it is a denial of 1992. Demographically it is simply untrue. For the 1989 evidence confirms British membership of a new demographic regime, centred on Western Europe and what had been the British colonial dominions, which has momentous potential for population and society in the world as a whole. From this point of view Britain is unremarkably European. Of course it remains, while the Channel Tunnel remains incomplete, what General de Gaulle insisted it was in vetoing its entry to the Common Market – *une Isle*. But communications and transport technology are fast destroying this anciently isolating characteristic which is, in any case, virtually irrelevant to the comings in and goings out of ideas about birth, marriage, divorce, family, age, gender and death which constitute the foundations of the new demographic order.

In its demographic essentials the new regime is a balance of low fertility and low mortality. It is, in other words, an historically unprecedented combination of fluctuating and small reproduction with steadily advancing large longevity. But there are contingent (i.e. not necessarily causal nor consequential) forces of an economic and social character which give the new demography its extraordinary significance. An ageing population is a necessary demographic consequence but economic affluence adds hitherto largely unrecognized implications and possibilities. The further social contingency of the relative decline of the family as a reproductive unit (which some contend is cause rather than correlate) must also be included as a defining characteristic of the new regime. Finally, *de facto* if not a necessary consequence of these demographic, economic and social forces, the new order is one of incipient population decline if the new well established trends of natural reproduction are not counteracted by an historic reversal of traditional patterns of international migration. Meanwhile low fertility, population ageing and family frailty together imply a changing structure of production and of distribution between age groups and the genders.

What then is new about the new demographic order? In one sense it is merely a modified description of the industrial population cycle as defined by demographers and sociologists earlier in the century. Agrarian societies had sparse populations balanced by high fertility and high mortality yielding relatively young populations adapting to the fluctuating conditions of survival, mainly food and disease. Britain and early European industrialism led the way out of the agrarian past with relatively reduced mortality and population explosion followed in the later nineteenth and early twentieth century by accelerated reduction in fertility, leading after the Second World War (admittedly with short term wobbles in the number of births) to the new low birth–death balance. So far then there is nothing dramatically new. But if the associated features of economic prosperity and the renegotiation of the division of labour between men and women were added then the new regime portends a new society, smaller in numbers, older in years and characterized by new egalitarian freedoms for women and a new political class of the 'Third Age'.

Population Size, Births and Deaths

Is the population in fact declining? At first glance the opposite appears to be the case. The population of the United Kingdom in 1988 was 57,065,000 – a highest recorded figure which had risen from 52,000,000 in 1961 through 56,460,000 in 1984. Of the 1988 total, England accounted for 47,536,000, Wales 2,857,000, Scotland 5,094,000, and Northern Ireland 1,578,000. The English figure shows continuous slow rise from 1961 as does the Welsh and Irish figure but the Scottish numbers have fallen slightly from their high point of 5,236,000 in 1971. The projection for the United Kingdom in 2001 is 59,266,000 which includes further small rises in England, Wales and Northern Ireland but a further small fall in Scotland. In relation to other European countries the United Kingdom has to be grouped with but ranked slightly below the German Federal Republic and Italy and slightly above France. It is less than half as big as the Japanese population and less than a quarter of the population of the USA.

Also at first glance the birth rate appears to be rising. There were 7,876,000 live births in the United Kingdom in 1988. This is an absolute increase compared with 1987 or 1978 but it is misleading. The total period fertility rate (TPFR) is the average number of children who would be born per woman if women were to experience current age-specific fertility rates throughout their child-bearing life. It was 1.84 in 1988 compared with 1.82 in 1987 and 1.76 in 1978. Only in Northern Ireland is fertility above the replacement level (at 2.39) but even there it is falling. In Scotland the figure is 1.69. On the other hand in West Germany it is as low as 1.38 and in Italy 1.28 while in the Irish Republic it remains at 2.35 (where again it has been declining rapidly in recent years).

The death rate meanwhile continues to decline. There were 649.2 thousand deaths in 1988 in the United Kingdom representing a rate of 11.4 per thousand population of all ages. This compares with 12.1 in the Britain of 1976, 11.1 in Sweden, 11.2 in Germany, 9.5 in France, 6.2 in Japan and 8.7 in the USA.

The British death rate is thus on the same evolving path as in advanced industrial countries generally. Its interest in 1989 lies rather in internal variation. Mortality varies geographically and by class. On the basis of figures from various sources Malcolm Britton[1] has shown that mortality was highest in the north and west of England and Wales, in urban areas, for people moving within a county, and for those born in Scotland and Ireland. Mortality rates for infants in the first month of life follow the overall regional pattern and was also higher among infants of mothers born in the Caribbean and Pakistan. Standardized mortality ratios (SMRs) are the observed number of deaths expressed as a percentage of the number expected during the specified period. The number of expected deaths is that which would occur if the national age-specific mortality rates were to obtain in a given region. Regional figures for males in 1979–83 were 112 in the North, 111 in the North–West but as low as 88 in East Anglia. Among local authorities the SMR for Manchester in 1979–83 (males) was as high as 125.

As to social class, Peter Goldblatt[2] has analysed the period 1971–85 in the light of controversy over previous analyses based on the British decennial supplement data. He uses data for men in the Office of Population, Censuses and Surveys (OPCS) longitudinal study (LS) and concludes that although biases inherent in decennial supplement figures contributed to the changes in the period from 1971–85, they were of insufficient magnitude to explain recent trends. Social class differences among men in the LS since 1981 have proved to be as great as those obtained using traditional methods once adjustment was made for differences in methods of study. Thus mortality differences are contin uing to widen for both men and women in the more and the less advantaged social classes.

Apart, however, from these indications of social polarization within Britain, the vital statistics up to 1989 confirm the emergence of the new demographic regime in potential if not actuality. The total number of births recorded in 1988 had risen by 12,000 compared with the previous year and indeed each year for the previous five years and the 1988 figure was the highest annual total since 1972. However, an increase in total births is not a direct indication of higher fertility. It can, and in this case does, reflect changes in the size or age structure of the female population. There have been substantial fluctuations in the TPFR over the past 30 years with a peak in 1964 of 2.93 in England and Wales followed by a consistent decline to a low of 1.66 in 1977. The significant enduring feature is that the TPFR has remained below 2.1 (the level leading to the long term 'natural' replacement of population) since 1972, although the 1988 TPFR is the highest recorded since 1980.

It should, however, be noted that TPFR is sensitive to short term changes in the timing of child-bearing. A more stable measure of fertility can be had from looking at average completed family size of individual birth cohorts. On this basis it is projected that the average family size for women born around 1960, who are currently in their peak child-bearing years, will be just below two. There are, in short, continuing conditions of incipient population decline in Britain as on the European Continent.

The Family and Reproduction

It follows that the fate of the family as the reproduction unit of society comes into question. A first conventional indicator is marital breakdown. There were 348,000 marriages in England and Wales in 1988, 1 per cent less than in 1987. But the number of divorces rose by 1,500 (1 per cent) to 153,000 in 1988, the first increase for two years.

Calculations are made from time to time as to the future proportions of marriages which will end in divorce. If the various marriage duration–specific divorce rates persist unaltered as they were in 1987, just under four in every ten marriages will ultimately end in divorce, though one in every two couples will celebrate their silver wedding and one in seven their golden wedding. Approximately one in ten couples are divorced before their fifth wedding anniversary, one in five before their ninth anniversary and one in four before their twelfth anniversary.

A second indicator is that of births outside marriage. In the United Kingdom in the March quarter of 1989, 27 per cent of all births occurred outside marriage compared with 25 per cent in the March quarter of 1988. There were considerable variations between counties and regions.[3] The lowest proportion of births outside marriage was in Northern Ireland (16 per cent) while in England proportions ranged from 19.7 in East Anglia to 31.3 in the North West. Internationally there is also considerable variation. Recent figures show nearly 50 per cent in Sweden and less than 10 per cent in Italy. But in most countries the proportions have increased by at least one- third since 1978. The British figure in that year was 10.0 compared with the 1988 figure of 25.1. In absolute numbers the 1988 figure was 177,000 which is 19,000 higher than the year before and continues an upward trend. Births outside marriage have almost trebled in number over a decade and thus account entirely for the rise in the total number of births in England and Wales in that births within marriage actually fell.

The number of births outside marriage increased for all age-groups but less for teenage girls than for older women. Even so, over three-quarters of teenage births in 1988 were outside marriage, almost double the proportion of ten years earlier. For women over 25, less than 16 per cent have their children outside marriage though the rate has also trebled over the last ten years.

Caution must attend the use of any statistic as a measure of the stability of the family. Helpful alternative information may be had from registration of births. There has been an increase in the number of joint registrations but a steady if slight increase in the proportion of sole registrations. In 1988, 70 per cent of births outside marriage were jointly registered and in a similar proportion of these cases the mother and father gave the same address as their usual place of residence. These figures suggest that at least half of the children born outside marriage during 1988 had parents who were living together in a stable relationship. We know in any case from the General Household Survey (GHS) that the incidence of cohabitation (living together as husband and wife without being legally married) has increased in recent years. The lastest GHS estimates show that in 1987 some 19 per cent of women aged 18 to 49 in Great Britain who were not legally married were cohabiting compared with 11 per cent in 1979.

There is considerable variation in the proportions of births outside marriage between ethnic groups as indicated by the mother's country of origin. In 1988 the highest figures (about 50 per cent) was among women born in the Caribbean commonwealth while, at the opposite end of the range, women born in the Indian subcontinent had extremely low rates (2 per cent among women of Indian origin and less than one per cent for women born in Pakistan or Bangladesh). For these latter groups the proportion of births outside marriage has remained fairly stable over the last ten years while the proportion for both UK born women and those born in the African commonwealth (excluding East Africa) have increased rapidly from around 10 per cent in 1978 to around 27 per cent in 1988 in both cases.

The 'shotgun marriage' is declining. Over the past ten years there has been a considerable decrease in the proportion of conceptions outside marriage leading to a maternity inside marriage (from 25 per cent in 1977 to 12 per cent in 1987), but there has been a corresponding increase in the proportion leading to jointly registered births outside marriage. Although there was a slight fall in the number of conceptions among girls aged under 16, conception rates rose for each single year of age and overall the number of conceptions to teenage girls rose by just under 4 per cent compared with 1986. For teenage conceptions as a whole some 35 per cent led to a legal abortion.

We have considered marriage and divorce and births inside and outside marriage. A third approach to the stability of the family as a reproductive unit is to consider one-parent families and their children. The best estimate of the number of one-parent families in Great Britain was 970,000 in 1985, and just over one million in 1986. In 1986 of all families containing dependent children, one in seven was a one-parent family and nine in every ten one-parent families was headed by a lone mother. It is also estimated that one-parent families in 1986 contained over 1.6 million dependent children, so that about one child in eight lives in a one-parent family. There are fewer dependent children, on average, in one-parent families than in married couple families; 1.6 and 1.8 respectively. Since the early 1970s the proportion of all dependent children who live with a divorced lone mother has trebled.

The number of one-parent families in Great Britain has grown from around 600,000 to just over a million since the early 1970s. This growth has been common to most industrialized countries although the largest increases have been reported in Great Britain, Australia and the United States; in other countries such as France, Japan and Switzerland the increase in numbers has been 20 per cent or less but for the majority of industrialized countries the range is between 30 and 50 per cent. Such reproductive circumstances are typically concentrated in the lower echelons of income with higher rates of unemployment and poorer housing conditions.

All in all, the evidence is of multiple instability of marriage and increasing frailty of support to mothers outside wedlock. It is however, a situation of great complexity and heated dispute. There are pessimistic traditionalists who believe that the family is collapsing with consequent chaos, crime and crisis of civilization. There are optimistic modernists who see a new dawn for opportunity and equality for women, the end of the stigma of illegitimate birth and the demise of male tyranny. And there are those who fear the approach of a world in which the interests of children are sacrificed on the altar of adult individualism. For example, are the gains of paid employment for wives made at the expense of quality in the care of children? While these disputes rage, the demographic observer can only note instability in the institutions of familial child-rearing and most especially the prospect of numerical decline through the weakening forces of natural increase. Demographers have been spectacularly wrong in past predictions of the twilight of par enthood and may be wrong again;[4] but it is difficult to anticipate any clear reversal of the present interests, male or female, which have evolved a fertility–mortality balance at less than replacement levels.

The Third Age

At all events the ageing of the British population, especially through fertility decline, is an established trend. There are multiple consequences. The problem of redistribution of resources over the life cycle will be an increasing preoccupation of social policy, calling into question the institution of retirement, the 'dependency' of the older age-groups, taxation and pension rights. In 1989 these issues are below the level of general political consciousness but are beginning to exercise sociologists and some politicians. One signal contribution to the discussion appeared in 1989 in Peter Laslett's *A Fresh Map of Life* and deserves some final remarks here.

Laslett distinguishes four phases of the modern and future life cycle for post-industrial societies. The first – childhood – has elongated with elaborated educational systems. The second – work and responsibility – has contracted with prosperity. Space has thereby opened for a third age of material comfort in good health and freedom from the need to follow paid employment before the fourth phase of decrepitude which ends in death. The third age is evolving a significant new political class. Its material existence is founded on the new demographic balance of low birth and death rates combined with economic growth. Its consciousness is founded on emerging recognition that people aged 25 have a better than evens chance of living beyond 70 while also anticipating retirement in the late 50s or early 60s. If the third age people (over 65 years of age) then constitute more than 10 per cent of the population a third age society comes into being. Britain qualified demographically at mid-century. Now she is beginning to qualify in her social psychology and in this she joins an international club of about 15 countries constituted by Western Europe, its descendant populations overseas and Japan.

So the prospect of population decline turns out also to be one of restructuring the relations between the genders and the age- groups – a period of both opportunity and conflict which will take us beyond 1989 and into the twenty-first century.

Key Statistics UK 1989

Population size (millions)	57.1 (mid 1988)
Birth rate (per 1,000 population)	13.4 (March 1989)
Births outside marriage (per cent)	27 (March quarter 1989)
Legal abortions in Great Britain (000s)	168.1 (1987)
Total Period Fertility Rate	1.84 (1988)
Marriages (000s)	398 (1987)
Marriage rate (persons marrying per 1000 population)	14.0 (1987)
Divorces (000s)	165 (1987)
Single-parent families with dependent children (percentage of all families)	13.9 (1986)
Emigration (000s)	210 (1987)
Immigration	212 (1987)
Net immigration	+2 (1987)
Death rate (per 1000 population)	12.1 (March 1989)
Still births rate (per 1000 births)	4.9 (1988)
Infant mortality rate (per 1000 live and still births)	9.0 (1988)
Perinatal and neonatal death rate (per 1000 live and still births)	14.0 (1988)
Life expectation at birth (years)	
Males	72.3 (1987)
Females	77.9 (1987)
Households (millions)	21.7 (1987)
Average household size	2.55 (1987)
Percentage of population between 16 and retirement age	61.5
Percentage of population over retirement age	18.2
Percentage of population over 75 years	6.6

Notes

1. Malcolm Britton, 'Mortality and geography', *Population Trends*, 56, summer 1989, p. 16.
2. Peter Goldblatt, 'Mortality by social class 1971–85', *Population Trends*, 56, summer 1989, p. 6.
3. cf. Gillian Dollamore, 'Live births in 1988', *Population Trends*, 57, autumn 1989, p. 20.
4. See for example, William Brass, 'Is Britain facing the twilight of parenthood', in H. Joshi (ed.), *The Changing Population of Britain*, Basil Blackwell, 1989.

Chronology

17 Feb: Backbench Bill to relax curbs on Sunday race meetings fails to progress to a second reading despite government support.

2 Mar: Heather Joshi (ed.) *The Changing Population of Britain*, a major survey, published by Basil Blackwell.

7 Apr: *Cost of Living – Regional Comparisons* published by the Reward Group. It draws attention to the soaring cost of housing and the great regional differences in the cost of living.

20 Apr: Epoch – End Physical Punishment of Children – launches its campaign to make physical punishment of children (not least by parents) illegal.

10 May: Mintel publishes a survey of European lifestyles.

14 Aug: Henley Centre report *Family Fortunes* predicts significant rise in divorce and illegitimate births by 1995. It also forecast that women will constitute more than half the workforce by 2000.

15 Aug: First county by county survey of household incomes published in *Economic Trends*. Surrey emerges as by far the most affluent county with Mid-Glamorgan as the least affluent.

11 Sept: European Parliament calls for EC-wide rules to end discrimination against transsexuals.

13 Sept: Marina Warner, *Into the Dangerous World: Some Reflections on Childhood and Its Costs*, Chatto and Windus, published. Part of the Counterblasts series, it attacks the government's policy on the family.

25 Sept: *Population Trends* published. It shows that there was a 2 per cent increase in births in England and Wales in 1988 to 694,000, though the figure was still below that required for long term replacement of the population. It also revealed that the rate of births outside marriage had risen to 25.6 per cent, with the rate of illegitimate conceptions (pregnancies leading to birth or legal termination) running at 40 per cent according to a survey conducted in 1987.

26 Sept: Annual report of Relate says two in five marriages end in divorce, the cost to the government of broken marriages being £1.25 billion per year.

28 Sept: *Cost of Living: Regional Comparisons September 1989*, Reward Group shows that Scotland is the best and Greater London the worst region in terms of costs of living.

Peter Lazlett, *A Fresh Map of Life: The Emergence of the Third Age*, Weidenfeld and Nicolson, published. It examines the growing number of active retired people and the implications of this for future population trends.

1 Oct: UK Forum on Young People and Gambling set up to help young people who are addicted to gambling.

2 Oct: Children who are smacked or beaten are more likely to become troublesome adolescents or to have a criminal record before they are twenty according to John and Elizabeth Newson, *The Extent of Physical Punishment in the UK*, Approach.

15 Nov: First case of maintenance being awarded to a man from the mother for the bringing up of their son under the Family Law Reform Act 1987.

16 Nov: *British Social Attitudes*, Gower, published.

29 Nov: *Young People in 1988*, Health Education Authority, surveys children's diet, drinking, pastimes and attitudes to health and drugs.

5 Dec: *General Household Survey*, OPCS, published for 1988. It showed a continued rise in one-parent families and cohabitation.

7 Dec: Robin Harris, *The Conservative Community*, Centre for Policy Studies, calls for government intervention in matters of conscience to strengthen the family and Christian values.

15 Dec: Study of Scottish diet published in *Scottish Medical Journal*.

Sport

PETER BILSBOROUGH

Ten years of Conservative government have been marked by a shift from a social democratic consensus about the role of the state in social policy to a more liberalist view placing responsibility for welfare on the individual. Social welfare policy has been influenced by a 'new right' ideology intent on: fostering firmer control by central government; encouraging greater intervention by private companies; reducing the importance of service provision by local authorities; giving greater emphasis to voluntarism. Sport, which has emerged as a significant aspect of social welfare over the past 20 years, has not been exempt from these trends.[1]

Historically the major providers of British sport – local authorities, the state, commercial operators and voluntary groups including national governing bodies of sport – have been locked in a complex web of negotiation and bargaining to influence sporting patterns. During the late 1980s the state has been dominant. To a greater extent than any other post-war administration, the present government has used legislation to reform sport and to reduce public sector investment in it. As an agent of reform it has stepped in to supervise aspects of law and order relating to hooliganism and crowd safety but its policies have been widely opposed. In an on-going drive to reduce state welfare spending and encourage self-help and commercial enterprise it has led local authorities to review their arrangements for sports provision and asked the governing bodies of sport to do more to help themselves. However, by encouraging commercial operators in particular to increase their influence, some of sports most cherished Corinthian values have been threatened.

Law and Order

The state has been involved in the supervision of sport for over 500 years. In recent times the major problem has been the regulation of crowds at football matches. In 1989 two issues have been to the fore: the establishment of safe facilities and crowd control practices; the battle against hooliganism.

Hooliganism continues to infest English football. The stadia and the surroundings provide the principal focal points. On the last weekend of the 1988–9 Football League season, hundreds of fans were arrested and dozens injured at seven

English grounds. The worst incident was at Selhurst Park where a pitch invasion by fighting Crystal Palace and Birmingham City fans interrupted the game for 26 minutes before order was restored by mounted police. The routes and transport to and from grounds also continue to be affected. In September riotous behaviour by hundreds of English fans on a North Sea ferry going to Sweden led to one death by drowning and dozens of arrests.

In January the government formally presented its ideas for a membership scheme to combat hooliganism. The details were published in the Football Spectators Bill. It proposed to appoint a body, the Football Membership Authority, to draw up a national membership scheme, only members of the scheme being allowed to enter a football ground. Any person convicted of a football-related offence would be disqualified from membership for 2–5 years. At an international level it also proposed restrictions on convicted football hooligans from travelling abroad at times when key matches were being played.

These attempts to regulate through restriction were widely criticized. The National Council for Civil Liberties was concerned about the wide exclusion powers with few civil liberties. Football's rulers described the Bill as 'bad for business' and 2,000 professional footballers and 430,000 spectators presented petitions to Parliament complaining about unacceptable restrictions and costs. There was widespread agreement that the scheme had been designed by people who did not understand football.[2]

Although the Bill was temporarily suspended following the Hillsborough disaster, the legislation was in place by November. However, it will not be implemented until season 1990–1. Doubts about electronic turnstile checks coupled with strict safety conditions at ground entrances, likely to be recommended by Lord Justice Taylor, have forced ministers to adopt a 'flexible' approach to the scheme's starting date.[3]

On the second Saturday in April, 95 spectators were killed and several hundred injured when thousands of soccer fans were crushed on an overcrowded terrace at a Football Sssociation (FA) Cup semi-final tie between Liverpool and Nottingham Forest at Hillsborough, Sheffield. It was the worst disaster in a grim catalogue of British soccer tragedies. The dead and injured were at the Liverpool end for the capacity all-ticket game. The incident was caused by a gate being opened on the instruction of the police just before the start of the game to let an uncontrolled build-up of fans into the ground. The sudden rush towards the terracing caused a crush of fans largely against the perimeter fencing.

Hillsborough is one of the finest football grounds in Britain. With tragic irony Sheffield Wednesday's chairman, Bert McGee, wrote in the match programme, 'As you look around Hillsborough you will appreciate why it has been regarded for so long as the perfect venue for all kinds of important matches.'[4] Events proved that even a ground of this standard which has consistently met the requirements of the 1975 Safety of Sports Grounds Act is not safe enough.

In response, as with previous incidents of this kind at Wembley in 1923 and Bolton in 1946, the government set up a judicial inquiry headed by Lord Justice Peter Taylor, an Appeal Court judge. An interim report containing 46 recommendations was published in August, in time for the start of the new season. The clubs responded immediately: more and clearer signs appeared at turnstiles; gates in perimeter fences were left open; a 15 per cent reduction in terrace capacity was implemented; turnstiles were closed when the permitted capacity of an area was about to be reached.[5] Remarkably the interim report steered a wide berth around the vexed problem of access. This remains the crux of the problem and the heart of the football spectators Bill.

It was widely agreed during the post-Hillsborough period of reflection and analysis that safety could be improved by providing more seats. But more seats means more cover which means more cost. The football authorities lobbied the clubs for a gradual change and the announcement in August of £4 million from the Football Grounds Improvement Trust, which receives £9 million a year from the 'Spot the Ball' competition run by pools companies, was good news. Nevertheless, the government tempered this aid with a call for self-help. It refused to budge on lowering the pools levy from its present 42.5 per cent which represented £280 million in 1987–8. It perceives the clubs to be more interested in buying players than making ground improvements. After the 1985 Heysel disaster, Mrs Thatcher asked 'How can the clubs plead poverty when one has just paid over £1 million for one player?'[6]

For their part the clubs have done little to deny this perception. An estimated £70 million has been spent on safety improvements since the enactment of the Safety of Sports Grounds Act in 1975 – £42 million came from the Football Grounds Improvement Trust and £28 million from the clubs themselves. In comparison they spent an estimated £70 million on players during the season 1988–9. The clubs cry 'poverty' when ground safety is mentioned but, as one City expert on the football industry noted, 'They are rather contemptuous of the fans – they tend to want to pack them in without too much thought for their comfort.'[7] Sadly, the fans have not helped either. Most hardcore supporters prefer their club to buy a new centre forward than a new stand, improve the defence instead of the toilets and have a good cup run than sit in comfort.

It is doubtful if the major grounds will meet the 1992 deadline set by the International Federation of Football Associations and supported by the government to have all-seated provision as there is little agreement on the way forward.

The Free Play of the Market and Self-Help

The state not only supervises but also facilitates sports development. It makes an enormous indirect contribution through the rate support grant to local authorities. This is largely spent on resources for sport in the community and physical education and sport in schools. During the 1980s spending on both forms of provision has been reduced by a Conservative government intent on 'rolling back the state', reducing public spending and encouraging the free play of market forces. In community sport, local authorities have been led to review their provision for sport and in particular to co-operate with commercial operators, while in schools, resources have been reduced and extramural voluntary assistance sought.

During 1989 two enabling measures have encouraged the free play of market forces on hitherto public provision for community sport. In August the Audit Commission focused the attention of local authorities on the effectiveness of their sports provision while in December the 1988 Local Government Act was extended to expose the management of sport and leisure facilities to competitive tendering.

The most noticeable feature of sports development during the last 25 years has been the massive expansion of publicly-owned facilities. Provision has centred upon a concern about access, underpinned by an ongoing debate about equality of sporting opportunity. Within the last twelve months the focus of attention has changed from what will be provided and where, to who will operate what is available. With the intention of increasing the efficiency, effectiveness and economy of local authority services, in December the government confirmed that the management of local authority sport and leisure facilities would be subject to compulsory competitive tendering (CCT) from 1 January 1992. Opposition has been voiced from two fronts. The political centre and left see it as another piece in the jigsaw of bitter right-wing hostility to local government while sports administrators and managers fear that the new 'contracting regime' will be inefficient, more expensive and less user orientated than existing arrangements. At the same time, as sport is increasingly exposed to the forces of the market, a new debate has begun about the balance between social equity and economic efficiency.[8]

With CCT already on the sporting agenda, in August the Audit Commission published *Sport for Whom* to encourage local authorities to review their provision for sport. It drew attention to numerous flaws in current practice and made a strong case for change. After studying practices in a wide range of local authorities over a 12-month period it reported that local authorities tended to concentrate on direct provision and underrate the potential for co-operation with the private and voluntary sectors. The report recommended changes designed to help authorities to improve their service and prepare for CCT. It was a timely publication. Its emphasis on co-operation, not competition, went a little way to relieve the tension between some local authorities and commercial operators.[9]

During the last 18 months, some forward-thinking local authorities have already reviewed their provision and voluntarily contracted out work. CCT has enabled them to realize that they are not necessarily the only providers of facilities and services. Deals have already been and continue to be struck with the private sector. One of the most notable was arranged by Doncaster Borough Council. In October it opened The Dome, Britain's largest leisure centre under one roof. It will be run by a private sector leisure company, Doncaster Leisure (Management) Limited. Moreover, its marketing has been contracted out to Heritage Projects Limited, who created the Jorvik Centre, York.[10] After 150 years of direct public provision local authorities are beginning to change their role from resource providers to 'resource gamekeepers' controlling sports development, allocating land, grants, amongst other things, to external, predominantly commercial, sports providers.

In attempts to improve efficiency and effectiveness in schools, the government has fought some acrimonious battles with teachers over pay and conditions of service. When it abolished teachers' negotiating rights in 1987 morale hit an all-time low. Subsequent industrial action has included withdrawal from voluntary involvement in extra-curricular school sport. It was not long before an articulate and influential sports lobby was expressing concern about a decline in the fitness of children and a deterioration in playing standards in traditional team games. As a result, the government wasted little time in establishing an inquiry into the state of sport in schools. The report, published in August 1988, contained 69 recommendations. The most controversial had major resource implications. These included: the reallocation of teachers' hours to ensure a full range of extracurricular activities; greater financial support to improve in-service training for club coaches and sports leaders; increases in the number of hours of instruction in physical education for trainee primary school teachers.[11]

Fifteen months later the government response indicated support for physical eduction by making it one of the ten statutory core subjects in the National Curriculum. In contrast, it based its support for sport on voluntarism and enterprise. In an attempt to emphasize that local clubs had an important role to play in the provision of school-aged sport, it launched a £1 million scheme, financed by the Midland Bank, to encourage participation among school leavers.[12]

Indirect funding to local authorities by the state is complemented by direct funding to the Sports Council which, amongst other things, develops 'arm's length' policy and grant aids the nation's governing bodies of sport. Just as local authorities have been required to review their provision, clear signals have been sent to the governing bodies that they must do more to support themselves. At the end of 1988 David Pickup, the Director General of the Sports Council, in his first speech to the Central Council of Physical Recreation (CCPR) said that the governing bodies must forget the begging bowl approach to sports funding and learn to stand on their own feet. In February he reiterated his message that the Sports Council expected sport to rely more on sponsorship and less on handouts from government. Towards the end of the year the Sports Council informed governing bodies that their Council grants would be cut by at least 50 per cent over the next three years but in return a minimum of £90,000 would be given over the same period to their umbrella body, the CCPR, to establish a sponsorship advisory service.

Not surprisingly, the governing bodies and the CCPR felt they had been unfairly treated particularly since in the last financial year the government received £2.4 billion in taxes from sport against an investment of only £545 million.[13] They were also fearful of being increasingly exposed to the enterprise culture and market forces. Those with little or no commercial potential predicted austerity and reductions in activity while some of those with televison and advertising appeal believe that a future based on sponsorship would threaten their authority.

Commercial Concerns

Governing bodies have supplemented their incomes through various commercial activities for a long time. Some have received revenue from a combination of sponsorship, radio and television fees and advertising for over 40 years. The process has been cautious and gradual but in the past decade of enterprise the pace has quickened considerably. At the same time governing bodies have found it increasingly difficult to control the demands from and effects of ever stronger links between sport and commerce. One of the most alarming trends in 1989 has been the ruthless pursuit of money shown by some leading players. Consequently some of sports most fundamental values such as honesty, loyalty and integrity have been threatened. Rugby and athletics have provided rich examples.

Rugby Union continues to resist the professional tide but there has been widespread speculation about covert payments to players. At the same time the home unions have been asked to consider ways of allowing players to profit from off-pitch activities. Stories of boots stuffed with notes are as old as the game itself, but at no time in the history of the game have allegations of shamateurism been so intense. In August, 25 players from some of the world's leading rubgy nations accepted invitations from the South African Rugby Football Union to join a centenary tour. It was reported that each had been offered $50,000. This was officially denied by the South African governing body. However, England's hooker, Brian Moore, confirmed that the sum he rejected to join the tour was 'very close' to £30,000. Similarly, Steve Sutton, a former Welsh lock, said that a Welsh Rugby Union (WRU) committee member had offered him money to tour. He had refused. However, the tour party contained ten Welsh players and six WRU committee men. Rumours of duplicity were rife in the valleys and Welsh rubgy has suffered considerable damage. The WRU president and secretary resigned in protest at their colleagues attitudes and latterly the Union set up an inquiry to look into what one former WRU treasurer called 'a sordid and devious affair'.[14] Further turmoil is expected when the inquiry reports.

Ironically, at the same time pressure has been put on the home unions by other members of the International Rugby Football Board to examine ways of relaxing the games amateur regulations. In December the Board published a consultative document recommending that players be allowed to earn money for some off-field activities and receive compensation for time lost from work through training for domestic internationals. Players have welcomed the recommendations although some believe they have not gone far enough. In contrast some administrators regard them as the start of a slide towards professionalism.[15]

Money has poured into athletics in recent years. To accommodate the market it has revised its Victorian definition of amateurism and introduced a new competitive calendar. As a result it has widened its spectator appeal, performances have improved and participation has increased. Athletes are able to receive money and make a full-time career from the sport. A small highly talented group have earned enormous sums of money but this has led to accusations of greed. There are several causes for concern. Some athletes have: suffered loss of form or injury by racing too often in an attempt to maximize income; spent the season trying to avoid head to head clashes with their major rivals in order to boost the purse for a future confrontation; preferred to compete in Grand Prix events rather than represent their country; made late withdrawals from events due to disagreements over appearance money.

Sponsorship, television and advertising have brought vast amounts of new money into many other sports besides athletics. Winners who have complied to the full with turning sport into media events and have made themselves available to press and sponsors for promotional purposes have received rich rewards. But there are some sportsmen and women who have not been prepared to respond to every request from sponsors. In January, Desmond Douglas, the country's best-known table tennis player, turned down the opportunity to earn some money when he chose not to compete in the English Table Tennis Association's 'Top Twelve' tournament, for which Stiga had given £3,500 prize money. The company was not pleased and in the previous year the Leeds Building Society had discontinued its sponsorship due to a similar episode. Ironically in 1989 it is Douglas and others like him who are no longer regarded as playing the game. Market forces have undermined the conventional code of 'playing the game for the game's sake'.

While top level sport has always had a business side to it, the ruthless pursuit of profit has not, generally, been the most important motive. However, after a decade of enterprise, reliance on business money has made it increasingly difficult for sport to resist business controls and values.

Notable Sporting Achievements 1989

7 Feb: Peter Scudamore breaks the record for the number of winners in a National Hunt season

22 Feb: Dennis Andries becomes only the third British boxer to regain a world title after winning the vacant WBC light-heavyweight championship

3 Mar: John Regis wins a gold medal at the World Indoor Athletic Championships. This British first was achieved in the 200m

12 Mar: Martine Le Moignan becomes the first British woman to win the world squash title

30 Mar: Martin Offiah (Widnes) becomes the first Rugby League player to score 50 tries in a season since Billy Boston (Wigan) in 1962

9 Apr: Nick Faldo wins the US Masters Open Golf Championship

7 June: Peter Shilton, the Derby County goalkeeper, sets a new record of 109 England caps

2 July: Nick Faldo wins the French Open Golf Championship – a record fourth successive European Tour victory

16 July: The British Lions win the Rugby Union test series in Australia, 2–1

1 Aug: Australia go 3–0 up in cricket test series and thus regain the Ashes. They went on to win the series 4–0

6 Aug: Britain's male athletes win the European Cup for the first time and qualify for the World Cup

10 Aug: Britain wins the Admiral's Cup, the premier trophy in international sailing, for the first time since 1981

15 Aug: Adrian Moorehouse becomes the first Briton for 13 years to set a world swimming record. He won gold in the 100m breast stroke at the European Championships

17 Aug: Britain and Ireland win the Walker Cup (amateur golf) against the USA

18 Aug: Nick Gillingham equals the world record for 200m breast stroke at the European Championships

10 Sept: Britain's male athletes come third in the World Cup. There are individual wins for: Linford Christie (100m); Tom McKean (800m); Steve Backley (javelin)

10 Sept: Virginia Leng wins a record third consecutive individual title in the European Three-Day Event Championships. The victorious British team also completes a hat-trick of titles

24 Sept: Europe's golfers retain the Ryder Cup after a 14–14 draw at The Belfry

18 Nov: Peter Scudamore surpasses John Francome's record career total of 1,138 winners for a jump jockey

25 Nov: New Zealand's All Blacks complete an undefeated tour of Wales and Ireland with a 21–10 win over the Barbarians

Winners of Major Events 1989
Association Football
    Football League: Arsenal
    FA Cup: Liverpool
    Littlewoods Cup: Nottingham Forest
    Scottish Football League: Rangers
    Scottish FA Cup: Celtic
Athletics
    GRE British League: Birchfield Harriers
    London Marathon(Men): Douglas Wakiihuri (Kenya)
    (Women): Veronique Marot (Great Britain)
Badminton
    All–England Championships (Men's singles): Yang Yang (China)
    (Women's singles): Li Lingwei (China)
Basketball
    National Champions: Glasgow Rangers
Cricket
    Britannic Assurance County Championship: Worcestershire
    NatWest Bank Trophy: Warwickshire
    Benson and Hedges Cup: Nottinghamshire
    Refuge Assurance League: Lancashire

Cycling
   Tour of Britain (Milk Race): Brian Walton (Canada)
Equestrian
   Badminton Three Day Event: Virgina Leng on Master Craftsman (Great Britain)
Golf
   British Open Championship: Mark Calcavecchia (USA)
   Dunhill British Masters Championship: Nick Faldo (England)
   Volvo PGA Championship: Nick Faldo (England)
Hockey
   Poundstretcher National League: Southgate
   Hockey Association Cup: Hounslow
   English Women's Champions: Ealing
Horse Racing
   1000 Guineas: Musical Bliss (Walter Swinburn)
   2000 Guineas: Nashwan (Willie Carson)
   Oaks: Aliysa (Walter Swinburn)
   St Ledger: Michelozzo (Steve Cauthen)
   Derby: Nashwan (Willie Carson)
   Grand National: Little Polveir (Jimmy Fost)
Motor Racing
   British Grand Prix: Alan Prost (Ferrari–France)
Rowing
   The University Boat Race: Oxford
Rugby League
   Silk Cut Challenge Cup: Wigan
   Stones Bitter League Champions: Widnes
Rugby Union
   Courage English League Champions: Bath
   McEwan's Scottish Club Champions: Kelso
   Whitbread Welsh Merit Table: Llanelli
   International Championship: France
Tennis
   All-England Championships
   (Men's singles): Boris Becker (West Germany)
   (Women's singles): Steffi Graf (West Germany)

Notes
1. P. Bramham and I. P. Henry. 'Political ideology and leisure policy in the United Kingdom', in *Leisure Studies* 4, 1985, pp. 1–9.
2. *The Times*, 28 October 1989. The legislation is not applicable to Scotland where in recent times the game has been relatively free of hooliganism.
3. *The Scotsman*, 31 October 1989; *The Times*, 1 November 1989.
4. *Sports Industry* 70, October 1989; *The Guardian*, 17 April 1989.
5. *The Glasgow Herald*, 5 August 1989.
6. The club was Everton and the player, Gary Lineker. *Sports Industry* 70, October 1989.
7. *Leisure Management*, 9, 6, 1989.
8. *The Times*, 7 December 1989; *Hansard*, 6 December 1989, cols 425–450.

9. *Audit Commission, Sport for Whom: Clarifying the Local Authority Role in Sport and Leisure*, HMSO, 1989.
10. *Leisure News* 5, October 1989.
11. *School Sport Forum, Sport and Young People: Partnership and Action*, The Sports Council, 1989.
12. Department of Education and Science/Department of the Environment, *The Government's Response to the School Sport Forum Report*, Department of Education and Science, 1989.
13. *The Times*, 22 November 1989.
14. *The Times*, 13 November 1989; 24 November 1989; 9 December 1989.
15. *The Times*, 14 December 1989; M. Clearly, (ed.), *The Rugby Union Yearbook*, Rugby Football Union, 1989, pp. 121–3.

Chronology

5 Jan: Welsh Rugby Union captain, Jonathan Edwards, signs for the Rugby League club, Widnes, for a record c£150,000.

17 Jan: The Football Supporters Bill begins its passage of the Lords.

18 Jan: Brian Clough, the Nottingham Forest manager, punches three youths when fans run onto the pitch after a Nottingham Forest v Queen's Park Rangers Littlewoods Cup tie.

24 Jan: The International Cricket Conference (ICC) decrees that any cricketer who has sporting links with South Africa after 1 April will not be selected for international teams until he has requalified. The ban is not retrospective. The requalification period is three years for the under-19s, four years for over-19s and five years for those over 19 who tour as members of a team. The ICC refused to discuss this with a delegation from South Africa. The new ban was criticized by the Cricketers' Association and leading English players and nearly 50 Tory MPs tabled a motion deploring the ICC decision.

31 Jan: A plan for a 180-mile footpath along the Thames is announced by the Countryside Commission.

1 Feb: Ted Dexter suggests year-long contracts for England cricketers to prevent them turning to South Africa for winter work.

9 Feb: Brian Clough is fined a record £5,000 and banned from Football League touchlines for the rest of the season after he is found guilty by the FA of bringing football into disrepute.

17 Feb: The Sports Council is criticized for serious weaknesses in its control of public money in a report by the National Audit Office.

20 Feb: There is a government setback on the football supporters national membership scheme when the Lords vote 124 to 121 for an amendment backing its phased rather than automatic introduction.

7 Mar: Ted Dexter is appointed chairman of the England cricket selectors.

22 Mar: John Emburey tells a sportswriters' lunch that two-year contracts for top players are needed to keep England cricketers from signing for lucrative tours of South Africa.

8 Apr: The death of two horses in the Grand National leads to calls to make the race safer.

15 Apr: Ninety-five people are crushed to death and hundreds more are injured in Britain's worst ever sporting tragedy in a crush at Sheffield Wednesday's Hillsborough ground at the FA cup semi-final tie between Liverpool and Nottingham Forest. A lengthy and emotional period of mourning on Merseyside begins.

17 Apr: In the wake of Hillsborough Douglas Hurd announces plans to require all leading football clubs to convert to all-seating stadiums. He also announces an inquiry into the disaster under Lord Justice Taylor. He meanwhile rejects backbench pressure for the postponement of the Football Supporters Bill. Perimeter fencing, blamed for the disaster, is taken down at Derby County with other clubs following their lead. Disparaging remarks about Liverpool supporters by the UEFA president, Jacques Georges, provoke furious responses from most quarters.

28 Apr: Fourteen Liverpool fans are sentenced to three years imprisonment (half of it suspended) by a Belgian court for their part in the Heysel riot in Brussels in 1985. The Taylor inquiry begins.

13 May: Hooliganism across the country on the final day of the football season leads to a renewal of government interest in pursuing the Football Supporters Bill. Hundreds of fans are arrested and dozens injured in incidents at eight English grounds.

3 July: The FA and the Football League call for the lifting of the ban on alcohol sales inside grounds in their submission to the Taylor inquiry.

7 July: A new code of practice on conservation, public access and recreation for the new water businesses announced.

10 July: Glasgow Rangers break more than a century of tradition by signing a Roman Catholic, Maurice Johnston, from FC Nantes. The Scottish striker also becomes only the second player in recent times to have played for both Celtic and Rangers.

28 July: Scottish FA agrees to allow a sponsor's name to be associated with the Scottish Cup for the first time in a £2.5 million deal with brewers Tennant Caledonian.

31 July: Announcement of the members of a 16-strong rebel cricket tour to South Africa, to be led by Mike Gatting.

4 Aug: The interim report on the Hillsborough disaster is published. It argues that a complacent police operation broke down under poor leadership. The officer in charge, Chief Superintendent David Duckenfield, is suspended on full pay. The Chief Constable of South Yorkshire, Peter Wright, offers his resignation. The club and local council are also criticized. Various recommendations to improve safety are made.

8 Aug: The two black cricketers on the rebel tour of South Africa quit having been condemned by leading black athletes.

Announcement that the Pennine Way is so eroded that it needs to be protected by a carpet covering.

Audit Commission report finds that though many councils assume that low prices at sports centres encourage poorer people to use them they are twice as likely to be used by professional people. It therefore concluded that 'many people are – through their rates – paying to subsidise the pastimes of the rich'.

13 Aug: Steve Ovett, one of Britain's most successful middle-distance runners, accuses Britain's athletic officials of underhand dealing at the Amateur Athletic Association's Championship.

14 Aug: Resignation of Peter Wright unanimously rejected by South Yorkshire Police Authority.

19 Aug: Rebel rugby tour of South Africa by a World Invitation XV (including some British players) begins.

28 Aug: Manchester United pay £2.3 million – a record between British clubs – for Gary Pallister, the Middlesborough and England defender.

4 Sept: Riotious behaviour on a ferry taking English fans to Sweden leads to one death by drowning.

6 Sept: More than 150 English football fans are arrested in Stockholm after outbreaks of violence and looting in the city centre after the World Cup game between England and Sweden.

7 Sept: Colin Moynihan, the Minister for Sport, tells the FA to cancel the scheduled friendly against the Netherlands in view of the behaviour of English fans in Sweden. The soft policing of the fans by the Swedes is criticized by British ministers.

16 Sept: Swansea fans gaoled after a game in Greece in the European Cup Winners Cup.

Nigel Mansell fined £50,000 after a controversial series of incidents in the Portuguese grand prix, from which he was disqualified. He subsequently (28 Sept) threatened to withdraw from motor racing.

27 Oct: A petition against the football membership scheme is presented by Denis Howell, the Labour spokesman on sport.

30 Oct: A petition signed by all 2,000 professional footballers, urging the government to abandon its membership scheme, is handed to Denis Howell.

31 Oct: The government makes several concessions during the final stages of the Football Spectators Bill. Concern about safety conditions at ground entrances forces ministers to adopt a 'flexible' attitude to the scheme's starting date.

Horse-racing on an all-weather track for the first time in Britain at Lingfield Park.

The National Playing Fields Association launches a campaign demanding immediate action by central and local government to combat a crisis in the provision of recreational playing space in Britain.

6 Nov: FA opens disciplinary proceedings against Arsenal and Norwich after a brawl on the pitch during the match on 4 Nov.

8 Nov: English Rugby Union opposes suggests that financial rewards for top players should be legalized.

12 Nov: The British Amateur Athletic Board discards its much maligned first-two-past-the-post selection system for major international events.

15 Nov: The government announces an increase in the grant to the Sports Council of £2.47 million for 1990, bringing the total to £43.74 million.

16 Nov: Colin Moynihan, the Minister for Sport, signs the European Anti-Doping Convention. Its intention is to put strong pressure on countries to close the net on sports cheats.

The Labour Party publishes a survey of school sport. It reports that a large majority of education authorities are worried about standards of physical education in their schools and that the decline in school sport is harming the health and fitness of children.

17 Nov: Steve Pinsent, a former Commonwealth Games weightlifting champion is gaoled for three months for supplying anabolic steroids to other lifters. The sentence was later reduced.

20 Nov: Seven British weightlifters are declared as having been positive in drug tests since April.

21 Nov: WRU announces the setting up of an independent inquiry into the events surrounding the South African Rugby Board's centenary celebrations.

23 Nov: Public Accounts Committee publishes a critical report on the CCPR.

FA charges West Ham and Wimbledon for bringing the game into disrepute during an ill-tempered Littlewoods cup-tie on 22 Nov during which six players were booked and the West Ham captain was sent off.

27 Nov: Norwich fined £50,000 and Arsenal £20,000 for the on-pitch brawl on 4 Nov.
The government publishes its response to the Sports Council's School Sport Forum Report.

30 Nov: Frank Warren, the boxing promoter, is shot as he arrives at an event in Barking Town Hall, London.
South Yorkshire Police agree compensation likely to total more than £50 million to victims of the Hillsborough disaster but deny responsibility for it.
English and Scottish FAs decide to cancel the 1990 Rous Cup competition.
Rugby Union's International Board announces that it is looking for a way to allow players to profit from their off-pitch activities while preserving the game's amateur status.

6 Dec: An Order is laid before Parliament to add the management of sports and leisure facilities to the list of 'defined activities' for compulsory competitive tendering.

7 Dec: For reasons of security FIFA decides to base England on the island of Sardinia for the opening matches of the 1990 World Cup.
Les Bettinson, team manager of the Great Britain Rugby League team, is sacked and replaced by Maurice Lindsey.

8 Dec: Centenary Way, a 83-mile footpath from York to Filey, is inaugurated.

13 Dec: The International Rugby Football Board publishes recommendations to relax the game's amateur regulations to be discussed further in Spring 1990.

28 Dec: To counteract cheating in sport the government confirms that it is to make the possession of muscle-enhancing anabolic steroids without a prescription a criminal offence.

Race Relations and Immigration

ZIG LAYTON-HENRY

The foundation on which race relations policy has been built under Mrs Thatcher's administration is the assumption that harmonious and improving community relations are dependent on firm but fair immigration controls. The 'firm but fair' formula is constantly reiterated by Conservative spokesmen to defend the government's tough policies towards aspiring immigrants and refugees.[1] In the Conservative Party document, 'Our first eight years', extolling the achievements of the government since May 1979, under the heading, 'Better race relations' the sole claim made was that fewer people had been accepted for settlement in the United Kingdom since the control of Commonwealth immigration began in 1962.[2] Mrs Thatcher has been determined to reassure public opinion that the British character will not be swamped by New Commonwealth immigration which will be brought to an end apart from a few compassionate cases.[3] The firm but fair government policy can be described as firm on immigration controls and fair to those who oppose immigration from the New Commonwealth. It is often unfair to genuine dependants and refugees seeking admission to the UK.

Since 1979 a series of measures have been taken to tighten controls over immigration. These have included changes in the immigration rules such as the introduction of the primary purpose rule,[4] tough action against illegal entrants and overstayers and, most important of all, a New Nationality Act, which was passed in 1981 and came into force on 1 January 1983. The Nationality Act abolished the imperial concept of the British subject and created a separate citizenship of the UK for those who had a close personal connection with the UK either because their parents or grandparents were born, adopted, naturalized or registered as citizens of the UK or through permanent settlement in the UK. British subjects in the remaining colonies and those who had no close connection with the UK were made citizens of the British Dependent Territories or British Overseas Citizens, neither of which carried the right of entry to, or abode in, the United Kingdom. The consequences of the Nationality Act (1981) and of previous restrictions on the rights of Commonwealth and colonial people to immigrate to the UK became a major issue in 1989 with the crisis over the crushing of the pro-democracy movement in China and its repercussions on the future of Hong Kong.

In the last few years the government has continued to give a high priority to 'keeping immigration control in good repair'.[5] In 1985 visas were required for visitors from Sri Lanka. In 1986 the visa requirement was extended to visitors from India, Pakistan, Bangladesh, Nigeria and Ghana. In 1987 the Immigration (Carriers' Liability) Act was passed making it an offence for airlines or shipping companies to bring people to the UK without proper documents, thus requiring these companies to enforce the visa regulations or face a possible fine of £1,000 per passenger. In 1988 a new Immigration Act was passed repealing the absolute right of men settled in Britain before 1 January 1973 to be joined by their families. The European Court of Human Rights had ruled that this discriminated against women and the government chose to comply with the ruling by abolishing the right for men rather than extending it to women. The right now became conditional on showing that dependants seeking entry to the UK would be provided with adequate accommodation and financial support and would thus not seek recourse to public funds. The Act restricted rights of appeal against refusal of entry and also against deportation on compassionate grounds. It made overstaying a continuing criminal offence and prohibited the entry of second or subsequent wives in a polygamous marriage. This latter measure appears to have been more an attempt to preserve the 'British character' than an attempt to close an immigration loophole as only 25 people were admitted under this provision in 1985.

Douglas Hurd appeared to confirm this in the debate when he stated 'Polygamy is not an acceptable social custom in this country.'[6]

Refugees and Asylum Seekers

Refugees with a well-founded fear of persecution are entitled to shelter and protection under the 1951 United Nations Convention on Refugees. All West European countries have experienced a rise in asylum applications in the 1980s and this is true for Britain where applications have risen from 1,563 in 1979 to 5,100 in 1988. This year applications have risen substantially. However, the numbers applying to Britain are relatively few compared with similar West European countries due to the discouraging attitude of the government. The Home Office view is that most applications are from economic migrants trying to evade immigration controls.[7] As applications have risen so have refusals. In 1980 about 40 per cent of asylum applications were refused, in 1988 the refusal rate was 75 per cent. Kurds from Turkey and Tamils from Sri Lanka have been two of the largest groups applying for asylum in recent years. In 1985 visa requirements were imposed on visitors from Sri Lanka after a steep rise in asylum applications from young male Tamils. In June 1989 a visa requirement was imposed on Turkey to discourage Kurdish applications after 3,500 Kurds arrived in Britain in May and June seeking political asylum. In October a Kurdish refugee, Dogan Arslan, committed suicide when told he would be deported back to Turkey. A considerable number of Kurds are likely to seek judicial review of Home Office decisions to refuse them asylum.

In May an Immigration Appeal Tribunal decided that the Home Office had illegally returned five Tamils to persecution, imprisonment and torture in Sri Lanka.[8] The tough policy of the government can also be seen in Hong Kong where over 50,000 Vietnamese refugees are held in appalling conditions in refugee camps. The government has allowed 20,000 Vietnamese refugees to come to Britain since 1979 but seems determined to treat those in the camps as economic migrants and repatriate almost all of them back to Vietnam.

The Case of Viraj Mendis

At dawn on 18 January 1989, police raided the church of the Ascension in Hulme, Manchester and arrested Viraj Mendis, a Singalese, who had come to Britain as a student in 1973. The raid ended the most publicized case of an immigrant faced with deportation seeking sanctuary in a church. Mr Mendis failed his college examinations in 1975 but stayed on in Britain in breach of the immigration laws. He claimed refugee status, arguing that as a supporter of Tamil separatism, his life would be in danger if he returned to Sri Lanka. However, there was no evidence that Mr Mendis was involved in politics before 1975 and the immigration adjudicator said that the appellant's public and open espousal of the separatist cause was nothing more than a deliberate and cynical attempt to avoid deportation.[9] The Home Secretary told the House of Commons that the woman he had married in 1984 had confirmed that the wedding was designed solely in an attempt to stay in Britain.[10] Viraj Mendis mobilized significant support and fought his case through the courts right up to the House of Lords. In spite of residing in Britain for 15 years, the Home Office felt he had flagrantly broken the immigration rules and were not prepared to allow him to stay. He was deported to Sri Lanka on 21 January 1989.

The Crisis over Hong Kong

A major concern of the government and the media has been over the future of Hong Kong and especially the campaign in the Colony for Britain to adopt a more generous attitude towards British passport holders. Over three million people in Hong Kong are citizens of the British Dependent Territories, but this citizenship does not give them the right to immigrate and settle in the UK. A great many people in Hong Kong desire full British passports as an insurance policy in case relations with China deteriorate after 1997. The suppression of the pro-democracy reform movement in China and especially the massacre in Tiananmen Square on 3 and 4 June 1989 greatly increased insecurity in Hong Kong and added to pressures to emigrate before the Chinese takeover.

However, neither the government, the Opposition nor the Foreign Affairs Select Committee were prepared to recommend that British passport holders in Hong

Table 1. Population, households, and families/persons not in families, by ethnic group, 1985−7, Great Britain

Ethnic group of person, head of household or family	Numbers (thousands)			Proportions (per thousand)			Percentages		
	Population	Households	Families/persons not in families	Population	Households	Families/persons not in families	Population	Households	Families/persons not in families
West Indian, Guyanese	521	191	216	10	9	9	21	27	26
African	105	42	51	2	2	2	4	6	6
Indian	745	192	242	14	9	10	30	28	29
Pakistani	404	88	111	7	4	5	16	13	13
Bangladeshi	111	21	30	2	1	1	4	3	3
Chinese	120	35	46	2	2	2	5	5	5
Arab	71	33	39	1	2	2	3	5	5
Mixed	255	47	58	5	2	3	10	7	7
Other	141	46	55	3	2	2	6	7	6
All ethnic minority groups	2473	694	848	45	33	36	100	100	100
White	51,333	20,358	22,199	944	959	955	−	−	−
Not stated	570	180	210	10	8	9	−	−	−
All ethnic groups	54,376	21,231	23,257	1000	1000	1000	−	−	−

Source: John Haskey, *Population Trends 57,* 1989, p. 9

Kong should be allowed the right of abode in the UK. The Foreign Secretary Sir Geoffrey Howe argued that the assessment made by the select committee and many other members of the House of Commons rested on the sheer scale of the numbers involved, which could be between 3–5 million people.[11] On 13 July he said, 'The practical difficulties of absorbing hundreds of thousands – possibly millions – of people make the granting of an open-ended right of abode to all British Dependent Territory citizens impossible to contemplate. It would be wrong to raise expectations that we could not possibly meet. I do not believe the House would support such a departure from the immigration policies pursued by successive British governments since the early 1960s.'[12] Mr Gerald Kaufman for the Opposition supported the government.[13] Only Mr Ashdown for the Liberal Democrats argued that citizens of the British Dependent Territories in Hong Kong should be offered the right of abode in Britain.[14]

The mass media and public opinion have been much more sympathetic to the plight of the Hong Kong Chinese and sensitive to Britain's moral obligations than the politicians. The quality press has strongly argued in favour of granting the right of abode to British passport holders and a gallup poll, carried out soon after the slaughter in Tiananmen Square, found as many as 42 per cent of the population believed that Hong Kong citizens should be given the legal right to settle in the UK. In 1983 a similar poll found that 44 per cent supported this, an almost identical proportion.[15] The government, however, has not been prepared to relax its generally tough controls on Commonwealth immigration. The Foreign Secretary, Sir Geoffrey Howe, interviewed on BBC1, warned of the scale of possible immigration and possible ethnic conflict if the right of abode was conceded. Some critics felt this policy smacked of racism.[16] In contrast to the British position, the Portuguese government granted full citizenship with the right of abode in Portugal and the European Community to the people in its colony of Macao.

On 20 December the new Foreign Secretary, Douglas Hurd, announced a government proposal to increase the confidence of key people in Hong Kong and reduce their emigration. He said the government would grant full British citizenship to 50,000 people and their dependants, a maximum of 225,000 people. These would be professional, business and technical experts, including crown servants, needed to run the Colony. Mr Kaufman reiterated the Opposition's belief that it would not be right to offer any commitment to British Dependent Territories passport holders in Hong Kong and stated that the Opposition was against the creation of specially favoured categories based on status or affluence.

Mr Tebbit supported the Opposition and opposed the government's decision, arguing it was a breach in the government's commitment to end large scale immigration. A significant number of Conservative MPs support Mr Tebbit's view and it is possible that a substantial rebellion against the proposed legislation will take place. Mr Tebbit made it clear that he believed immigration was one of the issues which drove traditional Labour voters to support Mrs Thatcher and that the government was in danger of driving them back to the Labour Party.

Table 2.　Percentage of the total population which belongs to the ethnic minority population by area of usual residence 1985 − 7 average, Great Britain

Region / Metropolitan county		%
(R)	(MC)	
1. North,R (total)		1.5
Tyne and Wear,MC		2.0
Remainder		1.2
2. Yorkshire & Humberside,R (total)		3.7
South Yorkshire,MC		2.2
West Yorkshire,MC		6.9
Remainder		0.7
3. East Midlands,R (total)		4.2
4. East Anglia,R (total)		2.2
5. South East,R (total)		7.7
Greater London		15.3
Remainder		2.8
6. South West,R (total)		1.1
7. West Midlands,R (total)		7.7
West Midlands,MC		13.3
Remainder		2.0
8. North West,R (total)		3.6
Greater Manchester,MC		5.3
Merseyside,MC		1.8
Remainder		2.9
England		5.2
Wales		1.2
Scotland		0.8
Great Britain		4.5

Source: OPCS

The Salman Rushdie Affair

Towards the end of 1988 British Muslims became actively involved in a campaign to ban *The Satanic Verses* by Salman Rushdie, which they regarded as an offensive and blasphemous attack on the Islamic faith. The book was published in September and quickly brought protests from Muslim groups. On 2 December they turned to direct action and 7,000 staged a demonstration in Bolton and a copy of the book was burned to gain publicity. This was unsuccessful. On 14 January 1989 a protest meeting was held outside Bradford Town Hall and, once again, a copy of the book was symbolically burned. This time the protest was widely reported and condemned.

A month later on 14 February the campaign against *The Satanic Verses* took a dramatic turn when the Ayatollah Khomeini urged Muslims throughout the world to execute Rushdie: 'I inform the proud Moslem people of the world that the author of *The Satanic Verses* book, which is against Islam, the Prophet and the Koran, and all those involved in its publication who were aware of its content, are sentenced to death.'[17]

There was widespread shock that a head of state could urge the death of a famous writer who was the citizen of another state. The Ayatollah's *fatwa* was immediately condemned in Western countries as Salman Rushdie went into hiding. Some Muslim leaders in Bradford, for example, supported the death sentence but the Council of Mosques in Britain condemned the violence and urged Muslims to obey the law. On 18 February Rushdie apologized for the distress he had caused to Muslims but this apology was not accepted by Ayatollah Khomeini. On 21 February the British government withdrew its diplomats from Tehran and sent Iran's representative home. This action was supported by the European Community. Many writers took the lead in supporting Rushdie and defending his right to publish.

On 24 February the Home Secretary, Douglas Hurd, addressed Muslims in the Central Mosque in Birmingham. He accepted that Muslims had been deeply hurt by the book but warned that violence or the threat of violence was wholly unacceptable and said that nothing would do more damage to racial harmony than the idea that British Muslims were indifferent to the rule of law in this country. Respect for the rule of law was a fundamental principle for which Britain stood as were freedom of speech and the toleration of different opinions.

The campaign against *The Satanic Verses* raised concern about the influence of Islamic fundamentalism in Britain and efforts by Muslim groups to set up their own educational institutions, especially single sex schools for girls. In July, John Patten, Minister of State at the Home Office responsible for Race Relations, spoke of the need for the Muslim community to integrate into British society. In a letter to the Advisory Council on Race Relations, he wrote, 'One cannot be British on one's own exclusive terms or on a selective basis.'[19]

Those sympathetic to the Muslim campaign, who included some members of Parliament with Muslim electors, deplored the fact that the blasphemy laws applied only to Christianity and condemned the unwillingness of many liberals to understand the intensity of the offence to practising Muslims. Some argued that British Muslims felt their values were being eroded in a hostile society, that only extreme actions enabled them to gain the attention of the media and politicians and generally their customs were not respected in British society. The action of the government in banning the polygamous wives could be cited as an example of this view.

The Rushdie affair has brought the peaceful, hard-working Muslim community into considerable political prominence. Issues of concern to Muslims such as education, problems of adjusting to British society and the role of the Islamic faith in a liberal secular country are receiving greater attention. The campaign divided those on the left, some of whom felt it was vital to preserve freedom of speech and publication, while others felt the campaign had unleashed considerable racist and anti-Muslim feelings which were legitimized by the actions of the Ayatollah and the threats by some protestors against the publishers and bookshops. Roy Hattersley argued forcefully that the proposition that Muslims are welcome in Britain if, and only if, they stop behaving like Muslims, is incompatible with the principles of a free society but in a free society the Muslim community can be allowed to do whatever it likes only as long as the choice it makes is not damaging to society as a whole.[20] The campaign against *The Satanic Verses* is continuing with few concessions to Muslim demands.

Immigration and DNA Testing

The invention of genetic fingerprinting has had a major impact on immigration as it is accepted that this is a conclusive way of proving family relationships. Immigration lawyers believe that there are thousands of cases of children, particularly from the Indian subcontinent, who have been wrongly refused entry to Britain because entry clearance officers and appeals adjudicators did not believe they were related to the British residents who claimed to be their parents. DNA testing should greatly speed up the resolution of such cases as lengthy interviews and hearings can be eliminated.

The Home Secretary, Douglas Hurd, announced on 14 June 1989 that a government scheme would be implemented later this year to provide for a DNA testing facility for first time applicants. The taxpayer would not be expected to pay for the scheme which would probably be paid for by a higher charge on all those seeking entry to the UK. Considerable controversy occurred over the position of children wrongly refused entry in the past but who were now too old (over 18 years) to qualify to enter as dependants. The Opposition argued all such men and women should be admitted. The government, however, refused to agree, arguing that it was their dependency status that was important. The Home Secretary said, 'In many cases over-age applicants are likely to have settled into independent adult life and may also have married and established a family of their own overseas and I do not propose to waive the requirements of the rules in these cases.'[21] It seems clear that the government's concern to keep as tight a control on immigration from the New Commonwealth outweighed any moral obligation to those who had been wrongly excluded in the past.

Conclusion

In recent years the predominant concern of the government has been to maintain strict controls over New Commonwealth immigration and to reduce the numbers of Third World people entering the UK to as small a figure as possible. This has been the emphasis of government policy in 1989. There has been a consistently tough policy towards visitors, students, immigrants and asylum seekers. The immigration laws have been tightened and rigorously enforced. Deportations have increased sharply since last August when the right of appeal for many deportees was removed and also as a result of increased powers for immigration officers. Unlike the Portuguese government in its treatment of Macao, the British government has been unwilling to concede the right of abode in the UK to citizens of the British Dependent Territories in Hong Kong despite considerable public sympathy for the Hong Kong Chinese. The government has been reluctant to remedy injustices caused by its tough policies such as the refusal to admit over-age dependants wrongly refused admission and the deportation of asylum seekers subsequently tortured by the Sri Lankan authorities. These 'firm but fair' immigration polices are justified on the grounds that they contribute to good race relations within Britain, though this seems to be a matter of appeasing anti-immigrant opinion among the majority rather than devoting resources to reducing racial discrimination and racial attacks, which the Home Office is well aware are major problems.[22]

Notes

1. Douglas Hurd: 'Harmony in our cities depends on maintaining a firm but fair immigration control', *The Guardian*, 7 November 1987.
Timothy Renton, Immigration Bill (3rd Reading), *Hansard*, Col.921, 16 February 1988.
Douglas Hurd, 'Firm but fair control on asylum builds harmony in our cities', *The Independent*, 27 July 1989.
2. *Our First Eight Years: The Achievements of the Conservative Government since May 1979*, Conservative Central Office, May 1987, p. 18.
3. Verbatim report of an interview by Gordon Burns with Mrs Thatcher, *World in Action*, Granada TV, 30 January 1978.
4. Any man or woman who wants to come to Britain to marry someone already settled here must prove that it is not the pri mary purpose of the marriage to gain entry to the UK. The rule was introduced in 1980.
5. Douglas Hurd, Immigration Bill, *Hansard*, Col.779, 16 November 1987.
6. *Hansard*, Col.785, 16 November 1987.
7. Douglas Hurd, *The Independent*, 26 June 1989.
8. *The Independent*, 17 May 1989.
9. *Hansard*, Col.340, 18 January 1989.
10. *Hansard*, Col.337, 18 January 1989.
11. Sir Geoffrey Howe, Statement on visit to Hong Kong, *Hansard*, Col.320, 5 July 1989.
12. *Hansard*, Cols.1170–1171, 13 July 1989.
13. Ibid., Col.1176.

14. Ibid., Col.1188.
15. *The Independent*, 1 July 1989.
16. Sir Geoffrey Howe interviewed on a BBC1 special programme: 'Hong Kong–a matter of honour', 12 June 1989.
    Peter Kellner, 'The less polite word for "social tension" is racism', *The Independent*, 3 July 1989.
17. *London Evening Standard*, 14 February 1989.
18. *The Independent*, 25 February 1989.
19. *The Independent*, 20 July 1989.
20. *The Independent*, 21 July 1989.
21. *Hansard*, Cols.463-465, 14 June 1989.
22. *The Response to Racial Attacks and Harassment: guidance for the statutory agencies.* Report of the Inter–Departmental Racial Attacks Groups, Home Office, 1989.

Chronology

14 Jan: British Muslims protest against *The Satanic Verses* outside Bradford Town Hall and symbolically burn a copy of the book.

18 Jan: Viraj Mendis, deemed to be illegally resident in the country, is seized from sanctuary in the Church of the Ascension, Manchester.

20 Jan: Viraj Mendis is deported to Sri Lanka.

14 Feb: Ayatollah Khomeini urges the execution of Salman Rushdie.

24 Feb: Douglas Hurd, addressing Muslims at Birmingham's Central Mosque, urges them not to break the law over the Rushdie affair and says that nothing will do more damage to racial harmony than the idea that British Muslims are 'indifferent to the rule of law in this country'.

27 Feb: NACRO report praises progress towards eliminating racism and discrimination from the criminal justice system.

13 Mar: *Towards a Whole School Policy: NUT Guidelines on Anti–Racism in Education* National Union of Teachers, draws attention to racism in schools and makes various recommendations for its elimination.

17 Mar: Inquiry by the Police Complaints Authority into allegations of racial harassment of a Sikh trainee at Ryton on Dunsmore Police College.

30 Mar: Rastafarian man wins victory in an industrial tribunal over his claim that he had been discriminated against at a job interview because he wore dreadlocks.

13 Apr: Government circular institutes ethnic monitoring of teachers.

24 Apr: The Home Office refuses to change, on grounds of cost, a police entrance exam which the Commission for Racial Equality argued was biased against ethnic minorities.

27 Apr: Home Office document argues that hundreds of people have been illegally deported since immigration rules were changed nine months previously.

16 May: Home Office report points out worrying levels of racial violence in Britain.
Release of the findings of the Immigration Appeals Tribunal that the Home Office has illegally returned five Tamils to Sri Lanka in breach of the 1951 Geneva Convention on Refugees.

17 May: The Labour leadership infuriates black supporters and imposes the white Kate Hoey as candidate for the Vauxhall by-election after local party activists abandoned the selection meeting to demand a black candidate.

20 May: Appeal for assistance from the Bishop of Stepney to the government for aid for the Kurdish refugees in the East End who have been arriving in considerable numbers since the beginning of May.

25 May: The Commission for Racial Equality finds the allocation of housing by Liverpool City Council has been discriminatory.

6 June: Roy Hattersley, deputy leader of the Labour Party, accuses the government of attempting to subvert immigration tribunals following leaks of letters from the Treasury Solicitor.

7 June: Amnesty International argues Britain is contravening UN guidelines over its treatment of Kurdish refugees.

9 June: Treasury Solicitor disbarred from giving advice to immigration tribunals.

13 June: The Commission for Racial Equality warns in its annual report that blacks and Asians in the inner cities are not benefiting from urban regeneration policies. It also points to the deleterious effects of the Rushdie affair.

14 June: Announcement that DNA testing facilities will be made available for first time applicants to the UK as dependants. The government also declared that relatives of immigrants who prove through DNA tests that they were wrongly barred from entering Britain will still not be allowed in if now over the age limit.

22 June: Home Office admits that aeroplanes carrying Kurds seeking asylum have been sent back to Istanbul.

3 July: Home Office report argues that the government should make high profile efforts to tackle racial disadvantage and fund special programmes for ethnic minorities.

18 July: Lord Gifford's report on race relations and policing in Toxteth, Liverpool, finds a 'uniquely horrific' level of racial discrimination.

Fay Weldon in her *Sacred Cows*, part of Chatto and Windus' Counterblasts series, calls for a re-thinking of the left's attitude to multiculturalism in the light of the Muslim response to the Rushdie affair, and accuses the left of being too ready to see ethnic minorities simply as victims.

20 July: Criticism of the government's relief schemes is voiced at the first national conference of the Vietnamese boat people.

27 July: Court of Appeal upholds the right of five deported Sri Lankan Tamils to reapply for asylum.

10 Aug: Conditions in immigrant detention centres are criticized by Penny Green in *Private Sector Involvement in Immigration Detention Centres* published by the Howard League.

23 Aug: Appeal Court ruling upholds the decision of Croydon's social services to take a child away from a white mother and place it with a black family in the light of the council's policy that every child should be brought up by families of the same ethnic group.

25 Aug: A report on the implications of the Croydon case is called for by David Mellor, Minister of State at the Department of Health, who also hints that the Children's Bill might be amended in the light of the case.

4 Sept: *English for Speakers of Other Languages–A Nation's Neglect*, Adult Literacy and Basic Skills Unit, calls for £3.5 million spending on language courses for ethnic minorities.

11 Sept: Black teachers call for a public inquiry into the alleged suppression of a report showing racial discrimination when teachers have been redeployed from overstaffed

schools in the ILEA area.

Row over the inability of a liaison officer at a Birmingham school to speak Urdu blows up.

7 Oct: Kurdish refugee, Siho Iyiguven, burns himself to death at Harmondsworth detention centre.

9 Oct: Kurdish refugee, Dogan Aslan, commits suicide rather than face deportation to Turkey.

13 Nov: Government announces that the next census will include questions about ethnic background.

20 Dec: Home Affairs Select Committee *Racial Attacks and Harassment*, HMSO, published. Douglas Hurd announces that the government proposes to grant full British citizenship to 50,000 key people and their dependants in Hong Kong to increase their confidence in the colony's future and reduce emigration.

21 Dec: Article by Norman Tebbit in the *Evening Standard* criticizing the government's plans to allow up to 225,000 Hong Kong people full British passports provokes fears of a Tory backbench revolt on the issue.

Women

SUSAN McRAE

Women's Employment and Social Inequality

The year 1989 was extraordinary, and not just in Eastern Europe. In Britain in 1989, the government, the media and employers discovered a demographic time bomb, and with it, the need to recruit and retain more women in the labour market. The consequences of this discovery are likely not only to bring dramatic changes in women's labour force participation in the 1990s, but may well also increase inequalities in living standards between families – social changes that were already discernible throughout 1989.

Demographic Change

British society at the end of the 1980s is on the edge of potentially momentous social changes. It is often the case that major changes in society occur only in response to crises,[1] and it is clear that a crisis labour market confronts Britain in the 1990s. Following a large surplus of 18–24 year olds during the mid-1980s, which resulted in unprecedented levels of youth unemployment, the number of young people available to employers over the first five years of the 1990s is expected to fall by about 30 per cent, representing a loss of around one million workers.[2] If British employers are to avoid restrictions on their ability to grow and compete in both domestic and international markets, then women must be encouraged to fill part of the gap in the labour market left by this impending demographic change.

Women are the most likely source of new labour force entrants. The number of women entering the labour market during the years to 1995 is expected to increase markedly, with women likely to account for about 80 per cent of a predicted 1.1 million new workers. Women aged 25–44, returning to work following breaks for childcare, are projected to make up the largest single group among these new labour force entrants.[3] The evidence suggests, however, that as many as one million more women would enter the labour force under the right conditions. These enabling conditions largely concern the provision of adequate childcare facilities. But women are also discouraged from returning to work because they do not have the opportunity to use their skills owing to inflexibility in the organization of work or to discrimination against women with young children.[4]

Facilitating Women's Employment

In anticipation of severe labour supply shortages, many employers are taking steps to encourage women to stay in, or return more quickly to, employment after having children. On one level, these steps are pragmatic and relate to the organization of workplaces. Thus, 1989 saw an increase in the availability of jobsharing arrangements, some extension of part-time working hours to senior level occupations (in the Civil Service, for example) and an acceleration in the implementation of career break or enhanced maternity leave schemes. Career break schemes allow women taking a break for childrearing to remain part of their former work organization and usually entail a few weeks of employment each year as well as re-entry or updating training. Some form of career break scheme is now available across a very wide range of organizations including NatWest, British Petroleum, Unilever plc, Shell UK, Boots, ICI, United Biscuits and so on. Although originally introduced for women with proven career potential, 1989 saw the beginning of an extension of eligibility for career break schemes to all staff at all occupational levels. In addition, a trend towards improved paternity leave arrangements could be discerned, in the absence of a statutory right for men to have time-off when they become fathers.

The year 1989 also witnessed an upsurge in interest in childcare facilities, and had, perhaps uniquely, the unexpected sight of the Secretary of State for Employment calling for husbands to do more housework and childcare. Although there were only about 100 private sector workplace nurseries by the end of the year, Midland Bank seemed to set a new standard by announcing they would be opening up to 300 workplace nurseries during the early 1990s. Childcare voucher schemes, operating on a principle similar to luncheon vouchers, were introduced in 1989, and the government signalled its support for employers and other organizations who wished to establish childcare facilities.

However, in keeping with current Conservative policy, the government offered little in the way of financial assistance to parents. Instead, a five-point strategy for improving childcare provision was announced. This plan places responsibility on employers, local authorities, and voluntary organizations. Employers are encouraged to claim available tax relief on the capital and running costs of workplace nurseries; local authorities and employers are invited to make use of school premises for after- school and holiday play schemes; and voluntary organizations are encouraged to set up local registers of childminders. The government agreed to provide 'pump-priming' funding for the establishment of a national association of childcare providers designed to improve the quality and standards of care, but showed no willingness to remove the tax liability that since 1983 has been levied against employees who have access to employer- subsidized childcare. At the end of the year, workplace nurseries continued to attract a higher level of taxation than company cars.

Alongside the actions outlined above, which are being taken by employers in order to increase the retention of women employees over their child-rearing years, many employers are taking steps to achieve greater equality of opportunity as between men and women, with the intention of using their female workers (current and future) more effectively. To this end, employers are attempting to eliminate discrimination against women by revising recruitment, selection and promotion procedures, by introducing women-only training and equal opportunity awareness courses, as well as by adopting a variety of other measures such as equal opportunity audits and continuous monitoring. A very few employers, such as British Rail and Littlewoods, introduced voluntary gender targets against which equal opportunity actions may be measured.[5]

The focus and outcome of these various actions by employers is likely to be uneven, however. Insofar as women have differential access to childcare facilities or flexible working arrangements, inequalities as between women in access to employment are likely to develop; insofar as men and women have more equal chances in the labour market, inequalities among women may deepen and inequalities between families be intensified. This is also likely to be one outcome of demographic changes bringing more women into employment.

Inequalities between Women

The need for women to fill some part of the gap in the labour force created by Britain's low birthrate during the 1970s is not monolithic. Workers will be needed both at the top of the labour market, to fill managerial and professional jobs, and in the lower reaches, to fill jobs in retail, catering and personal services. Women will be needed, in other words, to take the place of graduates and of less qualified school leavers. As more women enter employment to take up these diverse positions, inequalities between women – largely muted in the past by women's concentration in a very narrow band of occupations – seem set to increase.

Furthermore, there is likely to be more room for women at the top of the occupational hierarchy. Most observers believe that the marked post-war increase in higher-level and professional occupations will continue well into the next decade and beyond. Of the 1.7 million new jobs predicted by 1995, some one million will be in professional and related occupations, bringing the proportion of the labour force employed at this level to just under one-quarter by 1995.[6] The likelihood of women taking up a major share of these new jobs at the top is increased by the continuing trend among women to gain professional and higher-level qualifications,[7] and by past trends which suggest that the growth rate in representation of women in professional and related occupations has doubled that of men.[8]

However, not all women will have equal access to higher-level jobs, and the high incomes associated with these jobs. Rather, the evidence suggests that, like men, women from advantaged family backgrounds will do much better in the labour market than women from working class homes.[9] Social inequalities between women are likely to develop, therefore, as increasing numbers of women enter into disparate locations in the labour market.

As women have striven for equality of opportunity little attention has been paid to the attendant social inequalities between families that may derive from the increasing success of some groups of women in the labour market. Differential success in the labour market among women from differing class backgrounds is likely to exacerbate existing social inequalities.[10] Women tend to marry their 'sociological brothers'; only rarely marrying men from very different social class backgrounds.[11] As more women enter employment, then, the social and financial advantages brought into some families by men's higher-level or managerial occupations are likely to be augmented by wives' high earnings. While in other families, the inability of wives (or husbands) to obtain well-paid employment before having children, and their poorer access to childcare facilities after childbirth, is likely to lead to increased financial hardship over the years of family formation, especially when circumstances do not permit these wives to remain in the paid labour force.

Moreover, as it is the case in Britain that childbirth generally acts as a catalyst for women to take up part-time employment, the number of families experiencing financial hardship over family formation may be significant. Part-time employment is one of the few ways that women may readily balance paid work with family life. Research shows, however, that up to 30 per cent of women's life-time earnings can be lost post-motherhood, largely through a return to work part-time,[12] and that almost half of all women returning to part-time employment after breaks for childcare do so to jobs below the level for which they are qualified.[13] Differences between women in terms of their ability to return to work full-time, or to higher-level part-time work, carry important consequences for their families' economic prospects.

Moreover, the rate at which mothers are going back to work following the birth of a baby has been increasing rapidly. By the end of the 1970s about one quarter of mothers who were in work when they became pregnant returned to work within eight or nine months of having a baby.[14] Ten years later, in 1988, the proportion had doubled and nearly one-half of similar mothers went back to work. The increase in the rate of return to full-time work was even greater. All the indications are that this trend will continue during the 1990s as a result of the changing demographic composition of the labour supply, and may well accelerate. The rate and form of women's return to work varies, however, according to women's occupational status prior to childbirth. By the late 1980s, women in higher-level non-manual or professional and managerial occupations were almost twice as likely as women in skilled or unskilled manual work to return to employment within eight or nine months of having a baby, and almost five times as likely to return full-time. Nine out of ten of women in these higher-level jobs were able, moreover, to return to employment at the same occupational level, whether part- or full-time, while one in five of women in skilled jobs before having a baby dropped down into unskilled jobs upon their return which was generally on a part-time basis.[15]

Conclusion

It is possible that steps taken in 1989 to increase the participation of women in paid employment will lead to an increasing polarization in the labour market – between women and women, and between families with two high earners and those where women continue to work discontinuously over family formation in poorly paid, low-skilled jobs. It is also possible that 1992 will contribute to this polarization, although the impact of the single market on women is as yet unclear. The expected growth in service sector employment will benefit women by providing more opportunities for part-time employment, but to the extent that this employment continues to be associated with low wages and low skill development,[16] increased polarization between families may well result.

Marked changes in women's labour force participation over the 1990s, the beginnings of which were discernible during 1989, may well add up to little less than a social revolution. There are likely to be profound implications for roles and relationships within the family; for childcare practices and public provision of childcare; for fertility and population trends; for equity, differentials and relativities as between individuals and groups at work; for the distribution of income as between households and families in the community; as well as for the labour market itself.

Notes

1. Jean Lipman-Blumen, 'Role de-differentiation as a systems reponse to crisis: occupational and political roles of women', in *Sociological Inquiry*, 43, 2, 1973, pp. 105–29.
2. NEDO, *Young People and The Labour Market: A Challenge for the 1990s*, NEDO Books 1988.
3. Institute for Employment Research (IER), *Review of the Economy and Employment, Occupational Update 1988*, University of Warwick, 1988a.
4. Hilary Metcalf and Patricia Leighton, *The Under- utilization of Women in the Labour Market*, IMS Report No. 172, 1989.
5. For examples of the actions being taken by employers across a variety of occupations and companies, see *Women At The Top*, Hansard Society Report (Susan McRae, Rapporteur), January 1990.

6. Institute for Employment Research (IER), 'Review of the economy and employment', *Occupational Studies*, 2, University of Warwick, 1988.

7. Rosemary Crompton (with Kay Sanderson), 'Credentials and careers: some implications of the increase in professional qualifications amongst women', *Sociology*, 20, 1986, pp. 25–42.

8. Institute for Employment Research, *Review of the Economy and Employment*,1988, University of Warwick.

9. Robert Erikson and John Goldthorpe, 'Does the class mobility of women differ from that of men? Cross-sex comparisons' in *Cross-National Perspective*, Mannheim, CASMIN Working Paper No.114, 1988.

10. Westergaard and Resler, *Class in a Capitalist Society*, Harmondsworth, Penguin Books 1975.

11. Susan McRae, *Cross-Class Families*, Clarendon Press, Oxford, 1986.

12. Heather Joshi and M-L Newell, 'Family Responsibilities and Pay Differentials: Evidence from Men and Women born in 1946', CEPR Discussion Paper No.157, 1987.

13. Jean Martin and Ceridwen Roberts, *Women and Employment: A Lifetime Perspective*, HMSO, 1984.

14. W. W. Daniel, *Maternity Rights: The Experience of Women*, PSI Report No.588, June 1980.

15. Susan McRae, *Mothers at Work*, PSI, forthcoming 1990.

16. Duncan Gallie, 'Technological Change, Gender and Skill', ESRC Working Paper No.4, December 1988.

Chronology

20 Jan: Anne Widdicombe's Abortion (Amendment) Bill to reduce the time limit in which a pregnancy can be aborted to 18 weeks is talked out in the Commons.

24 Jan: A Department of Employment guideline that stipulates that only single parents can get allowances of up to £50 per week for childcare if they joined Employment Training is deemed unlawful by an industrial tribunal in that it discriminated against married mothers.

7 Feb: Equal Opportunities Commission publishes a five-year plan.

15 Feb: Peter Mottershead, *Recent Developments in Childcare: A Review*, HMSO, a study commissioned by the Equal Opportunies Commission, criticizes the lack of a coherent and positive childcare policy.

16 Feb: The government announces childcare measures for Civil Service staff.

9 Mar: Vasso Papandreou, the EC Commissioner for Social Affairs, criticizes the record of some EC members on childcare provision in a speech at the Women's TUC conference. She singles out Britain for criticism, not least for blocking an EC directive giving parents a legal right to time off work during the first two years of a child's life.

13 Mar: *Workplace Nurseries – Who Cares?* Workplace Nurseries Campaign points out only 20 private companies provide workplace nurseries.

21 Mar: Equal Opportunity Commission reviews the operation of equality legislation and describes it as ineffective, calling for simpler procedures and more substantive remedies.

18 Apr: Women's Legal Defence Fund launched to help women fight sex discrimination and equal pay cases on the same day that the Equal Opportunities Commission announces difficulties with funding.

18 May: The watchdog on test-tube baby clinics says offering free sterilization to women for donating their eggs should be illegal.

22 May: TUC report *Equality in Occupational Pension Schemes* argues that two-thirds of female workers do not benefit from these schemes.

13 June: The government is criticized by the Equal Opportunities Commission for vetoing a EC directive aimed at encouraging men and women to share work and family responsibilities.

14 June: Equal pay for work of equal value victory in an industrial tribunal by a woman working in the electricity industry.

20 June: Equal Opportunities Commission's annual report argues that blatant and offensive sexual discrimination is still rife in many firms.

19 July: PLP approves a rule change which increases the size of the shadow cabinet from 15 to 18 and requires that at least three votes must be cast for women candidates in a move to increase the number of women in the Shadow Cabinet.

16 Aug: Test case claim for equal pay won by a teacher against Doncaster education authority.

22 Aug: Launch of the TUC's Childcare Charter to encourage wider provision of nurseries to enable women to compete more successfully in the labour market.

1 Sept: *Women and the Labour Market* Income Data Services argues that employers are still doing little to attract or retain female workers.

4 Sept: The number of seats reserved for women on the General Council of the TUC is increased from 6 to 12.

11 Sept: *Survey* in Company says 1 woman in 10 was sexually attacked and 37 per cent claim to have suffered indecent exposure in the last year. It also reveals the strong fears of attack among women.

Female bank staff with Lloyds Bank win an industrial tribunal fight over pay inequality.

18 Sept: Hilary Metcalf and Patricia Leighton, *The Under-Utilization of Women in the Labour Market*, Institute of Manpower Studies, argues that more than 1 million women could be coaxed back into the labour market by better childcare and career prospects.

2 Oct: Midland Bank opens its first nursery in Sheffield with up to 300 more planned to open over the next four years to help the bank, whose staff is 56 per cent female, retain staff during the labour shortage of the 1990s.

16 Oct: Wage gap between men and women is wider now than at any time since the Equal Pay Act came into force according to the Equal Opportunities Commission report *Women and Men in Britain*, HMSO. Women in non-manual jobs earn on average only 61 per cent of their male counterparts (49 per cent if part-time). For manual workers the ratio is 72 per cent and 64 per cent respectively. The report also draws attention to the lack of childcare facilities at work and to sex-typing in education.

30 Oct: NUT launches its campaign to make it easier for female teachers to return to the classroom after having children, an important aspect of which is calls for improvements in nursery care.

14 Nov: Start of the Off the Shelf campaign against soft pornography in W. H. Smiths, spearheaded by Clare Short MP, the Campaign against Pornography and the National Union of Students.

22 Nov: Lord Houghton introduces an Abortion Act 1967 Amendment Bill to place a 24-week limit on legal terminations in an attempt to prevent pro-life MPs attempting

to amend the government's Human Fertilization and Embryology Bill with abortion clauses.

4 Dec: Gabriella Cox, *Working Women – A Study of Pay and Hours*, Greater Manchester Low Pay Unit, warns of increasing low pay, minimal employment rights and exploitation.

14 Dec: Houghton's Bill passes its second reading in Lords by 61 to 48.

Environmental Issues

ANDREW BLOWERS

During 1989 environmental issues became firmly entrenched on the British political agenda. Throughout the year the privatization of water aroused concerns about water quality and the impending privatization of electricity ensured that the environmental legacy of nuclear wastes remained a prominent issue. The blockage at Tilbury of a cargo of polychlorinated biphenyl (PCBs) from Canada destined for Pontypool and the refusal of other ports to accept such cargoes indicated the alarm that could be generated by toxic wastes. There were, too, more global concerns as attention remained focused on the depletion of the ozone layer and on climatic change through the 'greenhouse effect'.

A number of opinion polls registered the importance of the environment as a political issue. A Department of the Environment survey indicated that environment and pollution were regarded by 30 per cent of the population (unprompted) as one of the most important problems the government should deal with, second only to health and social services which attracted 32 per cent.[1] Practical confirmation of this concern was registered by the 15 per cent average vote (up to 20–25 per cent in the Conservative south of England) delivered to the Green Party in the June European elections, the highest in any country. 'For the first time, the electorally insignificant concerns of voters about local environmental issues have become linked with unease about events on a wider canvass, with startling political results.'[2]

There is no simple explanation for the emergence of the environment to political salience in the UK at the end of the 1980s. In particular there was an emphasis on global problems. None of the issues was particularly new. Scientists had been concerned about the ozone layer and the greenhouse effect for some time. The vast oil spillage from the *Exxon Valdez* off Alaska in March had riveted international attention on the consequences of pollution in a pristine environment. But, major incidents had occurred before such as Three Mile Island in 1979, Bhopal in 1984 and Chernobyl in 1986 and the routine but cumulative degradation of forests, soils, water and the atmosphere was a matter of scientific record and constant media attention.

It was the manner in which various environmental issues were consistently seized on across the political spectrum that made 1989 a year of the environment. The interesting question is whether the environment had become permanently established as a significant political issue or was of transitory interest and likely to fade when a deepening recession re-established the political priority of immediate economic concerns. Changes in public awareness, political ideology and international co-operation suggest that environmental issues will not easily be dislodged from the political agenda.

Responding To Public Awareness

Whereas the debates about limits to growth in the early 1970s were largely academic, the global concerns of 1989 achieved a widespread popular appeal as reflected in the media and public opinion. This was because such notions as a hole in the ozone layer letting in the deadly rays of the sun or global warming sufficient to bring about flooding, drought and other climatic changes were palpable. The link between fossil fuel power stations and the burning of tropical forests with the creation of greenhouse gases was clearly understood. People had already become familiar with the possibility of leukaemia clusters associated with nuclear installations or diseases caused by nitrates, lead or other pollutants in waste supplies. They were aware of the poisoning of forests, lakes and rivers by acid rain and the dangers of toxic chemicals and hazardous wastes. They were concerned about the damage to amenity and wildlife by development. Added to the 'new' global issues there was a growing awareness of cause and effect and recognition that future prosperity depended on environmental conservation and management.

Greater public understanding lent increased credibility to scientific evidence of environmental deterioration. In the previous upsurge of environmentalism during the 1970s the neo-Malthusian predictions of global environmental disaster were deservedly discredited for lack of empirical evidence and the assumption of exponential trends. Until recently governments and industry were dominated by a scientific elite concerned primarily with increasing production rather than with environmental conservation or protection. The authority of this elite has been diminishing partly because it has proved vulnerable to challenge by environmental counter expertise. The protestations that various industrial processes are safe and harmless have been progressively undermined by the evidence of nuclear accidents, pollution incidents and the discovery of environmentally related diseases. Conversely, the carefully researched and qualified scientific accounts of changes in the ozone layer and global warming have achieved both credibility and widespread attention. The contribution of scientific research has been an important factor in the growing concern about environmental problems.

The government, led by the Prime Minister herself, has responded to this public awareness. Beginning with her speech to the Royal Society in September 1988 announcing 'The Government espouses the concept of sustainable economic development'[3] the Prime Minister endeavoured to capture the environmental issue for the Conservatives. She presided over the international conference on the ozone layer in March 1989, held a Cabinet seminar on global warming in April and replaced Nicholas Ridley with Christopher Patten as Secretary of State in July to give a more environmentally acceptable image to her government. By the end of the year a Green Bill was promulgated to give some substance to the rhetoric. The Conservatives' concern for the environment was intended, in part, to prevent the issue being monopolized by their opponents but it also reflected a response to both general and specific public concerns.

It must be said that public concern was a mixture of general apprehension about a deteriorating environment and the specific expression of material self-interest. There was the general anxiety about the threats to the quality of life brought about by industrial pollution, population pressure and development. There was also the specific defence of amenity demonstrated during 1989 over the Channel Tunnel in Kent and the proposed new town at Foxley Wood in Hampshire. There was certainly an element of national 'not in my backyard' feeling in the protests over toxic waste imports. The fact that such wastes have to go somewhere, possibly to a poorer country where wastes cannot be so carefully handled, was largely ignored in the publicity generated by the issue in August. There is a cynical side to environmental protest. 'Who cares about the Third World – or the workers of Pontypool – when television can show Jonathan and Samantha daubing freighters from daddy's rubber dinghy?'[4]

The Impact of Political Ideology

The government's commitment to reduced public expenditure and its support for the market and deregulation provoked considerable controversy over environmental issues. There was concern that toxic waste management had been neglected through a lack of inspectors and too great a dependence on waste disposers who 'too often deploy the cheapest tolerable option'.[5] In its proposed re-examination of waste disposal the Government intended to end the 'poacher/gamekeeper' conflict of interest arising from local authorities having both waste regulation and disposal functions.[6] But the proposed establishment of 'arm's length' local authority waste disposal companies was 'likely to result in a progressive privatization of waste disposal'.[7] And it was the government's privatization proposals, notably for water and electricity, that caused the most widespread environmental concern during 1989.

In order to prepare the market for water privatization and to avoid big price rises for the consumer the government had to write off debts of £5 billion and to provide a so-called 'green dowry' of over £1 billion for investment in sewage and water treatment works. The new companies were granted immunity from prosecution while they upgraded polluting works to meet appropriate standards. In some cases this is likely to take another decade at least. It was also feared that in order to meet investment commitments while avoiding high price rises and paying shareholders the companies might be tempted to sell off their land assets for profitable but inappropriate development in attractive countryside. The introduction of a National Rivers Authority to police river quality was not matched by a similar inspectorate to police drinking water quality leaving this function to the enfeebled local authorities.

The government claimed that privatization would attract new capital and be 'good for our tap water, good for our rivers and good for the seas around our coasts'.[8] Opponents argued that privatization would not introduce competition into a natural monopoly industry like water. Public ownership and accountability was more likely to achieve environmental quality standards than private ownership where the overriding priority would be for profit and dividends.

The preparations for the even bigger (£20 billion) sell-off of the electricity industry in 1990 also had environmental implications. The massive financial liability in terms of decommissioning and waste disposal was the main reason for the withdrawal of the Maginox stations from the float in April, followed by the remaining nuclear plants in November, and the abandonment of plans for new pressurized water reactor (PWR) stations beyond Sizewell B. The government's support for nuclear power on the grounds that it reduced the greenhouse effect had been undermined by its own privatization plans.

Environmental problems arising from nuclear power remained. The reprocessing industry was surviving in Sellafield partly on foreign orders and consent was given in October for a fast breeder reprocessing plant at Dounreay (although this is unlikely to be built, if at all, until well into the next century). Reprocessing and the existing nuclear power stations would continue to create a vast burden of nuclear waste to be dealt with by future generations. In March Sellafield and Dounreay were identified as the two sites to be investigated for a deep repository for low and intermediate level nuclear wastes. The failure of the government to secure greenfield sites for nuclear waste disposal in the face of intense local opposition during 1983–7 had led, inevitably, to a pragmatic retreat to these two nuclear oases on the grounds that 'it would be best to explore first those sites where there is some measure of local support for civil nuclear activities'.[9]

The privatization of water and electricity engendered scepticism about the priority given to environmental matters by the government. By contrast, the publicity given by Secretary of State, Christopher Patten, to the publication of the Pearce Report in August was greeted with welcome and surprise by those interested in environmental issues. The report presented an economic approach to environmental management consistent with a market ideology.[10] It advocated placing a monetary value on 'free' environmental goods so that there was an incentive to conserve natural capital for present and future generations. 'Prices should reflect the true costs of production and use'[11] and could be applied in the form of taxes (for example, a carbon tax on fossil fuels) or incentives. Market-based incentives would supplement systems of environmental regulation and recover the increasing costs involved in conserving global environmental resources. Critics pointed out the problems in valuing future unknown environmental resources or those whose scarcity value might increase over time and the different valuations that might be placed by different societies over time. But the significance of the Pearce Report was that it indicated to government that environmental management is a necessary, and expensive, condition for future economic development.

There were other signs in the latter part of the year that the ideological tone of government thinking towards the environment was changing. For example, the Secretary of State in preparing his 'green plan' found the 142 per cent increase in vehicle mileage forecast over the next 40 years unacceptable in face of the need to reduce carbon dioxide levels. Statements of support for the town and country planning system and for new settlements after a decade of deregulation and developer power hinted at a shift in the government's ideological emphasis on the primacy of the market as the arbiter of urban development. But the more profound changes in the government's attitude to the environment were prompted by international changes and pressures.

International Concerns and Co-operation

During the past decade the EC has been especially vigorous in the prosecution of environmental policies for the reduction of pollution. Over 100 environmental directives have been adopted and around 50 are in the pipeline. Britain has tended to respond, often reluctantly, to initiatives but 'it has not succeeded in turning the tide'.[12] During the 1980s procrastination over the adoption of EC environmental directives on sulphur oxide emissions or dirty beaches had identified Britain as 'the dirty man of Europe'. During 1989 the first steps were taken in the programme of desulphurization of the major fossil fuel power stations. Of the 403 bathing beaches in England and Wales 34 per cent still failed the EC's bacteriological standard in 1989. Above all, water quality was the issue in 1989. Although British water quality had been steadily improving and legislation was 'remarkably broad and adaptable',[13] by 1989 evidence of declining standards was accumulating. The drinking water directive was signed in 1980 for compliance by 1985 but in 1989 the proposed standards were exceeded in many parts of the country. EC limits were breached in 298 supplies distributed to 1.7 million people in the case of nitrate, two million in the case of lead and a similar number in the case of aluminium. The relaxation of discharge consents in advance of privatization had delayed the timetable for clean-up well beyond 1995. Breaches of nitrate levels in Norfolk and lead levels in parts of Scotland led to legal action being taken against Britain in the European Court of Justice by the EC Environment Commissioner and further legal action was in prospect for delays in implementing clean-up of other polluting substances. Meanwhile Britain was challenging a proposed Environmental

Directive on prevention of nitrate pollution on the grounds that its general application failed to take into account local environments and farming practices. While it might not prevent nitrate leaching it would certainly result in 'severe cut-backs in output and disruption of rural society'.[14] The government introduced its own approach to the problem with a pilot scheme of 12 nitrate sensitive areas in East Anglia and the West Midlands where the effectiveness of land-use controls on leaching could be monitored.

Britain has shown more vigorous leadership in drawing international attention towards global environmental problems. The 'Saving the Ozone Layer' conference in London in March increased the support for phasing out certain CFCs by the end of the century, emphasized the development of substitutes and acknowledged the need for technology transfer and aid to the Third World. Even if planned reductions were achieved, the level of CFCs was likely to rise to six parts per billion by volume, three times the safe level. Similarly, the levels of greenhouse gases would inevitably rise as a result of the increase worldwide in fossil fuel power stations, vehicles, forest burning and other processes. According to a parliamentary report greater energy efficiency and conservation offered by far the best prospects of reducing the output of greenhouse gases.[15] Despite the warnings of global catastrophe, possibly within a generation, there was little urgency apparent in 1989 with the government content to await further research and to rely on market mechanisms and perhaps a resurgence of nuclear power to achieve modest reductions in the output of carbon dioxide.

A major reason for the development of global environmental concern during 1989 was the dramatic change in the political map of Europe. The general thawing in East West relations culminating in the astounding emancipation of the Eastern European states during 1989 reduced the fear of nuclear war. As fear of global war decreased attention began to turn to the possibility of global environmental disaster. The ending of the Cold War may encourage dialogue on global environmental problems which could eventually lead to action. If that is the consequence of events in Europe then 1989 will, indeed, be recorded as the year of the environment.

Environmental Issues – Ephemeral or Enduring?

It is unlikely that environmental issues will continue to command the attention lavished on them during 1989. As the economic boom ends and a period of economic retrenchment begins so we may expect a reversion to more immediate material concerns. Concern for the environment is more likely to flourish at times of relative prosperity among the relatively affluent with a material interest in defending their quality of life. An outcome of this has been the environmental inequalities which reinforce the patterns of social inequality in British life.

The apparently widespread interest in the environment during 1989 may not yet have resulted in a basic shift of attitudes. The environment has so far achieved enhanced political status only in a rhetorical sense. Provided it costs nothing everyone can subscribe to the idea of a better environment; it is a matter of consensus not conflict. The rise of green consumerism and the increased consumption of discount lead-free petrol are undemanding and passive responses to environmental problems. It is a relatively simple matter for political parties to emphasize their support in principle for environmental policies, as they all noticeably hastened to do in the wake of the success of the Green Party in 1989. Indeed the government promoted its green credentials by a strident emphasis on global environmental problems.

Meanwhile, on water quality and air pollution action has occurred only belatedly after continual pressure from the EC. Little has been done to encourage energy conservation which would make by far the biggest contribution to the problem of the greenhouse effect.[16] Indeed, any gains made on this front are likely to be wiped out by the anticipated growth in vehicle usage encouraged by the government's preference for road building over public transport. In other policy areas such as the proposed splitting up of the Nature Conservancy Council the government seemed to be pursuing a fragmented rather than an integrated approach to environmental matters.

It is highly likely that the political importance ascribed to the environment in 1989 will not be matched by early political action for three reasons. First, is the high economic costs involved. It is estimated that the costs of environmental controls required to reduce power station and vehicle emissions, to improve water quality and to mitigate global warming will double to 3 per cent of GDP in the 1990s. Recent political history suggests that the demands of industry, private consumers and investors will encourage delays in implementing clean-ups. Research, inspection and monitoring also require investment which has not been forthcoming hitherto. In the run-up to the next election both the government and their opponents will focus attention on short term economic issues with a high rate of return in votes. The environmental issues that will pay most dividends will be those which affect specific constituencies rather than those whose impact is barely perceptible in the short run.

Secondly, action to ameliorate environmental deterioration implies profound social changes. The pursuit of individual competition, self-interest and consumerism is not conducive to the conservation of environmental resources. During 1989 there was some recognition of this fact. 'What we need is not "no" but "green" growth. We need growth which doesn't sacrifice tomorrow in order to consume mindlessly today.'[17] But the social implications are profound. They include restrictions on the use of the car, prevention of population dispersal through planning constraints, strict regulation of pollution, changing agricultural practices and encouragement of energy conservation. Conservative ideology will resist the higher taxation and greater state intervention that will be necessary. And it will be difficult for any government to impose severe restrictions on travel. Furthermore, the social costs of environmental policy will be unevenly spread and are likely to be divisive.

The difficulty of achieving international co-operation is a third reason for deferring action. Nations are reluctant to surrender any sovereignty and even the EEC has made slow progress in implementing its environmental directives. Co-ordinated action involving rich and poor countries will prove much more difficult. Third World countries are naturally unwilling to forego the benefits of growth. Much of the future growth in fossil fuel consumption will come from major countries like China and India. The destruction of tropical forests provides resources, profits and growth for hard-pressed economies. The industrialized countries will find it difficult to cut their pollution and consumption of environmental resources while, at the same time, compensating the Third World for growth foregone. It is most improbable that countries with different living standards and ideologies will be able to act in concert to defend the global environment. The present costs of inaction are low and the future consequences uncertain.

There were, however, signs during 1989 that the political costs of avoiding action on the environment were rising. The interest in the environment appears to have broken out of its middle class, academic and pressure group confines and become a genuinely popular issue as reflected in the consistent attention reflected in the popular media and the responses to public opinion polls. The squalor of litter in town and country, of dirty rivers, polluted air, decaying and congested cities, repetitive design and built development and disfigured landscapes have become matters of heightened public awareness and concern. Furthermore attention has been focused on the 'environment' as the natural surroundings upon which we depend for resources, amenity, health and survival. Dominant issues in 1989 were the ozone layer and global warming which transcended political and national frontiers. The more specific and localized issues which emerged in 1989, notably water quality and toxic waste, also related to a general anxiety about environmental deterioration. Consciousness about the environment was raised during 1989. It remains to be seen whether concern can be translated into national and international action before it is too late to restore environmental deterioration and the damage to the global ecosystem.

Notes

1. ENDS (Environmental Data Services Ltd.) Report 176, September 1989, p. 3.
2. ENDS, Report 173, June 1989, p. 11
3. *Science and Public Affairs*, 1989, 4, pp. 3–9, p. 6.
4. Simon Jenkins, *The Sunday Times*, 13 August 1989.
5. House of Commons Environment Committee, Session 1988–89, Second Report, *Toxic Waste*, p. xiv.
6. Department of the Environment, *The Role and Functions of Waste Disposal Authorities*, a consultation paper.
7. ENDS, Report 176, September 1989, p. 25.

8. Secretary of State for the Environment, Christopher Patten, speech to the Conservative Party Conference, 11 October, 1989.
9. Secretary of State for the Environment, Nicholas Ridley, *Hansard*, 21 March, cols. 505–6.
10. D. Pearce et al, *Blueprint for a Green Economy*, London, Earthscan Publications, 1989.
11. Ibid, p. 170.
12. D. Baldock, 'The European Community and conservation in the Thatcher decade', *Ecos*, 10 (4), 1989, pp. 33–37, p.35.
13. N. Haigh, *EEC Environmental Policy and Britain*, London, Environmental Data Services, p. 293.
14. House of Lords, Select Committee on the European Communities, Session 1988–89, *Nitrate in Water*, para. 180.
15. House of Commons Energy Committee, Session 1988–89, 6th. Report, *Energy Policy Implications of the Greenhouse Effect*.
16. British Association of Nature Conservationists, *Ground Truth: A Report on the Prime Minister's First Green Year*, Media Natura, 1989.
17. See note 8.

Chronology

20 Jan: Government launches £50 million scheme to reafforest the bleak, despoiled countryside of central Scotland.

30 Jan: National Radiological Protection Board says that the radiation dose levels permitted by Parliament are intolerably high. It argues that the limit should be 15 millisieverts, not 50.

1 Feb: EC Commission rejects 'golden share' arrangements to prevent foreign takeovers of the water companies for five years after privatization.

3 Feb: Private water companies announce steep price rises in 1989.

5 Feb: EC Commission warns the government that the proposed post-privatization water quality controls may fall short of EC standards.

6 Feb: Government admits it has no powers to curb planned price rises by the private water companies of up to 70 per cent.

7 Feb: Flooding in Inverness.

8 Feb: Ministers refuse to back down on the water control immunity issue. EC Commission threatens to take the issue to the European Court.

20 Feb: Announcement that the privatized water companies are to be allowed to recoup the estimated £1.5 billion cost of installing water meters directly from the consumer.

24 Feb: Department of the Environment statistics reveal a large increase in toxic waste imports, water pollution and exhaust emissions.

Joan Ruddock's Control of Pollution (Amendment) Bill introduced in the Commons. It aims to set up a registration scheme for waste carriers and tighten up the laws on fly-tippers.

2 Mar: EC agrees to ban CFCs by 2000.

4–7 Mar: International conference on protecting the ozone layer in London. Urgent calls for restrictions on the use of CFCs made.

6 Mar: Natural Environment Research Council report warns that global resources are being depleted at an unsustainable rate and that waste is being deposited at rates that cannot be absorbed by the global system without damage.

7 Mar: Confirmation that a European Stratospheric Ozone Research Co-ordination Centre is to be set up at Cambridge.

8 Mar: Commons Environment Select Committee criticizes the inadequate management and supervision of toxic waste disposal and landfill sites by both local and central government since the 1974 Control of Pollution Act.

14 Mar: Unleaded petrol duty cut by 4p a gallon in the budget, making it 10p cheaper than ordinary petrol. The subsequent decision of the oil companies to raise the price of ordinary petrol by 4p rather than cut the price of unleaded is criticized as cynical.

1 Apr: Campaign for the reduction in emissions from diesel engines launched by Friends of the Earth.

11 Apr: Ark, a new environmental group, predicts that Britain will have a radically revised coastline by 2050 because of the greenhouse effect.

12 Apr: Commons Select Committee on Energy criticizes British Nuclear Fuels and warns against Britain becoming the world's nuclear dump.

13 Apr: European Parliament presses for catalytic converters to be compulsory for all new cars by 1993.

17 Apr: HM Pollution Inspectorate criticizes arrangements for the disposal of household and hazardous waste by metropolitan councils.

18 Apr: EC Commission orders Britain to clean up its drinking water, threatening action in the European Court if the government does not comply.

19 Apr: Vauxhall announces moves to fit catalytic converters to all models. Ford has already announced that these will be fitted to certain models.

20 Apr: Government announces plans to make polluters face charges for the cost of tackling the resulting pollution.

26 Apr: One day Cabinet seminar at Chequers of green experts on global warming.

2 May: New safeguards to protect environmentally sensitive land marked for sale by the water companies after privatization are announced as the Lords debates the Water Bill.

8 May: Attempts to amend Water Bill to prevent exploitation of land after privatization rejected in the Lords.

15 May: Lords Select Committee on Science and Technology criticizes the government's record on the handling of toxic waste.

Greenpeace report finds high levels of mercury contamination in the fish in the seas around the British coasts.

22 May: Write-offs of debt of £5.5 billion from the water industry before privatization announced by the government.

23 May: South West Water, which was responsible for the water supply poisoning at Camelford in July 1988 admits that there have been two more recent cases of poisoning of the water supply with aluminium sulphate.

ICI suggests a chlorine treatment to solve the problem of sewage affecting coastal bathing.

Leaked letter by Lord Marshall, the Chairman of the CEGB, written in 1987, published in *Time Out*. It confesses that the environmental lobby had been right about Sellafield and the nuclear industry wrong.

24 May: Heatwave ends in violent storms in which four die.

Britain backs EC demand for compulsory fitting of three-way catalytic converters to all new vehicles by 1993.

1 June: Water authorities reveal applications have been made to allow more than 900 sewage treatment plants to flout the law over the next three years.

5 June: Important speech by Sir Crispin Tickell, British Ambassador to the UN, to the Royal Society on global warming.

8 June: In the Lords the government rejects pleas to protect special conservation sites on land owned by the water authorities from development after privatization.

9 June: Nicholas Ridley, *Policies on Pollution*, Centre for Policy Studies, suggests taxes on fossil fuels to cover the cost of the environmental damage they cause.

EC environment ministers agree to cut exhaust emissions from smaller cars by two-thirds by the end of 1992.

22 June: Government drops £1 billion plan for replacing lead plumbing.

28 June: ICI agrees to stop dumping waste from Billingham in the Tees estuary and the North Sea by the mid-1990s.

2 July: *Solving the Greenhouse Dilemma*, Association for the Conservation of Energy, published. It argues that emissions could be cut by almost a quarter in the next 15 years without damaging the economy.

3 July: Because of water shortages 16 water bodies banned hosepipes, with 6 per cent of the population affected.

4 July: Antarctic Minerals Bill, which ratifies the Convention on the Regulation of Antarctic Mineral Resources, passes its second reading in the Commons.

6 July: Thirteenth report of the Royal Commission on Environmental Pollution (chaired by Lord Lewis), *The Release of Genetically Engineered Organisms to the Environment*, proposes strict new laws to control the environmental consequences of genetic engineering.

Water Bill becomes law.

Environmental guidelines for the privatized electricity industry announced.

7 July: Survey carried out under the aegis of the UN Economic Commission for Europe shows air pollution and insect attacks threaten the destruction of one-third of Britain's forests and two-thirds of its oak trees.

Code of practice on conservation, public access and recreation for the new water businesses announced.

11 July: Agreement between Chris Patten, the Minister for Overseas Development, and Brazil, under which Britain will make a contribution to the preservation of the rainforests.

Announcement that the Nature Conservancy Council is to be split up and put into the three national Countryside Commissions (including a new one for Wales).

17 July: Commons Select Committee on Energy report criticizes the government for its lack of policies to combat global warming by the burning of fossil fuels.

20 July: Report on the Camelford poisoning of the water supply in July 1988 is published.

Tighter anti-litter and dog-fouling laws proposed in a consultative paper.

21–24 July: Problems with contaminated water in London as well as hosepipe bans.

24 July: More areas introduce hosepipe bans.

25 July: Plan to create community forests on existing farmland, meadows and woodland is launched by the Countryside Commission and the Forestry Commission.

28 July: London weather centre reports that 1989 is the sunniest summer of the century so far.

Report by Dr Paul Ewings in the *British Medical Journal* indicates that the incidence of child leukaemia near the Hinkley Point nuclear power stations is nearly twice the national average but concludes that there is no evidence that radiation is to blame.

31 July: Pilot areas designated in a government campaign to reduce the flow of nitrates into the water supply.

2 Aug: Government provides £6 billion dowry to sweeten water-privatization (consisting of £4.4 billion write-off of debts and a £1 billion cash injection).

7 Aug: Friends of the Earth launch a nationwide scheme to provide comprehensive information on where people can take products for recycling.

Government's system for regulating pesticides is criticized by environmentalists.

9 Aug: *Greenpeace* blockades Tilbury to prevent a ship carrying hazardous waste from docking. This ship, with Canadian toxic waste on board, was told to leave the port without unloading.

10 Aug: Bristol joins Liverpool and Tilbury in refusing to handle toxic waste.

11 Aug: About 250 people evacuated from Aughton, near Ormskirk, Lancashire, after a chemical fire at a nearby factory sent a toxic gas cloud over the area.

15 Aug: Taxes on fossil fuels, pesticides, fertilizers and other products which pollute the biosphere are suggested in a report for the Department of the Environment by Professor David Pearce.

16 Aug: Britain is resisting a tough new EC directive to improve the safety of ships carrying toxic and other hazardous or polluting materials into EC ports. The Commons Select Committee on European Legislation reports on this issue.

18 Aug: Introduction of emergency standpipes in Devon and Cornwall threatened.

19 Aug: Thirty-mile oil slick in the Mersey estuary after 150 tonnes of crude oil escaped from a Shell pipeline under the river.

22 Aug: A man in Devon becomes the first to be fined for breaking the hosepipe ban.

Lords Select Committee on the European Communities report *Habitat and Species Protection*, HMSO, published. It deals with the environmental impact of the EC's agricultural policies and development policies in rural areas.

25 Aug: Announcement of £14 million sea defence building programme on the east coast of Norfolk.

Scathing attacks on water authorities as they reveal £22 million has already been spent on their seven-month campaign promoting the industry.

29 Aug: Critical responses to government plans to protect genetically manipulated organisms are voiced by the leading genetic scientist, John Beringer, and the Health and Safety Commission. A research programme into the impact of releasing such organisms into the environment is launched by a consortium headed by the Department of Trade and Industry.

31 Aug: *Integrated Pollution Control and Local Authority Air Pollution Controls: Public Access to Information* Green Paper published. It suggests a register of industrial pollution but would allow companies to avoid declaring commercially sensitive information.

Trond Iversen, Leanor Terrason and Anton Eliassen *Transatlantic Sulphur Transport: Preliminary Estimates from a Three-Dimension Euterian Model* Norwegian Meteorological Institute, finds significant quantities of acid rain in north Europe, not least the UK, are likely to have originated in north America.

1 Sept: Four families apply for writs against British Nuclear Fuels alleging radioactive emissions from Sellafield caused leukaemia in their children.

Details of the tough regulatory regime for policing the water industry when it is privatized in November are released. The National Rivers Authority becomes the responsible body for controlling pollution and improving the quality of waterways, lakes and coastal waters.

Consultative document on plans to cut harmful emissions from power stations issued.

8 Sept: Henley Centre calls for a 'green' tax on energy consumption.

12 Sept: New disaster database to provide vital information on how to cope with tragedies on a massive scale to be set up by disaster prevention and limitation unit at Bradford University.

Oil slick off Whitley Bay.

13 Sept: Nine tonnes of aluminium sulphate leak from a water treatment works in Wales.

14 Sept: Bryan Gould, Labour's trade and industry spokesman, warns investors in the water industry that they would face a steep financial loss on shares as a future Labour government returned the industry to state control.

Warning of rapid rise of global warming at the annual meeting of the BAAS.

Reservoirs in East Anglia closed for recreation because of spread of potentially toxic blue-green algae.

15 Sept: Three reservoirs in the South West closed for recreation for the same reason.

16 Sept: *Report on the Disposal of Waste at Sea 1986 and 1987* reports dumping of waste at sea is ecologically and economically sound.

17 Sept: Two oil tankers collide near the Humber estuary, leading to large oil slicks.

18 Sept: *Working Group on Ionising Radiation Report 1987–88*, Health and Safety Executive published. It deals with radiation levels in the tin mining and nuclear power industries.

Chris Patten has urgent talks with Carlo di Ripa Meana, the EC environment commissioner, in an attempt to prevent legal action over British water standards.

19 Sept: South West Water lifts hosepipe ban.

20 Sept: EC confirms it is to prosecute Britain over water standards.

24 Sept: Coastwatch UK, a week of checks on the state of Britain's beaches, is launched.

25 Sept: A further 19 reservoirs are found to contain blue-green algae according to the National Rivers Authority.

National Lead-Free Petrol Week begins with a call for a cut in road tax on cars fitted with catalytic converters by the Campaign for Lead-Free Air.

26 Sept: Environmentalists' critical assessment of the year's progress since Mrs Thatcher made her green speech to the Royal Society, *Ground Truth: The Prime Minister's First Green Year*, Media Natura, published.

Proposed changes to the system for the importation of waste announced.

28 Sept: Hundreds of gallons of diesel are split into Pipp Brook, a tributary of the River Mole, in Surrey.

1 Oct: Control of Substances Hazardous to Health regulations, governing the use of dangerous materials at the workplace, come into force.

Tanker spills 6,000 gallons of crude oil in Southampton Water.

11 Oct: Review of all government policy affecting the environment announced by Chris Patten.

20 Oct: Details of a £1.1 billion investment programme to clean up British coastal bathing waters announced.

28–29 Oct: Hurricane force winds cause widespread flooding and damage and at least six deaths.

2 Nov: Tests in the North Sea suggest that global warming may be proceeding up to 20 per cent faster than previously thought.

3 Nov: Prospectus for shares in the privatized water companies published.

7 Nov: Britain, USA and Japan at the environmental conference in the Netherlands block a proposed freeze on carbon dioxide emissions by 2000 at 1988 levels and a 20 per cent reduction by 2005.

8 Nov: Mrs Thatcher in a speech to the UN announces that Britain is to set up a centre for climate prediction and pledges £100 million aid to protect and regenerate the tropical rainforests.

21 Nov: Green Bill announced in the Queen's speech to deal with polluters.

22 Nov: Development is destroying many wildlife sites with the connivance of central and local government according to the Nature Conservancy Council in its annual report. Details of water privatization are announced.

24 Nov: New conservation group, *Plantlife*, is set up by David Bellamy to protect the wild plant life and habitats of Britain.

27 Nov: Sixth Report from the House of Lords Select Committee on Science and Technology: *The Greenhouse Effect* warns that research into climate change and the greenhouse effect is likely to be impeded by the shortage of scientists with relevant qualifications.

11 Dec: Performance report on the Pollution Inspectorate shows it has been falling short of its goals even though these have been set lower and lower.

12 Dec: Scheme to cut emissions of greenhouse gases, *Getting out of the Greenhouse*, published by Friends of the Earth.

13 Dec: Review of the National Parks and threats posed to them announced by Sir Derek Barber, chairman of the Coutryside Commission.

20 Dec: Environment Protection Bill published. It stipulates various pollution and litter controls and regulations on the release of the products of genetic engineering to the environment. It also entails the break-up of the Nature Conservancy Council.

28 Dec: Countryside Commission issues a ten-point manifesto for the 1990s.

Town and Country Planning

GORDON E. CHERRY

The social and economic context for planning in 1989 may be suggested by a number of indicators. Economic growth slackened, but industrial recovery continued in areas hard-hit earlier in the decade. The North–South divide in previous years had been drawn well to the South, but evidence suggested that the line dividing the prosperous southern half of the UK from the slower growing North, while still beginning at the Severn estuary, now extended further North East. A report by Cambridge Econometrics and the Northern Ireland Economic Research Centre, *Regional Economic Prospects: Analysis and Forecasts of the Year 2000* in January 1989, considered that the buoyant economic activity of the South East would decentralize to neighbouring regions, the future perhaps resembling the situation in the 1950s when the North, Scotland and Northern Ireland languished so much.

The 1989 edition of *Regional Trends* from the government's Statistical Service confirmed the economic dominance of the South East; the figure of 7.7 million in employment (in 1988), out of a population of 17 million, showed an increase of 500,000 since 1981. The South East now accommodates 30 per cent of the UK population on 11 per cent of the land area and has experienced a population increase of 1.8 per cent between 1981 and 1987. Inter-regional migration figures indicate that Wales is attracting more population than it is losing, while Scotland and Northern Ireland are experiencing a net loss. Regions showing a net increase in population include the East Midlands, East Anglia, the South East (excluding London) and the South West.

National population forecasts, published by the Office of Population, Censuses and Surveys (OPCS) in October 1989, indicated an increase of 4.4 million (8 per cent), to reach 61.3m for the UK by 2027. Within the same period the population of England is projected to increase by 10 per cent, Wales and Northern Ireland to rise by 6 per cent respectively, and Scotland to decrease by 11 per cent.

The South East

The South East can now be considered a problem region by virtue of the land use pressures occasioned by demand for new dwellings, the continued decentralization of population and jobs, the burgeoning service and 'high-tech' sectors, and the future impacts of the Single European Market and the Channel Tunnel. In this situation, the publications of Serplan (The London and South East Regional Planning Conference) have been significant. Early in 1988 the Secretary of State for the Environment asked Serplan for a re-examination of the dwellings required for the period 1991–2001, consequent upon the publication of new household formation projections. Serplan revised the figures upwards from 460,000 dwellings to 570,000 for the South East: 175,000 in London and 395,000 in the 12 South Eastern counties.

The Environment Secretary, Nicholas Ridley, published draft strategic planning guidance for London on 6 March. This consultation document covered a range of planning matters, including the number of houses, for which each borough should make provision in the 1990s. The guidance established the framework within which the London boroughs should prepare their Unitary Development Plans. It was widely criticized by professional bodies and special interest groups. The published guidance in July showed only insignificant changes from the draft of March, and criticisms of vagueness, lack of precision, and in particular an absence of policies which linked land use and transport, were pronounced.

Housing problems in the South East assumed a high political profile in July with Nicholas Ridley's announcement that he was 'minded to allow' the proposal of the Consortium Development's proposal for a new settlement at Foxley Wood in North East Hampshire. His appeal inspector had recommended refusal of this development because of its ecological impact, but contemporaneously the panel examining submitted Structure Plan alterations for the region which concluded that in the light of the new target for new dwellings in mid- and North East Hampshire by the year 2001, a new settlement was a better option than the expansion of existing towns and settlements. The Secretary of State agreed, but was roundly condemned by local residents.

Later that month the Secretary of State announced the refusal of planning permission for the building of a new settlement at Stone Bassett in South Oxfordshire. His appeal inspector had recommended refusal of the Consortium Development's proposal for a town of 6,000 dwellings, on the grounds, *inter alia*, that the County Structure Plan already provided for sufficient housing elsewhere. The joy of the local residents was halted the very next day when it was announced that a motorway service station would be built there instead.

In October Foxley Wood returned to centre stage when Nicholas Ridley's successor Christopher Patten overturned the previous announcement. Patten himself was now 'minded to dismiss' Consortium Development's appeal. The onus was placed before Hampshire County Council to come forward with fresh proposals. It is unlikely that this will be the end of the story; planning in the South East has been demonstrated to be inconsistent and characterized by uncertainty; and a more positive and determined approach is required. Serplan's consultation paper on South East Regional Planning Strategy, published in August, made comprehensive proposals for accommodating growth in places such as inner London, the East Thames Corridor and in certain northern and coastal towns. Meanwhile Consortium Developments could reflect on a number of years of trying to build new settlements beyond the London fringe; with an earlier refusal at Tillingham Hall in Essex, no approval from the government has yet been forthcoming.

Urban Affairs

The most prominent issue brought together the questions of housing, environment and quality of life in British cities. It focused very often on architecture and building styles, and conveyed responses to modernism and post-modernism; it produced a clash both between and within professions, notably architecture and planning; and Prince Charles took a lead in proclaiming the virtues of buildings of human scale, rather than the massive and the impersonal.

The architect Leon Krier unveiled his Master Planning Objectives in June for the Poundbury development on 200 acres of Duchy of Cornwall land at Dorchester; four separate quarters, all focusing on a new town centre, containing squares, avenues and civic buildings will comprise the new settlement which will increase the size of Dorchester by about one-third over a 15-year period. This proposal echoes the philosophy expressed in Prince Charles' book *A Vision of Britain: A Personal View of Architecture*, published in September, itself an expansion of his acclaimed BBC TV documentary shown in October 1988. His testament is based on 'ten principles on which we can build': the place, hierarchy, scale, harmony, enclosure, materials, decoration, art, signs and lights, and community. The Prince's message is that 'The skills, the crafts, the art that went into the architecture of the past are still there – just. But they need to be revived and put to work again, so that we can build cities, towns and villages which seem to have grown out of the historical fabric of Britain and which better reflect the true aspirations of its people. We must concentrate on creating environments in which people can prosper psychologically, as human beings, not merely as cogs in a mechanical process. We need design and layout which positively encourage neighbourliness, intimacy and, where possible, a sense of shared belonging to a recognized community.'[1]

The battle for architectural style did not eclipse other urban issues. The initial Urban Programme resource allocations, announced in February, amounted to £245 million for 1989–90; other DOE urban initiatives including the Urban Development Corporations, City Grant and Derelict Land Grant, would contribute to a total of £674 million for inner city regeneration for the year. However, the government announced in March that the Housing Action Trust (HAT) scheme would only go ahead in nine of the original 20 designated estates; estates in Sunderland, Leeds, Southwark and Lambeth are to be tackled first. The HAT programme was announced in July 1988 as a means of removing some run-down estates from council control, renovating them and selling them off to new owners. Another discouraging sign came with the publication of the 1986 English House Condition Survey (there is no Scottish equivalent) which revealed that, while the overall condition of the housing stock had improved since 1981, nearly 2.9 million dwellings (15 per cent) of the country's stock failed on one or more of three counts – unfitness, lack of basic amenities and serious disrepair.

Concern about the greening of the urban environment led to the Countryside Commission proposing a major initiative to improve countryside recreation opportunities for disadvantaged urban areas. Extensive urban forests were suggested for the outskirts of Walsall, Jarrow and Havering (East London), each forest site covering about 50 square miles. Later, the Countryside Commission and the Forestry Commission jointly amplified the proposals to create twelve community forests on fringes of major conurbations, sites including Cleveland, Sheffield, West Manchester, East Liverpool, Neath/Port Talbot and North Bristol.

Major development schemes in a number of cities were announced. Perhaps the most significant approval was that for the redevelopment of 1 Poultry in the City of London. An earlier proposal to replace the Victorian buildings (eight of them listed) with a steel and glass tower designed by Mies van der Rohe was refused after an inquiry in 1985. An alternative design by James Stirling, commissioned by Peter Palumbo, Chairman of the Arts Council, was the subject of a public inquiry in June 1988; approval was given by the Environment Secretary in June 1989.

Rural Questions

Arrangements to secure the release of land for low-cost housing development to meet local needs in rural areas were set out by Nicholas Ridley in February. Sites which would not normally be released for housing development could now, exceptionally, be released for low-cost schemes if the planning authority were satisfied as to the need for such housing. The proposal was well received, and a project at Penrith was subsequently approved.

Progress on countryside protection and landscape enhancement included the following. The Countryside Commission in March began the process of designating the Blackdown Hills on the borders of Devon and Somerset as the next Area of Outstanding Natural Beauty in England and Wales. In May, the extent of approved green belt in England stood at 4.5 million acres, compared with 1.8 million acres in 1979. In September two new long distance footpaths (now termed national trails) were proposed for central Wales (120 miles) and the Cotswolds (100 miles); these will add to the 1,676 miles covering the existing ten national trails in the country.

Proposals designed to benefit the landscape and wildlife through grants to farmers were announced in June. Environment 'top up payments' to farmers to encourage them to manage their set-aside fallow land are to be paid in a Countryside

Premium scheme launched for seven counties in the East of England, administered by the Ministry of Agriculture, Fisheries and Food. This represents an extension of a set of policies designed to assist farmers financially to take land out of cultivation.

The Planning System

The government's White Paper on *The Future of Development Plans* was published in January. It proposed the replacement of the present Country Structure Plans by new statements of county planning policies which would concentrate on the key issues which need to be dealt with at county level, taking into account any national and regional planning guidance issued by the Secretary of State. These statements would be accompanied by district-wide development plans. Response from professional bodies and environmental groups bemoaned the downgrading of strategic plan-making powers by county councils.

During the year unprecedented awards of costs were made to local authorities when they were faced with (and won) appeals against proposed development which was flagrantly opposed to government policy. In February Nicholas Ridley refused planning permission for a sub-regional shopping and leisure centre at the M1/M25 interchange between Watford and St Albans; he awarded costs to St Albans City Council against the developers, their proposal being an unacceptable breach of green belt policy. In March Bromley Borough Council were awarded costs against a developer for a similar shopping and leisure proposal – again, an unreasonable pursuit of a case to appeal despite clear policy statements about the need to protect green belts.

A report, commissioned by Nicholas Ridley in July 1988, from Robert Carnwath QC was published in April, and was put out for consultation. It advocated that tougher measures should be available to local planning authorities when the planning controls, which Parliament has laid down, have been breached. The package of measures might be anticipated to make enforcement more effective and remove any incentive for instances of unauthorized development and usage.

Another consultation paper from the Department of the Environment (DOE) and the Welsh Office in May, 'Permitted Use Rights in the Countryside', proposed to exempt a wide range of development in the countryside from the need for planning permission. The context for this was the White Paper published in May 1988, 'Releasing Enterprise', which announced a government review of the range of environmentally acceptable uses of open land, and existing buildings in rural areas, which could be undertaken without the need for planning permission. It was announced in October that the government had decided not to proceed with proposals to relax planning controls in the countryside in England and Wales.

The long running story of the future of County Hall, London, continued. In March 1988 the High Court upheld the view that the ex-GLC building should be retained for local government use. In August 1989 Nicholas Ridley lost his case in the Court of Appeal against Lambeth Council and the Inner London Education Authority and was ordered to pay costs. In the same month planning applications for a massive redevelopment of the County Hall site, which would turn the main building into a luxury hotel and private apartments, demolishing the North and South blocks and creating new office space, were rejected by Lambeth Council. A public inquiry began in September.

Finally, in a somewhat troubled year for the planning system when government was beset by housing and environmental problems particularly in the South East, and when it was accused by its detractors of failing to give adequate strategic guidance, there was a change of Secretary of State for the Environment in July. Nicholas Ridley was replaced by Christopher Patten, a move warmly received in many quarters, not least in Foxley Wood where Ridley's effigy had been burned by irate residents.

Note
1. Prince Charles, *A Vision of Britain: A Personal View of Architecture*, Doubleday, September 1989, pp. 155–6.

Chronology
3 Jan: *Regional Economic Prospects*, Cambridge Econometrics/Northern Ireland Economic Research Centre predicts deepening economic gulf between North and South in the run-up to 2000.

26 Jan: In *Ryeford Homes Ltd et al* v *Sevenoaks District Council et al* Judge John Newey QC declared a planning authority does not owe a duty to individual landowners to exercise care when granting applications for planning permission and accordingly is not liable for loss caused by permitted development by an adjoining landowner.

30 Jan: Government publishes plans for the reform of the development plan system.

16 Feb: Transport 2000 report warns of the danger that the Channel Tunnel will exacerbate the North–South divide and redirect investment into Northern France rather than to Britain.

22 Feb: Nicholas Ridley turns down plans for a major shopping and leisure complex in Hertfordshire and awards the inquiry costs to St Albans City Council against the developers, Town and City Properties (Development) Ltd, thus signalling his preparedness to defend the green belt.
Southgate estate in Runcorn designed by James Stirling in the 1970s is to be demolished.

8 Mar: Action for Cities programme on its first anniversary criticized as a public relations exercise masking failure by Friends of the Earth and, in a study of the North Peckham Task Force, by the Labour MP Harriet Harman.

28 Mar: Planning restrictions in the Lake District to become stricter, forcing house builders to sell only to local people.

31 Mar: Restrictions on the use of national park land after the privatization of the water industry announced, to be incorporated into the Water Bill.

7 Apr: The reshaping of the RIBA is agreed.

19 Apr: First national conference on urban renewal is held in London.

8 June: Peter Palumbo at last wins his battle for permission to redevelop the Mappin and Webb site in the City to a design by James Stirling.

3 July: Richard Rogers attacks the Prince of Wales' views on modern architecture.

7 July: Tacit approval from Nicholas Ridley for a private sector town of 12,500 people at Foxley Wood in Hampshire.

11 July: Attack on both neo-modernism and the Prince of Wales by the new president of the RIBA, Maxwell Hutchinson, in his inaugural address.

Plans to wind up the five Scottish new towns development corporations announced.

21 July: Plans for a new town at Stone Bassett in Oxfordshire turned down by Ridley.

28 July: *Efficient Planning* consultation paper published by the Department of the Environment to cut delays in development. It is criticized by planners and environmentalists.

3 Aug: Serplan (representing the South East's County and District Councils) publish *Into the Next Century* reviewing future planning and transport in the region.

6 Sept: Survey in *Architect's Journal* shows most British architects disagree with the Prince of Wales.

8 Sept: Attack on the Prince of Wales on the BBC Omnibus programme by Professor Peter Carolin of Cambridge.

16 Sept: Prince of Wales publishes his *A Vision of Britain*, Doubleday. This coincides with an exhibition of the same title at the V&A and a counterblast from Maxwell Hutchinson entitled *The Prince of Wales: Right and Wrong*.

20 Sept: Friction between local and central government is the main factor hampering progress on the regeneration of the inner cities according to the Audit Commission's report *Urban Regeneration and Economic Development: The Local Government Dimension*.

24 Sept: MORI poll in *The Sunday Times* finds that 87 per cent approve of Prince Charles' views on architecture.

29 Sept: Plan to redevelop the Lower Don Valley, creating a new airport, a supertram service, a new highway, new communities and 12,000 jobs are announced by Sheffield Development Corporation.

Christopher Patten turns down plans for a town of 4,800 houses at Foxley Wood in Hampshire.

27 Oct: Prince of Wales announces plans for his own summer school for civil architecture.

2 Nov: In a debate on architecture at the V&A Martin Pawley and Professor Colin St John Wilson link Prince Charles' attitudes to architecture with that of the Nazis, remarks which were subsequently condemned by the RIBA and, in Wilson's case, withdrawn. The audience at the debate agreed overwhelmingly that it was a good thing that the Prince had stimulated public debate on architecture, but disagreed by two to one with his solutions and held, by an even greater margin that he had not gone the right way about influencing planning and architectural decisions.

8 Nov: Plan for a National Architecture Centre at the London headquarters of the RIBA announced.

6 Dec: Nine junior ministers appointed to co-ordinate inner city policy in different centres.

Religion

GRACE DAVIE

An outsider who glanced at the chronology of religious events for Britain in 1989 would be understandably confused. Why is so much of it taken up with the reactions to a novel published in September 1988 by Salman Rushdie, a former Muslim? The Muslims are, after all, but a small minority (1.5 million) in British society. We have, in addition, to come to terms with the sheer violence of this episode given the normal expectations of our secularized Western society; a society in which debates – never mind threats to life – about blasphemy are, or so we thought, a thing of the past.

The first section of this essay will look at the religious context into which this storm broke at the beginning of 1989. The second will consider the Rushdie affair itself. The third will cover a range of issues, including questions about the establishment and the churches' involvement in contemporary political debate. A final section will consider the European dimension and some of its implications for the churches.

A Statistical Profile

Religious events always take place within a particular context. In our case, part of this context is determined by the particularities of British history. A second aspect derives from the current patterns of church membership in Britain and the way that these patterns relate to broader currents of religious beliefs. Both these variables (believing and belonging) need to be taken into consideration, for it is their precise combination which characterizes British religion at the end of the 1980s. The relationship between believing and belonging is not fixed; it was different in the past and may well be so in the future. All the more reason, then, to appreciate the particular pressures that derive from the way that these two variables interact at the present time.

We live in a society where only a minority (15 per cent) of our population attend their churches with any degree of regularity. On the other hand, two-thirds or more of British people continue to believe in some sort of God (table 1). The combination of believing *without* belonging has become for many people, if not most, the 'normal' form of religious life.

Table 1. Belief in God (numbers in percentages)

	Britain		Northern Ireland	
	1968	1987	1968	1986
I am certain there is a God	50	42	86	71
I believe there is a God but I am not certain	30	27	10	19
I am really not sure if there is a God or not	10	15	2	6
I do not believe that there is a God but				
I may be wrong	7	10	2	3
I am certain there is no God	2	4	< 1	1
Don't know	–	2	–	–

Source: Michael Svennevig, Ian Haldane, Sharon Spiers and Barrie Gunter, *Godwatching: Viewers, Religion and Television*, John Libbey, London 1988

Within this broad pattern, however, we need to note a number of variations. Wales, Scotland and Northern Ireland have very different religious histories from England. In addition, their populations maintain considerably higher levels of religious practice, notably the Northern Irish. Believing and belonging must, for them, be differently related. There are, in addition, a whole range of social factors – notably age, gender and social class – which affect this relationship and which cross cut national or regional differences. Women demonstrate a higher degree of religiosity than men on almost every indicator. The falling off of religious belief among the young (in addition to religious practice) has, perhaps, reached a critical point well beyond that anticipated by the life cycle. (If this is the case, the implications for the future of religious life in this country are considerable.) Social class factors are complex: what emerges is a closer correlation between believing and belonging among the middle class than elsewhere. Practice increases in higher social groups; paradoxically, so does unbelief.

Active church members in Britain are more or less equally divided between the three following groups: the Anglicans, the 'Other Protestants' and the Roman Catholics (table 2). Of the three the Anglicans are fractionally the smallest group. On the other hand, a very different picture emerges with respect to community size; nominal members of the Church of England form a very sizeable, and significant, section of the English population.

Religious growth, however, is likely to be found elsewhere: that is, among the smaller, evangelical communities (notably, the house–church movement), among the Orthodox and among the representatives of other faiths (table 2). Generalizations are, however, misleading. Each religious minority, Christian and non-Christian, must be looked at individually to grasp its essential characteristics. Not all groups within the 'other faith' category are growing; growth, moreover, takes place for a wide variety of reasons which must be separated out

Table 2.   Church membership 1987

Anglican	1,927,506
Methodist	516,739
Baptist	241,451
Presbyterian	1,346,366
Other	604,458
African/West Indian	65,211
Independent	331,344
Pentecostal	92,549
All others	115,354
Total Protestant	4,636,520
Roman Catholic	2,059,240
Orthodox	231,070
	6,926,830
(*Percentage of adult population*)	15%

Source: Peter Brierley (ed.), *UK Christian Handbook 1989/90*, MARC Europe, Bromley 1988, p. 144

systematically. Within this variety, the regional concentrations of certain religious minorities need particular underlining.

The situation can, perhaps, be summarized as follows: a considerable variety of religious activity (Christian and other) overlaying widespread – and, in England at least, largely Anglican – nominalism. Unbelief (a rather different phenomenon) remains a minority pursuit but is growing, particularly among the young.

The Rushdie Affair

A perceptive commentator linked two seemingly unconnected religious events: the disciplining of Lord MacKay of Clashfern by the Free Presbyterian Church of Scotland for attendance at a Roman Catholic requiem Mass and the withdrawal from display by W. H. Smith of Salman Rushdie's *The Satanic Verses*. The date is significant; it follows the book burnings in Bradford and anti-Rushdie demonstrations in Hyde Park, London, but precedes the deaths on the Indian subcontinent and, more importantly, the *fatwa* on Rushdie pronounced by the Ayatollah Khomeini. There was, therefore, at this stage, a certain symmetry about the two episodes; both, moreover, illustrated what many thought to be the unpleasant consequences of taking religion to extremes. British people do not 'take religion so seriously that they punish eminent members of their community for attending a competing religious event, nor to the extent that they burn and seek to ban certain books from sale in British shops'.[1]

On the other hand, and *The Times* article makes the point very precisely, each of these religious groups was, in fact, acting entirely reasonably within its own frame of reference. Their actions – intolerant and outmoded though they may seem to outsiders – follow from the principles by which their members have chosen to conduct their lives. The problem (if such it is) arises because the rest of us have elected to live according to very different rules of behaviour; strongly influenced, that is, the by the tradition in British society which refuses to think too deeply about religion. Indeed, most of us are, it seems, content with a somewhat tenuous attachment to our religious institutions; we believe without belonging and emphasize the private and individual nature of religious life. To live and to let live is very much part of this approach.[2]

The disciplining of Lord Mackay of Clashfern resolved itself by a schism in an already tiny church. The episode was over, and provoked little more than a raised eyebrow among the general public and a certain sadness among the religiously committed.

In contrast, the Rushdie affair has escalated out of all proportion, provoking not only national but international repercussions. The analysis of the affair by Appignanesi and Maitland[3] provides a helpful and detailed documentation, chronicling the early part of an astonishing sequence of events; this sequence includes the infamous *fatwa*, the rejection of Rushdie's apology and the reconfirming of the death sentence. (Later episodes are listed in the chronology.) Appignanesi and Maitland (in a brief comment on the back of their book) also highlight the inescapable tension beneath the whole episode: is it, in fact, possible to reconcile the basic right to free expression and the absolute claims of religion? Each of these threatens the other, if they are taken to their logical conclusion, but denying the right to a logical conclusion is, equally, self-defeating. There is, therefore, a certain sense in which the Rushdie affair is by its very nature insoluble, quite apart from the sheer violence inherent in the whole episode. Not only does this violence run counter to the religious sensibilities of the average Englishman, it quite plainly transgresses Western standards of behaviour.

Up to a point we might feel a similar uneasiness about any religious fundamentalism in Britain. (Many are, for example, concerned about the absolute claims of some para-Christian groups.) In other ways, however, the Rushdie episode demands separate consideration; not only does it invoke unacceptable levels of violence not found in other cases, it also concerns an Islamic, rather than Christian, minority. In consequence, it has become very difficult indeed to disentangle the racial from the religious elements in the whole affair. One fact is, however, beyond question. The presence of Islam is very much part of contemporary Britain (and indeed of contemporary Europe); it is not likely to go away in the near future. We must, therefore, confront the issues in these terms. The problem, whether we like it or not, is ours, not someone else's.

At this point we need to recall the regional factor so often overlooked in British religion. The Islamic population is concentrated in particular parts of the country.

There are, in consequence, those who feel threatened by this minority in a very direct sense and react accordingly. In contrast, there are very many British people who rarely, if ever, come into touch with representatives of other faiths. Not surprisingly, their reactions – though by no means unanimous – are very different indeed.

Establishment, Political Issues and the Ordination of Women

It is important to remember that the debate about establishment, though closely related to the Church of England's political activity, raises questions of a different order. Establishment is one particular arrangement – despite everything popular – between Church and State; it determines the context in which political initiatives takes place, but is not in itself an initiative. On the other hand, it is surely legitimate to ask whether establishment implies a certain connection between Church and State that in itself precludes political criticism. Is it, for example, possible for the Established Church to take pastoral responsibility for a government of whose policies it is openly critical?

In contrast there are those who argue the reverse: that the Church of England's established status enables rather than prevents this critical role. An Established Church organized on a parochial basis (and this includes manpower as well as buildings) can offer a unique contribution to a society that is increasingly divided both socially and regionally.

There are, clearly, differences of opinion. We must, however, acknowledge the fact that the leaders of the Church of England – despite (or because) of its established status, despite its declining membership and despite the evident misgivings of some of these members – continues to sustain a level of effective political criticism that many would have thought impossible a decade or so earlier. In so doing the Church (often in partnership with the other Christian denominations, and sometimes together with the representatives of other faiths) has a higher profile in public life than its active membership might suggest. The widely publicized article which the Archbishop of Canterbury published in the October edition of *The Director*, exemplifies this critical role and the repercussions that such a statement is likely to provoke.

There are, however, costs as well as advantages to almost any forms of Church/State connection. The cost of Establishment has been tangible in a very direct sense in the rejection by Parliament of the clergy (ordination) measure, a decision that – once again – raised queries about the viability of the whole Church/State arrangement. It is significant that the Measure is to be resubmitted to the House of Commons unamended. The whole episode epitomizes the difficult relationship between the maintenance of a principle (the lifelong nature of marriage) and the evident need for pastoral flexibility. If Parliament is insisting on the former, the Church is painfully aware of the latter.

The debate over the ordination of women has become the focus of a rather different tension: just how far, and in what ways, can (or should) the Church's teaching respond to the pressures of contemporary society. The conflict between an unchanging and unchangeable message and the pressure of the context in which this message has to be proclaimed is nothing new. It has occurred before and will occur again. The debate about the ordination of women is, however, particularly painful in that it calls into question the wider and very delicate issues of authority both within the Church of England and within the Anglican Communion. Who, for example, has the authority to decide changes of such magnitude? How are the decisions to be enforced, always assuming that they can be arrived at in the first place? What happens if episcopal and synodical expressions of authority come into conflict in any particular diocese? Which of these will take precedence? Is the Anglican Communion still a Communion if its bishops cannot mutually respect each other's authority?

Beneath these painful debates, however, there is evidence of a decisive shift in public opinion. Both within the Church and outside it, there is a growing acceptance of women's ordination. It is, it seems, an idea whose time has come.

The European Factor

Representatives of the British churches attended the European Conference 'Justice, Peace and the Integrity of Creation', an event of considerable significance which grouped together Christians from all denominations (including the Orthodox) from Eastern as well as Western Europe. Some of the British delegates were influential in its proceedings. On the other hand, the conference generated almost no interest in this country beyond the official representation and the British press chose, very largely, to ignore the whole undertaking.

Why this should be so prompts a number of questions. How ready are the churches to face the challenge of 1992, let alone the changes sweeping across Eastern Europe? Where do their fundamental loyalties lie? Do their institutional structures pull them too hard in a different direction, that is towards the Dominions, Africa and the New Commonwealth? Will some of our churches, for example, the Roman Catholics or the Presbyterians, find the European dimension easier than others?

The case of the Roman Catholics is particularly poignant. The Catholic minority is now a valued and permanent feature of British society, though the process whereby this assimilation has occurred has not always been an easy one. Moreover, popular reactions to the Archbishop of Canterbury's recent visit to Rome demonstrate just how close to the surface the old animosities remain. On the other hand, could it be that the very 'foreignness' – if we may use this term – of the Roman Church might enable Catholics to lead the way for church people in creating a more European type of consciousness in Britain? Clearly, they are better placed institutionally.

Perhaps the crucial question to ask is just how far will the Roman Catholics, or indeed anyone else, be permitted to fulfil such a role? For some of us the threat of Roman domination may well outweigh the advantages of thinking in a European perspective. For others neither idea is all that appealing; indeed, the two remain curiously confused for many British people, a confusion which goes some way to explaining why the maintenance of a discrete Protestant identity remains surprisingly significant in the late twentieth century. Once again, it would be foolish to ignore the reactions of those in the population who remain believers but who do not in any tangible way belong to their churches: for many of them anti-Papal (if not anti-Catholic) habits die particularly hard.

Notes

1. O. Leaman, *The Times*, 6 February 1989.
2. Such remarks do not, of course, apply to the Northern Irish. And if there is nothing else in common between the Northern Irish and the Muslim community, it is clear that both these groups not only affirm a specifically religious identity, but despise the majority of British people for their failure to do just this.
3. L. Appignanesi and S. Maitland, *The Rushdie File*, London, Fourth Estate, 1989.

Chronology

14 Jan: Salman Rushdie's *The Satanic Verses* burned by Muslim protesters in Bradford.

23 Jan: *Drift from the Churches: Secondary School Pupils Attitudes towards Christianity*, Christian Education Movement reveals increasing scepticism amongst pupils.

28 Jan: Muslim demonstration against *The Satanic Verses* in London.

1 Feb: Kenneth Baker defends the government's record before the Church of England General Synod.

14 Feb: Ayatollah Khomeini issues his *fatwa* (death penalty for blasphemy) against Salman Rushdie.

16 Feb: Poll in the evangelical *Church of England Newspaper* finds 60 per cent in favour of women priests and 50 per cent in favour of women bishops. Only 17 per cent would leave the Church because of women priests and 21 per cent if it had women bishops.

17 Feb: Cardinal Hume permits regular celebration of the Tridentine Mass in his archdiocese.

19 Feb: Ayatollah Khomeini rules out speculation that Salman Rushdie's apology could remove the death threat.

24 Feb: Douglas Hurd, in a speech at the Central Mosque, Birmingham, stresses that Muslims must obey the law, whilst recognizing the offence given to the Muslim community by *The Satanic Verses*.

27 Feb: The Government rejects call for the blasphemy laws to be extended to cover religions other than Christianity in the wake of the reaction to the Rushdie affair.

10 Mar: Two Sikh extremists are gaoled for life for the assassination of a rival Sikh religious leader.

13 Mar: Muslim attempt to summon Salman Rushdie for blasphemy and seditious libel fails.

26 Mar: The Bishop of Durham reaffirms his disbelief in the physical resurrection of Christ on Easter Sunday.

12 Apr: Tony Benn presents a Bill to abolish the common law offence of blasphemy.

27 Apr: Release of a letter (dated 8 Dec 1988) from the Pope to the Archbishop of Canterbury, Robert Runcie, threatening a serious deterioration in Anglican/Catholic relations if the Church of England decides to ordain women.

28 Apr: Eames Commission (chaired by Archbishop Robin Eames) designed to avert schism in the Anglican communion over women's ordination, reports.

6 May: Start of Luis Palau's evangelical mission to Wales.

11 May: The Bishop of Aston announces his resignation over the financial failure of the previous month's visit to Birmingham by Archbishop Desmond Tutu, which made a loss of about £200,000.

17 May: The Church of Ireland votes to allow the ordination of women as priests and bishops by large majorities.

21 May: Attack on the government by the retiring Moderator of the Church of Scotland.

25 May: Lord Mackay, the Lord Chancellor, is disciplined by the Synod of the Free Presbyterian Church of Scotland for attending a Catholic requiem mass.

27 May: Mass march of Muslims in London protesting against Rushdie is marred by violence.

29 May: Subsequent to the Mackay case defectors set up the Presbytery of the Associated Presbyterian Churches.

14 June: After a lengthy advertising campaign the Mission '89 Billy Graham evangelical crusade gets under way, ending on 8 July.

4 July: John Patten, the Minister of State at the Home Office, rules out the extension of the law of blasphemy to cover all religions and not just Christianity.

7 July: Controversy in the Church of England over allegations of homosexuality against Canon Brian Brindley, a senior figure in the General Synod, reopens the debate about the morality of homosexuality in the Church.

9 July: The Archbishop of Canterbury, preaching in York Minster, denounces all types of fundamentalism, whether Jewish, Christian or Muslim.

13 July: Labour backs plans for voluntary-aided Muslim schools providing they conform to the national curriculum.

18 July: Review of the financing of the redundant churches fund announced.

19 July: Anger in the Church of England after the Clergy Ordination Measure, to allow divorced men and women, and those who marry divorced people, to be ordained as priests and deacons at the discretion of the two archbishops, is defeated in the Commons by 51 to 46.

31 July: BBC go ahead with the broadcast of 'The Blasphemers' Banquet', a poem by Tony Harrison which defends Rushdie, in the face of pleas from the Archbishop of Canterbury and his advisers.

1 Aug: Archbishop of Canterbury sets up a joint working group with Muslim leaders to discuss the role of law in protecting religious sensibilities.

7 Aug: Brian Brindley resigns as Chairman of the General Synod's business sub-committee over allegations of homosexuality.

31 Aug: British Board of Film Classification refuses to give a certificate to a short video, *Visions of Ecstacy*, which contains erotic scenes involving Christ, reopening the blasphemy controversy.

3 Sept: Bombing of Liberty's department store in London by Muslim extremists over the Rushdie affair.

13 Sept: Muslim leaders are divided over the launch of the Islamic Party of Britain, which plans to contest parliamentary elections.

14 Sept: A York bookshop is damaged in a bomb attack by Muslim extremists. Three other devices were also left at other bookshops around the country.

16–17 Sept: Festival of Faith and the Environment in Canterbury. Protesters complain about the multi-faith nature of this exercise.

19 Sept: Remarks of Dr Runcie about his preparedness to accept some Papal authority draw a Protestant backlash.

28 Sept: Hundreds of secondary schools are still ignoring faiths other than Christianity in religious education lessons according to a survey from Culham College Institute.

29 Sept: The Archbishop of Canterbury goes to Rome for four days of talks on church unity with the Pope.

1 Oct: Dr Runcie speaks of recognizing the Pope as the central and leading figure in the church.

An attack by Dr Runcie on the 'Pharisees' of British society, who decry the unsuccessful, the jobless and the poor, is taken as a veiled criticism of the Thatcher government.

9 Oct: One in three would like blasphemy to be abolished as an offence and an equal proportion want it to be extended to cover all religions and not just Christianity according to a survey conducted by Public Attitude Survey.

15 Oct: English Churches Census – a comprehensive census of church attendance across the country – is held.

20 Oct: An opinion poll of British Muslims reveals strong support for the suppression of *The Satanic Verses* and the death threat to Rushdie.

25 Oct: *Call to Order*, published by Advisory Council for the Church's Ministry, suggests that the Church of England should recruit priests more vigorously.

30 Oct: Cost of Conscience conference of Anglo-Catholics in London pledges its opposition to women's ordination.

7 Nov: General Synod vote on the Priests (Ordination of Women) Measure is; Bishops 30 to 17, Clergy 149 to 85 and Laity 144 to 78.

8 Nov: General Synod decides to resubmit to Parliament legislation permitting divorced men or those married to divorcees to be ordained.

16 Nov: *British Social Attitudes*, Gower, shows that in Britain religious belief is lower than in any other western European country.

4 Dec: Leading church figures launch 'Cry for the Poor', an explicit attack on government policy as it affects the poor.

6 Dec: Methodist church leaders deliver a letter criticizing government policies to Downing Street.

7 Dec: *Church Statistics*, Central Board of Finance of the Church of England published.

14 Dec: The Video Appeals Committee upholds ban on 'Visions of Ecstacy'.

15 Dec: A Day of Muslim Solidarity, organized by the Association of Sunni Muslims, leads to renewed calls for death of Salman Rushdie and the withdrawal of his book.

19 Dec: Prince Charles attacks the standard of modern English and particularly the language of the *Alternative Service Book* and modern Bible translations in a Prayer Book Society speech.

The Literary Arts

DAVID MORGAN

The literary arts in 1989 showed more continuation and consolidation than innovation. The final year of the 1980s built upon the characteristic literary manners of the decade. The year saw few substantial new works. The 1980s had seen the character of modern writing modify in various ways. A new generation of novelists brought a sense of flair and narrative adventure to contemporary prose fiction. Their achievement led to the novel's predominance as a genre. These same novelists typically placed the contemporary world at one remove from the matter of fiction. Marketing and media manipulation gave poetry, at times, a surprisingly loud presence. It is, however, unlikely that the 1980s will earn a prominent place in the history of British poetry. The decade has seen a good deal of vigour in theatrical production; yet there has been a conspicuous downgrading of new writing for the theatre. In all this, 1989 was not untypical.

The reaction to a novel published the previous year will, however, ensure that 1989 is writ large in any future study of post-war literary history.

The Satanic Verses

The literary world in 1989 was the focus of an unusual degree of attention. The offence felt by many Muslims in Britain and abroad at Salman Rushdie's *The Satanic Verses* (originally published in September 1988) identified an extended context of reaction and consequence not previously brought into relationship with a British novelist. This large and complex novel attempted a literary fusion of modern metropolitan satire, myth and religious reference and in its aesthetic apartness alerted few early readers to the extent of possible offence caused. The situation reached a head in February 1989 when Ayatollah Khomeini called for the author to be killed. The campaign against the book continues; the knowledge that the writer is still in hiding has been a brooding presence, newly underwriting any pretension to importance in writing since that day.

The community of writers responded with great dignity in their pleas for principle and tolerance. Notable reactions came from Michael Foot MP, chairman of the Booker jury who had shortlisted the novel the previous year and novelists Carlos Fuentes and Fay Weldon were impressive in their sturdy defence of the work. The affair also re-emphasized the phenomenon of literary topicality. Tariq Ali and Howard Brenton promptly wrote their satire, *Iranian Nights*, for the stage and Tony Harrison, having produced a blunt-nosed piece of occasional verse in *The Observer*, followed with an elegant verse-essay for television on the same theme. These laudable artistic responses cannot, however, detract from the unimaginable burden which has been placed on one writer. The literary community has been irremediably changed by this threat to a writer's life because of writing a book.

Novels of Closure

Throughout the 1980s the contemporary novelist has shown the form to have a difficult relationship with the present times. As with previous years, the most acclaimed novels of 1989 were those which held our messy reality at arm's length. They might assert a distance of time or place or a combination of the two. The most accomplished examples of this literary inclination kept the current reality at bay by a force of style. They established an idiom substantial enough to achieve self-dependence for the novel in question.

Kazuo Ishiguro was awarded the Booker prize for his novel *The Remains of the Day*. Ishiguro's novel is a portrait of an uncertain narrator: an elderly butler who gradually reveals his emotional limitations to the reader. This work attracted much praise for 'subtlety' and the focus of such laudatory attention appeared to be the creation of a language for the butler. The plot progresses in well worn fashion but the reality which lies behind the style – the collaboration of a British peer with German anti-semitism in the years before the last war – is never allowed to threaten the quiet telling. This is a writer's ploy which often attracts praise. There is usually a critical relief that contemporary realities have been avoided.

A more substantial work was James Kelman's *A Disaffection*. This novel comprised a portrait of a week in the life of a school teacher. It is impressive principally for the language it employs. The idiom here is so substantial and vigorous as to be wonderfully present to the reader. The mood of the book, as the title suggests, is one of deeply felt alienation and the current political situation is forcefully implicated in this. It is easy to imagine the literary–historical force such a novel could take on for a future readership as a monument to the grievances inspired by late Thatcherism. Yet this exemplary possibility does not weaken the novel. Neither does it suggest an unqualified link with the present. Again it is the language which seals off as well as impresses. The spirit of the work is an emphatic demonstration of its contemporary stature but the narrative closure keeps the book at one remove once again. The week with which the novel is concerned is brought vividly before the reader but the final demand upon our sensibilities – a demand for essential recognition – is still not made.

This tendency to create within limits is seen *en bref* in Julian Barnes's *A History of the World in 10 Chapters*. This entertaining book takes an 1980s tendency to one logical extreme. Many recent novels have attempted to address, however playfully, large-scale subjects. Anthony Burgess's *Earthly Powers* was one of the first, dealing as it did with the protagonist's experience of a century. The year 1988 saw works of a similar sweep, notably William Boyd's *The New Confessions* and Graham Swift's *Out Of This World*.

Barnes's warm-hearted book offers different chapters on different moments in the world history he refers to. There are indeed supporting parallels and images but essentially the separate chapters are largely independent creations. The whole is enjoyable and thought-provoking but the linkages never genuinely trouble our sense of entertainment. We and they are allowed to remain in the elsewhere of fiction.

Now and in England

Of course there were fictional portraits of our times in 1989. Anita Brookner's *Lewis Percy* and Penelope Lively's *Passing On* charted the ways of a particular social milieu with characteristic accuracy. Margaret Forster's *Have the Men Had Enough?* was an impressively real, if modest, rendering of the social challenge of Alzheimer's Disease. Novels which attempted to paint the contemporary world over a broader canvas, such as Margaret Drabble's novel of this year, *A Natural Curiosity*, often attracted a good deal of unfavourable criticism. Here the delineation of the modern experience can seem too schematic. The fictional truth of the novel is brought into question by the weighty detail of the setting in time and place. At times the reader is forced to accept a realism founded upon naming and topical reference. It is worth noting that recent novels by Emma Tennant and Andrew Motion are to be the first volumes in fictional sequences depicting the post-war years. It is uncertain whether these more extensive projects will meet with greater success.

Unsurprisingly, the first fictions of the year did often tackle the present situation. Publishers Jonathan Cape gave extensive promotion to four first novelists in May of 1989. These young writers shared a testy relationship with the difficulty of now. Fictional debuts ranged from Brixton to Cumbria to Scotland in delineating Britain.

The more substantial first novels were again dependent upon otherness; Nicholas Shakespeare's *The Vision of Elena Silwes* (set in Peru) or James Hamilton-Paterson's *Gerontius* (centred upon the life of Elgar). In the continuum of the 1980s even the young novelist's urge to autobiography has found expression at a distance. Yet a year which saw first novels from several writers already known for their work in other genres, testifies to the strength of the form.

Senior Practitioners

Two noteworthy trilogies were completed in 1989. William Golding's *Fire Down Below* brought to a close the series begun with *Rites of Passage*. This very modern historical reconstruction of sea-board life is an enduring achievement, in particular the opening volume. With *The Open Door*, Alan Sillitoe brought to a close the depiction of Arthur Seaton, begun many years previously, in the now classic novel *Saturday Night and Sunday Morning*.

Many other distinguished writers published important novels in 1989 including Michael Frayn (*The Trick of It*), Beryl Bainbridge (*An Awfully Big Adventure*) and Anthony Burgess (*Any Old Iron*). Iris Murdoch celebrated her seventieth birthday with *The Message to the Planet*. Sybille Bedford, after a lengthy period without publishing a book, presented *Jigsaw*. This was an infectiously readable autobiographical account of the author's youth in Europe. Its portrayal of an earlier world seemed in its fragmentary inclusiveness to bridge successfully the era depicted and the time in which it was written. V. S. Pritchett continued to underline his role as senior practitioner of the short story with his collection, *A Careless Widow*. After numerous works in other forms a first set of stories came from Burgess, *The Devil's Mode*.

Qualified Experiment

Experiment at present is most often found in a form which ensures that the challenge to the reader is only partial. Typical of this is the fondness for historicism and pastiche demonstrated by many writers. Peter Ackroyd's work has made good use in the past of this forum for fusing tradition and change. His novel of 1989, *First Light*, enlisted Hardy's astrologically energized Dorset to this cause. The seventeenth century was anatomized in Rose Tremain's acclaimed *Restoration* and Jeanette Winterson's characteristically fabulous *Sexing the Cherry*.

As a rule, there are more pasts than futures in the contemporary novel but an honourable exception was Martin Amis's *London Fields*. Set in the near future it was once again apparent from the linguistic dexterity of the opening that this was a brilliantly provocative and ambitous book. This controversial work attracted fierce disapproval for its author – and not for the first time – for its treatment of female characters. Yet Amis's virtuoso engagement with the current language and with the widest implications of literary form (here the murder story is thoroughly decoded) seems certain to be a substantial force for the future.

200, 50, 10 Years Ago

Three anniversaries dominated the year's journalism. The bicentenary of the French Revolution encouraged many works of history from Simon Schama's embracing *Citizens* to many volumes of quieter scholarship. The fiftieth anniversary of the Second World War saw a similar rash of historical works and also provoked a varied fictional response: Allan Massie's politically centred *A Question of Loyalties* contrasted the domestic intimacy of John Fuller's *The Burning Boys*. Vernon Scannell's poems in *Soldiering On* were a notable retrospective addition to the poetry of that war.

It is arguable that the anniversary of greatest literary importance has been the tenth year of Mrs Thatcher's premiership. The political continuum which Britain has experienced during her time as Prime Minister has seen a redefinition (however impermanent) of many concepts and the introduction of a new rhetoric and new assumptions. At first the changed political situation was a challenge to be met by the literary artist. Now the sense of familiarity is such that writers can seem cramped by the consistency of the political climate. Often a sense of resignation seems predominant. It remains to be seen whether a sea-change in British politics would have a causal link to a parallel development in the arts.

One aspect of the literary establishment which is in keeping with the political consistencies, is the continued reluctance to welcome work from Europe and the wider non-English speaking literary world. Each year there are notable exceptions: in 1989 Umberto Eco's *Foucault's Pendulum* received extensive promotion; there were important novels from Carlos Fuentes, Heinrich Böll and Bohumil Hrabal; and a new version of the poems of Paul Celan. Nevertheless, translations of non-English writing occupy a shamefully small place in contemporary reading and publishing. As 1992 approaches it is to be hoped that positive moves will be made to remedy this.

The qualified acceptance of experimental work is also in keeping with the times and is still a feature at the end of this literary decade. Those few figures who achieve publication often appear strangely deviant from central concerns. Yet 1989 saw a wonderful reminder of the possibility for experiment and historical literary challenge in Samuel Beckett's *Stirrings Still*. This short piece saw more narrative underpinning than has been expected from late Beckett. The work also raised interesting questions about the material existence of the text in the late 1980s. *Stirrings Still* was available in a limited edition costing £1,000 but was also reprinted in full in *Guardian* (cost 30p). Beckett died on 22 December 1989 at the age of 83.

Similar ironies abounded when an interesting attempt to revive the pamphlet came from Chatto and Windus. This series, *Counterblasts*, included work from various notable figures but was most typical of its time in being thoroughly packaged and marketed; even more characteristically, substantial extracts were reprinted in the national press. It is difficult to decide whether such a relationship between certain newspapers and the literary arts speaks more of the health of those papers or the ultimate vulnerability of the book. With *Counterblasts* the topicality was never certain. The attempt has, however, to be welcomed. Yet it is typical of the age that the publisher dared not risk the real topicality and ephemerality which would then have allowed a possible, and earned, endurance for the works concerned such as that won by the historical pamphlets which have entered the literary canon.

Poetry and Accumulation

The year 1989 could not be thought a strong year for British poetry. The form had achieved a particular visibility in recent years but the quiet persistence of 1989 was a reminder of how vulnerable such a media dominated phenomenon is. Poetry has always to fight hard in an age of prose.

There were distinguished poems from Roy Fuller in *Available for Dreams* and Ted Hughes's *Wolf Watching* marked a return to his surer standard. One of the year's most characteristic and also individual volumes was Selima Hill's *The Accumulation of Small Acts of Kindness*. This extended sequence tells of a woman suffering from mental illness and takes as an idiom the very method of accumulation which also lightens the life of the protagonist. This is almost beyond criticism as a poetic style in that the arbitrary lies at its centre. The evocative power of the detail and the juxtaposition in Hill's poems depends upon nothing certain or universal. This almost random materialism is a typical late 1980s style. It may be seen also in those small narratives beloved by contemporary poets and the current tendency to employ the random image. What matters in such cases is the existence of an image as an image rather than any specific details of connotation. The question remains whether in placing her work beyond criticism Selima Hill may have also placed it beyond response.

Accumulation of a harsher sort is at the heart of Peter Reading's poetry. His volume in 1989, *Perduta Gente* was no exception. Reading focuses unstintingly upon the harsh concrete details of modern civilization albeit in a manner which is enlivened by formal wit. New collections from Elizabeth Jennings, George Mackay Brown and Peter Redgrove, and George MacBeth's *Collected Poems*, served as reminders of the quiet strength of current verse but the year saw no real highlights in the form. James Fenton's *Manila Envelope* had to be ordered direct from the Philippines and thus enacted its own irresistible pun. For all the delighted playfulness of this means of access to the writing, Fenton is still distinguished from most of his contemporaries by his challenging treatment of often terrible subjects, as here with modern war and revolution.

New Writing in the Theatre

New drama has still to fight for attention. Here, even more than for poetry, economic factors influence the degree to which the new writing can make its presence felt. Subsidy has become increasingly elusive throughout the decade. There is still a marginalization of new writing in the commercial theatre. It is not an assumed presence. There were new plays by established dramatists in 1989: David Storey, Caryl Churchill and Stephen Poliakoff were amongst those who had new works performed. For a playwright without the benefit of a solid catalogue of earlier successes, the challenge of gaining practical attention for one's work remains great. Writing in *The Guardian* at the end of May 1989, Michael Billington bemoaned the lack of good new British plays; the second half of the year saw little to contradict him.

New writing in the theatre is often found at smaller venues and festivals. The Edinburgh Festival did not feature many substantial new British pieces but John Clifford's *Ines de Castro* at the Traverse was a highlight of the proceedings and should help make Clifford's work known to a wider public. Jim Cartwright presented a chamber play, *To*, but this enjoyable work broke none of the new ground which had brought strength to the memorable *Road*.

There is a current theatrical tendency to focus upon the building up of characters without, often, an equally strong sense of structure. Often the notable performances which such works inspire overbalance the evening in the theatre and render the architecture of the play all the more vulnerable. It is difficult at present to envisage a time when a year in which two or three major new plays are produced (not the case in 1989) is not exceptional.

Literary Biography

The commonplace that this is a strong period for literary biography persists and with justification. The bicentenary of the French Revolution may have been the spur for the appearance in 1989 of several notable works on the romantics. Especially valuable are Stephen Gill's much needed *Wordsworth*, Richard Holmes's *Coleridge: Early Visions* which was awarded the Whitbread prize for 1989, and William St Clair's *The Godwins and The Shelleys*.

It is good to see that controversy can still be instigated by literary lives in an era when so many aesthetic sensibilities have been numbed. The year 1989 began with a furore surrounding Fiona MacCarthy's new life of Eric Gill. This book spoke of the sexual complexities of Gill's family life in a way which directly challenged the view of the artist as an ascetic religious craftsman. Martin Seymour-Smith's life of Kipling presented new speculations about that writer's sexual inclinations which never seem seriously to threaten the popular image of him, but entertained in its iconoclasm.

Probably the most characteristic and contemporary form of literary–biographical controversy came late in the year with the publication of Anne Stevenson's *Bitter Fame: A Life of Sylvia Plath*. Here the outcry centred upon Stevenson's attempt to demystify Plath who had long been something of a feminist icon. Allied to this was the apparently complex involvement of Plath's literary executor in the biography. The legal complications and financial pressures which underlay this portrait are again instances of a characteristic late 1980s mixing of art with money and the pitfalls of production. It seems inevitable that time must elapse before a fair picture of such an important modern writer can appear, but Stevenson's book in itself raised many questions of process and provided a necessary staging post on the way to a balanced account.

There were of course other notable biographies in 1989: David Cairns on Berlioz, Norman Sherry's very authorized portrait of Graham Greene and a suitably prompt flood of Warhol memorabilia. To expect an entirely rational portrait of Margaret Thatcher at this stage in her career would be to expect too much but Hugo Young's *One of Us* was a substantial act of synthesis and in its high-journalistic style demonstrated a perception of her contribution to recent politics, which is itself a central part of the more complete viewpoint to come.

The end of the political decade saw the publication of a number of political memoirs of which the most substantial (and perhaps most overtly literary) was probably Denis Healey's *The Time of My Life*.

A distinguished volume of autobiographical character was *What Am I Doing Here* by Bruce Chatwin. This collection of short pieces ranges over many subjects both close to and far from home. It was published in May after the author's death in January 1989. His death ended one of the most impressive and chameleon literary careers of the decade at an unreasonably early stage.

Literary Studies

In any year the vast majority of literary studies do not reach a wide readership. There were no conspicuous trends or movements in 1989 to facilitate a widening of exposure for the work in question. The influence of anniversaries which fuelled the Romantic emphasis on biography focused in the field of literary studies more upon the fiftieth anniversary of the war. Andrew Sinclair's *War Like a Wasp* attempted a necessary assessment of the wartime writing and Paul Fussell's *Wartime* tackled the topic with characteristic skill. Perhaps more truly illustrative, however, was the narrower focus of Michael Shelden's *Friends of Promise: Cyril Connolly and the World of Horizon*. Bryan Appleyard's *The Pleasures of Peace* was one of the first volumes to consider post-war writing in its peacetime context and managed an impressively broad sweep. There were notable books from Frank Kermode, *An Appetite for Poetry* and George Steiner, *Real Presences*.

The ultimate importance of 1989 for the annals of literary study is of an altogether weightier nature. The year will be central to any chronology of the English language and its literature because of the publication in March of the second edition of the *Oxford English Dictionary*. These twenty volumes enact a lasting embrace of the language. This was also the year when the last productions rolled off the historic Clarendon Press. With the *Oxford English Dictionary II*, the linguistic past seems safe but – what is perhaps the greater concern at the turn of the decade – is the same certainty appropriate to our hopes for security for our literary future?

The Political Economy of the Arts

ROBERT HEWISON

Until the Chancellor of the Exchequer's Autumn Statement, 1989 looked like being financially the grimmest of the decade for the arts, for museums and galleries and for organizations concerned with the cultural heritage. The Office of Arts and Libraries may be responsible for only one-third of 1 per cent of central government spending, but subsidy is vital to the political economy of the arts. The BBC and Independent Television are significant patrons, and the pop music industry is governed by market forces, but the engine of cultural activity is driven by a core of subsidized institutions. All of these in 1989 suffered attrition from rising inflation and government policy committed to reducing public expenditure.

The Enterprise Culture

At the end of January press briefings by Downing Street suggested that the Prime Minister was about to take a more visible interest in the arts, as demonstration of her government's new-found concern for the quality of life. In June 1988 the government had indeed been willing to reverse its policies on arts funding and release £150 million from the contingency reserve to secure the siting of the art collection of the Swiss industrialist, Baron Thyssen-Bornemisza in Britain, but in the event the money was not needed. The collection is to go to Madrid until the year 2000. Mrs Thatcher's higher profile in the arts did not emerge in 1989, and government policy remained that set out by her first Minister for the Arts, Norman St John Stevas, in 1979: 'The arts world must come to terms with the situation and accept the fact that government policy in general has decisively tilted away from the expansion of the public to the enlargement of the private sector. The government fully intends to honour its pledge to maintain public support for the arts as a major feature of policy, but we look to the private sphere to meet any shortfall and to provide immediate means of increase.'[1]

Since both those in the performing arts and museums had become used to a gradually rising level of public subsidy, ever since the creation of the Arts Council in 1945, this policy has led to persistent claims that the government now underfunds the arts and museums, and is allowing inflation to cut their budgets in real terms. In July 1987 Mrs Thatcher's fourth Minister for the Arts, Richard Luce, warned:

'Too many in the arts world have yet to be weaned away from the welfare state mentality.'

It would be wrong, however, to dismiss the government's attitude as mere philistinism. It sees the arts as playing a role in what Luce calls 'the culture of wealth creation'. It would also dispute claims of underfunding. In a debate on the arts on 15 June, Luce declared:

In real terms, the Arts Council receives three times as much from the government today as it did in the late 1960s. Since its creation by the government in 1980 the National Heritage Memorial Fund has received over £105 million from the tax-payer. The budgets of our national museums and galleries are also at record levels and central government spending on them has risen by 25 per cent in real terms since 1979–80. Funding for their building programmes has increased by about 50 per cent in real terms over the same period. Let us make no mistake about the achievement of the government. There has been an overall increase in arts funding of 39 per cent, in real terms, including abolition money, since 1979.[2]

The minister's calculations, however, must be treated with circumspection. A substantial element in his budget is the cost of the new British Library at St Pancras, a £400 million project due for completion (albeit in truncated form) in 1996. The abolition of the Greater London Council (GLC) and the six metropolitan county councils in April 1986 called for an increase in central government funding to replace their lost contributions to the arts – a transfer, rather than increase, in resources. Finally, the government calculates inflation on the Gross Domestic Product Deflator formula, not the Retail Price Index (RPI). A briefing paper from the National Campaign for the Arts in July argued that, using the RPI, the Arts Council has had a real increase of just 1 per cent in its grant between April 1979 (£63.125 million) and April 1989 (£134.3 million), exclusive of £21 million in replacement funding. For the eleven national museums and galleries funded by central government, the freezing of purchase grants since 1985 has meant a cut in real terms of 47 per cent. The only significant increase in their funding has been for building repairs, where immediate needs far exceed the resources available.

The case that the government has underfunded the arts throughout the decade is consistently argued by organizations that have the deficits to prove it. In practical terms, the new 'enterprise culture' has meant that organizations have had to pay more attention to marketing, management and the hunt for business sponsorship as an alternative source of funding. The latter has risen substantially to an estimated £30 million a year.

The Arts Council, which acquired a new chairman in January, the millionaire property developer, Peter Palumbo, had adapted to the new entrepreneurial style. At the beginning of the year it set up its own sponsorship unit to attract business sponsorship – not for its clients, but its own activities. It has also introduced 'incentive funding' in addition to revenue and project grants. The purpose of the scheme is to enable clients to develop economic self-sufficiency by increasing their earning capacity, and detailed plans must be submitted before the 'incentive' is awarded. In other words, the money is used for business, rather than artistic purposes. At the end of the first year of operation, 1988–9, in which £4.5 million had been distributed to 47 organizations in sums ranging from £5,000 to £250,000, the Arts Council claimed that £13 million in 'new money' had been raised by the organizations concerned.

By one measure, the policy of greater self-sufficiency appears to be working. In 1980–1 a client of the Arts Council received on average 45 per cent of its income as subsidy. In 1988–9 the average was 10 per cent less. The proportional change has, however, been largely achieved by increasing ticket prices. Similarly, no national museum receives 100 per cent of its running costs as grant aid, and all have to make up the difference through sponsorship, marketing, or increasingly, introducing entrance charges.

The effect of the new economic realism has been to hinder the long term aim – enshrined in the Arts Council charter – of increasing access to the arts. A report commissioned by the Arts Council from the British Market Research Bureau, published in October, showed that the arts and museums remain largely the privilege of the well-educated and the better-off. Those with an annual domestic household income of £20,000 or more have considerably higher levels of attendance than those in lower income groups, though as a whole we do not appear to be a very cultured nation. Based on a survey of 24,000 adults, the report found that during the period surveyed 6 per cent of the adult population went to the theatre, four per cent to an art gallery, 2 per cent to a classical music concert. Opera attracted 1 per cent of the population, but fewer than 1 per cent went to ballet or contemporary dance.

The Harrods of the Museum World

Although the most humiliating outcome of an attempt to adapt to the enterprise culture was the failure of Hereford Cathedral to raise funds by selling 'shares' in its treasure, the Mappa Mundi, as Mappa Mundi plc (the thirteenth-century map was withdrawn from auction at Sotheby's, and funds will now come from the National Heritage Memorial Fund and Paul Getty), the Victoria and Albert Museum has experienced the most controversial upheaval. The new director, Elizabeth Esteve-Coll, who took over in January 1988, has had to face enormous difficulties: a minimum of £50 million is needed for repairs, while salaries alone have threatened to outstrip the museum's grant.

Already embarked on a series of fund raising measures that led the museum's marketing director to describe it as 'the Harrods of the museum world', on 26 January the museum's trustees agreed to a proposal for restructuring the curatorial system, a proposal they had only half an hour to consider before their meeting. While the purely administrative staff were untouched, the individually managed collections were to be subsumed into two departments, one whose personnel were to be concerned exclusively with scholarship, the other with the physical management of the collections. Nine senior curatorial staff, including five heads of department, were offered 'voluntary' redundancy. Eight, under pressure, accepted. The initial £300,000 these redundancies cost was found, ironically in view of the V&A's problems, from its building budget.

The redundancies provoked protests both in the British and American museum worlds, and the controversy has proved severely damaging to the standing of the Director, who faced formal votes of no confidence from her staff. One trustee, Professor Martin Kemp of St Andrews University, resigned, protesting that trustee bodies have 'increasingly become mirrors of government policy'. Damage was done not only to reputation and morale, but also to scholarship. The V&A in May told the Museums and Galleries Commission that it 'no longer has any expertise' in the field of lace-work, or embroidery from 1560 to 1840, following the departure of a key curator. The November *The Times* reported that a sub-committee of trustees had concluded that the restructuring was unworkable. The individual collections would continue to be administered separately, under new heads of department appointed at a lower grade.

Ironically, the most successful example of private enterprise in the museum world also stems from the Victoria and Albert. In July the Design Museum opened at Butlers Wharf on the south bank of the Thames, below Tower Bridge. The Museum, devoted to all aspects of commercial and industrial design, had begun as the privately funded Boilerhouse Project at the V&A. Its principal capitalization of £7 million has come from Sir Terence Conran's private Conran Foundation; Butlers Wharf is a £200 million property development by a Conran company. The Design Museum has been very successful in attracting commercial sponsorship, and the title of the opening exhibition 'Commerce and Culture' has, in the museum's own phrase, 'set the agenda' for its approach.

The year 1989 was Museums Year, to mark the centenary of the foundation of the Museums Association, and the popular passion for the past – at least as a tourist attraction – showed no signs of weakening. According to the Museums and Galleries Commission, which has criticized the underfunding of national museums, in 1989 a new museum opened every 14 days.

Developments at the Royal Opera House

In February the Royal Opera House made another attempt to solve the problems of its cramped accommodation at Covent Garden. In 1975 the then Labour government had presented it with two acres of extra land to develop in its own way. In 1987 outline permission had been given for a scheme that involved the demolition of the adjacent Floral Hall and five other listed buildings. But the application to Westminster City Council for permission to proceed with the £150 million redevelopment, which would pay for improvements with the profits on offices, shops, apartments and parking on the rest of the site, was frustrated when it became known that the Opera House had been in negotiation with an American company proposing a 'Disney-style' theme for the development. Although the Board said it had rejected the proposal, Westminster deferred a decision, while the Covent Garden Community Association went to court.

In November the Board's architect, Jeremy Dixon, submitted a revised scheme, costing £175 million, with more space for technical facilities for the Opera House, and a reduced commercial element in the scheme. Half the Floral Hall would be preserved, and the other listed buildings restored and converted. The Royal Opera House plans to launch an appeal to cover the shortfall – estimated to be between £25 and £40 million – caused by the reduction in the profitability of the venture.

Both the Royal Opera and the English National Opera (ENO) announced deficits during the year. Peter Jonas, managing director of the ENO, made a point of announcing in March that he was budgeting for a deficit of £300,000, in order to highlight the company's funding difficulties. By the autumn, the Royal Opera House was facing a potential deficit of more than £2 million, in spite of raising ticket prices to as high as £90 a seat. Opera North and the Welsh National Opera also faced deficits of £300,000 and £100,000 respectively. In December the Arts Council withdrew funding from Kent Opera, a touring company with a deficit of £335,000 and the company went into liquidation.

Yet in 1988–9 opera audiences were the highest ever, with a total of more than 1.5 million. The popularity of opera, at least as a spectacle, was confirmed in June when the rock impresario Harvey Goldsmith mounted *Carmen* with a cast of more than 500 at Earl's Court, at a reported cost of £4.5 million, playing to more than 100,000 people in seven performances.

As suggested by the Arts Council's survey, the audience for ballet and contemporary dance appears to be declining, one reason being that nearly all companies are giving far fewer performances at the end of the 1980s than at the start of the 1970s. In February the Arts Council published a report on dance by Graham Devlin, *Stepping Forward*, which described dance as a 'deeply demoralized and nervous profession'. Devlin recommended stopping the £661,000 annual grant to the Manchester-based Northern Ballet Theatre, in order to free badly needed resources. The Council, however, declined this suggestion, granting the company a two-year stay of execution.

Theatre

For many leading members of the theatrical profession, the most important theatre in 1989 was one that had not presented a performance since 1606. The site of the Rose Theatre in Southwark was discovered during excavations prior to a redevelopment that would destroy it. Although a campaign to have the site scheduled as an ancient monument failed, the developers have, at considerable extra cost to themselves, agreed to preserve the remains beneath the new building and make them accessible to the public. English Heritage, the body responsible for supervising archaeological rescue, regards this as an example of the successful operation of the voluntary code of practice agreed with developers, by which developers themselves help to fund archaeology on their sites. The rarity value of uncovering the first authentic remains of an Elizabethan theatre was later diluted when traces of the Globe Theatre were discovered not far away.

Since part of the Globe Theatre lies beneath Southwark Bridge, it is unlikely to be excavated completely. The theatre's chief dramatist, however, enjoyed an unusual number of quality revivals. While the commercial theatre (whose activities remained almost entirely restricted to the West End) had its ration of justified flops – the musical *Metropolis* and Jeffrey Archer's second play, *Exclusive*, among them – Shakespeare was once more considered a 'bankable' playwright. This was proved both by Derek Jacobi's pairing of *Richard II* and *Richard III*, and Sir Peter Hall's production of *The Merchant of Venice*, starring Dustin Hoffman. But much of the credit must go to the efforts of the young actor-manager Kenneth Branagh, who had pioneered a Shakespeare repertory with his unsubsidized Renaissance Theatre Company at the Phoenix Theatre in 1988. In 1989 he seemed almost over eager to follow in the footsteps of Laurence Olivier (who died in July), when he released his own film version of *Henry V*. (In November the British Screen Advisory Council launched an inquiry into the declining fortunes of the British film industry, where investment has halved since 1986. Fewer than 40 films were made in Britain in 1989. The most notable film by a British director, Peter Greenaway's *The Cook The Thief His Wife And Her Lover* was largely funded with European money.)

The official home of the national playwright, the Royal Shakespeare Company (RSC), had another difficult year, in spite of recovering some of its artistic authority at the Barbican thanks to the presence of John Wood in a season that began with *The Tempest* and ended with *The Master Builder*. In November the RSC announced that in spite of presenting 40 productions to a million people in 1988–9, and raising more sponsorship than ever before, the company had a deficit of £1.163 million. The National Theatre was the only major company *not* to declare a deficit in 1989, although there were contingency plans to limit the repertory system if a shortfall occurred.

Theatres up and down the country were forced to economize by presenting fewer productions, with smaller casts, and in general the least popular theatrical form, the new play, appears to have suffered most, simply by not being produced. The touring company Foco Novo disbanded, and Avon Touring set out on its last tour. The most notable closures were the studio theatre of the Bristol Old Vic, and the Royal Court's Theatre Upstairs, although the latter was able to present some visiting productions. The only bright spot artistically was the success of the fifth London International Festival of Theatre in July, which presented a wide range of unfamiliar domestic and foreign work to a total audience of 60,000.

The South Bank

The South Bank Board which, funded by the Arts Council, took over responsibility for the Royal Festival Hall and other facilities on the South Bank from the GLC, announced in March plans for a £200 million redevelopment that would remove many of the concrete walkways and alter its 'new brutalist' appearance by encasing the existing buildings, and adding new ones, in a design by the 'post-modernist' architect Terry Farrell. The scheme, due for completion in 1993, is being paid for entirely by the developer Stuart Lipton, who will cover his costs from the commercial additions to the site.

As at Covent Garden, however, this entrepreneurial otpimism was blighted by the announcement that in the first year of operation, 1988–9, the Board had an operating deficit of £1.1 million and of £0.5 million on its capital account. Economies of £700,000 had to be made in the 1989–90 programme, including the cancellation of a major exhibition at the Hayward Gallery planned for March 1990. The chief cause of the deficit was the poor response to a Latin American music and arts programme, which was admitted to be a mistaken choice. The South Bank also experienced sporadic strikes when the Board refused to honour a nationally negotiated pay award for its staff on the grounds that it could not meet the increase. The Board agreed at the end of the year to pay the increase *pro tem*, until a new deal would be struck.

Conscious that the South Bank's music programme lacks coherence and identity, in June the Board invited applications from symphony orchestras for a 'residency' on the South Bank. (Small scale residencies are already held by the London Sinfonietta, the Academy of St Martins in the Fields, and the Berg Quartet.) The chosen orchestra would, at a cost to the South Bank of £500,000, enjoy increased rehearsal time and greater participation in planning and promotion. It would not, however, entirely escape the 34 per cent increases for use of the concert halls in the next two years. Only the London Philharmonic and the Philharmonia applied, and a decision is expected in 1990.

A Mounting Crisis

By midsummer – a hot one that adversely affected concert and theatre bookings – the rise in inflation and the lengthening toll of deficits led to a profound sense of impending crisis through the arts. Anxiety was compounded by the fact that the arts budget for 1990–1 was already known. In 1987 the Minister for the Arts had established a system of three-year funding, welcomed at the time because it allowed more time to plan. But the overall increase in the coming year was posted at 3.9 per cent (including the British Library building programme), a derisory figure in view of inflation at over 8 per cent. In July the chairmen of London's five leading museums and galleries wrote to the Prime Minister pleading for an increase in funds. The Secretary-General of the Arts Council, Luke Rittner, added his voice to the warnings of disaster, saying he had never seen 'quite so many arts organizations quite so near the edge of the precipice'. He was in a position to know, for the Council was drawing up contingency plans to cut off grants to up to 40 clients.

On 27 September the Council's chairman, Peter Palumbo, made a direct appeal to the Prime Minister at a private meeting, but the most persuasive case for a real increase in funds was made in a strategically placed contribution to the Arts Council's annual report, published on 10 October. Ian Rushton, chief executive of Royal Insurance, whose £1.1 million sponsorship over three years had kept the RSC afloat, warned the government that sponsors were happy to fund additional activities, but could not be expected to replace core funding. Sponsors were looking to the government to show a real commitment to the arts:

The arts have rightly been encouraged to follow an entrepreneurial course. But encouraging business attitudes requires in return business discipline and formal planning. No business could operate successfully when a major source of revenue – in this case the government – expects high standards of excellence and of quality of output but is not willing to offer forward guarantees on income. This is made even worse when the government allows that revenue to be reduced in real terms. A business faced with such a position would surely go bankrupt or have to debase its standards.

The Crisis Resolved (Temporarily)

As early as June the Minister for the Arts, who, as a minister without Cabinet rank carries little political weight, had written to the Chief Secretary to the Treasury, Norman Lamont, seeking to reopen his triennial agreement. Five meetings followed, and Luce's position may have been made easier by the resignation of Nigel Lawson as Chancellor. By all events on 16 November he was able to announce an increase of 12.9 per cent in his overall budget for 1990–1. The £494 million for next year will rise to £540 million in 1992–3. From this the Arts Council received an increase of 12.5 per cent (to £174.95 million) and the national museums and galleries 13.3 per cent (to £164.75 million). £180 million is to be spent over three years on their buildings. Their purchase grants, however, remain frozen.

The Arts Council followed swiftly by announcing increases of 11 per cent to the four 'flagship' companies, and 8 per cent for the South Bank Board. The budget for dance was increased by 17 per cent, the Scottish and Welsh Arts Councils received 11 per cent and the Regional Arts Associations (RAAs) 10 per cent. But both the RSC and the Royal Opera House pointed out that in spite of increases to £6.045 million and £14.896 million respectively, they would still have difficulty in balancing their budgets. The Minister for the Arts has had a notable, and unexpected success, but only the future path of inflation will show whether he has done anything more than maintain the status quo.

The Wilding Report

Anxiety about funding the arts served to distract attention from the publication in September of a review of the structure of arts funding commissioned by the minister from his former chief civil servant, Richard Wilding. *Supporting the Arts* made far-reaching proposals to change the relationship between the Arts Council and the RAAs, bringing them into a new 'federal' structure that would, Wilding argued, improve financial accountability and reduce bureaucracy. The price for the RAAs of a greater say, represented by seats on the Arts Council for their chairmen, would be a reduction in their number, possibly to six or seven. Wilding also proposed the absorption of the Crafts Council into the Arts Council. His proposals will form the basis of a White Paper, expected in 1990.

Overall, the recommendations appear to give greater power to the centre, with more decisions taken by Arts Council officers, and the Council itself run by a small executive committee. Such a change would be favoured by the new chairman, who has become, rather than the secretary-general, the most important figure in the Council. Palumbo's own tastes appear to favour support for the flagship companies and estabished art forms, over against 'community' arts.

A New Language, Little To Say

After ten years of Conservative government, it is still possible for the chairman of the Royal Opera House, Lord Sainsbury, to ask 'where is our national pride in the arts?' While the enterprise culture has made arts organizations more efficient, questions of money have occupied the energies of those who should be facing questions of creativity. The language of the arts has certainly changed: art is discussed in terms of 'product', its patrons are 'consumers', subsidy is 'investment'.

The problem remains as to what, in this language, it is possible to say. Long term, the treatment of culture as a commodity is likely to produce a more cautious, market-led climate in the arts, with genuine innovation limited to post-modernist exercises in 'style'. The only example of a display of vision in 1989 was the Prince of Wales's book, *A Vision of Britain*. But the Prince's architectural dream proved more a vision of the past than of the future.

Notes
1. Quoted in H. Baldry, *The Case for the Arts*, Secker and Warburg, 1981, p. 34.
2. *Hansard*, 15 June 1989, 1136.

Chronology
28 Jan: The Victoria and Albert Museum announces plans to open a branch housing its collection of South Indian art in Bradford.

30 Jan: Lord Strathclyde rules out tax incentives to help the British film industry.

3 Feb: Controversy about redundancies at the V&A begins.

9 Mar: £200 million proposal to turn London's South Bank complex into an even larger entertainments complex unveiled.

14 May: Protesters, including many famous actors, rally to the defence of the Rose Theatre, the only Tudor theatre to have been excavated, to protect it from developers.

22 May: Elizabeth Esteve-Coll, the Director of the V&A, says that the money the government gives to museums is totally inadequate and that this year the salary bill at her museum was greater than the grant towards running costs.

2 June: Developers at the Rose Theatre site talk of preserving the site and putting it on display in two years' time.

14 June: Nicholas Ridley turns down a plea to list the Rose Theatre as an ancient monument.

15 June: Richard Luce announces that there will be less secrecy over the price of works of art intended for export to give public galleries a better chance of keeping them in Britain, following a controversy over the granting of an export licence for Turner's 'Seascape, Folkstone'.

10 July: National Campaign for the Arts report calls for increased spending on the arts and argues that the Arts Council budget has been cut by 19 per cent in real terms since the Thatcher government came to office in 1979.

13 July: National Gallery faces £22 million expenditure on essential maintenance according to its Director, Neil MacGregor.

17 July: Call for the government to tackle the underfunding of the arts by the Chairman of the Arts Council, Luke Rittner.

20 July: Museums and Galleries Commission accuses the government of under-funding the largest museums and appointing inexperienced trustees to their boards in its annual report.

21 Aug: Announcement that the musical 'Metropolis' is to close in September, with expected losses of £2.5 million.

29 Aug: South Bank staff dispute over pay begins.

8 Sept: TUC presses its affiliated unions to devote up to 0.5 per cent of their subscriptions to sponsorship of the arts.

13 Sept: Policy Studies Institute publishes *Cultural Trends* on music, opera and dance. Among other points it shows a decline in the popularity of contemporary dance and that more than half government spending on music and opera goes on military bands. Royal Opera House, having just posted a £1 million deficit, announce plans to build a new opera house at Compton Verney, Warwickshire.

19 Sept: Richard Luce launches an initiative to restore the buildings of museums and art galleries.

The majority of the public are prepared to pay admission charges to museums according to a survey by the Museums Association.

9 Oct: Survey by British Market Research Bureau shows that going to the theatre, concerts or art galleries remains largely the preserve of the well-off and the well-educated.

12 Oct: Announcement that the remains of Shakespeare's Globe Theatre have been unearthed by archaeologists.

13 Oct: Charles Saatchi sells a major portion of his unique collection of contemporary art in New York.

17 Oct: British Museum, with an impending £1 million deficit, faces having to decide to charge its visitors, the director, Sir David Wilson warns.

18 Oct: Government-commissioned report by Richard Wilding claims that efficient funding of the arts is being stifled by excessive bureaucracy and duplication and recommends cutting the Arts Council staff and committees, merging some regional arts associations and making them more accountable and merging the Crafts and the Arts Council.

11 Nov: £3 million deal with the National Heritage Memorial Fund and John Paul Getty enables Hereford cathedral to keep the Mappa Mundi.

15 Nov: £66 million extra funding for the arts announced in the Autumn Statement.

21 Nov: Eleven per cent increase for the four national opera and theatre companies is announced by the Arts Council as well as increases of funding in other areas.

30 Nov: £10 million development of the National Portrait Gallery which will increase its gallery space by 37 per cent is announced.

Arts Council announce it is to end its £758,000 per year grant to Kent Opera.

2 Dec: Work to rule by the Royal Ballet begins.

21 Dec: Kent Opera liquidated.

South Bank dispute resolved.

Science

MICHAEL KENWARD

Science crept out of the 1980s and into the 1990s carrying a heavy burden of political baggage. It also shouldered several self-inflicted wounds.

The political baggage came in several shapes. The most obvious trend being the continued political influence on budgets. Long gone are the days when the funds available for science increased unchallenged. It was the last Labour administration, in the late 1970s, that first brought an end to this pattern of constant and unquestioned growth and began to cut into the science budget. The Conservative government continued the cuts with a vengeance, but now claims to have reversed the trend, something that many scientists find difficult to believe despite the figures.

One consequence of the perceived attack on science was the creation of Save British Science. This powerful group of academics solicited support from within the establishment. Indeed, 1989 saw several research heads within industry decrying the government's withdrawal from science funding. The propaganda seems to have worked and the message appears to have got across.

The most obvious statement of this about-face came at the end 1989 when the Prime Minister, Margaret Thatcher, gave the fiftieth anniversary lecture on 6 December 1989 to the Parliamentary and Scientific Committee, the body that brings together members of both houses of Parliament as well as industry and academia.

In its early days, the Conservative government urged its funding bodies, such as the research councils, to support research that offered short term returns. This was perhaps not an unreasonable response to an academic community that had previously shown remarkable lack of interest in research that might appeal to industry; but by the end of the decade the message had got across and the government had changed its mind. In recent years, university reseachers have bent over backwards to work with industry on research, perhaps so much so that the government will have to spell out its latest change of heart more clearly.

Back to Basics

In her anniversary address in December, Mrs Thatcher, a member of the Parliamentary and Scientific Committee for 30 years, went to great lengths to champion the cause of basic research: 'The truth is that the greatest economic benefits of scientific research have always resulted from advances in fundamental knowledge rather than the search for specific applications.' The Prime Minister went on to list areas where the science came before the technology, for example, 'transistors were not discovered by the entertainments industry seeking new ways of marketing of music, but by people working on wave mechanics and solid state physics.'

Mrs Thatcher spoke also of induction coils, electromagnetic waves and computers, whose binary logic circuits 'were not found by accountants seeking to store and rapidly process information, but by physicists in the 1930s wishing to count elementary particles'. She mentioned also nuclear energy – 'not discovered by oil companies with large budgets seeking alternative forms of energy, but by scientists like Einstein and Rutherford' – a technology that came to grief in 1989 not as a result of technical failure, but because its economics did not fit in with the government's privatization philosophy.

If political interference was outside the control of scientists, that cannot be said of the self-inflicted wounds. The most obvious case being the saga of cold fusion (see below) where the processes of science came adrift when the scientists involved failed to go through the usual channels of refereed journals and indulged in publication by press conference.

Embryonic Problems

One area where scientists worked hard to pre-empt trouble and to prepare for the inevitable political intervention was over the use of human embryos in research. In 1984, a Committee of Inquiry, chaired by Mary (now Baroness) Warnock, produced a report on the subject. The *Warnock Report* called for a statutory licensing authority to regulate research on in-vitro fertilization (IVF). Failing government action, the Medical Research Council (MRC) and the Royal College of Gynaecologists and Obstetricians (RCGO) jointly set up the Interim Licensing Authority (ILA), with guidelines modelled on the recommendations made in the *Warnock Report*. Since 1985, the ILA has monitored all IVF research carried out in Britain. The ILA regulated both research on IVF and its use in the treatment of infertility.

In November 1989, the government published the Human Fertilization and Embryology Bill that not only presented options for the control of IVF research, but also threw in new legislation on abortion. This muddying of the waters guaranteed a controversial passage of the Bill through Parliament.

On IVF, the Bill presented two options: a complete ban on all research, or research allowed up to 14 days after conception and controlled by a Statutory Licensing Authority. MPs were given a free vote on the subject. Mrs Thatcher, speaking the day before the House of Lords first debated the government's Bill, said that 'the capacity to do research is not in doubt, but some aspects dealt with in the *Warnock Report* – such as cloning, hybridization and research on the human embryo – give rise to very strong feelings on both sides of the argument.' Hybridization and cloning, she said, 'are not difficult to rule out'. However, 'the precise limits to research on the human embryo are more difficult to determine.'

The Prime Minister urged Parliament to 'study the best scientific advice in the consequences of a particular course of action'. However, 'in the end it will be personal conviction, in the light of all the facts, that will determine the result of the vote on the limits we set to research on the human embryo'.

The MRC and RCGO responded to the Bill with a report offering that scientific advice and warning that a ban on IVF research would halt work to improve the technique; it would also hamper the study of infertility, contraception and work on the diagnosis of genetic abnormalities before an embryo is transferred to the womb. This call came hot on the heels of a similar statement from the Royal Society which said, 'To permit research in this area to continue under control of a Statutory Authority, empowered to restrict it in accordance with the changing views of society, would provide adequate safeguards without neglecting the interests of those who stand to benefit from its clinical application.'

Britain was not alone in experiencing difficulties with its position on embryo research. For ten years the US has banned the use of federal funds for work on human embryos. Earlier in the year the West German government also threatened to ban such work.

Cystic Fibrosis

These moves on the political front came in the same year that scientists announced considerable progress in the understanding of one genetic disease, cystic fibrosis (CF). In August, Lap-Chee Tsui and Jack Riordan, of the University of Toronto, and Francis Collins, of the University of Michigan, announced that they had found the gene that leads to this inherited lung disease.

Tsui and Collins compared the DNA from individuals with and without cystic fibrosis. They found the CF gene using a new technique to cut up and process the DNA. If both parents possess this gene, their offspring can inherit the disease.

Discovery of the CF gene does not mean that a cure is imminent. It does mean that scientists can screen people to see if they carry the defective CF gene. In the longer term, this knowledge will also help those working on drugs to treat the disease. Knowledge of the gene may also lead to methods of eliminating the disease through gene therapy, a controversial technique that will not be possible if all work stops on IVF research.

The idea of gene therapy is to remove cells from a 'pre-embryo' – the stage in the development of the human conceptus after conception but before implantation in the womb – and to detect and correct such genetic defects as CF. Gene therapy would inevitably raise numerous ethical questions. In December the government set up a committee, chaired by Sir Cecil Clothier QC, to draft ethical guidelines for doctors who might want to use the technique.

Cold Fusion

The story of the research on cystic fibrosis has one thing in common with one of the more bizarre scientific episodes of 1989, cold fusion. In both cases the story hit the newspaper headlines before it appeared in the scientific literature. However, this happened to the cystic fibrosis team by accident rather than design. After the researchers had sent their papers to the journal, *Science*, news leaked out to the press. In the case of cold fusion, the press announcements came before the scientific papers.

In March, two respected scientists, Professor Stanley Pons, of the University of Utah, and Professor Martin Fleischmann, of the University of Southampton, announced that they had achieved what was later dubbed 'fusion in a jam jar'. They had, they said, persuaded atoms of deuterium, an isotope of hydrogen, to fuse into a heavier atom, releasing energy in the process. In the event, the argument as to whether they had achieved anything of the sort rumbled on for the rest of the year. Despite mounting scepticism, tales of confirmation of cold fusion continued to appear in newspapers, if not in scientific journals. The last, from two separate teams in Japan, came in December.

The saga caused so much amazement because for nearly 50 years physicists had been struggling to achieve controlled fusion, that is, to mimic the sun and the hydrogen bomb. This work had involved ever more sophisticated and expensive machines, culminating in such devices as the Joint European Torus (JET), an EEC project based at Culham in Oxfordshire. These fusion machines use complex arrangements of magnetic fields to hold together 'a plasma', a gas so hot, around 100 million degrees, that its ions and electrons are separated.

Here, too, the aim is to make isotopes of hydrogen fuse together. The favoured fuels for fusion are deuterium and tritium. Deuterium occurs naturally in water. Tritium is a radioactive isotope of hydrogen: it is created in minute quantities on the edge of space, but a reactor would have to breed its own tritium in nuclear reactions.

It costs something like £100 million a year to operate JET. Fleischmann and Pons said that they had achieved fusion for just a few thousand pounds. They did this by passing an electric current through deuterium, using palladium as an electrode. The pair said that this arrangement has produced far more heat than they could explain through ordinary electrochemistry. They theorized that fusion reactions were taking place within the palladium.

Widespread scepticism greeted the revelation first. Then came 'confirmation' from various laboratories – Poland and Hungary were among the first countries to jump on the bandwagon. But as the months passed, many of these earlier results were withdrawn and other laboratories failed in attempts to detect either energy or any of the tell-tale chemical products that would go with nuclear fusion.

Why did anyone take the idea at all seriously? Perhaps because high-temperature superconductors were still fresh in the minds of the scientific community. Here, too, a pair of scientists, Alex Müller and Georg Bednorz, had come up with a result that had previously seemed unlikely, but they were more circumspect in how they revealed the news.

Müller and Bednorz, two scientists at IBM's research centre in Zurich, quietly tucked their paper away in a relatively obscure German journal, knowing that they would have several months in which to confirm their work before the paper appeared. Fleischmann and Pons first revealed their results at a press conference, later publishing a paper that convinced no one.

Just as companies rushed to buy the rights to exploit the research of some of the scientists who worked on superconductors, others hurried to Fleischmann and Pons. In the event, they probably wasted their time and money. A few scientists championed cold fusion, most notably Edward Teller, but the consensus was that if anything odd had happened in those jam jars, and it was a very big 'if', it was no energy panacea.

Hot Fusion

Ironically, in the year that cold fusion got scientists hot under the collar, conventional magnetic fusion passed an important milestone. Magnetic fusion has to reach three important targets if it is to work. In November the scientists on JET announced that they had reached all three. The trouble is that they had not reached them all at the same time. That will take a bigger machine and more time. However, the prospects for hot fusion looked so good that the JET team asked the Common Market for a four-year extension to its scientific programme, which was due to end in 1992.

Particles

Behaviour that would once have raised eyebrows also reared its head in the more conventional areas of science. A slightly undignified squabble marred what should have been a momentous point in the history of particle physics.

Scientists at the Stanford Linear Collider (SLC) in California and the Large Electron Positron accelerator (LEP) in Switzerland argued over which team was first to measure the mass of the Z° particle. The scientific importance of this measurement is that it sets limits on the number of different fundamental types of matter. This, in turn, sets limits for the theoreticians trying to come up with a 'theory of everything'.

Both SLC and LEP, at the European Laboratory for Particle Physics (CERN), came into operation in 1989. SLC was a 'quick and dirty' project, with an innovative design that cost around $120 million to build. CERN was a far more ambitious machine that cost nearer $1000 million.

SLC could not hope to breed $Z°$ particles in the same profusion as LEP; but had the project not experienced delays it could have made a large enough number of particles to answer the important question of the number of types of matter much earlier. In the event, SLC beat LEP to the punch, producing its first particles in April, about a year late. LEP started up in July and produced its first $Z°$ particles in the middle of August.

It is the mass of the $Z°$, and how accurately we can measure it, that tells us about the types of matter that exist. The SLC team had already produced 250 $Z°$'s before LEP made its first particle. Nor was the Stanford group the only one in the United States to make $Z°$'s. In Chicago, the Collider Detector at Fermilab had conjured 500 particles into existence by the beginning of July.

The results from SLC and Fermilab were such that even before LEP arrived on the scene, physicists had a pretty good idea that there were but three generations of quarks, and therefore three types of matter.

This much was clear in August, the acrimony set in in October when scientists at CERN accused the SLC team of trying to upstage them. The Californians provoked the ire of CERN by holding a press conference just a day before the European project announced its conclusive measurements on the mass of the $Z°$. By the time of CERN's announcement on 13 October, LEP had clocked up 11,000 particles against 500 from SLC. The SLC team admitted that its measurements were not conclusive, but put the odds at 25–1 against there being a fourth family of matter.

Particle physicists may have set a limit on the number of types of matter, they have not, though, run out of ideas for new machines. During 1989, the US announced that its next accelerator, the Superconducting Supercollider, would be built in Texas. This machine would, the official announcement said, cost some $5.9 billion. But by the end of the year technical problems loomed large and this estimate began to look decidedly optimistic, with talk of their needing an extra $2 billion.

Health Warning

It goes without saying that any assessment of the most significant scientific advances in any one year is even more likely to be proved wrong than assessments of political or economic events. Not for nothing do the Nobel committees wait for some years before awarding their prizes, despite Alfred Nobel's stricture that they be awarded for the year's most significant event. This does not, however, guarantee they they avoid controversy. Another odd event of 1989 was the squabble that blew up over the Nobel prize for medicine.

The medicine prize for 1989 went to J. Michael Bishop and Harold E. Varmus of the University of California. The two Americans received their award for work on cancer genes. Dominique Stehelin, a French researcher, complained that his contribution had been ignored, a complaint supported by Hubert Curien, the French Minister for Research and Technology.

For all this strange behaviour within science, researchers can console themselves with the knowledge that the public respects them even if it does not understand what they are up to. Two polls conducted during the year showed that people find science interesting and they believe that science does more good than harm.

A team at Oxford University found that people in Britain are far more interested in medicine, technology and science (decreasing in that order) than in sport, films or politics. A poll by *New Scientist* magazine showed that the scientific community comes after 'medicine' and 'the military' in terms of public respect, far above Parliament, unions, organized religion, the Civil Service, and, last and least, the press. Sadly, the Oxford study also revealed an appalling ignorance of basic science among the British public. More than half the population believes that nuclear power stations cause acid rain, and less than a third know that electrons are smaller than atoms.

Chronology

9 Jan: Plessey announce their new phased array radar systems.

13 Jan: New evidence of a statistical link between levels of aluminium in drinking water and increased risk of Alzheimer's Disease is published in *The Lancet*.

19 Jan: British Aerospace and Rolls Royce announce their decision to go ahead with plans to rescue the revolutionary space plane Hotol.

7 Feb: Scientific research spending by the government is raised by £125 million in 1989–90 to £825 million.

17 Feb: The announcement of the development by Ivor Catt of super memory chips based on wafer-scale integration technology by the chip company Anamartic.

23 Feb: Animal Liberation Front bombing of laboratories at Bristol.

28 Feb: European Space Agency satellite Hipparcos is unveiled in Turin. It is intended to measure accurately the motions and positions of the stars.

8 Mar: Duke of Norfolk's Unborn Children (Protection) Bill's second reading in the Lords. The Bill is designed to curb experiments on human embryos.

9 Mar: New evidence of links between the pill and breast cancer is published.

17 Mar: British Biotechnology's pioneering work in the use of collayanese inhibitors to arrest arthritis is announced.

23 Mar: Professor Paul Davies of Newcastle University criticizes the growing North–South divide in science and technology, which he says is exaggerated by patterns of governing funding.

23 Mar: Race to claim success in nuclear fusion begins with the claim of Stanley Pons of Utah and Martin Fleischmann of Southampton that they have produced controlled nuclear fusion in a test tube at room temperature.

25 Mar: Arson attacks on two animal research centres in Edinburgh.

7 Apr: Fleischmann and Pons publish their paper in *The Journal of Electroanalytical Chemistry and Interfacial Electrochemistry*.

19 Apr: The Duke of Norfolk drops his backbench Bill banning embryo research following hints that the government intends to act.

24 Apr: The Advisory Board for the Research Councils of the Department of Education and Science meets to consider proposals to abolish the five individual research councils and replace them with a single council in the light of the report of the committee chaired by Richard Morris.

26 Apr: A £9 million programme to develop technology for exploiting the ocean's commercial potential is announced.

27 Apr: Doubts are cast on the chances of getting any energy from cold fusion in an article in *Nature* by John Davies of Birmingham and James Cohen of Los Alamos Laboratory.

3 May: The Advisory Council for Science and Technology criticizes the Ministry of Defence for not fully exploiting its vast research and development spending in the civil sector.

8 May: The research ship *Discovery* sets off to examine the role of the oceans in global warming.

12 May: Claims of spectacular results in treating the rare child cancer, Neuroblastoma, with the new drug meta iodo benzyl guanadine.

16 May: The new drug Eminase is released. It can help to reduce deaths caused by heart attacks.

9 June: In *The Lancet* Julian Hopkin and William Cookson publish their discovery of an abnormal gene which leads to a range of allergic reactions – including hay fever and asthma.

26 June: British scientists have made a breakthrough in the study of the greenhouse effect by demonstrating a link between the photosynthesis of tiny plants in oceans and the amount of carbon dioxide in the atmosphere.

5 July: A survey in *Nature* shows widespread ignorance of science amongst the general public.

7 July: A report in *The Lancet* confirms successful tests with a birth cushion for easing childbirth developed by Jason Gardosi.

11 July: Department of Trade and Industry says millions of pounds of science and technology money could go back to the Treasury because companies and universities are too slow to agree joint research projects. The slow take-up of joint European research projects is also criticized.

16 July: Alfonso Molina, *Transputers and Parallel Computers: Building Technological Capabilities through Socio-Technical Constituencies*, Economic and Social Research Council, on the importance of the development of transputer technology, is published.

25 July: A strict new code of practice governing the use of the foetus and foetal material in treatment and research is approved by the government. This was the result of the Polkinghorne committee's report, instantly accepted by the government.

27 July: Science and Public Expenditure *1989: A Report to the Secretary of State for Education and Science* from the Advisory Board for the Research Councils, Department of Education and Science, warns that British science is so starved of funds that basic research is having to be dropped and is lagging behind that of European competitors.

4 Aug: Doctors in Scotland in an article in *The Lancet* link cot deaths to low blood sugar
levels.

Report published in the *British Medical Journal* of successful experiments with use of
lasers to kill cancer tissue in vital organs.

Evidence that Wellcome's AZT drug slows the progress of Aids in its early stages is
announced.

8 Aug: The Hipparcos satellite is launched. Unfortunately it took up the wrong orbit after
its booster rockets failed to respond properly.

10 Aug: Breakthrough in the early detection of heart disease announced in *British Medical
Journal*.

Alan Bond, the inventor of the revolutionary space plane Hotol announces plans to set
up his own company to develop a revolutionary new space engine.

14 Aug: CERN's Large Electron Positron Collider begins preliminary work.

25 Aug: A research team at Cambridge led by Graham Burton explains how smoking during
pregnancy harms the unborn child.

11 Sept: More than 200 British scientists living in the USA have signed an open letter to
Thatcher calling for reform and more funding of science policy. This was organized by
British Scientists Abroad.

12 Sept: Announcement that the first computer chip that can think for itself has been
developed in Britain by a team led by Simon Jones of Bangor. This is hailed as the
world's first neural chip.

Sir Douglas Hague condemns the administrators of British science as arrogant,
amateurish and unprofessional before the BAAS's annual meeting in Sheffield.

14 Sept: A new study of brain disease at Strathclyde announced.

15 Sept: Announcement of progress towards finding a treatment of Alzheimer's disease by
Dr Ray Baker of Merck Sharp and Dohme's Neuroscience Research Centre at Harlow.

18 Sept: CERN's new Large Electron Positron Collider, the largest in the world, starts work.

18–19 Sept: Scientists at the end of a three- year round the world voyage on the Natural
Environment Research council ship, *Charles Darwin*, announce their discoveries.

29 Sept: First baby born in Britain from the intra vaginal culture technique, a simplification
of normal test tube techniques.

9 Oct: Success in developing computers that can recognize continuous speech announced
by Dr Roger Moore of the Royal Signals and Radar Establishment.

12 Oct: Computer Conservation Society formed.

13 Oct: CERN announces that tests with its Large Electron Positron Collider have shown
that all matter is made from just three families of sub-atomic particles.

25 Oct: Royal Society report on research priorities suggests that 'The universities should
abandon tenure and encourage research with increased research funding rather than
increases in salary.'

Annual Review of Government-Funded Research and Development 1989, HMSO
shows that government support for civil R&D is set to decline in real terms over the
next few years and that many researchers, particularly at the Agriculture and Food
Research Council, will lose their jobs.

2 Nov: Tests in the North Sea suggest that the oceans absorb only about 30 per cent of
man-made carbon dioxide, rather than 50 per cent as previously thought and that
therefore global warming is proceeding up to 20 per cent faster than previously
imagined.

3 Nov: Article in *The Lancet* suggests researchers at the Royal Free Medical School, London have established the cause of Crohn's Disease.

14 Nov: Official figures on Britain's civil research and development spending published.
A study for the Science and Engineering Research Council argues that universities need to spend £240 million on new equipment simply to teach contemporary science properly.
Sir David Phillips, chairman of the Advisory Board for the Research Councils, warns of a large-scale movement of scientists across European frontiers and an internal EC brain drain from regions with poorer scientific resources after 1992.

21 Nov: Human Fertilization and Embryology Bill announced in the Queen's speech.

23 Nov: Human Fertilization and Embryology Bill published.
Hundreds of top rated science projects are being turned down because of lack of funds according to the Science and Engineering Council's annual report.

28 Nov: A committee on the ethics of gene therapy is set up under the chairmanship of Sir Cecil Clothier.

2 Dec: A new technique of screening for ovarian cancer developed at Kings College Hospital, South London, is announced in the *British Medical Journal*.

6 Dec: Mrs Thatcher gives the fiftieth anniversary lecture of the Parliamentary and Scientific Committee at the House of Lords.

Scotland

JAMES G. KELLAS

The Scottish Constitutional Convention

In 1989 a Scottish Constitutional Convention met twice, on 30 March and on 7 July. The origins of the Convention can be traced to the failure in 1979 to establish a Scottish Assembly. This led, in 1980, to the formation of the Campaign for a Scottish Assembly (CSA), made up of devolutionists from a wide spectrum of Scottish politics. It was officially shunned by the Conservative Party from the start, and only latterly supported by Labour. In July 1988, a special Constitutional Steering Committee appointed by the CSA produced *A Claim of Right for Scotland* which recommended the establishment of a Scottish Constitutional Convention 'to draw up a scheme of devolution; to mobilize Scottish opinion behind that scheme'; and 'to deal with the government in securing approval of that scheme, or an acceptable modification of it'.

When the CSA proceeded to organize the Convention it was clear that its terms of reference and its proposed composition would be controversial. The Conservatives refused to participate, as they were opposed to devolution. The Scottish National Party (SNP) went only as far as a planning session on 27 January 1989 before pulling out three days later. This action was later endorsed by the Party's National Council. The SNP objected to the terms of reference, which excluded independence for Scotland; to the indirect election method of selecting delegates to the Convention; and to the absence of any provision for a referendum on the proposals.

It was thus apparent that the Convention represented only the devolutionist part of Scottish political opinion. Nevertheless, the opening meeting in the Church of Scotland General Assembly Halls on 3 March was attended by most of the Labour and the Social and Liberal Democrat (SLD) MPs, who amounted to 50 out of the total of 72 MPs in Scotland, and by representatives of the Green Party and the Communist Party. Many local authorities also sent delegates, and the Churches were well represented. Harry Ewing, a former Labour minister, and David Steel, former Liberal leader, were elected joint chairmen. The Convention proceeded to endorse the *Claim of Right for Scotland*, amidst considerable media publicity.

The follow-up meeting in Inverness on 7 July was less sensational. There was no clear focus to the deliberations, and divisions among the delegates became apparent. The SLD vice-chairman, Bob McCreadie, complained that Labour was using the Convention as a 'convenient fig leaf' for its party policy, and was excluding the SLD federal solution. Proportional representation for the proposed Assembly was another issue dividing Labour from the other parties, and by October the SLD (now 'Liberal Democrats'), and the Green Party, were threatening to pull out of the Convention. The proposed meeting in Glasgow in December was postponed to January 1990 to allow time for more ideas to be submitted from individuals and organizations. It was beginning to look as if Scotland was again showing its divisions on the constitutional issue, thereby allowing the government to continue to 'divide and rule'.

Elections and Parties

The Conservatives might congratulate themselves on the troubles facing the Constitutional Convention, but they had little else to be happy about. Their standing in opinion polls was exceptionally low (well under the 24 per cent obtained in the 1987 general election), and their showing in elections was abysmal. At the Glasgow Central by-election in June they obtained only 7.6 per cent of the vote, and at the European elections in the same month, 21 per cent, losing both their Scottish seats. The Conservative Party organization in Scotland was blamed for this poor performance, and a big shake-up was ordered by Mrs Thatcher. In July, the right-wing Scottish Office minister, Michael Forsyth, was appointed Chairman of the Party in Scotland, and he proceeded to introduce new young blood from the radical right. In September, the President of the Scottish Conservative and Unionist Association, Professor Ross Harper, resigned as the result of an alleged sex scandal reported in the *Sun* newspaper. He was succeeded in October by Michael Hirst, a former MP defeated at the 1987 election. The Conservatives even brought back Teddy Taylor, MP for Southend, to campaign in Scotland. He had lost his seat in Glasgow as long ago as 1979. All this indicated the difficulty facing the party in Scotland in providing a credible campaigning force from their 10 MPs.

The SNP meanwhile was alternating between euphoria and despair. The Glasgow Govan by-election victory of November 1988, which returned Jim Sillars to Parliament on a 33 per cent swing from Labour, gave the party a new confidence which it had not possessed since 1977. Its policy of 'Independence in Europe' was apparently very popular with the Scottish electorate, reaching 61 per cent support in a System Three poll in the *Glasgow Herald* (14 April 1989). But polls also saw a majority supporting continuing membership of the United Kingdom. While SNP leaders played up these polls, actual elections did not favour the party so much. The Glasgow Central by-election was not a repeat of Govan, for the SNP lost to Labour. It trebled its vote from 10 to 30 per cent, but this time its lesser-known candidate and the better Labour campaign denied it the seat. In the European elections, the SNP won 25.6 per cent of the vote, and narrowly missed winning the

Scotland North East seat. But its sole Euro-MP remained 'Madame Ecosse', Mrs Winifred Ewing in the Highlands and Islands. In 1989 the SNP pursued two policies with doubtful electoral advantage. As noted in the previous section, it withdrew from the Constitutional Convention, and attacked it from the outside. This antagonized moderate nationalist opinion ('gradualists') and those parts of the general public concerned to achieve a consensus on devolution. Second, it pursued a campaign of non-payment of the community charge (poll tax), and sought to promulgate a list of 100,000 non-payers. The campaign faltered when around 80 per cent of the eligible population paid up on time, and the list of non-payers was never published. The credibility of its 'direct action' campaign was dented, and opinion poll ratings of SNP support dropped from 32 per cent in early January 1989 to 17 per cent in November. The SNP has to demonstrate that it has the support of the Scottish nation to make its nationalism effective. In 1989, that support rose and fell in an uncertain fashion.

The Labour Party recovered quickly from its loss of Govan to the SNP. Its remaining 49 MPs benefited from the SNP's failures and from the growing popularity of the party in England. In 1989 the 'Doomsday Scenario' (which predicted a Labour Scotland interminably facing a Conservative government elected by English voters) faded away as Labour overtook the Conservatives in British opinion polls. In Scotland, the party rose from its 42 per cent level at the 1987 election to 55 per cent in the System Three poll of November 1989. In March it rejected the idea of pacts with other parties to create a 'Tory-free Scotland'. Yet its vote at Glasgow Central, despite victory, was well down on 1987 (55 per cent compared with 65 per cent). In the Euroelections it moved up from only 40.7 per cent in 1984 to 41.9 per cent in 1989, while gaining two seats from the Conservatives.

Labour was now strongly committed to devolution, which the Shadow Scottish Secretary Donald Dewar described as 'Independence in the United Kingdom', an obvious rejoinder to the SNPs 'Independence in Europe'. Whatever that meant, the party's domination of the Constitutional Convention and its new electoral credibility as the next government persuaded the militants of Scottish Labour Action to keep quiet by the end of 1989. Earlier in 1989, these activists had promoted the notion of a 'dual mandate', whereby voting Labour in Scotland meant a mandate to form the British government *and* to form a Scottish government, even if Labour lost the British election, which then seemed likely. This was a kind of 'unilateral declaration of independence' by a section of Scottish Labour. By late 1989, all eyes were back on London.

For the Scottish Democrats, it was a poor year. Their Eurovote was only 4.3 per cent, and they lost their deposit at Glasgow Central. Their opinion poll ratings hovered around 5 per cent for most of the year, but they were better off than the SDP, who did not contest any European seats at all, and whose opinion poll ratings sank to 1–3 per cent. The two Scottish SDP MPs had already crossed to join the SLD in 1988. The Greens made less of an impact in Scotland than in England, for they won only 7.2 per cent of the Eurovote compared with 15 per cent in Britain as a whole. In February 1989, a Scottish Socialist Party was launched to try to bridge the gap between far-left politics and Scottish nationalism. It did not contest elections, however, and its impact was minimal.

The Poll Tax and School Boards

Scotland started to pay the poll tax (community charge) in April 1989, one year ahead of England and Wales. The tax was deeply unpopular with around three-quarters of the Scottish electorate, including some Conservatives, according to surveys, and various campaigns were established to attack the charge, and some sought non-payment. As we have seen, the SNP tried to produce a list of non-payers, but this did not materialize. In fact, many Scots (as high as 25 per cent in Glasgow) did not pay on time, but by the end of the year the non-payers had dropped to about 12 per cent across Scotland. In Glasgow, however, the figure was 22 per cent, and in Strathclyde Region (Scotland's largest) 14.4 per cent.[1] At the same time, fines and 'warrant sales' of the property of non- payers proved highly embarrassing to those Labour, Democrat and SNP councils whose legal duty it was to collect the tax. The concessions made by the government at the 1989 Conservative Party Conference in advance of the English/Welsh collection only served to underline the point that Scotland alone was politically unable to affect the government's policies, even if it retrospectively benefited from the concessions made for the South.

School boards were introduced in Scotland in August. These had been strongly opposed by the teachers' organizations, and the public was largely uninterested. Nevertheless, the government was determined to introduce 'parent power' into Scotland, and in a different form from that in England and Wales. In the event, in most regions around half of School Boards, with around 30 per cent of all Scottish pupils, could not be formed for lack of parent candidates, and the Scottish Office had to use an advertising campaign to promote a round of by-elections to fill the vacancies. Once more, Scotland proved resistant to the policies of the Thatcher government. 'Opting-out' of schools from local government control became law in November, despite the absence of that policy from the 1987 Conservative manifesto. It was a backbench Conservative, Allan Stewart, who had been able to carry this clause in committee, with the tacit support of the right-wing elements in the government.

SDA, HIDB, SSHA and the Electricity Boards

During 1989, the government continued to move towards the transformation of the public sector in Scotland. The Scottish Development Agency (SDA) was set to become Scottish Enterprise, and the Highlands and Islands Development Board to become the Highland and Islands Enterprise. Each body was to gain manpower training functions from the Training Agency, and was to be run by local businessmen in regional agencies. Meanwhile, the Scottish Special Housing Association became Scottish Homes on 1 April, and proceeded to sell off its housing stock to housing associations and private owners. The two electricity boards (North of Scotland Hydro-Electric and South of Scotland Electricity) were to be privatized, but with nuclear power remaining in public ownership. The net effect of these changes was to shift control of the Scottish economy from the public to the private sector, but not on the scale originally intended. The viability of a non-nuclear private electricity in Scotland was in question, since the nuclear component accounts for about half of the assets of the electricity boards.

Needless to say, Scottish political opinion outside the Conservative Party was largely hostile to these changes, although Labour was ambivalent about Scottish Enterprise, which gave training powers to a body based in Scotland instead of one based in England. This seemed to be an addition to the powers of the Scottish Office, and a diminution of control from the south, which Labour supported. In general, Scottish politics in 1989 moved in opposing directions: towards nationalism and devolution with a left-wing bias, and towards a Thatcherite 'enterprise culture'. The resolution of this conflict was not in sight, and would have to await the next general election.

Note

1. *The Scotsman*, 16 January 1990.

Chronology

27 Jan: Cross-party talks in Edinburgh between Labour, the SLD and the SNP to plan a Scottish constitutional convention.

30 Jan: SNP pulls out of the proposed Convention on the grounds that the Convention members will be unelected.

26 Feb: Scottish Socialist Party launched. One of its leaders, Alex Wood, and Jim Sillars, the SNP MP for Govan, allege that Labour manoeuvred the SNP into withdrawing from the Convention.

1 Mar: A research centre for promoting Scottish political ideas, the Scottish Centre for Economic and Social Research, is launched.

12 Mar: Proposals for electoral pacts to get rid of the ten remaining Scottish Tory MPs are rejected by Labour.

24 Mar: Western Isles Island Council gives notice it intends to seek approval for a local by-law preventing ferries using Lochmaddy pier on Sundays to frustrate Caledonian MacBrayne's plans to start a Sunday ferry from Skye to North Uist in May.

30 Mar: Scottish Convention's inaugural gathering. Harry Ewing and David Steel are elected as chairmen.

31 Mar: Four Scottish Labour councillors burn poll tax books outside the Scottish Office in Edinburgh.

1 Apr: Poll tax introduced in Scotland. Demonstrations against the tax in Edinburgh.

8 May: Malcolm Rifkind announces reform of business rates in Scotland.

12 June: First appeal in Scotland against fines for failure to register for poll tax is dismissed as 'incompetent and irrelevant'.

27 June: Western Isles Island Council fails to prevent the new Sunday ferry service to North Uist.

7 July: Second meeting of the Scottish Convention.

26 July: Rule changes to the Scottish poll tax announced by Mr Rifkind.

13 Sept: Policy Studies Institute survey points out that the campaign against the poll tax in Scotland has actually contributed to its success by publicizing it and highlighting the penalties for defiance.

21 Sept: At its conference at Dunoon the SNP promise lower taxes and increased social security benefits. It also demands that the government uses its golden share in BP to block the oil company's plan to make 1,000 workers in Scotland redundant.

28 Oct: Joint conference of the Shetland Movement and the Orkney Movement in Kirkwall, Orkney.

7 Nov: Report of the Standing Committee on the Scottish Economy suggests that a 'white knight' should be set up to protect Scottish companies from hostile takeover bids.

21 Dec: Enterprise and New Towns (Scotland) Bill published. It replaces the Scottish Development Agency and the Highlands and Islands Development Board with Scottish Enterprise and Highlands and Islands Enterprise.

Wales

DENIS BALSOM

Continuity and Change

Wales and England were joined by Act of Parliament in 1536. Although remaining geographically and culturally distinct, the broad political and historical development of Wales was indistinguishable from that of England. The early *Encyclopaedia Britannica* entry, now considered highly patronizing, 'For Wales see England' was essentially correct. With the extension of the franchise and the growth of democracy in the nineteenth century, the impact of the industrial revolution in Wales and the mass adoption of non-conformity however, Wales' claim for greater recognition acquired validity. Confronting the uniformity of modern industrialized society the uniqueness of Wales began to take more concrete political form. A radical tradition in political thought and behaviour was established and, many claim, persists to this day.

The passage through Parliament of the first wholly Welsh legislation, the Welsh Intermediate Education Act, took place in 1889. The centenary of this Act coincided with the silver jubilee of the creation of the Welsh Office and with it the establishment of a Cabinet ranking Secretary of State for Wales. In 1989 this post was held, for the first time, by an Englishman, Peter Walker MP for Worcester. The prevailing issue of contemporary social concern is in-migration and cultural erosion and yet, in the midst of this tangible reaction to integration and assimilation, Wales is administratively and politically more autonomous than ever before. An underlying theme of Welsh politics for many years has been the achievement of such political autonomy, culminating in the referendum of the proposed Welsh Assembly in March 1989. But although this modest measure towards Welsh self-determination was resoundingly defeated at the polls, structural and administrative autonomy flourishes.

The Welsh industrial economy, so long the archetypal coal and steel community, has been transformed through closure and redundancy into a patchwork of light assembly plants, often foreign owned, often highly dependent upon female labour. With such changes have come parallel adjustments in community structure, shared values and trade union membership.

The proportion of those in Wales speaking Welsh has fallen consistently from 50 per cent at the turn of the century to perhaps a mere 18 per cent today. But 1989 saw the announcement that Welsh was to form a compulsory element, for all children up to age 16, in the new national curriculum. Since 1982 the fourth television channel in Wales, Sianel Pedwar Cymru, provides around 30 hours a week of prime time broadcasting in Welsh at an annual cost in excess of £50 million.

For a century or more the features and themes of Welsh politics and society have remained curiously consistent: the struggle to achieve an equilibrium in the face of immense social and political change.

Is There a Welsh Politics?

The national rhythm of political affairs, dominated by Whitehall and Westminster, prevails even within Wales. Yet accurate assessment requires events to be viewed 'bi-focally'. Wales is not immune to the currents of British politics nor totally subsumed within them. Thus, the national two-party struggle, and the emergence of the Labour Party from its period of electoral retreat, can be played out before the nation in the Pontypridd and Vale of Glamorgan by-elections. The former, although popularly assumed to be a typical coal mining valley, fortress Labour constituency, is, today, a complex community of new industries, aspiring dormitory neighbourhoods servicing Cardiff and gentrified former council estates, which still contains areas of economic decline and social deprivation. A strong showing by Labour was expected and required to confirm their political revival. The former Alliance parties were given an opportunity to abuse each other in the glare of national publicity, whilst Plaid Cymru, the Nationalist Party of Wales, endeavoured to demonstrate its relevance to an electorate in Wales that did not speak Welsh and was not contained within the mountain fastness of Gwynedd. Labour retained the seat and Plaid Cymru polled a quarter of the votes. A highly satisfactory result for those focused on Westminster politics, as it was too for those whose concern was Wales. One could acclaim or disclaim the result according to taste.

Such indifference was not possible at the subsequent Vale of Glamorgan by-election. An established Conservative majority was being defended in a part of Wales with no great cultural or industrial distinctiveness. This was pure two-party, Westminster politics being fought out in a constituency typical of those, common throughout southern England, which will determine the outcome of the next election. Labour won. Extravagant extrapolation from this result immediately transformed the tenor of mid-1989 British political analysis. A Labour government, led by a Welsh MP, was suddenly 'electable' but such interpretation of the by-election result was from a wholly British perspective and largely outside any sense of there being a Welsh politics.

The results of the local elections in May, and the European elections in June, all furthered discussion of a Labour revival in Britain. In Wales, Labour had regained much of its former dominance at the 1987 election, but substantial local government gains and capturing a monopoly of Euro-seats reinforced the case. The national upsurge of the Green Party at the Euro-elections was also noted in Wales, but the party most endangered by this trend was, probably, Plaid Cymru. Irrespective of policy, Plaid Cymru had long been the beneficiary of any protest vote in Wales. The potential of the Greens to usurp this role was deeply disturbing to the Nationalists. But the uniformity of support for the Green Party across all of Britain suggests that ecological politics is an issue, highly salient to the 1990s, not to be contained by the national borders within the United Kingdom.

During 1989 two further instances of national political significance, but with a Welsh dimension, further illustrate the integration of Wales in British politics. The Secretary of State for Wales, Peter Walker, very publicly questioned the broad economic philosophy of the government and extolled the virtues of his own more interventionist approach in Wales. Evidence of such dissent within the Cabinet captured the attention of the country for some days to the extent that Mr Walker was fully expected to be relieved of office at the July reshuffle. This did not happen, but Mr Walker remains a somewhat isolated figure whose policies in Wales are applauded almost more loudly by his opponents than by those in his own party.

Later in the year another maverick figure from the Conservative Party in Wales, Sir Anthony Meyer, MP for Clwyd North West and a long time critic of Mrs Thatcher, achieved notoriety. By putting himself forward at the annual Conservative leadership election, Sir Anthony forced a contest for the first time since Mrs Thatcher's own election as leader in 1975. The challenge was purely nominal, and of no especial Welsh connection other than in Sir Anthony's seat, but indicative of a shift in opinion in Parliament, as well as in the country, for political change. A British phenomenon with which Wales would be at one.

Pyres of Protest

In a year of anniversaries, 1989 completed a decade since the arson attacks in Wales, largely attributed to Meibion Glyndwr, had first occurred. In the intervening years over 200 incendiary attacks have been recorded without any successful prosecution of the perpetrators. The arson campaign, initially aimed at second homes in Wales, has more recently focused upon estate agents advertising property in Wales to the wider British market. Attacks on estate agents have occurred throughout Wales but also in Liverpool, Chester, Shrewsbury and London. Many of these incidents have been relatively minor, yet the premises of an estate agent in central London were entirely gutted. August saw the commemoration of the Investiture of Prince Charles as Prince of Wales at Caernarfon in 1969. At a time of high political tension, the dignified ceremonial of the Investiture had been marred by the deaths of two nationalists at Abergele, killed by the premature explosion of a bomb they were attempting to lay in the path of the Royal train. The twentieth anniversary of this event in 1989 saw a larger than usual remembrance and the appearance, for the first time, of a 'colour guard' clothed, IRA style, in berets and dark glasses. Such demonstrations could be dismissed as pure histrionics were there not still a violent dimension to Welsh politics, as seen in the continued arson campaign.

The underlying issues, cited in justification by the arsonists and other militants, are those of linguistic decline and cultural erosion in large parts of rural Wales. These are not new concerns and have long been themes in Welsh politics. Concern over in-migration, however, did peak in 1989. The economic boom recently enjoyed in the South of England produced a correspondingly large appreciation of property values. In Wales, recovery from the industrial recession of the early 1980s was sporadic and very uneven. Consequently over a large part of Wales, especially in rural Wales, property values did not rise relative to those in southern England. This discrepancy made property in Wales an increasingly attractive purchase. The long established pattern in Wales of youth depopulation and the inflow of the more elderly for retirement has now been graphically supplemented by large-scale in-migration.

The present migration tends to be families able to exploit better roads and commute to their work in England, to utilize modern telecommunications and work remotely from their former base or merely wishing to 'drop-out' into a more attractive environment. In all such cases the move to Wales is likely to have been accompanied by a substantial capital gain achieved through the differential in property values. The restoration of remote cottages as second homes created work and supplemented the tourist industry but rarely threatened the local community. Permanent migration changes the character of communities more fundamentally and more rapidly. Nowhere is this more apparent than in primary schools, where the positive benefits of enhanced enrolments have been severely tempered by the overwhelming predominance of monolingual English speaking children over their Welsh speaking neighbours.

One political response to this heightened consciousness, regarding the frailty of the Welsh language, was the creation, in July 1988, of the Welsh Language Board – a body explicitly charged to promote the language and advise the Secretary of State of the need for administrative or legislative action concerning the wellbeing of Welsh. In 1989 the Board published guidelines designed to promote the use of Welsh in both the private and public sectors of the economy, as well as a draft Bill outlining proposals for a new Welsh Language Act. Welsh already enjoys certain legal guarantees of status and usage, but many linguistic activists have urged the need for more comprehensive legislation giving Welsh similar rights to those of minority languages elsewhere. Debate of all linguistic issues is highly contentious in Wales and concessions to Welsh speakers can be resented by non-Welsh speaking Welshmen. The Language Board, clearly attempting to retain the confidence of the government as well as that of the general public, has proceeded cautiously and in turn has, itself, become a target of protest from Cymdeithas yr Iaith Gymraeg and other linguistic campaigners. Any assessment of provision for the Welsh language in 1989 however, must conclude there has been considerable progress and that many concessions have been made in recent years. A fine line must be trod, lest the protests lose tacit public support and, literally, burn themselves out.

The Third Industrial Revolution

The industrial economy of Wales is one of the oldest in the world. The development of the coal, iron and steel industries in Wales in the late eighteenth and nineteenth centuries laid the foundation for modern industrial practice throughout the world. This industrial economy reached its peak, perhaps, in the inter-war years. Always highly susceptible to trade and business cycles, the shift from coal to oil, as the principal source of fuel, finally heralded an era of economic decline in Wales. Government regional policies encouraged the growth of manufacturing and secondary industries and the Welsh economy diversified into other sectors, such as engineering, chemicals, glass, textiles, and oil refining, but this second industrial revolution did not fully compensate for the importance of coal and steel to Wales. The economic recessions of the 1970s and 1980s saw the final rationalization of the steel industry, to a small element of an integrated European economy. Coal production also declined progressively with heavy closure in the 1960s. The miner's strike of 1984–5, however, was in defence of a Welsh coal industry based upon 28 pits, by 1989 this had been reduced to six. Much of Wales' manufacturing capacity was also lost at this time as Britain adjusted to major changes in the global distribu tion of economic capacity. Recent Welsh unemploy ment peaked in 1985 and the subsequent recovery has seen major new industrial investment in both South and North East Wales.

The economy created in this third industrial revolution is highly dependent upon the tertiary and service sector, in addition to its introducing substantial light engineering and assembly opportunities. Much of this development has been financed by Japanese, American and German capital with considerable 'official' encouragement through the Welsh Development Agency and other bodies. Underlying such economic adjustment has also been an 'official' view determined to promote the market and the private sector over and above the public sector economy. A decade ago it was often maintained that Wales had the largest public sector economy west of the iron curtain, in the political climate of the 1980s such restructuring was inevitable.

Such change has had profound social impact. There has been a substantial shift of population from traditional industrial communities to the developing areas adjacent to the new communication links, the M4 corridor in the South and the A55 expressway in the North. Such shifts alone have substantial political impact through redefining parliamentary constituency boundaries and creating more competitive two party seats from the previously solid Labour heartland. Working practices are no longer based upon mass membership of militant trade unions but often upon single union agreements in plants employing a very high proportion of female labour. The impact upon community and family social structure has totally transformed the conventional image of Wales as typically populated by workers and miners supported by long-suffering, but all competent, 'mams'. Although heralded as a high technology revolution, this third era of industrial development in Wales is, perhaps, the least well-rooted. The output of Wales today is often based upon high technology, but the skilled research and development work, and even component manufacture, is often undertaken elsewhere. Many of the new jobs in Wales are dependent upon low technology assembly of 'hi-tech' products. Wales may have gained by diversifying from an overdependence upon a few heavy industries, but the newly diverse, fragmented economy has yet to demonstrate its ability to support the integrated communal fabric upon which the proud identity and traditions of Wales were based.

Imperfect Allegiance

Wales remains a fully integrated, yet ever more acculturated part of the United Kingdom. Distinctive traits remain but, for the English speaking population, the pressures of conformity bring increasing homogenization with the rest of the country. For the Welsh speaking population new structures and institutional reform have created an environment where the status and security of Welsh has never been better founded. The growth and demand for Welsh medium primary and secondary schools, the addition of Welsh to the national curriculum, the Welsh fourth channel and the acceptance by a growing number of public and commercial authorities that fluency in Welsh is a valuable career asset, all attest to recognition of the place of Welsh today. For this group the pressures to conformity are even stronger. Fluency in Welsh allows access to a distinctive, but often ancient, culture. All Welsh speakers are bilingual and are thus able to enjoy and participate in the powerful and all pervasive sense of Anglo-American culture as they wish. What ever there was of an Anglo-Welsh culture is even more fragile in the face of this global phenomenon.

Thus, although Welsh Wales is somewhat better defended in 1989, the cultural attrition continues. This process need not be deliberate nor malicious, young people everywhere appear to share common tastes in pop music and soap opera. The pressures of such conformity cannot be legislated away but inevitably question the longevity of any distinct minority language or cultural grouping. The year 1989 will be noted for another uniquely Welsh event – the septennial referendum on the opening of licensed premises on Sundays. Such polls are mounted in response to public petition and the area of Wales temperate on a Sunday has diminished steadily since 1961. Prior to the 1989 referendums just two areas, Dwyfor and Ceredigion both heartland areas of Y Fro Gymraeg, remained 'dry'. Although votes were requested in 14 local authorities in 1989 the Sabbatarians retained their hold only in Dwyfor.

Some argue that the progressive extension of the Sunday Opening frontier has marked the final demise of the distinct Welsh culture group. Such an issue is clearly more complex and cannot be reduced to a single measure, but across the full range of social, cultural and political life modern Wales is almost totally assimilated into the United Kingdom. Such variance as remains does not fundamentally undermine this relationship but merely suggests a slightly imperfect allegiance.

Chronology

5 Jan: Jonathan Davies, Llanelli and Wales outside-half, signed for Widnes Rugby League club. Four-year contract worth at least £200,000.

20 Jan: Labour Party announce plans for regional assemblies including a Welsh Assembly with legislative and taxation powers.

3 Feb: Welsh sports personality of the year (1988) Colin Jackson, Olympic silver medalist.

10 Feb: British Steel announce 1,000 further job losses.

23 Feb: Pontypridd by-election following death of Brynmor John. Dr Kim Howells, (Labour) elected.

24 Feb: Meibion Glyndwr attacks in Gwynedd.

27 Feb: Further attacks in Gwynedd.

1 Mar: Plaid Cymru reject devolution as a future option for Wales

Peter Walker announces 40 per cent increase in grants for the Welsh language to £4.6 million.

18 Mar: Wales finish bottom of the five nations Rugby championships.

10 Apr: Welsh Office announce three-year, £1 billion roads development programme.

Peter Walker publicly critical of government economic policy.

3 May: Tai Cymru – Housing for Wales – launched, replacing the Housing Corporation in Wales, with a budget of £72 million for 1989–90.

4 May: County Council elections. Labour gain control of Clwyd County Council, there being no change in the control of the other seven authorities.

Vale of Glamorgan by-election following the death of Sir Raymond Gower. John Smith (Labour) elected.

6 May: Neath beat Llanelli 14–13 in WRU cup final.

18 June: Labour win all four Welsh seats in the elections to the European Parliament.

1 July: Appearance of the Meibion Glyndwr colour guard at the Abergele Martyrs March commemorating the death of two men at the time of the investiture of the Prince of Wales at Caernarfon, 1969.

4 July: Toyota confirm plans to build a £104 million engine plant at Shotton in Clwyd. Toyota is the 25th Japanese manufacturing company to establish a plant in Wales.

5 July: Final report of a national curriculum working party recommends that Welsh be taught in all schools up to age 16.

20 July: Secretary of State announces that the community charge in Wales (poll tax) will be, on average, £100 lower than that for England.

27 July: Welsh Tourist Board announce that earnings from tourism in 1988 totalled £1,115 million.

5–13 Aug: Record attendance of 162,100 at the National Eisteddfod in Llanrwst. The Chair was won by Idris Rowlands of Lampeter, the Crown by Selwyn Griffiths of Caernarfon.

17 Aug: Publication of the Agricultural Census revealed an increase of 5 per cent in the total number of sheep and lambs in Wales – 11 million, four times the human population and a record level.

23 Aug: Further colliery closures announced by British Coal. Only six pits, employing 3,500 remain in South Wales.

10 Sept: Police announce investigation of possible links between Meibion Glyndwr and the IRA.

15 Sept: Final volume of the first Welsh language encyclopaedia, *Chwilota*, published by University of Wales Press.

13 Oct: Michael Foot, MP for Blaenau Gwent, announces his retirement at the next election.

26–29 Oct: Dafydd Ellis Thomas re-elected president of Plaid Cymru, at the Party's annual challenge, following considerable criticism of his leadership.

8 Nov: Referendum on the opening of licensed premises on Sundays held in 14 local authority areas.

Northern Ireland

PAUL ARTHUR

The year 1989 marks the twentieth anniversary of the arrival of the British Army on the streets of Northern Ireland, and the seventeenth year of the continuation of the policy of direct rule. We could continue with reference to anniversaries – the tercentenary of the Siege of Derry, for example – but it would be to make a simple, but profound, point. Northern Ireland has its own sense of the contemporaneity of the past. Measuring movement from one year to the next does not hold much interest for those who think in terms of historical epochs. A second difficulty arises from the unusual nature of the political system inside Northern Ireland. Since the imposition of direct rule in 1972 it lacks a political forum of any real stature – the 566 local councillors exercise the minimum of power on the 26 district councils and the 17 MPs (in reality, 16 since Gerry Adams of Sinn Fein has never taken his place at Westminster) are swamped within the two-party system. An absence of political power carries with it a concomitant lack of responsibility. Thus, while there is an appearance of political movement in fact it is little more than shadow boxing.

During the year two elections – one for the district councils and one for the European Parliament – were contested; there was a change in the ministerial team at the Northern Ireland Office; a general election was held in the Republic of Ireland; and a formal review of the working of the Anglo-Irish Conference was published. It will be noted that already we have strayed outside the territory of Northern Ireland in our reference to the Irish election and to the Anglo-Irish Agreement. That is as it should be because it is impossible to contain the politics of the province within its territory. What has been referred to as the Northern Ireland problem is really a problem of Anglo-Irish relations writ small.

The Anglo-Irish Dimension

A new realism was imposed on Northern Ireland on 15 November 1985 when the Anglo-Irish Agreement was signed at Hillsborough Castle. This is not the place to rehearse all the nuances of the Agreement but to mark its significance four years later. Its continuing existence was an affront to the unionist community and a stark signal of the isolation of the Northern Ireland political process: important political decisions bypassed Belfast and flowed through London and Dublin. It was hardly surprising that unionists perceived it as an insidious form of joint rule aiming, ultimately, at Irish unity as the solution to the Northern Ireland problem.

We should note that between 1921–72 unionists appeared to enjoy untrammelled power; even after direct rule was imposed unionist politicians exercised their veto in that they were able to block British proposals for a form of power sharing within Northern Ireland. Four years of concentrated protest against the Agreement demonstrated that that veto was redundant. Moreover, unionists had forfeited political alliances at Westminster: their militant activities within Northern Ireland and their seeming constitutional intransigence was out of place in the more sedate surroundings of the Commons. By 1989 their protest campaign had failed – that was the first time in a history of resistance that they had not had their way with a British government – and their sense of estrangement from the British political process was complete.

Secondly, despite several serious controversies involving the British and Irish governments, the Agreement had held during 1988 and 1989. Dublin–London relations encountered major problems including perceived miscarriages of justice, strong differences on extradition and concerns about improving the quality of life in Northern Ireland. Constant complaints by the Irish government and sections of the British establishment about the Guildford Four led to their release from prison in October 1989 after serving 15 years in prison for a crime they did not commit. Their release had 'a very positive effect' on Anglo-Irish relations according to the Irish Foreign Minister, Gerry Collins.

The authorities may not have agreed altogether since they were concerned with Irish extradition procedures. In the first year of its operation in 1988–9, the Irish authorities extradited five people (two to Great Britain and three to Northern Ireland) but they returned 32 warrants; and the (Irish) Director of Public Prosecutions announced in October 1989 that there was insufficient evidence to convict Father Patrick Ryan – sought by Britain as an alleged republican conduit of weapons and money from the European mainland. Finally during 1989 the government introduced a Fair Employment Bill which met with the general approval of the Irish authorities since it was recognized that it was a serious attempt to correct the grave imbalance in employment patterns which operated against the Catholic community in Northern Ireland.

All this frenetic activity has been described as a form of conflict management. However it be described there was little doubt that increased contact through the permanent Anglo-Irish secretariat had reduced the risk of misunderstanding between the two governments and had enhanced security co-operation. The closer relationship was reflected in the review of the working of the conference published in May 1989. The two governments stood by the principles of the Agreement and built on them by displaying a healthy measure of flexibility in the penultimate paragraph (29) of the Review: 'If in future it were to appear that the objectives of the Agreement could be more effectively served by changes in the scope and nature of the working of the Conference, consistent with the basic provisions and spirit of the Agreement, the two governments would be ready in principle to consider such changes.' In other words, only an arrangement which would meet with the approval of both governments and transcended the Agreement in importance would be considered.

Thirdly, the fact that the Agreement remained in place four years on was an indication of one of its real motivations. The point was made by the British Ambassador to Ireland when he addressed a group of businessmen in London in June: Sir Nicholas Fenn said that whatever the present uncertainties in Northern Ireland there could be 'no return to the dictatorship of the majority'. He acknowledged that it had, in some respects, profoundly alienated the unionist population but 'it reflected a fundamental change in the politics of the North. I have no hesitation in saying that it was one of those rare diplomatic instruments which changes the game thereafter.' The change in the game envisaged by the signatories was attitudinal change and that is difficult to achieve – or to measure – within a short time span.

Electoral Politics in Northern Ireland: A Phoney War?

Since 1972, elections in Northern Ireland have been conducted as much within the two communities as between them. Unionists have experimented in coalition formation from time to time as in the United Ulster Unionist Coalition (UUUC) in January 1974. But they have always been uneasy affairs and the UUUC had collapsed by 1977. Similarly, a pact was entered into after the signing of the Agreement but by 1989 it was under severe strain. The march of the more militant Democratic Unionist Party (DUP) towards unionist domination had been stifled inside the pact and some of its younger, more talented, souls deserted the party in 1988–9 because they believed that the party had conceded too much to the more staid Ulster Unionist Party (UUP), led by Jim Molyneaux. This was reflected in the May local council elections when the DUP lost 33 seats and the UUP held its own. To some extent the battle between them was personal and ideological. It boiled down to a dispute over the merits of integration versus devolution. The UUP leadership favoured the former whereas the DUP was committed wholeheartedly to the latter. In any case the debate was ersatz. Devolution could not be obtained unless and until unionists indicated their willingness to share power with the minority. Integration ran against the grain of history. There was no evidence that it enjoyed any deep rooted popularity in Britain and it became fashionable in Northern Ireland, only after the signing of the Agreement – a curious exercise in escaping the implications of the Agreement. Nevertheless, a tenacious and well organized campaign within Northern Ireland led to the affiliation of four constituency associations in Northern Ireland by the Conservative Party's National Union in November 1989. It is too early to judge what impact this will have on local politics but it is yet another example of the erosion of traditional values especially in the unionist community.

In many respects Northern Ireland was becoming more integrated into the British system with the advance of Thatcherism and the absence of a local parliamentary forum to resist it. In 1989 industrial output in the province rose by an estimated 8 per cent while unemployment fell by almost 10,000. But it would be foolish to construct a bright future on the back of these figures. Gross Domestic Product per head in Northern Ireland was still the lowest of any region in the UK and exactly the same as it was in 1979 (78 per cent of the UK average). Unemployment at the end of 1989 was 14.6 per cent, almost twice the level of 7.9 per cent in 1979 and higher than any other UK region. This tendency was confirmed by a Central Statistical Office report in July 1989 which found that Northern Ireland had the highest unemployment, lowest earnings, most still births, largest families and lowest output per head in the United Kingdom. Health, education and welfare were becoming more standardized along the British model. Even the two most prestigious industries – Harland and Woolf's shipyard and Short's aircraft factory (the bastions of Protestant working class Ulster) were privatized during 1989. All of this might seem appropriate for a region of the United Kingdom but since Northern Ireland had enjoyed a large measure of autonomy between 1921 and 1972, political 'interference' was resented by the former ruling majority.

Less resentment was felt by the minority – at least by those who supported the constitutionalist party, the Social Democratic and Labour Party (SDLP). Catholics had not expected a fair deal from the system and the more militant Sinn Fein (SF) made no secret of its support for the IRA campaign of terrorism. But the Hillsborough Agreement brought about a sea change in minority attitudes. In the first place SF electoral growth was arrested. By 1983 it could call on as much as 40 per cent of the Catholic vote. By 1989, as the implications of the Agreement began to bite, and the IRA campaign was perceived as being more abhorrent, it had lost 16 of its 59 council seats and was managing to hold its own only in the West Belfast constituency of Gerry Adams. However, slowly and painfully, British attempts at the reform of the system was winning grudging support in the Catholic community.

The Security Dimension

Curiously, the Catholic community was conscious of another form of integration – the Northern Irish apparatus of law and order and of the administration of justice was becoming more visible in the British system. Widespread concern about possible miscarriages of justice in the Birmingham Six and the Guildford Four cases received widespread publicity; the introduction of a more draconian security package led the Standing Advisory Committee on Human Rights to complain in January that they 'might cumulatively be eroding confidence in the impartiality of the Northern Ireland administration' and led the government to decide to derogate temporarily from the European Convention on Human Rights; the imposition of a broadcasting ban on Sinn Fein and other organizations led to protests from the National Union of Journalists and threats to take their case to Europe: all of these were indicative of the poisonous effects of the Northern Ireland problem on the British system and of the growing difficulties of quarantining it from mainland politics.

Above all of this was the continuing terrorist threat. Loyalist terrorism had become more visible in the aftermath of the signing of the Agreement and in April three loyalists were charged in Paris with transporting 'first category arms' after they had been found with representatives of the South African government. Moreover, in the latter half of 1989 there was growing evidence of collusion between some members of the Ulster Defence Regiment (a regiment of the British Army) and loyalist paramilitaries. A senior British police officer was called in to investigate but he had not completed his inquiries by the end of the year.

Republican terrorism took on a new turn. A series of bloody 'mistakes' – the IRA admitted to killing 11 innocent civilians in 1988 – was carried on into 1989, further alienating the very community it claimed to be protecting. But it shifted much of its campaign away from Northern Ireland and struck out at British security personnel on the mainland and the Continent leading to, among others, the deaths of 11 bandsmen at Deal, Kent, in September and to the infant child of an army officer in West Germany in October. Indeed, such was the threat to army personnel abroad that the Secretary of State, Peter Brooke, announced in West Germany in December that the IRA would probably be responsible for more security deaths there than in Northern Ireland.

The year 1989 was a year of false dawns. A new Secretary of State, Peter Brooke, and a new Chief Constable of the Royal Ulster Constabulary, Hugh Annesley, brought with them new thinking but the same priorities and it is too early to judge their impact. The redundant nature of the political process within Northern Ireland is demonstrated by the fact that the one possible breakthrough in political dialogue occurred at Duisburg in West Germany in October 1988 when a meeting of two representatives of the four main constitutional parties in Northern Ireland (UUP, SDLP, DUP and the Alliance Party) was convened by a lawyer and Lutheran ecumenist. The original agenda was abandoned in favour of seeking ways of breaking the political impasse but unanimity was impossible to reach. When word leaked out that the meeting had taken place there was uproar – 'How close is Duisburg to Munich?' was a familiar refrain.

Several appeals during the year by the Irish Prime Minister, Charles Haughey, to unionists to discuss the future were all rebuffed. Indeed two prominent Northern Ireland politicians, Austin Currie of the SDLP and John Cushnahan of the Alliance Party, left Northern Ireland and started new political careers in the Republic as Fine Gael members of the Irish and European Parliaments respectively. Their departure symbolized the sense of despair which pervaded political life. It was not a promising year in Northern Ireland.

Chronology

4 Jan: Huge haul of Semtex bomb-making equipment found in Londonderry.

18 Jan: Catholic man shot dead by Protestant extremists.

23 Jan: IRA announce the disbanding of the Donegal active service unit after the killing of two Protestant civilians.

Guillotine of the Prevention of Terrorism (Temporary Provisions) Bill in the Commons.

31 Jan: Fair Employment (Northern Ireland) Bill, which replaces the existing equality agency with a Fair Employment Commission with enhanced powers, funding and staff, is given a second reading in the Commons by 272 to 192.

1 Feb: Two bombs in Belfast. One soldier is killed.

2 Feb: BBC reveals secret talks have been under way between the SDLP, the DUP, the UUP and the Alliance Party in West Germany since October 1988. Ian Paisley then distances himself from these talks which subsequently founder.

8 Feb: Anglo-Irish conference in London. The British demand new extradition procedures.

12 Feb: Republican solicitor Pat Finucane is murdered in Belfast. Remarks by Douglas Hogg, Minister of State at the Home Office, that some solicitors were 'unduly sympathetic' to terrorist organizations were felt to have contributed to his death.

14 Feb: UN report finds that detainees have been maltreated in Belfast.

A Sinn Fein councillor is shot dead.

16 Feb: The Irish People's Liberation Organization shoot and injure five people in a loyalist club in the Stonewall Road area.

20 Feb: Bombing of the Parachute regiment barracks in Shropshire by the IRA.

Catholic security guard shot dead in Armagh.

25 Feb: Charles Haughey, the Irish Prime Minister, offers talks with the unionists.

IRA killing in West Belfast.

26 Feb: Unionists reject Haughey's offer.

7 Mar: Three Protestants killed by IRA gunmen.

10 Mar: One man killed and another wounded in West Belfast.

13 Mar: Disciplinary hearings begin into the County Armagh shootings of 1982 and their aftermath involving 22 RUC officers.

Spanish government contradicts the British version of the killing of three IRA terrorists in Gibraltar in 1988.

16 Mar: Senior loyalist paramilitary figure shot dead in North Belfast.

17 Mar: Catholic man killed in what appears to be a tit-for-tat killing.

19 Mar: Catholic man killed in North Belfast.

20 Mar: IRA murders two senior RUC policemen and seize confidential documents from their car.

25 Mar: A soldier is run down and killed in the Falls Road, West Belfast.

4 Apr: IRA man murdered by loyalist gunmen.

11 Apr: Ban on broadcasting of interviews with republican and loyalist groups which openly support terrorism is lifted in the run-up to local government elections in Ulster.

12 Apr: Woman killed in a bomb attack at Warrenpoint, County Down.

13 Apr: Wanted IRA man, Paul Kane, extradicted from the Irish Republic.

21 Apr: Protestant taxi driver killed in North Belfast.

Arrest in Paris of three loyalists reveals evidence of a trade in arms between South Africa and Ulster loyalists.

4 May: Soldier and ex-soldier killed in IRA bomb attacks.

9 May: Shorts, the aerospace and defence contractors, to axe 700 jobs.

18 May: Northern Ireland council elections. SDLP wins 20 seats, Sinn Fein loses 19 and the DUP loses ground. Four unofficial Conservative candidates are elected.

1 June: Two men gaoled for life for the murder of two soldiers who inadvertently drove into the path of a republican funeral in 1988.

6 June: A 400lb IRA bomb causes considerable damage to Castle Court, Belfast's £60 million new shopping development.

7 June: In an interview in *The Independent* Garret Fitzgerald argues that Britain is incapable of producing a co-ordinated policy on Northern Ireland and blames the failure of the Irish to understand how stupidly 'the British can act as one of the major sources of misunderstanding between our two countries'.

Shorts sold to Bombardier of Canada, with a £780 million cash injection from the government.

14 June: Britain persuades the UN Security Council to take action aimed at stopping terrorists obtaining plastic explosives such as the Czech manufactured Semtex.

19 June: IRA attempt to bomb the barracks at Osnabruck, West Germany, is foiled.

2 July: IRA bomb attack in Hanover kills an army corporal.

7 July: Three RUC officers are seriously injured in an IRA bomb attack.

17 July: Police and Criminal Evidence (Northern Ireland) Order becomes law.

3 Aug: Army tours in Northern Ireland to be extended.

9 Aug: Controversy over RUC use of plastic bullets reopens after the death of a Catholic boy in Belfast.

22 Aug: RUC move to crackdown on drinking clubs, which are regarded as a major source of revenue for terrorist organizations.

23 Aug: Catholic Bishop of Down and Connor says he would give unqualified endorsement of a Catholic's decision to join the RUC, marking a major advance in the hierarchy's view of the force.

27 Aug: Catholic man shot dead by loyalist gunmen in County Down.

28 Aug: Review of weapons policy in Northern Ireland ends in a decision to give the Ulster Defence Regiment (UDR) plastic baton rounds for the first time and to give the RUC more modern firearms.

Announcement of a plan to phase out part-time soldiers in the UDR and make it a full-time force.

30 Aug: Loyalist paramilitary sources claim information on republican suspects has been given to them over the years by contacts in the security forces.

1 Sept: Two soldiers shot and wounded by the IRA in Munster, West Germany.

2 Sept: Catholic man killed in Belfast. One of his killers is shot dead by the army and the other is apprehended.

7 Sept: Wife of a British soldier killed by the IRA in Dortmund.

8 Sept: Successful management buy-out at Harland and Woolf shipyards with the backing of its workers.

10 Sept: Disclosure that a list of IRA suspects has disappeared from a military establishment in Northern Ireland.

14 Sept: RUC admits confidential documents on IRA suspects have been stolen.

15 Sept: Investigation into collusion between the security forces and the Protestant paramilitary launched under John Stevens, deputy chief constable of Cambridgeshire.

19 Sept: Disappearance of two more confidential security force documents disclosed.

22 Sept: IRA bomb kills ten (the death toll eventually rose to 11) at a Royal Marines base at Deal, Kent.

Latest and largest cache of documents on republican suspects leaked.

25 Sept: SDP becomes the first mainland party to decide to contest elections in Northern Ireland.

2 Oct: Claims of an unofficial loyalist 'force within a force' in the RUC are made in the Belfast newspaper, the *Irish News*.

Gerry Adams, the Sinn Fein president, addressing a fringe meeting at the Labour Party conference, defends the Deal bombing.

4 Oct: Man killed by the IRA in Belfast.

8 Oct: 28 members of the UDR are arrested as part of an investigation into links between security force personnel and the loyalist paramilitary.

RUC superintendent killed by a booby trap bomb as he drove to church.

Attempted gaol break by IRA prisoners at Crumlin Road gaol foiled.

10 Oct: Model Conservative association in North Down to be allowed to affiliate to the Conservative Party.

12 Oct: The Irish refuse to prosecute Patrick Ryan, wanted in Britain for IRA activities.

26 Oct: RAF corporal and his baby daughter killed by a gunman at Wildenrath, West Germany.

3 Nov: Peter Brooke indicates willingness to talk to Sinn Fein if they renounce violence and recognizes that there is no military solution to the Northern Ireland problem.

18 Nov: IRA bombs kill three soldiers in County Down and injures one in Colchester.

21 Nov: Lord Donaldson, Master of the Rolls, denounces government restrictions on broadcasting interviews with organizations supporting terrorism in Northern Ireland as 'half- baked' at a hearing into the legality of the restrictions in the Court of Appeal.

29 Nov: Two Catholics killed in a loyalist attack on a bar in County Tyrone.

6 Dec: Legal challenge to the government's ban on direct-speech broadcast interviews with members of Northern Ireland terrorist groups decisively rejected in the Court of Appeal.

Twelve suspected loyalist extremists arrested in Belfast by the team inquiring into collusion between Protestant paramilitaries and security force members.

7 Dec: 20 people injured by a 500lb car bomb left in Lisburn town centre by the IRA.

13 Dec: Two soldiers killed in an attack on a border post in County Fermanagh.

20 Dec: Report shows that Catholics are seriously under-represented on the staff at Queens' University, Belfast.

Index